CONNECTICUT PRACTICE SERIES™

RULES OF APPELLATE PROCEDURE

2014-2015 Edition
Issued in December 2014

By

WESLEY W. HORTON
of the Connecticut Bar

and

KENNETH J. BARTSCHI
of the Connecticut Bar

THOMSON REUTERS™

For Customer Assistance Call 1-800-328-4880

Mat #41419836

ISBN: 978–0–314–61624–1

DEDICATIONS

To my wife, Chloe, for her patience and understanding.

Wesley W. Horton

To my partner, Jim, for his support and good humor.

Kenneth J. Bartschi

PREFACE TO 2014–2015 EDITION

This 2014–2015 edition includes all appellate rules and forms in effect as of January 1, 2015 for the Supreme Court and Appellate Court. It also takes into account all statutes in effect on that date and court decisions reported in the Connecticut Law Journal and the Connecticut Law Reporter through September 30, 2014.

The only major changes in the rules adopted in 2014 were the various amendments to § 67-2, effective September 1, 2014, concerning the right to file double-sided appendices and the requirements and procedure for the electronic filing of briefs and appendices.

Appeals filed after July 1, 2013 no longer include a printed record. Instead, the appellant will be required to file an appendix (previously an appendix was optional) that contains certain documents formerly included in the printed record. A number of rules have been amended to make reference to this new requirement. The rules also clarify that the term "record" for purposes of appeal encompasses everything presented in the proceedings below. This major change has resulted in amendments throughout the appellate rules.

Because the old rules will apply to appeals filed prior to July 1, 2013, and because it can take some time for briefing to be completed, the old rules will still be relevant, at least for a while. Therefore this volume includes both the old and new rules.

Wesley W. Horton
Kenneth J. Bartschi
Hartford, Connecticut
November 2014

WestlawNext™

THE NEXT GENERATION OF ONLINE RESEARCH

WestlawNext is the world's most advanced legal research system. By leveraging more than a century of information and legal analysis from Westlaw, this easy-to-use system not only helps you find the information you need quickly, but offers time-saving tools to organize and annotate your research online. As with Westlaw.com, WestlawNext includes the editorial enhancements (e.g., case headnotes, topics, key numbers) that make it a perfect complement to West print resources.

- FIND ANYTHING by entering citations, descriptive terms, or Boolean terms and connectors into the WestSearch™ box at the top of every page.

- USE KEYCITE® to determine whether a case, statute, regulation, or administrative decision is good law.

- BROWSE DATABASES right from the home page.

- SAVE DOCUMENTS to folders and add notes and highlighting online.

SIGN ON: next.westlaw.com
LEARN MORE: store.westlaw.com/westlawnext
FOR HELP: 1–800–WESTLAW (1–800–937–8529)

RELATED PRODUCTS

West's CONNECTICUT PRACTICE SERIES™

Superior Court Civil Rules
Horton and Knox

Juvenile Law
Levesque and Hrelic

Rules of Appellate Procedure
Horton and Bartschi

Civil Practice Forms
Kaye and Effron

Criminal Procedure
Borden and Gold, formerly Borden and Orland

Criminal Jury Instructions
Borden and Gold, formerly Borden and Orland

Trial Practice
Yules

Family Law and Practice with Forms
Rutkin, Hogan and Oldham

Land Use Law and Practice
Fuller

Criminal Law
Borden and Gold, formerly Borden and Orland

Unfair Trade Practices
Langer, Belt and Morgan

Construction Law
David E. Rosengren

Employment Law
Stephen B. Harris and Lawrence Peikes

Environmental Protection Act
David F. Sherwood and Janet P. Brooks

Elements of an Action
Thomas B. Merritt

Motions in Limine
David N. Finley and Thomas P. Boggess

Summary Judgment
Erin Carlson

Workers' Compensation Law
Robert F. Carter, et al.

Elder Law
Kate McEvoy

DUI Law
Steven A. Tomeo and Johnathan R. Sills

The History of the Connecticut Supreme Court
Wesley W. Horton

Connecticut General Statutes Annotated

Connecticut Digest

Connecticut Rules of Court Pamphlet

Connecticut Reporter

Westlaw®

Thomson Reuters® thanks you for subscribing to this product. Should you have any questions regarding this product please contact Customer Service at 1-800-328-4880 or by fax at 1-800-340-9378. If you would like to inquire about related publications or place an order, please contact us at 1–800–344–5009.

 **THOMSON REUTERS™**
Thomson Reuters
610 Opperman Drive
Eagan, MN 55123

legalsolutions.thomsonreuters.com

Summary of Contents

Table of Contents

CHAPTER 62 CHIEF JUDGE, APPELLATE CLERK AND DOCKET: GENERAL ADMINISTRATIVE MATTERS

CHAPTER 63 FILING THE APPEAL; WITHDRAWALS

CHAPTER 64 PROCEDURE CONCERNING MEMORANDUM OF DECISION

CHAPTER 65 TRANSFER OF CASES

CHAPTER 66 MOTIONS AND OTHER PROCEDURES

CHAPTER 67 BRIEFS

CHAPTER 68 CASE FILE

CHAPTER 69 ASSIGNMENT OF CASES FOR ARGUMENT

CHAPTER 70 ARGUMENTS AND MEDIA COVERAGE OF COURT PROCEEDINGS

CHAPTER 71 APPELLATE JUDGMENTS AND OPINIONS

CHAPTER 72 WRITS OF ERROR

CHAPTER 73 RESERVATIONS

CHAPTER 74 APPEALS FROM JUDICIAL REVIEW COUNCIL

CHAPTER 75 APPEALS FROM COUNCIL ON PROBATE JUDICIAL CONDUCT

CHAPTER 80 APPEALS IN HABEAS CORPUS PROCEEDINGS FOLLOWING CONVICTION

CHAPTER 81 APPEALS TO APPELLATE COURT BY CERTIFICATION FOR REVIEW IN ACCORDANCE WITH GENERAL STATUTES CHAPTERS 124 AND 440

CHAPTER 82 CERTIFIED QUESTIONS FROM COURTS OF OTHER JURISDICTIONS

FORMS

INTRODUCTION AND CHECK LIST FOR APPEALS

Introduction

The Connecticut appellate rules were greatly revised in 1996 and included in the completely new numbering system of the loose-leaf 1998 Practice Book. The Connecticut appellate rules bear little resemblance to the Federal Rules of Appellate Procedure.

The history of each of the current rules is included in a Historical Note immediately after the individual rule, followed by any relevant Cross Reference and the Authors' Comments.

Table 1
Place Where Documents Are Filed

Document	Place	Authority
Unless Otherwise Indicated	Appellate Clerk	§ 62-7
Appeal Form	Superior Court (Endorsed Copy to Appellate Clerk)	
63-4 Papers	Appellate Clerk	§§ 63-4, 62-7
Transcript	Appellate Clerk	§ 63-8
Briefs and Appendix	Appellate Clerk	§ 67-2
Motion for Extension of Time to File Appeal under § 66-1	Superior Court	§ 66-1
Motion to Superior Court for Rectification or Articulation	Appellate Clerk	§§ 62-7, 66-5
Preappeal Motion to Superior Court to Terminate Stay of Execution	Superior Court	§ 61-11
Post Appeal Motion to Trial Court to Terminate Stay of Execution	Appellate Clerk	§§ 62-7, 61-11
Motion for Stay Pending Appeal	Superior Court	§ 61-12
Motion to Superior Court under Appellate Rules	Appellate Clerk	§ 62-7
Motion to Superior Court under Superior Court Rules	Superior Court	§ 4-3
Petition for Certification to Supreme Court	Appellate Clerk (Copy to Superior Court)	§ 84-4
Petition for Certification to Appellate Court	Appellate Clerk (Copy to Superior Court)	§ 81-1

The clerk's office for both the Appellate Court and Supreme Court is located in the Supreme Court building. The mailing address for the Appellate and Supreme Courts is 231 Capitol Avenue, Hartford, CT 06106. However, the Appellate Court hears oral argument and its judges have chambers at 75 Elm Street, Hartford, CT 06106.

Table 2
Number of Copies
(filed with Appellate Clerk unless otherwise noted)

Document	Number	Authority
Unless Otherwise Indicated	Original plus 15 with Appellate Clerk	§ 62-7
Appeal (Form JD-SC-28 or JD-SC-29)	Original with Trial Clerk; With Appellate Clerk: 1 Endorsed Copy	§ 63-3
§ 63-4 Papers	Original only	§ 63-4
§ 64-1 Notice	Original plus 3	§ 64-1
Certification that opposing counsel were sent Transcript Completion Form	Original only	§ 63-8
Transcript	One nonreturnable copy	§§ 62-7, 63-8
Motion for Extension of Time	Original only	§ 66-1
Motion for Extension of Time to file Petition for Certification	Original only	§§ 66-1, 84-7, 81-5
Motion to Superior Court for Rectification	Original plus 3	§ 66-5
Motion to Superior Court to Terminate Stay of Execution	Original plus 3	§ 61-11
Motion for Reargument	Original plus 15	§§ 62-7, 71-5
Other Motion and Application	Original plus 15	§ 62-7
Petition for Certification to Appellate or Supreme Court	Endorsed original plus 15 with Appellate Clerk: One copy to Trial Clerk	§§ 81-1, 84-4
Statement opposing Petition	Original plus 15	§§ 81-3, 84-6
Brief and Appendix	Appellate Court cases: Original plus 10	§ 67-2
	Supreme Court cases: Original plus 15	§ 67-2
	Transferred cases: Follow Clerk's Instructions	§ 65-1
Record (Appeals filed before July 1, 2013)	Follow Clerk's Instructions	§ 68-7

Table 3
Fees

Document	Fee	Authority
Appeal to Appellate Court	$250 entry fee	C.G.S. § 52-259
Appeal to Supreme Court from Superior Court	$250 entry fee	C.G.S. § 52-259
Appeal to Supreme Court from Appellate Court	$250 entry fee	C.G.S. § 52-259
Writ of Error to Supreme Court	$250 entry fee	C.G.S. § 52-259
Case transferred to Supreme Court via § 65-1	$0	§ 65-1

Document	Fee	Authority
Case improperly in Appellate Court transferred to Supreme Court	$0	§ 65-4
Case improperly in Supreme Court transferred to Appellate Court	$0	§ 65-4
Joint Appeal	one fee	§ 61-7
Cross Appeal	$0	§ 61-8
Petition for Certification	$75	C.G.S. § 52-259
Motion to Reargue (Civil cases only)	$125	C.G.S. § 52-259c(b)

The entry fee for all appeals and the fee for a petition for certification to the Appellate Court from a trial court in a zoning case are paid to the trial court clerk. §§ 63-5, 81-1. The fee for a motion to reargue and for a petition for certification to the Supreme Court can be paid to any trial court clerk in the state.

Table 4
Format

Document	Format	Authority
Motions, Applications, Petitions and Statements in Opposition	12-point font, Arial or Univers only	§§ 66-3, 81-2,
	certification of compliance with above requirements double spaced single sided 27 lines to page Minimum Margin Requirements: Top-1" Left-1¼" Right-½" Bottom-1"	§§ 81-3, 84-5, 84-6
Briefs	Same as above	§ 67-2
Appendices	In General Single Sided	§ 67-8 § 67-2
	Parts one and two bound together and bound with brief, if possible.	§ 67-2
	If either part of appendix is over 150 pages, parts of appendix must be separately bound.	§ 67-2
Records (Appeals filed before July 1, 2013)	Follow Clerk's Instructions	§§ 67-2, 68-7
Signature of Counsel	Include your typed name, mailing address, telephone and facsimile numbers, and juris number	§§ 62-6, 67-2

Document	Format	Authority
Certification to other Counsel	Include name, address and telephone and facsimile numbers of all counsel served	§ 62-7

Table 5
Time to File
(from filing by opponent or notice of decision by clerk unless otherwise noted)

Document	Time	Authority
Appeal to Appellate or Supreme Court		
Generally	20 days	§ 63-1, and various other Statutes and Rules
Summary Process	5 days from decision (some days excluded)	C.G.S.A. § 47a-35
Mechanics Lien	7 days from decision	C.G.S.A. § 49a-35c
Prejudgment Remedy	7 days from decision	C.G.S.A. § 52-278l
Lis Pendens	7 days from decision	C.G.S.A. § 52-325c
Non Final Judgment	14 days	C.G.S.A. § 52-265a
Temporary Injunction in Labor Case	14 days from decision	C.G.S.A. § 31-118
Cross Appeal	10 days from appeal	§ 61-8
Petition for Certification		
to Appellate Court	20 days	§ 81-1
to Supreme Court	20 days	§ 84-4
Opposition to Petition for Certification	10 days	§§ 81-3; 84-6
Action Following Grant Of Certification	20 days	§§ 81-4; 84-9
Amended Appeals	20 days	§ 61-9
Stay Motions	None	See §§ 61-11, 61-12; but see § 61-13
Review of Stay Order	10 days	§ 61-14

Document	Time	Authority
Papers Appellant Must File Under § 63-4	10 days from appeal	§ 63-3
Response to § 63-4 Papers	20 days	§ 63-4
Motion for Rectification or Articulation	See rule	§ 66-5, para. 8
Motion for Review	10 days	§§ 66-6, 66-7
Motion to Dismiss	10 days after ground arose	§ 66-8
Appellant's Brief and Appendix	45 days after appeal or transcript sent	§ 67-3, para. 1
Appellee's Brief	30 days	§ 67-3, para. 4
Reply Brief	20 days	§ 67-3, para. 5
Cross Appeal -Briefing	See rule	§ 67-3, para. 6
Motion for Reconsideration	10 days	§ 71-5
Motion for Reconsideration of Costs	10 days	§ 71-3
Time to Pay Fees	With Appeal	§ 63-5
Time to Order Transcripts	With Appeal	§ 63-8
How to Compute Time	First day no; last day yes	§ 63-2
Extensions of Time	Generally 10 days before	§ 66-1 (a)(4) deadline

Check List

I. Before Trial

1. Review every adverse ruling of the trial court to determine whether it is a final judgment (see § 4 of commentary to § 61-1). If it arguably is, file an appeal or see §§ 61-2 through 61-5.

2. If a motion to strike is granted against you, do not replead unless the decision is harmless, Royce v. Town of Westport, 183 Conn. 177, 439 A.2d 298 (1981); Good Humor Corp. v. Ricciuti, 160 Conn. 133, 135, 273 A.2d 886, 887–888 (1971).

3. A motion to reargue a final judgment filed within the time to appeal generally extends the appeal period, § 11-11; Springfield-De Witt Gardens, Inc. v. Wood, 143 Conn. 708, 125 A.2d 488 (1956). This is risky for speedy statutory proceedings, however; see part 3 of commentary to § 63-1.

II. During Trial

1. Mark all rejected exhibits for identification.
2. Make specific objection to all adverse rulings (§ 5-5).
3. In court cases, file a written statement of all questions of law before the end of argument or when trial briefs are filed (§§ 5-1, 60-5).
4. In jury cases, file a motion for directed verdict at the close of evidence, or you cannot claim judgment N.O.V. (§ 16-37).
5. In jury cases, make specific requests to charge, and take specific exceptions to the charge (§§ 16-20 to 16-23, 60-5).
6. If appeal is a certainty, make arrangements for ordering transcript during trial. Make sure the court reporter takes down opening and closing arguments.
7. Make sure you know what will constitute the trial judgment to start the appeal period running (§ 61-1 and commentary). Generally speaking, in a jury case, the judgment comes into existence on the day the judge denies the losing party's motion to set aside the verdict; in a court case, the judgment comes into existence on the day the judge files the memorandum of decision or rules from the bench after trial. At that time there is no document entitled "judgment," however a "judgment" does exist and it can be appealed.

III. After Jury Verdict

1. In all cases, file a motion to set aside verdict within 10 calendar days of the verdict (§ 16-35). Small v. South Norwalk Sav. Bank, 205 Conn. 751, 756–759, 535 A.2d 1292, 1295–1296 (1988). An appeal directly from the verdict, while now permissible; Santopietro v. City of New Haven, 239 Conn. 207, 211–212, 682 A.2d 106, 108–113 (1996); is still a poor idea. See Horton & Knox, Superior Court Civil Rules, § 16-35, section 1 of Authors' Comments.
2. If you have moved for a directed verdict, move for judgment N.O.V. at the same time you file your motion to set aside the verdict (§ 16-37).
3. If the complaint is insufficient, or the verdict defective, an alternative to judgment N.O.V. is the motion in arrest of judgment; see II Stephenson, Conn.Civ.Proc. § 201(b) and (f). (This may be useful if you forgot to move for a directed verdict.) Evidence of jury improprieties can also be raised on a motion in arrest. Id. § 276. See Horton & Knox, Superior Court Civil Rules, § 16-35, section 3 of Authors' Comments.
4. If new evidence, evidence of fraud, or evidence of jury improprieties, turns up within 10 days of the verdict or

judgment by the trial court, move for a new trial (§§ 16-35; 17-4A).

5. If new evidence turns up more than 10 days after the verdict, file a petition (a separate law suit) for a new trial.

IV. After Judgment and Before Appeal

1. Decide how long you have to appeal:
    i. In general, you have 20 calendar days from issuance of notice of judgment, which means from the date the decision was orally announced or sent to you by the clerk, whichever is earlier (see § 63-1 and commentary). (Note the postmark on the envelope from the trial court).
    ii. You have 5 days (some days excluded) from the date of judgment in summary process cases (C.G.S.A. § 47a-35).
    iii. You have 7 days from the date of decision in mechanic's lien, prejudgment remedy and lis pendens cases (C.G.S.A. §§ 49-35c, 52-278l, 52-325c).
    iv. You have 20 days from issuance of notice by the clerk to obtain a signature from a clerk or judge on a writ of error, which must then be served and returned to court (§ 72-3).
    v. You have 14 days from issuance of notice of judgment to attempt an appeal of a non-final judgment (C.G.S.A. § 52-265a, § 83-1; see § 1 of commentary to § 61-1).
    vi. You have 20 days from issuance of notice of judgment in juvenile matters (§ 79-1).
    vii. You have 14 days from the grant or denial of a temporary injunction in a labor case (C.G.S.A. § 31-118).
    viii. You have 20 days from issuance of notice of judgment to request certification to appeal (§§ 84-4, 81-1).
    ix. You have 20 days from issuance of notice of granting of certification by the Appellate Court from a trial court decision in a zoning case (§ 81-4).
    x. You have 20 days from issuance of notice of certification from an Appellate Court decision to pay the fees (§ 84-9).

    (Note that these are calendar, not working, days (§ 63-2)).

2. Decide whether you have the right to appeal:
    i. Is judgment final? (See § 4 of commentary to § 61-1.)
    ii. Are you an aggrieved party? (See § 2 of commentary to § 61-1.)
    iii. Is subject matter appealable? (See § 1 of commentary to § 61-1.)

      (a) criminal contempt (see writ of error, § 72-1);

      (b) small claims (see commentary to § 72-1);

      (c) verdict of acquittal (see § 1(v) of commentary to § 61-1).

3. Decide to what court the appeal goes:

    i. Most Superior Court decisions go to the Appellate Court as of right (C.G.S.A. § 51-197a).

    ii. The following Superior Court decisions go directly to the Supreme Court as of right (C.G.S.A. § 51-199):

        (1) [for original jurisdiction of Supreme Court, see § iv below];

        (2) decision declaring state (but not federal) statute or constitutional provision unconstitutional;

        (3) conviction of capital felony, class A felony or any other felony where the maximum penalty that may be imposed exceeds 20 years (P.A. 98-81, § 5);

        (4) sentence of death;

        (5) election or primary dispute under C.G.S.A. §§ 9-323, 9-325 (§ 9-323 case bypasses Superior Court);

        (6) reprimand or censure of (but not the failure to reprimand or censure) a probate judge under C.G.S.A. § 45a-65 (bypasses Superior Court);

        (7) decision on judicial removal or suspension under C.G.S.A. § 51-51j (bypasses Superior Court);

        (8) decision of judicial review counsel under C.G.S.A. § 51-51r (bypasses Superior Court);

        (9) important cases accepted by the Supreme Court under C.G.S.A. § 52-265a;

        (10) writ of error under C.G.S.A. § 51-199(b)(10);

        (11) any other matter provided by law.

    iii. Workers' Compensation cases bypass the Superior Court entirely and go directly to the Appellate Court (§ 76-1).

    iv. Reapportionment cases bypass the Superior and Appellate Courts and are decided pursuant to the Supreme Court's grant of original jurisdiction (Constitutional Amendment, Art. 16, § 2).

    v. If appeal goes to Appellate Court, consider whether to move the Supreme Court to transfer the case to itself under §§ 65-1 and 65-2.

4. If applicable, decide from whom permission to appeal is required.

    i. No permission is needed except as noted.

    ii. Permission from trial court or an Appellate or Supreme Court judge is needed for appeals in habeas corpus appeal by prisoner (C.G.S.A. § 52-470).

    iii. Permission from trial court is needed for certain appeals in criminal cases (C.G.S.A. §§ 54-95, 54-96).

    iv. Zoning and inland wetlands cases under C.G.S.A. §§ 8-8, 8-9, 8-30a, and 22a-43(d) go from the Superior Court to the Appellate Court only after certification by two judges of the Appellate Court.

    v. Appeals decided by the Appellate Court may be appealed to the Supreme Court only on certification by three justices of the Supreme Court (§ 84-8).

5. Decide if you wish or need to file a motion for reargument. (See §§ 11-11, 60-5 and 63-1 and Authors' Comments).

6. If new evidence or other grounds arise within the appeal period, file a motion to open judgment, except as noted in commentary to § 63-1. This will generally extend the appeal period.

7. Decide if you will need clarification of the decision.

8. Decide if there is any basis for a pre-appeal motion for review. (See § 66-6).

9. Decide what portion of the transcript to order and order it (§ 63-8).

10. If you are indigent, take advantage of § 63-6 or § 63-7.

11. If you do not intend to appeal, decide whether you will want to cross appeal if the other side appeals. (See commentary to § 61-8).

V. Filing Appeal

1. File appeal preferably in person or by e-filing when available, see P.B. § 63-3, as soon as possible. Do not wait until the last day. (See § 5 of commentary to § 63-1).

2. Draft appeal papers carefully:

    i. Fill out Form JD-SC-28 or JD-SC-29 carefully. See annotated forms in this book.

    ii. Jurisdictional statement should include the following language:

        (a) "final judgment";

        (b) "decision setting aside a verdict"; or

        (c) other statutorily authorized ruling.

    iii. Security no longer required (§ 63-5).

3. Where to file:

The appeal is filed with the clerk of the trial court (§ 63-3). Use the Superior Court docket number.

4. Copies:

      i. Give original to trial court clerk, who will endorse it and give you an endorsed copy for you to file with the appellate clerk's office in Hartford (§ 63-3).

      ii. Certification to opposing counsel is necessary (§ 63-3).

5.   Fees: (See C.G.S.A. § 52-259).

Appellate Court: $250 entry fee.

Supreme Court: $250 entry fee.

Make sure clerk notes on the appeal papers that the fee has been paid. The fee may be paid with a check payable to the Clerk of the Superior Court.

6.   Documents to be filed (in person or by mail) with the appellate clerk's office in Hartford when the appeal is filed with the trial court:

      i.   In all cases, a preliminary statement of the issues to be raised on appeal (§ 63-4(a)(1)).

      ii.   In all cases, either a transcript acknowledgment form or a certificate that none is deemed necessary (§ 63-4(a)(2)). For suggested format of above documents, see Forms 3000.1-A and JD-ES-38 at the back of this book.

      iii. In all cases, a docketing statement with various information (§ 63-4(a)(3)).

      iv. In all civil cases, a preargument conference statement (§ 63-4(a)(4)).

      v.   In most civil cases, a draft judgment file (§ 63-4(a)(5)).

      vi. In most civil cases when the constitutionality of a state statute is in issue, a notice so stating (§ 63-4(a)(6)).

      vii. Trial court sealing order, if any (§ 63-4(a)(7)).

      viii. If trial judge did not comply with § 64-1(a), file § 64-1(b) notice.

7.   Copies and certification:

      i. Original only for items i-vi. Original and 3 copies for the § 64-1 notice.

      ii. Certification to opposing counsel (give name, address and telephone and fax numbers) is necessary (§ 62-7).

8.   When transcript is received, send completion form to all counsel of record (§ 63-8(d)).

9.   If transcript is delayed past the estimated delivery date, obtain and file amended transcript form. (§ 63-8(b)).

10. If applicable, file motion for articulation or rectification at least 10 days before brief is initially due (§ 66-5).

VI. Transferring Appeal

1. If you think the appeal filed in the Appellate Court ought to be heard by the Supreme Court, so state on Preargu-

ment Conference Form. Ask the judge at the Preargument Conference (if there is one) to recommend transfer. If transfer still does not happen, file a motion for transfer (§ 65-2).

VII. Duty of Appellee

1. If appeal period runs without notice of an appeal, check file in trial court clerk's office to be sure none has been filed.

2. As soon as appeal is filed, it is a good idea, but not mandatory if you had an appearance in the trial court, to file appearance with appellate clerk. If you do not have an appearance in the trial court at the time an appeal is taken, you must file an appearance with the appellate clerk.

3. Check for defects in jurisdictional statement:
    i. Appeal from proper decision (§ V, 2).
    ii. Proper party appealing.

4. If defective or untimely, file motion to dismiss within 10 days (§ 66-8; see XVIII, infra).

5. File cross appeal within 10 days of the appeal as follows:
    i. If trial court did not grant all relief requested;
    ii. When the trial court granted too much relief to the opposing party.
    For suggested format of cross appeal, see Form 3000.1-A.

6. If cross appeal is filed, follow § V except that there is no entry or record fee (§ 61-8).

7. Documents to be filed with Appellate or Supreme Court clerk in Hartford in response to appellant's appeal within 20 days of the appeal:
    i.   (optional) A preliminary statement of the issues if appropriate (see § 63-4(a)(1)).
    ii. (optional) If the appellant orders only a portion of the transcript, the appellee should order any other parts (§ 63-4(a)(2)).
    iii. (optional unless additional information needed) A docketing statement (§ 63-4(a)(3)).
    iv. The appellee does not file a preargument conference statement (§ 63-4(a)(4)).
    v.   (optional) Response to draft judgment file (§ 63-4(a)(5)).

8. If you want an appeal in the Appellate Court transferred to the Supreme Court, file a motion for transfer (§ 65-2).

9. If you think the appellant has filed the appeal in the wrong court, file a motion to transfer (§ 65-4).

10. If applicable, file motion for articulation or rectification at least 10 days before appellant's brief is initially due (§ 66-

5). (If you ask for an extension of time to file brief be sure to ask also for an extension of time to file motion for articulation.)

VIII. Preargument Conference
A settlement conference is normally set up before briefs are due. See § 63-10. Often the clerk extends the brief deadline for the appellee until 45 days after the conference. This also extends the deadline for a motion for articulation or rectification (§ 66-5).

IX. Briefs and Appendix
1. Timetables (§ 67-3).
    i. File transcript completion forms as soon as received (§ 63-8(d)).
    ii. Where a transcript has been ordered, the appellant's brief and appendix are due 45 days after the transcript ordered by the appellant is mailed (or preferably hand-delivered) to him.
    iii. With no transcript or with the transcript received prior to the filing of appeal, the appellant's brief and appendix are due 45 days after the filing of the appeal.
    iv. The appellee's brief is due 30 days after the appellant's brief is filed.
    v. The appellant's optional reply brief is due 20 days after the appellee's brief is filed.
    vi. If there is a cross appeal, the cross appellant's brief must be filed with the appellee's brief and there is no additional time allowed.
    vii. If there is a cross appeal, the cross appellee's brief must be filed with the appellant's reply brief, and 30 rather than 20 days are allowed.
    viii. The cross appellant's optional reply brief is due 20 days after the cross appellee's brief.
2. Copies and Certification (§ 67-1).
    i. Supreme Court: The original and 15 copies of the brief and the appendix must be filed with a certification of service on counsel of record and to any trial judge whose decision is the subject of the appeal. The certification must also indicate that the brief complies with the applicable formatting requirements.
    ii. Appellate Court: The original and 10 copies.
    iii. With certain exceptions, briefs and appendices must now be filed electronically in addition to the paper copies as noted. Note the requirements requiring proof of filing, redacting personal information and the certification requirements.

3. Form (§ 67-2).
    i. Briefs are typewritten or photocopied from a typewritten original. Be sure there are no sharp staple points showing, or the clerk will lend you a hammer and order you to blunt them.
    ii. Briefs must be single sided (§ 67-2).
    iii. Appendices may be double sided (§ 67-2).
    iv. Parts one and two of the appendices should be bound together and bound with the brief, if possible. If either part of an appendix exceeds 150 pages, the parts must be separately bound (§ 67-2).
4. Transcripts
    i. Be sure to file the transcript with your brief (§ 63-8(e)(1), (2)).
    ii. Also file Form JD-CL-62 with number and dates of transcripts (§ 63-8(e)(3)).
5. Designation of Pleadings (Appeals filed before July 1, 2013)
    A revised designation of the specific pleadings must be filed with the brief (§ 63-4(a)(2)).
6. Page Limits (§ 67-3):
    i. Appellant's brief: 35 pages
    ii. Appellee's brief: 35 pages
    iii. Appellant's reply brief: 15 pages
    iv. If cross appeal, combined cross appellant's and appellee's brief: 50 pages
    v. If cross appeal, combined cross appellee's brief and appellant's reply brief: 40 pages
    vi. If cross appeal, cross appellant's reply brief: 15 pages
    The appendix, statement of issues, table of authorities and table of contents, if any, are not included in the page limitations.
    There is a 5-page bonus if a state constitutional issue is briefed, but the party must make a request to the clerk (§ 67-3).

X. Appendix to Briefs
1. Part one of the appendix is required in most cases. Part two is optional in most cases (§ 67-8). The appendix is filed with the brief (§ 67-3).

XI. Record
1. The appellant should review the file of the lower court or tribunal to make sure it is complete (§ 61-10). If something is missing, file a motion for rectification (§ 66-5).

XII. What to Do if You Missed a Deadline
1. If it is anything except the appeal itself, file a motion to file

documents late with the appellate clerk in Hartford (§§ 60-2, 60-3). If possible, file any late documents at the same time.

2. If it is the appeal, and more than 20 days have run from issuance of notice of judgment, do not file a motion under § 66-1, because the trial court cannot grant it, and you only alert your opponent to the defect. Either file the late appeal without a motion and hope for the best (if there is no motion to dismiss in 10 days, you may be safe), or ask the Appellate or Supreme Court for permission to file a late appeal under § 60-2. If you took the former route and a motion to dismiss is filed within 10 days, move in the Appellate or Supreme Court under § 60-2 for permission to appeal late.

XIII. What to Do if You Filed the Wrong Document

1. Ask for permission to file the proper document.
2. Try to convince the Court to treat it as if it were the proper document. State v. Ayala, 222 Conn. 331, 342, 610 A.2d 1162, 1168 (1992) (petition for certification treated as petition under § 52-265a); AirKaman, Inc. v. Groppo, 221 Conn. 751, 755 n.5, 607 A.2d 410, 412 n.5 (1992) (§ 61-8 papers treated as § 63-4(a)(1) papers); Novak v. Levin, 287 Conn. 71, 81, 951 A.2d 514, 519 (2008) (motion for reconsideration treated as motion for permission to file motion for reconsideration).

XIV. Expediting the Appeal

1. Use § 60-3. See commentary.
2. Request an early preargument conference if that may be useful (§ 63-10).
3. Consider asking for argument en banc (§ 70-7).

XV. Stays of Execution and Bail

1. Generally speaking, the appellant in civil cases is automatically entitled to a stay pending appeal (§§ 61-11, 61-13).
2. If there is or will be no automatic stay, file a motion for stay (§ 61-12).
3. If a § 61-11 stay is not effective (as in administrative appeals), move for a stay in the Appellate or Supreme Court (§ 61-12).
4. If an ancillary case ought to be stayed pending the principal appeal, move for a stay in the Appellate or Supreme Court (§ 60-2).
5. If a stay ought to be terminated, so move either before or after judgment (§ 61-11).
6. Move for review within 10 days of the decision (§ 66-6),

which itself generally operates as a stay (§ 61-14). Make sure trial judge explained the decision (§ 64-1).

7. If the trial judge makes an adverse ruling on bail in a criminal case pending appeal, move for review under § 61-14.

8. Concerning injunction and p.j.r. appeals, see commentary to § 61-11.

XVI. After Decision on Merits

1. As to when to file a motion for reconsideration or reconsideration en banc (they can now be combined), see § 71-5 and commentary. A motion for reconsideration generally continues the stay of execution. Motions for reconsideration are usually decided within two weeks. Pay fee of $125.00 to any trial court clerk in the state (C.G.S.A. § 52-259c).

2. As to who taxes costs and what costs can be taxed, see commentary to § 71-3.

3. Within 20 days after decision of Appellate Court, or after denial of motion to reargue (§ 84-4), file petition for certification in Supreme Court (§§ 84-1 to 84-7).

XVII. Petition for Certification to Supreme Court

1. This applies only to appeals from Appellate Court.

2. For grounds, see § 84-2.

3. For form, see § 84-5.

4. Within 20 days of Appellate Court decision or denial of motion for reconsideration:
   a. file 1 copy with trial court and get original endorsed;
   b. pay $75.00 fee with any trial court clerk in the state;
   c. file original and 15 copies of petition with Supreme Court (§ 84-4).

5. Opponent should file opposition statement and, if desired, cross petition within 10 days (§§ 84-4(b), 84-6).

6. If petition is granted, pay $250.00 to trial court within 20 days of issuance of notice of granting (§ 84-9).

XVIII. Petition for Certification to Appellate Court

1. This applies only to zoning or similar appeals from Superior Court.

2. For grounds, see § 81-1.

3. For form, see § 81-2.

4. Within 20 days of the trial court's decision:
   a. file 1 copy with trial court and get original endorsed;
   b. pay $75.00 fee to trial court;
   c. file endorsed original and 15 copies of petition with appellate clerk (§ 81-1).

5. Opponent should file opposition statement (cross petition not mentioned in rules) within 10 days (§ 81-3).
6. If petition is granted, file appeal in usual way within 20 days of issuance of notice of granting (§ 81-4).

XIX. Miscellaneous References to Authors' Commentary

1. Standard of Appellate Review. "Clear error" and "plain error", which are entirely different concepts, are discussed in the commentary to § 60-5.
2. Issue not raised or improperly raised in trial court. The possibility of raising such issues also is discussed in the commentary to § 60-5.
3. Writ of Error. The viability of this relic is discussed in § 72-1. See our Form 3000.24-A.
4. Motion to Dismiss or for Judgment. The usefulness and interrelationship of these motions are considered in the commentary to §§ 85-1 and 66-8.
5. Copies of Motions. Motions addressed to the Appellate or Supreme Court (except for extensions of time) require the original and 15 copies; motions addressed to the trial judge but filed in the Appellate or Supreme Court, such as under §§ 61-11 and 66-5, are filed in quadruplicate.
6. Administrative Appeals. The record is governed by § 68-10. The brief and appendix are governed by § 67-1. Exhibits before the administrative agency are governed by § 68-1.

CHAPTER 60

GENERAL PROVISIONS RELATING TO APPELLATE RULES AND APPELLATE REVIEW

AUTHORS' COMMENTS

The rules in Chapters 60 through 86 generally apply in both the Supreme Court and the Appellate Court. Prior to October 1, 1992, the Appellate Court had some separate rules of its own.

§ 60-1. Rules to Be Liberally Interpreted

The design of these rules being to facilitate business and advance justice, they will be interpreted liberally in any case where it shall be manifest that a strict adherence to them will work surprise or injustice.

Historical Note

Derivation:
    1978 P.B. (1996–97), § 4182
    1978 P.B. (1986–96), § 4187
    1978 P.B., § 3164
    1963 P.B., § 762
    1951 P.B., § 471
    1934 P.B., § 423
    1922 P.B., § 74
    1908 P.B., § 69
    1899 P.B., § 69

Prior to 1963, the first sentence read in part: " * * * they will be interpreted liberally by this court in any case * * * " Prior to 1922, the first sentence read in part: " * * * they may be relaxed or dispensed with by the Court in any case * * * ".

AUTHORS' COMMENTS

This rule has been primarily used to expedite appeals, Buckman v. People Exp., Inc., 205 Conn. 166, 169, 530 A.2d 596, 598 (1987); Miller v. Schaffer, 164 Conn. 8, 9, 320 A.2d 1, 2 (1972); City of Hartford v. Hartford Elec. Light Co., 172 Conn. 71, 372 A.2d 131 (1976). This rule, along with §§ 60-2 and 60-3, should be cited for motions for permission to file a late document, such as a brief, appeal, or transcript statement. For an example of circumstances in which the court permitted a late appeal, see Connecticut Light and Power Co. v. Lighthouse Landings, Inc., 279 Conn. 90, 104–06, 900 A.2d 1242, 1250–52 (2006) (subsequent decision changed significance of earlier decision).

The Appellate Court cited this section and P.B. § 60-2 in Somers v. Chan, 110 Conn.App. 511, 955 A.2d 667 (2008), to vacate a stipulated judgment concerning attorneys fees where a prior judge found the fees to be unreasonable, and in State v. Jimenez-Jaramill, 134 Conn.App. 346, 380–82, 38 A.3d 239, 260-61, cert. denied, 305 Conn. 913, 45 A.3d 100 (2012), to vacate a dismissal of a criminal proceeding in the middle of the defendant's testimony.

The Appellate Court cited this section in allowing a writ of error in a small claims case where the defense pressed a claim at trial exceeding the small claims limit and the magistrate ordered it. Newtown Pool Service, LLC v. Pond, 140 Conn.App. 514, 59 A.3d 378 (2013).

§ 60-2. Supervision of Procedure (Applicable to appeals filed before July 1, 2013)

The supervision and control of the proceedings on appeal shall be in the court having appellate jurisdiction from the time the appeal is filed, or earlier, if appropriate, and, except as otherwise provided in these rules, any motion the purpose of which is to complete or perfect the trial court record for presentation on appeal shall be made to the court in which the appeal is pending. The court may, on its own motion or upon motion of any party, modify or vacate any order made by the trial court, or a judge thereof, in relation to the prosecution of the appeal. It may also, for example, on its own motion or upon motion of any party, (1) order a judge to take any action necessary to complete the trial court record for the proper presentation of the appeal; (2) when it appears that by reason of omission from the prepared record of matters of record in the trial court the questions of law in the case are not properly presented, order the appellant to cause to be photocopied the portions so omitted; (3) order improper matter stricken from the record or from a brief or appendix; (4) order a stay of any proceedings ancillary to a case on appeal; (5) order the addition to the prepared record of parts of the file necessary to present correctly or fully the matters comprehended by Sections 67-4 and 67-5; (6) order that a party for good cause shown may file a late appeal, petition for certification, brief or any other document, unless the court lacks jurisdiction to allow the late filing; (7) order that a hearing be held to determine whether it has jurisdiction over a pending matter; (8) order an appeal to be dismissed unless the appellant complies with specific orders of the trial court, submits to the process of the trial court, or is purged of contempt of the trial court; (9) remand any pending matter to the trial court for the resolution of factual issues where necessary; (10) correct technical or other minor mistakes in a published opinion which do not affect the rescript.

§ 60-2. Supervision of Procedure (Applicable to appeals filed on or after July 1, 2013)

The supervision and control of the proceedings on appeal shall be in the court having appellate jurisdiction from the time the appeal is filed, or earlier, if appropriate, and, except as otherwise provided in these rules, any motion the purpose of which is to complete or perfect the record of the proceedings below for presentation on appeal shall be made to the court in which the appeal is pending. The court may, on its own motion or upon motion of any party, modify or vacate any order made by the trial court, or a judge thereof, in relation to the prosecution of the appeal. It may also, for example, on its own motion or upon motion of any party: (1) order a judge to take any action necessary to complete the trial court record for the proper presentation of the appeal; (2) consider any matter in the record of the proceedings below necessary for the review of the issues presented by any appeal, regardless of whether the matter has been included in the appendix of any party; (3) order improper matter stricken from a brief or appendix; (4) order a stay of any proceedings ancillary to a case on appeal; (5) order that a party for good cause shown may file a late appeal, petition for certification, brief or any other document, unless the court lacks jurisdiction to allow the late filing; (6) order that a hearing be held to determine whether it has jurisdiction over a pending matter; (7) order an appeal to be dismissed unless the appellant complies with specific orders of the trial court, submits to the process of the trial court, or is purged of contempt of the trial court; (8) remand any pending matter to the trial court for the resolution of factual issues where necessary; or (9) correct technical or other minor mistakes in a published opinion which do not affect the rescript.

Historical Note

Derivation:
   1978 P.B. (1986–97), § 4183
   1978 P.B., § 3096
   1963 P.B., §§ 675, 692
   1951 P.B., §§ 402, 435

Effective July 1, 2013, this rule was amended to delete references to the printed record and to make clear that the court may consult anything in the proceedings below.

Effective September 3, 1996, the reference to correcting the record was deleted, (6) was amended to add the reference to the petition, brief or other document and the "unless" clause, and old (8) (sanctions) was deleted.

Section (1) was amended to refer only to the trial court record and (3) was amended to refer explicitly to striking a brief effective October 1, 1986.

Sections (6) through (10) were added effective January 1, 1985, as was the phrase "for example" before (1).

The sections labeled (4) and (5) were added effective July 1, 1978. Also effective July 1, 1978 is the reference in the second line to pre-appeal proceedings.

Sections (2) and (3) were added in 1963. Section 402 of the 1951 Practice

Book refers to § 358 of the 1934 Practice Book, but that refers only to the trial court's refusal or neglect to make a finding.

Cross References

Maltbie, Conn.App.Proc.2d, §§ 269–70 (supervision of procedure); § 271 (perfection of record); § 279 (orders to trial judge); §§ 270, 329 (motions to strike)

AUTHORS' COMMENTS

Novak v. Levin, 287 Conn. 71, 80–81, 951 A.2d 514 (2008), states that this section grants broad authority to the appellate courts over management of their dockets. In *Novack* the Supreme Court permitted the Appellate Court to treat an untimely motion for reconsideration as a motion for permission to file a motion for reconsideration.

a. Pre-appeal motions

The reference to pre-appeal proceedings is important. Even before the rule was so amended, this section had been used to order a judge to decide a motion to set aside a verdict, Tough v. Ives, 159 Conn. 605, 607, 268 A.2d 371, 372 (1970), and to review a decision on a denial of waiver of the costs to take an appeal, State v. Hudson, 154 Conn. 631, 228 A.2d 132 (1967); cf. State v. Casiano, 282 Conn. 614, 922 A.2d 1065 (2007) (review of request for counsel); Valluzzo v. Valluzzo, 103 Conn. 265, 130 A. 126 (1925) (review of ruling concerning counsel fees to take domestic appeal). The court has also reviewed the trial court's denial of an extension of time to file an appeal, Johl v. Town of Groton, 172 Conn. 689, 365 A.2d 631 (1976). The court has said this rule can be invoked to permit the filing of a late appeal where the trial judge lacks that power under § 66-1, State v. Stead, 186 Conn. 222, 227–28, 440 A.2d 299, 301 (1982); DeTeves v. DeTeves, 202 Conn. 292, 299 n.10, 520 A.2d 608, 611 n.10 (1987). State v. Audet, 170 Conn. 337, 343, 365 A.2d 1082, 1086 (1976), holding that the prior Supreme Court rules apply only after an appeal is filed, appears to have overlooked *Tough*, although *Audet* was written before the rule included the "pre-appeal" language. Unfortunately, Simms v. Warden, 229 Conn. 178, 186–89, 640 A.2d 601, 606–07 (1994), casts some doubt in dictum whether an appellate court has any jurisdiction without an appeal being filed. See especially note 13 in *Simms*. But see the 1996 Official Commentary to § 66-6.

b. Section 1

Section 1 can be used to compel the trial judge to file a memorandum of decision; State v. Pressley, 59 Conn.App. 77, 80, 755 A.2d 929, 931 (2000); or to sign the transcript of its oral decision, State v. Jagat, 111 Conn.App. 173, 176–77, 958 A.2d 206, 208 (2008); State v. Fontanez, 37 Conn.App. 205, 207, 655 A.2d 797, 798 (1995); or to take further evidence and order further findings, Johnson v. Sourignamath, 75 Conn.App. 403, 426, 816 A.2d 631, 633–34 (2003); and should be used to compel the trial judge to take whatever action is necessary to indicate the disposition of matters pending in the trial court; Wynn v. Metropolitan Property and Cas. Ins. Co., 30 Conn.App. 803, 809 n.8, 623 A.2d 66, 70 n.4, aff'd, 228 Conn. 436, 635 A.2d 814 (1994); State v. Lawler, 30 Conn.App. 827, 830 n.2, 622 A.2d 1040, 1042 n.2 (1993); or to rule on overlooked claims; Gennarini Const. Co., Inc. v. Messina Painting & Decorating Co., 5 Conn.App. 61, 66, 496 A.2d 539, 542 (1985); or to enter a judgment; American Bank of Connecticut v. Eagle Const. Co., 10 Conn.App. 251, 255–56, 522 A.2d 835, 838 (1987); or to articulate its decision, In re Brian T., 134 Conn.App. 1, 8, 38 A.3d 114, 119 (2012); Clark v. Clark, 127 Conn.App. 148, 153 n.5, 13 A.3d 682, 685 n.5, cert. denied, 301 Conn. 914, 13 A.3d 682 (2011); or to rule on a motion for contempt, see Lambert v. Donahue, 78 Conn.App. 493, 511–12, 827 A.2d 729, 742 (2003) (noting in dictum that this rule and not an appeal is the proper way to challenge the trial court's failure to rule on a motion).

In D'Appollonio v. Griffo-Brandao, 138 Conn.App. 304, 311 n.4, 53 A.3d 1013, 1019 n.4 (2012), the court after oral argument ordered the trial court to clarify whether its references to the "factual situation" were findings of fact.

c. Section 3

The motion to strike, section 3, has been used to attack the propriety of a brief even before the 1986 rule changes; Ravitch v. Stollman Poultry Farms, Inc., 165 Conn. 135, 138 n.2, 328 A.2d 711, 713 n.2 (1973); Yale Literary Magazine v. Yale University, 4 Conn.App. 592, 603 n.4, 496 A.2d 201, 208 n.4 (1985), aff'd, 202 Conn. 672, 522 A.2d 818 (1987); cf. Pierce v. Norton, 82 Conn. 441, 442, 74 A. 686, 687 (1909); of a document that was not properly made a part of the trial court record, Cunningham v. Planning and Zoning Com'n of Town of Plainville, 90 Conn.App. 273, 278–79, 876 A.2d 1257, 1261, cert. denied, 276 Conn. 915, 888 A.2d 83 (2005); of an issue in a brief when that issue was dismissed; Gibson v. Gibson, 34 Conn.App. 139, 640 A.2d 145 (1994); or of a draft finding, State v. Brown, 166 Conn. 203, 204, 353 A.2d 721, 721 (1974); of an unnecessary request for finding; Morici v. Jarvie, 136 Conn. 370, 71 A.2d 556 (1950); of an appendix; St. John v. Commissioner of Transp., 172 Conn. 234, 235–36, 374 A.2d 190, 190–91 (1977); see also O'Hara v. State, 218 Conn. 628, 639 n.8, 590 A.2d 948, 954 n.8 (1991).

The motion to strike should not be used to strike something filed late if a motion to dismiss is in order, Maykut v. Plasko, 170 Conn. 310, 313, 365 A.2d 1114, 1116 (1976); Crozier v. Zaboori, 14 Conn.App. 457, 460, 541 A.2d 531, 533 (1988) (defect in motion excused). On the other hand, in Rice v. Housing Authority of City of Meriden, 129 Conn.App. 614, 20 A.3d 1270 (2011), a motion to strike a late-filed transcript was the proper motion because the Appellate Court still had to consider after striking the transcript whether the issues on appeal could be decided without a transcript. (In fact it could not.)

Perhaps this section could also be used to strike an improper or untimely notice of intention to appeal under § 61-5, where failure to have the notice stricken might leave a dismissed party uncertain whether he could safely close his file while the other parties awaited trial.

d. Section 4

The first reported uses of Section 4 are Madison Hills Ltd. Partnership v. Town of Madison, 38 Conn.App. 168, 659 A.2d 744 (1995), and State v. Garcia, 235 Conn. 671, 675, 669 A.2d 573, 574 (1996). The Supreme Court granted a stay in an administrative appeal under this section in Semerzakis v. Commissioner of Social Services, 274 Conn. 1, 10 n.5, 873 A.2d 911, 916 n.5 (2005). In Sullivan v. McDonald, 281 Conn. 122, 913 A.2d 403 (2007) (en banc), the Supreme Court stayed a trial court order quashing a subpoena to testify before the legislature's Judiciary Committee.

e. Section 5

Section 5 (formerly 6) has been successfully used to file a late writ of error in Francis v. Fonfara, 303 Conn. 292, 295 n.6, 33 A.3d 185, 188 n.6 (2012) (this subsection not cited); and a late appeal in State v. Reid, 277 Conn. 764, 894 A.2d 963 (2006), and Connecticut Light and Power Co. v. Lighthouse Landings, Inc., 279 Conn. 90, 102-06, 900 A.2d 1242, 1249–51 (2006). See also Janulawicz v. Commissioner of Correction, 310 Conn.265, 273–74, 77 A.3d 113, 119 (2013) (last petition for certification will be generously considered). An interesting commentary by Justice Norcott in *Reid* points out that Connecticut is in a very small minority in giving judges discretion to allow late appeals. 277 Conn. at 793, 894 A.2d at 982. A motion under this subsection failed, however, in Alliance

Partners, Inc. v. Voltarc Technologies, Inc., 263 Conn. 204, 820 A.2d 224 (2003) (en banc) (affirming Appellate Court's denial of permission to appeal one day late), and in Perricone v. Perricone, AC 27052 (order entered Feb. 8, 2006), cert. denied, 278 Conn. 913, 899 A.2d 38 (2006). See also dictum in Zamstein v. Marvasti, 240 Conn. 549, 556, 692 A.2d 781, 785 (1997).

It has also been used to file a late petition for certification. Shelby Mut. Ins. Co. v. Ghelfa, 196 Conn. 812, 495 A.2d 280 (1985); Fong v. Planning and Zoning Bd. of Appeals of Town of Greenwich, 212 Conn. 628, 563 A.2d 293 (1989) (November 23, 1988 order).

This section does not authorize the trial court to grant permission to file a late appeal. Gordon v. Gordon, 148 Conn. App. 59, 62 n.5, 84 A.3d 923, 926 n.5 (2014).

f. Unlisted motions

Note that before listing the 9 subsections, the rule says "for example." Thus, citing its supervisory powers, the Appellate Court instructed trial courts not to use a particular jury instruction in future criminal trials, even though the court did not err in the case on appeal. State v. Sitaras, 106 Conn.App. 493, 507–08, 942 A.2d 1071, 1080, cert. denied, 287 Conn. 906, 950 A.2d 1283 (2008).

Supervisory powers also include the power to make appropriate post appeal orders, such as custody pending the new trial ordered by the Appellate Court. O'Neill v. O'Neill, 13 Conn.App. 300, 304, 536 A.2d 978, 980 (1988). It also includes the power to order the trial court to enter judgment if, after remand the trial court refused to do so; Wilson v. Security Ins. Co., 213 Conn. 532, 569 A.2d 40 (1990); and also includes the power to decide an issue in spite of procedural violations if the record is adequate. Monk v. Temple George Associates, LLC, 273 Conn. 108, 122–23, 869 A.2d 179, 189 (2005). The trial court cannot interfere with these supervisory powers. Galland v. Bronson, 16 Conn.App. 54, 57, 546 A.2d 935, 936, cert. denied, 209 Conn. 820, 551 A.2d 755 (1988). Both the Supreme and Appellate Courts have used their supervisory powers to consider an issue not properly raised below; West Hartford Interfaith Coalition, Inc. v. Town Council of Town of West Hartford, 228 Conn. 498, 507, 636 A.2d 1342, 1347 (1994); Harley v. Indian Spring Land Co., 123 Conn.App. 800, 833, 3 A.3d 992, 1014–15 (2010); even where it is also inadequately briefed, Argentinis v. Fortuna, 134 Conn.App. 538, 547, 39 A.3d 1207, 1217 (2012) (reviewing claim by self-represented party); State v. Jimenez-Jaramill, 134 Conn.App. 346, 381-82, 38 A.3d 239, 261, cert. denied, 305 Conn. 913, 45 A.3d 100 (2012). Section 60-5 seems like a more appropriate authority. However, the Appellate Court reviewed an unpreserved claim of judicial bias citing this section, which arguably does fall under the court's supervisory powers. Sapper v. Sapper, 109 Conn.App. 99, 102–03, 951 A.2d 5, 7–8 (2008). See also Senk v. Senk, 115 Conn.App. 510, 515, 973 A.2d 131, 134 (2009) (plain error review of unpreserved judicial bias claim).

The Supreme Court has used its supervisory powers to decide an uncertified issue. State v. James, 261 Conn. 395, 410–11, 802 A.2d 820, 831 (2002). Citing this section, the Supreme Court, in the interests of judicial economy, decided an issue the Appellate Court had not reached where no party objected and the issue was fully briefed. State v. Martinez, 295 Conn. 758, 766 n.3, 991 A.2d 1086 n.3 (2010).

In State v. Webster, 308 Conn. 43, 60 n.13, 60 A.3d 259, 269 n.13 (2013), the court on grounds of judicial economy certified an issue raised in the Appellate Court but not decided there.

The Supreme Court has exercised its supervisory powers to hold that compelling a defendant to appear in court in prison garb was per se reversible error. State v. Rose, 305 Conn. 594, 46 A.3d 146 (2012). The court has also used its supervisory powers to limit jury instructions. State v. Medrano, 308 Conn. 604, 65 A.3d 503 (2013).

This rule demonstrates the wide power the Supreme Court has to supersede contrary trial court rulings, Chanosky v. City Bldg. Supply Co., 152 Conn. 449, 451, 208 A.2d 337, 338–39 (1965) (extensions of time); State v. Reddick, 139 Conn. 398, 94 A.2d 613 (1953) (waiver of expenses). It also can be used to dismiss an appeal for contemptuous conduct by the appellant, Greenwood v. Greenwood, 191 Conn. 309, 464 A.2d 771 (1983); and to decide an issue that should have been decided by the Appellate Court, Matza v. Matza, 226 Conn. 166, 189, 627 A.2d 414, 425 (1993). It cannot, however be used to decide an is-sue that should first be decided by the trial court. National Elevator Industry Pension, Welfare and Educational Funds v. Scrivani, 229 Conn. 817, 644 A.2d 327 (1994). In State v. Sinchak, 17 Conn. L. Rptr. 544, 1996 WL 537908 (Conn. Super. Ct. 1996), Judge Murray held that this section meant that the Supreme Court should rule in the first instance on a motion to unseal exhibits.

This section or § 66-5 can be used to complete the record, such as if the mem-orandum of decision fails to dispose of all issues. J.M. Lynne Co., Inc. v. Geraghty, 204 Conn. 361, 376, 528 A.2d 786, 793 (1987).

Citing this section and P.B. § 60-1, the Appellate Court reviewed a claim the trial court did not address, even though the parties did not seek articulation. McCann Real Equities Series XXII, LLC v. David McDermott Chevrolet, Inc., 93 Conn.App. 486, 521 n.30, 890 A.2d 140, 163 n.30, cert. denied, 277 Conn. 928, 895 A.2d 798 (2006).

The court in Somers v. Chan, 110 Conn.App. 511, 955 A.2d 667 (2008), vacated a stipulated judgment for attorney's fees where a prior court found the fees unreasonable. The court entering the stipulated judgment was unaware of the earlier ruling.

Where the Supreme Court reversed its earlier decision in a criminal case and the defendant had served the maximum sentence on the only remaining count, the court ordered the immediate release of the defendant citing this section. State v. Miranda, 272 Conn. 430, 432, 864 A.2d 1 (2004).

Section 8 (formerly 9) could have been but was not used in Douglas v. Warden, State Prison, 218 Conn. 778, 783–87, 591 A.2d 399, 402–05 (1991). It was used in State v. Douros, 87 Conn.App. 122, 864 A.2d 57 (2005), Campbell v. Commis-sioner of Correction, 121 Conn.App. 576, 581, 997 A.2d 543, 546 (2010), and State v. Ryder, 111 Conn.App. 271, 277, 958 A.2d 797, 800 (2008). In *Ryder* it was used suo motu to determine whether the appeal was moot.

This section may also be used to remove a court-appointed attorney, State v. Brown, 166 Conn. 203, 204, 353 A.2d 721, 721 (1974), and may well be broad enough to remove any attorney.

In City of Hartford v. Hartford Elec. Light Co., 172 Conn. 71, 73–74, 372 A.2d 131, 133 (1976), the court denied a request that all subsequent motions concern-ing the appeal be filed with it.

An appellee may move to stay the appeal until the appellant complies with trial court orders concerning alimony. Heard v. Heard, 116 Conn. 632, 637, 166 A. 67, 69 (1933). A motion to dismiss under this section was denied in Broderick v. Broderick, 20 Conn.App. 145, 146, 565 A.2d 3, 4 (1989).

Motions may be filed in the Supreme Court or Appellate Court in many areas other than those specifically mentioned here:

(i)   motion to dismiss or for judgment, see §§ 66-8, 85-1, 85-2;

(ii)   motion to review an order concerning a stay of execution, see §§ 61-14, 66-6;

(iii)   motion for a stay of execution, see §§ 61-12, 71-7;

(iv)   motion concerning bail, see § 61-13;

(v)   motion for extension of time to file papers, see § 66-1;
(vi)   motion to submit case on briefs only, see § 70-2;
(vii)   motion to reargue, see § 71-5;
(viii)   motion to reconsider costs, see § 71-3;
(ix)   motion for review of rectification of appeal, see §§ 66-5 and 66-6;
(x)   motion of attorney to withdraw appearance, see §§ 62-8 and 62-9; Douglas v. Warden, State Prison, 218 Conn. 778, 783, 591 A.2d 399, 402 (1991);
(xi)   motion to amend § 63-4 papers;
(xii)   motion to vacate improper procedural order of trial court, see State v. Robinson, 10 Conn.App. 520, 525, 523 A.2d 1365, 1367–68, cert. denied, 204 Conn. 807, 528 A.2d 1154 (1987).

As to whether a trial judge may be ordered to perfect the appeal record even if he is no longer a judge, see State v. Palmieri, 143 Conn. 569, 124 A.2d 911 (1956).

In In re Juvenile Appeal, 189 Conn. 66, 81, 454 A.2d 1262, 1270 (1983), the Supreme Court found error and ordered further proceedings within 60 days.

g. Summary Decisions

A motion for summary reversal appears to be an appropriate motion. State v. Rodriguez, 151 Conn. App. 120, 93 A.3d 1186 (2014); Mandillo v. Hawley Sweeping & Co., A.C. 20718 (order entered April 25, 2001); Lynes v. Janazzo Heating & Air Conditioning, A.C. 21568 (order entered September 19, 2001). A motion for summary affirmance would probably be favorably received in a clear case. Huguenin v. Commissioner of Correction, 271 Conn. 806, 807, 861 A.2d 472, 473 (2004). Del Toro v. City of Stamford, 270 Conn. 532, 535 n.3, 853 A.2d 95, 97–98 n.3 (2004); Connecticut Bank of Commerce v. Giordano, A.C. 23927 April/May 2003 Appellate Court docket, p. 7.

§ 60-3. Suspension of the Rules

In the interest of expediting decision, or for other good cause shown, the court in which the appeal is pending may suspend the requirements or provisions of any of these rules in a particular case on motion of a party or on its own motion and may order proceedings in accordance with its direction.

Historical Note

Derivation:
    1978 P.B. (1986–1997), § 4187
    1978 P.B. § 3164 (second paragraph)
    1963 P.B. § 762 (second paragraph)
This section was new in 1969.

Cross References
Statute on Expedited Appeals, § 52-265a

AUTHORS' COMMENTS

In Francis v. Fonfara, 303 Conn. 292, 295 n.6, 33 A.3d 185, 188 n.6 (2012), the Supreme Court cited this section and § 60-2 in permitting the plaintiff to file a late writ of error. See also Janulawicz v. Commissioner of Correction, 310 Conn. 265, 273–74, 77 A.3d 113, 119 (2012) (standard for late petition for certification). In Novak v. Levin, 287 Conn. 71, 80–81, 951 A.2d 514, 519 (2008), the Supreme Court allowed the Appellate Court to treat an untimely motion for reconsideration as a motion for permission to file a motion for reconsideration.

When all else fails this section should not be overlooked. For example, when the appeal has been filed one day late and a motion to dismiss is timely filed, relief might be considered under this rule if there is good cause, although § 60-2 may serve as well, State v. Stead, 186 Conn. 222, 227–28, 440 A.2d 299, 301–02 (1982). A late appeal was allowed in *United Food & Commercial Workers Local 919 v. Record Journal Publishing Co.* (Appellate Court order entered January 4, 1995). However, this section cannot be used to create jurisdiction in the Supreme Court where it does not otherwise exist. State v. Ellis, 224 Conn. 711, 720–21, 621 A.2d 250, 253–54 (1993) (motion for review of Appellate Court order dismissed where case on the merits is still in the Appellate Court).

The Supreme Court is more likely to show lenity concerning a litigant's failure to follow proper procedure when new rules have just been adopted, State v. Kreske, 130 Conn. 558, 560 n.1, 36 A.2d 389, 391 n.1 (1944). The court may also follow the trial court's and counsel's handling of the record even if there are defects in the record, State v. Van Keegan, 132 Conn. 33, 35, 42 A.2d 352, 353 (1945).

While C.G.S.A. § 52-265a was passed to permit appeals to be expedited, the constitutionality of it was questioned in State ex rel. Kelman v. Schaffer, 161 Conn. 522, 529–31, 290 A.2d 327, 331–32 (1971). However, the statute, unlike this rule, also gives a party a substantive right to appeal a non-final judgment in rare situations. See Laurel Park, Inc. v. Pac, 194 Conn. 677, 678–79 n.1, 485 A.2d 1272, 1273 n.1 (1984).

This section was used to imply an extension of time when the rules did not explicitly allow one, Morici v. Jarvie, 136 Conn. 370, 372, 71 A.2d 556, 557 (1950). It was also used when the issue was briefed in spite of the procedural problems. Monk v. Temple George Associates, LLC, 273 Conn. 108, 122–23, 869 A.2d 179, 189 (2005). It was not permitted to request the Appellate Court to articulate its decision; Nicoll v. State, 38 Conn.App. 333, 661 A.2d 101 (1995) (no further proceedings); although the court did so anyway.

Compare Fed.R.App.P. 2.

§ 60-4. Definitions (Applicable to appeals filed before July 1, 2013)

"Appellant" shall mean the party, or parties if an appeal is jointly filed, taking the appeal. "Appellee" shall mean all other parties in the trial court at the time of judgment, unless after judgment the matter was withdrawn as to them or unless a motion for permission not to participate in the appeal has been granted by the court.

"Counsel of record" shall also include all parties appearing pro se, and "court reporter" shall refer to all court reporters and court reporting monitors.

"Administrative appeal" shall mean an appeal from a judgment of the superior court concerning the appeal to that court from a decision of any officer, board, commission or agency of the state or of any political subdivision of the state.

"Motion" should be read to include applications and petitions other than petitions for certification.

"Petition" does not include petitions for certification unless the context clearly requires.

§ 60-4. Definitions (Applicable to appeals filed on or after July 1, 2013)

"Appellant" shall mean the party, or parties if an appeal is jointly filed, taking the appeal. "Appellee" shall mean all other parties in the trial court at the time of judgment, unless after judgment the matter was withdrawn as to them or unless a motion for permission not to participate in the appeal has been granted by the court. "Counsel of record" shall also include all self-represented parties. "Court reporter" shall refer to all court reporters and court reporting monitors. "Administrative appeal" shall mean an appeal from a judgment of the superior court concerning the appeal to that court from a decision of any officer, board, commission or agency of the state or of any political subdivision of the state.

"Motion" shall include applications and petitions other than petitions for certification. "Issues" shall include claims of error, certified questions and questions reserved.

"Petition" does not include petitions for certification unless the context clearly requires.

"Record" shall include the case file, any decisions, documents, transcripts, recordings and exhibits from the proceedings below, and, in appeals from administrative agencies, the record returned to the trial court by the administrative agency.

Historical Note

Derivation: 1978 P.B. (1996–97), § 4001A

This rule was amended effective January 1, 2013 to define "issues" and "record" and to clarify that the latter refers to the proceedings below.

The definitions of motion and petition are new effective September 3, 1996.

AUTHORS' COMMENTS

In Wesley v. Schaller Subaru, Inc., 277 Conn. 526, 529 n.1, 893 A.2d 389, 392 n.1 (2006), the court, citing the second sentence of the first paragraph, held that a winning party in the trial court as to whom the appellant is not appealing has the right to file a brief in support of the appellant.

§ 60-5. Review by the Court; Plain Error; Preservation of Claims

The court may reverse or modify the decision of the trial court if it determines that the factual findings are clearly erroneous in view of the evidence and pleadings in the whole record, or that the decision is otherwise erroneous in law.

The court shall not be bound to consider a claim unless it was distinctly raised at the trial or arose subsequent to the trial. The court may in the interests of justice notice plain error not brought to the attention of the trial court.

In jury trials, where there is a motion, argument, or offer of proof or evidence in the absence of the jury, whether during trial or before, pertaining to an issue that later arises in the presence of the jury, and counsel has fully complied with the requirements for preserving any objection or exception to the judge's adverse ruling thereon in the absence of the jury, the matter shall be deemed to be distinctly raised at the trial for purposes of this rule without a further objection or exception provided that the grounds for such objection or exception, and the ruling thereon as previously articulated, remain the same.

If the court deems it necessary to the proper disposition of the cause, it may remand the case for a further articulation of the basis of the trial court's factual findings or decision.

It is the responsibility of the appellant to provide an adequate record for review as provided in Section 61-10.

Historical Note

Derivation (first, fourth and fifth paragraphs):
    1978 P.B. (1986–97), § 4061
    1978 P.B., § 3060D

This rule was clarified effective October 1, 1986 to indicate that the clear error rule applies to factual findings. See Metropolitan Dist. v. Housing Authority of City of Hartford, 12 Conn.App. 499, 501, 531 A.2d 194, 200, cert. denied, 205 Conn. 814, 533 A.2d 568 (1987).

The last sentence was added effective January 1, 1985. Entirely new rule effective July 1, 1979. Contrast prior §§ 3034 and 3039, which provided for narrower review.

Derivation (second and third paragraphs):
    1978 P.B. (1996–97), § 4061
    1978 P.B. (1986–96), § 4185
    1978 P.B., § 3063
    1963 P.B., § 652
    1951 P.B., § 409
    1934 P.B., § 363
    1930 Rules Change, § 15

The second and third paragraphs were moved here from § 4185 effective September 3, 1996.

The third paragraph was added effective October 1, 1986.

Major changes were made effective July 1, 1979. The prior rule was as follows:

"The supreme court shall not be bound to consider any errors on an appeal unless they are specifically assigned or claimed and unless it appears on the record that the question was distinctly raised at the trial and was ruled upon and decided by the court adversely to the appellant's claim, or that it arose subsequent to the trial."

This prior rule was substantially unchanged since 1930. Although there is no specific rule in the 1922, 1908 and 1899 Practice Books, this was the practice previously. See, e.g., 1890 rules in 58 Conn. 561, 584, §§ 1, 2; 1870 Rules, 37 Conn. 619, § III. A vaguer rule adopted in 1826, 6 Conn. 327, was also so construed in Flint v. Clark, 13 Conn. 361, 367, 1839 WL 140 (1839). The constitutionality of § 652 is discussed in State v. Evans, 165 Conn. 61, 66–70, 327 A.2d 576, 579–82 (1973), and State v. Simms, 170 Conn. 206, 211–12, 365 A.2d 821, 824 (1976).

Cross References

Maltbie, Conn.App.Proc.2d, §§ 304–308

AUTHORS' COMMENTS

Both the clearly erroneous and plain error provisions were adopted in 1978 and derive from the Fed. R. Civ. P. 52 (clear error) and 51 (plain error). Clear error and plain error are entirely different concepts. Clear error concerns the standard of review given on appeal to findings of fact made by trial judges; plain error concerns whether the court should reverse on an issue that was not raised or not raised properly in the trial court. Do not say "clear" when you mean "plain" or "plain" when you mean "clear," and do not use either word informally. They are technical words in appellate law and you will confuse appellate judges as to what you are claiming if you misuse them.

A. Clearly Erroneous Test

1. Background

Before 1979, a finding of fact by the trial court could be reviewed on appeal only if it fit into one of three rather narrow categories: (1) it was without evidence; (2) it was in language of doubtful meaning; or (3) an omitted fact was admitted or undisputed. So if there was evidence, the finding was sustained even when it was against the weight of the evidence, Plastic & Metal Fabricators, Inc. v. Roy, 163 Conn. 257, 268, 303 A.2d 725, 730–31 (1972); King v. Travelers Ins. Co., 123 Conn. 1, 3, 192 A. 311, 312 (1937).

A discussion of the Supreme Court's constitutional power to correct trial court findings is found in Horton, "The Connecticut Supreme Court—On Becoming Supreme Again", 52 Conn.B.J. 45, 46–52 (1978). See also Styles v. Tyler, 64 Conn. 432, 30 A. 165 (1894), stating the rule followed in the nineteenth century that questions of fact could not be reviewed at all on appeal. The old rule made some sense in the nineteenth century when there were no transcripts; see Papallo v. Meriden Sav. Bank, 128 Conn. 289, 290–91, 22 A.2d 637, 638 (1941); Lynahan v. Church, 82 Conn. 132, 72 A. 726 (1909); Mattatuck Motors, Inc. v. Barbieri, 8 Conn.Supp. 75, 79, 1940 WL 663 (C.P. 1940); but it makes little sense today, except perhaps in those situations where a transcript is unavailable or inadequate, such as in the demeanor of a witness or in an observation of the premises; Dadio v. Dadio, 123 Conn. 88, 92–93, 192 A. 557, 559 (1937); or in an observation in the courtroom, such as the plaintiff's scar, Goldberg v. Mertz, 122 Conn. 308, 309, 194 A. 721, 723 (1937).

While the rule is unclear (unlike § 64-1, which by its terms applies only to bench trials), the authors' opinion is that the clearly erroneous test applies only to hearings to the court. Rule 52 of the federal civil rules, from which this language derives, applies only to court trials.

2. Test since 1979

The best definition of "clearly erroneous" is found in Stutz v. Shepard, 279 Conn. 115, 124–26, 901 A.2d 33, 39–40 (2006). "A finding is 'clearly erroneous' when there is no evidence in the record to support it or when, although there is evidence to support it, the reviewing court on the entire evidence is left with the definite and firm conviction that a mistake has been committed." Many cases state the test in this fashion.

The Supreme Court attempted to explain the difference between clear error and abuse of discretion in TES Franchising, LLC v. Feldman, 286 Conn. 132, 138 n.6, 943 A.2d 406, 412 n.6 (2008). The authors discuss this distinction, as well as the distinction between law and fact, in detail in their comments to § 67-4 concerning the standard of review statement required in appellate briefs. The important point here is while the "clearly erroneous" test provides for a broader review of trial court factual determinations then the pre-1979 rules, it is still a difficult test to meet. However, the court in administrative appeals has construed the "clearly erroneous" rule to be broader than the "substantial evidence test." New England Cable Television Ass'n, Inc. v. Department of Public Utility Control, 247 Conn. 95, 118, 717 A.2d 1276, 1289 (1998); Briggs v. State Employees Retirement Com'n, 210 Conn. 214, 217, 554 A.2d 292, 294 (1989); see also Brunswick v. Statewide Grievance Committee, 103 Conn.App. 601, 931 A.2d 319, cert. denied, 284 Conn. 929, 934 A.2d 244 (2007).

Because the clearly erroneous test requires a review of all the evidence, the appellant should make sure there is a reporter for all proceedings and order all conceivably relevant transcripts. Stutz v. Shepard, 279 Conn. 115, 124–26, 901 A.2d 33, 39–40 (2006).

The Supreme Court and Appellate Court have applied the clearly erroneous test in countless cases, usually to hold that there wasn't any. Clear error was found in the following cases: O'Connor v. Larocque, 302 Conn. 562, 597–98, 31 A.3d 1, 23–24 (2011) (insufficient evidence of intent to claim exclusive possession in tenancy); Naples v. Keystone Bldg. and Development Corp., 295 Conn. 214, 225–26, 990 A.2d 326, 335–36 (2010) (finding on damages clearly erroneous); Fleming v. City of Bridgeport, 284 Conn. 502, 513–14, 935 A.2d 126 (2007) (finding that plaintiff is not in possession clearly erroneous, as conceded by defendant at oral argument); Smith v. Muellner, 283 Conn. 510, 516–26, 932 A.2d 382, 388–94 (2007) (finding that right-of-way was extinguished clearly erroneous); Wesley v. Schaller Subaru, Inc., 277 Conn. 526, 893 A.2d 389, 392 (2006) (finding of agency relationship clearly erroneous); Echavarria v. National Grange Mut. Ins. Co., 275 Conn. 408, 419, 880 A.2d 882, 889 (2005) (finding of actual notice clearly erroneous); Miller v. Town of Westport, 268 Conn. 207, 219 n.20, 842 A.2d 558, 565–66 n.20 (2004) (seller of lot a different person); Bernstein v. Nemeyer, 213 Conn. 665, 570 A.2d 164 (1990) (testimony of several witnesses improperly not credited); Kuras v. Kope, 205 Conn. 332, 533 A.2d 1202 (1987) (numerous clearly erroneous factual findings); Noble v. White, 66 Conn.App. 54, 60, 783 A.2d 1145, 1150 (2001) (whether the defendant received a document); Murphy v. Buonato, 42 Conn.App. 239, 246, 679 A.2d 411, 416 (1996), aff'd, 241 Conn. 319, 696 A.2d 320 (1997) (evidence required finding that defendant was keeper of dog); Kubeck v. Foremost Foods Co., Inc., 190 Conn. 667, 672 n.4, 461 A.2d 1380, 1383 n.4 (1983) (no evidence to support inference); Reynolds v. Soffer, 190 Conn. 184, 189, 459 A.2d 1027, 1030 (1983) (authenticity of deeds contradicts finding of no evidence of adverse possession); Jackson v. Jackson, 2 Conn.App. 179, 478 A.2d 1026, cert. denied, 194 Conn. 805, 482 A.2d 710 (1984) (trial court's findings unreasonable); Oakland Heights Mobile Park, Inc. v. Simon, 36 Conn.App. 432, 437–40, 651 A.2d 281, 284 (1994) (failure to find arrearage clear error); Weisman v. Kaspar, 233 Conn. 531, 540–47, 661 A.2d 530, 534–37 (1995) (knowledge of fraudulent representations).

3. Negative Findings

Disbelief of the testimony of a witness generally does not justify the trier in finding the contrary, Paige v. Saint Andrew's Roman Catholic Church Corp., 250 Conn. 14, 29, 734 A.2d 85, 93 (1999); State v. Hart, 221 Conn. 595, 605, 605 A.2d 1366, 1371 (1992); State v. Mayell, 163 Conn. 419, 427, 311 A.2d 60, 64 (1972) (criminal appeal); Bisogno v. Connecticut State Bd. of Labor Relations, 149 Conn. 4, 7, 174 A.2d 797, 799 (1961) (administrative appeal); Dzenutis v. Dzenutis, 200 Conn. 290, 303, 512 A.2d 130, 137 (1986) (civil appeals); unless there is some basis for the court to make an "affirmative finding of a negative," Badela v. Karpowich, 152 Conn. 360, 361, 206 A.2d 838, 839 (1965). But see Hotkowski v. Hotkowski, 165 Conn. 167, 172, 328 A.2d 674, 677 (1973), where the trial court did not believe that a party had only a certain asset. The Supreme Court in *Hotkowski* implicitly permitted the trial court to find to the contrary without evidence. And in Gilpatric v. National Sur. Co., 95 Conn. 10, 17, 110 A. 545, 547 (1920), the court commented favorably on the evidential quality of negative facts (what one fails to do). But see Kiessling v. Kiessling, 134 Conn. 564,

566, 59 A.2d 532, 533 (1948). In Brodsky v. Brodsky, 153 Conn. 299, 301–02, 216 A.2d 180, 181 (1966), a finding based on ambiguous testimony was stricken. See also Schmidt v. Schmidt, 180 Conn. 184, 429 A.2d 470 (1980).

4. Duty of Appellee

An appellant claiming that the factual basis of the memorandum of decision is without evidence must file whatever evidence exists in the case, such as transcript, for the Supreme Court to consider the issue, Perrotti v. Massa, 183 Conn. 16, 438 A.2d 806 (1981); see Calo-Turner v. Turner, 83 Conn.App. 53, 56, 847 A.2d 1085, 1086–1087 (2004) (declining to review trial court's findings as to fault in a dissolution case where the appellant did not provide all the trial transcripts). If the appellant does that, the appellee's brief should refer to all the evidence supporting the memorandum of decision, or risk reversal). See Connecticut Emp. Union Independent, Inc. v. Connecticut State Emp. Ass'n, Inc., 183 Conn. 235, 439 A.2d 321, 329 (1981); Duksa v. City of Middletown, 192 Conn. 191, 196 n.4, 205–06, 472 A.2d 1, 3 (1984). Compare Neal v. Shiels, Inc., 166 Conn. 3, 7 n.1, 347 A.2d 102, 105 n.1 (1974), decided under the old rules. In certain types of cases, such as dissolutions and motions at short calendar, affidavits or representations of counsel may possibly be used to substantiate the trial court's decision. Compare Fitzgerald v. Fitzgerald, 169 Conn. 147, 149 n.1, 205–06 362 A.2d 889, 891 n.1 (1975), also decided under the old rules. In general, however, oral statements of counsel are not considered evidence, Cologne v. Westfarms Associates, 197 Conn. 141, 154, 496 A.2d 476, 484 (1985); nor are unsupported statements of fact in a brief, Reynolds v. Soffer, 183 Conn. 67, 438 A.2d 1163 (1981).

If there is no evidence to support a vital fact found by the trial judge, there is varying authority on the proper result: in Thomas F. Rogers, Inc. v. Hochberg, 143 Conn. 22, 25, 118 A.2d 910, 911 (1955), a new trial was ordered; but in Scinto v. Derman, 33 Conn.Supp. 754, 370 A.2d 1093 (App. Sess. 1976), judgment was directed by a 2-1 vote. Where there is no evidence to support a finding, proving clear error is easy. Where there is some evidence to support a finding, proving clear error is difficult. However, one example is that even if there is some evidence to support the trial court, an appellant sometimes can attack a finding of fact if the evidence has "insufficient probative value." Marshall v. Kleinman, 186 Conn. 67, 72, 438 A.2d 1199, 1202 (1982); Cochran v. McLaughlin, 128 Conn. 638, 646, 24 A.2d 836, 839 (1942). Formal logic will sometimes bridge the evidentiary gap, Gra Rock Spring Co. v. Central New England Ry. Co., 93 Conn. 77, 80, 105 A. 350, 351 (1918).

5. Failure to Contradict Testimony

A failure to contradict testimony did not make it undisputed under the pre-1979 rules. Under the new rule, this will often still be the case, Guaranty Bank and Trust Co. v. Dowling, 4 Conn.App. 376, 384, 494 A.2d 1216, 1219, cert. denied, 197 Conn. 808, 499 A.2d 58 (1985), although the trial judge may be under some obligation to explain satisfactorily why critical and uncontradicted testimony was not accepted, or risk having the decision held clearly erroneous, as occasionally happens. Blaker v. Planning and Zoning Com'n of Town of Fairfield, 219 Conn. 139, 149, 592 A.2d 155, 159–60 (1991); Riccio v. Waterbury Foundry Co., 118 Conn. 468, 470–71, 173 A. 106, 106–07 (1934). In Norton v. American Bank & Trust Co., 5 Conn.Supp. 226, 228–29, 1937 WL 1310 (1937), Judge O'Sullivan discussed at some length examples of evidence that might be held undisputed even though it was not explicitly admitted. Thus, if a fact is of such a nature that contradictory evidence would certainly be offered if it was available, it might be deemed undisputed if not contradicted.

Also, the manner in which one side presents the case might implicitly indicate that a fact is not controverted. This is what the court concluded in State v.

Winfrey, 302 Conn. 195, 204 n.6, 207–08, 24 A.3d 1218, 1225 n.6, 1226–27 (2011). If the memorandum of decision is silent on key uncontradicted testimony, the Supreme Court has the power under the second paragraph of the rule to remand for a supplemental memorandum. Be sure to urge the court to use this rule in appropriate cases to show whether the trial judge overlooked a fact or deliberately did not find it, Gutowski v. City of New Britain, 165 Conn. 50, 56–57, 327 A.2d 552, 556 (1973). That a lawyer makes a representation in court and opposing counsel is silent does not convert the representation into a stipulation. Irizarry v. Irizarry, 90 Conn.App. 340, 345 n.2, 876 A.2d 593, 596 n.2 (2005).

The appellant should bolster any claim that the judge's failure to credit evidence in the appellant's favor was clearly erroneous by any available means. Cases under both the pre-1978 and post-1978 rules show such success in the following areas:

1. helpful statement in opponent's brief, State v. Townsend, 167 Conn. 539, 561 n.6, 356 A.2d 125, 138 n.6 (1975); Basta v. U. S. Fidelity & Guar. Co., 107 Conn. 446, 448, 140 A. 816, 817 (1928); Krawiec v. Kraft, 163 Conn. 445, 451–52, 311 A.2d 82, 85–86 (1972); but see Windham Community Memorial Hospital v. City of Willimantic, 166 Conn. 113, 115, 348 A.2d 651, 653 (1974);

2. opponent's financial affidavit, Sanchione v. Sanchione, 173 Conn. 397, 401, 378 A.2d 522, 525 (1977);

3. recital in deed, Corsino v. Grover, 148 Conn. 299, 307, 170 A.2d 267, 270–71 (1961); Schwager v. Buzanosky, 101 Conn. 186, 189–90, 125 A. 373, 374 (1924);

4. recitation of procedures followed by an administrative agency in conducting a hearing, Town of Waterford v. Connecticut State Bd. of Ed., 148 Conn. 238, 247, 169 A.2d 891, 896 (1961);

5. physical evidence, State v. Hammond, 221 Conn. 264, 267–70, 604 A.2d 793, 795–96 (1992); Cappiello v. Haselman, 154 Conn. 490, 492, 227 A.2d 79, 80 (1967); Mlynar v. A. H. Merriman & Sons, 114 Conn. 647, 650, 159 A. 658, 659 (1932); Budaj v. Connecticut Co., 108 Conn. 474, 476, 143 A. 527, 528 (1928); Essam v. New York, N. H. & H. R. Co., 140 Conn. 319, 99 A.2d 138 (1953); Wadlund v. City of Hartford, 139 Conn. 169, 91 A.2d 10 (1952); Hamel v. Chase Cos., 112 Conn. 286, 289–90, 152 A. 59, 60 (1930); cf. State v. Avcollie, 178 Conn. 450, 452, 423 A.2d 118, 120 (1979);

6. exhibits or other documentary evidence, State Nat. Bank of Connecticut v. Dick, 164 Conn. 523, 525–26, 325 A.2d 235, 237 (1973); such as a picture, Middlesex Theatre v. Commissioner of State Police, 128 Conn. 20, 24, 20 A.2d 412, 414 (1941); or an unimpeached medical record or death certificate, Russo v. Metropolitan Life Ins. Co., 125 Conn. 132, 135–36, 3 A.2d 844, 846 (1939); but see Greenwich Contracting Co. v. Bonwit Const. Co., 156 Conn. 123, 129, 239 A.2d 519, 522 (1968);

7. acceptance by the trial judge of other closely related testimony of the same witness, Fidelity & Cas. Co. of New York v. Constitution Nat. Bank, 167 Conn. 478, 488–89, 356 A.2d 117, 123 (1975); State v. Skinner, 132 Conn. 163, 167, 43 A.2d 76, 78 (1945); Sanford v. Dimes, 3 Conn.App. 639, 642, 491 A.2d 398, 400 (1985);

8. inability to find another reasonable explanation of an opponent's evasive response, Gelinas v. Nelson, 165 Conn. 33, 35–38, 327 A.2d 565, 566–68 (1973);

9. corroboration from witnesses on both sides, Pappaceno v. Picknelly, 135 Conn. 660, 663, 68 A.2d 117, 118 (1949) (jury case); or by a clearly impartial witness, German v. German, 125 Conn. 84, 90, 3 A.2d 849, 851 (1938); or oc-

casionally even by the uncontradicted testimony of several witnesses, Skladzien v. W. M. Sutherland Bldg. & Const. Co., 101 Conn. 340, 125 A. 614 (1924); Dupuis v. Dupuis, 100 Conn. 96, 99–100, 122 A. 904, 905 (1923); see also Russo v. Seleit, 98 Conn. 398, 412, 119 A. 569, 573 (1922);

10.   indications that the trial judge inadvertently overlooked rather than deliberately did not find a fact, Fidelity & Cas. Co. of New York v. Constitution Nat. Bank, 167 Conn. 478, 488–89, 356 A.2d 117, 123 (1975); Gutowski v. City of New Britain, 165 Conn. 50, 56–57, 327 A.2d 552, 556 (1973) (*Fidelity* was considered a "rare occasion" in Steinman v. Maier, 179 Conn. 574, 576, 427 A.2d 828, 830 (1980)); and Swenson v. Dittner, 183 Conn. 289, 439 A.2d 334 (1981);

11.   sheriff's return in another case, Jenkins v. Bishop Apartments, Inc., 144 Conn. 389, 390, 132 A.2d 573, 574 (1957);

12.   proof that evidence to the contrary was presented in bad faith, Driscoll v. Jewell Belting Co., 96 Conn. 295, 300, 114 A. 109, 110 (1921) (the language is dictum, and how bad faith is to be conclusively proved is not clear);

13.   the inference claimed by the appellant is the only one that is consistent with other facts found, Ford Bros. v. Frederick M. Ward Co., 107 Conn. 425, 430, 140 A. 754, 755 (1928); cf. Grayson v. Grayson, 4 Conn.App. 275, 292, 494 A.2d 576, 585 (1985);

14.   oral admissions of opposing counsel, Abbott v. Lee, 86 Conn. 392, 401, 85 A. 526, 529 (1912); cf. State v. McNellis, 15 Conn.App. 416, 441, 546 A.2d 292, 304, cert. denied, 209 Conn. 809, 548 A.2d 441 (1988);

15.   arbitrary disregard of an expert's testimony, Builders Service Corp., Inc. v. Planning & Zoning Com'n of Town of East Hampton, 208 Conn. 267, 294, 545 A.2d 530, 544 (1988). This case was narrowly read in State v. Holloway, 22 Conn.App. 265, 276–81, 577 A.2d 1064, 1070–72, cert. denied, 215 Conn. 819, 576 A.2d 547 (1990);

16.   failure of opposing counsel to contest representations of fact in a motion, Ramos v. Commissioner of Correction, 248 Conn. 52, 62, 727 A.2d 213, 217–18 (1999);

17.   finding in language of doubtful meaning, New Haven Sav. Bank v. Valley Investors, 174 Conn. 77, 81, 384 A.2d 321, 323 (1977), or to findings in a distorted order, Walsh v. Turlick, 164 Conn. 75, 77, 316 A.2d 759, 761 (1972). Just because something is not explicit does not mean it is doubtful. See Czarnecki v. Plastics Liquidating Co., Inc., 179 Conn. 261, 267 n.6, 425 A.2d 1289, 1292 n.6 (1979). However, a judge's finding is "justifiably criticized" if it states a fact in an ambiguous fashion, such as by saying that "the plaintiff relied on 'some or all' of these representations." Taylor v. Lounsbury-Soule Co., 106 Conn. 41, 48, 137 A. 159, 162 (1927);

18.   Finding based on a misreading of a statute. St. Joseph's Living Center, Inc. v. Town of Windham, 290 Conn. 695, 728–29, 966 A.2d 188, 211 (2009).

Nevertheless, the above areas are still the exception. The rule is that the trial judge can reject uncontradicted testimony, State v. Watson, 165 Conn. 577, 589 n.1, 345 A.2d 532, 539 n.1 (1973); even of two experts, Colonial Finance Co. v. Brodsky, 140 Conn. 391, 394–95, 100 A.2d 568, 569–70 (1953); and the existence of a document does not necessarily make its contents indisputable physical facts, Greenwich Contracting Co. v. Bonwit Const. Co., 156 Conn. 123, 129, 239 A.2d 519, 522 (1968). See also Goldblatt v. Ferrigno, 138 Conn. 39, 41, 82 A.2d 152, 154 (1951).

A very long delay before ruling may weaken the presumption of correctness that a decision might otherwise have. Lewis v. Healey, 73 Conn. 136, 139, 46 A. 869, 870 (1900).

6. Admissions

In general a trial court finding contrary to an uncontradicted admission of a party is clearly erroneous. Alcorn v. Fellows, 102 Conn. 22, 27, 127 A. 911, 913 (1925). There are certain exceptions the authors have uncovered. The trial court can reject an admission if the evidence shows the party is confused and her knowledge of English is limited. Kanopka v. Kanopka, 113 Conn. 30, 39, 154 A. 144, 147 (1931). The trial judge can reject the literal admission that a party makes if the judge concludes that something less damaging was meant, Kapilonuz v. Sundman, 123 Conn. 214, 216, 193 A. 749, 750 (1937). ("I was blinded by the lights" really meant "my vision was momentarily interfered with"). It can also reject an admission if it is merely an opinion and there is contrary evidence from other witnesses, or if there appears to be collusion. King v. Spencer, 115 Conn. 201, 161 A. 103 (1932). Likewise the appeals court can overlook the literal (and unsupported) meaning of what the trial judge said and interpret it in accordance with "the gist of the [trial] court's conclusion"; Vaiuso v. Vaiuso, 2 Conn.App. 141, 150, 477 A.2d 678, 684, cert. denied, 194 Conn. 807, 482 A.2d 712 (1984). Also, the mere fact that a witness for a party testifies to a certain fact does not make that fact binding on that party; Weiner v. E. M. Loew's Enterprises, 120 Conn. 581, 584, 181 A. 921, 922 (1935); except possibly when that witness's testimony was not controverted; McCue v. McCue, 100 Conn. 448, 453, 123 A. 914, 916 (1924). Even a stipulation of facts may not be binding on the trial court in certain circumstances, Northeastern Pharmaceutical and Chemical Co., Inc. v. Heffernan, 179 Conn. 363, 368, 426 A.2d 769, 772 (1979). In an extreme case, the appellee not only did not contest the draft finding but even admitted it in testimony. The trial court said he was obviously mistaken and refused to find it. This action was upheld in Humphrys v. Beach, 149 Conn. 14, 20, 175 A.2d 363, 366 (1961).

7. Evidence Not on Record

In general a finding is erroneous if it is based on evidence not on the record. State v. Cuvelier, 175 Conn. 100, 106, 394 A.2d 185, 188 (1978); Castellani v. Criscuolo, 39 Conn.Supp. 485, 487, 466 A.2d 812, 813 (Super. Ct. Appellate Sess. 1983). Matters not on the record will be disregarded. State v. Sinclair, 197 Conn. 574, 586 n.14, 500 A.2d 539, 546 n.14 (1985).

There are certain exceptions to this rule. If a finding is based on a view of the premises, the court should state what it saw. Cartenovitz v. Conti, 92 Conn. 546, 548–49, 103 A. 629, 630 (1918). Obviously such a finding would be virtually impossible to attack. Lupinacci v. Planning and Zoning Commission of Town of Darien, 153 Conn. 694, 700, 220 A.2d 274, 276–77 (1966). The rule is the same when demonstrations are performed in court, unless the demonstration is adequately described in the record. Mongillo v. New England Banana Co., 115 Conn. 112, 114, 160 A. 433, 434 (1932). However a trial court should not abuse this rule by making findings based on an inspection of premises that only an expert could make. G. F. Heublein, Inc. v. Second Nat. Bank, 115 Conn. 168, 175–76, 160 A. 898, 900 (1932). The court might also find that the jurors assented to a verdict nonverbally. State v. Mosca, 90 Conn. 381, 384–85, 97 A. 340, 342 (1916).

8. Heightened Standard of Proof

Where a litigant has a heightened standard of proof, such as clear and convincing evidence, a finding pursuant to that standard may be more susceptible to clear error. Spector v. Konover, 57 Conn.App. 121, 127, 747 A.2d 39, 43, cert. denied, 254 Conn. 913, 759 A.2d 507 (2000).

9. Testimony

It serves little purpose for a court to find that a witness testified to something. The issue is whether the court believed it, Meshberg v. Bridgeport City Trust Co., 180 Conn. 274, 277 n.4, 429 A.2d 865, 867 n.4 (1980); Scott v. Scott, 190 Conn. 784, 788 n.5, 462 A.2d 1054, 1056 n.5 (1983). See State v. Kendrick, 132

Conn.App. 473, 479 n.5, 31 A.3d 1189, 1193 n.5 (2011), cert. granted, 303 Conn. 925, 35 A.3d 1076 (2012) (recitation of witness testimony should not be construed as factual findings). However, in one case, it was evident that the court credited certain testimony even though the finding was not explicit, Velsmid v. Nelson, 175 Conn. 221, 225, 397 A.2d 113, 116 (1978). In order to avoid this problem, when a finding states that certain testimony was given, a motion for articulation should be used to make it clear whether the court believed the testimony. However, beware of the judge who finds that there was evidence for something when there was not. This may lead to reversal, as in Dixon v. Lewis, 94 Conn. 548, 109 A. 809 (1920). Articulation might have solved this problem too.

However, if credibility is not an issue, factual issues can be more appropriately reviewed on appeal, State v. Thompson, 191 Conn. 360, 373 n.12, 464 A.2d 799, 808 n.12 (1983).

It is also improper for the trial court to say that certain evidence is "highly suggestive" of a fact or to say that a fact "possibly" or "perhaps" happened; the court should unequivocally state whether it finds something to be the case or not, In re Williamson's Estate, 123 Conn. 424, 429–30, 432, 196 A. 770, 772, 773 (1937).

10. Certified Appeals

In cases on certification from the Appellate Court, the Supreme Court seems to have given little if any deference to the Appellate Court's review of the trial court's fact finding. See State v. Cofield, 220 Conn. 38, 44, 595 A.2d 1349, 1352 (1991).

B. **Plain Error, *Golding* and Supervisory Powers Tests**

The plain error doctrine applies only if the issue was not properly preserved in the lower court. If it was properly preserved, plain error review is not needed. See Cima v. Sciaretta, 140 Conn.App. 167, 173 n.5, 58 A.3d 345, 349 n.5 (motion in limine preserved issue), cert. denied, 308 Conn. 912, 61 A.3d 532 (2013).

Section 60-5 refers to plain error but not review under State v. Golding, 213 Conn. 233, 567 A.2d 823 (1989), but it is appropriate to discuss both here because they both concern appellate review of unpreserved or improperly preserved issues in the trial court. Although the two types of review overlap somewhat, there are many areas where *Golding* but not plain error review will work, and vice versa. In the normal appeal, however, succeeding in either is an uphill battle. While plain error is derived from the federal rules, *Golding* is a home-grown concept that has grown like kudzu in criminal cases since it was created in 1989. For both tests, if an issue is not raised at trial or not properly raised at trial, an appellate court generally will not review it unless a claim is made for plain error review. In re Emerald C., 108 Conn.App. 839, 851–53 n.9, 949 A.2d 1266, 1274–75 n.9, cert. denied, 289 Conn. 923, 958 A.2d 150 (2008). This requirement no longer exists for *Golding* review. State v. Elson, 311 Conn. 726, 748–55, 91 A.3d 862, 876–80 (2014). Query whether it should continue to apply to plain error claims. One exception is that it is not necessary to seek *Golding* review of claims of prosecutorial impropriety where there was no objection at trial. State v. Fauci, 282 Conn. 23, 33–34, 917 A.2d 978, 986 (2007).

Note that if the record is inadequate for Golding review, it is also inadequate for plain error review. State v. Shields, 124 Conn.App. 584, 601 n.12, 5 A.3d 984, 995 n.12 (2010), aff'd, 308 Conn. 678, 69 A.3d 293 (2013). But see State v. Webster, 308 Conn. 43, 63-64, 60 A.3d 259, 271 (2013) (Rogers, C.J. concurring) (query whether *Golding* waiver doctrine applies here).

Under the appellate courts' supervisory powers test, an appellate court can order a trial court to adopt a rule of procedure necessary for the "perceived fairness of the judicial system as a whole." State v. Medrano, 308 Conn. 604, 629–31, 65 A.3d 503, 519–20 (2013) (trial judges not to comment on the interest of a testifying defendant in criminal cases); Tanzman v. Meurer, 309 Conn. 105, 117, 70 A.3d 13, 21 (2013) (trial judges in family cases basing an award on a party's earning capacity must state what the capacity is).

Regardless of the type of unpreserved error claimed, the appellate court may on its own raise that issue under certain conditions as described in Blumberg Assoc. Worldwide, Inc. v. Brown & Brown of Connecticut, Inc., 311 Conn. 123, 84 A.3d 840 (2014).

That the trial court cannot grant the relief requested is no excuse for failing to ask that court to do so. Ulbrich v. Groth, 310 Conn. 375, 427–29, 78 A.3d 76, 111–12 (2013) (trial court must be asked to overrule Supreme Court precedent in order to preserve issue for appeal).

1. Plain Error Test

According to Cogswell v. American Transit Ins. Co., 282 Conn. 505, 521, 923 A.2d 638, 650 (2007), and numerous prior cases, plain error is not a rule of reviewability; it is a rule of reversibility. It is a stringent test, invoked sparingly to avoid manifest injustice, when the trial court's error is, to use the literal meaning of "plain," obvious to any fair-minded observer. Such review is extraordinary and should be used sparingly. State v. Griggs, 288 Conn. 116, 123 n.11, 951 A.2d 531, 538–39 n.11 (2008); In re Yasiel R., 151 Conn. App. 710, 715–19, 94 A.3d 1278, 1282–84, cert. granted, 314 Conn. 907, __ A.3d __ (2014). Plain error, however, was found in Mueller v. Tepler, 312 Conn. 631, 644 n.11, 95 A.3d 1011, 1020, n.11 (2014), where the Appellate Court failed to allow the plaintiff to replead under P.B. § 10-44 after affirming the grant of a motion to strike.

Plain error must also be harmful as well as obviously wrong. State v. Miller, 150 Conn.App. 667, 679 n.4, 92 A.3d 986, 995 n.4 (2014), If there is no true error to correct, there is no plain error. Reville v. Reville, 312 Conn. 428, 69, 93 A.3d 1076, 1104 (2014) (court refused to create an exception to which party bears the burden of proving fraud when claim not raised below).

While the above situation may arise occasionally, the more frequent use of the plain error rule in the past has been to review issues of statutory construction, such as in *Cogswell*, where there is no need for further fact-finding and no party is prejudiced. Presumably prejudice is avoided by giving an opportunity to brief the issue adequately. State v. Falcon, 68 Conn.App. 884, 793 A.2d 274, cert. denied, 260 Conn. 924, 797 A.2d 521 (2002) (overruled on other grounds, State v. D'Antonio, 274 Conn. 658, 877 A.2d 696 (2005)); State v. Prat, 66 Conn.App. 91, 101 n.4 784 A.2d 367, 374 n.4 (2001). In such cases the error need not be plain at all. In short the plain error rule has been largely a misnomer. Not only that, while *Cogswell* is silent, the Supreme Court in fact will decide all manner of issues not properly preserved, and statutory construction is just one of them. We have gathered scores of cases in 26 categories in section 2 of this authors' comment. Only a few of them would meet the definition of "plain" error in the literal sense.

We say plain error "has been" largely a misnomer because, as we read the *Blumberg Assoc.* case decided in early 2014, the authors believe "supervisory powers" will in the future largely displace plain error review when the error is not literally plain. The authors recommend reading our discussion of the plain error cases with the caveat that it may be best to refer to both plain error and supervisory powers when referring to nonconstitutional issues not properly preserved.

In any event plain error review only infrequently succeeds. In *Cogswell*, for example, the statutory construction question foundered on an inadequate factual record. See also State v. Myers, 290 Conn. 278, 290–91, 963 A.2d 11, 18–19 (2009) (failure to comply with rules of practice is not per se plain error). And even if the error is "plain," plain error cannot be invoked if silence was a strategic choice. Gay v. Safeco Ins. Co. of America, 141 Conn.App. 263, 268–69, 60 A.3d 1046, 1049 (2013).

Plain error can be raised by both appellants and appellees. For example, the appellee may raise as plain error an alternate basis to affirm not properly preserved. City of New Haven v. Bonner, 272 Conn. 489, 498, 863 A.2d 680, 685 (2005).

The court employs a two-step analysis to determine plain-error claims: did the court make an error and was it obvious in the sense that it is not debatable. Zuberi v. Commissioner of Correction, 140 Conn. App. 839, 844, 60 A.3d 337, 341, cert. denied, 308 Conn. 931, 64 A.3d 330 (2013).

A ruling by the Appellate Court that there is or is not plain error is subject to plenary review by the Supreme Court. State v. Sanchez, 308 Conn. 64, 78–80, 60 A.3d 271, 280–81 (2013) (failure to give *Ledbetter* instruction concerning misidentification was not plain error).

A party raising plain error has at least two tactical decisions to make. First: Was the issue properly preserved below? This question is often difficult to answer. See, for example, Rowe v. Superior Court, 289 Conn. 649, 960 A.2d 256 (2008), where the court divided 3-2 on that very point, and State v. Coccomo, 302 Conn. 664, 31 A.3d 1012 (2011), where the court divided 4-3 on it. And in Morgan v. Hartford Hosp., 301 Conn. 388, 394 n.7, 21 A.3d 451, 455 n.7 (2011), the court said that whether the defendant had waived the right to file a motion to dismiss was within the scope of the defendant's motion, hardly a self-evident proposition. Second, if you cannot figure out the answer to the first question: Do you take a chance in just saying it was properly raised and wait to see what the other side says? But plain error cannot be raised for the first time in a reply brief. SS-II, LLC v. Bridge Street Associates, 293 Conn. 287, 302, 977 A.2d 189, 199 (2009). This is a harsh position for the court to take if the injustice is manifest, but it is the rule. Since plain error, unlike clear error, does not affect the standard of review if the court decides to consider the issue, the authors advise briefing plain error (or, if applicable, *Golding*) in the opening brief whenever there is any significant chance that the issue was not properly preserved. The only downside of doing so is the remote possibility that both the opponent and the appellate court won't spot the potential problem.

Since plain error cannot be raised in a reply brief, a fortiori the courts will not consider an unpreserved issue that is not briefed at all. Pestey v. Cushman, 259 Conn. 345, 373, 788 A.2d 496, 514 (2002). However, the Supreme Court raised such an issue suo motu at oral argument and decided the issue in Genovese v. Gallo Wine Merchants, Inc., 226 Conn. 475, 480 n.6, 628 A.2d 946, 948 n.6 (1993), and Joe's Pizza, Inc. v. Aetna Life and Cas. Co., 236 Conn. 863, 868 n.1, 675 A.2d 441, 444 n.1 (1996). In both cases the appellee did not oppose consideration of the new issue (*Joe's Pizza*) or at least a major part of the new issue (*Genovese*).

It is clear to the authors what is going on: if the unpreserved issue is not important, the general rule of *Pestey* will be enforced; if the issue is important, it may be considered on the merits—if the record is adequate and there is no need for further fact-finding.

If a party expressly or implicitly waives the issue in the trial court, the law is unsettled as to whether plain error review is possible. While the Appellate Court says no; State v. Charles, 134 Conn.App. 242, 252 n.6, 39 A.3d 750, 756 n.6, cert. denied, 304 Conn. 930, 42 A.3d 392 (2012); the Supreme Court has left the issue open; State v. Coleman, 304 Conn. 161, 175–76, 37 A.3d 713, 722 (2012).

To return now to the first tactical decision we raised: Was the issue properly preserved below? The rule merely says the issue has to be "raised" below. This leads to five subsidiary issues: (a) Does the issue also have to be decided below? (b) When does the issue have to be raised below? (c) How does it have to be raised below? (d) What does the opponent do? and (e) Will the appellate tribunal remand on its own?

(a)

As for the first question, the authors are of the opinion that it depends on the nature of the case. In cases involving a pure issue of law, it may not matter whether the trial court ever decided the issue. DDS Wireless International, Inc. v. Nutmeg Leasing, Inc., 145 Conn.App. 520, 524 n.2, 75 A.3d 86, 90 n.2 (2013). But see Pike v. Bugbee, 115 Conn.App. 820, 974 A.2d 743 (2009) (refusing to consider theory of legal sufficiency of complaint where not made to trial court deciding motion to strike). In issues involving discretion or a finding of facts, it should not matter whether the trial court decides the issue at trial, as long as the appellant asks for articulation during the appeal. State v. Mullins, 288 Conn. 345, 357, 952 A.2d 784 (2008) (abrogated on other grounds by, State v. Polanco, 308 Conn. 242, 61 A.3d 1084 (2013)). In issues involving how the case is presented to the jury, it may be crucial that the trial court decided the issue during the trial. In general, however, a case cannot be tried on one theory and appealed on another. Afkari-Ahmadi v. Fotovat-Ahmadi, 294 Conn. 384, 395, 985 A.2d 319, 326 (2009); State v. Johnson, 288 Conn. 236, 287–88, 951 A.2d 1257, 1259, 1290 (2008).

In Hicks v. State, 287 Conn. 421, 442 n.7, 948 A.2d 982, 997 n.7 (2008), and Bingham v. Department of Public Works, 286 Conn. 698, 704, 945 A.2d 927, 930 (2008), the court held that a request for a continuance was not preserved for appellate review because the appellant never sought an articulation to obtain a ruling. This implies that the defect was not the failure to obtain a ruling during trial but the failure to obtain a ruling during the appeal, i.e., the failure to use § 66-5. King v. Sultar, 253 Conn. 429, 448–49, 754 A.2d 782, 793–94 (2000), holds that the trial court need not rule on a statutory construction issue for it to be reviewable (as long as a finding is not required because of the nature of the issue). Willow Springs Condominium Ass'n, Inc. v. Seventh BRT Development Corp., 245 Conn. 1, 52–53, 717 A.2d 77, 104 (1998), a jury case, held that a claim of insufficiency of evidence must be both raised and decided by the trial court. The court noted the absence of a motion for directed verdict and also the lack of a motion for articulation. The lack of both barred review, although the lack of the former alone undoubtedly would have barred a directed judgment (but not a new trial). In Hull v. Fonck, 122 Conn.App. 286, 291 n.5, 999 A.2d 775, 778 n.5 (2010), the court refused to review a claim of insufficient evidence where the defendant had not raised the issue in his motion for JNOV. So if the trial court fails to rule on an issue at trial, the party raising the issue on appeal should move for an articulation so that the trial judge rules on the issue unless the nature of the issue is such that the judge's decision is of no significance.

It appears that an alternate basis to affirm properly raised in the trial court does not have to be decided there in order to be reviewable. Hudson Valley Bank v. Kissel, 303 Conn. 614, 627 n.10, 35 A.3d 260, 268 n.10 (2012). The court will not decide an alternate basis to affirm that was not raised in the trial court. Perez-Dickson v. City of Bridgeport, 304 Conn. 483, 498–501, 43 A.3d 69, 82–85. 279 Ed. Law Rep. 1015, 114 Fair Empl. Prac. Cas. (BNA) 1461 (2012).

The Appellate Court holds that the trial court must rule on the issue. Bragdon v. Sweet, 102 Conn.App. 600, 605, 925 A.2d 1226, 1229 (2007); State v. Moody, 77 Conn.App. 197, 204, 822 A.2d 990, 998, cert. denied, 264 Conn. 918, 827 A.2d 707, cert. denied, 540 U.S. 1058, 124 S. Ct. 831, 159 L.Ed. 2d 714 (2003) appeal from dismissal of habeas corpus dismissed, 108 Conn.App. 96, 946 A.2d 1268

(2008), See also State v. Stephen O., 106 Conn.App. 717, 723 n.4, 943 A.2d 477, 481 n.4, cert. denied, 287 Conn. 916, 951 A.2d 568 (2008) (failure to rule on pretrial motion in limine). The Appellate Court rule is too rigid in light of *Hicks*.

(b)

As for the second question, the problem is whether the issue was raised either too early or too late in the trial court. It is risky to rely only on a pretrial ruling and not reraise the issue at trial.

However, a pretrial ruling is sufficient in jury cases if you fit within the third paragraph of this rule. West Haven Sound Development Corp. v. City of West Haven, 207 Conn. 308, 311 n.2, 541 A.2d 858, 860 n.2 (1988).

In addition, pretrial rulings suffice if the issue decided was a legal question "and no further evidence on the question was presented at trial." Pelletier v. Sordoni/Skanska Const. Co., 286 Conn. 563, 577, 945 A.2d 388, 398 (2008); Doe v. Yale University, 252 Conn. 641, 661 n.19, 748 A.2d 834, 848 n.19 (2000).

Other than those exceptions you had best claim plain error if the issue was not reraised and decided at trial or if further evidence was introduced at trial. Gurliacci v. Mayer, 218 Conn. 531, 541 n.7, 590 A.2d 914, 920 n.7 (1991).

The next question is whether an issue raised after trial is too late. In general the answer is yes, especially in a jury trial where it is too late to bring back the jury. For example, if the issue involves improper final argument to the jury, raising the issue for the first time in a postverdict motion is untimely. Cavaliere v. Olmsted, 98 Conn.App. 343, 346 n.2, 909 A.2d 52, 55 n.2 (2006). Presumably this reasoning would also apply to evidentiary issues and the charge to the jury. However, the court will review claims arising after trial, such as the passage of the statute claimed to apply retroactively. Town of Middlebury v. Department of Environmental Protection, 283 Conn. 156, 172 n.13, 927 A.2d 793, 803 n.13 (2007).

Finally, there apparently is a special rule for burden of proof questions. If the trial court applied a burden of proof that a party disputes, that party must move for reconsideration on that precise issue. Kaczynski v. Kaczynski, 294 Conn. 121, 131, 981 A.2d 1068, 1074–75 (2009). It is possible (but hopefully it will not come to pass) that Kaczynski applies to other questions as well. See BNY Western Trust v. Roman, 295 Conn. 194, 210 n.13, 990 A.2d 853, 863 n.13 (2010).

(c)

The third subsidiary question is how to raise the issue below. The court will not review new legal grounds raised for the first time on appeal. Corrarino v. Corrarino, 121 Conn.App. 22, 993 A.2d 486 (2010). In order to avoid plain error review, the issue must be "distinctly" raised at trial, not just "briefly suggested"; McKiernan v. Caldor, Inc., 183 Conn. 164, 438 A.2d 865 (1981); State v. Faison, 112 Conn.App. 373, 380, 962 A.2d 860, 865, cert. denied, 291 Conn. 903, 967 A.2d 507 (2009) ("*precise* matter must be raised"); Yale Literary Magazine v. Yale University, 4 Conn.App. 592, 597, 496 A.2d 201, 204 (1985), judgment aff'd, 202 Conn. 672, 522 A.2d 818, 38 Ed. Law Rep. 237 (1987). Cf. Union Carbide Corp. v. Aetna Cas. and Sur. Co., 212 Conn. 311, 316, 562 A.2d 15, 18 (1989); Greenberg, Rhein and Margolis, Inc. v. Norris-Faye Horton Enterprises, Inc., 218 Conn. 162, 169, 588 A.2d 185, 189 (1991). This is particularly important for evidentiary issues as review will be limited to the grounds asserted at trial. Connecticut Bank and Trust Co. v. Munsill-Borden Mansion, LLC, 147 Conn.App. 30, 36–37, 81 A.3d 266, 271 (2013). Requesting interest in a trial brief was not adequate to raise the issue where the plaintiffs failed to make the request in their postverdict motions in Schoonmaker v. Lawrence Brunoli, Inc., 265 Conn. 210, 265, 828 A.2d 64, 101 (2003). If the matter concerns a motion to strike evidence, it must be clear what evidence was stricken. Skelly v. Pleasure Beach Park Corp., 115 Conn. 92, 94–95, 160 A. 309, 310 (1932).

However, if the claim was "functionally made" at trial even if articulated in a different manner, review may be had. Rowe v. Superior Court, 289 Conn. 649, 661–62, 960 A.2d 256, 264 (2008) (trial court appears to have understood and ruled on an inartful objection that possibly was internally inconsistent) (3-2 decision); Fadner v. Commissioner of Revenue Services, 281 Conn. 719, 729 n.12, 917 A.2d 540, 547 n.12 (2007); State v. Dabkowski, 199 Conn. 193, 198, 506 A.2d 118, 121 (1986); Salmon v. Department of Public Health and Addiction Services, 259 Conn. 288, 305, 788 A.2d 1199, 1210 (2002) (claim "functionally raised"). Also, a claim may be "distinctly raised" even though it is "not well articulated"; Mather v. Griffin Hosp., 207 Conn. 125, 138, 540 A.2d 666, 673 (1988); especially if the trial judge understood the grounds for the objection; State v. Deptula, 31 Conn.App. 140, 146, 623 A.2d 525, 528 (1993); or if it is within the scope of the issue that was raised, Morgan v. Hartford Hosp., 301 Conn. 388, 394 n.7, 21 A.3d 451, 455 n.7 (2011); and even if the focus of the legal argument has shifted; Neuhaus v. DeCholnoky, 280 Conn. 190, 216 n.18, 905 A.2d 1135, 1151 n.18 (2006); State v. Munoz, 233 Conn. 106, 119 n.7, 659 A.2d 683, 690 n.7 (1995); State v. Lonergan, 16 Conn.App. 358, 362–63, 548 A.2d 718, 720 (1988). See also Sgueglia v. Milne Const. Co., 212 Conn. 427, 432 n.5, 562 A.2d 505, 508 n.5 (1989). If the issue is important, the court may excuse the failure to articulate the issue as clearly as required. Daily v. New Britain Mach. Co., 200 Conn. 562, 576 n.11, 512 A.2d 893, 901 n.11 (1986). Reviewing courts have discretion to consider legal theories that differ from those presented at trial if the theories relate to a properly preserved issue. State v. Allen, 311 Conn. 1, 10 n.5, 83 A.3d 326, 332 n.5 (2014).

In some circumstances, no objection at trial is necessary to secure review. For instance a party is not required to raise and anticipate that a trial court will apply the wrong legal standard to its evidence. Moss v. Foster, 96 Conn.App. 369, 376, 900 A.2d 548, 554 (2006). Nor is it always necessary to object more than once during the trial on a point. State v. Person, 20 Conn.App. 115, 129, 564 A.2d 626, 634 (1989), aff'd, 215 Conn. 653, 577 A.2d 1036 (1990). Further, a party need not object on the grounds of parol evidence because that is not strictly a rule of evidence. Capp Industries, Inc. v. Schoenberg, 104 Conn.App. 101, 110 n.6, 932 A.2d 453, 460 n.6, cert. denied, 284 Conn. 941, 937 A.2d 696, 697 (2007). On the other hand, an issue does not arise "subsequent to the trial" merely because the Supreme Court first considers an issue in another case after the trial, if the issue has been considered previously in other jurisdictions. Atlantic Richfield Co. v. Canaan Oil Co., 202 Conn. 234, 241 n.1, 520 A.2d 1008, 1013 n.1 (1987).

In courtside cases it is normally timely if the issue is raised in the posttrial briefs. Season-All Industries, Inc. v. R.J. Grosso, Inc., 213 Conn. 486, 495, 569 A.2d 32, 37 (1990). See P.B. § 5-1. A motion for mistrial for judicial misconduct was timely as long as it was filed before the judge ruled on the merits of the case. Kane v. Kane, 43 Conn.App. 508, 511, 683 A.2d 1034, 1035–36 (1996).

The "plain error" rule no longer applies in a jury case involving money damages (see C.G.S.A. § 52-228b) when the losing party has failed to file a motion to set aside the verdict but has appealed directly from the verdict; Santopietro v. City of New Haven, 239 Conn. 207, 211–12, 682 A.2d 106, 108–13 (1996); although the rule may be otherwise if the issue had not previously been passed on by the trial judge (e.g., excessiveness of verdict).

(d)

Once a party (usually the appellant) has raised and briefed a plain error issue, the appellee then has a tactical decision to make. Even if it is likely that the Supreme Court will not review an issue, it is risky for the appellee not to brief the issue on the merits. In Ralto Developers, Inc. v. Environmental Impact Com'n of City of Danbury, 220 Conn. 54, 60, 594 A.2d 981, 984 (1991), the appellee relied exclusively on the argument that the issue was not properly preserved. The Supreme Court agreed, but gave the issue plain error review and reversed. See also Nielsen v. Kezer, 232 Conn. 65, 73 n.15, 652 A.2d 1013, 1018 n.15 (1995). On the other hand, briefing the issue on the merits increases the odds that the court will reach the merits.

(e)

Finally, § 60-5 gives the Supreme Court the power to remand the cases to the trial court for a further articulation on the basis of its decision. However the Supreme Court rarely does so. Mazzone v. Connecticut Transit Co., 240 Conn. 788, 798, 694 A.2d 1230, 1234–35 (1997); Larsen Chelsey Realty Co. v. Larsen, 232 Conn. 480, 489–90, 656 A.2d 1009, 1016–17 (1995) (generous reading of rule where constitutional right to jury trial is implicated because motion to set aside a verdict was granted); Connecticut Bank and Trust Co., Inc. v. Winters, 225 Conn. 146, 163–65, 622 A.2d 536, 544–45 (1993); Lauer v. Zoning Com'n of Town of Redding, 220 Conn. 455, 471 n.16, 600 A.2d 310, 318 n.16 (1991); Rostain v. Rostain, 213 Conn. 686, 569 A.2d 1126, decision after remand, 214 Conn. 713, 573 A.2d 710 (1990); and twice in State v. Lafferty, 191 Conn. 73, 463 A.2d 238 (1983), appeal after remand, 192 Conn. 571, 472 A.2d 1275 (1984). The Appellate Court did so in Mackie v. Hull, 69 Conn.App. 538, 549, 795 A.2d 1280, 1288, cert. denied, 261 Conn. 916, 806 A.2d 1055 (2002), and Markarian v. Markarian, 2 Conn.App. 14, 475 A.2d 337 (1984). See also State v. Whitney, 37 Conn.Supp. 864, 440 A.2d 987 (Super. Ct. Appellate Sess. 1981).

Normally, however, the Supreme and Appellate Courts will not do this, and have made it clear that it is the appellant's duty to provide an adequate record where the memorandum is inadequate, Stutz v. Shepard, 279 Conn. 115, 123–26, 901 A.2d 33, 38–40 (2006) (no transcripts of arbitration proceedings). The proper way to do so is to order the proper transcripts or to file a motion for rectification under § 66-5. Id.

2. Types of Plain Error

The appellate courts have considered error not raised below for many reasons. While the Supreme Court often says the error must be obvious to be entitled to plain error review, see, e.g., State v. Coccomo, 302 Conn. 664, 678–97, 31 A.3d 1012, 1022–32 (2011); State v. Fagan, 280 Conn. 69, 89 n.14, 905 A.2d 1101, 1114 n.14 (2006), in many of the categories listed below the error is not necessarily obvious. Also, many of the categories are similar to the reasons the Supreme Court gives for invoking its supervisory powers. State v. Schiappa, 248 Conn. 132, 175–76 n.47, 728 A.2d 466, 490 n.47 (1999).

As noted earlier, plain error cases tend to break down into two broad categories: (1) extraordinary situations affecting the fairness or integrity of the proceedings; State v. Taylor, 101 Conn.App. 160, 165 n.1, 921 A.2d 617, 621 n.1, cert. denied, 283 Conn. 903, 927 A.2d 915 (2007); State v. Fitzgerald, 257 Conn. 106, 111, 777 A.2d 580, 583–84 (2001); and (2) statutory construction claims; State v. Velasco, 253 Conn. 210, 218–19 n.9, 751 A.2d 800, 806–07 n.9 (2000). *Velasco* says nothing about the statutory construction claim being extraordinary, presumably because such a claim affects society as a whole, and in any event many of the cases cited below are not statutory construction claims.

Here, in any event, are all the categories of plain error review the authors have found:

   1. When the public welfare was involved, Kavanewsky v. Zoning Bd. of Appeals of Town of Warren, 160 Conn. 397, 401, 279 A.2d 567, 569–70 (1971) (large part of town rezoned two acres); Jaser v. Jaser, 37 Conn.App. 194,

196–97 n.2, 655 A.2d 790, 793 n.2 (1995); cf. Perricone v. Perricone, 292 Conn. 187, 218–20, 972 A.2d 666, 688–89 (2009) (no violation of public policy found);

2.   Where the issue was important, Riccio v. Abate, 176 Conn. 415, 418 n.1, 407 A.2d 1005, 1007 n.1 (1979); Columbus Industrial Bank v. Miller, 125 Conn. 313, 315–16, 6 A.2d 42, 43 (1939); Daley v. Gaitor, 16 Conn.App. 379, 383, 547 A.2d 1375, 1377, cert. denied, 209 Conn. 824, 552 A.2d 430 (1988) (issue raised at trial but not properly preserved);

3.   Where the claim involved judicial integrity, Wiegand v. Wiegand, 129 Conn.App. 526, 532–33, 21 A.3d 489, 493 (2011); but see 129 Conn.App. at 541–44 (Lavine, J., concurring)); Cameron v. Cameron, 187 Conn. 163, 168, 444 A.2d 915, 918 (1982); or public confidence in attorneys, Golembeski v. Metichewan Grange No. 190, 20 Conn.App. 699, 701, 569 A.2d 1157, 1159 (1990); In re Shana M., 26 Conn.App. 414, 416, 600 A.2d 1385, 1386 (1992); or public confidence in jury deliberations, State v. Robins, 34 Conn.App. 694, 705–07, 643 A.2d 881, 887–88 (1994), judgment aff'd, 233 Conn. 527, 660 A.2d 738 (1995) (improper charge about what jurors could discuss with others not on the jury); but see Frauenglass & Associates v. Enagbare, 149 Conn.App. 103, 104 n.1, 88 A.3d 1246, 1248 n.1 (2014);

4.   Where "the interests of justice" require it, Magnan v. Anaconda Industries, Inc., 193 Conn. 558, 577–78, 479 A.2d 781, 791 (1984); State v. Eric T., 8 Conn.App. 607, 614, 513 A.2d 1273, 1277 (1986); G.S. v. T.S., 23 Conn.App. 509, 510–11, 582 A.2d 467, 467–68 (1990) (failure to appoint lawyer for minor child in custody dispute); Bartley v. Bartley, 27 Conn.App. 195, 198, 604 A.2d 1343, 1345 (1992) (manifest injustice); Jaser v. Jaser, 37 Conn.App. 194, 196–97 n.2, 655 A.2d 790, 793 n.2 (1995) ("fundamental justice between the parties"); State v. Harris, 54 Conn.App. 18, 25, 734 A.2d 1027, 1030, 1031, cert. denied, 250 Conn. 925, 738 A.2d 660 (1999) ("serious constitutional ramifications"); Argentinis v. Fortuna, 134 Conn.App. 538, 539–40, 39 A.3d 1207, 1213 (2012) (need "to ensure the fair and just administration of the courts");

5.   When both court and counsel overlooked controlling common law precedent, State v. Gelinas, 160 Conn. 366, 368–69, 279 A.2d 552, 554 (1971) (testimony of character witness);

6.   When both court and counsel overlooked a controlling statute, Collins v. Colonial Penn Ins. Co., 257 Conn. 718, 727, 778 A.2d 899, 906 (2001); Connecticut Nat. Bank v. Giacomi, 242 Conn. 17, 39, 699 A.2d 101, 115 (1997); Genovese v. Gallo Wine Merchants, Inc., 226 Conn. 475, 480 n.6, 628 A.2d 946, 948 n.6 (1993); Smith v. Zoning Bd. of Appeals of Town of Greenwich, 227 Conn. 71, 86 n.9, 629 A.2d 1089, 1098 n.9 (1993); State v. Cotton, 69 Conn.App. 505, 506, 794 A.2d 1116, 1117 (2002); Dionne v. Markie, 38 Conn.App. 852, 857, 663 A.2d 420, 422 (1995); Cunningham v. Cunningham, 72 Conn. 157, 160, 44 A. 41, 42 (1899) ("the law of the land"); or even a portion of a statute, Ralto Developers, Inc. v. Environmental Impact Com'n of City of Danbury, 220 Conn. 54, 59, 594 A.2d 981, 984 (1991); State v. Guckian, 27 Conn.App. 225, 246, 605 A.2d 874, 885, aff'd, 226 Conn. 191, 627 A.2d 407 (1993); or improperly relied entirely on a statute, State v. Thornton, 55 Conn.App. 28, 31–32, 739 A.2d 271, 273 (1999). However, the issue must have a proper factual foundation for the application of the statute or the issue will not be considered. Cogswell v. American Transit Ins. Co., 282 Conn. 505, 522, 923 A.2d 638, 650 (2007);

7.   When both court and counsel overlooked a controlling Practice Book rule, R.I. Waterman Property, Inc. v. Misiorski, 51 Conn.App. 659, 725 A.2d 340 (1999); State v. Pina, 185 Conn. 473, 440 A.2d 962, 967 (1981); Campbell v. Rockefeller, 134 Conn. 585, 588, 59 A.2d 524, 526 (1948); or overlooked

"established practice," State v. Martin, 189 Conn. 1, 2 n.1, 454 A.2d 256, 257 n.1 (1983);

8. Because "of the large sum involved and the interest of the municipality in the matter," Delaney v. City of Hartford, 125 Conn. 587, 592, 7 A.2d 659, 662 (1939) (dicta); but see City of Norwich, Dept. of Public Utilities v. Town of Lebanon, 193 Conn. 342, 349, 477 A.2d 115, 119 (1984);

9. When both parties briefed the issue, Scott v. General Iron & Welding Co., Inc., 171 Conn. 132, 139, 368 A.2d 111, 116 (1976); Nauss v. Pinkes, 2 Conn.App. 400, 409 n.7, 480 A.2d 568, 574 n.7, cert. denied, 194 Conn. 808, 483 A.2d 612 (1984); Genovese v. Gallo Wine Merchants, Inc., 226 Conn. 475, 480 n.4, 628 A.2d 946, 948 n.4 (1993) (supplemental briefs); Madison Hills Ltd. Partnership II v. Madison Hills, Inc., 35 Conn.App. 81, 84, 644 A.2d 363, 366, cert. denied, 231 Conn. 913, 648 A.2d 153 (1994); Jaser v. Jaser, 37 Conn.App. 194, 196–97 n.2, 655 A.2d 790, 793 n.2 (1995);

10. When the error was apparent on the face of the record, Riggs v. Zaleski, 44 Conn. 120, 121, 1876 WL 1765 (1876); Crandall v. State, 10 Conn. 339, 370–71, 1834 WL 102 (1834) (Prudence Crandall);

11. Where the error was clear or manifest or went to a vital issue, Batick v. Seymour, 186 Conn. 632, 641, 443 A.2d 471, 475 (1982) (jury charge); State v. Rogers, 18 Conn.App. 104, 111, 556 A.2d 1030, 1033 (1989) (suppression of evidence); Bonner v. Winter, 175 Conn. 41, 392 A.2d 436 (1978) (evidentiary ruling); or where the error truly was plain, State v. Shaw, 24 Conn.App. 493, 500, 589 A.2d 880, 884 (1991); Prishwalko v. Bob Thomas Ford, Inc., 33 Conn.App. 575, 636 A.2d 1383 (1994) (plain error to take case from jury); or "obvious"; Herrera v. Madrak, 58 Conn.App. 320, 325, 752 A.2d 1161, 1165, cert. denied, 239 Conn. 901, 682 A.2d 1007 (2000); Equity Mortg., Inc. v. Niro, 44 Conn.App. 471, 475, 690 A.2d 407, 409 (1997);

12. Where the court considered the issue in previous cases although not raised below, State v. King, 187 Conn. 292, 309 n.13, 445 A.2d 901, 910 n.13 (1982);

13. Where the record is complete and the question is essentially one of law, so that the trial court's opinion makes no difference and neither party is prejudiced; State v. Velasco, 253 Conn. 210, 219 n.9, 751 A.2d 800, 806 n.9 (2000); Genovese v. Gallo Wine Merchants, Inc., 226 Conn. 475, 480 n.6, 628 A.2d 946, 948–49 n.6 (1993); Cochran v. McLaughlin, 128 Conn. 638, 644, 24 A.2d 836, 839 (1942); Amica Mut. Ins. Co. v. Woods, 48 Conn.App. 690, 696 n.7, 711 A.2d 1208, 1211 n.7, cert. denied, 245 Conn. 916, 719 A.2d 900 (1998); Biller Associates v. Rte. 156 Realty Co., 52 Conn.App. 18, 25, 725 A.2d 398, 402, aff'd, 252 Conn. 400, 746 A.2d 785 (2000); Madison Hills Ltd. Partnership II v. Madison Hills, Inc., 35 Conn.App. 81, 84, 644 A.2d 363, 366, cert. denied, 231 Conn. 913, 648 A.2d 153 (1994);

14. Where the trial court considered the issue even if it was not raised by counsel in the trial court, DeSena v. City of Waterbury, 249 Conn. 63, 72 n.10, 731 A.2d 733, 737 n.10 (1999); Society for Sav. v. Chestnut Estates, Inc., 176 Conn. 563, 568 n.2, 409 A.2d 1020, 1022 n.2 (1979); Konover Development Corp. v. Zeller, 228 Conn. 206, 215, 635 A.2d 798, 803 (1994); or in their assignment of errors (now statement of issues) on appeal, Bright v. Zoning Bd. of Appeals of Town of Fairfield, 149 Conn. 698, 703, 183 A.2d 603, 605 (1962);

15. Where counsel made no objection in the trial court because it would have been futile in light of the trial court's prior rulings, see State v. Higgs, 143 Conn. 138, 145, 120 A.2d 152, 155 (1956);

16. If the matter concerns subject matter jurisdiction, Monroe v. Monroe, 177 Conn. 173, 177, 413 A.2d 819, 823 (1979); Town of Bristol v. Tucker, 39 Conn.Supp. 454, 575, 466 A.2d 336, 338 (Super. Ct. Appellate Sess. 1983); Mayor v. Mayor, 17 Conn.App. 627, 629 n.2, 554 A.2d 1109, 1110 n.2 (1989);

17. If the court is going to order a new trial anyway because of another issue properly raised, Sanderson v. Steve Snyder Enterprises, Inc., 196 Conn. 134, 143, 491 A.2d 389, 394 (1985); Mourison v. Hansen, 128 Conn. 62, 67, 20 A.2d 84, 86–87 (1941);

18. When the claimed error resulted in an unreliable verdict, injustice or a miscarriage of justice, State v. Ortiz, 71 Conn.App. 865, 871–72, 804 A.2d 937, 942, cert. denied, 261 Conn. 942, 808 A.2d 1136 (2002); Smith v. Czescel, 12 Conn.App. 558, 533 A.2d 223, cert. denied, 206 Conn. 803, 535 A.2d 1316 (1987) (jury charge); State v. Knight, 29 Conn.App. 675, 676–77, 617 A.2d 913, 914–15 (1992);

19. Where there was a recent statutory change, State v. Preyer, 198 Conn. 190, 198–99, 502 A.2d 858, 862–63 (1985);

20. Where the basic rules concerning summary judgment are involved, Walker v. Lombardo, 2 Conn.App. 266, 268–69, 477 A.2d 168, 169–70 (1984);

21. When the opposing party does not object to consideration of the issue, Genovese v. Gallo Wine Merchants, Inc., 226 Conn. 475, 480 n.6, 628 A.2d 946, 948 n.6 (1993);

22. Without specifying a reason, State v. Henning, 220 Conn. 417, 427, 599 A.2d 1065, 1070 (1991); see Justice Berdon's dissent, 220 Conn. at 432, 599 A.2d at 1072;

23. Where opposing counsel did not object to the issue being raised at oral argument(!), Joe's Pizza, Inc. v. Aetna Life and Cas. Co., 236 Conn. 863, 868 n.1, 675 A.2d 441, 444 n.1 (1996);

24. Where an issue is "so interwoven" with a properly raised issue, State v. Chapman, 227 Conn. 616, 618–19 n.3, 632 A.2d 674, 676 n.3 (1993), on reconsideration, 229 Conn. 529, 643 A.2d 1213 (1994); but see Crawford v. Commissioner of Correction, 294 Conn. 165, 203–04, 982 A.2d 620, 642–43 (2009), where it was not;

25. Where a claim is made that the trial court violated a supervisory directive of the Supreme Court, State v. Malave, 47 Conn.App. 597, 605 n.5, 707 A.2d 307, 311 n.5 (1998), aff'd, 250 Conn. 722, 737 A.2d 442 (1999);

26. Where it would be inconsistent to leave an unappealed part of a judgment intact where the rest of the judgment is reversed, Magnan v. Anaconda Industries, Inc., 193 Conn. 558, 577–78, 479 A.2d 781, 791 (1984);

27. Where the claim is that a recent U.S. Supreme Court case has overruled the Connecticut Supreme Court case the trial court was relying on, Hartford Steam Boiler Inspection and Ins. Co. v. Underwriters at Lloyd's and Companies Collective, 121 Conn.App. 31, 44–45, 994 A.2d 262, 273, cert. denied, 297 Conn. 918, 996 A.2d 277 (2010);

28. Where the issue relates to an issue preserved for appeal, State v. Allan, 311 Conn. 1, 10 n.5, 83 A.3d 326, 332 n.1 (2014).

It is helpful if more than one of these twenty-six categories apply. Genovese v. Gallo Wine Merchants, Inc., 226 Conn. 475, 480 n.6, 628 A.2d 946, 948 n.6 (1993) (categories 5, 9, 13 and 21) (1993). See West Hartford Interfaith Coalition, Inc. v. Town Council of Town of West Hartford, 228 Conn. 498, 507, 636 A.2d 1342, 1347 (1994) (categories 1, 2 and apparently 13); Jaser v. Jaser, 37 Conn.App. 194, 196–97 n.2, 655 A.2d 790, 793 n.2 (1995) (categories 1, 4 and 9); Imperial Cas. and Indem. Co. v. State, 246 Conn. 313, 320–23, 714 A.2d 1230, 1234–36 (1998) (numerous categories).

Note that the plain error doctrine cannot revoke an otherwise valid waiver. State v. Velez, 113 Conn.App. 347, 361 n.8, 966 A.2d 743, 753 n.8, cert. denied, 291 Conn. 917, 970 A.2d 729 (2009); but see State v. Coleman, 304 Conn. 161, 175–76, 37 A.3d 713, 722 (2012) (leaving the issue open).

3. Golding Test

If the unpreserved issue is a constitutional one, *Golding* review generally is a more promising approach than plain error review. State v. Golding, 213 Conn. 233, 239–40, 567 A.2d 823, 827 (1989), created the following four-prong test:

> [A] defendant can prevail on a claim of constitutional error not preserved at trial only if all of the following conditions are met: (1) the record is adequate to review the alleged claim of error; (2) the claim is of constitutional magnitude alleging the violation of a fundamental right; 3) the alleged constitutional violation clearly exists and clearly deprived the defendant of a fair trial; and (4) if subject to harmless error analysis, the state has failed to demonstrate harmlessness of the alleged constitutional violation beyond a reasonable doubt. In the absence of any one of these conditions, the defendant's claim will fail.

While the test sounds very stringent and the tone is harsh, in practice the test is not harsh at all. If the defendant has a meritorious constitutional issue and can get by the first prong of an adequate record, the sailing is usually clear. While the second and third prongs, in addition to requiring the issue to be of constitutional magnitude, require that the right be "fundamental," that the violation "clearly" exists and that the defendant was "clearly deprived of a fair trial," these additional requirements add little to the defendant's burden when the appellate decisions applying *Golding* are examined. Good examples are State v. Griggs, 288 Conn. 116, 122–23 n.11, 951 A.2d 531, 538–39 n.11 (2008); State v. Salamon, 287 Conn. 509, 569 n.49, 949 A.2d 1092, 1133 n.49 (2008); State v. Brewer, 283 Conn. 352, 358–61, 927 A.2d 825, 830–32 (2007); and State v. Perry, 108 Conn.App. 788, 791, 949 A.2d 537, 539–40 (2008). In all of these cases, once the record was found adequate, the court analyzed the constitutional question exactly as it would have if the question had been raised in the trial court.

Of course, getting by the first prong is often impossible because, no matter how creative the appellate lawyer is, the record for an issue not raised in the trial court often is inadequate. This point is discussed in detail in In re Azareon Y., 309 Conn. 626, 72 A.3d 1074 (2013).

That *Golding* review, where applicable, is much less stringent than plain error review, which generally (but not always) requires the appellant to prove a manifest injustice, is shown by Rowe v. Superior Court, 289 Conn. 649, 960 A.2d 256 (2008), where the 3-justice majority stretches to find that the issue was properly preserved. Justices Palmer and Zarella concurred, concluding that the issue was *not* properly preserved but that it succeeds under *Golding*. None of the justices said a word about plain error review.

Note that the applicability of *Golding* no longer need be briefed. State v. Elson, 311 Conn. 726, 91 A.3d 862 (2014).

The only real teeth *Brewer* put into the *Golding* test is the concept of waiver or induced error. In State v. Kitchens, 299 Conn. 447, 10 A.3d 942 (2011), the court in a 4-3 decision held that, concerning jury charge issues, if the trial court prepares a draft charge and circulates it to counsel in sufficient time to review it carefully, any unraised constitutional issue is implicitly waived. In addition, if the defendant takes some affirmative action to waive the issue at trial, such as by his counsel expressing satisfaction with how the trial judge was handling the issue, *Golding* review will fail. In addition to *Brewer*, see State v. Foster, 293 Conn. 327, 342, 977 A.2d 199, 208 (2009); Mozell v. Commissioner of Correction, 291 Conn. 62, 73, 967 A.2d 41, 50 (2009); State v. Holness, 289 Conn. 535, 543, 958 A.2d 754, 759 (2008); State v. Mish, 110 Conn.App. 245, 257–58, 954 A.2d 854, 862–63, cert. denied, 289 Conn. 941, 959 A.2d 1008 (2008); State v. Diaz, 109 Conn.App. 519, 535–37, 952 A.2d 124, 135–36, cert. denied, 289 Conn. 930, 958 A.2d 161 (2008). However, mere participation in a hearing later challenged on appeal is not an implicit waiver. State v. Madigosky, 291 Conn. 28, 35 n.7, 966 A.2d 730, 735 n.7 (2009); State v. Arthur H., 288 Conn. 582, 602–03, 953 A.2d 630 (2008); nor is acquiescence, State v. Reynolds, 118 Conn.App. 278, 304–06, 983 A.2d 874, 891–92 (2009), cert. denied, 294 Conn. 933, 987 A.2d

1029 (2010). And some waivers must be made personally, not by counsel. State v. Gore, 288 Conn. 770, 789–90, 955 A.2d 1, 14 (2008). Whether a *Golding* waiver would also waive plain error has not been decided. See State v. Webster, 308 Conn. 43, 63–64, 60 A.3d 259, 271 (2013) (Rogers, C.J., concurring). Since plain error usually involves a miscarriage of justice or the like, the authors would say no.

As to the relationship between prongs 2 and 3 in generalized due process claims, see State v. Crespo, 303 Conn. 589, 609 n.15, 35 A.3d 243, 257 n.15 (2012) (possible problem in *Golding* jurisprudence).

Golding applies to civil cases. Ackerman v. Sobol Family Partnership, LLP, 298 Conn. 495, 498, 530–32, 4 A.3d 288, 311 (2010); Perricone v. Perricone, 292 Conn. 187, 212 n.24, 972 A.2d 666, 683 n.24 (2009).

While some of the language of *Golding* has to be modified slightly for civil cases ("defendant"; the fourth prong; see the parentheticals in *Smith*), the authors agree *Golding* should apply in civil cases. After all, the constitution gives lots of important rights that have nothing to do with criminal cases.

The constitution *Golding* was referring to was the federal constitution. The court applied *Golding* review to a state constitutional claim in State v. Waz, 240 Conn. 365, 371 n.11, 692 A.2d 1217, 1279 n.11 (1997).

The *Golding* test is a review of a test initially adopted in State v. Evans, 165 Conn. 61, 70, 327 A.2d 576, 581–82 (1973). Most of that test is now obsolete, but *Golding* explicitly preserved one aspect of *Evans* that gives litigants another basis to claim review: "where a new constitutional right not readily foreseeable has arisen between the time of trial and appeal." *Golding*, 213 Conn. at 239 n.8. This route should be claimed if the record is inadequate because it has no such requirement.

4. Possible Reargument Requirement

It is unlikely but possible that certain issues clearly resolved by the trial court will not be properly preserved for appellate review unless the losing party first moves for reargument under P.B. § 11-11. See Authors' Comments to that section of the rules in light of Kaczynski v. Kaczynski, 294 Conn. 121, 131, 981 A.2d 1068, 1074–75 (2009), and BNY Western Trust v. Roman, 295 Conn. 194, 210 n.13, 990 A.2d 853, 863 n.13 (2010).

5. Time of Plainness

In interpreting the federal plain error rule, the U.S. Supreme Court recently held in a 6-3 opinion that the plainness of the trial court's error need not be apparent at the time of the trial court's ruling. It is sufficient if the error is plain at the time of the appellate court's ruling. Henderson v. U.S., __ U.S. __, 133 S. Ct. 1121, 185 L. Ed. 2d 85 (2013).

6. Supervisory Powers

An appellate court may exercise its supervisory powers when necessary to the "perceived fairness of the judicial system as a whole." State v. Medrano, 308 Conn. 604, 65 A.3d 503 (2013) and Tanzman v. Meurer, 309 Conn. 105, 70 A.3d 13 (2013), (*supra* at § 60-5 (Authors' Comments in Subdivision B. Plain Error, Golding and Supervisory Powers Tests)). The use of supervisory powers is discussed in great detail in Blumberg Associates Worldwide, Inc. v. Brown and Brown of Connecticut, 311 Conn. 123, 84 A.3d 840 (2014), supra. See also the extensive discussion in State v. Elson, 311 Conn. 726, 763–85, 91 A.3d 862, 884–98 (2014).

C. Harmful Error

In order to be reversible the error must also be harmful.

The test for determining whether error is harmful in civil cases is "whether the harmful ruling would likely affect the result." George v. Ericson, 250 Conn. 312, 327, 736 A.2d 889, 899 (1999). If the evidence in question would "tend to affect" the trier's decision, the erroneous ruling is harmful, Swenson v. Sawoska, 215 Conn. 148, 153, 575 A.2d 206, 208 (1990); Berndston v. Annino, 177 Conn. 41, 45, 411 A.2d 36, 39 (1979). See also Higgins v. Karp, 243 Conn. 495, 507, 706 A.2d 1, 6–7 (1998) ("may well have affected the trial court's conclusion"); Borkowski v. Borkowski, 228 Conn. 729, 747, 638 A.2d 1060, 1069 (1994); and Pelarinos v. Henderson, 34 Conn.App. 726, 643 A.2d 894, 897, cert. denied, 231 Conn. 909, 648 A.2d 155 (1994). To some extent this will probably overlap the definition of an abuse of discretion. See State v. Onofrio, 179 Conn. 23, 30, 425 A.2d 560, 565 (1979).

In criminal cases involving nonconstitutional error, such error is harmless when "an appellate court has a fair assurance that the error did not substantially affect the verdict." State v. Sawyer, 279 Conn. 331, 357, 904 A.2d 101, 117 (2006) (overruled on other grounds by, State v. DeJesus, 288 Conn. 418, 953 A.2d 45 (2008)) (quoting a Second Circuit case). For constitutional cases, see the fourth prong of *Golding*.

An older case adopting a broad test for harmful error is Bosworth v. Bosworth, 131 Conn. 389, 391, 40 A.2d 186, 187 (1944). In State v. Camera, 132 Conn. 247, 251, 43 A.2d 664, 665 (1945), and Peck v. Pierce, 63 Conn. 310, 320, 28 A. 524, 528 (1893), the court disapproved a statement by the trial court that its conclusion would have been the same even if certain inadmissible evidence was excluded. The same result was reached when the trial judge said he was not influenced by an improperly filed brief. Spiro v. Nitkin, 72 Conn. 202, 207, 44 A. 13, 14–15 (1899). See also In Re Samantha C., 268 Conn. 614, 675, 847 A.2d 883, 920 (2004) (unlikely court would have spent so much time discussing improper evidence if it made no difference). But see Leddy v. Raccio, 118 Conn.App. 604, 984 A.2d 1140 (2009), giving a narrow reading to the Peck line of cases.

Error induced by the appellant generally cannot be a ground for finding error. State v. Cruz, 269 Conn. 97, 105, 848 A.2d 445, 450 (2004); Sachs v. Sachs, 60 Conn.App. 337, 345, 759 A.2d 510, 515 (2000); State v. Boyd, 36 Conn.App. 516, 520–21, 651 A.2d 1313, 1316, cert. denied, 232 Conn. 912, 654 A.2d 356 (1995).

Another case suggests in dictum that the burden of showing prejudice may shift to the appellee if he was responsible for the error. Williams v. Salamone, 192 Conn. 116, 119–22, 470 A.2d 694, 697–98 (1984).

Harmful error is more difficult to prove if the general verdict rule applies. This rule is best explained in Curry v. Burns, 225 Conn. 782, 626 A.2d 719 (1993). See also New England Estates, LLC v. Town of Branford, 294 Conn. 817, 853 n.27, 988 A.2d 229 (2010) (footnote not in Atlantic Reporter); Kunst v. Vitale, 42 Conn.App. 528, 535 n.4, 680 A.2d 339, 343 n.4 (1996).

§ 60-6. Appellate Jurists Sitting as Superior Court Judges

Without the permission of the chief justice, the justices of the supreme court and the judges of the appellate court will not, as judges of the superior court, in vacation, or when the superior court is not in session, pass orders which may be the subject of an appeal, unless it appears that there is a necessity for prompt action, and that no other judges having jurisdiction over the matter can conveniently act.

Historical Note

Derivation:

1978 P.B. (1986–97), § 4186
1978 P.B., § 3072
1963 P.B., § 669
1951 P.B., § 468
1934 P.B., § 420
1922 P.B., § 69
1908 P.B., § 67
1899 P.B., § 67

This rule is substantially unchanged since 1899. The reference to the permission of the chief justice was added effective September 3, 1996.

Cross Reference

C.G.S.A. § 51-205.

CHAPTER 61

REMEDY BY APPEAL

§ 61-1. Right of Appeal

An aggrieved party may appeal from a final judgment, except as otherwise provided by law.

Historical Note

Derivation:

　1978 P.B. (1986–97), § 4000

　1978 P.B., § 3000

This rule was greatly simplified in 1996 to avoid referring to special-purpose appeals but leaving a catch-all exception that would include statutes that permit appeals from non-final judgments or forbid them from final ones. The definition of a final judgment is not self-evident, as the extensive commentary to § 61-1 shows. The leading definitional case, however, is State v. Curcio, 191 Conn. 27, 463 A.2d 566 (1983).

Prior to October 1, 1986, § 3000 stated as follows:

Sec. 3000. Right of Appeal

　The right of appeal is a statutory privilege accorded only upon compliance with the requirements of the applicable statutes and the rules of court.

　If a party is aggrieved by the decision of the court or judge upon any question or questions of law arising in the trial, including the denial of a motion to set aside the verdict, or in arrest of judgment, or the granting or denial of a motion under Sec. 321 for judgment notwithstanding the failure of the jury to return a verdict, he may appeal from the final judgment of the court or of such judge, or he may appeal from a decision setting aside a verdict or from the denial of a motion to set aside a nonsuit or from the denial of a motion for judgment notwithstanding the failure of the jury to return a verdict.

　If any party against whom a verdict is rendered at the direction of the court shall desire to appeal therefrom, he shall, within the time specified in Sec. 320 for filing such motions, file a motion to set aside and if such a motion is denied, he may appeal from the final judgment and claim as error the refusal to set the verdict aside in the manner provided in regard to other motions to set verdicts aside.

The following history refers to old § 3000:

The first paragraph of § 3000 was added effective January 1, 1985.

Derivation (second paragraph):

　1963 P.B., § 600

　1951 P.B., § 377

　1934 P.B., § 334

　1930 Rules Change, § 1

Derivation (third paragraph):

　1963 P.B., § 605

　1951 P.B., § 381

　1934 P.B., § 340

　1930 Rules Change (1932 Rule)

The second paragraph of § 3000 was amended in 1975 to change "assign" to "claim".

Otherwise, the second and third paragraphs of § 3000 were unchanged from 1963 to 1986. In 1963, changes were made concerning the types of decisions appealable. From then until 1986, one could appeal from the denial of a motion for judgment notwithstanding the failure of the jury to return a verdict, although the Supreme Court questioned its legality in Gold v. Newman, 211 Conn. 631, 560 A.2d 960 (1989).

The following sentence in the 1951 rule was omitted in the 1963 rule:

"There shall be but one appeal in any such case."

Prior to a 1943 amendment, one could appeal if he "shall consider himself aggrieved", but this language was held to mean substantially the same thing as the present "An aggrieved party". Waterbury Trust Co. v. Porter, 130 Conn. 494, 498–99, 35 A.2d 837, 838–39 (1944). But see Yudkin v. Gates, 60 Conn. 426, 427–28, 22 A. 776 (1891).

The need for a final judgment has existed since the early 1800's, E. J. Hansen

Elevator, Inc. v. Stoll, 167 Conn. 623, 626, 356 A.2d 893, 895 (1975); Gleason v. Chester, 1 Day 27 (1802); Id.1 Day 152 (1803). In the nineteenth century, appellate review was usually accomplished by a writ of error or motion for new trial. 3 Day 27.

The filing of the appeal was substantially changed in 1930. Previously the first document filed was usually a "notice of appeal"; the appeal itself, which included a recognizance and a statement of the reasons of appeal, did not need to be filed until after a finding was made by the court.

In 1996 this rule was broadened so that it applied to the judgment of a judge (e.g., a decision in chambers) as well as of a court. Previously this situation was covered by § 4001. Prior to 1864, decisions of a judge were not appealable. Brown v. Cray, 88 Conn. 141, 147, 89 A. 1123, 1124 (1914).

Cross References

Statutes authorizing appeals, C.G.S.A. §§ 51-197a to c, e to f; § 51-199; § 52-263; § 52-265a; § 42-110h, Arduini v. Automobile Ins. Co. of Hartford, 23 Conn.App. 585, 583 A.2d 152 (1990); § 47a-35 (summary process); § 49-35c (mechanic's liens); § 52-325b (lis pendens), but not § 52-325d, Dunham v. Dunham, 217 Conn. 24, 33–40, 584 A.2d 445, 449–53 (1991); § 52-278l (p.j.r.'s), Greenberg, Rhein and Margolis, Inc. v. Norris-Faye Horton Enterprises, Inc., 218 Conn. 162, 163 n.2, 588 A.2d 185 (1991), § 46b-142 (juvenile matters); § 52-400d (various post-judgment procedures, including § 52-356c but apparently *not* including § 52-356b)

Writ of Error, §§ 72-1 to 72-4

Forms JD-SC-28 and JD-SC-29

Maltbie, Conn.App.Proc.2d, § 1 (right to appeal); §§ 6–7 (party aggrieved); §§ 113, 182, 185 (decisions appealable); §§ 10–15 (final judgment); § 113 (appeal from directed verdict)

AUTHORS' COMMENTS

1. Right to Appeal

(i) What Is Appealable

An appeal is a proceeding authorized by statute since 1882 by which a case is transferred from a trial (Superior) court to a higher (Appellate or Supreme) court for relief from alleged error committed in the trial court. The appeal substituted for the motion in error and the motion for new trial, which existed before 1882. Zaleski v. Clark, 45 Conn. 397, 1877 WL 1954 (1877); White v. Howd, 66 Conn. 264, 266, 33 A. 915, 916 (1895); State v. Vaughan, 71 Conn. 457, 42 A. 640 (1899). For the difference between the two motions, see Wilson v. Peck, 39 Conn. 54, 63, 1872 WL 1442 (1872); Mead v. Dayton, 28 Conn. 33, 36, 1859 WL 1246 (1859).

An appeal is purely a statutory right. State v. S & R Sanitation Services, Inc., 202 Conn. 300, 307, 521 A.2d 1017, 1021 (1987); In re Judicial Inquiry No. 85-01, 221 Conn. 625, 605 A.2d 545 (1992); Newman v. Newman, 235 Conn. 82, 94, 663 A.2d 980, 986 (1995). So if there is no statutory right to appeal, there can be no appeal; Aston Motor Car Co. v. Mannion, 92 Conn. 568, 103 A. 655 (1918); In re Woodruff, 83 Conn. 330, 76 A. 294 (1910); even if there had previously been a right to appeal while the case was pending in the trial court, Neilson v. Perkins, 86 Conn. 425, 85 A. 686 (1913). In dictum, *Neilson* goes even further, and says the legislature can destroy jurisdiction on an existing appeal. The authors question this dictum.

The legislature generally has limited the right to appeal to the final judgment, although there are many exceptions. BNY Western Trust v. Roman, 295 Conn. 194, 202, 990 A.2d 853, 858 (2010) (citing this book). Thus by statute, an appeal can be taken as of right in the following cases:

(1) from final judgments or actions of Superior Court (C.G.S.A. §§ 51-197a), § 52–263. The appeal for the purpose of C.G.S.A. § 52–263 must be from a judicial proceeding. Board of Educ. of City of New Haven v. Tavares Pediatric Center, 276 Conn. 544, 555, 888 A.2d 65, 71 (2006). This Rule does not apply to:

(a) small claims, which are not appealable (C.G.S.A. § 51-197a);

(b) zoning and inland wetlands appeals, which are appealable only on certification by the Appellate Court (C.G.S.A. §§ 8-8, 8-9, 8-30a, 22a-43(d)); Christensen v. Zoning Bd. of Appeals of Town of Avon, 78 Conn.App. 378, 827 A.2d 716 (2003); except that a direct appeal may be taken from the action of a zoning board pursuant to C.G.S.A. § 14-321; Hendel's Investors Co. v. Zoning Bd. of Appeals of the Town of Montville, 62 Conn.App. 263, 269, 771 A.2d 182, 186 (2001);

(c) decisions of the Appellate Court, which are appealable to the Supreme Court only on certification by the Supreme Court (C.G.S.A. § 51-197f);

(d) habeas corpus appeals, which are appealable only with the permission of the trial judge or a judge of the Appellate or Supreme Court (C.G.S.A. § 52-470) (10 day period to petition); Hunnicutt v. Commissioner of Correction, 83 Conn.App. 199, 200 n.1, 848 A.2d 1229, 1230 n.1, cert. denied, 270 Conn. 914, 853 A.2d 527 (2004); this statute applies to the state as well as to the prisoners, Laws v. Warden, State Prison, 218 Conn. 479, 590 A.2d 436 (1991); note that action is to be taken by a judge or justice and not by a court; see Swanson v. Reincke, 151 Conn. 746, 201 A.2d 670 (1964); and note also that prisoners routinely appeal from the denial of permission to appeal, which yields almost the same review of the merits that granting permission would have yielded.

(e) criminal appeals by the state, which may be taken only with the permission of the trial judge (C.G.S.A. § 54-96; see commentary following);

(2) from decisions concerning mechanic's liens, prejudgment remedies, and lis pendens (C.G.S.A. §§ 49-35c; 52-278*l*; 52-325c); note carefully the 7-day appeal period, see authors' comments to § 63-1;

(3) from summary process decisions (C.G.S.A. § 47a-35; note carefully the 5-day appeal period);

(4) from temporary injunctions in labor cases (C.G.S.A. § 31-118) (14 days);

(5) from any order or decision (including non-final ones) which "involves a matter of substantial public interest and in which delay may work a substantial injustice" (C.G.S.A. § 52-265a; but see § vi following; note carefully the 14-day appeal period);

(6) from a judgment ordering an accounting (C.G.S.A. § 52-405; Karanian v. Maulucci, 185 Conn. 320 n.1, 440 A.2d 959 n.1 (1981));

(7) from election disputes under C.G.S.A. § 9-325 (see Wrinn v. Dunleavy, 186 Conn. 125, 132–35, 440 A.2d 261, 265–66 (1982));

(8) from some court closure and sealing orders (C.G.S.A. § 51-164x and P.B. § 11-20A(g); note carefully the 72-hour appeal period and query whether 72 hours is different from 3 days);

(9) from an evidentiary nonsuit (C.G.S.A. § 52-211); Grondin v. Curi, 262 Conn. 637, 648 n.13, 817 A.2d 61, 69 n.13 (2003).

(10) from decision of Workers' Compensation Commissioner on wrongful discharge (C.G.S.A. § 31-290a);

(11) from a decision on class action certification in CUTPA cases (C.G.S.A. § 42-110h).

(12) from the granting of a motion to set aside a verdict, but not from the

granting of a motion for a new trial (G.G.S.A. § 52-263); note that this statute applies to both civil and criminal cases. State v. Morrissette, 265 Conn. 658, 830 A.2d 704 (2003).

If a ruling is not immediately appealable, it may be appealed later when there is an appealable judgment, for the phrase "arising in the trial" has been construed broadly to include all trial court rulings. Breen v. Phelps, 186 Conn. 86, 90 n.6, 439 A.2d 1066, 1071 n.6 (1982). If a statute makes a judge's decision "conclusive", it is not appealable. In re Woodruff, 83 Conn. 330, 76 A. 294 (1910). The authors question the reasoning of *Woodruff*. "Conclusively" could as plausibly simply mean "final," in other words, "appealable." Trial court decisions should not be completely insulated from appellate review unless the legislature makes its intent to the contrary absolutely clear.

On the other hand, if a ruling is immediately appealable, it may be that it cannot be appealed later. See State v. Kelly, 208 Conn. 365, 370–71, 545 A.2d 1048, 1051 (1988) (court closure order); In re Shamika F., 256 Conn. 383, 773 A.2d 347 (2001) (temporary custody order). See § 61-2 and comments.

(ii) Where to Appeal

All appeals go directly to the Appellate Court except that the following appeals go to the Supreme Court (C.G.S.A. § 51-199):

(1) [for original jurisdiction of Supreme Court, see below];
(2) decision declaring state (but apparently not federal) statute or constitutional provision unconstitutional;
(3) conviction of capital felony, class A felony or any other felony where the maximum punishment that may be imposed exceeds 20 years (P.A. 98-81, § 5, effective October 1, 1998);
(4) sentence of death;
(5) election or primary dispute under C.G.S.A. §§ 9-323, 9-325;
(6) reprimand or censure (but apparently not the failure to reprimand or censure) a probate judge under C.G.S.A. § 45a-65;
(7) decision regarding judicial removal or suspension under C.G.S.A. § 51-51j;
(8) decision of judicial review counsel under C.G.S.A. § 51-51r;
(9) important cases accepted by the Supreme Court under C.G.S.A. § 52-265a;
(10) writ of error (a writ is not an appeal; see Chapter 72);
(11) any other matter provided by law.

Even if an appeal can be taken directly to the Supreme Court, that Court may still transfer it to the Appellate Court. Vasquez v. Superior Court, 102 Conn.App. 394, 395 n.1, 925 A.2d 1112, 1115 n.1, cert. denied, 284 Conn. 915, 931 A.2d 935 (2007).

Counsel who would like an appeal filed in the Appellate Court to be heard by the Supreme Court should make a motion to the Supreme Court under § 65-2.

Reapportionment cases bypass the Superior and Appellate Courts and are decided pursuant to the Supreme Court's grant of original jurisdiction (C.G.S.A. § 51-199; Constitutional Amendment, Art. 16, § 2); Fonfara v. Reapportionment Com'n, 222 Conn. 166, 610 A.2d 153 (1992); *In re Petition of Reapportionment Commission, S.C. 16642* (Order entered December 7, 2001 granting petition); In re Petition of Reappointment Commission, 303 Conn. 798, 36 A.3d 661 (2012) (adopting report of special master).

(iii) Writ of Error

If no specific statutory appellate rights are provided, an alternate method of testing the jurisdiction of the lower court is the common law writ of error. Such a writ is independent of the statutory appellate process, State v. Assuntino, 173

Conn. 104, 376 A.2d 1091 (1977). For further discussion of the writ of error, see commentary to § 72-1.

(iv) Contempt Appeals

In spite of statutory authority to take appeals from final judgments, there appears to be no right of appeal from a judgment of summary criminal contempt for actions in the courtroom. In that situation the defendant must apply for a writ of error, In re Dodson, 214 Conn. 344, 346, 572 A.2d 328, 330 (1990); Banks v. Thomas, 241 Conn. 569, 589, 698 A.2d 268, 279 (1997). This appears to be so even when the issue is the effectiveness of counsel during the criminal contempt proceeding. Robinson v. Commissioner of Correction, 62 Conn.App. 429, 440, 771 A.2d 952, 959, cert. denied, 257 Conn. 902, 777 A.2d 194 (2001). The authors do not agree with this decision.

Civil contempts, and criminal contempts occurring outside the courtroom, are appealable but apparently limited to "questions of jurisdiction such as whether the court had authority to impose the punishment inflicted and whether the act or acts for which the penalty was imposed could constitute a contempt." Friedlander v. Friedlander, 191 Conn. 81, 84–85, 463 A.2d 587, 590 (1983); although an early case holds that nonjurisdictional issues may be raised, Baldwin v. Miles, 58 Conn. 496, 497–98, 20 A. 618, 618–19 (1890), and recent cases seem to expand review. See Hardy v. Superior Court, Judicial Dist. of Fairfield, 305 Conn. 824, 831–34, 48 A.3d 50, 56–57 (2012) (expanding review for criminal contempt cases); In re Leah S., 284 Conn. 685, 692–93, 935 A.2d 1021, 1026–27 (2007) (child protection appeal). It is difficult to understand why contempt judgments are entitled to such insulation from review. The issue was finessed in Papa v. New Haven Federation of Teachers, 186 Conn. 725, 731, 444 A.2d 196, 200, 3 Ed. Law Rep. 998, 116 L.R.R.M. (BNA) 2368 (1982), and again in Barbato v. J. & M. Corp., 194 Conn. 245, 250–51, 478 A.2d 1020, 1023 (1984). In Bryant v. Bryant, 228 Conn. 630, 636, 637 A.2d 1111, 1114 (1994), the court held that a civil contempt finding based on an arrearage under a dissolution decree was a final appealable order, overruling Perry v. Perry, 222 Conn. 799, 611 A.2d 400 (1992). *Bryant* was followed in Tomasso Bros., Inc. v. October Twenty-Four, Inc., 230 Conn. 641, 650 n.9, 646 A.2d 133, 138 n.9 (1994), and Khan v. Hillyer, 306 Conn. 205, 49 A.3d 996 (2012), holds that a civil contempt finding accompanied by a coercive action is a final order.

Compare the federal rules, which are that a civil contempt ruling against a party is not immediately appealable; Commodity Futures Trading Com'n v. Armstrong, 269 F.3d 109 (2d Cir.2001); International Business Machines Corp. v. U.S., 493 F.2d 112 (2d Cir. 1973); whereas criminal contempt and civil contempt rulings against a nonparty (for example, a refusal to be deposed) are, Application of American Tobacco Co., 866 F.2d 552 (2d Cir.1989); International Business Machines Corp. v. U.S., 493 F.2d 112 (2d Cir. 1973).

In any event, a contempt order is not appealable until the penalty is set. N.D.R. Liuzzi v. Lighthouse Litho, LLC, 144 Conn.App. 613, 75 A.3d 694 (2013).

(v) Criminal Appeals by Permission

Habeas corpus decisions can be appealed by either party only if the trial judge or an appellate judge gives permission. C.G.S.A. § 52-470(b). However, an appeal from a denial of a right to appeal may be filed, and the threshold question will be whether there was an abuse of discretion in the denial. Simms v. Warden, 229 Conn. 178, 186–89, 640 A.2d 601, 606–07 (1994); Simms v. Warden, 230 Conn. 608, 646 A.2d 126 (1994) (no abuse of discretion found); Rivera v. Commissioner of Correction, 254 Conn. 214, 226–28, 756 A.2d 1264, 1272–73 (2000) (abuse of discretion found where appeal was not frivolous). If lack of frivolity is the test, the Supreme Court should directly say so.

A denial of a petition for a new trial requires permission to appeal. C.G.S.A. § 54-95; Santiago v. State, 261 Conn. 533, 804 A.2d 801 (2002).

The state cannot appeal in a criminal case unless the trial court permits it, C.G.S.A. § 54-96; State v. Anonymous, 55 Conn.App. 250, 739 A.2d 298 (1999). The constitutionality of this statute was upheld in State v. Audet, 170 Conn. 337, 342, 365 A.2d 1082, 1085 (1976). However, the trial court cannot limit such an appeal only to certain issues, State v. Berry, 156 Conn. 651, 652, 240 A.2d 97, 97 (1968). Also, the action of the trial judge on the request for permission to appeal has been held reviewable on a motion for review (§ 66-6) to determine whether the trial court abused its discretion, State v. S & R Sanitation Services, Inc., 202 Conn. 300, 521 A.2d 1017 (1987) (no); State v. Bergin, 214 Conn. 657, 660–63, 574 A.2d 164, 166–68 (1990) (yes). However, Simms v. Warden, 229 Conn. 178, 186–89, 640 A.2d 601, 606–07 (1994), which concerns C.G.S.A. § 52-470(b), holds that an appeal from the denial of permission to appeal, and not a motion for review, is the proper remedy.

If a judge suppresses evidence, the state can move for dismissal and then appeal, State v. Ross, 189 Conn. 42, 454 A.2d 266 (1983). It appears that a pretrial appeal by the state generally must be only after the case is dismissed. State v. Southard, 191 Conn. 506, 467 A.2d 920 (1983).

Prior to 1985, the predecessor of § 63-1 explicitly permitted the state to appeal a judgment on a verdict of not guilty. Although this procedure had previously been upheld, State v. Palko, 122 Conn. 529, 538–42, 191 A. 320, 324–26 (1937), aff'd Palko v. State of Connecticut, 302 U.S. 319, 58 S. Ct. 149, 82 L. Ed. 288 (1937); *Palko* was overruled in Benton v. Maryland, 395 U.S. 784, 89 S. Ct. 2056, 23 L. Ed. 2d 707 (1969). For state cases applying *Benton*, see State v. Flower, 176 Conn. 224, 405 A.2d 655 (1978); State v. Jacobowitz, 182 Conn. 585, 594, 438 A.2d 792, 796 (1981), overruled in part by State v. Welch, 224 Conn. 1, 615 A.2d 505 (1992).

However, if reversal on appeal would not require further proceedings, such as when the trial court enters an acquittal in spite of a verdict of guilty, an appeal by the state is permitted, State v. Avcollie, 174 Conn. 100, 384 A.2d 315 (1977). *Flower*, which was a non-jury case, also suggests that if there is a sufficient record so that the appellate court can make a determination of guilty without further proceedings, that also would be permitted.

If the court grants a motion for accelerated rehabilitation and the defendant successfully completes the program, the state can appeal from the dismissal and claim that the original motion should not have been granted. State v. Angelo, 25 Conn.App. 235, 239-40, 594 A.2d 24, 25-26, cert. denied, 220 Conn. 911, 597 A.2d 335 (1991).

(vi) Non-final Judgments

C.G.S.A. § 52-265a, (see §§ 83-1 to 83-4), states in relevant part:

"Notwithstanding the provisions of sections 52-264 and 52-265, any party to an action who is aggrieved by an order or decision of the Superior Court in an action involving a matter of substantial public interest and in which delay may work a substantial injustice, may appeal under this section from such order or decision to the Supreme Court within two weeks from the date of the issuance of the order or decision. The appeal shall state the question of law on which it is based."

The chief justice must grant certification to appeal and does so two or three times a year. See Lopez v. Board of Education, 310 Conn. 576, 579, 81 A.3d 184, 186 (2013) (removal of Bridgeport superintendent); State v. Komisarjevsky, 302 Conn. 162, 165, 25 A.3d 613 (2011) (unsealing defendant's witness list); State v. Elias G., 302 Conn. 39, 40 n.1, 23 A.3d 718, 719 n.1 (2011) (youthful offender transfer to regular docket); State v. B.B., 300 Conn. 748, 750 n.1, 17 A.3d 30, 32 n.1 (2011) (denial of such transfer); Foley v. State Elections Enforcement Com'n, 297 Conn. 764, 2 A.3d 823 (2010) (dispute over public funding of primary for governor); Missionary Soc. of Connecticut v. Board of Pardons and Paroles, 272

Conn. 647, 866 A.2d 538 (2005) (one of several cases involving death-row inmate Michael Ross); Office of Governor v. Select Committee of Inquiry, 271 Conn. 540, 858 A.2d 709 (2004). If the case affects only the parties to the case, the chief justice is unlikely to grant the application. State v. Fielding, 296 Conn. 26, 35 n.7, 994 A.2d 96, 101 n.7 (2010). In Wiseman v. Armstrong, 269 Conn. 802, 807, 850 A.2d 114, 117 (2004), Chief Justice Sullivan granted certification while an appeal in the Appellate Court was pending. Apparently, he excused the failure to file the application timely. See also Fielding. In Del Toro v. City of Stamford, 270 Conn. 532, 535–36 n.3, 853 A.2d 95, 97–98 n.3 (2004), he granted certification sua sponte one day after oral argument in the Supreme Court. In *Komisarjevsky*, a 5-2 majority treated a petition for certification as an application under § 52-265a, after which the chief justice granted review.

If the right involved is colorable and is the right not to be subjected to a trial, the denial is immediately appealable. State v. Moeller, 178 Conn. 67, 420 A.2d 1153 (1979); (double jeopardy); State v. Seravalli, 189 Conn. 201, 455 A.2d 852 (1983) (same) Shay v. Rossi, 253 Conn. 134, 749 A.2d 1147 (2000), overruled in part by Miller v. Egan, 265 Conn. 301, 828 A.2d 549 (2003) (sovereign immunity); Chadha v. Charlotte Hungerford Hosp., 272 Conn. 776, 865 A.2d 1163 (2005) (absolute immunity of defendants); Hopkins v. O'Connor, 282 Conn. 821, 925 A.2d 1030 (2007) (same); Young v. Metropolitan Property and Cas. Ins. Co., 60 Conn.App. 107, 112-13, 758 A.2d 452, 454-55, cert. denied, 255 Conn. 906, 762 A.2d 912 (2000) (collateral estoppel). Note, however, that the denial of a motion to dismiss where governmental or municipal immunity is claimed is not a final judgment. Vejseli v. Pasha, 282 Conn. 561, 923 A.2d 688 (2007).

However, reservations do not require a final judgment. State v. Sanabria, 192 Conn. 671, 681–85, 474 A.2d 760, 767–69 (1984). See also Kinsella v. Jaekle, 192 Conn. 704, 709–11, 475 A.2d 243, 247–48 (1984).

The statute governing probate appeals to the superior court allows virtually any decree or order to be appealed. Doyle v. Reardon, 11 Conn.App. 297, 527 A.2d 260 (1987).

(vii) Small Claims

No appeal may generally be taken from a small claims judgment (C.G.S.A. § 51-197a); State v. Sanabria, 192 Conn. 671, 683, 474 A.2d 760, 768 (1984), but there are narrow exceptions. A lower court has held (2-1) that the accidental failure of suit statute (§ 52-592) may apply if the small claims judgment was not on the merits. New Milford Block Co. v. Ericson, 3 Conn. Cir. Ct. 1, 206 A.2d 487 (App. Div. 1964). The same court also stated in dictum that a motion to reopen the judgment (C.G.S.A. § 52-212) is proper, 3 Conn.Cir. at 7, 206 A.2d at 490. A third possibility not mentioned in *Ericson* is the writ of error. Cannavo Enterprises, Inc. v. Burns, 194 Conn. 43, 48, 478 A.2d 601, 604 (1984). This option was narrowed in 1986. See § 72-1; Beizer v. Dobrowolski, 11 Conn. L. Rptr. 71, 1994 WL 51040 (Conn. Super. Ct. 1994).

(viii) Certification from Federal Courts

Effective October 1, 1985, the Supreme Court is authorized to accept questions from the federal courts where Connecticut law is dispositive of the federal case. C.G.S.A. § 51-199(a). Tribal courts were added in 2005. See §§ 82-1 to 82-7.

(ix) Miscellaneous Appeals

A judgment entered by consent or stipulation is not subject to appeal even if improperly entered, although the denial of a motion to correct such a judgment is appealable, William G. Major Const. Co. v. DeMichely, 166 Conn. 368, 375, 349 A.2d 827, 830–31 (1974); Sergeant v. Sergeant, 39 Conn.App. 57, 62 n.9, 663 A.2d 445, 448 n.9 (1995); as is a granting of a motion to enforce a judgment;

Bernet v. Bernet, 56 Conn.App. 661, 745 A.2d 827, cert. denied, 252 Conn. 954, 749 A.2d 1202 (2000). But see some careless language in Connecticut Pharmaceutical Ass'n, Inc. v. Milano, 191 Conn. 555, 558, 559–60, 468 A.2d 1230, 1232, 1233 (1983). A motion for a new trial after a stipulated judgment has been considered on the merits. Sparaco v. Tenney, 175 Conn. 436, 399 A.2d 1261 (1978). If the stipulated judgment reserved certain rights, a motion to set it aside is not a prerequisite to an appeal. Mulligan v. Hall, 229 Conn. 224, 640 A.2d 108 (1994).

The jurisdiction of the Supreme Court must not be confused with the jurisdiction of the lower court, for the Supreme Court must always first decide whether it has jurisdiction of the appeal before it can decide whether the lower court had jurisdiction. Belden v. Sedgwick, 68 Conn. 560, 567, 37 A. 417, 418 (1897). Likewise, lack of trial court jurisdiction does not deprive the Supreme Court of appellate jurisdiction. State v. Johnson, 301 Conn. 630, 641–42, 26 A.3d 59 (2011). Contrast Application of Smith, 133 Conn. 6, 8, 47 A.2d 521, 523 (1946), where the Supreme Court said the trial court lacked jurisdiction and then, in a *non sequitur,* dismissed the appeal on that basis. See also Lusas v. St. Patrick's Roman Catholic Church Corp. of Waterbury, 123 Conn. 166, 193 A. 204 (1937) (jurisdiction of trial court decided on merits even though Supreme Court lacked jurisdiction). The authors would advise not relying on *Lusas.* See Girard v. Carbones Auto Body, Inc., 35 Conn.Supp. 625, 626–27, 403 A.2d 281, 282 (Super. Ct. Appellate Sess. 1978). In the authors' opinion, the correct rule is found in Reardon v. Department of Public Health and Addiction Services, 37 Conn.App. 694, 657 A.2d 702 (1995), holding that a trial court order dismissing a case for lack of jurisdiction is an appealable final judgment.

There are three unusual situations peculiar to criminal appeals. A defendant who is a fugitive is disentitled to an appeal, State v. Leslie, 166 Conn. 393, 349 A.2d 843 (1974); even in some circumstances if the fugitive returns, State v. Brabham, 301 Conn. 376, 21 A.3d 800 (2011); and an appeal by a defendant who dies is normally moot, State v. Trantolo, 209 Conn. 169, 549 A.2d 1074 (1988); State v. Grasso, 172 Conn. 298, 299, 374 A.2d 239, 240 (1977), although the Court's reliance on State v. Raffone, 161 Conn. 117, 119–20, 285 A.2d 323, 325–26 (1971), appears somewhat dubious. Finally, a lower court has held that a defendant may appeal from a judgment of not guilty by reason of insanity, State v. Marzbanian, 2 Conn. Cir. Ct. 312, 315–17, 198 A.2d 721, 724–25, cert. denied, 151 Conn. 730, 197 A.2d 944 (App. Div. 1963).

If the Appellate Court denies certification in a zoning appeal, that denial cannot be appealed by certification to the Supreme Court. Grieco v. Zoning Com'n of Town of Redding, 226 Conn. 230, 627 A.2d 432 (1993).

An appeal can be taken directly from the judgment accepting a verdict; Santopietro v. City of New Haven, 239 Conn. 207, 211–21, 682 A.2d 106, 108–13 (1996); but it is still unwise and may in some circumstances, such as when the issue first arises when the verdict is rendered, be fatal to bypass the motion to set aside the verdict. While an appeal can be taken directly from the verdict in 20 days under P.B. § 63-1(b), if one wishes to file a postverdict motion before considering an appeal, such a motion generally must be filed in 10 days under P.B.§ 16-35.

It is important that the trial court specifically render judgment if there is going to be an appeal. However, in Northeast Elec. Contractors v. Udolf, 1 Conn.App. 169, 171 n.3, 469 A.2d 419, 420 n.3 (1984), the Appellate Court excused the lack of a formal judgment where the trial court found the facts necessary for a judgment.

2. Who Can Appeal

(i) Party in Lower Court

The Supreme Court has held that a nonparty to the Superior Court proceedings does not have the right to appeal under C.G.S.A. § 52-263. State v. Salmon, 250 Conn. 147, 735 A.2d 333 (1999) (forfeiture of bond in criminal case; bondsman has no right to appeal). See also Security Mut. Life Ins. Co. of New York v. Kings West Ltd. Partnership, 56 Conn.App. 44, 741 A.2d 329 (1999), cert. denied, 252 Conn. 928, 746 A.2d 789 (2000) (receiver); Leydon v. Town of Greenwich, 57 Conn.App. 727, 750 A.2d 492 (2000) (sanctions against amicus curiae). The proper mechanism to obtain review is by a writ of error under Chapter 72. However, an appeal is still possible from the denial of a motion to intervene if the claim is made of an absolute right to do so. King v. Sultar, 253 Conn. 429, 436, 754 A.2d 782, 787 (2000).

(ii) Aggrievement, Standing and Mootness

In order for someone to appeal, the appellant must have standing, and the appellant must be aggrieved. Electrical Contractors, Inc. v. Department of Educ., 303 Conn. 402, 411–14, 35 A.3d 188, 197–98, 192 L.R.R.M. (BNA) 2954, 2012-1 Trade Cas. (CCH) ¶ 77768 (2012). In addition, the appeal must be ripe. Keller v. Beckenstein, 305 Conn. 523, 537–38, 46 A.3d 102, 100–11 (2012). A case is not ripe if the questions raised are merely hypothetical unless some future event occurs. Esposito v. Specyalski, 268 Conn. 336, 844 A.2d 211 (2004) (indemnification appeal not ripe until responsibility for accident decided).

The Supreme Court clearly distinguished between standing and aggrievement in Gladysz v. Planning and Zoning Com'n of Town of Plainville, 256 Conn. 249, 773 A.2d 300 (2001). Standing is the broader concept, and thus a litigant who has standing may not be aggrieved. A litigant who *may* have a specific interest in a controversy has standing, Wilcox v. Webster Ins., Inc., 294 Conn. 206, 216–17, 982 A.2d 1053, 1062 (2009) ("colorable claim of injury") whereas a litigant is aggrieved only if he *does* have a specific interest in the controversy and is injured by it. Id. Put another way, standing may get you through the courthouse door but it won't get you a judgment unless you prove aggrievement. However, a litigant who is not the proper person to seek an adjudication lacks standing as a matter of law. Goodyear v. Discala, 269 Conn. 507, 511, 849 A.2d 791 (2004). Occasionally the Supreme Court confuses standing with aggrievement, as in Soracco v. Williams Scotsman, Inc., 292 Conn. 86, 97, 971 A.2d 1, 8 (2009) ("the litigant" has failed to demonstrate the requisite aggrievement to establish standing").

Both standing and aggrievement generally require a specific and personal interest in the subject matter rather than a general interest that any member of the community might have. Town of New Hartford v. Connecticut Resources Recovery Authority, 291 Conn. 511, 519, 970 A.2d 583, 589 (2009); Eder Bros., Inc. v. Wine Merchants of Connecticut, Inc., 275 Conn. 363, 368–70, 880 A.2d 138, 142–43 (2005). State v. Anonymous, 237 Conn. 501, 680 A.2d 956 (1996) (obligation to destroy criminal records); Connecticut Business and Industries Ass'n, Inc. v. Commission on Hospitals and Health Care, 214 Conn. 726, 573 A.2d 736 (1990) (public cannot appeal hospital rate decision). See also Community Collaborative of Bridgeport, Inc. v. Ganim, 241 Conn. 546, 698 A.2d 245 (1997) (co-chair not authorized to sue); Connecticut Post Ltd. Partnership v. South Cent. Connecticut Regional Council of Governments, 60 Conn.App. 21, 758 A.2d 408 (2000) (appeal withdrawn (2001)) (no property interest in protection from competition). Likewise, where no practical relief can be granted on appeal, the appeal must be dismissed. Clement v. Clement, 34 Conn.App. 641, 643 A.2d 874 (1994). An appellant who obtained the relief sought in the trial court lacks aggrievement. Patriot Nat. Bank v. Braverman, 134 Conn.App. 327, 38 A.3d 267 (2012).

In addition to classical aggrievement, which requires a specific and personal interest, there is statutory aggrievement. The plaintiff in Burton v. Commissioner of Environmental Protection, 291 Conn. 789, 970 A.2d 640 (2009), was statutorily aggrieved as a member of the public because the environmental statute in question so provided.

As might be expected, this generality does not solve all specific problems. In zoning cases, the appellant's real property values must ordinarily be affected by the decision, Sheridan v. Planning Bd. of City of Stamford, 159 Conn. 1, 13, 266 A.2d 396, 402–03 (1969), but in liquor cases anyone in the community is deemed to be affected by it, Macaluso v. Zoning Bd. of Appeals of Town of Windsor, 167 Conn. 596, 600–01, 356 A.2d 885, 887 (1975). The Supreme Court has held that the requirement of a pecuniary interest "is too narrow" in probate cases, Gaucher (Estate of Camp) v. Camp's Estate, 167 Conn. 396, 400–401, 355 A.2d 303, 306 (1974). See also the broad test of Maloney v. Pac, 183 Conn. 313, 439 A.2d 349, 353–54 (1981). Taxpayer standing was allowed in American-Republican, Inc. v. City of Waterbury, 183 Conn. 523, 526–28, 441 A.2d 23, 25 (1981), but denied in Sadloski v. Town of Manchester, 235 Conn. 637, 668 A.2d 1314 (1995). Parent standing concerning an adult mentally disabled child was allowed in Buchholz's Appeal From Probate, 9 Conn.App. 413, 519 A.2d 615 (1987). The interest involved must be direct, Urrata v. Izzillo, 1 Conn.App. 17, 467 A.2d 943 (1983) (creditor of heir cannot challenge will).

Associational standing was permitted in Connecticut Ass'n of Health Care Facilities, Inc. v. Worrell, 199 Conn. 609, 508 A.2d 743 (1986), and reaffirmed in Connecticut Ass'n of Not-For-Profit Providers for the Aging v. Department of Social Services, 244 Conn. 378, 709 A.2d 1116 (1998). Associational standing and aggrievement were also discussed in Gay and Lesbian Law Students Ass'n at University of Connecticut School of Law v. Board of Trustees, University of Connecticut, 236 Conn. 453, 463–71, 673 A.2d 484, 490–93 (1996) (denial of assistance in securing employment provides aggrievement).

The definition of aggrievement has historically varied depending on when the issue is raised during the appeal. If there is any possibility that an appellant may or will suffer injury because of a judgment, it is clear that he is "aggrieved" within the meaning of §61-1 for the purpose of avoiding a motion to dismiss, Waterbury Trust Co. v. Porter, 130 Conn. 494, 499, 35 A.2d 837, 839 (1944). However, when the merits of the appeal are determined, the old rule was that the appeal would be dismissed unless the appellant has shown that he is actually harmed by the judgment, McWilliams v. Morton, 97 Conn. 514, 519, 117 A. 557, 558–59 (1922). This appears no longer to be the case. See Hartford Kosher Caterers, Inc. v. Gazda, 165 Conn. 478, 486, 338 A.2d 497, 502 (1973), where the "possibility" test was applied on the merits of the appeal. Gazda was reaffirmed in Merrimac Associates, Inc. v. DiSesa, 180 Conn. 511, 429 A.2d 967 (1980), where an unsuccessful bidder at a probate sale was given the right to appeal. See also Hall v. Planning Commission of Town of Ledyard, 181 Conn. 442, 435 A.2d 975 (1980). In Lord v. Lord, 44 Conn.App. 370, 373 n.2, 689 A.2d 509, 511 n.2, cert. denied, 241 Conn. 913, 696 A.2d 985 (1997), the Appellate Court stated that the defendant's stipulation in satisfaction of a contempt motion did not render the appeal moot because the finding of contempt could have future collateral consequences. Similarly, even though a defendant stipulated to the terms of an inevitable foreclosure, the defendant remained aggrieved where it had contested liability at trial. Barasso v. Rear Still Hill Road, LLC, 81 Conn.App. 798, 842 A.2d 1134 (2004).

A proper party in the trial court is not necessarily a proper party on the appeal. Connecticut Resources Recovery Authority v. Planning and Zoning Com'n of Town of Torrington, 46 Conn.App. 563, 565, 699 A.2d 314, 315, cert. denied, 243 Conn. 936, 702 A.2d 640 (1997). In Waterbury Trust Co. v. Porter, 130 Conn. 494, 500, 35 A.2d 837, 839 (1944), concerning the validity of a private trust funding a trade school in Waterbury, the City of Waterbury was held to be a proper defendant in the trial court, because of the possibility that the trust would be held valid, but when the trust was declared invalid, the city was held not to be aggrieved of the decision, because it is not the function of the city to represent the public interest in such a case. The Freedom of Information Commission was likewise held not aggrieved of a Superior Court decision modifying a ruling of the FOIC Local 1303 and Local 1378 of Council No. 4, AFSCME, AFL-CIO v. Freedom of Information Com'n, 191 Conn. 173, 463 A.2d 613 (1983). The standing of the FOIC in such appeals was reinstated by P.A. 84-311. The State Board of Mediation and Arbitration apparently lacks standing to appeal in a *Local 1303* situation. City of Danbury v. International Ass'n of Firefighters, I.A.F.F., Local 801, 221 Conn. 244, 248 n.4, 603 A.2d 393, 395 n.4 (1992).

The removal of a fiduciary from office provides aggrievement, Stanley v. Stanley, 175 Conn. 200, 397 A.2d 101 (1978); however, an executor is not aggrieved by a judgment construing a will when the contesting beneficiaries have appeared, Jacobs v. Button, 79 Conn. 360, 362, 65 A. 150, 151 (1906); nor is a trustee in insolvency when a claim the trustee allowed is disallowed by the Superior Court, Appeal of Woodbury, 70 Conn. 455, 39 A. 791 (1898); nor is an administrator of an intestate estate aggrieved because his authority is revoked when a will is found and admitted, Gaucher (Estate of Camp) v. Camp's Estate, 167 Conn. 396, 401, 355 A.2d 303, 306 (1974). A testamentary trustee is aggrieved if a later will is found, O'Leary v. McGuinness, 140 Conn. 80, 98 A.2d 660 (1953); Zempsky's Appeal From Probate, 6 Conn.App. 521, 506 A.2d 1050, cert. denied, 200 Conn. 808, 512 A.2d 231 (1986). Minority trustees also have the right to appeal, Belcher v. Conway, 179 Conn. 198, 205 n.1, 425 A.2d 1254, 1257 n.1 (1979).

A party that is not factually aggrieved of a decision may nevertheless appeal if the legislature authorizes it, Weigel v. Planning and Zoning Commission of Town of Westport, 160 Conn. 239, 278 A.2d 766, 770 (1971) (abutting owner).

A person may be aggrieved of a refusal to answer a question in a declaratory judgment action, Town of West Hartford v. Willetts, 125 Conn. 266, 268 n.1, 5 A.2d 13, 14 n.1 (1939).

On the other hand, a litigant who fails to appeal from the final judgment against him cannot later claim to be aggrieved of an order setting a time for compliance with the judgment in order to test the underlying order. Willocks v. Klein, 38 Conn.App. 317, 660 A.2d 869 (1995).

A case normally becomes moot if an appellant is no longer aggrieved. Lichtman v. Beni, 280 Conn. 25, 905 A.2d 647 (2006) (appellant failed to move to stay the discharge of a mechanic's lien pending appeal); Peart v. Psychiatric Sec. Review Bd., 41 Conn.App. 688, 678 A.2d 488 (1996) (Board changed its mind pending appeal); or there is no longer an actual controversy; In re Kiara R., 129 Conn.App. 604, 21 A.3d 883 (2011) (appeal by mother claiming visitation once she is awarded custody); Rosengarten v. Downes, 71 Conn.App. 372, 802 A.2d 170, appeal dismissed, 261 Conn. 936, n.*, 806 A.2d 1066, n* (2002) (appeal of civil union dissolution case dismissed as moot where plaintiff died while appeal was pending); Chimblo v. Monahan, 265 Conn. 650, 829 A.2d 841 (2003); see First Trust Nat. Ass'n v. Hitt, 36 Conn.App. 171, 649 A.2d 798 (1994).

A case is moot if the court cannot grant practical relief, such as where a defendant fails to seek review of a ruling holding he lacked standing to challenge a search. State v. Jevarjian, 307 Conn. 559, 58 A.3d 243 (2012) (mooting certified appeal on the propriety of the search); see also Wyatt Energy, Inc. v. Motiva Enterprises, LLC, 308 Conn. 719, 66 A.3d 848 (2013) (failure to challenge alternate findings that would affirm judgment mooted appeal).

An issue that is capable of repetition, yet evading review, is an exception to the mootness rule. In re Jeffrey M., 307 Conn. 640, 59 A.3d 165 (2013) (doctrine not applied); In re Emoni W., 305 Conn. 723, 729–33, 48 A.3d 1, 4–6 (2012) (doctrine applied). Loisel v. Rowe, 233 Conn. 370, 660 A.2d 323 (1995) thoroughly discussed this exception. See Dutkiewicz v. Dutkiewicz, 289 Conn. 362, 957 A.2d 821 (2008) (requirement to attend parental education program); Putman v. Kennedy, 279 Conn. 162, 167, 900 A.2d 1256, 1260 (2006) (distinguishing the collateral consequences doctrine); Conetta v. City of Stamford, 246 Conn. 281, 715 A.2d 756 (1998) (case dismissed as moot); In re Steven M., 264 Conn. 747, 754–56, 826 A.2d 156, 163–64 (2003) (transfer order for juvenile in custody of Department of Children and Families was reviewable despite mootness); Russo v. Common Council of City of Middletown, 80 Conn.App. 100, 832 A.2d 1227 (2003) (requirement for exception not met). Also, a case is not moot if "there is a reasonable possibility that prejudicial consequences will occur." Williams v. Ragaglia, 261 Conn. 219, 226, 802 A.2d 778, 782–83 (2002); Town of Wallingford v. Department of Public Health, 262 Conn. 758, 767, 817 A.2d 644 (2003).

If a case becomes moot on appeal, the appellant may be able to have the lower court decision or decisions vacated. In re Jessica M., 250 Conn. 747, 738 A.2d 1087 (1999); State v. Charlotte Hungerford Hosp., 308 Conn. 140, 60 A.3d 946 (2013). Similarly, where a criminal appeal is not moot because of collateral consequences even though the defendant has served the sentence, the defendant may have the conviction vacated. Monsam v. Dearington, 82 Conn.App. 451, 844 A.2d 927 (2004). For a discussion of the grounds for vacatur, see State v. Singleton, 274 Conn. 426, 876 A.2d 1 (2005).

(iii) Plaintiff Accepting Remittitur

A plaintiff accepting a remittitur cannot appeal another aspect of the damages if the issue is not separable from the ruling on the remittitur. Cohen v. Yale-New Haven Hosp., 260 Conn. 747, 800 A.2d 499 (2002).

3. Decisions Appealable

The following are appealable in the jurisdictional statement on forms JD-SC-28 and JD-SC-29:

    a.   a final judgment (§ 61-1; C.G.S.A. § 52-263);

    b.   a decision granting a motion to set aside a verdict (C.G.S.A. § 52-263), Stern v. Allied Van Lines, Inc., 246 Conn. 170, 173–75, 717 A.2d 195, 197–98 (1998); State v. Morrissette, 265 Conn. 658, 830 A.2d 704 (2003); but see, Cheryl Terry Enterprises, Ltd. v. City of Hartford, 262 Conn. 240, 248 n.13, 811 A.2d 1272, 1277 n.13 (2002) (remainder of case must be disposed of too);

    c.   the denial of a motion to set aside an evidentiary nonsuit (§ 52-211), Minicozzi v. Atlantic Refining Co., 143 Conn. 226, 227–28, 120 A.2d 924, 925 (1956);

    d.   the grant of a nonsuit (§§ 52-210, 52-212); but a generally more practical alternative is to move to set it aside first, Jaquith v. Revson, 159 Conn. 427, 430–31, 270 A.2d 559, 561 (1970)); and

    e.   possibly certain other nonfinal judgments (see § 1 above);

Because the jurisdictional block in the appeal form, JD-SC-28 (labeled "Appeal"), now includes the word "judgment," the authors are confident that older cases holding that an appeal from a memorandum of decision or a motion to set aside a verdict is vulnerable to dismissal are now bad law. See such obsolete cases as Angier v. Barton, 160 Conn. 204, 207, 276 A.2d 782, 784 (1970); Maciejewska v. Lombard Bros., Inc., 171 Conn. 35, 37 n.1, 368 A.2d 206, 208 n.1 (1976); Windham Community Memorial Hospital v. City of Willimantic, 166 Conn. 113, 348 A.2d 651 (1974); Sharkey v. City of Stamford, 196 Conn. 253, 254, 492 A.2d 171, 172 (1985); Edward Sutt Associates, Inc. v. D & S Concrete Products, Inc., 3 Conn.App. 179 n.2, 485 A.2d 1358, 1359 n.2 (1985); and Serby v. Serby, 4 Conn.App. 398, 399 n.1, 494 A.2d 617, 618 n.1 (1985). In any event, the Supreme

Court held in Pritchard v. Pritchard, 281 Conn. 262, 275, 914 A.2d 1025, 1033 (2007), that the appeal forms do not implicate subject matter jurisdiction. Thus, if there is an error, it should be correctable. For example, if a party appeals from a nonfinal judgment, but the preliminary statement of issues shows the party is really appealing from a final judgment, the appeal is likely to be treated as an appeal from the final judgment. State v. Lanasa, 141 Conn.App. 685, 687, n.1, 62 A.3d 572, 575 n.1, cert. denied, 308 Conn. 945, 66 A.3d 885 (2013).

Under old § 3000, the granting of a directed verdict was not appealable; rather a motion to set aside the verdict had to be made. While such a motion is no longer mandatory, it should be filed as a matter of course. If it is granted, an appeal lies from that decision; if it is denied, an appeal lies from the final judgment, Bogart v. Tucker, 164 Conn. 277, 283, 320 A.2d 803, 806–07 (1973). On the denial of a motion to set aside a verdict, the entry of judgment is "a matter of course", Gordon v. Feldman, 164 Conn. 554, 557, 325 A.2d 247, 249–50 (1973), so a final judgment exists from which an appeal can be taken as soon as the motion to set aside is denied. It would appear that granting a motion for a new trial or a motion in arrest of judgment is not appealable, see § 40 of this commentary.

The defendant can appeal from a plaintiff's verdict that the court set aside as inadequate. Steinert v. Whitcomb, 84 Conn. 262, 268, 79 A. 675, 677 (1911).

From 1963 until 1986, this rule permitted an appeal from the denial of a motion for judgment notwithstanding the failure of the jury to return a verdict. Such a ruling is no longer immediately appealable, and the rule from 1963 until 1986 may have been invalid. Gold v. Newman, 211 Conn. 631, 560 A.2d 960 (1989).

4. Final Judgment

Although many judgments are clearly final (and therefore appealable) or interlocutory (and therefore not appealable unless a statutory exception exists) the gray area between these two ends of the finality spectrum has spawned endless litigation. The Supreme Court's standard definition is set forth in State v. Curcio, 191 Conn. 27, 31, 463 A.2d 566, 569 (1983). The *Curcio* test provides that an aggrieved party may bring an interlocutory appeal where either "the order or action terminates a separate and distinct proceeding . . . [or] the order or action so concludes the rights of the parties that further proceedings cannot affect them." *Id.* at 31, 463 A.2d at 569–70. Stating the rule, however, is easier than applying it. See Abreu v. Leone, 291 Conn. 332, 968 A.2d 385 (2009) (first prong met in an independent discovery proceeding); Woodbury Knoll, LLC v. Shipman and Goodwin, LLP, 305 Conn. 750, 755–69, 48 A.3d 16, 20–29 (2012) (same); Metropolitan Dist. v. Housing Authority of City of Hartford, 12 Conn.App. 499, 502–03, 531 A.2d 194, 196, cert. denied, 205 Conn. 814, 533 A.2d 568 (1987) (both tests met); Steiner v. Bran Park Associates, 216 Conn. 419, 582 A.2d 173 (1990) (case bifurcated); Papa v. Thimble Creek Condominium Ass'n, Inc., 50 Conn.App. 139, 716 A.2d 947 (1998) (neither test met); Montanaro v. Aspetuck Land Trust, Inc., 137 Conn.App. 1, 7 n.5, 48 A.3d 107, 113 n.5, cert. denied, 307 Conn. 932, 56 A.3d 715 (2012) (second test met). If the order fits into one of those categories, the order is appealable regardless of the fact that proceedings continue or that there may be a multiplicity of appeals. For example, Hartford Acc. and Indem. Co. v. Ace American Reinsurance Co., 279 Conn. 220, 901 A.2d 1164 (2006), established that *Curcio* applies to an order to post security because the plaintiff's loss would be irreparable. Dewart v. Northeastern Gas Transmission Co., 139 Conn. 512, 514, 95 A.2d 381, 382 (1953), established that an order to proceed to arbitration, being separate and distinct from the hearing before the arbitrator, is appealable. On the other hand, an order that does not fit into one of these categories is not appealable regardless of the urgency of relief requested, Planning and Zoning Comn of

Town of Middlefield v. Zemel Brothers, Inc., 159 Conn. 638, 268 A.2d 248 (1970); or irreparability of the harm, Olcott v. Pendleton, 128 Conn. 292, 295, 22 A.2d 633, 634–35 (1941) (both involving temporary injunctions); or the public policy requiring speedy adjudication of the issue, Prevedini v. Mobil Oil Corp., 164 Conn. 287, 294, 320 A.2d 797, 800–01 (1973) (stay of summary process proceeding).

Even an appellee's willingness to withdraw a portion of the case in order to make the judgment final is futile, since an appeal from a nonfinal judgment is void ab initio, Stroiney v. Crescent Lake Tax Dist., 197 Conn. 82, 86 n.3, 495 A.2d 1063, 1066 n.3 (1985). While the precise result in *Stroiney* may still have vitality today, its broad "void ab initio" reasoning no longer is valid in light of the last paragraph of § 61-9 added in 2010.

The parties and the trial court cannot manipulate the rules to create an artificial final judgment by withdrawing unadjudicated claims subject to reinstatement after the appeal is decided. Mazurek v. Great American Ins. Co., 284 Conn. 16, 33–34, 930 A.2d 682, 692 (2007). However, if the unadjudicated portion of the case that would destroy finality had been abandoned by the time of judgment, the trial papers could be amended to reflect that fact without affecting the finality of the original judgment. Zamstein v. Marvasti, 240 Conn. 549, 554–57, 692 A.2d 781, 784–86 (1997).

An especially clear discussion of the nature of a final judgment is found in State v. Kemp, 124 Conn. 639, 1 A.2d 761 (1938). Compare the discussion in the Gillespie v. United States Steel Corp., 379 U.S. 148, 85 S. Ct. 308, 13 L. Ed. 2d 199 (1964).

That an immediate appeal is available in an independent action does not make a similar but interlocutory order in an ongoing action immediately appealable. Ackerson v. Stramaglia, 225 Conn. 102, 105, 621 A.2d 1315, 1317 (1993).

It is very important to recognize a final judgment when it occurs, for if the aggrieved party fails immediately to appeal, or reserve right to appeal under § 61-5, the party will not be able to appeal at a later time, New Milford Water Co. v. Watson, 75 Conn. 237, 245, 52 A. 947, 950–51 (1902); City of Stamford v. Stephenson, 78 Conn.App. 818, 824-25, 829 A.2d 26, 29-30, cert. denied, 266 Conn. 915, 833 A.2d 466 (2003). Cf. Haynes v. Power Facility Evaluation Council, 177 Conn. 623, 629, 419 A.2d 342, 345 (1979).

WARNING! Prior to In re Shamika F., 256 Conn. 383, 773 A.2d 347 (2001), the authors' opinion was that rulings that were immediately appealable as final judgments even though they did not end the whole case gave the appellant an option: the ruling could be appealed immediately or it could be appealed later when the whole case was disposed of. *Shamika F.* makes deferring the appeal vulnerable to a res judicata claim, except in those few cases when a § 61-5 notice of intent to appeal can be filed. It may be that *Shamika F.* will, as it should, be eventually limited to child custody cases. In re Stephen M., 109 Conn.App. 644, 953 A.2d 668 (2008), explains the rationale underlying *In re Shamika F.* and offers a way to distinguish it from other appealable interlocutory orders. The authors' advice in the meantime is: Be safe rather than sorry; appeal all arguably final judgments, whether or not they dispose of the whole case, now. *Shamika F.* was cited in 2004, but fortunately only in the custody context, Sweeney v. Sweeney, 271 Conn. 193, 209, 856 A.2d 997, 1007 (2004).

Also, one must not be misled by the trial judge's opinion as to appealability. Thus an order labeled as a "temporary injunction" may in fact function as a permanent injunction and be appealable, Town of Bozrah v. Chmurynski, 303 Conn. 676, 681–82, 36 A.3d 210, 214–15 (2012); an order entitled "interlocutory judgment" may be appealable, Kerite Co. v. Alpha Employment Agency, Inc.,

166 Conn. 432, 436–37, 352 A.2d 288, 290 (1974); even if the Supreme Court labels it "interlocutory", Fitzgerald v. Fitzgerald, 169 Conn. 147, 151, 362 A.2d 889, 891 (1975); and a judgment made "without prejudice" may also be appealable, Foley v. Foley, 140 Conn.App. 490, 492 n.1, 58 A.3d 977, 978 n.1 (2013); Varanelli v. Luddy, 130 Conn. 74, 80, 32 A.2d 61, 64 (1943); Wojick v. Wojick, 164 Conn. 552, 553, 325 A.2d 288, 288 (1973) (issue of finality not discussed). See also Raudat v. Leary, 88 Conn.App. 44, 48–49, 868 A.2d 120, 123 (2005) ("partial judgment" held to be a final judgment). On the other hand, the trial judge's statement that he is entering a final judgment does not necessarily make it such. Wells Fargo Bank of Minnesota, N.A. v. Jones, 85 Conn.App. 120, 123 n.4, 856 A.2d 505, 508 n.4 (2004). Doublewal Corp. v. Toffolon, 195 Conn. 384, 390, 488 A.2d 444, 448 (1985); Paranteau v. DeVita, 208 Conn. 515, 519 n.7, 544 A.2d 634, 637 n.7 (1988).

The label on the order or motion also does not usually determine appealability. In In re Brianna F., 50 Conn.App. 805, 811–12, 719 A.2d 478, 482 (1998), the appellant filed a "Motion for Advice," a dubious sounding motion which the trial court nevertheless granted. The Appellate Court looked at the substance of the motion and order and held the ruling to be a final judgment.

The existence of a formal judgment file is not necessary before a final judgment exists. The judgment file simply is a reflection that a ruling already exists that constitutes a final judgment. Howarth v. Northcott, 152 Conn. 460, 462, 208 A.2d 540, 542 (1965), overruled on other grounds by Hao Thi Popp v. Lucas, 182 Conn. 545, 438 A.2d 755 (1980).

If the facts and legal argument of an order that is not final is inextricabley intertwined with an order that is final, the court will exercise jurisdiction over both claims. Aqleh v. Cadlerock Joint Venture II, L.P., 299 Conn. 84, 89–90, 10 A.3d 498, 502 (2010).

Whether particular orders were held to be final judgments or not are discussed below. Note that lack of a final judgment does not mean the ruling is never appealable but only that it is not appealable at that time.

A. *Administrative Agency Appeals*

The Supreme Court has held, overruling cases to the contrary, that *any* remand order in an appeal governed by C.G.S.A. § 4-183(j), the Uniform Administrative Procedure Act is immediately appealable. Commission on Human Rights and Opportunities v. Board of Educ. of Town of Cheshire, 270 Conn. 665, 855 A.2d 212 (2004).

However, the older cases not involving § 4-183(j), primarily appeals from local agencies and in workers' compensation cases, presumably are still viable. See Hummel v. Marten Transport, 282 Conn. 477, 923 A.2d 657 (2007) (affirming finality requirement for appeals pursuant to C.G.S.A. § 31-301b). Thus, unless § 4-183(j) applies, or error has been found and a new administrative hearing is ordered; Schieffelin and Co., Inc. v. Department of Liquor Control, 202 Conn. 405, 410, 521 A.2d 566, 568 (1987); O'Donnell v. City of Waterbury, 111 Conn.App. 1, 4 n.1, 958 A.2d 163, 165 n.1, cert. denied, 289 Conn. 959, 961 A.2d 422 (2008); an order that the administrative agency determine the merits of the plaintiff's claim; Gerte v. Logistec Connecticut, Inc., 283 Conn. 60, 924 A.2d 855 (2007); hear further evidence to complete the administrative record, Matey v. Estate of Dember, 210 Conn. 626, 556 A.2d 599 (1989); prepare the record properly; France v. Munson, 123 Conn. 102, 109, 192 A. 706, 709 (1937); or correct its finding; Luliewicz v. Eastern Malleable Iron Co., 126 Conn. 522, 12 A.2d 779 (1940); are not appealable. This rule also applies to a remand to an attorney trial referee for further proceedings. OCI Mortg. Corp. v. Marchese, 48 Conn.App. 750, 712 A.2d 449 (1998). In Levarge v. General Dynamics Corp., Elec. Boat Div., 282 Conn. 386, 920 A.2d 996 (2007), an appeal could not be taken from the compensation commissioner's decision before apportionment of liability.

The Supreme Court has held that an order remanding a case to a local zoning agency for a wholly new hearing is appealable. Watson v. Howard, 138 Conn. 464, 467, 86 A.2d 67, 68 (1952); see also Barry v. Historic Dist. Com'n of Borough of Litchfield, 108 Conn.App. 682, 687–701, 950 A.2d 1, 6–14, cert. denied, 289 Conn. 942, 959 A.2d 1008 (2008), which exhaustively discusses numerous other decisions in this area including Westover Park, Inc. v. Zoning Bd. of City of Stamford, 91 Conn.App. 125, 881 A.2d 412 (2005).

A remand directing a particular result in a zoning appeal is clearly appealable. Finley v. Inland Wetlands Com'n of Town of Orange, 289 Conn. 12, 24, 959 A.2d 569, 578–79 (2008); Kaufman v. Zoning Com'n of City of Danbury, 232 Conn. 122, 129–30, 653 A.2d 798, 803–04 (1995); see also Children's School, Inc. v. Zoning Bd. of Appeals of City of Stamford, 66 Conn.App. 615, 618–19, 785 A.2d 607, 611–12 (remand to consider only conditions of approval appealable), cert. denied, 259 Conn. 903, 789 A.2d 990 (2001). And if the remand is solely to perform a ministerial act, that decision is appealable. Birnie v. Electric Boat Corp., 288 Conn. 392, 394–95 n.1, 953 A.2d 28 (2008).

The granting of a motion to preclude defenses is not a final judgment when a further evidentiary hearing is necessary that will require more than a ministerial and uncontested calculation of benefits. Rodriguez v. Bruce Mfg. and Molding Co., 30 Conn.App. 320, 620 A.2d 149 (1993).

B. *Appellate Court Judgments*

The relevant statute, C.G.S.A. § 51-197f, states that cases in the Appellate Court may be taken to the Supreme Court on certification "upon final determination of *any appeal*" (emphasis added); see also § 84-1. The final determination of the appeal turns on whether the Appellate Court has conclusively resolved the issues before it and "disposes of the cause such that no further action is necessary on *its* part." In re Judicial Inquiry Number 2005-02, 293 Conn. 247, 257, 977 A.2d 166, 172 (2009) (emphasis in original). Thus, a decision by the Appellate Court reversing summary judgment, which returns the case to the procedural posture it would have been in if the trial court denied summary judgment, is a final determination by the Appellate Court for purposes of Supreme Court review. Gold v. Town of East Haddam, 290 Conn. 668, 966 A.2d 684 (2009). A fortiori, an Appellate Court decision ordering further proceedings in the trial court, such as reversing the grant of a motion to strike or a motion to dismiss, should be appealable to the Supreme Court.

Where the Appellate Court decides a motion or petition, the finality turns on the language of the statute authorizing appellate review. Where the order under review is an interlocutory order, such as revocation of bail, the petition for review of such order is not an appeal for purposes of § 51-197f. State v. Ayala, 222 Conn. 331, 338–41, 610 A.2d 1162, 1166–68 (1992). Where, however, a statute authorizes an *appeal* of an interlocutory order, the Appellate Court's decision on the appeal is subject to Supreme Court review. In re Judicial Inquiry Number 2005-02, 293 Conn. 247, 258, 977 A.2d 166, 173 (2009) (statute specifically provided that party aggrieved by decision of grand jury panel has "the right to appeal").

Interlocutory orders by the Appellate Court, such as striking part of a brief, are not immediately appealable to the Supreme Court. State v. Ellis, 224 Conn. 711, 719–21, 621 A.2d 250, 253–55 (1993).

C. *Arbitration Cases*

An appeal may be taken from an order confirming, vacating, modifying or correcting an arbitration award. C.G.S.A. § 52-423; Board of Educ. of Town of East

Haven v. East Haven Educ. Ass'n, 66 Conn.App. 202, 208–09, 784 A.2d 958, 963–64 (2001). However, an order remanding the case back to the arbitrator for clarification is not immediately appealable. Hartford Steam Boiler Inspection and Ins. Co. v. Underwriters at Lloyd's and Companies Collective, 271 Conn. 474, 496–97, 857 A.2d 893, 906–07 (2004), cert. denied, 544 U.S. 974, 125 S. Ct 1826, 161 L.Ed. 2d 723 (2005).

An order to proceed with arbitration under C.G.S.A. § 52-410 is appealable under the "separate and distinct proceeding" category, Dewart v. Northeastern Gas Transmission Co., 139 Conn. 512, 514, 95 A.2d 381, 382 (1953); Merrill Lynch and Co. v. City of Waterbury, 34 Conn.App. 11, 14 n.7, 640 A.2d 122, 124 n.7 (1994). However, an order refusing to stay arbitration under C.G.S.A. § 52-409 is not appealable. Travelers Ins. Co. v. General Elec. Co., 230 Conn. 106, 644 A.2d 346 (1994). The granting of a motion to stay a court proceeding is not appealable, Gores v. Rosenthal, 148 Conn. 218, 169 A.2d 639 (1961); Flynn v. Town of Newington, 2 Conn.App. 230, 234 n.6, 477 A.2d 1028, 1031 n.6, cert. denied, 194 Conn. 804, 482 A.2d 709 (1984). This means a race to the courthouse in many cases depending on whether one wants an appealable or an unappealable order.

An order collateral to an arbitration proceeding ordering reinstatement of a worker is immediately appealable because it is a separate and distinct proceeding and because the pay could not be retrieved after it is paid. Goodson v. State, 228 Conn. 106, 112–14, 635 A.2d 285, 287–88 (1993). A judgment answering questions under C.G.S.A. § 52-415, is not immediately appealable, but should be raised on a motion to vacate the arbitrator's award; Daginella v. Foremost Ins. Co., 197 Conn. 26, 495 A.2d 709 (1985). "Award" is defined in State v. Connecticut Emp. Union Independent, 184 Conn. 578, 440 A.2d 229 (1981).

D. *Attachments and the Like*

The granting or denial of a prejudgment remedy was held appealable, E. J. Hansen Elevator, Inc. v. Stoll, 167 Conn. 623, 628–30, 356 A.2d 893, 895–96 (1975), even before C.G.S.A. § 52-278*l* was passed. Also held appealable is the reducing or dissolving of an attachment, Sachs v. Nussenbaum, 92 Conn. 682, 686, 104 A. 393, 394–95 (1918); Potter v. Appleby, 136 Conn. 641, 643, 73 A.2d 819, 820 (1950). The reduction of a mechanic's lien bond was reviewed on the merits without discussion of this issue in Six Carpenters, Inc. v. Beach Carpenters Corp., 172 Conn. 1, 372 A.2d 123 (1976). However, the denial of a motion to vacate a prejudgment remedy under C.G.S.A. § 52-278*l* was held not appealable in City Nat. Bank of Connecticut v. Davis, 181 Conn. 42, 434 A.2d 310 (1980); and a denial of a motion to discharge a lien was held not appealable in Pistorio v. Metro Productions, Inc., 14 Conn.App. 157, 540 A.2d 111 (1988).

An order to post a bond to secure the payment of periodic alimony was held appealable in Phares v. Phares, 1 Conn.App. 172, 174, 469 A.2d 791, 792 (1984); see Olive Elec. Supply Co., Inc. v. Brewery Square Ltd. Partnership, 6 Conn.App. 443, 505 A.2d 1280 (1986), for rulings on bond orders under C.G.S.A. § 49-37.

A denial of a motion to dissolve a judgment lien in a foreclosure action is not appealable. Ackerson v. Stramaglia, 225 Conn. 102, 621 A.2d 1315 (1993).

In an action to foreclose a judgment lien, an order determining priorities is not immediately appealable. Moran v. Morneau, 129 Conn.App. 349, 19 A.3d 268 (2011).

E. *Attorneys*

The denial of admission of an out-of-state attorney under § 2-16 is not a final judgment. Yale Literary Magazine v. Yale University, 202 Conn. 672, 522 A.2d 818 (1987).

The disqualification of an attorney for a party generally is not immediately appealable; Burger and Burger, Inc. v. Murren, 202 Conn. 660, 522 A.2d 812 (1987); apparently even in a criminal case; State v. Vumback, 247 Conn. 929, 719 A.2d 1172 (1998) (see dissenting opinions on denial of certification); nor is the denial of a motion disqualifying an attorney; State v. Powell, 186 Conn. 547, 442 A.2d 939 (1982), cert. denied sub nom. Moeller v. Connecticut, 459 U.S. 838, 103 S. Ct. 85, 74 L. Ed. 2d 80 (1982). Only the client, not the lawyer individually, has the right to raise this issue (after the trial). Crone v. Gill, 250 Conn. 476, 736 A.2d 131 (1999). An exception is if the disqualification order is intended as a punishment of the attorney for misconduct. Briggs v. McWeeny, 260 Conn. 296, 313–16, 796 A.2d 516, 529–31 (2002). Such a claim, however, should be raised by a writ of error. Amity Regional School Dist. No. 5 v. Atlas Const. Co., 258 Conn. 923, 782 A.2d 1241 (2001).

The disqualification of a lawyer for a witness is immediately reviewable (by a writ of error), Bergeron v. Mackler, 225 Conn. 391 n.1, 623 A.2d 489, 490 n.1 (1993).

An award of attorney's fees pendente lite is not immediately appealable except in a family case; Pendiman Corp. v. White Oak Corp., 195 Conn. 393, 488 A.2d 449 (1985). See subsection K for family cases.

If there is a claim for attorneys' fees in a case that is ancillary to the main action and only the main action is resolved, that may be a final judgment even though a ruling on attorneys' fees remains to be made. The losing party cannot wait until the ruling on attorneys' fees to appeal the ruling on the main action. Paranteau v. DeVita, 208 Conn. 515, 544 A.2d 634 (1988). In Roemmele v. Haymond, A.C. 21519 (order entered February 21, 2001), the Appellate Court granted a motion to dismiss an appeal as to all issues except attorneys' fees when no appeal was taken until after the fees order had been entered. *Paranteau* has been extended to a strict foreclosure case in Benvenuto v. Mahajan, 245 Conn. 495, 715 A.2d 743 (1998), which rejects the contrary result in Connecticut Nat. Bank v. L & R Realty, 40 Conn.App. 492, 671 A.2d 1315 (1996); and to a case in which the right to and amount of punitive damages have not been determined; Hylton v. Gunter, 313 Conn. 472, 2014 WL 4258270 (2014), which rejects the contrary result in Lord v. Mansfield, 50 Conn. App. 21, 717 A.2d 267, cert. denied, 247 Conn. 943, 723 A.2d 321 (1998).

An order regarding attorney's fees is not final until the court determines the amount. Sullivan v. Brown, 116 Conn.App. 660, 662–63, 975 A.2d 1289, 1290, cert. denied, 294 Conn. 914, 983 A.2d 852 (2009).

A member of the Bar of the county involved can appeal from the admission or readmission of a lawyer to the Bar on motion. Application of Dodd, 131 Conn. 702, 42 A.2d 36 (1945) (admission); Application of Pagano, 207 Conn. 336, 339–41, 541 A.2d 104, 106–07 (1988) (readmission). The state bar examining committee can appeal an applicant's admission to the bar. Scott v. State Bar Examining Committee, 220 Conn. 812, 818–19, 601 A.2d 1021, 1025 (1992). A grievance committee can appeal a Superior Court decision refusing to discipline a lawyer. Grievance Committee of Hartford County Bar v. Broder, 112 Conn. 263, 112 Conn. 269, 152 A. 292 (1930). A lawyer cannot appeal from the statewide grievance committee's decision to file a presentment in Superior Court. Miniter v. Statewide Grievance Committee, 122 Conn.App. 410, 998 A.2d 268, cert. denied, 298 Conn. 923 4 A.3d 1228 (2010).

Treating the bar examining committee as an administrative agency, the Supreme Court held that an order remanding consideration of a bar application for further proceedings before the local standing committee was an appealable final judgment. Doe v. Connecticut Bar Examining Committee, 263 Conn. 39, 44–49, 818 A.2d 14, 20–23 (2003).

The imposition of a sanction against a party's attorney should be raised by a writ of error and not in an appeal from a judgment as to the parties. Conte v. Conte, 45 Conn.App. 235, 236, 695 A.2d 32, 33 (1997).

F. *Class Action Certification*

C.G.S.A. § 42-110h allows an immediate appeal from decisions in CUTPA cases on class certification. See Marr v. WMX Technologies, Inc., 244 Conn. 676, 711 A.2d 700 (1998). An order denying class certification, however, is not immediately appealable. Palmer v. Friendly Ice Cream Corp., 285 Conn. 462, 940 A.2d 742 (2008). A decertification order may be appealed. Rivera v. Veterans Memorial Medical Center, 262 Conn. 730, 818 A.2d 731 (2003).

G. *Condemnation Cases*

The granting or denial of immediate possession is appealable, Northeastern Gas Transmission Co. v. Brush, 138 Conn. 370, 374, 84 A.2d 681, 682–83 (1951). An order appointing a committee to assess damages in condemnation cases is appealable, Antman v. Connecticut Light & Power Co., 117 Conn. 230, 235, 167 A. 715, 717 (1933); New Milford Water Co. v. Watson, 75 Conn. 237, 241–42, 52 A. 947, 949 (1902); as is an order refusing to revoke such an appointment, State v. Fahey, 146 Conn. 55, 59, 147 A.2d 476, 478 (1958). However, the committee must actually be appointed before the order is appealable, Town of Branford Sewer Authority v. Williams, 159 Conn. 421, 427, 270 A.2d 546, 549 (1970). On the other hand, an order appointing a committee to determine if a road should be discontinued is not final, Cone v. Darrow, 148 Conn. 109, 167 A.2d 852 (1961), which distinguishes the *Brush* case.

H. *Criminal Cases*

See (N) as to pleadings, and (I) as to discovery. Since the state cannot appeal a judgment of not guilty (see § 1(v) to this comment), it may wish to move for dismissal after an order suppressing evidence and then appeal, State v. Ross, 189 Conn. 42, 454 A.2d 266 (1983).

State v. Curcio, 191 Conn. 27, 31, 463 A.2d 566, 569–70 (1983), establishes two alternate tests for allowing an immediate appeal of interlocutory orders in both civil and criminal cases. One is whether the order "terminates a separate and distinct proceeding;" the second is whether the order "so concludes the rights of the parties that further proceedings cannot affect them."

Examples of cases meeting the second prong of the *Curcio* test are State v. Jenkins, 288 Conn. 610, 954 A.2d 806 (2008), holding that a claim that an 18-month period for determining competency to stand trial was exceeded is immediately appealable, and State v. Garcia, 233 Conn. 44, 62–66, 658 A.2d 947, 956–57 (1995), holding that an order to administer medication involuntarily is immediately appealable.

State v. Roberson, 165 Conn. 73, 81–82, 327 A.2d 556, 560–61 (1973), holds that an order terminating probation is appealable. See also State v. Cooley, 3 Conn.App. 410, 411 n.1, 488 A.2d 1283, 1284 n.1, cert. denied, 196 Conn. 805, 492 A.2d 1241 (1985). Two lower courts have held a nolle not to be appealable, State v. Barnes, 4 Conn. Cir. Ct. 464, 234 A.2d 649 (App. Div. 1967); State v. Anonymous (1975-2), 32 Conn. Supp. 501, 337 A.2d 336 (App. Sess. 1975); but they are probably bad law in the light of State v. Lloyd, 185 Conn. 199, 206–08, 440 A.2d 867, 871 (1981); and State v. Herring, 209 Conn. 52, 547 A.2d 6 (1988). Likewise, State v. Talton, 209 Conn. 133, 547 A.2d 543, 545 (1988), allows the defendant to appeal from a dismissal without prejudice. Dismissal appears to be a prerequisite to any appeal by the state in a criminal case, State v. Southard, 191 Conn. 506, 467 A.2d 920 (1983). The granting of a motion for acquittal in a court case is an appealable final judgment for the State. State v. Paolella, 210 Conn. 110, 118–21, 554 A.2d 702, 706–07 (1989). So is the trial court's granting of the defendant's motion to vacate his conviction. State v. Malcolm, 257 Conn.

653, 657–58, 778 A.2d 134, 136–37 (2001). For general discussion of criminal appeals by the state, see § 1(v), above.

If the defendant enters a nolo contendere plea, his right to appeal previous rulings in the case will be severely circumscribed, State v. Satti, 2 Conn.App. 219, 477 A.2d 144 (1984) (appeal dismissed concerning denial of accelerated rehabilitation application).

The denial of a reward under C.G.S.A. § 54-52 is appealable, State v. Malm, 143 Conn. 462, 123 A.2d 276 (1956).

A bail bondsman does not have the right to appeal in a criminal case from an order forfeiting the bond. The remedy is a writ of error. State v. Salmon, 250 Conn. 147, 735 A.2d 333 (1999).

The following are not appealable: the denial of a motion for specific performance of a plea agreement, State v. Thomas, 106 Conn.App. 160, 941 A.2d 394, cert. denied, 287 Conn. 910, 950 A.2d 1286 (2008); a denial of a motion to dismiss for lack of a speedy trial, State v. Rhoads, 122 Conn.App. 238, 999 A.2d 1, cert. denied, 298 Conn. 913, 4 A.3d 836 (2010); State v. Ahern, 42 Conn.App. 144, 678 A.2d 975 (1996); a decision denying youthful offender status, State v. Longo, 192 Conn. 85, 469 A.2d 1220 (1984), overruling State v. Bell, 179 Conn. 98, 425 A.2d 574 (1979); a decision denying application for accelerated rehabilitation, State v. Spendolini, 189 Conn. 92, 454 A.2d 720 (1983) (3-2 decision); or for participation in a pretrial alcoholic education program, State v. Dionne, 38 Conn.Supp. 675, 460 A.2d 503 (App. Sess. 1983) (2-1 decision); or to submit to a competency examination, State v. O'Connell, 36 Conn.App. 135, 648 A.2d 168, cert. denied, 231 Conn. 943, 653 A.2d 824 (1994); and a denial of a motion for suspension of prosecution and for treatment under C.G.S.A. §§ 17a-695 and 17a-696, State v. Russo, 53 Conn.App. 781, 732 A.2d 783 (1999). A decision refusing dismissal under the accelerated rehabilitation program was held not appealable, State v. Parker, 194 Conn. 650, 485 A.2d 139 (1984). *Parker* was legislatively overruled by C.G.S.A. § 54-56e. The denial of a motion to transfer to the criminal docket is not appealable. In re Juvenile Appeal (85-AB), 195 Conn. 303, 488 A.2d 778 (1985), superseded by statute as stated in In re Michael S., 258 Conn. 621, 784 A.2d 317 (2001). However, an order transferring a juvenile case to Superior Court is appealable when the criminal court finalizes the transfer. State v. Jamar D., 300 Conn. 764, 18 A.3d 582 (2011).

A motion to dismiss an appeal from a decision ordering the withdrawal of blood from the defendant's body has been denied, State v. Acquin, 174 Conn. 784, 381 A.2d 1368 (1978). But see State v. Grotton, 180 Conn. 290, 429 A.2d 871 (1980).

The defendant cannot appeal from an order to unseal a police report on which probable cause was found. State v. Figueroa, 22 Conn.App. 73, 576 A.2d 553 (1990). A defendant can appeal from the denial of a colorable motion claiming double jeopardy. State v. Tate, 256 Conn. 262, 276, 773 A.2d 308, 319 (2001); State v. Kasprzyk, 255 Conn. 186, 188 n.1, 763 A.2d 655, 657 n.1 (2001); State v. Seravalli, 189 Conn. 201, 455 A.2d 852 (1983). However, that rule applies only when the double jeopardy claim involves successive prosecutions, not multiple punishments. State v. Crawford, 257 Conn. 769, 778 A.2d 947 (2001).

In reliance on the defendant's representations, the state destroyed evidence after he pleaded guilty in State v. Malcolm, 257 Conn. 653, 657–58, 778 A.2d 134, 137–38 (2001). When the trial court later granted the defendant's motion to withdraw his plea, *Malcolm* held the state could appeal under the second prong of *Curcio*.

I. *Discovery and Sanction Orders*

In general, rulings on discovery motions are not final. Green Rock Ridge, Inc. v. Kobernat, 250 Conn. 488, 736 A.2d 851 (1999); Melia v. Hartford Fire Ins.

Co., 202 Conn. 252, 520 A.2d 605 (1987) (violation of attorney-client privilege concerning a party not a basis to avoid rule); but see Woodbury Knoll, LLC v. Shipman and Goodwin, LLP, 305 Conn. 750, 754–55, 48 A.3d 16, 20–21 (2012) (violation of privilege concerning a nonparty reviewed); State v. Kemp, 124 Conn. 639, 646–47, 1 A.2d 761, 763–64 (1938) (denial of motions to examine minutes of grand jury); Chrysler Credit Corp. v. Fairfield Chrysler-Plymouth, Inc., 180 Conn. 223, 429 A.2d 478 (1980) (imposition of sanctions for failure to comply with notice of deposition); Rosa Bros., Inc. v. Mansi, 61 Conn.App. 412, 767 A.2d 116 (2001) (sanctions for refusal to answer questions at deposition); State v. Grotton, 180 Conn. 290, 429 A.2d 871 (1980) (blood, saliva, and urine test); Cruz v. Gonzalez, 40 Conn.App. 33, 668 A.2d 739 (1995) (payment order for blood test); Ruggiero v. Fuessenich, 237 Conn. 339, 676 A.2d 1367 (1996) (attempt to discover erased criminal records); cf. Barbato v. J. & M. Corp., 194 Conn. 245, 478 A.2d 1020 (1984) (order compelling testimony not appealable); Resnik v. Muir, 4 Conn. Cir. Ct. 293, 230 A.2d 622 (App. Div. 1967) (ruling re deposition). An exception exists if the underlying case is in an out-of-state court and the discovery order terminates the Connecticut proceedings. Lougee v. Grinnell, 216 Conn. 483, 486–87, 582 A.2d 456, 458 (1990) (overruled on other grounds by, State v. Salmon, 250 Conn. 147, 735 A.2d 333 (1999)). However, if the person seeking review is a non-party, review should be by a writ of error under P.B. § 72-1, not by appeal. Woodbury Knoll, LLC v. Shipman and Goodwin, LLP, 305 Conn. 750, 754–55, 48 A.3d 16, 20–21 (2012); State v. Salmon, 250 Conn. 147, 152–62, 735 A.2d 333, 336–41 (1999). The Appellate Court also made an exception when the sole issue is whether the witness can appear in an administrative proceeding with counsel. The court's affirmative ruling was final. City of Middletown v. von Mahland, 34 Conn.App. 772, 776–77, 643 A.2d 888, 890 (1994).

While postjudgment discovery pursuant to C.G.S.A. § 52-351b is a separate and distinct proceeding, a denial of protective orders is not appealable. Presidential Capital Corp. v. Reale, 240 Conn. 623, 692 A.2d 794 (1997).

An extreme way to raise an appealable issue on discovery is to refuse to comply, be defaulted, and appeal after the hearing in damages, Kiessling v. Kiessling, 134 Conn. 564, 59 A.2d 532 (1948). See also Pavlinko v. Yale-New Haven Hosp., 192 Conn. 138, 470 A.2d 246 (1984) (dismissal for failure to answer questions at deposition); Grondin v. Curi, 262 Conn. 637, 817 A.2d 61 (2003) (appeal from nonsuit). The Supreme Court acknowledged that failing to comply with an interlocutory order in order to obtain a final judgment is an appropriate way to raise an issue. Usowski v. Jacobson, 267 Conn. 73, 95, 836 A.2d 1167, 1179 (2003). See also Honan v. Dimyan, 85 Conn.App. 66, 856 A.2d 463 (2004). Another way is for the deponent to be held in contempt. Green Rock Ridge, Inc. v. Kobernat, 250 Conn. 488, 498, 736 A.2d 851, 856 (1999); Nowacki v. Nowacki, 129 Conn.App. 157, 163 n.3, 20 A.3d 702, 706 n.3 (2011). However, review via § 52-265a was successful in Metropolitan Life Ins. Co. v. Aetna Cas. and Sur. Co., 249 Conn. 36, 730 A.2d 51 (1999). (Justice Berdon, the senior qualified justice, certified the appeal.)

Even though discovery rulings are theoretically appealable after the trial is over, the trial usually makes such rulings harmless or moot. Counsel should make an offer of proof before or during trial to show how the ruling was harmful.

Note, that the rule is different when the proceeding itself is a discovery proceeding. Blumenthal v. Kimber Mfg., Inc., 265 Conn. 1, 3 n.2, 826 A.2d 1088, 1091 n.2 (2003).

J. Dismissals, Nonsuits, and Defaults

A dismissal under § 14-3 is final, Jenkins v. Ellis, 169 Conn. 154, 157–60, 362 A.2d 831, 832–34 (1975), and so is a discontinuance of a dormant case, Lake

Garda Co. v. Lake Garda Imp. Ass'n, 156 Conn. 61, 64–65, 238 A.2d 393, 395–96 (1968). In Lo Sacco v. Parmelee, 18 Conn.App. 808, 556 A.2d 1058 (1989), a § 14-3 dismissal was reversed. In Usowski v. Jacobson, 267 Conn. 73, 836 A.2d 1167 (2003), a dismissal for failure to comply with a discovery sanctions order was reversed. A denial of a motion to dismiss generally is not appealable. See subsection N, *Pleadings.*

A default is not a final judgment; G.F. Const., Inc. v. Cherry Hill Const., Inc., 42 Conn.App. 119, 679 A.2d 32 (1996); rather the judgment entered upon the default after a hearing in damages is the final judgment, Automotive Twins, Inc. v. Klein, 138 Conn. 28, 33, 82 A.2d 146, 149 (1951). The propriety of the default can be raised on the appeal from the final judgment, Kiessling v. Kiessling, 134 Conn. 564, 565 n.1, 59 A.2d 532, 534–35 n.1 (1948).

A nonsuit is appealable, Burgess v. Vanguard Ins. Co., 192 Conn. 124, 125 n.1, 470 A.2d 244, 245 n.1 (1984). Norton v. Petrie, 59 Conn. 200, 20 A. 199 (1890), to the contrary, is thus presumably bad law. The denial of a motion to reopen a nonsuit also is appealable. Jaquith v. Revson, 159 Conn. 427, 430–31, 270 A.2d 559, 560–61 (1970). However, if a motion to open is filed more than 20 days after the nonsuit, an appeal from the denial of the motion to open tests only the motion to open ruling. Conway v. City of Hartford, 60 Conn.App. 630, 635, 760 A.2d 974, 977 (2000). The denial of a nonsuit is not appealable, Adamsen v. Adamsen, 151 Conn. 172, 177, 195 A.2d 418, 421 (1963); Reynolds v. Molitor, 184 Conn. 526, 440 A.2d 192, 194 (1981). An order setting aside a nonsuit is not appealable. Wann v. Lemieux, 36 Conn.App. 138, 648 A.2d 889 (1994), unless there is a colorable claim that the court lacked authority to set aside the nonsuit. PRI Capital Group, LLC v. Eastern Capital Funding, LLC, 90 Conn.App. 1, 878 A.2d 342 (2005).

K. *Family Cases*

Pendente lite orders for alimony are appealable, Litvaitis v. Litvaitis, 162 Conn. 540, 548, 295 A.2d 519, 523 (1972). However, a judgment on the merits of the dissolution action pending appeal may moot the appeal. LaFaci-Zitzkat v. Zitzkat, 19 Conn.App. 805, 562 A.2d 527 (1989). The authors question the overly broad language in this opinion. Rulings on motions to modify divorce judgments as to support are also appealable, Howarth v. Northcott, 152 Conn. 460, 463, 208 A.2d 540, 542 (1965), overruled on other grounds by Hao Thi Popp v. Lucas, 182 Conn. 545, 438 A.2d 755 (1980); In re Haley B., 262 Conn. 406, 815 A.2d 113 (2003) (modification of visitation). Temporary orders of custody are appealable; Madigan v. Madigan, 224 Conn. 749, 620 A.2d 1276 (1993); In re Emoni W., 129 Conn.App. 727, 730 n.5, 21 A.3d 524, 533 n.5 (2011), rev'd on other grounds, 305 Conn. 723, 48 A.3d 1 (2012); as is the granting of an extension of commitment of a minor child to the Department of Children and Families. In re Todd G., 49 Conn.App. 361, 713 A.2d 1286 (1998); as is the granting of a motion to cease reunification, In re Paul M., 148 Conn.App. 654 659-63, 85 A.3d 1263, 1266 (2014). A pendente lite order concerning enrollment in a school was held appealable in Sweeney v. Sweeney, 271 Conn. 193, 856 A.2d 997 (2004). *Madigan* and *Sweeney* were cited in Dutkiewicz v. Dutkiewicz, 289 Conn. 362, 369 n.8, 957 A.2d 821, 828 n.8 (2008) (concerning parenting education programs). Similarly, the Appellate Court held in a 2-1 decision that temporary custody and visitation orders entered pending a full hearing on a family relations report was not a final judgment. Strobel v. Strobel, 73 Conn.App. 428, 808 A.2d 698 (2002).

A civil contempt order concerning an arrearage is an appealable order. Bryant v. Bryant, 228 Conn. 630, 636 n.5, 637 A.2d 1111, 1115 n.5 (1994). So is an order requiring a contemnor to pay for the family relations program even though the court continued the contempt proceeding. Khan v. Hillyer, 306 Conn. 205, 49 A.3d 996 (2012).

An order compelling disclosure of a financial affidavit is not immediately appealable, although a finding of contempt on such failure would be. Nowacki v. Nowacki, 129 Conn.App. 157, 20 A.3d 702 (2011).

It is unclear whether a pendente lite attorneys' fee award is immediately appealable, although Hotchkiss v. Hotchkiss, 143 Conn. 443, 123 A.2d 174 (1956), and England v. England, 138 Conn. 410, 85 A.2d 483 (1951), in fact reviewed such orders on the merits. The Supreme Court granted certification on this issue in Perricone v. Perricone, 271 Conn. 919, 859 A.2d 569 (2004), but the appeal was withdrawn. The Appellate Court held that a pendente lite counsel fees award was immediately appealable in Rostad v. Hirsch, 128 Conn.App. 119, 124, 15 A.3d 1176, 1179 (2011).

An order vacating a contempt ruling is appealable even though the court set the motion for a further hearing on the subject. Pritchard v. Pritchard, 281 Conn. 262, 914 A.2d 1025 (2007).

A domestic violence restraining order is immediately appealable. Putman v. Kennedy, 279 Conn. 162, 167-68 n.9, 900 A.2d 1256, 1260–61 n.9 (2006).

Because they are akin to temporary injunctions, a decision to modify the automatic orders set forth in P.B. § 25-5 is not immediately appealable. Parrotta v. Parrotta, 119 Conn.App. 472, 988 A.2d 383 (2010).

L. *Foreclosure and Receivers*

A foreclosure case is not appealable until the amount of the debt and the method of foreclosure are set; City of Danbury v. Hovi, 34 Conn.App. 121, 640 A.2d 609 (1994); Chase Manhattan Mortg. Corp. v. Machado, 83 Conn.App. 183, 185 n.3, 850 A.2d 260, 262 n.3 (2004) (summary judgment); nor until the law days are set in a strict foreclosure case; Connecticut Nat. Bank v. L & R Realty, 40 Conn.App. 492, 671 A.2d 1315 (1996). However, in a foreclosure by sale, the appellant need not await the setting of a date for a foreclosure sale. Willow Funding Co. v. Grencom Associates, 63 Conn.App. 832, 835–38, 779 A.2d 174, 177–79 (2001), and in any foreclosure case the appellant need not await the determination concerning attorneys' fees. Benvenuto v. Mahajan, 245 Conn. 495, 715 A.2d 743 (1998). Neither denial nor the grant of an application for protection from foreclosure under C.G.S.A. § 49-31g is immediately appealable. Savings Bank Life Ins. Co. v. Linthicum, 43 Conn.App. 467, 683 A.2d 737 (1996) (denial); Wells Fargo Bank of Minnesota, N.A. v. Jones, 85 Conn.App. 120, 856 A.2d 505 (2004) (grant).

An order reopening a judgment confirming the sale at a foreclosure auction is appealable, Banca Commerciale Italiana Trust Co. v. Westchester Artistic Works, 108 Conn. 304, 308, 142 A. 838, 839 (1928) (facts require close reading).

Where a new law date was set pending appeal, this constituted a new judgment requiring a second appeal, Felletter v. Thompson, 133 Conn. 277, 50 A.2d 81 (1946). But see RAL Management, Inc. v. Valley View Associates, 278 Conn. 672, 899 A.2d 586 (2006) (because execution on judgment was stayed on appeal, trial court had no authority to set new law days).

For the effect of C.G.S.A. § 49-31d on mootness, see Citicorp Mortg., Inc. v. Hairston, 34 Conn.App. 138, 640 A.2d 146 (1994).

The appointment of a receiver of rents is not appealable; Hartford Nat. Bank and Trust Co. v. Tucker, 195 Conn. 218, 223, 487 A.2d 528, 531 (1985); nor is an order refusing to revoke the appointment; Silver v. Kingston Realty Corp., 114 Conn. 349, 350, 158 A. 889, 890 (1932); nor is an order to disburse rents to the first mortgagee over objection of the second mortgagee; New England Sav. Bank v. Nicotra, 230 Conn. 136, 644 A.2d 909 (1994). However, the Appellate Court has held the denial of the appointment of a receiver to be final. Brey v. Brey, 1 Conn.App. 397, 398 n.4, 472 A.2d 354, 355 n.4, cert. denied, 193 Conn. 806, 477

A.2d 659 (1984); noted in *Hartford National case*, 195 Conn. at 223 n.4, 487 A.2d at 531 n.4. Instructions given by the Court to the receiver are not appealable; More v. Western Connecticut Title & Mortgage Co., 129 Conn. 464, 29 A.2d 450 (1942); though how this case is reconcilable with Guarantee Trust & Safe-Deposit Co. v. Philadelphia, R. & N.E.R. Co., 69 Conn. 709, 714, 38 A. 792, 793 (1897), is a bit difficult to see. That parties were involved in the *Guarantee* appeal that were not involved in the main action may explain the difference.

M. *Parties*

An order to drop a party is appealable, Harris v. First Nat. Bank & Trust Co. of New Haven, 139 Conn. 749, 753, 97 A.2d 260, 261–62 (1953); but the denial of an order to add or cite in a party has been held not appealable, Guthrie v. Hartford Nat. Bank & Trust Co., 146 Conn. 741, 742, 156 A.2d 192, 192 (1959). If a new party seeks to intervene, the test whether the denial is appealable appears to be whether each party had at least a "colorable claim to intervene as a matter of right." King v. Sultar, 253 Conn. 429, 434–35, 754 A.2d 782, 786–87 (2000); Rosado v. Bridgeport Roman Catholic Diocesan Corp., 60 Conn.App. 134, 758 A.2d 916 (2000). Where the claim to intervene is not colorable, the appeal will be dismissed. Clark v. Clark, 115 Conn.App. 500, 974 A.2d 33 (2009). The authors' opinion is that *Guthrie* is of questionable validity today. The granting of a motion to intervene is not appealable. Rocque v. Sound Mfg., Inc., 76 Conn.App. 130, 818 A.2d 884, cert. denied, 263 Conn. 927, 823 A.2d 1217 (2003).

An order imposing sanctions is not appealable until the amount of the sanctions is fixed. Fattibene v. Kealey, 12 Conn.App. 212, 216, 530 A.2d 206, 208 (1987).

For review by nonparties use the writ of error. P.B. § 72-1.

An appeal from a judgment concerning one party is appealable even if the case continues as to another party. Bunnell v. Berlin Iron Bridge Co., 66 Conn. 24, 37, 33 A. 533, 536 (1895); Coble v. Maloney, 34 Conn.App. 655, 660 n.7, 643 A.2d 277, 280 n.7 (1994). The authors do not understand why § 61-2 was not referred to in *Coble*.

N. *Pleadings*

The granting of a motion to dismiss (formerly erase) is appealable. Wells Laundry & Linen Supply Co. v. ACME Fast Freight, 138 Conn. 458, 464, 85 A.2d 907, 910 (1952). *Wells* illustrates the point that parties must be alert to protect their appellate rights. In that case, what appears to be a third-party defendant had that party action erased, and the original defendant failed to file an appeal or notice of appeal until after judgment on the original action was entered in favor of the plaintiff. However, in Canty v. Otto, 304 Conn. 546, 555–56, 41 A.3d 280, 287–88 (2012), the court reviewed the denial of a motion to dismiss where another judge based his decision to grant a prejudgment remedy on the reasoning denying the motion to dismiss. The denial of a motion to dismiss is generally not appealable; LaSalle Bank, Nat. Ass'n v. Bialobrzeski, 123 Conn.App. 781, 786 n.12, 3 A.3d 176, 180 n.12 (2010), although an appeal from such a denial may be entertained in a double jeopardy case; Sasso v. Aleshin, 197 Conn. 87, 90, 495 A.2d 1066, 1068 (1985); and in immunity cases not involving a factual dispute; Conboy v. State, 292 Conn. 642, 974 A.2d 669, 186 L.R.R.M. (BNA) 3167, 158 Lab. Cas. (CCH) P 60862 (2009). See subsection O., Post-Judgment Orders, para. 2; see also subsection V., *Miscellaneous,* para. 2.

The "overruling" of a special defense is not appealable. Sillman v. Sillman, 168 Conn. 144, 145, 358 A.2d 150, 151 (1975); Sewer Commission of Borough of Colchester v. Norton, 164 Conn. 2, 5, 316 A.2d 775, 777 (1972).

A party may not appeal directly from an order granting a motion to strike.

Breen v. Phelps, 186 Conn. 86, 89, 439 A.2d 1066, 1070–71 (1982). Judgment must first enter on the stricken complaint. Where, however, the plaintiff does not replead a stricken count and later proceedings dispose of the action, the court has jurisdiction over the appeal, DeCorso v. Calderaro, 118 Conn.App. 617, 624, 985 A.2d 349, 354 (2009), cert. denied, 295 Conn. 919, 991 A.2d 564 (2010).

The motion to strike retains certain features of the old demurrer, so demurrer case law may still be valid. If an entire cause of action is stricken, great care must be taken to preserve review. Repleading may eliminate the right to review; Good Humor Corp. v. Ricciuti, 160 Conn. 133, 135, 273 A.2d 886, 888 (1971); just as amending a complaint after unsuccessfully resisting a request to revise, State v. McLaughlin, 132 Conn. 325, 337, 44 A.2d 116, 122 (1945). See Authors' Comments to § 61-2 for a party's options following a decision on a motion to strike complaints or counts of a complaint (or counterclaim).

If it is only an order striking a special defense, further action may or may not be needed to preserve review. This problem has been discussed in detail in Nowak v. Nowak, 175 Conn. 112, 394 A.2d 716 (1978). Contrast Scott v. Scott, 83 Conn. 634, 636, 78 A. 314, 315 (1910), and Carabetta v. City of Meriden, 145 Conn. 338, 341–42, 142 A.2d 727, 729–30 (1958), with Panaroni v. Johnson, 158 Conn. 92, 103, 256 A.2d 246, 254 (1969). Probably the safest course is for the defendant to refuse to remove the special defense from his answer, whereupon the plaintiff would be forced to request that it be revised out of the complaint. When the Court orders the special defense removed pursuant to the order striking it, no argument can later be raised that the defendant voluntarily repleaded. See Mirci v. Ford Motor Co., 23 Conn. L. Rptr. 211, 1998 WL 867256 (Conn. Super. Ct. 1998).

If a motion to strike is denied, a losing party that has no factual defense can refuse to plead further, whereupon judgment will be entered against the party, State v. DeWitt School, Inc., 151 Conn. 631, 632–33, 201 A.2d 472, 473 (1964) (civil case); State v. Tyrell, 100 Conn. 101, 122 A. 924 (1923) (criminal case!). However, if the judgment is affirmed, that is the end of the case and there will be no further proceedings. Stamford Dock & Realty Corp. v. City of Stamford, 124 Conn. 341, 342 n.1, 200 A. 343, 345–46 n.1 (1938). On the other hand, although one might think the losing party on a motion to strike overruled waives nothing by pleading further, the ruling may become unreviewable if the essential facts of the cause of action are later proved, Mechanics' Bank v. Woodward, 74 Conn. 689, 691, 51 A. 1084, 1085 (1902); Putnam, Coffin & Burr, Inc. v. Halpern, 154 Conn. 507, 517, 227 A.2d 83, 89 (1967). However, simply appealing from the denial of a motion to strike will not work; it is not appealable. White v. White, 42 Conn.App. 747, 680 A.2d 1368 (1996).

Since a motion to quash is equivalent to the old demurrer, Adamsen v. Adamsen, 151 Conn. 172, 175, 195 A.2d 418, 420 (1963), the denial of a motion to suppress or quash has been held not appealable, Varanelli v. Luddy, 132 Conn. 113, 117, 42 A.2d 656, 658 (1945); State v. Chapnick, 30 Conn.Supp. 518, 297 A.2d 77 (C.P. App. Div. 1972). But see State v. Rao, 171 Conn. 600, 370 A.2d 1310 (1976), where *Adamsen* was ignored. And an order granting the old motion to expunge a paragraph of a complaint which effectively removes the cause of action is also appealable, Harris v. First Nat. Bank & Trust Co. of New Haven, 139 Conn. 749, 753, 97 A.2d 260, 261–62 (1953); see also Jackson v. Conland, 171 Conn. 161, 368 A.2d 3 (1976) (expunging cross-claim) and Springfield-De Witt Gardens, Inc. v. Wood, 143 Conn. 708, 709 n.1, 125 A.2d 488, 489 n.1 (1956) (expunging counterclaim). But see Middlesex Mut. Assur. Co. v. Massare, 32 Conn.Supp. 508, 338 A.2d 505 (Super. Ct. Appellate Sess. 1975), where the Appellate Session of the Superior Court held that the granting of a motion to expunge the first count of a complaint was not appealable. Such a decision may now be appealable pursuant to P.B. § 61-2 if certain conditions are met.

O. *Post-Judgment Orders*

An order reopening a final judgment is not appealable, Citibank, N.A. v. Lindland, 310 Conn. 147, 173, 75 A.3d 651, 666 (2013); and in addition, the final judgment that was reopened generally can no longer be appealed, Byars v. FedEx Ground Package System, Inc., 101 Conn.App. 44, 46 n.2, 920 A.2d 352, 353 n.2 (2007); Clover Farms v. Kielwasser, 134 Conn. 622, 59 A.2d 550 (1948); Ostroski v. Ostroski, 135 Conn. 509, 66 A.2d 599 (1949) (divorce judgment). This rule does not apply to existing appeals if the underlying judgment is subsequently opened, although further proceedings may moot the appeal, which generally is not the case if the judgment is opened for reasons unrelated to the appeal. RAL Management, Inc. v. Valley View Associates, 278 Conn. 672, 899 A.2d 586 (2006); Burton v. City of Stamford, 115 Conn.App. 47, 971 A.2d 739, 747, cert. denied, 293 Conn. 912, 978 A.2d 1108 (2009).

However, the order is immediately appealable if the question is whether the lower court's reopening the judgment was outside its power, *Citibank v. Lindland*, supra; Novak v. Levin, 287 Conn. 71, 77, 951 A.2d 514, 517–18 (2008); Connecticut Light and Power Co. v. Costle, 179 Conn. 415, 426 A.2d 1324 (1980); Smith v. Reynolds, 54 Conn.App. 381, 382 n.1, 735 A.2d 827, 828 n.1 (1999). Whether a motion to open was timely filed raises such a question and constitutes a final judgment. Johnson v. Atlantic Health Services, P.C., 83 Conn.App. 268, 849 A.2d 853 (2004); Richards v. Richards, 78 Conn.App. 734, 829 A.2d 60 (2003). In order to be appealable, the jurisdictional claim must at least be colorable. Cantoni v. Xerox Corp., 251 Conn. 153, 740 A.2d 796 (1999) (jurisdictional claim not colorable); Rosenfield v. Rosenfield, 61 Conn.App. 112, 762 A.2d 511 (2000) (Peters, J.) (same). For a discussion of the meaning of jurisdiction, see Amodio v. Amodio, 247 Conn. 724, 724 A.2d 1084 (1999).

Likewise, the granting of a motion for a new trial is not appealable. Hoberman v. Lake of Isles, 138 Conn. 573, 575, 87 A.2d 137, 138 (1952). This also is the federal rule. Ortiz-Del Valle v. N.B.A., 190 F.3d 598 (2d Cir. 1999). If the trial court's jurisdiction is not at issue, the proper way to test the court's order is to appeal from the judgment after the second trial. Note that, if the basis of the opposition to the new trial is that the Court had lost jurisdiction over the case because of passage of time, this issue will be waived if the opponent files substituted pleadings at the second trial. Ferguson v. Sabo, 115 Conn. 619, 623, 162 A. 844, 845 (1932). The authors question the wisdom of a rule making the reopening of a final judgment after a trial on the merits nonfinal. If there is a reversible error in the granting of the motion, it seems a pity to force the parties to go through another unnecessary trial before raising that issue, especially since a party is permitted under § 61-1 to appeal from the granting of a motion to set aside a verdict.

In a jury case, the denial of a motion for judgment notwithstanding the verdict is not appealable where the denial is coupled with the granting of a motion for a mistrial or for a new trial. Gold v. Newman, 211 Conn. 631, 560 A.2d 960 (1989) (mistrial before verdict); Robbins v. Van Gilder, 225 Conn. 238, 622 A.2d 555 (1993) (mistrial after verdict); White v. Edmonds, 38 Conn.App. 175, 177 n.2, 659 A.2d 748, 749 n.2 (1995) (verdict set aside). In the *White* case, the party against whom the verdict had been set aside had a statutory right to appeal from the granting of the opponent's motion to set aside the verdict. C.G.S.A. § 52-263.

The denial of a motion to open a judgment, whether the judgment was a dismissal under § 14-3 or any other type of judgment, is a final judgment and therefore appealable regardless of whether the motion was filed within 20 days of the judgment. Morelli v. Manpower, Inc., 226 Conn. 831, 628 A.2d 1311 (1993). A motion to open that is granted as to some claims but denied as to others is not appealable. McKeon v. Lennon, 131 Conn.App. 585, 595, 27 A.3d 436, 443, cert. denied, 303 Conn. 901, 31 A.3d 1178 (2011).

If the motion to reopen is filed during the 20-day appeal period on the underlying judgment, the motion clearly extends the appeal period on that judgment. P.B. § 63-1. In that situation, if the litigant appeals from the denial of the motion when he meant to appeal from the underlying judgment, the Appellate Session has considered it as an appeal from the latter in the absence of timely objection. Norfolk and Dedham Mut. Fire Ins. Co. v. Sagnella, 37 Conn.Supp. 806, n.1, 437 A.2d 150, 151 n.1 (App. Sess. 1981). However, if the motion to reopen is filed outside the appeal period, Snow v. Calise, 174 Conn. 567, 392 A.2d 440 (1978), holds that a motion to open filed within four months postpones the time for appealing from the underlying judgment. The authors do not agree with *Snow*. If the motion to open is filed more than 20 days after the judgment, the later appeal should test only the propriety of the denial of the motion, not the propriety of the underlying judgment. This is the position of the Appellate Court. Conway v. City of Hartford, 60 Conn.App. 630, 635, 760 A.2d 974, 977 (2000); Altberg v. Paul Kovacs Tire Shop, Inc., 31 Conn.App. 634, 626 A.2d 804 (1993). Otherwise *Snow* in effect has extended the appeal period from 20 days to four months without any basis in § 63-1 or elsewhere in the rules or statutes. Without mentioning *Snow*, the Supreme Court cited the Appellate Court view in Flater v. Grace, 291 Conn. 410, 419–20, 969 A.2d 157, 162 (2009). The denial of a motion for a new trial is not appealable. State v. Asherman, 180 Conn. 141, 429 A.2d 810 (1980). The rationale of *Asherman* is that the motion was an interlocutory matter in an ongoing case. The Appellate Court relied (improperly, in the authors' opinion) on *Asherman* to hold that the denial of a motion for new trial is not appealable even if that terminates the proceedings, as it did in Waterworks v. Audet, 29 Conn.App. 722, 617 A.2d 932 (1992).

If a petition for a new trial is brought in a separate and distinct action, the granting or denial of the petition is appealable, Husted v. Mead, 58 Conn. 55, 19 A. 233 (1889); Palverari v. Finta, 129 Conn. 38, 41, 26 A.2d 229, 230 (1942) (cross-complaint for a new trial).

Unlike the federal rule, a Connecticut trial court can open a judgment without appellate permission while the appeal is pending. Ahneman v. Ahneman, 243 Conn. 471, 482–83, 706 A.2d 960, 965–66 (1998); Krasowski v. Fantarella, 51 Conn.App. 186, 720 A.2d 1123, (1998), cert. denied, 247 Conn. 961, 723 A.2d 815 (1999); Hewitt v. Wheeler School and Library, 82 Conn. 188, 194–95, 72 A. 935, 937–38 (1909) (trial court cannot put off deciding an issue to see if there is an appeal). That the trial court has inherent post-judgment powers is implicit in the language of § 61-9. See *Ahneman, 243 Conn. at 482, 706 A.2d at 965.* The trial court also has the power to rule on other motions properly before it pending the appeal. Walsh v. Laffen, 131 Conn. 358, 360, 40 A.2d 689, 690 (1944).

A motion to open that is filed and granted after an appeal from a final judgment does not destroy the finality of the original judgment for purposes of appellate jurisdiction. RAL Management, Inc. v. Valley View Associates, 278 Conn. 672, 899 A.2d 586 (2006).

If a remand order is issued and the agency does not address that order, any other order the agency issues that is intertwined with issues on remand is not appealable until it addresses the remand order. Matey v. Estate of Dember, 85 Conn.App. 198, 856 A.2d 511 (2004).

An order supposedly clarifying a prior judgment is appealable, if the claim is that the order actually makes a change in the judgment under the guise of clarification, Harrison v. Harrison, 94 Conn. 280, 108 A. 800 (1920); Miller v. Miller, 16 Conn.App. 412, 547 A.2d 922, cert. denied, 209 Conn. 823, 552 A.2d

430 (1988). See also Holcombe v. Holcombe, 22 Conn.App. 363, 366–67, 576 A.2d 1317, 1319 (1990); Barnard v. Barnard, 214 Conn. 99, 570 A.2d 690 (1990); Cattaneo v. Cattaneo, 19 Conn.App. 161, 561 A.2d 967 (1989); Schott v. Schott, 18 Conn.App. 333, 557 A.2d 936 (1989), and Eisenbaum v. Eisenbaum, 44 Conn.App. 605, 606 n.1, 691 A.2d 25, 27 n.1 (1997). Some of the cases say flat-out that a clarification order is appealable, but the decisions show that the appeal is limited as noted above.

P. *Probate*

Appeals from the acceptance of the inventory, refusal to remove executor and approval of final account were held final orders in Ramsdell v. Union Trust Co., 202 Conn. 57, 63 n.3, 519 A.2d 1185, 1188 n.3 (1987). Contrast C.G.S.A. § 45a-186, which does not require that a Probate Court order be final in order to appeal to the Superior Court. See Curtiss v. Beardsley, 15 Conn. 518, 523, 1843 WL 393 (1843).

Q. *References*

An order referring a case to a referee is not appealable, Castle v. Planning and Zoning Commission of Town of Stonington, 155 Conn. 617, 620, 236 A.2d 460, 461 (1967). An order "referring" a case to the insurance commissioner has been held not appealable, Bartelstone v. Blue Cross and Blue Shield of Connecticut, Inc., 3 Conn.App. 627, 491 A.2d 417, cert. denied, 196 Conn. 808, 494 A.2d 905 (1985), relying on *Castle*. Since the effect of this referral is to dismiss the action, the authors do not agree with this decision. An order sustaining a remonstrance to the report of a committee is not appealable. Cothren v. Atwood, 63 Conn. 576, 29 A. 13 (1894). Likewise, an order rejecting the report of an attorney trial referee, revoking the reference, and placing the case on the trial list is not appealable. Douglas-Mellers v. Windsor Ins. Co., 68 Conn.App. 707, 714-15, 792 A.2d 899, 904 (2002). This holding would apply to objections sustained to the reports of attorney referees under § 19-14 unless the Court also entered judgment under § 19-17. How *Cothren* squares with In re Application of Oyster Ground Committee of Town of Clinton, 52 Conn. 5, 6, 1884 WL 1055 (1884), is difficult to see. The authors' opinion is that the Supreme Court would not follow *Clinton Oyster* today. See Gold v. Newman, 211 Conn. 631, 560 A.2d 960 (1989).

R. *Stays of Proceedings*

A stay of proceedings pending resolution of another case is not appealable, Prevedini v. Mobil Oil Corp., 164 Conn. 287, 293–94, 320 A.2d 797, 800–01 (1973); Gores v. Rosenthal, 148 Conn. 218, 221–22, 169 A.2d 639, 640–41 (1961). But see Associates Discount Corp. v. Burns, 2 Conn. Cir. Ct. 386 n.1, 199 A.2d 572 n.1 (1963), cert. denied, 151 Conn. 737, 200 A.2d 553 (1964), concerning the denial of a permanent stay of proceedings in a bankruptcy case. A denial of a stay was held not appealable in Waterbury Teachers Ass'n v. Freedom of Information Com'n, 230 Conn. 441, 645 A.2d 978 (1994). The authors do not disagree with the precise holding. However, trial court rulings, whether final or not, should be stayable by an appellate court under §§ 61-11 and 61-12 on motion if necessary to preserve eventual appellate review.

The denial of a stay of consolidated habeas proceedings challenging the death penalty on grounds of racial disparity was not a final judgment where the petitioners were permitted to make their challenge in a separate habeas proceeding In re Claims of Racial Disparity, 135 Conn.App. 756, 42 A.3d 401, cert. denied, 305 Conn. 917, 46 A.3d 170 (2012).

S. *Summary Judgments*

A summary judgment on liability only where the question of damages remains is not appealable, Stroiney v. Crescent Lake Tax Dist., 197 Conn. 82, 84, 495

A.2d 1063, 1065 (1985). IBM Credit Corp. v. Mark Facey and Co., Inc., 44 Conn.App. 490, 690 A.2d 410 (1997) (prejudgment interest not ruled on; summary judgment not final). The denial of a summary judgment is generally not appealable, Brown and Brown, Inc. v. Blumenthal, 288 Conn. 646, 954 A.2d 816 (2008). Moreover, the denial generally is not even appealable later when there is a final judgment, especially if an intervening trial produced more evidence on the subject. Smith v. Town of Greenwich, 278 Conn. 428, 465, 899 A.2d 563, 585 (2006). But see Heritage Village Master Ass'n, Inc. v. Heritage Village Water Co., 30 Conn.App. 693, 697–98, 622 A.2d 578, 581 (1993), making a narrow exception in a case involving a question of collateral estoppel; Chadha v. Charlotte Hungerford Hosp., 77 Conn.App. 104, 822 A.2d 303 (2003), aff'd, 272 Conn. 776, 865 A.2d 1163 (2005), holding that the denial of summary judgment on a claim of absolute immunity was immediately appealable; and Manifold v. Ragaglia, 94 Conn.App. 103, 891 A.2d 106 (2006) (same; immunity claim must be colorable). The denial of summary judgment in First Merchants Group, Ltd. Partnership v. Fordham, 138 Conn.App. 220, 50 A.3d 963, cert. denied, 307 Conn. 937, 56 A.3d 716 (2012), was final where the plaintiff was prevented from putting on evidence to prove his claim that an arbitration award was not final.

If there are motions for summary judgment filed by both sides and one is granted and the other is denied, the appeal can often consider both rulings and result in reversing the denial of summary judgment. Connecticut Ins. Guar. Ass'n v. Drown, 134 Conn.App. 140, 143 n.1, 37 A.3d 820, 823 n.1, cert. granted, 305 Conn. 908, 44 A.3d 183 (2012); Levine v. Advest, Inc., 244 Conn. 732, 756, 714 A.2d 649, 661 (1998); Ocsai v. Exit 88 Hotel, LLC, 127 Conn.App. 731, 732 n.1, 17 A.3d 83, 84 n.1 (2011). However, Town of Westbrook v. ITT Hartford Group, Inc., 60 Conn.App. 767, 775 n.13, 761 A.2d 242, 247 n.13 (2000) (Peters, J.), ruled otherwise where the issues on the motion denied apparently were different from those on the motion granted but were not separately addressed.

In Mount Vernon Fire Ins. Co. v. Morris, 90 Conn.App. 525, 533–34 n.8, 877 A.2d 910, 916–17 n.8 (2005), an order granting partial summary judgment was immediately appealable because resolution of the issue on appeal would not have affected resolution of the outstanding issues.

T. *Temporary Injunctions*

Except as authorized by statute (such as in labor disputes; see C.G.S.A. § 31-118), or by a very narrow Curcio window, rulings on temporary injunctions are generally not final judgments; Massachusetts Mut. Life Ins. Co. v. Blumenthal, 281 Conn. 805, 811, 917 A.2d 951, 955 (2007); Rustici v. Malloy, 60 Conn.App. 47, 758 A.2d 424 (2000) (labor dispute exception not applicable; *Curcio* test not met); Olcott v. Pendleton, 128 Conn. 292, 295, 22 A.2d 633, 634–35 (1941); although *Olcott* does in dicta state that the dissolution of a temporary injunction might be appealable if it caused irreparable damage. This dicta was cited with approval in Hiss v. Hiss, 135 Conn. 333, 338, 64 A.2d 173, 175 (1949); Board of Ed. of City of Shelton v. Shelton Ed. Ass'n, 173 Conn. 81, 88, 376 A.2d 1080, 1083 (1977). A temporary injunction that orders mandatory restorative relief is also generally not appealable. City of Stamford v. Kovac, 228 Conn. 95, 634 A.2d 897 (1993). In Brown v. Brown, 69 Conn.App. 209, 210 n.1, 794 A.2d 550, 552 n.1 (2002), a temporary injunction concerning relocation of children was construed as a temporary custody request and therefore appealable (although the case was held to be moot).

Since a ruling on a temporary injunction is generally not appealable, a ruling on a motion for reconsideration of such a ruling is also not appealable. Clinton v. Middlesex Mut. Assur. Co., 37 Conn.App. 269, 655 A.2d 814 (1995).

A creative attempt to treat a temporary injunction as a prejudgment remedy failed in Rhode Island Hosp. Trust Nat. Bank v. Trust, 25 Conn.App. 28, 592 A.2d 417 (1991).

A motion to enjoin the ejectment of a tenant in a foreclosure action was a final judgment under the second prong of *Curcio*. Tappin v. Homecomings Financial Network, Inc., 265 Conn. 741, 752, 830 A.2d 711, 718–19 (2003).

Federal case law is generally not helpful because 28 U.S.C.A. § 1292(a)(1) permits appeals from the granting or denial of temporary injunctions. However, even in the federal courts rulings on temporary restraining orders are generally not appealable, Hoh v. Pepsico, Inc., 491 F.2d 556, 560 (2d Cir. 1974).

U. *Transfers*

An order by the Superior Court transferring the case to another court, such as the old Court of Common Pleas, is not appealable. Felletter v. Thompson, 133 Conn. 277, 279, 50 A.2d 81, 82 (1946). *A fortiori*, a transfer to another district or geographical area would not be appealable. This in general is the federal rule as to transfers from one district to another, A. Olinick and Sons v. Dempster Bros., Inc., 365 F.2d 439 (2d Cir. 1966).

V. *Miscellaneous*

A denial of a res judicata or collateral estoppel claim is immediately appealable. Santorso v. Bristol Hospital, 308 Conn. 338, 346 n.7, 63 A.3d 940, 946 n.7 (2013). However, review of denial of a prejudgment remedy on a collateral estoppel issue must await the final ruling on the prejudgment remedy. State v. Bacon Const. Co., 300 Conn. 476, 15 A.3d 147 (2011). In addition, a claim of a contractual right to avoid trial is not the same as collateral estoppel. Soracco v. Williams Scotsman, Inc., 128 Conn.App. 818, 19 A.3d 209, cert. denied, 302 Conn. 903, 23 A.3d 1244 (2011).

A denial of sovereign immunity is also a final judgment. Kizis v. Morse Diesel Intern., Inc., 260 Conn. 46, 49 n.6, 794 A.2d 498, 500 n.6 (2002); as is a colorable claim of absolute immunity. Chadha v. Charlotte Hungerford Hosp., 77 Conn.App. 104, 822 A.2d 303, aff'd, 272 Conn. 776, 865 A.2d 1163 (2005). But a claim of municipal immunity is not. Vejseli v. Pasha, 282 Conn. 561, 923 A.2d 688 (2007).

The finality of a decision from the workers' compensation review board where a remand had been ordered depends on the scope of the remand. Byars v. Whyco Chromium Co., 33 Conn.App. 667, 637 A.2d 805 (1994); Conetta v. City of Stamford, 246 Conn. 281, 289–91, 715 A.2d 756, 761–62 (1998). A denial of a motion to dismiss based on a colorable claim of ministerial immunity is appealable. Dayner v. Archdiocese of Hartford, 301 Conn. 759, 23 A.3d 1192 (2011).

A judgment ordering parties to interplead is final, Kerite Co. v. Alpha Employment Agency, Inc., 166 Conn. 432, 436–37, 352 A.2d 288, 290 (1974). But see Yankee Millwork Sash and Door Co. v. Bienkowski, 43 Conn.App. 471, 683 A.2d 743 (1996). Since the rationale for this is that interpleader is a separate and distinct proceeding, presumably a judgment denying interpleader would also be final. An order for an accounting is appealable under C.G.S.A. § 52-405; and a refusal to order an accounting is appealable under Preston v. Preston, 102 Conn. 96, 122, 128 A. 292, 301 (1925).

A judgment for the plaintiff by the trial court on the equitable issues in the case is appealable even though the legal issues as to damages have yet to be considered by the jury. Ricci v. Naples, 108 Conn. 19, 142 A. 452 (1928). The authors question the correctness of this decision. The Appellate Court followed *Ricci* in Wilcox v. Ferraina, 100 Conn.App. 541, 546 n.6, 920 A.2d 316, 320 n.6 (2007). More correct is American Factors, Inc. v. Foreign Intrigue, Inc., 6 Conn.App. 656, 506 A.2d 1085 (1986), holding that a ruling for the plaintiff on liability only is not a final judgment. The authors also question Glasson v. Town of Portland, 6 Conn.App. 229, 231 n.3, 504 A.2d 550, 551 n.3 (1986), holding that a ruling issuing an injunction but not passing on damages is final. See also Walton v. Town of New Hartford, 223 Conn. 155, 162 n.9, 612 A.2d 1153, 1157 n.9 (1992) (holding that ordering indemnification but not determining the amount is immediately appealable). *Glasson* and *Walton* were relied on to find appealability in Wilcox v. Ferraina, 100 Conn.App. 541, 546 n.6, 920 A.2d 316, 320–21 n.6 (2007), leaving the law in this area in some confusion.

Granting a protective order is not appealable. Holyoke Mut. Ins. Co. in Salem v. Papa, 13 Conn.App. 808, 534 A.2d 917 (1987). An appeal from bifurcated trial on title to stock is final. Neri v. Neri, 35 Conn.App. 812, 647 A.2d 1, 3 n.8, cert. denied, 231 Conn. 916, 648 A.2d 154 (1994).

If a ruling is made in final disposition of an ancillary but independent proceeding, then the ruling is appealable, Wardell v. Town of Killingly, 96 Conn. 718, 722, 115 A. 539, 540–41 (1921). However, if the ruling, even if made in the ancillary proceeding, does not terminate that ancillary proceeding, then it is not appealable, Guerin v. Norton, 167 Conn. 282, 283, 355 A.2d 255, 255 (1974).

An order striking a case from the jury list is not appealable, Franchi v. Farmholme, Inc., 191 Conn. 201, 209, 464 A.2d 35, 39 (1983).

A finding on disclosure that a garnishee has or has not property of debtor is not appealable. Tweedy v. Nichols, 27 Conn. 518, 1858 WL 1081 (1858) (has); Welles v. Schroeder, 67 Conn. 257, 34 A. 1051 (1896) (has not). Wait for the judgment on scire facias.

The Appellate Session of the Superior Court has held the following orders not appealable: denial of a motion to extend time to comply with judgment (a mandatory injunction) and granting of motion for an order of execution in accordance with judgment, Iannotti v. Turner, 32 Conn.Supp. 573, 575, 346 A.2d 114, 115 (1975).

Judge Corradino has suggested that his denial of anonymous party status is immediately appealable. Doe v. Diocese Corp., 11 Conn. L. Rptr. 519, 524, 1994 WL 174693 (Conn. Super. Ct. 1994). The authors doubt it.

The denial of a writ of error coram nobis is appealable. State v. Henderson, 259 Conn. 1, 3, 787 A.2d 514, 515 (2002).

A denial of a motion for judgment based on an alleged settlement is not immediately appealable. Sharon Motor Lodge, Inc. v. Tai, 82 Conn.App. 148, 842 A.2d 1140, cert. denied, 269 Conn. 908, 852 A.2d 738 (2004).

A denial of a motion for an order of weekly payments is appealable, Hartford Federal Sav. and Loan Ass'n v. Bowen, 3 Conn. Cir. Ct. 86, 87, 208 A.2d 364, 365 (App. Div. 1964), as is the granting of such a motion. Bergen v. Belfonti, 7 Conn.Ops. 181 (2001) (West, J.). Cf. State v. Florence, 35 Conn.Supp. 598, 401 A.2d 65 (Super. Ct. Appellate Sess. 1978) (appeal from denial of wage execution allowed). *Bower* and *Florence* were mentioned in In re Dean, 246 Conn. 183, 204 n.19, 717 A.2d 176, 186 n.19 (1998).

A judgment for the plaintiff on liability only with the question of damages remaining to be resolved is not appealable, Palmer v. Hartford Nat. Bank & Trust Co., 157 Conn. 597, 253 A.2d 28 (1968); Paranteau v. DeVita, 208 Conn. 515, 524 n.11, 544 A.2d 634, 639 n.11 (1988). Likewise, a failure to decide a claim for punitive damages makes the judgment nonfinal. Perkins v. Colonial Cemeteries, Inc., 53 Conn.App. 646, 734 A.2d 1010 (1999). A failure to rule on a claim of prejudgment interest pursuant to C.G.S.A. § 37-3a also makes the judgment nonfinal. Balf Co. v. Spera Const. Co., Inc., 222 Conn. 211, 608 A.2d 682 (1992). However, interest awarded pursuant to C.G.S.A. § 52-192a (offer of judgment/offer of compromise) is severable from the main action; therefore the lack of a ruling on a claim for such interest does not deprive the court of appellate jurisdiction on an otherwise final judgment. Earlington v. Anastasi, 293 Conn. 194, 196–97 n.3, 976 A.2d 689, 692 n.3 (2009). A decision determining the validity of a lien in a petition action is not appealable until a decision is made on a distribution of funds, Levay v. Levay, 137 Conn. 92, 75 A.2d 400 (1950).

Although subsequent events do not generally destroy finality of judgment, RAL Management, Inc. v. Valley View Associates, 278 Conn. 672, 899 A.2d 586 (2006), that rule does not apply where the "subsequent event" is discovery of claims encompassed by the complaint that existed but were not know at the time summary judgment entered. Liberty Mutual Ins. Co. v. Lone Star Industries, Inc., 290 Conn. 767, 794 n.32, 967 A.2d 1, 20 n.32 (2009).

When the judgment on the complaint necessarily implies a judgment on the counterclaim, there is a final judgment on both, apparently by implication. Martin v. Martin's News Service, Inc., 9 Conn.App. 304, 306 n.2, 518 A.2d 951, 953 n.2 (1986); Zirinsky v. Zirinksy, 87 Conn.App. 257, 865 A.2d 488, 493, cert. denied, 273 Conn. 916, 871 A.2d 372 (2005) (failure to consider motion is functional equivalent of denial); Russell v. Russell, 91 Conn.App. 619, 628, 882 A.2d 98, 105 n.8, cert. denied, 276 Conn. 924, 925, 888 A.2d 92 (2005) (same); Rudder v. Mamanasco Lake Park Ass'n, Inc., 93 Conn.App. 759, 767, 890 A.2d 645, 653 n.9, cert. denied, 278 Conn. 904, 896 A.2d 108 (2006) (same). Likewise, when counts of a complaint are antagonistic, judgment for the plaintiff on one implies judgment for the defendant on the rest. Liberty Plumbing Supply Co. v. Paul S. Yoney, Inc., 41 Conn.App. 594, 595 n.1, 677 A.2d 13, 14 n.1 (1996). See also Poulin v. Yasner, 64 Conn.App. 730, 781 A.2d 422, 425–27, cert. denied, 258 Conn. 911, 782 A.2d 1245 (2001).

A final judgment does not enter until after the collateral source payment issue is decided. Smith v. Otis Elevator Co., 33 Conn.App. 99, 633 A.2d 731 (1993). On the other hand, the filing of a motion for a remittitur does not affect the finality of the judgment. Preston v. Phelps Dodge Copper Products Co., 35 Conn.App. 850, 854–55, 647 A.2d 364, 367 (1994). *Preston* is an unusual case because there a motion to set aside the verdict was untimely. Normally, the trial court should dispose of such a motion at the same time it rules on the remittitur to avoid appellate complications.

If the trial court awards prejudgment interest but does not fix the amount, there is no final judgment. Gianetti v. Meszoros, 268 Conn. 424, 844 A.2d 851 (2004). Likewise, if a court finds a wrongful withholding of partnership funds but does not decide how the funds are to be divided, there is no final judgment. Gorelick v. Montanaro, 94 Conn.App. 14, 891 A.2d 41 (2006).

Before you withdraw or stipulate to judgment concerning a portion of the complaint, be sure that that action will not affect the resolution of issues in the rest of the complaint on appeal. See Highgate Condominium Ass'n v. Watertown Fire Dist., 210 Conn. 6, 17–18, 553 A.2d 1126, 1132–33 (1989).

5. Defective Appeal

When an appeal is jurisdictionally defective, the defect generally cannot be cured by amending the appeal. Nolan v. City of Milford, 86 Conn.App. 817, 862 A.2d 879 (2005) (withdrawal of claim); Galgano v. Metropolitan Property and Cas. Ins. Co., 64 Conn.App. 25, 31 n.10, 779 A.2d 229, 233 n.10 (2001). Holyoke Mut. Ins. Co. in Salem v. Papa, 13 Conn.App. 808, 534 A.2d 917 (1987). However, if an amended appeal is taken from a final judgment, the amended appeal will not fall along with the original appeal. See P.B. § 61-9.

If the appeal form shows an appeal from the wrong judgment, an amended appeal may (and should) save the day if the § 63-4 papers show the proper judgment. See Lewis v. Commissioner of Correction, 121 Conn.App. 693, 698 n.6, 996 A.2d 1214, 1218 n.6 (2010), appeal dismissed, 304 Conn. 315, 39 A.3d 1104 (2012), leaving the issue open.

The authors recommend that, when in doubt as to which of two judgments is the final one, file two appeals and then move to consolidate them under P.B. § 61-7.

6. Original Jurisdiction

The Connecticut Supreme Court generally does not have original jurisdiction, *Winchester Repeating Arms Co. v. Radcliffe*, 134 Conn. 164, 170, 56 A.2d 1, 4 (1947) (trial costs); *In re Ansonia Water Co.*, 80 Conn. 326, 68 A. 378 (1907) (mandamus). The usual way to invoke the Court's appellate power is by appeal, although occasionally the writ of error (§§ 72-1 to 72-4) or the reservation (§ 73-1) can be used. Very rarely one might try filing a motion to invoke the Court's power under § 60-2 even though an appeal is not yet pending, although one would have to be careful to avoid the holding in *Radcliffe*.

§ 61-2. Appeal of Judgment on Entire Complaint, Counterclaim or Cross Complaint

When judgment has been rendered on an entire complaint, counterclaim or cross complaint, whether by judgment on the granting of a motion to strike pursuant to Section 10-44, by dismissal pursuant to Section 10-30, by summary judgment pursuant to Section 17-44, or otherwise, such judgment shall constitute a final judgment.

If at the time a judgment referred to in this section is rendered, an undisposed complaint, counterclaim or cross complaint remains in the case, appeal from such a judgment may be deferred (unless the appellee objects as set forth in Section 61-5) until the entire case is concluded by the rendering of judgment on the last such outstanding complaint, counterclaim or cross complaint.

If the judgment disposing of the complaint, counterclaim or cross complaint resolves all causes of action brought by or against a party who is not a party in any remaining complaint, counterclaim, or cross complaint, a notice of intent to appeal in accordance with the provisions of Section 61-5 must be filed in order to preserve the right to appeal such a judgment at the conclusion of the case.

Historical Note to §§ 61-2 through 61-5

Derivation:
  1978 P.B. (1996–97), §§ 4002A, 4002B, 4002C, 4002D
  1978 P.B. (1986–95), § 4002
  1978 P.B., § 3061
  1963 P.B., § 604
  1951 P.B., § 380
  1934 P.B., § 372
  1922 P.B., § 16
  1908 P.B., § 15
  1899 P.B., § 15

Prior to 1996 this rule, along with current §§ 61-3, 61-4 and 61-5, was a part of § 4002 and only applied to rulings on specified motions. The 1996 amendments also limited the notice of intent to appeal to those situations where a particular party is entirely removed from the case.

Prior § 4002 was subject to numerous revisions in 1986 and 1992. Before 1951 this section could be used only when the judgment disposed "of the cause as between one or more plaintiffs and one or more of the defendants"; although Cronin v. Gager-Crawford Co., 128 Conn. 401, 23 A.2d 149 (1941), in fact permitted an appeal outside the language of the 1934 rule. Before the advent of Practice Book rules, the disposal of a counterclaim (cross-bill) was not a final judgment until the complaint (bill) was disposed of. Treadway v. Coe, 21 Conn. 283, 1851 WL 580 (1851).

Cross References

Maltbie, Conn.App.Proc.2d §§ 16, 119

Form 3000.17

AUTHORS' COMMENTS

Sections 61-2 through 61-5 are very useful, as they will often permit the losing party to take an immediate appeal to the Supreme Court on one portion of the case; see Ace Equipment Sales, Inc. v. Buccino, 273 Conn. 217, 223 n.4, 869 A.2d 626, 630 n.4 (2005) (counterclaim); Rocque v. DeMilo and Co., Inc., 85 Conn.App. 512, 514 n.1, 857 A.2d 976, 979 n.1 (2004) (same); Cronin v. Gager-Crawford Co., 128 Conn. 401, 23 A.2d 149 (1941) (supplemental judgment); or as to one party, Bunnell v. Berlin Iron Bridge Co., 66 Conn. 24, 37, 33 A. 533, 536 (1895); Esposito v. Wethered, 4 Conn.App. 641, 496 A.2d 222 (1985); or in the alternative to reserve an appeal until the whole case is over. As to the latter alternative, see Leary v. Stylarama of New Haven, Inc., 174 Conn. 217 n.1, 384 A.2d 377 n.1 (1978). As to the former alternative, see Redmond v. Matthies, 149 Conn. 423, 430, 180 A.2d 639, 643 (1962). A useful discussion of relevant cases involving this section prior to the 1986 changes can be found in Jackson v. Conland, 171 Conn. 161, 164–65, 368 A.2d 3, 5 (1976).

These sections are also a danger, however, as they often require the losing party to take some action under this section within twenty days of a ruling that falls within the complex and uncertain category of "final judgment" (see commentary to § 61-1) especially if a party is completely removed from the case. A party that fails to do so cannot appeal at a later time absent waiver. Wells Laundry & Linen Supply Co. v. ACME Fast Freight, 138 Conn. 458, 464, 85 A.2d 907, 910 (1952); Birnbaum v. Ives, 163 Conn. 12, 23, 301 A.2d 262, 268 (1972) (cross appeal); Sorteberg Controls Corp. v. Field, 2 Conn.App. 413, 415, 478 A.2d 1051, 1052 (1984); Willocks v. Klein, 38 Conn.App. 317, 660 A.2d 869 (1995). Thus, when in doubt whether a party has been completely removed from the case, one should file a notice of intention to appeal with the trial clerk.

Before 1986, it was possible to appeal as of right from a judgment on one count even if all parties remained in the case. Burgess v. Vanguard Ins. Co., 192 Conn. 124, 125 n.1, 470 A.2d 244, 245 n.1 (1984). *Burgess* is no longer good law.

If judgment remaining outstanding as to one party would affect the result as to the parties for whom there is already a judgment, the latter judgment is not final and appealable until the case is disposed of as to all parties. T.P. Brewer Const. Co. v. F and G Associates, 34 Conn.App. 714, 643 A.2d 308 (1994); Southport Manor Convalescent Center, Inc. v. Kundrath, 41 Conn.App. 747, 677 A.2d 977 (1996). The decisions make no mention of this section and the authors do not agree with them. The rationale justified reversal of the partial judgment, not dismissal for lack of jurisdiction.

No longer is there a special exception for the motion to strike. Prior to October 1, 1986, because of the unfortunate language of P.B. § 10-44 the Supreme Court previously held that a partial judgment could not be entered so as to invoke an immediate right of appeal where only a portion of a complaint is stricken. Kilbride v. Dushkin Pub. Group, Inc., 186 Conn. 718, 443 A.2d 922 (1982).

If a partial judgment is entered on a motion to strike and an appeal is taken and lost, the losing party does not have the right to replead under P.B. § 10-44. Zeller v. Mark, 14 Conn.App. 651, 542 A.2d 752 (1988).

The following chart may help explain the complexities of these rules:

Action by Trial Court	**Response by Losing Party**
i. Dismissal or Summary or other Judgment on Whole Case	Appeal within 20 days.
ii. Dismissal or Summary or other Judgment on Whole Complaint where Counterclaim (or a portion of it) remains, or vice versa	If remaining case applies to all parties, appeal or do nothing; if otherwise, appeal or file notice of intention to appeal. Lord v. Mansfield, 50 Conn.App. 21, 717 A.2d 267, cert. denied, 247 Conn. 943, 723 A.2d 321 (1998) (appeal taken from complaint proper although part of counterclaim remained); Connecticut Bank and Trust Co., N.A. v. Reckert, 33 Conn.App. 702, 711-12, 638 A.2d 44, 49-50 (1994) (summary judgment on a third party complaint appealable even though counterclaim still pending.)
iii. Whole Case stricken	Replead within 15 days (§ 10-44) or move for judgment and then appeal within 20 days.
iv. Whole Complaint stricken where Counterclaim remains, or vice versa	Replead within 15 days or move for judgment and then act as in ii.
v. All Claims against one Party in a Complaint or Counterclaim Dismissed	Either appeal or file notice of intention to appeal within 20 days; Burns v. Board of Educ. of City of Stamford, 228 Conn. 640, 644 n.3, 638 A.2d 1, 3 n.3 (1994).
vi. All Claims against one Party in a Complaint or Counterclaim stricken	Replead within 15 days or move for judgment and then either appeal or file notice of intention to appeal within 20 days. The former was done in Tolchinsky v. Town of East Lyme, 43 Conn.App. 456, 457 n.2, 683 A.2d 747, 748 n.2 (1996); the latter was done in Bernhard-Thomas Building Systems, LLC v. Dunican, 286 Conn. 548, 551, 944 A.2d 329, 333 (2008).
vii. Special Defense stricken	Do nothing until court orders defense removed from answer. Then do so and do nothing further until final judgment. Mirci v. Ford Motor Co., 23 Conn. L. Rptr. 211, 212, 1998 WL 867256 (Conn. Super. Ct. 1998).

Action by Trial Court	Response by Losing Party
viii. All Claims against one Party in a Complaint or Counterclaim Disposed of by Summary or other Judgment	Appeal or file notice of intention to appeal within 20 days. Anderson v. Gordon, Muir and Foley, LLP, 108 Conn.App. 410, 949 A.2d 488, 490 n.2, cert. denied, 289 Conn. 927, 958 A.2d 156 (2008) (summary judgment); Connecticut Nat. Bank v. Rytman, 241 Conn. 24, 34, 694 A.2d 1246, 1252 (1997) (same).
ix. Some Claims in Complaint or Counterclaim Dismissed, or stricken or Disposed of by Summary or other Judgment where other Claims remain against the same Party	If you wish to appeal immediately, ask the trial judge for an express determination in favor of appealability; and request additional permission from the chief judge; if both permissions are granted, appeal; Royal Indem. Co. v. Terra Firma, Inc., 287 Conn. 183, 188–89, 947 A.2d 913, 915–16 (2008).

The Appellate Court has held this provision also may apply to a separate cause of action within one count. Zeller v. Mark, 14 Conn.App. 651, 652 n.2, 542 A.2d 752, 753 n.2 (1988). |

§ 61-3. Appeal of Judgment on Part of Complaint, Counterclaim or Cross Complaint That Disposes of All Claims in That Pleading Brought by or against One or More Parties

A judgment disposing of only a part of a complaint, counterclaim, or cross complaint is a final judgment if that judgment disposes of all causes of action in that complaint, counterclaim, or cross complaint brought by or against a particular party or parties.

Such a judgment shall be a final judgment regardless of whether judgment was rendered on the granting of a motion to strike pursuant to Section 10-44, by dismissal pursuant to Section 10-30, by summary judgment pursuant to Section 17-44, or otherwise. The appeal from such judgment may be deferred (unless an objection is filed pursuant to Section 61-5) until the final judgment that disposes of the case for all purposes and as to all parties is rendered. If the appeal from such a judgment is to be deferred, a notice of intent to appeal must be filed in accordance with the provisions of Section 61-5.

A party entitled to appeal under this section may appeal regardless of which party moved for the judgment to be made final.

Historical Note

Before 1996, this rule was a part of § 4002. See historical note to § 61-2. Prior to 1996, the judgment had to include *all counts against* a particular party. In 1996 "counts" was replaced with "causes of action" and "against" with "by or against".

AUTHORS' COMMENTS

This section was applied in Hartford Acc. and Indem. Co. v. Ace American Reinsurance Co., 284 Conn. 744, 752 n.8, 936 A.2d 224, 229 n.8 (2007); and Tyler v. Tyler, 151 Conn.App. 98, 93 A.3d 1179 (2014). A judgment is not final if the ruling does not dispose of an entire complaint or all claims against a party. Harnage v. Commissioner of Correction, 141 Conn.App. 9, 60 A.3d 308 (2013).

A notice of intent to appeal is unnecessary if the order entered is not immediately appealable. Chase Manhattan Mortg. Corp. v. Machado, 83 Conn.App. 183, 185 n.3, 850 A.2d 260, 262 n.3 (2004). However, DeCorso v. Calderaro, 118 Conn.App. 617, 985 A.2d 349, (2009), cert. denied, 295 Conn. 919, 991 A.2d 564 (2010), seems to say that a litigant should move for judgment on a stricken count even if he is planning to appeal later after a final judgment. The authors do not agree that a judgment on the motion to strike is necessary in that situation.

§ 61-4. Appeal of Judgment That Disposes of At Least One Cause of Action While Not Disposing of Either (1) An Entire Complaint, Counterclaim or Cross Complaint, or (2) All The Causes of Action in a Pleading Brought by or against a Party

(a) Judgment not final unless trial court makes written determination and chief justice or chief judge concurs

This section applies to a trial court judgment that disposes of at least one cause of action where the judgment does not dispose of either of the following: (1) an entire complaint, counterclaim, or cross complaint, or (2) all the causes of action in a complaint, counterclaim or cross complaint brought by or against a party. If the order sought to be appealed does not meet these exact criteria, the trial court is without authority to make the determination necessary to the order's being immediately appealed.

This section does not apply to a judgment that disposes of an entire complaint, counterclaim, or cross complaint (see Section 61-2); and it does not apply to a trial court judgment that partially disposes of a complaint, counterclaim, or cross complaint, if the order disposes of all the causes of action in that pleading brought by or against one or more parties (see Section 61-3).

When the trial court renders a judgment to which this section applies, such judgment shall not ordinarily constitute an appealable final judgment. Such a judgment shall be considered an appealable final judgment <u>only if</u> the trial court makes a written determination that the issues resolved by the judgment are of such significance to the determination of the outcome of the case that the delay incident to the appeal would be justified, and the chief justice or chief judge of the court having appellate jurisdiction concurs.

If the procedure outlined in this section is followed, such judgment shall be an appealable final judgment, regardless of whether judgment was rendered on the granting of a motion to strike pursuant to Section 10-44, by dismissal pursuant to Section 10-30, by summary judgment pursuant to Section 17-44, or otherwise.

A party entitled to appeal under this section may appeal regardless of which party moved for the judgment to be made final.

(b) Procedure for obtaining written determination and chief justice's or chief judge's concurrence; when to file appeal

If the trial court renders a judgment described in this section without making a written determination, any party may file a motion in the trial court for such a determination within the statutory appeal period, or, if there is no applicable statutory appeal period, within twenty days after notice of the partial judgment has been sent to counsel. Papers opposing the motion may be filed within ten days after the filing of the motion.

Within twenty days after notice of such a determination in favor of appealability has been sent to counsel, any party intending to appeal shall submit an original plus three copies of a motion for permission to file an appeal with the clerk of the court having appellate jurisdiction. The motion shall state the reasons why an appeal should be permitted. Papers opposing the motion may be filed within ten days after the filing of the motion. The motion and any opposition papers shall be referred to the chief justice or chief judge to rule on the motion. If the chief justice or chief judge is unavailable or disqualified, the most senior justice or judge who is available and is not disqualified shall rule on the motion.

The appellate clerk shall send notice to the parties of the decision of the chief justice or chief judge on the motion for permission to file an appeal. For purposes of counting the time within which the appeal must be filed, the date of the issuance of notice of the decision on this motion shall be considered the date of issuance of notice of the rendition of the judgment or decision from which the appeal is taken.

Historical Note

Before 1996 this rule was a part of § 4002. See historical note to § 61-2. In 1996 the same changes made to what is now § 61-3 were made here. See historical note to § 61-3. In addition, in 1996, consent of the trial judge and chief judge of the Appellate Court was added and consent of the opposing party was deleted.

AUTHORS' COMMENTS

This rule was applied in Royal Indem. Co. v. Terra Firma, Inc., 287 Conn. 183, 188–89, 947 A.2d 913, 915–16 (2008), and American Progressive Life and Health Ins. Co. of New York v. Better Benefits, LLC, 292 Conn. 111, 114, 971 A.2d 17, 18 (2009).

Good discussions of the factors a trial judge should take into account in deciding whether to permit an appeal under this section are ShareAmerica, Inc. v. Ernst & Young LLP, 25 Conn. L. Rptr. 160, 1999 WL 566930 (Conn. Super. Ct. 1999), and Moore v. Brower, 41 Conn. L. Rptr. 730, 2006 WL 2411382 (Conn. Super. Ct. 2006). See also Fortin v. Hartford Underwriters Ins. Co., 42 Conn. L. Rptr. 353, 2006 WL 3524562 (Conn. Super. Ct. 2006), and a reference to the trial court's decision in Deming v. Nationwide Mut. Ins. Co., 279 Conn. 745, 752, 905 A.2d 623, 629 (2006).

The authors have some question whether the Supreme Court can create jurisdiction to appeal. See LaReau v. Reincke, 158 Conn. 486, 492, 264 A.2d 576, 579 (1969); Psaki v. Karlton, 97 Conn.App. 64, 70–71, 903 A.2d 224, 227–28 (2006). But see id. at 69, 903 A.2d at 226.

§ 61-5. Deferring Appeal until Judgment Rendered That Disposes of Case for All Purposes and as to All Parties

(a) When notice of intent to appeal required; procedure for filing

An appeal of a judgment described in Sections 61-2 or 61-3 may be deferred until the judgment that disposes of the case for all purposes and as to all parties is rendered. In the following two instances only, a notice of intent to appeal must be filed in order to defer the taking of an appeal until the final judgment that disposes of the case for all purposes and as to all parties is rendered:

 (1) when the deferred appeal is to be taken from a judgment that not only disposes of an entire complaint, counterclaim or cross complaint but also disposes of all the causes of action brought by or against a party or parties so that that party or parties are not parties to any remaining complaint, counterclaim or cross complaint; or

 (2) when the deferred appeal is to be taken from a judgment that disposes of only part of a complaint, counterclaim, or cross complaint but nevertheless disposes of all causes of action in that pleading brought by or against a particular party or parties.

In the event that the party aggrieved by a judgment described in (1) or (2) above elects to defer the taking of the appeal until the disposition of the entire case, the aggrieved party must, within the appeal period provided by statute, or, if there is no applicable statutory appeal period, within twenty days after issuance of notice of the judgment described in (1) or (2) above, file in the trial court a notice of intent to appeal the judgment, accompanied by a certification that a copy thereof has been served on each counsel of record in accordance with the provisions of Section 62-7.

When a notice of intent to appeal has been filed in accordance with this subsection, an objection to the deferral of the appeal may be made by (1) any party who, after the rendering of judgment on an entire complaint, counterclaim or cross complaint, is no longer a party to any remaining complaint, counterclaim, or cross complaint, or (2) any party who, by virtue of a judgment on a portion of any complaint, counterclaim, or cross complaint, is no longer a party to that complaint, counterclaim, or cross complaint. Objection shall be filed in the trial court, within twenty days of the filing of the notice of intent to appeal, accompanied by a certification that a copy thereof has been served on each counsel of record in accordance with the provisions of Section 62-7.

When such a party has filed a notice of objection to the deferral of the appeal, the appeal shall not be deferred, and the appellant shall file the appeal within twenty days of the filing of such notice of objection.

(b) Effect of failure to file notice of intent to appeal when required; effect of filing notice of intent to appeal when not required

If an aggrieved party, without having filed a timely notice of intent to appeal, files an appeal claiming that a judgment described in (1) or (2) of subsection (a) of this section was rendered improperly, the issues relating to such earlier judgment will be subject to dismissal as untimely.

The use of the notice of intent to appeal is abolished in all instances except as provided in subsection (a) of this section, which sets forth the two instances in which a notice of intent must be filed. Except as provided in subsection (a), the filing of a notice of intent to appeal will preserve no appeal rights.

Historical Note

Before 1996 this rule was a part of § 4002. See historical note to § 61-2. In 1996 the notice of intent to appeal was limited to those situations where a party is entirely removed from the case. Also in 1996, the opponent of a notice of intent to appeal was permitted to object to the notice, thus forcing the other side to file an immediate appeal or abandon the issues

AUTHORS' COMMENTS

This rule was used in Wilderman v. Powers, 110 Conn.App. 819, 826 n.3, 956 A.2d 613, 617 n.3 (2008).

The Appellate Court declined to review the plaintiff's claim of error on a stricken count of its complaint because, based on P.B. § 4002(a) in effect at the time of the ruling, the plaintiff failed to move for judgment on that one count or to file a notice of intent to appeal in Tuthill Finance v. Greenlaw, 61 Conn.App. 1, 762 A.2d 494 (2000). That result seems harsh in view of the current rule, which abolishes the need for a notice of intent to appeal under the facts of *Tuthill*.

A notice of intent to appeal is unnecessary if the order entered is not immediately appealable. Chase Manhattan Mortg. Corp. v. Machado, 83 Conn.App. 183, 185 n.3, 850 A.2d 260, 262 n.3 (2004).

§ 61-6. Appeal of Judgment or Ruling in Criminal Case

(a) Appeal by Defendant

(1) Appeal From Final Judgment.

The defendant may appeal from a conviction for an offense when the conviction has become a final judgment. The conviction becomes a final judgment after imposition of sentence. In cases where a final judgment has been rendered on fewer than all counts in the information or complaint, the defendant may appeal from that judgment at the time it is rendered.

(2) Appeal of Ruling Following Judgment Rendered Upon Conditional Plea of Nolo Contendere

(i) On Motion to Dismiss or Suppress

When a defendant, prior to the commencement of trial, enters a plea of nolo contendere conditional on the right to take an appeal from the court's denial of the defendant's motion to suppress or motion to dismiss, the defendant, after the imposition of sentence, may file an appeal within the time prescribed by law. The issue to be considered in such appeal shall be limited to whether it was proper for the court to have denied the motion to suppress or the motion to dismiss. A plea of nolo contendere by a defendant under this subsection shall not constitute a waiver by the defendant of nonjurisdictional defects in the criminal prosecution. The court shall not accept a nolo contendere plea pursuant to this subsection where the denial of the motion to suppress or motion to dismiss would not be dispositive of the case in the trial court. The court shall also decline to accept such a nolo contendere plea where the record available for review of the denial of the motion to suppress or motion to dismiss is inadequate for appellate review of the court's determination thereof.

(ii) On Any Motion Made Prior to Close of Evidence

With the approval of the court, after a hearing to consider any objections thereto, a defendant may enter a conditional plea of guilty or nolo contendere, reserving in writing the right, on appeal from the judgment, to review of the adverse determination of any motion made prior to the close of evidence, which motion must be specified in such written reservation. If the defendant prevails on appeal, the judgment shall be set aside and the defendant shall be allowed to withdraw the conditional plea of guilty or nolo contendere after the case has been remanded to the trial court. A plea of guilty or nolo contendere under this subsection shall not constitute a waiver of nonjurisdictional defects in the criminal prosecution. The court shall not accept a plea of guilty or nolo contendere pursuant to this subsection where the adverse determination of the specified motion would not be dispositive of the case in the trial court. The court shall also decline to accept such a nolo contendere or guilty plea where the record available for review of the ruling upon the specified motion is inadequate for appellate review of the court's determination thereof.

(b) Appeal by State

The state, with the permission of the presiding judge of the trial court and as provided by law, may appeal from a final judgment. In cases where an appealable judgment has been rendered on fewer than all counts of the information or complaint, the state may appeal from the judgment at the time it is rendered.

(c) Appeal From a Ruling

To the extent provided by law, the defendant or the state may appeal from a ruling that is not a final judgment or from an interlocutory ruling deemed to be a final judgment.

Historical Note

Derivation:
    1978 P.B. (1986–97), § 4003

Amendments were made in 1996 and 2001 to track C.G.S.A. § 54-94a. Amendments in 2001 were made to collect in one place the various types of criminal appeals. Sections 61-2 through 61-5 should not be used for criminal cases.

Amendments were made June 17, 2008, effective January 1, 2009.

This rule is new effective October 1, 1986. Section (b) is referred to in State v. Chung, 202 Conn. 39, 44 n.5, 519 A.2d 1175, 1178 n.5 (1987), and State v. Kelley, 206 Conn. 323, 336, 537 A.2d 483, 490 (1988).

AUTHORS' COMMENTS

This rule was used in State v. Rutledge, 17 Conn.App. 250, 251 n.1, 552 A.2d 435, 436 n.1 (1989). Query whether jurisdiction to appeal can be created by rule. See Gold v. Newman, 211 Conn. 631, 560 A.2d 960 (1989), and Simms v. Warden, 229 Conn. 178, 183–86, 640 A.2d 601, 604–06 (1994).

Subsection (a)(2) was read broadly in State v. Piorkowski, 236 Conn. 388, 413–21, 672 A.2d 921, 935–39 (1996), to allow appellate review if the defendant attaches conditions to his plea not found in the rule. This subsection was also used in State v. Vincente, 44 Conn.App. 249, 688 A.2d 359, 362 (1997); and State v. Turner, 267 Conn. 414, 417 n.4, 838 A.2d 947, 951 n.4 (2004).

The court used the reasoning of this rule in concluding that the state's appeal from the dismissal of three of six charges was from a final judgment, even though this rule was not yet in effect at the time the appeal was filed. State v. Joyner, 255 Conn. 477, 487–89, 774 A.2d 927, 933–34 (2001).

The 2001 amendments were discussed in State v. Joyner, 255 Conn. 477, 488, 774 A.2d 927, 934 (2001). The purpose was merely to collect all the ways one could appeal, not to break new ground.

Subsection (b) was applied in State v. Henry, 90 Conn.App. 714, 720–21, 881 A.2d 442, 447, cert. denied, 276 Conn. 914, 888 A.2d 86 (2005).

§ 61-7. Joint and Consolidated Appeals (Applicable to appeals filed before July 1, 2013)

(a) (1) Two or more plaintiffs or defendants in the same case may appeal jointly or severally. Separate cases heard together and involving at least one common party may as of right be appealed jointly, provided all the trial court docket numbers are shown on the appeal form (JD-SC-28 and JD-SC-29).

(2) Prior to the filing of an appeal the trial court, on motion of any party or on its own motion, may order that a joint appeal be filed in any situation not covered by the preceding paragraph.

(3) In the case of a joint appeal, only one entry fee is required.

(b) (1) The supreme court, on motion of any party or on its own motion may order that appeals pending in the supreme court be consolidated.

(2) When an appeal pending in the supreme court involves the same cause of action, transaction or occurrence as an appeal pending in the appellate court, the supreme court may, on motion of any party or on its own motion, order that the appeals be consolidated in the supreme court. The court may order consolidation at any time before the assignment of the appeals for hearing.

(3) The appellate court, on motion of any party or on its own motion, may order that appeals pending in the appellate court be consolidated.

(4) There shall be no refund of fees if appeals are consolidated.

(c) Whenever appeals are jointly filed or are consolidated, only a single record shall be prepared. In addition, all appellants must file a single, consolidated brief and all appellees must file a single, consolidated brief; provided, however, that any party may file a request in writing to the chief justice or chief judge, as the case may be, for permission to file a separate brief if the joint parties cannot agree upon the contents of the joint brief or to brief issues which are not common to the joint parties.

§ 61-7. Joint and Consolidated Appeals (Applicable to appeals filed on or after July 1, 2013)

(a) (1) Two or more plaintiffs or defendants in the same case may appeal jointly or severally. Separate cases heard together and involving at least one common party may as of right be appealed jointly, provided all the trial court docket numbers are shown on the appeal form (JD-SC-28 and JD-SC-29).

(2) Prior to the filing of an appeal the trial court, on motion of any party or on its own motion, may order that a joint appeal be filed in any situation not covered by the preceding paragraph.

(3) In the case of a joint appeal, only one entry fee is required.

(b) (1) The supreme court, on motion of any party or on its own motion may order that appeals pending in the supreme court be consolidated.

(2) When an appeal pending in the supreme court involves the same cause of action, transaction or occurrence as an appeal pending in the appellate court, the supreme court may, on motion of any party or on its own motion, order that the appeals be consolidated in the supreme court. The court may order consolidation at any time before the assignment of the appeals for hearing.

(3) The appellate court, on motion of any party or on its own motion, may order that appeals pending in the appellate court be consolidated.

(4) There shall be no refund of fees if appeals are consolidated.

(c) Whenever appeals are jointly filed or are consolidated, all appellants shall file a single, consolidated brief and appendix. All appellees shall file a single, consolidated brief or, if applicable, a single, consolidated brief and appendix. If the parties cannot agree upon the contents of the joint brief and appendix, or if the issues to be briefed are not common to the joint parties, any party may file a motion for permission to file a separate brief and appendix.

Historical Note

Derivation:
  1978 P.B. (1986–97), § 4004, 4026
  1978 P.B., § 3002
  1963 P.B., § 606
  1951 P.B., § 382

The language in (c) about permission to file a separate brief was added in 1996.

This rule was entirely rewritten effective January 1, 1985 and again effective October 1, 1986 to clarify numerous ambiguities in the previous language. The last paragraph was clarified effective October 1, 1992.

This rule was first adopted in 1951.

Cross References

Form 3000.19
Maltbie, Conn.App.Proc.2d, § 124

AUTHORS' COMMENTS

A party appealing two different rulings in the same appeal should use Section 61-9. But see Rocque v. DeMilo and Co., Inc., 85 Conn.App. 512, 526, 857 A.2d 976, 986 (2004), where one appeal from two orders was permitted without comment.

In the authors' opinion, if the court's second ruling occurs within the appeal period for the first order, it is proper to use one appeal form for both orders provided the appeal is filed within the time to do so for the first order.

Consolidation of appeals is unlikely to affect a litigant's substantive rights.

See Plante v. Charlotte Hungerford Hosp., 300 Conn. 33, 58, 12 A.3d 885 (2011), where such an issue was raised but not decided.

Occasionally a cautious lawyer, being uncertain which of two decisions is final, will file a separate appeal from both decisions and move to consolidate them. It makes no sense for the Appellate Court suo motu to put the more vulnerable appeal on its motion calendar and then dismiss it. The cautious lawyer then has to file a petition for certification and, if the Appellate Court chooses the wrong appeal to dismiss, the parties may be stuck briefing an avoidable jurisdictional issue. The proper result is to allow the consolidation so that the jurisdictional issue can be ignored. That is exactly what the Supreme Court did in State v. Lombardo Bros. Mason Contractors, Inc., 307 Conn. 412, 419–20 n.13, 54 A.3d 1005, 1012 n. 13 (2012).

§ 61-8. Cross Appeals (Applicable to appeals filed before July 1, 2013)

Any appellee or appellees aggrieved by the judgment or decision from which the appellant has appealed may jointly or severally file a cross appeal within ten days from the filing of the appeal. Except where otherwise provided, the filing and form of cross appeals, extensions of time for filing them, and all subsequent proceedings shall be the same as though the cross appeal were an original appeal. No entry or record fee need be paid.

§ 61-8. Cross-Appeals (Applicable to appeals filed on or after July 1, 2013)

Any appellee or appellees aggrieved by the judgment or decision from which the appellant has appealed may jointly or severally file a cross appeal within ten days from the filing of the appeal. Except where otherwise provided, the filing and form of cross appeals, extensions of time for filing them, and all subsequent proceedings shall be the same as though the cross appeal were an original appeal. No entry or record fee need be paid.

Historical Note

Derivation:
    1978 P.B. (1986–97), § 4005
    1978 P.B., § 3003
    1963 P.B., § 607
    1951 P.B., § 383

This rule was clarified effective January 1, 1985 to indicate that a cross appellant must be aggrieved of the judgment or decision.

Prior to 1951 the cross appeal was simply an independent appeal, according to the Maltbie reference noted below, although his citations neither support nor refute that statement.

Cross appeals are less important now than under the finding system, where the only assignments of error an appellee could make under old § 623 were those "directed to the finding of any fact or refusal to find the fact." Without a cross appeal, it has been held under § 623 that an appellee cannot raise issues of law, Farmers and Mechanics Sav. Bank v. First Federal Sav. and Loan Ass'n of Meriden, 167 Conn. 294, 303 n.4, 355 A.2d 260, 264 n.4 (1974); Akin v. City of Norwalk, 163 Conn. 68, 70, 301 A.2d 258, 259 (1972). These considerations do not apply in light of § 63-4(a)(1).

Cross References

Maltbie, Conn.App.Proc.2d §§ 122, 287

AUTHORS' COMMENTS

1. Need for Cross Appeal

Although this rule was not amended in 2013, commentary was added to make clear that a cross appellant has the same obligations as the appellant with respect to part one of the appendix. While this may result in some redundancy, putting the onus on cross-appellants ensures a proper appendix if the appeal is withdrawn and only the cross appeal remains.

An appellee who wishes to attack the judgment in any way *must* file a cross appeal. Gagne v. Vaccaro, 311 Conn. 649, 661, 90 A.3d 196, 198 (2014); Connole v. Babij, 140 Conn.App. 494, 496 n.5, 59 A.3d 334, 335 n.5 (2013); Centimark Corp. v. Village Manor Associates Ltd. Partnership, 113 Conn.App. 509, 537 n.10, 967 A.2d 550, 569 n.10, cert. denied, 292 Conn. 907, 973 A.2d 103 (2009); Board of Educ. of Town of Plainfield v. Local R1-126, Nat. Ass'n of Government Employees, 108 Conn.App. 35, 36 n.1, 947 A.2d 371, 373 n.1 (2008). An appellee who does not file a cross appeal will be limited in the issues that can be discussed on appeal, although § 63-4(a)(1) substantially broadens the old § 623 as to what issues an appellee may raise. See Scoville v. Scoville, 179 Conn. 277, 278 n.1, 426 A.2d 271, 272 n.1 (1979). Specifically, if an appellee would be claiming a different result from what the trial court ordered, a cross appeal rather than an alternate basis to affirm must be filed. Mitchell v. Silverstein, 67 Conn.App. 58, 60 n.5, 787 A.2d 20, 21 n.5 (2001). On the other hand, an appellee claiming the trial court should have reached the same result on a different ground should raise this claim as an alternative basis to affirm, not as a cross appeal. Electrical Contractors, Inc. v. Department of Educ., 303 Conn. 402, 455–56, 35 A.3d 188, 223–24, 192 L.R.R.M. (BNA) 2954, 2012-1 Trade Cas. (CCH) ¶ 77768 (2012); Connecticut State Medical Society v. Connecticare, Inc., 272 Conn. 482, 484 n.3, 863 A.2d 652, 683 n.3 (2005); Jones v. Town of Redding, 296 Conn. 352, 363–67, 995 A.2d 51, 58–60 (2010).

In State v. Albino, 312 Conn. 763, 770-71, 97 A.3d 478, 484–85 (2014), the Court treated a cross appeal as an alternate basis to affirm where the issue was intertwined with the appeal and it was fully briefed by the parties.

If neither a cross appeal under this section nor a preliminary statement of issues under § 63-4(a)(1) is filed by the appellee, the appellee clearly cannot raise any issue of law. Lynch v. Davis, 181 Conn. 434, 437, 435 A.2d 977, 978 (1980). In the authors' view, the two situations where § 63-4(a)(1) is inadequate without a cross appeal are (1) (as to plaintiff) the failure of the trial court to grant all the relief or full damages claimed; Blue Cross/Blue Shield of Connecticut, Inc. v. Gurski, 47 Conn.App. 478, 481, 705 A.2d 566, 567, cert. denied, 247 Conn. 920, 722 A.2d 809 (1998); and (2) (as to defendant) the failure of the trial court to deny all relief to the plaintiff. In National Harmony, Inc. v. Normand, A.C. 6671 (1988), the plaintiff claimed defendant appealed from the award of specific performance and damages. The trial court awarded only specific performance. The defendant appealed from the award of specific performance, and the plaintiff filed a § 63-4 appellee's statement claiming damages. The Appellate Court struck the plaintiff's statement in an order dated February 24, 1988, presumably on the ground that the plaintiff should have cross appealed. In Futterleib v. Mr. Happy's, Inc., 16 Conn.App. 497, 499, 548 A.2d 728, 730 (1988), the defendant appealed after trial and the plaintiff in his § 63-4 papers raised the issue whether one count should have been stricken before trial. The Appellate Court refused to consider the issue in the absence of a cross appeal. Thus, a litigant who wishes to change the judgment in any way must cross appeal. Housing Authority of Hartford, 82 Conn.App. at 19, n. 1, 842 A.2d at 603 n. 1. But see LaCroix v. Board of Educ. of City of Bridgeport, 2 Conn.App. 36, 38, 475 A.2d 1110, 1111–12 (1984), rev'd on other grounds, 199 Conn. 70, 505 A.2d 1233 (1986), where the Appellate Court, in an unusually generous mood, considered an issue under situation (2) without a cross appeal but with a § 63-4 statement. See also DeBeradinis v. Zoning Com'n of City of Norwalk, 228 Conn. 187, 198 n.7, 635 A.2d 1220, 1225 n.7 (1994) (issue considered where fully briefed by both sides).

See Nowell v. Nowell, 163 Conn. 116, 121–23, 302 A.2d 260, 263–65 (1972), for problems arising if the case is remanded and the appellee attempts to raise issues in the trial court that should have been raised in a cross appeal.

When in doubt, file both a cross appeal and a § 63-4 appellee's statement.

P.B. § 61-10 also applies to cross appeals. Suffield Development Associates Ltd. Partnership v. National Loan Investors, L.P., 60 Conn.App. 842, 851–52, 763 A.2d 1049, 1054 (2000).

The authors vigorously disagree with Cunningham v. Planning and Zoning Com'n of Town of Plainville, 90 Conn.App. 273, 277–78, 876 A.2d 1257, 1260–61, cert. denied, 276 Conn. 915, 888 A.2d 83 (2005), holding that failure to cross appeal bars an appellee from claiming that the appellants waived their issue on appeal by inadequately briefing them in the trial court. The authors do not think the appellee had to raise that claim as an alternative basis to affirm; a fortiori the Appellate Court is simply wrong to require a cross appeal when the appellee is not asking that the judgment be altered in any way.

2. Response if No Cross Appeal Filed

If there is no cross appeal, and the appellee briefs an issue of law not encompassed within § 63-4(a)(1), the appellant should attempt to strike this material under § 60-2. The risk in filing such a motion is that the Court may allow the appellee to file a late § 63-4 statement; the appellant may then respond in a reply brief. See Cristofaro v. Planning and Zoning Com'n of Town of Burlington, 11 Conn.App. 260, 262 n.4, 527 A.2d 255, 256 n.4 (1987). If the appellant files a reply brief discussing the issue on the merits, the Supreme Court may excuse the defect. If the appellant refrains from discussing the issue, the Supreme Court is less likely to rule on it, Prokolkin v. General Motors Corp., 170 Conn. 289, 304, 365 A.2d 1180, 1187 (1976). However, in Nielsen v. Kezer, 232 Conn. 65, 73 n.15, 652 A.2d 1013, 1018 n.15 (1995), the Supreme Court excused the appellee even though the appellant did not discuss the issue on the merits in his reply brief. Thus, not only did the appellee get the alternate issue reviewed, but it was done with briefing from only one side.

3. Right to File Cross Appeal

A party must be aggrieved of the lower court judgment in order to cross appeal. However, the courts frequently treat a cross appeal as an alternate basis to affirm under § 63-4. Kortner v. Martise, 312 Conn. 1, 5 n.4, 59 n.17, 91 A.3d 412, 417 n.4, 446 n.17 (2014); Pelletier v. Sordoni/Skanska Const. Co., 286 Conn. 563, 589–90, 945 A.2d 388, 405 (2008); State v. Preston, 286 Conn. 367, 373 n.4, 944 A.2d 276, 292 n.4 (2008); Wesley v. Schaller Subaru, Inc., 277 Conn. 526, 529 n.1, 893 A.2d 389, 392 n.1 (2006); Bower v. D'Onfro, 45 Conn.App. 543, 547 n.5, 696 A.2d 1285, 1287 n.5 (1997). What this means is: When in doubt file a cross appeal.

4. Cross Appeal as to Non-Appealing Party

A cross appeal may be filed against a non-appealing party. Wickes Mfg. Co. v. Currier Elec. Co., Inc., 25 Conn.App. 751, 754 n.3, 596 A.2d 1331, 1332 n.3 (1991).

5. Withdrawal or Dismissal of Original Appeal

This does not affect the viability of the cross appeal, Schurman v. Schurman, 188 Conn. 268, 269–70, 449 A.2d 169, 170–71 (1982) (withdrawal); CFM of Connecticut v. Chowdhury, 38 Conn.App. 745 n.1, 662 A.2d 1340 n.1 (1995) (dismissal).

§ 61-9. Decisions Subsequent to Filing of Appeal; Amended Appeals (Applicable to appeals filed before July 1, 2013)

Should the trial court, subsequent to the filing of a pending appeal, make a decision that the appellant desires to have reviewed, the appellant shall file an amended appeal in the trial court within twenty days from the issuance of notice of the decision as provided for in Section 63-1.

The amended appeal shall be filed in the trial court in the same manner as an original appeal pursuant to Section 63-3. No additional fee is required to be paid upon the filing of an amended appeal.

Within ten days of filing the amended appeal, the appellant shall file with the appellate clerk an original and one copy of either a certificate stating that there are no changes to the Section 63-4 papers filed with the original appeal or any amendments to those papers. Any other party may file an original and one copy of responsive Section 63-4 papers within twenty days of the filing of the certificate or the amendments.

If the original appeal is dismissed for lack of jurisdiction, the amended appeal shall remain pending if it was filed from a judgment or order from which an original appeal properly could have been filed.

After disposition of an appeal where no amended appeals related to that appeal are pending, a subsequent appeal shall be filed as a new appeal.

If the amended appeal is filed after the filing of the appellant's brief but before the filing of the appellee's brief, the appellant may move for leave to file a supplemental brief. If the amended appeal is filed after the filing of the appellee's brief, either party may move for such leave. In any event, the court may order that an amended appeal be briefed or heard separately from the original appeal.

If the appellant files a subsequent appeal from a trial court decision in a case where there is a pending appeal, the subsequent appeal shall be treated as an amended appeal and there shall be no refund of the fees paid.

§ 61-9. Decisions Subsequent to Filing of Appeal; Amended Appeals (Applicable to Appeals filed on or after July 1, 2013)

Should the trial court, subsequent to the filing of a pending appeal, make a decision that the appellant desires to have reviewed, the appellant shall file an amended appeal in the trial court within twenty days from the issuance of notice of the decision as provided for in Section 63-1.

The amended appeal shall be filed in the trial court in the same manner as an original appeal pursuant to Section 63-3. No additional fee is required to be paid upon the filing of an amended appeal.

Within ten days of filing the amended appeal, the appellant shall file with the appellate clerk the original and one copy of the endorsed amended appeal form and an original of either a certificate stating that there are no changes to the Section 63-4 papers filed with the original appeal or any amendments to those papers. Any other party may file an original of responsive Section 63-4 papers within twenty days of the filing of the certificate or the amendments.

If the original appeal is dismissed for lack of jurisdiction, the amended appeal shall remain pending if it was filed from a judgment or order from which an original appeal properly could have been filed.

After disposition of an appeal where no amended appeals related to that appeal are pending, a subsequent appeal shall be filed as a new appeal.

If the amended appeal is filed after the filing of the appellant's brief and appendix but before the filing of the appellee's brief and appendix, the appellant may move for leave to file a supplemental brief and appendix. If the amended appeal is filed after the filing of the appellee's brief and appendix, either party may move for such leave. In any event, the court may order that an amended appeal be briefed or heard separately from the original appeal.

If the appellant files a subsequent appeal from a trial court decision in a case, where there is a pending appeal, the subsequent appeal shall be treated as an amended appeal, and there shall be no refund of the fees paid.

Historical Note

Derivation:
   1978 P.B., (1986–97), § 4006
   1978 P.B., § 3062
   1963 P.B., § 639
   1951 P.B., § 403
Effective August 1, 2014, the appellant must file both an original and one

copy of the endorsed appeal form with the appellate clerk. This rule was almost completely rewritten effective January 1, 2013 to eliminate numerous ambiguities. What is now the fourth paragraph was added in 2010.

Effective July 1, 1979, all reference to the finding system has been eliminated. Previously there had been no substantial change since the rule was adopted in 1951.

Cross References

Maltbie, Conn.App.Proc.2d, § 180

Form 3000.18

AUTHORS' COMMENTS

Prior to January 1, 2010, an amended appeal could not cure a jurisdictional defect in the original appeal. Broadnax v. City of New Haven, 294 Conn. 280, 298 n.33, 984 A.2d 658, 669 n.33 (2009). Consequently, if there was any question about the court's jurisdiction over an appeal, it was necessary to file a separate appeal from a later order. See *Broadnax*, 984 A.2d. at 668 n.32. The last paragraph, added in 2010, should reduce the need for such prophylactic measures. For the use of the amended rule, see Cunniffe v. Cunniffe, 150 Conn.App. 419, 420 n.1, 91 A.3d 497, 501 n.1, cert. denied, 314 Conn. ___, ___ A.3d ___ (2014); Rosa v. Lawrence and Memorial Hosp., 145 Conn.App. 275, 282 n.9, 74 A.3d 534, 542 n.9 (2013). McKeon v. Lennon, 131 Conn.App. 585, 611–12, 27 A.3d 436, 452, cert. denied, 303 Conn. 901, 31 A.3d 1178 (2011); Midland Funding, LLC v. Tripp, 134 Conn.App. 195, 196 n.1, 38 A.3d 221, 222 n.1 (2012). However, if the amended appeal also is from a nonfinal judgment, the 2010 change will not save the appeal. Morgan v. Morgan, 136 Conn.App. 371, 373, 46 A.3d 255, 256 (2012).

Unlike the federal trial courts, the Connecticut trial courts have plenary authority to issue orders otherwise within their jurisdiction while appeal is pending. See Ahneman v. Ahneman, 243 Conn. 471, 482–83, 706 A.2d 960, 965–66 (1998). If the subsequent order grants the relief sought on appeal, the appeal may become moot. RAL Management, Inc. v. Valley View Associates, 278 Conn. 672, 899 A.2d 586 (2006). In Kendall v. Amster, 108 Conn.App. 319, 948 A.2d 1041 (2008), the trial court's post-appeal order granting some but not all relief sought on appeal did not moot the appeal. The court in *Kendall* suggested that the appellant should file an amended appeal pursuant to this rule.

An amended appeal (Form 3000.1) is filed with the trial court clerk; at the same time a copy should be filed with the appellate clerk along with § 63-4 papers. The amended appeal box should be checked when filing an amended appeal form under this rule. The corrected/amended appeal box should be checked when errors in the original appeal are being corrected.

While the rule is unclear, the authors' opinion is that the subsequent decision is subject to §§ 61-11 and 61-12 (the stay rules) and § 66-5 (the articulation/ rectification rule) independent of their applicability to the judgment originally appealed.

Note, however, that amending an appeal, even if additional transcripts are ordered, does not extend the briefing deadline. File a motion for extension of time pursuant to P. B. § 66-1(c), if necessary.

A failure to comply with this section is grounds for the Court to refuse review; Schaghticoke Indian Tribe v. Rost, 138 Conn.App. 204, 214, 50 A.3d 411, 417 (2012); Rocque v. DeMilo and Co., Inc., 85 Conn.App. 512, 527, 857 A.2d 976, 986 (2004); Jewett v. Jewett, 265 Conn. 669, 672-73 n.4, 830 A.2d 193, 198–99 n.4 (2003); even if a supplemental statement of issues is filed; Brown v. Brown, 190 Conn. 345, 350, 460 A.2d 1287, 1290 (1983) (counsel fees to defend dissolution appeal); Fisher v. Fisher, 4 Conn.App. 97, 101, 492 A.2d 525, 528 (1985) (same). The rule was complied with in Friedlander v. Friedlander, 191 Conn. 81, 84, 463 A.2d 587, 590 (1983).

Denials of motions to reopen the judgment and similar matters can be reviewed without the necessity of a second appeal, Freccia v. Martin, 163 Conn. 160, 162, 302 A.2d 280, 282 (1972). All that is needed is to amend the original appeal, and if necessary, amend other § 63-4 papers. Failure to do so was fatal in Juliano v. Juliano, 96 Conn.App. 381, 386, 900 A.2d 557, 560, cert. denied, 280 Conn. 921, 908 A.2d 544 (2006). Review of post-appeal motions often arises in dissolution cases. See Saunders v. Saunders, 140 Conn. 140, 145, 98 A.2d 815, 817 (1953) (denial of attorneys' fees to defend against appeal); Mailly v. Mailly, 13 Conn.App. 185, 187–88, 535 A.2d 385, 387 (1988) (grant of attorneys' fees to defend against appeal). In *Mailly* the appellant also used the amended appeal to appeal from an earlier judgment. Since the appellee did not move to dismiss within 10 days the untimeliness was waived. Sometimes the subsequent ruling may moot out the whole appeal, Reynolds v. Vroom, 130 Conn. 512, 515, 36 A.2d 22, 23–24 (1944).

This section does NOT apply to orders that can be reviewed only under § 66-6 as a motion for review, such as on a stay order. Scagnelli v. Donovan, 88 Conn.App. 840, 871 A.2d 1084 (2005); or a motion pursuant to P.B. § 66-5 to perfect the record. Cunniffe v. Cunniffe, 150 Conn.App. 419, 420 n.1, 91 A.3d 497, 501 n.1, cert. denied, 314 Conn. ___, ___ A.3d ___ (2014). This makes sense because there are certain motions that should be disposed of before the appeal is heard.

This section is obviously meant for the typical situation of an order subsequent to the appeal from the final judgment. However, what happens if the reverse occurs, that is, the first appeal is from a ruling *before* the final judgment (such as under § 61-2)? Thereafter filing an amended appeal from the final judgment seems like the tail wagging the dog. And what happens if a trial court order is issued after oral argument on appeal or in the midst of appellate reargument or certification proceedings? In these situations, unless the later trial court ruling would directly affect the existing appeal, the authors' advice is to use the last paragraph of the rule to file a wholly independent appeal, and to refer to the existence of the first appeal in the docketing statement. This advice should be followed cautiously, however; unless there is a good reason to file a separate appeal, an amended appeal should be filed.

In a case prior to the enactment of this rule in 1951, the Court held that it was not necessary to amend the appeal in order to raise issues concerning the denial of counsel fees and disbursements to prosecute the appeal and for temporary alimony. Rather, it was only necessary to amend the assignment of errors (now statement of issues). Mathurin v. City of Putnam, 136 Conn. 361, 363, 71 A.2d 599, 601 (1950); Cf. Valluzzo v. Valluzzo, 103 Conn. 265, 130 A. 126 (1925); Bielan v. Bielan, 135 Conn. 163, 164, 62 A.2d 664, 666 (1948). Whether that decision survives is questionable. Beware of pre-1951 decisions permitting an independent appeal from post-judgment orders while an appeal from the judgment is pending. Cases such as Dochelli v. Dochelli, 125 Conn. 465, 3 A.2d 666 (1939), probably do not survive the adoption of this rule in 1951. Double appeals were criticized even before 1951 in Mathurin v. City of Putnam, 136 Conn. 361, 363, 71 A.2d 599, 601 (1950). Post-judgment orders can still be immediately challenged or put into immediate effect under §§ 61-11 to 61-14.

Rulings under this section do not have to be final judgments; Young v. Polish Loan & Indus. Corp., 126 Conn. 714, 11 A.2d 395 (1940) (appointment of receiver of rents after final judgment), although the ruling would have been a final judgment if no appeal were then pending.

It appears that in at least exceptional cases this section can be invoked right up to the time of oral argument. In Chamber of Commerce of Greater Waterbury, Inc. v. Murphy, 179 Conn. 712, 722, 427 A.2d 866, 871 (1980), the Supreme Court heard oral argument on February 27, 1980 and reviewed a motion that had only been denied by the trial court on February 20, 1980. The court in State v. Legnani, 109 Conn.App. 399, 408 n.4, 951 A.2d 674, 681, cert. denied, 289 Conn. 940, 959 A.2d 1007 (2008), granted a motion for permission to file a late amended appeal after oral argument (!) where the state did not object.

If a motion for a new trial is filed and denied pending appeal, the denial should be reviewed by an amended appeal under this section rather than by a motion for review under § 66-6. See Season-All Industries, Inc. v. R.J. Grosso, Inc., A.C. 7202 (1989).

The Appellate Court has held that an appeal need not be amended following an order granting a remittitur while an appeal is pending. Preston v. Phelps Dodge Copper Products Co., 35 Conn.App. 850, 854–55, 647 A.2d 364, 367 (1994). The authors do not agree. Appellate review must consider the remittitur, not just the original judgment, but the order on the remittitur is not before the Appellate Court.

§ 61-10. Responsibility of Appellant to Provide Adequate Record for Review (Applicable to appeals filed before July 1, 2013)

(a) It is the responsibility of the appellant to provide an adequate record for review. The appellant shall determine whether the entire trial court record is complete, correct and otherwise perfected for presentation on appeal. For purposes of this section, the term "record" is not limited to its meaning pursuant to Section 63-4(a)(2), but includes all trial court decisions, documents and exhibits necessary and appropriate for appellate review of any claimed impropriety.

(b) The failure of any party on appeal to seek articulation pursuant to Section 66-5 shall not be the sole ground upon which the court declines to review any issue or claim on appeal. If the court determines that articulation of the trial court decision is appropriate, it may remand the case pursuant to Section 60-5 for articulation by the trial court within a specified time period. After remand to the trial court for articulation, the trial court may, in its discretion, require assistance from the parties in order to provide the articulation. Such assistance may include, but is not limited to, supplemental briefs, oral argument and provision of copies of transcripts and exhibits.

§ 61-10. Responsibility of Appellant to Provide Adequate Record for Review (Applicable to appeals filed on or after July 1, 2013)

(a) It is the responsibility of the appellant to provide an adequate record for review. The appellant shall determine whether the entire record is complete, correct and otherwise perfected for presentation on appeal.

(b) The failure of any party on appeal to seek articulation pursuant to Section 66-5 shall not be the sole ground upon which the court declines to review any issue or claim on appeal. If the court determines that articulation of the trial court decision is appropriate, it may remand the case pursuant to Section 60-5 for articulation by the trial court within a specified time period. After remand to the trial court for articulation, the trial court may, in its discretion, require assistance from the parties in order to provide the articulation. Such assistance may include, but is not limited to, supplemental briefs, oral argument and provision of copies of transcripts and exhibits.

Historical Note

Derivation:
    1978 P.B. (1996–97), § 4007
The first sentence was transferred from § 4061. The remainder of the rule is new.

Subsection (B) was announced in the Connecticut Law Journal of November 6, 2012 effective January 1, 2013.

Cross References
    P.B. § 61-10 (Motion for Rectification; Motion for Articulation)

AUTHORS' COMMENTS

Subsection (b), effective January 1, 2013, abolishes the forfeiture practice the appellate courts had adopted for many years if a litigant failed to move for articulation pursuant to § 66-5 of an arguably ambiguous decision. The court followed the new rule in Smith v. Commissioner of Correction, 141 Conn.App. 626, 638, 62 A.3d 554, 562, cert. denied, 308 Conn. 947, 67 A.3d 947 (2013). The commentary, however, makes clear that the rule change does not preclude the court from refusing review because the record is inadequate for other reasons such as the failure to obtain *any* memorandum of decision or to designate and file necessary transcripts. See Murcia v. Geyer, 151 Conn.App. 227, 231 n.1, 93 A.3d 1189, 1191 n.1, cert. denied, 314 Conn. 917, _ A.3d _ (2014) (judgment affirmed where appellant failed to procure memorandum of decision); State v. Pearson, 139 Conn.App. 521, 56 A.3d 722 (2012) (record "bereft of facts" and claims inadequately briefed); Cleford v. Bristol, 150 Conn.App. 229, 90 A.3d 998 (2014) (inadequate brief and failure to provide transcripts precluded review). While the court will review a claim in the absence of an articulation, the court will read an ambiguous record to support rather than undermine the judgment. State v. Richard S., 143 Conn.App. 596, 70 A.3d 1110, cert. denied, 310 Conn. 912, 2013 WL 5774869 (2013); Shamitz v. Taffler, 145 Conn.App. 132, 142, 75 A.3d 62, 68 (2013) (in the absence of an adequate record for review, court will not presume error); D'Ascanio v. Toyota Industries Corp., 309 Conn. 663, 72 A.3d 1019 (2013) (McDonald, J., concurring).

However, the appellant does not have a duty to prepare an adequate record to review a defensive argument put forward by the appellee. State v. Ruocco, 151 Conn. App. 732, 741–43, 95 A.3d 573, 579–81 (2014).

Note that the last sentence of (b) explains the meaning of the word "record." See Holmes v. Hartford Hospital, 147 Conn.App. 713, 721 n.4, 84 A.3d 885, 890 n.4 (2014); see also P.B. § 60-4.

Since subsection (b) is a dramatic change in appellate procedure adopted after several years of consultation between the courts and the appellate bar, we will offer our advice here for applying the general language of (b) to specific situations.

To begin with, the new provision must mean more than "If the decision is unclear, we will now affirm the decision instead of refusing to consider the issue." While that approach is an improvement to the extent that the court will afford review, a default rule that an ambiguity requires affirmance is substantively not much better than the prior forfeiture rule, especially if the result is an uncorrected error.

Our view is that an appellate court should first determine if the trial court's reasoning (if there is any) is clear, either from the language taken in isolation or in the context of the decision as a whole. If the reasoning is still unclear, the court should review any other relevant considerations the record discloses. One relevant consideration should be the strength of the appellee's case at trial. If the trial court's ambiguous reasoning could be either (a) or (b), (a) being proper and (b) being not proper, a strong case presented by the appellee should yield an affirmance; a weak case should yield a remand to the trial court to give its reasoning clearly. Another relevant consideration should be how seriously the parties at trial argued each of the possible reasons for what ultimately became the trial court's decision. If the parties spent a lot of time on (b) at trial but hardly mentioned (a), a remand should be considered.

Two cases decided under the new rule demonstrate this approach. In *Smith* the petitioner in a habeas corpus action claimed that the state failed to turn over some photographs of the crime scene that showed a hat. The trial court said the petitioner failed to prove that the failure to disclose was a *Brady* Comments from page 97 continued on next page violation. The trial court made no further explanation of its decision. Since the basis of the decision was ambiguous, the Appellate Court might simply have affirmed, but it did not. Rather it examined the photographs itself and determined that the existence of the hat would likely not have affected the result.

Likewise in *D'Ascanio*, Justice McDonald's concurring opinion stated in dictum that an ambiguous decision should be read in favor of the judgment, but then went into considerable detail to explain why the evidence most persuasively supported reading the ambiguous decision in favor of the result reached by the trial court.

In short, the trial court decision should always be reviewed in the context of the whole record. While language viewed by itself might be ambiguous, the context of the record may well make one reading of the decision the better one. And if the context still leaves the trial court reasoning in doubt, the appellate court should liberally use the second sentence of (b) to order an articulation rather than affirm on a basis that, while just barely justifiable, seems to the appellate court to require confirmation by the trial court of what it really meant.

The cases to follow should be read with some caution because they were issued before (b) was added to this rule on January 1, 2013.

For an example of the court ordering an articulation sua sponte, see Aliano v. Aliano, 148 Conn.App, 267, 273, 85 A.3d 33, cert. denied, 311 Conn. 939, 89 A.3d 350 (2014).

To the extent that any of the following cases were decided prior to January 1, 2013, and concern the failure to seek articulation, they should be read with caution.

Both the Supreme Court and Appellate Court have made it abundantly clear that if this responsibility is not acted on, review is jeopardized. Carmichael v. Stonkus, 133 Conn.App. 302, 306, 34 A.3d 1026, 1028–29, cert. denied, 304 Conn. 911, 39 A.3d 1121 (2012) (no transcript of ruling provided); Quaranta v. King, 133 Conn.App. 565, 569–71, 36 A.3d 264, 267–68 (2012) (only partial transcript provided); State v. Bonner, 290 Conn. 468, 493, 964 A.2d 73, 89 (2009) (failure to correct record about in camera discussions); Desrosiers v. Henne, 283 Conn. 361, 366–68, 926 A.2d 1024, 1026–28 (2007) (inadequate transcript, so review denied); O'Halpin v. O'Halpin, 144 Conn.App. 671, 675–76, 74 A.3d 465, 469 (failure to order transcripts of discovery proceeding precluded review), cert. denied, 310 Conn. 952, 81 A.3d 1180 (2013); Rice v. Housing Authority of City of Meriden, 129 Conn.App. 614, 20 A.3d 1270 (2011) (failure to file paper transcripts timely and failure to file electronic version at all; transcripts stricken on motion and appeal lost); Forrestt v. Koch, 122 Conn.App. 99, 111, 996 A.2d 1236, 1243 (2010) (expense of obtaining lengthy transcript does not relieve appellant of burden of providing adequate record); Stutz v. Shepard, 279 Conn. 115, 901 A.2d 33 (2006) (failure to provide transcript of arbitration proceedings); State v. Lugo, 266 Conn. 674, 685–86, 835 A.2d 451, 459 (2003) (failure to clarify decision; review limited); Cedar Mountain, LLC v. D and M Screw Machine Products, LLC, 135 Conn.App. 276, 287, 41 A.3d 1131, 1138 (2012) (failure to seek review of inadequate articulation); Wells Fargo Bank of Minnesota, N.A. v. Morgan, 105 Conn.App. 856, 860–61, 941 A.2d 943, 945–946 (2008) (lack of written or signed oral decision; issue not decided); Daigle v. Metropolitan Property and Cas. Ins. Co., 257 Conn. 359, 364–65, 777 A.2d 681, 684–85 (2001) (exhibits not entered into record for identification); Gentile v. Carneiro, 107 Conn.App. 630, 655 n.22, 946 A.2d 871, 888 n.22 (2008) (child support guidelines worksheet not in court file); State v. Hannah, 104 Conn.App. 710, 714–15, 935 A.2d 645, 648 (2007), cert. denied, 285 Conn. 916, 943 A.2d 475 (2008) (failure to have excluded recording marked as exhibits or transcribed on the record); In re Diamond J., 121 Conn.App. 392, 996 A.2d 296, cert. denied, 297 Conn. 927, 998 A.2d 1193 (2010) (unsigned transcript and no articulation precluded review).

Among these things the appellant must insure the record is clear about is that the alleged error is harmful. Chester v. Morris, 150 Conn.App. 57, 63, 89 A.3d 1034, 1038 (2014).

If the appellant has attempted to complete the record and has moved unsuccessfully for review under § 66-7, then the appellant cannot be faulted under § 61-10. Kenny v. Banks, 289 Conn. 529, 532 n.5, 958 A.2d 750, 752 n.5 (2008).

The death of the trial judge does not excuse the failure to file a motion for articulation. Lawton v. Weiner, 91 Conn.App. 698, 882 A.2d 151 (2005). The authors disagree with *Lawton*.

In State v. Linarte, 107 Conn.App. 93, 107 n.8, 944 A.2d 369, 381 n.8, cert. denied, 298 Conn, 901, 957 A.2d 873 (2008), the Appellate Court held that the record was inadequate to review the denial of an order to disclose the victim's medical records because the defendant was free to subpoena them and had not done so. That the records were not privileged and subject to subpoena strikes the authors as a reason to rule on the merits rather than find the record inadequate.

However, review was permitted in Mickey v. Mickey, 292 Conn. 597, 609–10, 974 A.2d 641, 651 (2009) (transcripts unnecessary to decide issue raised); Taylor v. King, 121 Conn.App. 105, 112 n.5, 994 A.2d 330, 335 n.5 (2010) (same); Finan v. Finan, 287 Conn. 491, 494–95, 949 A.2d 468, 471 (2008) (record showed adequate substitute for missing exhibit); State v. Wilson, 111 Conn.App. 614, 621–22, 960 A.2d 1056, 1063 (2008), cert. denied, 290 Conn. 917, 966 A.2d 234 (2009) (finding obvious even though not explicitly stated); American Sav. Bank v. Lukas, 106 Conn.App. 460, 463 n.4, 942 A.2d 1041, 1043 n.4 (2008) (representation of the parties before Appellate Court); Mazzone v. Connecticut Transit Co., 240 Conn. 788, 797–98, 694 A.2d 1230, 1234–35 (1997) (issue remanded); Community Action for Greater Middlesex County, Inc. v. American Alliance Ins. Co., 254 Conn. 387, 395, 757 A.2d 1074 (2000) (one sentence trial court decision adequate but not preferable); Loricco Towers Condominium Ass'n v. Pantani, 90 Conn.App. 43, 876 A.2d 1211, cert. denied, 276 Conn. 925, 888 A.2d 93 (2005) (reviewing claim trial court lacked subject matter jurisdiction despite explanation of factual basis for court's decision); In re Anthony E., 96 Conn.App. 414, 417, 900 A.2d 594, 596, cert. denied, 280 Conn. 914, 908 A.2d 535 (2006) (unsigned transcript sufficient); Gordon v. H.N.S. Management Co., Inc., 272 Conn. 81, 101, 861 A.2d 1160, 1174 (2004) (undisputed facts), and Lorthe v. Commissioner of Correction, 103 Conn.App. 662, 931 A.2d 348, cert. denied, 284 Conn. 939, 937 A.2d 696 (2007) (deciding ineffective assistance of counsel claim not decided by trial court because it was a legal question and the parties had briefed the claim on appeal).

This section also applies to the cross appellant. Griffin Hosp.v. Commission on Hospitals and Health Care, 200 Conn. 489, 520, 512 A.2d 199, 216 (1986); Suffield Development Associates Ltd. Partnership v. National Loan Investors, L.P., 60 Conn.App. 842, 851–52, 763 A.2d 1049, 1054 (2000),rev'd in part on other grounds, 260 Conn. 766, 802 A.2d 44 (2002).

Appellees, *not* appellants, are responsible for an adequate record for issues appellees raise. Skuzinski v. Bouchard Fuels, Inc., 240 Conn. 694, 704 n.7, 694 A.2d 788, 793 n.7 (1997); Zahringer v. Zahringer, 262 Conn. 360, 369–371, 815 A.2d 75, 80–81 (2003).

The burden to provide an adequate record includes appeals from the Workers Compensation Commission. Cable v. Bic Corp., 270 Conn. 433, 442–43, 854 A.2d 1057, 1064 (2004).

The appellant now has to present an adequate record to support a claim that a material fact was found without evidence. State v. Spillane, 257 Conn. 750, 757–58, 778 A.2d 101, 105 (2001). Prior to *Spillane*, the appellant could simply make that claim and it was the appellee's burden to provide the supporting evidence.

In a jury case, the appellant should always insure that the trial court gives its reasons when it decides a motion to set aside the verdict even if the motion is denied. Boretti v. Panacea Co., 67 Conn.App. 223, 231–32, 786 A.2d 1164, 1170 (2001), cert. denied, 259 Conn. 918, 791 A.2d 565 (2002). Use P.B. §§ 66-5 and 64-1.

One notable (and commendable) exception to the duty being put solely on the appellant is the trial court's duty to explain any deviation from the child support guidelines. In Wallbeoff v. Wallbeoff, 113 Conn.App. 107, 110–13, 965 A.2d 571, 573–75 (2009), the Appellate Court blamed the trial judge for not doing so rather than the appellant for not moving for articulation where the guidelines require the court to state its findings on the record.

§ 61-11. Stay of Execution in Noncriminal Cases

(a) Automatic stay of execution

Except where otherwise provided by statute or other law, proceedings to enforce or carry out the judgment or order shall be automatically stayed until the time to take an appeal has expired. If an appeal is filed, such proceedings shall be stayed until the final determination of the cause. If the case goes to judgment on appeal, any stay thereafter shall be in accordance with Section 71-6 (motions for reconsideration), Section 84-3 (petitions for certification by the Connecticut supreme court), and Section 71-7 (petitions for certiorari by the United States supreme court).

(b)   Matters in which no automatic stay is available under this rule

Under this section, there shall be no automatic stay in actions concerning attorneys pursuant to chapter 2 of these rules, in juvenile matters brought pursuant to chapters 26 through 35a, or in any administrative appeal except as otherwise provided in this subsection.

Unless a court shall otherwise order, any stay that was in effect during the pendency of any administrative appeal in the trial court shall continue until the filing of an appeal or the expiration of the appeal period, or any new appeal period, as provided in Section 63-1. If an appeal is filed, any further stay shall be sought pursuant to Section 61-12.

For purposes of this rule, "administrative appeal" means an appeal taken from a final judgment of the trial court or the compensation review board rendered in an appeal from a decision of any officer, board, commission, or agency of the state or of any political subdivision thereof. In addition to appeals taken pursuant to the Uniform Administrative Procedure Act, "administrative appeal" includes, among other matters, zoning appeals, teacher tenure appeals, tax appeals and unemployment compensation appeals.

(c)   Stays in family matters

Unless otherwise ordered, no automatic stay shall apply to orders of relief from physical abuse pursuant to General Statutes § 46b-15, to orders for exclusive possession of a residence pursuant to General Statutes §§ 46b-81 or 46b-83 or to orders of periodic alimony, support, custody or visitation in family matters brought pursuant to Chapter 25 or to any later modification of such orders. The automatic orders set forth in Section 25-5 (b) (1), (2), (3), (5) and (7) shall remain in effect during any appeal period and, if an appeal is taken, until the final determination of the cause unless terminated, modified or amended further by order of a judicial authority upon motion of either party.

Any party may file a motion to terminate or impose a stay in matters covered by this subsection, either before or after judgment is rendered, based upon the existence or expectation of an appeal. Such a motion shall be filed in accordance with the procedures in subsection (e) of this rule or Section 61-12. The judge hearing such motion may terminate or impose a stay of any order, pending appeal, as appropriate, after considering (1) the needs and interests of the parties, their children and any other persons affected by such order; (2) the potential prejudice that may be caused to the parties, their children and any other persons affected, if a stay is entered, not entered or is terminated; (3) if the appeal is from a judgment of dissolution, the need to preserve, pending appeal, the mosaic of orders established in the judgment; (4) the need to preserve the rights of the party taking the appeal to obtain effective relief if the appeal is successful; (5) the effect, if any, of the automatic orders under Section 25-5 on any of the foregoing considerations; and (6) any other factors affecting the equities of the parties.

The judge who entered the order in a family matter from which an appeal lies may terminate any stay in that matter upon motion of a party as provided in this subsection or sua sponte, after considering the factors set forth in this subsection or if the judge is of the opinion that an extension of time to appeal is sought or the appeal is taken only for delay. Whether acting on a motion of a party or sua sponte, the judge shall hold a hearing prior to terminating the stay.

(d) Termination of stay

In all cases not governed by subsection (c), termination of a stay may be sought in accordance with subsection (e) of this rule. If the judge who tried the case is of the opinion that (1) an extension to appeal is sought, or the appeal is taken, only for delay or (2) the due administration of justice so requires, the judge may at any time upon motion or sua sponte, order that the stay be terminated. Whether acting on a motion of a party or sua sponte, the judge shall hold a hearing prior to terminating the stay.

(e) Motions to terminate stay

A motion to terminate a stay of execution may be filed before judgment; if it is, it may be ruled upon when judgment is entered. If such a motion is filed before judgment, or after judgment but before an appeal, it shall be filed in triplicate with the clerk of the superior court. If it is filed after an appeal is filed, an original and three copies shall be filed with the appellate clerk, who shall forward the motion to the judge who tried the case. That judge shall file any ruling thereon with the appellate clerk and with the clerk of the trial court where the matter was tried. If the judge who tried the case is unavailable, the motion shall be forwarded to the clerk of the court in the judicial district where the case was tried, who shall assign the motion for a hearing and decision to any judge of the superior court.

(f) Motions to request stay

Requests for a stay pending appeal where there is no automatic stay shall be governed by Section 61-12.

(For stays of execution in criminal cases, see Section 61-13; for stays in death penalty cases, see Section 61-15.)

(g) Strict Foreclosure—Motion Rendering Ineffective a Judgment of Strict Foreclosure

In any action for foreclosure in which the owner of the equity has filed, and the court has denied, at least two prior motions to open or other similar motion, no automatic stay shall arise upon the court's denial of any subsequent contested motion by that party, unless the party certifies under oath, in an affidavit accompanying the motion, that the motion was filed for good cause arising after the court's ruling on the party's most recent motion. Such affidavit shall recite the specific facts relied on in support of the moving party's claim of good cause. If, notwithstanding the submission of such an affidavit of good cause, the plaintiff contends that there is no good cause to stay the court's judgment of strict foreclosure pending resolution of the appeal, the plaintiff may seek termination of the automatic stay by filing a motion requesting such relief accompanied by an affidavit stating the basis for the plaintiff's claim. In the event such a motion to terminate stay is filed, it shall be set down for argument and the taking of evidence, if necessary, on the second short calendar next following the filing of the motion. There shall be no automatic stay in the event that the court grants the motion to terminate the stay and, if necessary, sets new law dates. There shall be no automatic stay pending a motion for review of an order terminating a stay under this subsection.

(h)   Foreclosure by Sale—Motion Rendering Ineffective a Judgment of Foreclosure by Sale

In any action for foreclosure in which the owner of the equity has filed a motion to open or other similar motion, which motion was denied fewer than twenty days prior to the scheduled auction date, the auction shall proceed as scheduled notwithstanding the court's denial of the motion, but no motion for approval of the sale shall be filed until the expiration of the appeal period following the denial of the motion without an appeal having been filed. The trial court shall not vacate the automatic stay following its denial of the motion during such appeal period.

Historical Note

Derivation:
  1978 P.B. (1986–97), § 4006
  1978 P.B., § 3065
  1963 P.B., § 661
  1951 P.B., § 411
  1934 P.B., § 366
  1930 Rules Change, § 19A
  1922 P.B., § 17
  1908 P.B., § 16
  1899 P.B., § 16

Effective October 1, 2013, subsections (g) and (h) were added to address stays in foreclosure cases.

Effective January 1, 2013, this rule was amended to add what is now subsection (c) and to clarify further that a hearing is required prior to terminating a stay.

In 2002, the reference to § 46b-15 was added to (b).

This entire rule was rewritten for clarity effective January 1, 2000. The second and third paragraphs of subsection (b), concerning administrative appeals, are new, and overrule Schallenkamp v. DelPonte, 29 Conn.App. 576, 577 n.4, 616 A.2d 1157, 1158 n.4 (1992), aff'd, 229 Conn. 31, 639 A.2d 1018 (1994).

In 1996 (e) was added.

This rule was amended effective May 10, 1993 to add "other than any transfer orders to the regular criminal docket" at the end of the first paragraph.

This rule was amended effective October 1, 1992 to require motions to be filed in quadruplicate rather than triplicate, and to require the ruling to be filed with both the appellate and trial clerks.

The first paragraph was amended effective October 1, 1986 to expand the types of cases and orders not subject to an automatic stay of execution. At the same time, the second paragraph was added and the word "automatic" was added to the title. Before 1986 only criminal and certain juvenile matters were not subject to an automatic stay.

The beginning of this rule was amended effective January 1, 1985 to eliminate conflicts with various statutes on stays.

The reference in the first paragraph to certain juvenile matters was added effective October 1, 1979. Prior to September 3, 1968 the stay lasted two weeks rather than twenty days, to conform to the appeal period.

Prior to 1930, the rule only applied "in a civil action providing for the recovery of damages or requiring the performance of an act," but there was no provision for termination of the stay.

Cross References

Maltbie, Conn.App.Proc.2d, §§ 292–94

P.J.R. appeals, C.G.S.A. § 52-278*l*

AUTHORS' COMMENTS

1. Judgments Subject to Automatic Stay

This rule has been amended twice to address the issues that arise in family matters. In 2013, a new subsection (c) was added to set out factors courts should consider in making stay rulings in family matters. The commentary makes clear that the list is not exhaustive and the courts can consider other factors such as whether the appeal was taken solely for delay.

When in doubt whether an order is stayed, the best course is often to be proactive. For example, a party filing a motion to terminate a stay of execution does not by doing so concede that the order is automatically stayed. Eisenbaum v. Eisenbaum, 44 Conn.App. 605, 608 n.5, 691 A.2d 25, 28 n.5 (1997).

The general rule is that an appeal stays enforcement of a civil judgment. Bauer v. Waste Management of Connecticut, Inc., 239 Conn. 515, 530, 686 A.2d 481, 488 (1996). A timely § 63-1 motion or a timely motion for extension of time to appeal under § 66-2 will continue an automatic stay.

An order that is not immediately appealable is not subject to an automatic stay. Cunniffe v. Cunniffe, 150 Conn.App. 419, 430, 91 A.3d 497, 506, cert. denied, 314 Conn. ___, ___ A.3d ___ (2014).

Pendente lite orders do not survive the judgment even if the judgment is appealed, Saunders v. Saunders, 140 Conn. 140, 146, 98 A.2d 815, 818 (1953). Thus there used to be a judicial gap between the date of the judgment, when the pendente lite order expires, and the termination of the automatic stay of execution, when the final judgment could take effect pending appeal, Yontef v.

Yontef, 185 Conn. 275, 291, 440 A.2d 899, 907–09 (1981). The Court suggested that the trial court enter temporary protective orders which would go into immediate effect pending the taking of an appeal or the resolution of § 61-11 motions. Since the basis of this authority was a dissolution statute, C.G.S.A. § 46b-56, it would appear that this case was not authority for such orders in other types of cases. *Sua sponte* orders under *Yontef* were very explicitly limited to custody matters in Garrison v. Garrison, 190 Conn. 173, 181–83, 460 A.2d 945, 949–50 (1983). The 1986 amendments address this problem.

Many family orders are not subject to an automatic stay. See Champagne v. Champagne, 35 Conn. L. Rptr. 241, 2003 WL 22078527 (Conn. Super. Ct. 2003). For that reason, counsel are going to have to be cognizant of this section during trial and ask the trial court for temporary stay orders contingent on the decision on the merits. See § 61-12. On the facts of the case in McCabe v. McCabe, 42 Conn. L. Rptr. 520, 2006 WL 3860762 (Conn. Super. Ct. 2006), an order for payment of household expenses was held not in the nature of alimony and support. An attorneys' fee award in a family case is stayed on appeal. There is a disagreement between two trial judges on the subject of counsel fees. Zelotes v. Zelotes, 44 Conn. L. Rptr. 552, 2007 WL 4634072 (Conn. Super. Ct. 2007). An award of counsel fees to a spouse is stayed, according to Judge Pickard. Rostad v. Hirsch, 49 Conn. L. Rptr. 793, 2010 WL 2574126 (Conn. Super. Ct. 2010), However, an award of counsel fees to the attorney for the minor child is not stayed because it is in the nature of child support, according to Judge Conway, Brown v. Brown, 49 Conn. L. Rptr. 129, 2009 WL 5698518 (Conn. Super. Ct. 2009). The authors agree with Judge Pickard; the rule has a clear list of the domestic orders that are not stayed, and counsel fees is absent from the list.

An order to transfer an automobile is not considered periodic alimony, so an appeal stays such an order. Tessitore v. Tessitore, 31 Conn.App. 40, 46, 623 A.2d 496, 499 (1993), overruled on other grounds by, Kaczynski v. Kaczynski, 294 Conn. 121, 981 A.2d 1068 (2009). An order to sell the residence also is automatically stayed. Golden v. Mandel, 110 Conn.App. 376, 383 n.7, 955 A.2d 115, 120 n.7 (2008).

There is also no automatic stay in juvenile cases. In re Bromell G., 214 Conn. 454, 572 A.2d 352 (1990). In In re Amy H., 56 Conn.App. 55, 61, 742 A.2d 372, 377 (1999), the respondent's visitation rights were terminated along with his parental rights pending appeal. His visitation rights were extinguished when he failed to move for a stay pending appeal. In re Elijah J., 54 Conn. L. Rptr. 778, 2012 WL 5447897 (2012). This rule does not apply to civil contempts, Papa v. New Haven Federation of Teachers, 186 Conn. 725, 731, 444 A.2d 196, 200 (1982); Tyler v. Hamersley, 44 Conn. 393, 412, 1877 WL 1881 (1877); but see Bryant v. Bryant, 228 Conn. 630, 637 n.5, 637 A.2d 1111, 1115 n.5 (1994) (noting that unwarranted appeals of contempt findings would be subject to termination of the automatic stay); although the question of what is a contempt is not always clear, see Catlin v. Baldwin, 47 Conn. 173, 1879 WL 1560 (1879). If the section does not apply to civil contempts, *a fortiori* it does not apply to criminal contempts. If the trial court will not rule on motion to stay its contempt order pending appeal, a motion for review pursuant to § 61-14 is in order.

This rule has no exception for injunctions, but C.G.S.A. §§ 52-476 and 52-477 have stay provisions that are arguably different from the general language of this rule. Barber v. Barber, 15 Conn.Supp. 271, 272–73, 1948 WL 640 (1948). There is a rather casual holding on this important subject that "injunctions continue in effect pending appeal unless the trial court, upon application, orders their stay"; Hartford Federal Sav. & Loan Ass'n v. Tucker, 192 Conn. 1, 7, 469 A.2d 778, 782 (1984). However, *Tucker* cites C.G.S.A. § 52-477 as its authority and that statute only concerns mandatory injunctions. In a well-reasoned opinion Justice Borden, for a unanimous court in Tomasso Bros., Inc. v. October

Twenty-Four, Inc., 230 Conn. 641, 652–58, 646 A.2d 133, 139–42 (1994), held that both prohibitory and mandatory injunctions are in effect pending appeal unless the enjoined party obtains a stay from the trial court. See also Sullivan v. McDonald, 281 Conn. 122, 126 n.2, 913 A.2d 403, 406 n.2 (2007). In the light of *Tomasso*, Cott Beverage Corp. v. Canada Dry Ginger Ale, Inc., 21 Conn.Supp. 244, 154 A.2d 140, 141 (1959), is presumably bad law although *Tomasso* does not expressly say so. *Tomasso* was followed in Friends of Hillhouse Ave. v. Yale University, 24 Conn. L. Rptr. 515, 1999 WL 311362 (Conn. Super. Ct. 1999). Note that the dissolution of a temporary injunction is not stayed pending appeal, Chasnoff v. Porto, 140 Conn. 267, 272, 99 A.2d 189, 192 (1953); *cf.* Laurel Park, Inc. v. Pac, 194 Conn. 677, 684 n.11, 485 A.2d 1272, 1276 n.11 (1984). *Tomasso* was applied in Ferris v. Clark, 12 Conn. L. Rptr. 505, 1994 WL 563976 (Conn. Super. Ct. 1994).

Orders disciplining attorneys are not subject to one automatic stay. Disciplinary Counsel v. Snaider, 149 Conn.App. 738, 741 n.2, 90 A.3d 286, 289 n.2 (2014). Thus, the suspension of a lawyer's license to practice law is not stayed pending appeal. Statewide Grievance Committee v. Egbarin, 26 Conn. L. Rptr. 548, 2000 WL 278532 (Conn. Super. Ct. 2000). Nor does the denial of a motion to dismiss a presentment stay further proceedings in the trial court. Disciplinary Counsel v. Johnson, 52 Conn. L. Rptr. 110, 2011 WL 2536501 (Conn. Super. Ct. 2011).

A lis pendens may not be discharged under C.G.S.A. § 52-325a while an appeal is pending from a judgment in favor of the party against whom the lis pendens was granted because of these provisions. Bennett v. Hegarty, 8 Conn. L. Rptr. 377, 1993 WL 53597 (Conn. Super. Ct. 1993).

While this section apparently applies to probate appeals, a probate court decision reversed by the Superior Court has no effect whatever until and unless the Appellate Court reverses the Superior Court. Kerin v. Stangle, 209 Conn. 260, 550 A.2d 1069 (1988). Thus, a motion to terminate the stay pending an appeal in the Appellate Court can put the Superior Court decision in effect pending appeal, but nothing (except an Appellate Court reversal) can put a reversed Probate Court decision in effect.

Probate decisions, however, are not automatically stayed. C.G.S.A. § 45a-186(f); In re Zukovs, 49 Conn. L. Rptr. 170, 2010 WL 525629 (Conn. Super. Ct. 2010) (Peck, J.).

This section apparently applies to writs of mandamus, State ex rel. Bonoff v. Evarts, 115 Conn. 98, 101–02, 160 A. 294, 295–96 (1932). In *Bonoff* the Supreme Court criticized the trial court for issuing a writ to be complied with before the appeal period had run. But see Tyler v. Hamersley, 44 Conn. 419, 1877 WL 1882 (1877) (mandamus after Supreme Court decision not stayed pending second appeal).

For administrative appeals, see Sikand v. Wilson–Coker, 276 Conn. 618, 632 n.13, 888 A.2d 74, 82 n.13 (2006).

This section applies to mortgage foreclosures. First Connecticut Capital, LLC v. Homes of Westport, LLC, 112 Conn.App. 750, 762, 966 A.2d 239, 246 (2009) (perpetual motion machine); Hartford Nat. Bank and Trust Co. v. Tucker, 181 Conn. 296, 435 A.2d 350 (1980); Farmers and Mechanics Sav. Bank v. Sullivan, 216 Conn. 341, 349, 579 A.2d 1054, 1057 (1990). An appeal from a foreclosure judgment does not automatically stay a rent receivership. Hartford Federal Sav. & Loan Ass'n v. Tucker, 192 Conn. 1, 6–7, 469 A.2d 778, 781–82 (1984). A trial court may also appoint a receiver pending appeal if appropriate. Fedor v. Taylor, 26 Conn. L. Rptr. 396, 2000 WL 177298 (Conn. Super. Ct. 2000); LaSalle National Bank v. Shook, 29 Conn. L. Rptr. 462, 2001 WL 358901 (Conn. Super. Ct. 2001). An appeal from a writ of restitution ordering a landlord to return personal property to a tenant does not automatically stay the judgment, which is in the nature of an injunction. Murphy v. Burke, 16 Conn. L. Rptr. 201, 1995 WL 790582 (Conn. Super. Ct. 1995). See also City of Middletown v. P & G Enterprises Ltd. Partnership, 45 Conn.Supp. 435, 437, 718 A.2d 90, 91 (Super. Ct. 1998). An order for weekly payments is stayed pending appeal. Bergen v. Belfonti, 29 Conn. L. Rptr. 130, 2001 WL 88258 (Conn. Super. Ct. 2001) (West, J.).

This section applies to habeas corpus appeals, Moulthrop v. Walker, 12 Conn.Supp. 35, 1942 WL 833 (1942). In one case the prisoner was admitted to bail on the ground of due administration of justice when the warden appealed, Redway v. Walker, 13 Conn.Supp. 240, 1945 WL 580 (Super. Ct. 1945). In Krynski v. Connecticut Adult Probation Services, 56 Conn. L. Rptr. 5, 2013 WL 1943939 (Conn. Super. Ct. 2013), the court terminated the stay where it granted habeas relief so the petitioner would not be deported pending appeal. It also applies to habeas corpus appeals in family cases, Barber v. Barber, 15 Conn.Supp. 271, 1948 WL 640 (1948). Query whether the 1986 rule changes apply.

The filing of a writ of error also effects a stay of execution, Geddes v. Sibley, 116 Conn. 22, 25, 163 A. 596, 598 (1932), unless it is brought for the purpose of delay. Brewster v. Cowen, 55 Conn. 152, 10 A. 509 (1887). Query whether this rule or C.G.S.A. § 52-278 applies to an attempt to terminate the stay of execution. The authors believe either can be used as they are not inconsistent. This commentary is quoted in Whitaker v. Howard, AC 21046 (2000) (ruling on motion to terminate stay by trial judge).

It is probable although not certain that this section applies to amended appeals from § 61-9 rulings. See Hotchkiss v. Hotchkiss, 143 Conn. 443, 444 n.1, 123 A.2d 174, 175 n.1 (1956). This footnote is also a good discussion of when to grant a termination of stay in a dissolution appeal.

Various statutory provisions concerning specialized appeals affect the operation of this rule. An appeal concerning a mechanic's lien automatically stays the order, but the appeal must be taken in 7 days; C.G.S.A. § 49-35c; an appeal concerning summary process also automatically stays the order except for nonpayment of rent, but the appeal must be taken in 5 days, excluding certain days; C.G.S.A. § 47a-35; see DeCorso v. Calderaro, 118 Conn.App. 617, 625–26, 985 A.2d 349, 355 (2009), cert. denied, 295 Conn. 919, 991 A.2d 564 (2010); an appeal concerning a prejudgment remedy does not automatically stay the order; C.G.S.A. § 52-2781. But Pryor v. Tavana, 49 Conn. L. Rptr. 657, 2010 WL 2106225 (Conn. Super. Ct. 2010), holds that an order directing payment of a sum into a receivership is automatically stayed.

An appeal from class action certification automatically stays only discovery proceedings concerning information on that subject. Macomber v. Travelers Property & Cas. Corp., 37 Conn. L. Rptr. 349, 40 Conn. L. Rptr. 29, 2004 WL 1559183 (Conn. Super. Ct. 2004).

2. Effect of Filing § 63-1 Motion

A § 63-1 motion filed within the appeal period automatically stays the judgment if an appeal from the judgment would do so. Farmers and Mechanics Sav. Bank v. Sullivan, 216 Conn. 341, 349, 579 A.2d 1054, 1057 (1990). In Farmers and Mechanics Bank v. Kneller, 40 Conn.App. 115, 670 A.2d 324 (1996), the defendant failed to file a motion to open within 20 days and the Appellate Court correctly held that there was no stay upon the filing of the untimely motion. See also Perkins v. Stop & Shop Companies, Inc., 1998 WL 422135 (Conn. Super. Ct. 1998). But what happens when the trial court denies the motion to open? In Brooklyn Sav. Bank v. Frimberger, 29 Conn.App. 628, 617 A.2d 462, 464 (1992), the Appellate Court held that, even though a motion filed outside the 20 days did not yield an automatic stay, the court's denial of the motion did automatically stay enforcement of *the underlying judgment*. Judge Curran was required to follow *Frimberger* in Housekey Financial Corp. v. Creed, 22 Conn. L. Rptr. 454, 1998 WL 420695 (Conn. Super. Ct. 1998). The authors disagree with *Frimberger*. It makes no sense to construe a rule so that the denial of a motion yields a better result for the movant than inaction on the motion. The Appellate Court wrongly equates a ruling on an untimely motion to open with the underlying judgment. Because the motion was filed outside the 20 days, the ruling on the motion merely stayed proceedings to enforce the denial of the motion. The ruling should have had no staying effect on the judgment itself.

3. Effect of Stay

A stay affects the entire judgment, even those parts that are not attacked on appeal. Valentine v. Valentine, 57 Conn.L.Rptr. 269, 272, 2013 WL 6698035 (Conn. Super. Ct. 2013); Town of Stratford v. Ross & Roberts, Inc., 54 Conn. L. Rptr. 527, 2012 WL 3854597 (Conn. Super. Ct. 2012) (appeal from dissolution judgment stays lump sum alimony order even though appeal pertains only to other issues).

The automatic stay only applies to "proceedings to enforce or carry out the judgment or order." Thus where a judgment did not order that an election be held, the holding of the election was not stayed by a judgment that the plaintiff did not win a primary. Caruso v. City of Bridgeport, 284 Conn. 793, 937 A.2d 1 (2007). Likewise, Judge Jennings held that an appeal from the granting of class action certification stayed further proceedings only involving the potential class members. Artie's Auto Body, Inc. v. Hartford Fire Ins. Co., 44 Conn. L. Rptr. 535, 2007 WL 4411083 (Conn. Super. Ct. 2007).

In Pavliscak v. Bridgeport Hosp., 48 Conn.App. 580, 586–89, 711 A.2d 747, 750–52, cert. denied, 245 Conn. 911, 718 A.2d 17 (1998), the Appellate Court held that this rule prevents a trial judge from granting a motion which dramatically changes the judgment while the appeal is pending. *Pavliscak* is clearly wrong. Under Ahneman v. Ahneman, 243 Conn. 471, 706 A.2d 960 (1998), the trial court has the power to open a judgment and enter a wholly new one even though an appeal is pending. The Appellate Court wrongly equated execution on the judgment (which this rule governs) with significant alteration of the judgment (which this rule does not govern). The Supreme Court may have denied certification because the trial judge was prevented for other valid reasons from granting the motion.

In RAL Management, Inc. v. Valley View Associates, 278 Conn. 672, 899 A.2d 586 (2006), the Supreme Court held that the trial court should not have set new law days because, even though it had terminated the automatic stay, the appellate proceedings reviewing that order were not complete and the stay remained in place. *Id. at 684–85, 899 A.2d at 593.* Thus, the order opening the judgment to set new law days was a nullity. *Id. at 685, 899 A.2d at 593.* The Court reaffirmed the trial court's general authority to decide motions while the case is on appeal and noted that in some situations, i.e., when the appellant gets complete relief from the trial court, the appeal may become moot. *Id. at 682, 692, 899 A.2d at 592, 598.*

One trial judge granted an execution notwithstanding the pendency of an appeal on the ground that it was taken solely for delay. Cerne v. Zahariades, 2 Conn.Supp. 87, 1935 WL 659 1935), aff'd, 121 Conn. 702, 183 A. 748 (1936).

Because an appeal stays execution of a judgment, an appellant cannot be held in contempt for not complying with an order that is stayed on appeal. Pryor v. Tavana, 49 Conn. L. Rptr. 657, 2010 WL 2106225 (Conn. Super. Ct. 2010).

If an appeal is taken from a portion of a judgment, the appeal does not stay execution on the remainder, Cronin v. Gager-Crawford Co., 128 Conn. 401, 404, 23 A.2d 149, 150 (1941); Roper v. City of New Britain, 70 Conn. 459, 466, 39 A. 850, 853 (1898); Messer v. Wildman, 53 Conn. 494, 2 A. 705 (1885). In addition, if the order appealed from is not appealable, the order is not stayed pending appeal. Hartford Federal Sav. & Loan Ass'n v. Tucker, 192 Conn. 1, 5, 469 A.2d 778, 781 (1984); Quinlan v. City Nat. Bank of South Norwalk, 105 Conn. 424, 429, 135 A. 435, 437 (1926); Cunniffe v. Cunniffe, 150 Conn.App. 419, 430, 91 A.3d 497, 506, cert. denied, 314 Conn. ___, ___ A.3d ___ (2014). See Yale Literary Magazine v. Yale University, 202 Conn. 672, 674, 522 A.2d 818, 819 (1987). However, a brave trial judge is required who will act before the Supreme Court has dismissed the appeal. By analogy, if an appeal is taken by one defendant only, the judgment should not be stayed against any other defendant if the judgment is severable. See Donnarumma v. Korkin, 97 Conn. 223, 116 A. 178 (1922); Middlesex Hosp. v. Town of Hamden, 33 Conn.App. 247, 635 A.2d 313 (1993). But the holding of Preisner v. Aetna Cas. and Sur. Co., 203 Conn. 407, 525 A.2d 83 (1987), appears to be the contrary. See Berger v. Cuomo, 9 Conn. L. Rptr. 409, 1993 WL 280308 (Conn. Super. Ct. 1993), in which the trial court held that this section always stays a judgment as to a non-appealing defendant while an appeal by another defendant is pending. Logically, a partial appeal should stay only the portion of the judgment appealed unless the judgment is inseverable. Also, one judge has held that a sanctions order is not a judgment and therefore is not stayed even if a § 61-5 notice is properly filed. Barnes/Science Associates Ltd. Partnership v. Edo Corp., 3 Conn. L. Rptr. 485, 1991 WL 65816 (Conn. Super. Ct. 1991).

An appeal does not automatically stay orders that are ancillary to the order from which the appeal was taken. Thus, an action to discharge a lis pendens is not automatically stayed because the judgment in the underlying action has been appealed. Allen v. Peterson, 50 Conn.L.Rptr. 383 (2010). An appeal from the denial of a motion to nullify a contract for the sale of land pursuant to a partition judgment did not stay enforcement of the committee's motion for approval of the deeds. Mitchell v. Silverstein, 33 Conn. L. Rptr. 199, 2002 WL 31440882 (Conn. Super. Ct. 2002), aff'd, 80 Conn.App. 903, 836 A.2d 1280, cert. denied, 267 Conn. 916, 884 A.2d 981 (2003). In Rosado v. Bridgeport Roman Catholic Diocesan Corp., 276 Conn. 168, 884 A.2d 981 (2005), the trial court violated this provision by adjudicating the merits of a protective order while an appeal on the propriety of the motion to open was pending.

The appellate stay does not prevent determination of offer of compromise interest. Brennan v. Brennan Associates, 55 Conn. L. Rptr. 731, 2013 WL 1407822 (2013). Nor does it prevent the running of post judgment interest. DiLieto v. County Obstetrics and Gynecology Group, P.C., 310 Conn. 38, 74 A.3d 1212 (2013); Rostad v. Hirsch, 148 Conn. App. 441, 85 A.3d 1212, cert. granted, 311 Conn. 948, 949, 91 A.3d 463 (2014). If a marshal has partially executed a judgment at the time a stay of execution goes into effect, an ancient case holds that the marshal may complete the execution notwithstanding the stay. Phelps v. Landon, 2 Day 370, 1806 WL 200 (Conn. 1806). One judge refused to follow *Phelps* in Kaplan and Jellinghaus, P. C. v. Newfield Yacht Sales, Inc., 179 Conn. 290, 426 A.2d 278 (1979). The fact that a judgment is fully satisfied does not bar the appeal, as the money would have to be repaid if the appeal succeeds. Reilly v. State, 119 Conn. 217, 222–23, 175 A. 582, 585 (1934). *Cf.* Bock v. Meriden Trust & Safe Deposit Co., 135 Conn. 94, 95 n.1, 60 A.2d 918, 919 n.1 (1948). However, in some cases termination of the stay will moot the appeal. Connecticut Sav. Bank v. Howes, 9 Conn.App. 446, 519 A.2d 1216 (1987) (foreclosure). A trial judge's order under this section is reviewable under § 61-14. However the trial court's discretion is very broad. In Northeastern Gas Transmission Co. v. Benedict, 139 Conn. 36, 41, 89 A.2d 379, 381 (1952), the Court construed the language "if the judge who tried the case is of the opinion * * * " to give the judge very broad discretion.

This section does not toll the period during which a judgment lien is filed or post judgment discovery can be pursued. All Seasons Services, Inc. v. Guildner,

89 Conn.App. 781, 878 A.2d 370 (2005). See also Kendall v. Amster, 39 Conn. L. Rptr. 902, 2005 WL 2364862 (Conn. Super. Ct. 2005) (disclosure of assets allowed); Presidential Capitol v. Reale, 12 Conn. L. Rptr. 111, 1994 WL 373166 (Conn. Super. Ct. 1994) (post judgment discovery); Conrad v. Erickson, 12 Conn. L. Rptr. 543, 1994 WL 590579 (Conn. Super. Ct. 1994). The authors also agree with these decisions. The Appellate Court has held that a plaintiff may obtain a prejudgment remedy to protect the verdict pending an appeal. Gagne v. Vaccaro, 80 Conn.App. 436, 454, 835 A.2d 491, 502–03 (2003), cert. denied, 268 Conn. 920, 846 A.2d 881 (2004), quoted in Town of New Hartford v. Connecticut Resources Recovery Authority, 291 Conn. 502, 506 n.4, 970 A.2d 578, 581 n.4 (2009). In any event, a court can avoid the legal uncertainty by terminating the automatic stay in order to allow the taking of discovery and filing of liens. Jones v. Ippoliti, 15 Conn. L. Rptr. 484, 1995 WL 779091 (Conn. Super. Ct. 1995). Judge Parker has pointed out a serious gap in this rule, and his reasoning would also apply to § 61-12. In Borden v. North Stonington Planning & Zoning Com'n, 23 Conn. L. Rptr. 10, 1998 WL 727769 (Conn. Super. Ct. 1998), he points out that a motion to stay enforcement of a judgment dismissing a zoning appeal would stay nothing because a dismissal of a case leaves nothing to carry out or be enforced. What the appellant is looking for is an order restraining the agency from carrying out its decision. Likewise in Earlington v. Anastasi, 44 Conn. L. Rptr. 98, 2007 WL 2596877 (Conn. Super. Ct. 2007), Judge Tanzer held that an appeal from judgment on a jury verdict does not stay proceedings on a motion for offer of judgment interest.

4. Effect of Reconsideration or Certification Proceedings

There is a possible conflict between subsection (e), and §§ 71-6 and 84-3. The authors' opinion is that the latter provisions are trumps and no trial court should exercise its power under § 61-11(e) after the Supreme Court or Appellate Court rules on the merits of the appeal but before the appellate proceedings are completed.

5. Terminating the Stay

The court can terminate the automatic stay if the appeal is taken solely for delay; See also Ameriquest Mortg. Co. v. DeLulio, 2008 WL 5540456 (Conn. Super. Ct. 2008) (prospective termination of stay under both prongs); see Labow v. Labow, 2008 WL 1971389 (Conn. Super. Ct. 2008), aff'd, 115 Conn.App. 419, 973 A.2d 127, cert. denied, 293 Conn. 918, 979 A.2d 489; Pinnacle Financial Services, LLC v. Matava, 2008 WL 1914432 (Conn. Super. Ct. 2008); or where justice so requires. See Alderman & Alderman v. Millbrook Owners' Ass'n, Inc., 2004 WL 2397361 (Conn. Super. Ct. 2004). There, the trial court, citing Griffin Hosp. v. Commission on Hospitals and Health Care, 196 Conn. 451, 493 A.2d 229 (1985), terminated the stay in an appeal from an interpleader action because the failure to do so would have jeopardized a complicated settlement concerning cleanup of toxic waste on the defendant's property. One trial court split the baby by denying a motion to terminate the stay in a foreclosure case conditioned on the defendant paying taxes and interest. Mun v. Vincent R. Doria, LLC, 2008 WL 2345909 (Conn. Super. Ct. 2008). Generally, the trial court must decide whether to terminate a stay in the first instance. JP Morgan Chase Bank v. Gianopoulos, 131 Conn.App. 15, 23, 30 A.3d 697, 702, cert. denied, 302 Conn. 947, 30 A.3d 2 (2011).

Other examples of termination of stays for due administration of justice are election cases, Miller v. Schaffer, 164 Conn. 8, 17, 320 A.2d 1, 5–6 (1972); condemnation cases, Northeastern Gas Transmission Co. v. Benedict, 139 Conn. 36, 89 A.2d 379 (1952); see also Iroquois Gas Transmission System, L.P. v. Candlewood Valley Country Club, 3 Conn. L. Rptr. 196, 1991 WL 25529 (Conn. Super. Ct. 1991); family cases to which the automatic stay applies, Tyler v.

Tyler, 2008 WL 4683906 (Conn. Super. Ct. 2008) (distribution of assets); and discovery proceedings where a person's identity must be obtained before the statute of limitations runs out, Muti v. Collins, 24 Conn.Supp. 455, 456–57, 194 A.2d 450, 451, aff'd, 150 Conn. 729, 197 A.2d 935 (1963). See also City of Hartford v. Hartford Elec. Light Co., 172 Conn. 13, 14, 372 A.2d 130, 131 (1976) (utility rate case); West Haven Housing Authority v. Simmons, 5 Conn. Cir. Ct. 282, 288, 250 A.2d 527, 531 (App. Div. 1968) (summary process). On the other hand, a stay was not terminated in Ziyadeh v. Majarian, 2 Conn.L.Trib. No. 60, p. 3 (1976) (Healey, J.) (action on note); Vandal v. Vandal, 31 Conn.App. 561, 626 A.2d 784 (1993) (payment of real estate taxes), and Town of Southbury v. Colonial Land Investors, 11 Conn. L. Rptr. 486, 1994 WL 197714 (Conn. Super. Ct. 1994) (foreclosure). For a particularly detailed decision denying a motion to terminate the stay in a quo warranto action, see Bateson v. Weddle, 2010 WL 5064481 (Conn. Super. Ct. 2010).

If the trial court terminates the stay before the appeal is filed, the prospective appellant should file a motion for review with the Appellate Court. That strategy succeeded in Webster Trust v. Mardie Lane Homes, LLC, 93 Conn.App. 401, 404 n.6, 891 A.2d 5, 7 n.6 (2006). But see Brycki v. Brycki, 91 Conn.App. 579, 881 A.2d 1056 (2005) (dismissing pre-appeal motion for review of a motion for articulation). The authors disagree with *Brycki*, which does not cite P.B. § 60–2.

§ 61-12. Discretionary Stays

In noncriminal matters in which the automatic stay provisions of Section 61-11 are not applicable and in which there are no statutory stay provisions, any motion for a stay of the judgment or order of the superior court pending appeal shall be made to the judge who tried the case unless that judge is unavailable, in which case the motion may be made to any judge of the superior court. Such a motion may also be filed before judgment and may be ruled upon at the time judgment is rendered unless the court concludes that a further hearing or consideration of such motion is necessary. A temporary stay may be ordered sua sponte or on written or oral motion, ex parte or otherwise, pending the filing or consideration of a motion for stay pending appeal. The motion shall be considered on an expedited basis and the granting of a stay of an order for the payment of money may be conditional on the posting of suitable security.

In the absence of a motion filed under this section, the trial court may order, sua sponte, that proceedings to enforce or carry out the judgment or order be stayed until the time to take an appeal has expired or, if an appeal has been filed, until the final determination of the cause. A party may file a motion to terminate such a stay pursuant to Section 61-11.

In determining whether to impose a stay in a family matter, the court shall consider the factors set forth in Section 61-11(c).

Historical Note

Derivation:
   1978 P.B. (1986–97), § 4047
This rule was amended effective January 1, 2013 to add the last paragraph

providing that the factors set forth in P.B. § 61-11(c) courts must consider when deciding whether to terminate a stay in family matters also apply when deciding whether to impose discretionary stays.

The caption was changed from "Nonautomatic Stays" and the second paragraph was added effective January 1, 2000.

This rule is new effective October 1, 1986. See § 4050. "Application" was changed to "motion" throughout the rule effective September 3, 1996.

AUTHORS' COMMENTS

The failure to seek a stay may moot the appeal. See Stash v. Commissioner of Motor Vehicles, 297 Conn. 204, 209 n.7, 999 A.2d 696, 698 n.7 (2010) (license suspension expired, but claimed reviewed because of collateral consequences).

The leading case concerning the test for discretionary stay is Griffin Hosp. v. Commission on Hospitals and Health Care, 196 Conn. 451, 493 A.2d 229 (1985), which discusses four prongs. See In re Alexander T., 33 Conn. L. Rptr. 586, 2002 WL 31957474 (Conn. Super. Ct. 2002) (stay denied where success on appeal is only a possibility, not a probability); Garavel v. Garavel, 52 Conn. L. Rptr. 213, 2011 WL 3276719 (Conn. Super. Ct. 2011) (stay of alimony increase denied where no irreparable harm shown); Hammonasset Holdings, LLC v. Drake Petroleum Co., Inc., 54 Conn. L. Rptr. 27, 2012 WL 2044586 (Conn. Super. Ct. 2012) (stay of temporary mandatory injunction in environmental case denied).

This section was used in a juvenile case in In re Bromell G., 214 Conn. 454, 572 A.2d 352 (1990). Denial of the stay was held to be an abuse of discretion. A stay was denied in In re Elijah J., 54 Conn. L. Rptr. 778, 2012 WL 5447897 (Conn. Super. Ct. 2012); In re Kiarra S., 2009 WL 765938 (Conn. Super. Ct. 2009), aff'd sub nom. In re Dairrah D., 122 Conn.App. 903, 996 A.2d 320, cert. denied, 298 Conn. 915, 4 A.3d 830 (2010); in Friends of Hillhouse Ave. v. Yale University, 24 Conn. L. Rptr. 515, 1999 WL 311362 (Conn. Super. Ct. 1999); and in Moye v. Credit Acceptance Corp., 31 Conn. L. Rptr. 265, 2001 WL 1763979 (Conn. Super. Ct. 2001) (class certification). A stay was granted in Rodriquez v. Anderson, 26 Conn. L. Rptr. 543, 2000 WL 276988 (Conn. Super. Ct. 2000) (continuing a temporary injunction), and in Statewide Grievance Committee v. Pinsky, 31 Conn. L. Rptr. 171, 2002 WL 112405 (Conn. Super. Ct. 2002).

One trial court cited this section to stay the trial court proceedings as to the remaining defendants after the plaintiffs appealed from the dismissal of the action as to two defendants. Morgan v. Hartford Hosp., 2010 WL 1667304 (Conn. Super. Ct. 2010). The authors question whether this section would apply to such situations, although the court probably has inherent authority to stay proceedings pending appeal.

§ 61-13. Stay of Execution in Criminal Case

Except as otherwise provided in this rule, a judgment in a criminal case shall be stayed from the time of the judgment until the time to take an appeal has expired, and then, if an appeal is filed, until ten days after its final determination. The stay provisions apply to an appeal from a judgment, to an appeal from a judgment on a petition for a new trial and to a writ of error, where those matters arise from a criminal conviction or sentence. Unless otherwise provided in this rule, all stays are subject to termination under subsection (d).

(a) Appeal by defendant arising from a sentence

(1) Sentence of imprisonment

A sentence of imprisonment shall be stayed automatically by an appeal, provided the defendant is released on bail.

(2) Sentence of probation or conditional discharge

Upon motion by the defendant to the trial court, a sentence of probation or conditional discharge may be stayed if an appeal is taken. If the sentence is stayed, the court shall fix the terms of the stay. If the sentence on appeal is not stayed, the court shall specify when the term of probation shall commence. If the sentence is not stayed and a condition of the sentence is restitution or other payment of money, the court shall order that such payments be made to the clerk of the trial court to be held by said clerk until ten days after final determination of the appeal.

(3) Sentence of a fine

A sentence to pay a fine shall be stayed automatically by an appeal, and the stay shall not be subject to termination.

(4) Sentencing sanctions of restitution and forfeiture

The execution of a sanction of restitution or forfeiture of property, which was imposed as part of a sentence, shall be stayed automatically by an appeal. Upon motion by the state or upon its own motion, the trial court may issue orders reasonably necessary to ensure compliance with the sanction upon final disposition of the appeal.

(5) Other sentencing sanctions

Upon motion by the defendant, other sanctions imposed as part of a sentence, including those imposed under General Statutes §§ 53a-40c, 53a-40e, 54-102b, 54-102g, and 54-260, may be stayed by an appeal. If the sanction is stayed, the trial court may issue orders reasonably necessary to ensure compliance with the sanction upon final disposition of the appeal.

(b) Appeal by defendant from presentence order

In an appeal from a presentence order where the defendant claims that an existing right, such as a right not to be tried, will be irreparably lost if the order is not reviewed immediately, the appeal shall stay automatically further proceedings in the trial court.

(c) Appeal by the state from a judgment

In an appeal by the state, the appeal shall stay automatically further proceedings in the trial court until ten days after the final determination of the appeal. The defendant shall be released pending determination of an appeal by the state from any judgment not resulting in a sentence, the effect of which is to terminate the entire prosecution.

(d) Motion for stay or to terminate a stay

If a motion for a stay or a motion to terminate a stay is filed before the appeal is taken, the original motion and three copies shall be filed with the trial court. After the appeal is taken, the motion and three copies shall be filed in the appellate court; motions filed in the appellate court shall be forwarded by the clerk of the appellate court to the trial court for a decision. If the judge who tried or presided over the case is unavailable, the motion shall be forwarded to the clerk of the court in which the case was tried and shall be assigned for a hearing and decision to any judge of the superior court. Upon hearing and consideration of the motion, the trial court shall decide the motion by filing with the court clerk a written or oral memorandum of decision that shall include the factual and legal basis therefor. If oral, the decision shall be transcribed by the court reporter and signed by the trial court. Pending the filing or consideration of a motion for stay, a temporary stay may be ordered sua sponte or on written or oral motion.

In appeals by defendant from a presentence order and appeals by the state from a judgment, the judge who tried the case may terminate any stay, upon motion and hearing, if the judge is of the opinion that (1) an extension to appeal is sought, or the appeal is taken, only for delay, or (2) the due administration of justice so requires.

(For stays of execution in death penalty cases, see Section 61-15.)

Historical Note

This rule was completely rewritten effective January 1, 2000. Concerning death sentences see new § 61-15.

New rule effective July 1, 1978. The second paragraph was added effective January 1, 1985.

AUTHORS' COMMENTS

For when the order on a petition for certification takes effect, see Authors' Comments to § 71-1.

§ 61-14. Review of Order concerning Stay; When Stay May Be Requested From Court Having Appellate Jurisdiction

The sole remedy of any party desiring the court to review an order concerning a stay of execution shall be by motion for review under Section 66-6. Execution of an order of the court terminating a stay of execution shall be stayed for ten days from the issuance of notice of the order, and if a motion for review is filed within that period, the order shall be stayed pending decision of the motion, unless the court having appellate jurisdiction rules otherwise.

A motion for extension of time to file a motion for review of a ruling concerning a stay of execution must be filed in the trial court but shall not automatically stay the execution after the ten days has expired, except that the trial judge may order a stay pending a ruling on the motion for extension of time.

A ruling concerning a stay is a judgment in a trial to the court for purposes of Section 64-1, and the trial court making such a ruling shall state its decision, either orally or in writing, in accordance with the requirements of that section.

In any case in which there is no automatic stay of execution and in which the trial court denies, or refuses to rule on, a motion for stay, an aggrieved party may request a stay of execution of the judgment from the court having appellate jurisdiction pending the filing of and ruling upon a motion for review. The request must be filed with the appellate clerk.

Historical Note

Derivation:
　1978 P.B. (1986–97), § 4049
　1978 P.B., § 3067
　1963 P.B., § 662
　1951 P.B., § 411

In 1996 the time to file a motion was extended from 5 to 10 days.

The fourth paragraph was amended effective October 1, 1992 to add the last sentence and to delete the provision expressly giving one justice the power to grant a stay. However, this is still provided for in § 66-2(d).

The second and fourth paragraphs were added effective October 1, 1986.

This rule was amended effective January 1, 1985 to make the five day period start to run from the clerk's notification. This means when the clerk mails it. See Sec. 63-1. The second paragraph and last phrase of the first paragraph were effective July 1, 1979. The second sentence was added effective July 1, 1978 and conforms the rule to prior practice, Northeastern Gas Transmission Co. v. Benedict, 139 Conn. 36, 38, 89 A.2d 379, 380 (1952). The word "terminating" was changed to "concerning" in the first sentence at the same time to provide for review if the trial judge refuses to terminate the stay. Previously that was apparently not reviewable, Broadriver, Inc v. City of Stamford, 155 Conn. 731, 235 A.2d 663 (1967).

This rule was substantially unchanged since 1951. Prior to 1951, there was no specific provision for review of a termination order.

Cross Reference

Maltbie, Conn.App.Proc.2d, § 292

AUTHORS' COMMENTS

This section, and not an appeal, is the appropriate way to obtain review of the denial or granting of a stay of decision. Sikand v. Wilson–Coker, 276 Conn. 618, 632 n.13, 888 A.2d 74, 82 n.13 (2006); Scagnelli v. Donovan, 88 Conn.App. 840, 871 A.2d 1084 (2005); Powers v. Farricelli, 43 Conn.App. 475, 476 n.2, 683 A.2d 740, (1996) (issue as to denial of stay in preliminary statements of issues stricken).

Note that the stay remains in effect during the pendency of a motion for review or a motion for reconsideration of an order on a motion for review. RAL Management, Inc. v. Valley View Associates, 278 Conn. 672, 899 A.2d 586 (2006); First Connecticut Capital, LLC v. Homes of Westport, LLC, 112 Conn.App. 750, 966 A.2d 239 (2009).

Once the Appellate Court has ruled on a motion for review, the Supreme Court apparently lacks jurisdiction to review the ruling on a petition for certification. State v. Carter, 212 Conn. 811, 564 A.2d 1072 (1989) (petition from review of bond decision dismissed). In the authors' opinion, there has to be a way for the Supreme Court to review Appellate Court decisions on stays, for the harm may be irreparable. We recommend filing a motion for reconsideration of the Appellate Court's decision on the motion for review along with a motion to transfer the case to the Supreme Court.

The failure to seek review of an order terminating a stay of an order discharging a judgment lien rendered the appeal moot in Lucas v. Deutsche Bank Nat. Trust Co., 103 Conn.App. 762, 931 A.2d 378, cert. denied, 284 Conn. 934, 935 A.2d 151 (2007).

§ 61-15. Stay of Execution in Death Penalty Case

If the defendant is sentenced to death, the sentence shall be stayed for the period within which to take an appeal. If the defendant has taken an appeal to the supreme or appellate court of this state or to the United States supreme court or brought a writ of error, writ of certiorari, writ of habeas corpus, application for a pardon or petition for a new trial, the taking of the appeal, the making of the application for a writ of certiorari or for a pardon, or the return into court of the writ of error, writ of habeas corpus, or petition for a new trial shall, unless, upon application by the state's attorney and after hearing, the supreme court otherwise orders, stay the execution of the death penalty until the clerk of the court where the trial was had has received notification of the termination of any such proceeding by decision or otherwise, and for thirty days thereafter. Upon application by the defendant, the supreme court may grant a stay of execution to prepare a writ of error, a writ of certiorari, writ of habeas corpus, application for a pardon or petition for a new trial. Upon application by the defendant and after hearing, the supreme court may extend a stay of execution beyond the time limits stated within this rule for good cause shown. No appellate procedure shall be deemed to have terminated until the end of the period allowed by law for the filing of a motion for reconsideration, or, if such motion is filed, until the proceedings consequent thereon are finally determined. When execution is stayed under the provisions of this section, the clerk of the court shall forthwith give notice thereof to the warden of the institution in which such defendant is in custody. If the original judgment of conviction has been affirmed or remains in full force at the time when the clerk has received the notification of the termination of any proceedings by appeal, writ of certiorari, writ of error, writ of habeas corpus, application for a pardon or petition for a new trial, and the day designated for the infliction of the death penalty has then passed or will pass within thirty days thereafter, the defendant shall, within said period of thirty days, upon an order of the court in which the judgment was rendered at a regular or special criminal session thereof, be presented before said court by the warden of the institution in which the defendant is in custody or his deputy, and the court, with the judge assigned to hold the session presiding, shall thereupon designate a day for the infliction of the death penalty and the clerk of the court shall issue a warrant of execution, reciting therein the original judgment, the fact of the stay of execution and the final order of the court, which warrant shall be forthwith served upon the warden or his deputy. (For stays of execution in other criminal cases, see Section 61-13.)

Historical Note

This rule is new effective January 1, 2000. The prior provisions on the subject were found in the third paragraph of § 61-13.

AUTHORS' COMMENTS

A defendant can waive the stay of execution pending resolution of habeas cases initiated by others. In re Ross, 272 Conn. 676, 866 A.2d 554 (2005).

§ 61-16. Notification of (1) Bankruptcy Filing, (2) Disposition of Bankruptcy Case and (3) Order of Bankruptcy Court Granting Relief from Automatic Stay

(a) If a party to an appeal files a bankruptcy petition, that party shall immediately notify the appellate clerk in writing. The notification shall set forth the date the bankruptcy petition was filed, the bankruptcy court in which the petition was filed, the name of the bankruptcy debtor and the docket number of the bankruptcy case.

(b) Upon resolution of the bankruptcy case, the party who filed for bankruptcy protection shall immediately notify the appellate clerk in writing that the case has been resolved in the bankruptcy court. If the bankruptcy court grants relief from the automatic bankruptcy stay, the party obtaining such relief shall immediately notify the appellate clerk in writing of the termination of the automatic stay.

Historical Note

This rule is new effective October 1, 2002.

CHAPTER 62

CHIEF JUDGE, APPELLATE CLERK AND DOCKET: GENERAL ADMINISTRATIVE MATTERS

§ 62-1. Chief Judge

(a) The chief justice shall designate one of the judges of the appellate court as chief judge of the appellate court.

(b) With the approval of the chief justice, the chief judge shall (1) schedule such sessions as may be necessary, at such locations as the facilitation of court business requires, (2) designate as many panels as may be necessary, and assign three judges to each panel, and (3) designate a presiding judge for each panel on which the chief judge does not sit.

Historical Note

Derivation:
    1978 P.B. (1992–97), § 4028
    1978 P.B. (1983–92), § 2001
Entirely new rule effective August 23, 1983. The title originally was "Chief Presiding Judge."

Cross References
    C.G.S.A. § 51-197c

§ 62-2. Clerk

The justices of the supreme court shall appoint an appellate clerk who shall be the chief clerk of the supreme court and of the appellate court, but who shall not be the chief clerk of any judicial district. As used in these rules, the clerk of any trial court from which an appeal is taken shall be referred to as the clerk of the trial court.

Historical Note

Derivation:
    1978 P.B. (1986–97), § 4029
    1978 P.B., § 3005 (first paragraph)
New rule effective July 1, 1978.

§ 62-3. Entry of Cases

The appellate clerk, upon receipt of an appeal, reservation, or writ of error, shall enter the case upon the docket of the court to which the appeal was taken.

Historical Note

Derivation:
    1978 P.B. (1986–97), § 4031
    1978 P.B., § 3093
    1963 P.B., § 683
    1951 P.B., § 431
    1934 P.B., § 375
    1930 Rules Change (1932 rule)
Effective July 1, 1978, the trial clerk's function was removed.

Prior to September 15, 1975, notice of the appeal was not even given to the Clerk of Hartford County until the assignment of errors was filed.

Previously the rule was substantially unchanged since it was first enacted in 1932.

§ 62-4. Case to Remain on Docket of Trial Court

A case that has been appealed shall remain on the docket of the court where it was tried until the appeal is decided or terminated.

Historical Note

Derivation:
    1978 P.B. (1986–97), § 4032
    1978 P.B., § 3132
    1963 P.B., § 737
    1951 P.B., § 466
    1934 P.B., § 417
    1930 P.B., § 18
This rule is substantially unchanged since it was adopted in 1930.

AUTHORS' COMMENTS

This rule does not provide independent authority to open a judgment after four months have passed. Nelson v. Dettmer, 49 Conn. L. Rptr. 805, 2009 WL 6383056 (Conn. Super. Ct. 2009), aff'd on other grounds, 305 Conn. 654, 46 A.3d 916 (2012).

§ 62-5. Changes in Parties

Any change in the parties to an action pending an appeal shall be made in the court in which the appeal is pending. The appellate clerk shall notify the clerk of the trial court of any change.

Historical Note

Derivation:
    1978 P.B. (1986–97), § 4033
    1978 P.B., § 3074
    1963 P.B., § 707
    1951 P.B., § 434
There has been no substantial change since the rule was adopted in 1951.

AUTHORS' COMMENTS

See Negro v. Metas, 110 Conn.App. 485, 493–94, 955 A.2d 599, 604–05, cert. denied, 289 Conn. 949, 960 A.2d 1037 (2008); Hayes Family Ltd. Partnership v. Planning and Zoning Com'n of Town of Manchester, 98 Conn.App. 213, 215 n.1, 907 A.2d 1235, 1237 n.1 (2006), cert. denied, 281 Conn. 903, 904, 916 A.2d 44 (2007); 289 Conn. 949, 960 A.2d 1038; Schoolhouse Corp. v. Wood, 43 Conn.App. 586, 684 A.2d 1191, cert. denied, 240 Conn. 913, 691 A.2d 1079 (1996).

§ 62-6. Signature on Papers

All papers including original copies of briefs shall be signed by counsel of record. Each pleading or other document filed shall set forth the signer's telephone and facsimile numbers, mailing address, and, if applicable, the signer's juris number.

Historical Note

Derivation:
    1978 P.B. (1986–97), § 4030
    1978 P.B., § 3005
Most of this section was transferred to § 60-4 effective September 3, 1996. At the same time the remaining paragraph was amended to add fax numbers.

§ 62-7. Matters of Form; Filings; Certification to Counsel (Applicable to appeals filed before July 1, 2013)

It is the responsibility of counsel of record to submit papers for filing in a timely manner and in the proper form.

The appellate clerk may refuse to accept for filing any papers presented in a form not in compliance with these rules; in refusing, the appellate clerk shall indicate how the papers have failed to comply. The clerk shall stamp any papers refused with the date on which they were received before returning them, and shall retain a copy thereof. Any papers correcting a noncomplying filing shall be deemed to be timely filed if resubmitted to the appellate clerk within fifteen days. The time for responding to any such paper shall not start to run until the correcting paper is filed.

Except for the transcript of evidence or where otherwise indicated, an original and fifteen copies of all papers shall be filed with the appellate clerk. For copies of the initial appeal papers, see Sections 63–3 and 63–4; for copies of papers withdrawing an appeal or writ of error, see Section 63–9; for copies of motions and opposition papers, see Section 66–3 (motions in general), Section 66–1 (extension of time), Section 61–11 (termination of stay of execution), and Section 66–5 (rectification); for copies of briefs, see Section 67–2; for copies of the record, see Section 68–7; for copies of petitions for certification and opposition papers, see Sections 84–4 and 84–6; for copies of certified questions from courts of other jurisdictions, see Section 82–4.

All papers except the transcript and regulations filed pursuant to Section 81–6 shall contain a certification that a copy has been served on each other counsel of record, including the names, addresses and telephone and facsimile numbers of all counsel served. The certification concerning briefs may be signed by counsel of record or the printer on the last page of one of the briefs or on a separate typewritten document filed with the briefs. All service and filing by mail shall be by first class or express United States mail, postage prepaid, or by hand delivery.

If a document must be filed by a certain date under these rules or under any statutory provision, the document must be received by the appellate clerk by the close of business on that date; it is not sufficient that a document be mailed by that date to the appellate clerk unless a rule or statutory provision expressly so computes the time.

The signed original of documents filed pursuant to Sections 66–3, 67–2, 81–2, 813, 84–5 and 84–6 shall bear an attached certificate indicating that the document is in compliance with all of the requirements of the rule under which it is being filed.

§ 62-7. Matters of Form; Filings; Certification to Counsel (Applicable to appeals filed on or after July 1, 2013)

It is the responsibility of counsel of record to submit papers for filing in a timely manner and in the proper form.

The appellate clerk may refuse to accept for filing any papers presented in a form not in compliance with these rules; in refusing, the appellate clerk shall indicate how the papers have failed to comply. The clerk shall stamp any papers refused with the date on which they were received before returning them, and shall retain a copy thereof. Any papers correcting a noncomplying filing shall be deemed to be timely filed if resubmitted to the appellate clerk within fifteen days. The time for responding to any such paper shall not start to run until the correcting paper is filed.

Except for the transcript of evidence or where otherwise

indicated, an original and fifteen copies of all papers shall be filed with the appellate clerk. For copies of the initial appeal papers, see Sections 63–3 and 63–4; for copies of papers withdrawing an appeal or writ of error, see Section 63–9; for copies of motions and opposition papers, see Section 66–3 (motions in general), Section 66–1 (extension of time), Section 61–11 (termination of stay of execution), and Section 66–5 (rectification); for copies of briefs and appendices, see Section 67–2; for copies of petitions for certification and opposition papers, see Sections 84–4 and 84–6; for copies of certified questions from courts of other jurisdictions, see Section 82–4.

All papers except the transcript and regulations filed pursuant to Section 81–6 shall contain a certification that a copy has been served on each other counsel of record, including the names, addresses and telephone and facsimile numbers of all counsel served. The certification concerning briefs may be signed by counsel of record or the printer on the last page of one of the briefs or on a separate typewritten document filed with the briefs. All service and filing by mail shall be by first class or express United States mail, postage prepaid, or by hand delivery.

If a document must be filed by a certain date under these rules or under any statutory provision, the document must be received by the appellate clerk by the close of business on that date; it is not sufficient that a document be mailed by that date to the appellate clerk unless a rule or statutory provision expressly so computes the time.

The signed original of documents filed pursuant to Sections 66–3, 67–2, 81–2, 813, 84–5 and 84–6 shall bear an attached certificate indicating that the document is in compliance with all of the requirements of the rule under which it is being filed.

Historical Note

Derivation:
  1978 P.B. (1986–87), § 4014
  1978 P.B., § 3013

Effective September 1, 2014, noncomplying papers must be refiled within 15 days.

Effective January 1, 2004, the last paragraph was added. Effective in 1999 the last sentence of the second paragraph was added. Effective September 3, 1996, counsel certification must include fax numbers.

This rule is almost entirely new effective October 1, 1986. It greatly simplifies the copy rules. Prior to 1978, most papers did not have to be certified to other counsel.

A major change effective October 1, 1992 is that the name, address and telephone number of all counsel served must be stated.

AUTHORS' COMMENTS

It is the current practice of the clerk's office to date stamp upon receipt any document which is then returned as defective. If the document is corrected and promptly refiled within two or three days, the time of filing will probably relate back to the original filing date.

§ 62-8. Names of Counsel; Appearance

Counsel for all parties in the trial court shall be deemed to have appeared in the appeal unless permission to withdraw has been granted pursuant to Section 62-9 or unless an in lieu of appearance pursuant to Section 3-8 has been filed by other counsel. Counsel who filed the appeal or filed an appearance in the Appellate Court after the appeal was filed shall be deemed to have appeared in the trial court for the limited purpose of prosecuting or defending the appeal. Unless otherwise provided by statute or rule, counsel who have so appeared shall be entitled to review all trial court docket sheets and files, including sealed files, and shall be entitled to participate in proceedings in the trial court on motions filed in the trial court pursuant to Section 66-1 and motions filed in the appellate court but referred to the trial court for decision. Where counsel did not file the appeal but have appeared in the appellate court, a copy of an appearance form stamped by the appellate clerk's office shall be satisfactory evidence of an appearance in an appeal. This rule shall not be deemed to permit appellate counsel to review records that were sealed as to trial counsel but retained in the trial court file for appellate review.

This rule shall not be deemed to excuse trial counsel with respect to preserving a defendant's right to appeal pursuant to Section 63-7; nor shall this rule prevent trial counsel from moving for a withdrawal of appearance pursuant to Section 62-9.

No change, substitution or withdrawal of counsel shall be permitted after the due date of the final reply brief without leave of the court.

Historical Note

Derivation:
    1978 P.B., (1986–97), § 4034
    1978 P.B., § 3094
    1963 P.B., § 684
    1951 P.B., § 432
    1934 P.B., § 391
    1922 P.B., § 35
    1908 P.B., § 34
    1899 P.B., § 34

The last sentence of the rule was added in 2008. The pro hac vice provisions were revised and moved to new § 62-8A in 2007. The second sentence was added in 2005 to allow appellate counsel to review trial files to the extent trial counsel could.

This rule was completely rewritten effective July 16, 1990 to return essentially to the practice before 1986, which was that the trial lawyers were automatically deemed also to be the appellate lawyers. Between 1986 and 1990, the rule stated as follows:

Counsel who files the appeal shall be deemed to have appeared for the appellant in the supreme court. Appearances shall be filed for other parties in the supreme court within fourteen days from the filing of the appeal accompanied by a certification that a copy thereof has been served on each counsel of record in accordance with the provisions of Sec. 10-12. Failure to appear in the appeal may invoke the sanctions of §§ 85-1 to 85-3.

The appearance of counsel pro hac vice should be allowed only by permission of the supreme court.

This rule was completely rewritten effective October 1, 1986. Old § 3094 stated as follows:

> The clerk of the trial court shall note upon the copy of the file furnished by him to the chief clerk of the supreme court the names and addresses of the counsel of record on each side who appeared in the trial court, and the chief clerk of the supreme court will enter the names of the same counsel of record other than counsel appearing pro hac vice, unless otherwise instructed or advised, on the docket of the supreme court, as appearing therein for the parties for whom they appeared in the trial court. The appearance of counsel pro hac vice shall be allowed only by permission of the supreme court. Appearances may be withdrawn in accordance with Sec. 3114.

The following history refers to old § 3094:

This rule is substantially unchanged since 1899 except that the portion about withdrawal of counsel was added in 1951 and the pro hac vice reference was added in 1985.

Cross References

Maltbie, Conn.App.Proc.2d, § 302

AUTHORS' COMMENTS

The Appellate Clerk will mail notices to counsel to the address on record with the Statewide Grievance Committee and Barmaster, not the address on appeal papers, so it is important to make sure the contact information with these sources is accurate.

Even under the old rule, new counsel who was handling the appeal was supposed to file an appearance. Willard v. Town of West Hartford, 135 Conn. 303, 304 n.1, 63 A.2d 847 (1949). Counsel appearing only on the appeal should file an appearance at the Appellate or Supreme Court Clerk's Office. Counsel may or may not wish to file an appearance in the trial court at the same time. Note that the appearance of counsel in the trial court after an appeal has been filed does not carry over to the Appellate Court and such counsel should file an appearance at the appellate level too, if they wish to participate in the appeal. In the authors' opinion, the last sentence of the first paragraph shows that no trial clerk can force a lawyer to file an appearance at the Superior Court for the sole purpose of filing an appeal.

Counsel may be admitted on appeal pro hac vice. An admission pro hac vice in the trial court now carries over on appeal. See P.B. § 62-8A. An application on appeal should comply with the general requirements of P.B. § 2-16, but follow the format of P.B. § 66-2.

The appearance of counsel on behalf of amicus curiae in the trial court does not carry over to the Appellate Court. This rule assumes that only parties appear and participate as of right in the appeal. City of Norwalk v. Farrell, 80 Conn.App. 399, 405, 835 A.2d 117, 121 (2003). However, one habeas court held that because the lawyer had an appearance at the time of an Appellate Court decision, his failure to file a petition for certification or determine whether a petition had not merit was deficient. Janulawicz v. Warden, 2009 WL 4916510 (Conn. Super. Ct. 2009).

This rule does not require a trial lawyer to file an appeal on behalf of a client. Davis v. Commissioner of Correction, 109 Conn.App. 92, 950 A.2d 587, cert. denied, 289 Conn. 930, 950 A.2d 587 (2008).

§ 62-8A. Attorneys of Other Jurisdictions Participating Pro Hac Vice on Appeal

(a) An attorney, who upon written application pursuant to Section 2-16 has been permitted by a judge of the superior court to participate in the presentation of a cause or appeal pending in this state, shall be allowed to participate in any appeal of said cause without filing a written application to the court having jurisdiction over the appeal. All terms, conditions and obligations set forth in Section 2-16 shall remain in full effect. The chief clerk of the superior court for the judicial district in which the cause originated shall continue to serve as the agent upon whom process and notice of service may be served.

(b) Any attorney who is in good standing at the bar of another state and who has not appeared pro hac vice in the superior court to participate in the cause now pending on appeal, may for good cause shown, upon written application presented by a member of the bar of this state, be permitted in the discretion of the court having jurisdiction over the appeal to participate in the presentation of the appeal, provided, however, that:

(1) such application shall be accompanied by an affidavit

(A) stating whether an application was filed pursuant to Section 2-16 in the superior court and, if so, the disposition of said application;

(B) certifying whether such applicant has a grievance pending against him or her in any other jurisdiction, has ever been reprimanded, suspended, placed on inactive status, disbarred or otherwise disciplined, or has resigned from the practice of law and, if so, setting forth the circumstances concerning such action;

(C) certifying that the applicant has paid to the clerk of the superior court any fee required by the General Statutes for admission pro hac vice;

(D) certifying that the applicant has paid the client security fund fee due for the calendar year in which the application is made;

(E) designating the chief clerk of the superior court for the judicial district in which the cause originated as his or her agent upon whom process and notice of service may be served;

(F) certifying that the applicant agrees to register with the statewide grievance committee in accordance with the provisions of chapter 2 of the rules of practice while appearing in the appeal and for two years after the completion of the matter in which the attorney appeared and to notify the statewide grievance committee of the expiration of the two year period;

(G) identifying the number of attorneys in his or her firm who are appearing pro hac vice in the cause now on appeal or who have filed or intend to file an application to appear pro hac vice in this appeal; and

(H) identifying the number of cases in which the attorney has appeared pro hac vice in any court of this state since the attorney first appeared pro hac vice in this state.

(2) a member of the bar of this state must be present at all proceedings and arguments and must sign all motions, briefs and other papers filed with the court having jurisdiction over the appeal and assume full responsibility for them and for the conduct of the appeal and of the attorney to whom such privilege is accorded. Said application shall be made to the court having jurisdiction over the appeal. The application shall be filed in accordance with Sections 66-2 and 66-3. Good cause for according such privilege may include a showing that by reason of a long-standing attorney-client relationship, predating the cause of action or subject matter of the appeal, the attorney has acquired a specialized skill or knowledge with respect to issues on appeal or to the client's affairs that are important to the appeal, or that the litigant is unable to secure the services of Connecticut counsel. Upon the granting of an application to appear pro hac vice, the clerk of the court in which the application is granted shall immediately notify the statewide grievance committee of such action.

(c) No application to appear pro hac vice shall be permitted after the due date of the final reply brief as set forth in Section 67-3 without leave of the court.

Historical Note

New rule in 2007. Subsection (c) was added in 2008.

This rule was revised October 1, 2013, to make it consistent with P.B. § 2-16, which governs pro hac vice appearances in the trial court.

AUTHORS' COMMENTS

The statutory application fee is $600, which is currently set to expire on July 1, 2015. (C.G.S.A. § 52-259(i)).

§ 62-9. Withdrawal of Appearance

(a) An attorney or party whose appearance has been filed shall be deemed to have withdrawn such appearance upon failure to file a written objection within ten days after written notice has been given or mailed to such attorney or party that a new appearance has been filed in lieu of the appearance of such attorney or party in accordance with Section 62-8.

(b) An attorney may, by motion, withdraw his or her appearance for a party after an additional appearance representing the same party has been entered on the docket. A motion to withdraw pursuant to this subsection shall state that an additional appearance has been entered on appeal. The appellate clerk may as of course grant the motion if the additional appearance has been entered.

(c) Except as provided in subsections (a) and (b), no attorney whose appearance has been entered on the docket shall withdraw his or her appearance without leave of the court. A motion for leave to withdraw shall be filed with the appellate clerk in accordance with Sections 66-2 and 66-3. The motion shall include the current address of the party as to whom the attorney seeks to withdraw. No motion for leave to withdraw shall be granted until the court is satisfied that reasonable notice has been given to the party being represented and to other counsel and self-represented parties of record. Reasonable notice to the party or parties may be satisfied by filing along with the motion, a certified or registered mail return receipt signed by the individual party or parties represented by the attorney.

(d) A motion for leave to withdraw appearance of appointed appellate counsel pursuant to Section 43-34 shall be filed with the appellate clerk. The form of the motion shall comply with Sections 66-2 and 66-3, except that only an original and one copy shall be filed. The brief accompanying the motion, as required under Section 43-35, shall comply with Section 43-35 in form and substance. The original of the brief and the transcript of the pertinent proceedings shall be filed with the appellate clerk with the motion to withdraw. The motion, brief and transcript shall be referred to the trial court for decision. That decision may be reviewed pursuant to Section 66-6.

Historical Note

Derivation:
   1978 P.B. (1986–97), § 4035
   1978 P.B., § 3114
   1963 P.B., § 708
   1951 P.B., § 432

This rule was completely rewritten effective July 16, 1990 and then clarified in 1996, but the content is very similar to the pre-1990 rule, which stated as follows:

Subject to the provisions of Secs. 4000 and 4037, the clerk of the court where the case was tried and the chief clerk of the supreme court or its messenger having custody of the files, evidence and exhibits in any case shall make them available for the use of any party.

In 1978, the first paragraph was amended to transfer from the trial court to the Supreme Court all decisions under this section after the appeal is filed, and in 1986 the last sentence was added.

The second and fourth paragraphs were added in 1976 to standardize the practice with the rules of the Superior Court. The third paragraph was added in 1985.

AUTHORS' COMMENTS

A motion to withdraw in a criminal case because the lawyer was fired was granted in Douglas v. Warden, State Prison, 218 Conn. 778, 783, 591 A.2d 399, 402 (1991).

The procedure for filing an *Anders* brief was discussed in Vazquez v. Commissioner of Correction, 88 Conn.App. 226, 869 A.2d 234 (2005).

§ 62-9A. Hybrid Representation; Removal or Substitution of Counsel in Criminal and Habeas Corpus Appeals

On appeal, a defendant or habeas petitioner has no right to self-representation while represented by counsel. If an indigent defendant or habeas petitioner wishes to replace appointed counsel or remove appointed counsel and appear as a self-represented, in lieu of such counsel, the defendant or habeas petitioner shall file a motion with the appellate clerk making such request and setting forth the reasons therefor. An original and three copies of the motion shall be filed. A copy of such motion shall be served, in accordance with Section 62-7, upon the attorney sought to be removed or replaced and upon the state.

The appellate clerk shall forward the motion to the trial judge, who shall conduct a hearing and enter appropriate orders consistent with the relevant provisions of chapter 44 of these rules. The decision on the motion shall be filed with the appellate clerk.

Historical Note

This rule is new effective January 1, 2005. It was amended in 2009 to add the reference to habeas petitioners.

AUTHORS' COMMENTS

This rule was cited in State v. Pires, 310 Conn. 222, 244 n.2, 77 A.3d 87, 102 n.2 (2013).

§ 62-10. Files to Be Available to Parties

Subject to the provisions of Section 62-11, the clerk of the trial court and the appellate clerk or the appellate messenger having custody of the files, evidence and exhibits in any case shall make them available for the use of any party or counsel to that party, whether or not the file is sealed. This provision applies to counsel who have appeared in either the trial court or the appellate court. This rule shall not be deemed to permit appellate counsel to review records that were sealed as to trial counsel but retained in the trial court file for appellate review.

Historical Note

Derivation:
    1978 P.B. (1986–97), § 4036
    1978 P.B., § 3070
    1963 P.B., § 667
    1951 P.B., § 419
The last two sentences were added in 2005.
"Clerk of the court where the case was tried" was changed to "clerk of the trial court" effective September 3, 1996.

The title, but not the language, of the rule was changed in 1963 from "Files to Be Available to Attorneys".

AUTHORS' COMMENTS

The court cited this section in State v. Crespo, 114 Conn.App. 346, 377, 969 A.2d 231, 251 (2009), aff'd, 303 Conn. 589, 35 A.3d 243 (2012).

§ 62-11. Files and Records Not to Be Removed

No files, records or exhibits in the custody of officers of the court shall be removed from the court except by the appellate clerk, the reporter of judicial decisions or by order or permission of an appellate jurist.

Historical Note

Derivation:
  1978 P.B. (1986–97), § 4037
  1978 P.B., § 3071
  1963 P.B., § 668
  1951 P.B., § 467
  1934 P.B., § 418
  1922 P.B., § 66
  1908 P.B., § 64
  1899 P.B., § 64
  58 Conn. at 586, § 1 (1890)
  1879 P.B., ch. XV, § 1

This rule was amended in 1985 to add the chief clerk. Prior to 1951 the files could not be removed by a party except for use in the courtroom. However, prior to 1899, the rule was substantially as it is now.

CHAPTER 63

FILING THE APPEAL; WITHDRAWALS

§ 63-1. Time to Appeal

(a) General provisions

Unless a different time period is provided by statute, an appeal must be filed within twenty days of the date notice of the judgment or decision is given. The appeal period may be extended if permitted by Section 66-1(a). If circumstances give rise to a new appeal period as provided in subsection (c) of this rule, such new period may be similarly extended as long as no extension of the original appeal period was obtained.

If a motion is filed within the appeal period that might give rise to a new appeal period as provided in subsection (c) of this rule, the appeal may be filed either in the original appeal period, which continues to run, or in the new appeal period.

As used in this rule, "appeal period" includes any extension of such period obtained pursuant to Section 66-1(a).

(b) When appeal period begins

If notice of the judgment or decision is given in open court, the appeal period shall begin on that day. If notice is given only by mail, the appeal period shall begin on the day that notice was mailed to counsel and self-represented parties of record by the trial court clerk. The failure to give notice of judgment to a nonappearing party shall not affect the running of the appeal period.

In criminal cases where the appeal is from a judgment of

conviction, the appeal period shall begin when sentence is pronounced in open court.

In civil jury cases, the appeal period shall begin when the verdict is accepted.

(c) New appeal period

(1) How new appeal period is created

If a motion is filed within the appeal period that, if granted, would render the judgment, decision or acceptance of the verdict ineffective, either a new twenty-day period or applicable statutory time period for filing the appeal shall begin on the day that notice of the ruling is given on the last such outstanding motion, except as provided for additur or remittitur in the next paragraph.

If a motion for additur or remittitur is filed within the appeal period and granted, a new twenty-day appeal period shall begin upon the earlier of (A) acceptance of the additur or remittitur or (B) expiration of the time set for the acceptance. If the motion is denied, the new appeal period shall begin on the day that notice of the ruling is given.

Motions that, if granted, would render a judgment, decision or acceptance of the verdict ineffective include, but are not limited to, motions that seek: the opening or setting aside of the judgment; a new trial; the setting aside of the verdict; judgment notwithstanding the verdict; reargument of the judgment or decision; collateral source reduction; additur; remittitur; or any alteration of the terms of the judgment.

Motions that do not give rise to a new appeal period include those that seek: clarification or articulation, as opposed to alteration, of the terms of the judgment or decision; a written or transcribed statement of the trial court's decision; or reargument of a motion listed in the previous paragraph.

If, within the appeal period, any motion is filed, pursuant to Section 63-6 or 63-7, seeking waiver of fees, costs and security or appointment of counsel, a new twenty-day appeal period or statutory period for filing the appeal shall begin on the day that notice of the ruling is given on the last such outstanding motion. If a party files, pursuant to Section 66-6, a motion for review of any such motion, the new appeal period shall begin on the day that notice of the ruling is given on the motion for review.

(2) Who may appeal during new appeal period

If a new appeal period arises due to the filing of a motion that, if granted, would render a judgment, decision or acceptance of the verdict ineffective, any party may take an appeal during the new appeal period regardless of who filed or prevailed upon such motion. If, however, a new appeal period arises due to the filing of a motion for waiver of fees, costs and security or a motion for appointment of counsel, only the party who filed such motion may take an appeal during the new appeal period.

(3) What may be appealed during new appeal period

The new appeal period may be used for appealing the original judgment or decision and/or for appealing any order that gave rise to the new appeal period. Such period may also be used for amending an existing appeal pursuant to Section 61-9 to challenge the ruling that gave rise to the new appeal period. Rulings on motions for waiver of fees, costs and security or motions for appointment of counsel may not be appealed during the new appeal period, but may be challenged by motion for review in accordance with Section 66-6.

(d) When motion to stay briefing obligations may be filed

If, after an appeal has been taken but before the appeal period has expired, any motion is filed that, if granted, would render the judgment, decision or acceptance of the verdict ineffective, any party may move to stay the briefing obligations of the parties in accordance with Section 67-12.

(e) Simultaneous filing of motions

Any party filing more than one motion that, if granted, would render the judgment, decision or acceptance of the verdict ineffective, shall file such motions simultaneously insofar as simultaneous filing is possible.

Historical Note

Derivation:
  1978 P.B. (1986–97), § 4009
  1978 P.B., §§ 3007, 3008
  1963 P.B., § 601
  1951 P.B., § 378
  1934 P.B., § 335
  1930 Rules Change, § 2

This section was completely rewritten primarily for clarity in both 1996 and 2000. The changes also resolve certain ambiguities, such as the effect of failure to give notice of the judgment to the nonappearing party (subsection (b)), the effect of waiver of fees motions on opposing parties (subsection (c)(2)), and the handling of certain adverse postjudgment rulings (subsection (c)(3)). It also provides for a motion for stay briefing obligations (subsection (d)).

Prior to 1951, there was no explicit provision that the filing of a motion which, if granted would nullify the judgment extended the appeal period, but this was implied. De Lucia v. Home Owners' Loan Corp., 130 Conn. 467, 470, 35 A.2d 868, 870 (1944).

Cross References

Maltbie, Conn.App.Proc.2d § 117

AUTHORS' COMMENTS

1. Time to Appeal

With certain exceptions to be discussed, an appeal must be filed "within twenty days of the issuance of notice of the rendition of the judgment," which is the date the clerk mails it, not the date the lawyer receives it. See Table 5, "Time to File" in the introduction.

In calculating the appeal period, the date the clerk sent notice to counsel is day zero. Thus the 20 days excludes that date. Section 63-2; MacCalmont v. MacCalmont, 6 Conn.App. 117, 503 A.2d 624 (1986). Cf. Austin, Nichols & Co. v. Gilman, 100 Conn. 81, 123 A. 32 (1923). So if day zero is, say, July 1, the last day to appeal is July 21. But the authors' opinion is: never wait until the 20th day to appeal; too many things can go wrong.

The 20-day rule is set by this section and not by statute. Missing the deadline will render the appeal vulnerable to a timely motion to dismiss under P.B. § 66-8, but it is not a jurisdictional defect leading to automatic dismissal. Parlato v. Parlato, 134 Conn.App. 848, 850 n.1, 41 A.3d 327, 329 n.1 (2012); Kelley v. Bonney, 221 Conn. 549, 559 n.4, 606 A.2d 693, 699 n.4, 74 Ed. Law Rep. 896 (1992). Note that if the lawyer has changed mailing address, the new address must be given in compliance with P.B. §§ 2-26 and 3-12 or lack of actual notice may be fatal. See Yaremich v. Lam, 71 Conn.App. 650, 654–55, 803 A.2d 369, 372 (2002). The clerk's office will use the address on file with the Statewide Grievance Committee and Barmaster, so keep this information up to date.

Note that the second paragraph of Section 63–1(a) provides that the original appeal period continues to run if a Section 11–11 motion is filed. However, in Weinstein v. Weinstein, 275 Conn. 671, 699, 882 A.2d 53, 70–71 (2005), the court held that filing a motion for reconsideration suspends finality. If that is so, then the second paragraph of Section 63–1(a) is a nullity and counsel should be wary of relying on it. *Weinstein* is a 3–2 decision.

Following Weinstein, the Supreme Court held that the four-month period for opening a judgment under C.G.S.A. § 52-212a starts to run when a timely motion to reargue is decided. Nelson v. Dettmer, 305 Conn. 654, 46 A.3d 916 (2012).

If the judgment is entered on one date, but the clerk neglects to issue notice of it to the parties until later, the later date starts the appeal period, Tilo Co. v. Fishman, 164 Conn. 212, 214, 319 A.2d 409, 410 (1972). See also Noethe v. Noethe, 18 Conn.App. 589, 595–96, 559 A.2d 1149, 1152–53 (1989).

If a party has been defaulted for failure to appear, the appeal period starts to run from the date the judgment is entered. Falls Mill of Vernon Condominium Ass'n, Inc. v. Sudsbury, 49 Conn. L. Rptr. 314, 2010 WL 937268 (Conn. Super. Ct. 2010), aff'd, 128 Conn.App. 314, 15 A.3d 1210 (2011). *Falls Mill* is a thorough discussion of the judicial history of the last sentence of the first paragraph of subsection (b). Likewise, if the clerk notifies some but not all opposing parties on one date, and the remainder on another date, the later notified party can appeal after the later notice. Notestrine v. Farmington Town Plaza & Zoning Commission, PAC 95-11 (Order entered October 11, 1995, see petitioner's brief). See also Dime Sav. Bank v. Saucier, 44 Conn.App. 812, 692 A.2d 1288 (1997) (oral decision applies to parties in court at the time; notice of a written decision applies to those who were not).

In Williams v. Citizens Utilities Co., 2 Conn. Cir. Ct. 227, 228, 197 A.2d 541, 542 (App. Div. 1963), no criticism was made that the motion was filed on the last day at 5:10 p.m., or that it was handwritten, with typed copies filed the following day. 2 Conn.Cir.Ct. at 228–29, 197 A.2d at 542. Note, however, that this is a lower court opinion. The clerk's office currently will stamp in on the next day documents received after 5:00 p.m. Appeals filed electronically after 5:00

p.m. are deemed filed on the next day the court is open. P.B. § 7-17. If the electronic system is down for more than 30 minutes prior to 3:00 p.m. or anytime between 3:00 p.m. and 5:00 p.m., the filing will be timely if made on the next day the court is open. P.B. § 7-17.

If no post-trial motions are filed in a jury case, the time runs from when the verdict is accepted, Grzys v. Connecticut Co., 123 Conn. 605, 607, 198 A. 259, 261 (1938).

The failure first to file a motion to set aside the verdict does not limit the Supreme Court review to claims of plain error; Santopietro v. City of New Haven, 239 Conn. 207, 211–21, 682 A.2d 106, 108–13 (1996); but it is usually unwise to bypass the motion.

If the judgment is issued in open court, the rule is clear in criminal cases: the appeal period starts running from the date sentencing is pronounced. In civil cases, the rule is surprisingly ambiguous. If the appeal is from a civil verdict, the appeal period starts running from the date the verdict is accepted. But litigants rarely appeal from that; rather appeals in civil jury cases are almost always taken from the judgment or decision on the motion to set aside the verdict. If the decision on the motion to set aside the verdict is rendered orally, the authors' opinion is that the appeal period starts to run on that date, not on the date when a postcard is sent out by the clerk announcing the decision the parties already know. The same rule should apply to non-jury civil cases where the decision is rendered orally.

A decision on a mechanics lien and a pre-judgment remedy must be appealed within seven days of "the order" or "the rendering of the order"; C.G.S.A. §§ 49-35c, 52-278*l*; although the Appellate Court has held that the relevant date is when the clerk notifies the parties; Second Injury Fund of the State Treasurer v. Lupachino, 45 Conn.App. 324, 695 A.2d 1072 (1997); and an appeal from a summary process decision must be taken within five days, excluding Sundays and legal holidays, of the rendering of judgment, C.G.S.A. § 47a-35. *Lupachino* is a risky precedent to rely on, because there is no indication of the date the order was actually filed with the clerk. Obviously the date the judge signs the order in chambers is of no legal significance. Under no circumstances should counsel follow some dicta in *Lupachino* suggesting that the appeal period runs from when counsel *receives* the decision.

The 20-day rule applies to discharge of a mechanics' lien after a trial on the merits. New England Sav. Bank v. Meadow Lakes Realty Co., 235 Conn. 663, 668 A.2d 712 (1996).

Since Saturdays are not excluded from the time period in summary process actions, if the fifth day falls on Saturday, the appeal should be filed on Friday, although the Appellate Session has held that filing the appeal the following Monday is timely, Evergreen Co-op, Inc. v. Michel, 36 Conn.Supp. 541, 542–44, 418 A.2d 99, 100 (App. Sess. 1980). Until the Supreme Court rules, however, better safe than sorry.

In calculating the appeal period in a summary process case, beware of the reasoning of Small v. South Norwalk Sav. Bank, 205 Conn. 751, 756–58, 535 A.2d 1292, 1295–96 (1988). The illogic of *Small* might lead to a conclusion that Sundays and legal holidays are excluded only if they are terminal days.

There used to be a ten-day appeal period in juvenile cases, but these cases are now governed by the general 20-day rule. See § 79a-2. Temporary injunctions in a labor dispute are governed by C.G.S.A. § 31-118 (14 days from decision).

Because the state in a criminal case needs the trial court's permission to appeal, the appeal period does not start to run until the state is granted permission to appeal. State v. Tucker, 23 Conn.App. 559, 583 A.2d 139 (1990). Whether this applies if the trial court denies permission and the state files a motion for review remains open. Laws v. Warden, State Prison, 218 Conn. 479, 481 n.2, 590 A.2d 436 (1991).

The filing of a bankruptcy petition obviously stays the appeal period. Knutson Mortg. Corp. v. Salata, 55 Conn.App. 784, 740 A.2d 918 (1999).

2. What Constitutes the Judgment

Oral judgments are clearly discussed in the rule. Written judgments must be carefully distinguished from the judgment file, which is a clerical document of no significance in computing the appeal period. Do not wait for the judgment file before appealing. Lucisano v. Lucisano, 200 Conn. 202, 206, 510 A.2d 186, 189 (1986); LaPre v. Nibo Films, Ltd., 10 Conn.App. 669, 673 n.4, 525 A.2d 140, 143 n.4 (1987). A written judgment is the document, usually entitled the "Memorandum of Decision," which states the court's decision in the case, Grzys v. Connecticut Co., 123 Conn. 605, 607, 198 A. 259, 261 (1938), and it is entered when it is filed with the clerk. Appeal of Bulkeley, 76 Conn. 454, 456, 57 A. 112, 113 (1904). However, it is the notice of the filing of this document that starts the appeal period running. Bogaert v. Zoning Bd. of Appeals of Town of North Branford, 162 Conn. 532, 535 n.2, 294 A.2d 573, 575 n.2 (1972). See Tough v. Ives, 159 Conn. 605, 268 A.2d 371 (1970).

However, the memorandum of decision may not constitute the judgment, such as if it does not entirely dispose of the case. In those cases a separate judgment is needed and that is not a mere clerical document. See § 61-2; Web Press Services Corp. v. New London Motors, Inc., 203 Conn. 342, 343 n.1, 525 A.2d 57, 58 n.1 (1987).

In a civil jury case, the date of judgment is the date of the decisions on the postverdict rulings filed pursuant to P.B. §§ 16-35 and 16-36. If no such motions are filed, the date of judgment is the date the verdict was accepted. P.B. § 17-2.

3. Extension of Time

Extension of time to file an appeal may generally (but see next three paragraphs) be granted under § 66-1, or by filing one of the various motions listed in § 63-1(c)(1), such as a motion to open the judgment. Wells Fargo Bank of Minnesota, N.A. v. Morgan, 98 Conn.App. 72, 909 A.2d 526 (2006). However, the motion must be filed within 20 days of the mailing of the notice of judgment to create a new appeal period for the underlying judgment. Yanow v. Teal Industries, Inc., 196 Conn. 579, 582, 494 A.2d 573, 575 (1985); Worth v. Korta, 132 Conn.App. 154, 158–59, 31 A.3d 804, 807–08 (2011), cert. denied, 304 Conn. 905, 38 A.3d 1201 (2012); Stephen v. Hoerle, 39 Conn.App. 253, 664 A.2d 817 (1995). Presumably a motion to reopen a judgment would be treated as a motion to open it. A motion to open is not a substitute for an appeal, so a motion filed after the expiration of the appeal period will not preserve for appeal the issues litigated in the earlier rulings, Alix v. Leech, 45 Conn.App. 1, 692 A.2d 1309 (1997). Where a party files a motion to open after the appeal period has run, review is limited to the correctness of the ruling on the motion to open. Chapman Lumber, Inc. v. Tager, 288 Conn. 69, 94–95, 952 A.2d 1, 20 (2008); Farren v. Farren, 142 Conn.App. 145, 152, 64 A.3d 352, 357, cert. denied, 309 Conn. 903, 64 A.3d 352 (2013). A motion to reargue the denial of a motion to open does create a new appeal period as to the motion to open, but not as to the underlying judgment. Gibbs v. Spinner, 103 Conn.App. 502, 506 n.4, 930 A.2d 53, 56 n.4 (2007).

A motion for articulation or clarification does NOT extend the appeal period, because it is not a motion which if granted would render the judgment ineffective. Light v. Grimes, 136 Conn.App. 161, 168–70, 43 A.3d 808, 812–14, cert. denied, 305 Conn. 926, 47 A.3d 885 (2012); Matka Corp. v. Automated Material Handling, Inc., 34 Conn.App. 723, 643 A.2d 276 (1994). The 1996 amendments to this rule now make this clear. If you combine such a motion with a motion to reargue or open (which the authors do not recommend), make sure the text of the motion actually asks for a change in the judgment. Otherwise it will be functionally treated as only a motion to articulate or clarify, which can lead to dismissal of a late appeal, as happened in Levine v. State Teachers' Retirement Board, A.C. 18264 (order of dismissal entered June 17, 1998). Cf. Jaser v. Jaser, 37 Conn.App. 194, 200–05, 655 A.2d 790, 794–97 (1995) (practical effect of trial court, rather than label of motion, determines its nature). For a good discussion of the difference between a motion that extends the appeal period and a motion that does not, see In re Haley B., 262 Conn. 406, 815 A.2d 113 (2003).

A motion to reargue a motion to open also does NOT extend the appeal period for the underlying decision even if the motion to open was filed within the 20-day appeal period. Waldman v. Jayaraj, 89 Conn.App. 709, 874 A.2d 860 (2005); Opoku v. Grant, 63 Conn.App. 686, 693–94, 778 A.2d 981, 985–96 (2001).

The general 20-day appeal period set by this section is not jurisdictional. Wells Fargo Bank of Minnesota, N.A. v. Jones, 85 Conn.App. 120, 123 n.5, 856 A.2d 505, 508 n.5 (2004). On the other hand, many statutory appeal periods *are* jurisdictional, so extensions of time are prohibited in those cases. Since the prejudgment remedy statute provides that "no such appeal shall be taken except within seven days . . . ," the Supreme Court has prohibited the granting of a timely motion for extension of time to file the appeal, Ambroise v. William Raveis Real Estate, Inc., 226 Conn. 757, 628 A.2d 1303 (1993), overruling Giordano Const. Co., Inc. v. Ross, 182 Conn. 577, 438 A.2d 772 (1980). *Ambroise* was applied to § 52-325c (lis pendens appeals) in Srager v. Koenig, 36 Conn.App. 469, 651 A.2d 752 (1994); to summary process appeals in HUD/Barbour-Waverly v. Wilson, 235 Conn. 650, 668 A.2d 1309 (1995), and Gayle v. Young, 41 Conn.App. 913, 676 A.2d 434 (1996); and to mechanics liens in Burke Const., Inc. v. Smith, 41 Conn.App. 737, 677 A.2d 15 (1996). Also, the 20-day period set forth in C.G.S.A. § 31-301(a) to appeal from the decision of a workers' compensation commissioner to the compensation review board is jurisdictional. Stec v. Raymark Industries, Inc., 299 Conn. 346, 10 A.3d 1 (2010). On the other hand, the 10-day period for filing a petition for certification to appeal from a habeas corpus judgment is not jurisdictional. Iovieno v. Commissioner of Correction, 242 Conn. 689, 694–700, 699 A.2d 1003, 1006–09 (1997).

An automatic extension can also generally be obtained by filing a motion to reargue within the appeal period in accordance with P.B. § 11-11 (not § 11-12). Such motions were previously proper under the common law. Steele v. Town of Stonington, 225 Conn. 217, 219, 622 A.2d 551, 553 (1993); Tiber Holding Corp. v. Greenberg, 36 Conn.App. 670, 671 n.1, 652 A.2d 1063, 1064 n.1 (1995); Springfield-De Witt Gardens, Inc. v. Wood, 143 Conn. 708, 709 n.1, 125 A.2d 488, 489 n.1 (1956); apparently even if the motion to reargue could not itself be granted by the trial court, Whitney Frocks v. Jaffe, 138 Conn. 428, 429-30 n.1, 85 A.2d 242, 243 n.1 (1951). Both the Supreme Court and Appellate Court have allowed a motion to reargue to toll the appeal period in a summary process case; Young v. Young, 249 Conn. 482, 733 A.2d 835 (1999); Lopez v. Livingston, 53 Conn.App. 622, 731 A.2d 335 (1999). This has the remarkable result of confining *HUD* and *Gayle*, supra, to motions for extension of time to appeal. The authors strongly advise lawyers not to attempt to apply *Young* and *Lopez* to pre-judgment remedy appeals. The statutory language is much harsher.

If the appeal period is less than 20 days, reargument must be requested within the shorter appeal period. *Young* and *Lopez* do not expressly say so, but that conclusion appears to be implied in the reasoning. If the motion is filed outside the appeal period, the time to appeal is not extended. In re Dalands, 81 Conn. 249, 70 A. 449 (1908); Tiber Holding Corp. v. Greenberg, 36 Conn.App. 670, 652 A.2d 1063 (1995); Charbonneau v. Charbonneau, 51 Conn.App. 311,

721 A.2d 565 (1998), cert. denied, 247 Conn. 964, 724 A.2d 1125 (1999). If the motion has procedural defects and the trial court denies the motion on that basis, query whether § 63-1 extends the time. Signore v. Signore, 216 Conn. 806, 580 A.2d 60 (1990) (certification granted, but appeal thereafter withdrawn).

Prior to 1996, a motion by one party did not extend the appeal period for any other party. See Farmers and Mechanics Sav. Bank v. Sullivan, 216 Conn. 341, 579 A.2d 1054 (1990), in which a timely motion to open by one party did not extend the time for another party to file a motion to open. However, the 1996 and 2000 revisions to what is now subsection (c)(2) overrule *Sullivan*. An appeal by one party does not stay the liability as to other parties. Middlesex Hosp. v. Town of Hamden, 33 Conn.App. 247, 251, 635 A.2d 313, 315 (1993) (warning: an inseverable judgment is entirely reversed if it is reversed as to one appellant, Rowell v. Ross, 89 Conn. 201, 213, 93 A. 236, 240 (1915)). Query whether *Middlesex* and *Rowell* are entirely reconcilable.

The Appellate Division has held that a motion to stay proceedings for stay of execution does not extend the time to appeal (pro se appellant), Continental Nat. Am. Group v. Majeske, 30 Conn.Supp. 567, 305 A.2d 291 (C.P. App. Div. 1973).

What happens if a prospective appellant dies during the 20-day appeal period? In light of Barton v. City of New Haven, 74 Conn. 729, 52 A. 403 (1902), the appeal period probably stops running until an executor or administrator of the estate is appointed. However, the authors would take the conservative approach of appealing during the 20-day period. Better to have an appeal dismissed as premature than as late.

Once a § 63-1 motion has been denied a repetitive § 63-1 motion will not extend the appeal period. Brooklyn Sav. Bank v. Frimberger, 29 Conn.App. 628, 630–31, 617 A.2d 462, 464 (1992).

Note that P.B. § 35a-21 prohibits extensions of time in juvenile matters for more than 40 days from the judgment.

Note too that, while a motion to open a judgment can be filed within four months of the denial of a motion that would extend the appeal period under § 63-1; Nelson v. Dettmer, 305 Conn. 654, 680, 46 A.3d 916, 933 (2012); the ruling on the motion to open will not relate back to the underlying judgment unless the motion was filed within 20 days of the notice of the judgment. *Nelson*, 305 Conn. at 680, 46 A.3d at 933.

4. Appeals After Expiration of Time Limits

If the time for filing an appeal has run before a motion for extension has been filed, the trial court lacks the power to grant it under § 66-1(c)(4). In re Karen R., 45 Conn.Supp. 255, 257, 717 A.2d 856, 857 (1998). However, the Supreme Court may grant it under § 60-2(6). See also State v. Stead, 186 Conn. 222, 440 A.2d 299 (1982). This is a motion that should be sparingly filed.

If an appeal is not timely filed, the appeal in the past was usually dismissed if the appellee filed a motion to dismiss within ten days of the filing of the appeal. See cases cited in Authors' Comments to P.B. § 66-8. If the appellee fails to file a timely motion to dismiss, the lateness of the appeal has been considered waived. This issue is discussed in detail in LaReau v. Reincke, 158 Conn. 486, 490–95, 264 A.2d 576, 578–80 (1969), cited in Connelly v. Doe, 213 Conn. 66, 69–70 n.5, 566 A.2d 426, 428 n.5 (1989), and McCarthy v. City of Bridgeport, 21 Conn.App. 359, 361, 574 A.2d 226, 227, cert. denied, 215 Conn. 814, 576 A.2d 543 (1990). See also Tarzia v. Great Atlantic and Pacific Tea Co., 52 Conn.App. 136, 727 A.2d 219 (1999). Waiver may not apply to statutory time periods. Ambroise v. William Raveis Real Estate, Inc., 226 Conn. 757, 628 A.2d 1303 (1993).

The Supreme Court permitted a late appeal where a subsequent order altered the premise of the earlier decision. Connecticut Light and Power Co. v. Lighthouse Landings, Inc., 279 Conn. 90, 900 A.2d 1242 (2006). See also State v. Reid, 277 Conn. 764, 894 A.2d 963 (2006) (permitting appeal seven years after guilty plea).

If there are two judgments, and an appeal is filed that is timely as to the second judgment but not timely as to the first, the untimeliness is waived unless a motion to dismiss is filed within 10 days attacking the attempt to appeal from the earlier judgment. Savage v. Savage, 25 Conn.App. 693, 694, 596 A.2d 23, 24 (1991). See also Cowles v. Cowles, 71 Conn.App. 24, 25 n.1, 799 A.2d 1119, 1120 n.1 (2002). Deshpande v. Deshpande, 142 Conn.App. 471, 475 n.7, 65 A.3d 12, 14 n.7 (2013).

In the federal courts, the appeal period is jurisdictional. See Cardillo by Cardillo v. U.S., 767 F.2d 33 (2d Cir. 1985).

The appellee succeeded in striking issues from an earlier judgment by timely filing a motion to dismiss in Buehler v. Buehler, 117 Conn.App. 304, 978 A.2d 1141 (2009).

In any event it is not clear that the court would grant any motion by the state to dismiss in a criminal case. Since it is highly unlikely that a criminal defendant would deliberately file a late appeal, any federal constitutional issues could be raised in a later habeas corpus petition if the appeal were dismissed, State v. Brown, 157 Conn. 398, 402, 254 A.2d 570, 572–73 (1969); Fredericks v. Reincke, 152 Conn. 501, 508, 208 A.2d 756, 759 (1965), citing federal law.

Whatever you do, do not try to induce the trial judge to vacate the judgment and to reenter it at a later date to allow a timely appeal. Connecticut Mortgage & Title Guaranty Co. v. Di Francesco, 112 Conn. 673, 151 A. 491 (1930). Finally, appealing from a deficiency judgment does not extend the time to appeal from the underlying judgment of strict foreclosure. N.E. Leasing, LLC v. Paoletta, 89 Conn.App. 766, 768 n.1, 877 A.2d 840, n.1, cert. denied, 275 Conn. 921, 883 A.2d 1245 (2005).

The Appellate Court will not review claims that should have been raised in an earlier appeal. Fernandes v. Rodriguez, 90 Conn.App. 601, 613, 879 A.2d 897, 905, cert. denied, 275 Conn. 927, 883 A.2d 1243 (2005).

5. Avoiding Motion to Dismiss

Since a motion to dismiss based on a technical defect in the appeal (wrong decision appealed from, defective recognizance or bond, papers filed in wrong court, no signature on papers, fees not paid, wrong parties, and the like) must be filed within ten days of the filing of the appeal, the appellant can avoid a lot of anguish by either filing the appeal at least eleven days before the appeal period runs out, or by moving for an extension of time to file the appeal, and then filing it at least eleven days before the extension runs out. Then the appellee will have to file a motion to dismiss within the appeal period.

If the motion to dismiss is well taken and the appeal period has not run, the authors' advice previously was for appellant to withdraw the defective appeal and file a new one within the appeal period. Presumably, although not certainly, the Appellate Court would treat a second appeal to it as the lower courts would treat any ordinary case which has been withdrawn and brought again within the statute of limitations. There is some helpful dicta on the subject in Zachs v. Public Utilities Commission, 171 Conn. 387, 394, 370 A.2d 984, 988 (1976). It may be significant that § 377 of the 1951 Practice Book stated "There shall be but one appeal in any such case", but this language is omitted in the present § 63-1. See State v. Cullum, 1 Conn. Cir. Ct. 120, 23 Conn.Supp. 20, 176 A.2d 583, cert. denied, 149 Conn. 728, 176 A.2d 587 (1961), decided under the 1951 rule.

The authors now think it is probably wiser, whether or not the appeal period has run, for the appellant to file an appropriate motion. A motion under § 66-1 for extension of time to file a corrected or amended appeal may be proper if the appeal period has not run; a motion under § 60-2 to the Appellate Court to "complete, correct or otherwise perfect the record" may be proper in all situations; cf. Mims v. Kingsley, 145 Conn. 7, 8 n.1, 138 A.2d 520, 522 n.1 (1958). Finally, a motion to the Appellate Court under § 60-2(6) to permit filing an amended appeal may succeed. See Huber v. Pudim, 143 Conn. 567, 124 A.2d 219 (1956).

6. Effect on Appeal if § 63-1 Motion is Granted

If a motion for reargument is granted, an appeal cannot be filed until a new decision is entered following the reargument. Gardner v. Falvey, 45 Conn.App. 699, 697 A.2d 711 (1997). *Gardner* also held that if the trial court grants a motion to reargue while an appeal is pending, the judgment apparently is destroyed and the appeal is subject to dismissal. Gardner v. Falvey, 45 Conn.App. 699, 697 A.2d 711 (1997). The Supreme Court has held, however, that if the appeal was from a final judgment, a subsequent order opening the judgment will not destroy jurisdiction over the appeal. RAL Management, Inc. v. Valley View Associates, 278 Conn. 672, 899 A.2d 586 (2006).

§ 63-2. Expiration of Time Limitations; Counting Days

In determining the last day for filing any papers, the last day shall, and the first day shall not, be counted. Time shall be counted by calendar, not working, days.

When the last day of any limitation of time for filing any paper under these rules or an order of the court falls on a day when the office of the trial court or of the appellate clerk is not required to be open, the paper may be filed on the next day when such office is required so to be open.

Historical Note

Derivation:
  1978 P.B. (1986–97), § 4010
  1978 P.B., § 3069
  1963 P.B., § 664
  1951 P.B., § 412

Effective September 3, 1996, the first sentence was broadened to refer to filings in all courts.

The first paragraph was added effective October 1, 1986. The second paragraph is essentially unchanged since 1951, and conforms to two earlier decisions. Sommers v. Adelman, 90 Conn. 713, 714, 99 A. 50, 51 (1916); Alderman Bros. Co. v. Westinghouse Air Brake Co., 91 Conn. 383, 385, 99 A. 1040, 1041 (1917).

Cross References

Maltbie, Conn.App.Proc.2d, § 295

AUTHORS' COMMENTS

This rule is similar to § 7-17, which was applied in Village Green Apartments v. Foster, 36 Conn.Supp. 565, 566–67, 420 A.2d 1173, 1174 (Super. Ct. 1980), and misapplied in Small v. South Norwalk Sav. Bank, 205 Conn. 751, 756–58, 535 A.2d 1292, 1295–96 (1988). How to count days was discussed in Stephen v. Hoerle, 39 Conn.App. 253, 664 A.2d 817 (1995).

The trial court in Torniero v. Allingtown Fire Dist., 45 Conn. L. Rptr. 433, 2008 WL 2096868 (Conn. Super. Ct. 2008), applied this rule to a motion to reargue.

The Supreme Court affirmed the Appellate Court's dismissal of an appeal filed one day late because the lawyer misread this section. Alliance Partners, Inc. v. Voltarc Technologies, Inc., 263 Conn. 204, 820 A.2d 224 (2003).

The chief clerk has interpreted the second paragraph to allow for filing the next day the clerk's office is open if the office closed early on the last day for filing a document. 56 Conn.L.J.No. 35, p. 1E.

§ 63-3. Filing of Appeal; Number of Copies

Any appeal may be filed in the original trial court or the court to which the case was transferred or in any judicial district court in the state, except that juvenile appeals and appeals from interlocutory orders, if permitted by law, must be filed with the clerk of the original trial court or the court to which the case was transferred. Procedures for appeals in e-filed cases are governed by Section 63-3A. An application for a fee waiver pursuant to Sections 63-6 or 63-7 must be filed with the clerk of the court in which the case was tried or otherwise resolved.

The original appeal form shall be accompanied by a certification that a copy thereof has been served on each counsel of record, as defined in section 60-4, in accordance with the provisions of section 62-7. At the time the appeal is filed, the appellant shall, as set forth in section 63-5, pay to the clerk of the trial court all required fees. The clerk shall: (1) endorse on the original appeal form the date and time of filing and the receipt or waiver of fees; (2) return the original endorsed appeal form to the appellant; and (3) immediately notify the clerk of the original trial court that an appeal has been filed. In addition, in noncriminal matters, the clerk shall, without cost, provide the appellant with a copy of the docket sheet (DS1) listing the counsel for all parties. In criminal and habeas corpus matters, the clerk shall also send a copy of the endorsed appeal form to the office of the chief state's attorney, appellate bureau. If an appeal is e-filed, the paper confirmation of e-filing, together with the appeal form, shall be used in lieu of the endorsed appeal form for purposes of this rule.

On the same day on which the original appeal form is endorsed by the trial court clerk, the appellant shall deliver a copy of the endorsed appeal form to the clerk of the trial court in which the case was originally filed and the clerk of any trial court to which the case was subsequently transferred. The copy may be delivered by hand, fax or any other electronic means permitted by section 4-4. The appellant shall obtain proof that the original trial court and any subsequent trial court received the copy on the same day on which it was delivered.

Within ten days of filing the appeal, the appellant shall file with the appellate clerk the original and one copy of the endorsed appeal form; the docket sheet, if any; the papers required by section 63-4; and proof that a copy of the endorsed appeal form was transmitted to the original trial court and to any trial court to which the case subsequently was transferred. The appellant shall certify that a copy of the endorsed appeal form was served on: (1) the clerk of the original trial court; (2) the clerk of any other trial court to which the case was transferred; and (3) any trial court whose decision is the subject of the appeal. The appellant shall also certify that a copy of the endorsed appeal form and all other papers required by section 63-4 was served on (1) every other party in the manner set forth in section 62-7 and (2) in criminal and habeas corpus matters, the office of the chief state's attorney, appellate bureau.

The appellate clerk, upon receipt of the foregoing, shall docket the appeal, affix to the endorsed appeal form the docket number assigned to the appeal and send one copy to the trial judge and one copy to each party to the appeal and, in criminal and habeas corpus matters, to the office of the chief state's attorney, appellate bureau.

Historical Note

Derivation:
   1978 P.B. (1986–97), § 4012
   1978 P.B., § 3011

This rule was amended effective October 1, 2013 to move the rules for electronically filed appeals to a new section, § 63-3A.

Effective May 1, 2010, appeals in certain civil cases may be e-filed. Effective January 1, 2010, most appeals may be filed in any judicial district court in the state. Notable exceptions are juvenile matters and interlocutory orders. Also on January 1, 2010, the deadline for filing appeal papers with the appellate clerk is 10 days after filing the appeal, no longer "forthwith."

Effective September 3, 1996, counsel are no longer required to provide extra copies to the clerk to mail to all counsel of record. Also, the trial court clerk is now required to photocopy the endorsed appeal form and give a copy to the appellant for filing with the appellate clerk.

The second sentence of the third paragraph was added effective October 1, 1992, the fourth sentence was added effective May 10, 1988 and the third sentence was added effective October 1, 1992. In the first paragraph, the second sentence was added and the last sentence was clarified effective October 1, 1986.

Basically this is a new rule effective July 1, 1978, except that the last paragraph was added effective July 1, 1979. Before 1978, the appeal was filed in quadruplicate and no certification to counsel of record was required (§ 638). The requirement that a copy of the appeal be sent to the chief clerk of the Supreme Court is new.

AUTHORS' COMMENTS

The 2010 amendments allow parties to file appeals at any courthouse or electronically in most cases. Note that now the endorsed appeal form must be served on self represented parties and counsel of record. Electronically filed appeals are governed by P.B. § 63-3A, effective October 1, 2013.

By requiring the appellant to obtain an endorsed copy of the appeal from the trial clerk and to send it to the appellate clerk, with the § 63-4 papers, the appellate clerk can quickly determine whether the appeal has been properly filed. Note that this rule also requires an appellant to obtain from the trial court a copy of the DS1 docket sheet, which is a list of counsel, and file it with the appellate clerk along with the § 63-4 papers. Counsel may want to get the DS2 docket sheet, which is the list in chronological order of all papers filed with the trial court (except exhibits and transcripts), prior to filing the appeal to avoid potential delays in completing the § 63-4 papers, especially (a)(2). Unless the appeal is filed electronically, the appellant should file the papers in both courts in person so that any defects, if spotted by the clerks, can be corrected before the appeal period passes. Unless the file is sealed, the DS-1 and DS-2 forms are available on line for civil, family, and some housing cases. See www.jud.ct.gov. It is usually easier to download these forms than to get them from the clerk.

A technical violation of this rule or § 63-4 will usually be excused if promptly corrected. Norwich v. Shelby-Posello, 140 Conn.App. 383, 385 n.1,59 A.3d 239, 240 n.1 (2013). Note, however, that the appellant was self represented.

The rule now provides a 10-day window to file appeal papers with the Appellate Clerk.

§ 63-3a. Appeals in E-Filed Cases

An appeal may be e-filed in any case in which e-filing is permitted in the trial court. The appeal form shall be e-filed in accordance with Section 4-4 and shall contain a certification that a copy has been served on each counsel of record, as defined in Section 60-4, in accordance with the provisions of Section 62-7.

All required fees shall be paid at the time of e-filing by any method specified by Judicial Branch E-Services. The appellant shall print a copy of the confirmation of e-filing and affix it to the original appeal form. The original appeal form and the confirmation of e-filing together are deemed to be the endorsed appeal form.

Within ten days of e-filing the appeal, the appellant shall file with the appellate clerk the original and one copy of the endorsed appeal form, with a certification that a copy was served on each party as required by Section 63-3; two print copies of the electronic docket sheet for the case as it appears on the Judicial Branch website; and the papers required by Section 63-4.

Upon receipt of the foregoing, the appellate clerk shall docket the appeal and proceed in accordance with Section 63-3.

Historical Note

This rule was new effective October 1, 2013, to address the procedure for filing appeals electronically. These rules previously appeared in Practice Book § 63-3.

§ 63-4. Additional Papers to Be Filed by Appellant and Appellee when Filing Appeal (Applicable to appeals filed before July 1, 2013)

(a) At the time the appellant sends a copy of the endorsed appeal form and the docket sheet to the appellate clerk, the appellant shall also send the appellate clerk an original and one copy of the following:

(1) A preliminary statement of the issues intended for presentation on appeal. If any appellee wishes to: (A) present for review alternative grounds upon which the judgment may be affirmed, (B) present for review adverse rulings or decisions of the court which should be considered on appeal in the event the appellant is awarded a new trial, or (C) claim that a new trial rather than a directed judgment should be ordered if the appellant is successful on the appeal, that appellee shall file a preliminary statement of issues within twenty days from the filing of the appellant's preliminary statement of the issues.

Whenever the failure to identify an issue in a preliminary statement of issues prejudices an opposing party, the court may refuse to consider such issue.

(2) A preliminary designation of the specific pleadings in the trial court case file which the appellant deems necessary to include in the record including their dates of filing in the trial court, and, if applicable, their number as listed on the docket sheet. If any other party objects to the inclusion of any pleadings in the trial court case file designated by the appellant or deems it necessary to include other pleadings in the record, that party may, within twenty days from the filing of the appellant's designation of the record, file an objection to the designation of the appellant, or file a designation of those other pleadings deemed necessary. No portion of the transcript of evidence shall be designated for inclusion in the record. Any objection or proposed supplemental designation shall be reviewed by the appellate clerk pursuant to Section 68-3. The appellant shall file a revised designation of the specific pleadings at the time the brief of the appellant is filed.

(3) A certificate stating that no transcript is deemed necessary, or a copy of the transcript order acknowledgment form (JD-ES-38) with section I thereof completed, filed with the official reporter pursuant to Section 63-8. If any other party deems any other parts of the transcript necessary that party shall, within twenty days from the filing of the appellant's transcript papers, file a copy of the order form (JD-ES-38) which that party has placed in compliance with Section 63-8.

If the appellant is to rely on transcript delivered prior to the taking of the appeal, an order form (JD-ES-38) shall be filed stating that an electronic version of a previously delivered transcript has been ordered. The detailed statement of the transcript to be relied on required by Section 63-8 also must be filed. If any other party deems any other parts of the transcript necessary, and those parts have not been delivered at the time of the taking of the appeal, that party shall have twenty days to order those additional parts. If any other party is to rely on transcript delivered prior to the taking of the appeal, an order form (JD-ES-38) shall be filed within twenty days stating that an electronic version of a previously delivered transcript has been ordered.

(4) A docketing statement containing the following information to the extent known or reasonably ascertainable by the appellant: (A) the names and addresses of all parties to the appeal and their trial and appellate counsel and the names and addresses of all persons having a legal interest in the cause on appeal sufficient to raise a substantial question whether a judge should be disqualified from participating in the decision on the case by virtue of that judge's personal or financial interest in any such persons; (B) the case names and docket numbers of all pending appeals to the supreme court or appellate court which arise from substantially the same controversy as the cause on appeal, or involve issues closely related to those presented by the appeal; (C) whether there were exhibits in the trial court; and (D) in criminal cases, whether or not the defendant is incarcerated as a result of the proceedings in which the appeal is being taken. If additional information is or becomes known to, or is reasonably ascertainable by the appellee, the appellee shall file a docketing statement supplementing the information required to be provided by the appellant.

(5) In all noncriminal matters, except for matters exempt from a preargument conference pursuant to Section 63-10, a preargument conference statement.

(6) Except for (A) habeas corpus matters based on criminal convictions, (B) pre-and postjudgment orders in matters claiming dissolution of marriage, legal separation or annulment, (C) prejudgment remedies under chapter 903a of the General Statutes and (D) actions of foreclosure of title to real property, in all noncriminal cases a draft judgment file prepared in the form prescribed by Section 6-2 et seq. If any appellee disagrees in any respect with the draft judgment file, that appellee shall file either a statement specifying the disagreement or a separate draft judgment file within twenty days of the filing of the appellant's draft. The appellate clerk shall transmit the appellant's draft judgment file and any disagreeing statements or other drafts to the trial court clerk. The trial court clerk shall, within twenty days of receipt of such documents and, if necessary, after consultation with the judge who tried the case, file the original judgment file, sending copies, in the manner prescribed by Section 68-1, to the appellate clerk. The appellate clerk shall send copies to all counsel of record on the appeal. Any objections to the form of the judgment file may thereafter be raised only by a motion for rectification under Section 66-5.

If the trial court clerk fails to file the original judgment file within twenty days as required, the appellant may file with the appellate clerk a notice that the judgment file has not been so filed. The appellate clerk shall notify the trial court clerk and the trial judge of the pending appeal and the fact that the disagreement over the judgment file has not been resolved, after which the trial court clerk shall promptly file the judgment file as prescribed above.

(7) Except for habeas corpus matters based on criminal convictions, and all cases in which the attorney general is a party, has appeared on behalf of a party or has filed an amicus brief in proceedings prior to the appeal, in all noncriminal cases where the constitutionality of a state statute has been challenged, a notice identifying the statute, the name and address of the party challenging it, and whether the statute's constitutionality was upheld by the trial court. The appellate clerk shall send a copy of such notice to the Attorney General.

(8) In matters in which documents are under seal, conditionally or otherwise, or limited as to disclosure, a copy of the time, date, scope and duration of sealing order form (JD-CL-76) shall be attached to the appeal form. (See Sec. 77-2.)

(b) Except as otherwise provided, a party may as of right file amendments to the preliminary statement of issues or the designation of the pleadings in the trial court case file at any time until that party's brief is filed. Amendments to the docketing statement may be filed at any time. Amendments to the transcript statement may be made only with leave of the court. If leave to file such an amendment is granted, the adverse party shall have the right to move for permission to file a supplemental brief and for an extension of time. Amendments to the preargument conference statement shall not be presented in writing but may be presented orally at the preargument conference, if one is held.

(c) Failure to comply with this rule shall be deemed as sufficient reason to schedule a case for sanctions under Section 85-3 or for dismissal under Section 85-1.

§ 63-4. Additional Papers to Be Filed by Appellant and Appellee when Filing Appeal (Applicable to appeals filed on or after July 1, 2013)

(a) At the time the appellant sends a copy of the endorsed appeal form and the docket sheet to the appellate clerk, the appellant shall also send the appellate clerk an original of the following:

(1) A preliminary statement of the issues intended for presentation on appeal. If any appellee wishes to: (A) present for review alternative grounds upon which the judgment may be affirmed;

(B) present for review adverse rulings or decisions of the court which should be considered on appeal in the event the appellant is awarded a new trial; or (C) claim that a new trial rather than a directed judgment should be ordered if the appellant is successful on the appeal, that appellee shall file a preliminary statement of issues within twenty days from the filing of the appellant's preliminary statement of the issues.

Whenever the failure to identify an issue in a preliminary statement of issues prejudices an opposing party, the court may refuse to consider such issue.

(2) A certificate stating that no transcript is deemed necessary, or a copy of the transcript order acknowledgment form (JD-ES-38) with section I thereof completed, filed with the official reporter pursuant to Section 63-8. If any other party deems any other parts of the transcript necessary, that party shall, within twenty days from the filing of the appellant's transcript papers, file a copy of the order form (JD-ES-38), which that party has placed in compliance with Section 63-8.

If the appellant is to rely on transcript delivered prior to the taking of the appeal, an order form (JD-ES-38) shall be filed stating that an electronic version of a previously delivered transcript has been ordered. The detailed statement of the transcript to be relied on required by Section 63-8 also must be filed. If any other party deems any other parts of the transcript necessary, and those parts have not been delivered at the time of the taking of the appeal, that party shall have twenty days to order those additional parts. If any other party is to rely on transcript delivered prior to the taking of the appeal, an order form (JD-ES-38) shall be filed within twenty days, stating that an electronic version of a previously delivered transcript has been ordered.

(3) A docketing statement containing the following information to the extent known or reasonably ascertainable by the appellant: (A) the names and addresses of all parties to the appeal and their trial and appellate counsel and the names and addresses of all persons having a legal interest in the cause on appeal sufficient to raise a substantial question whether a judge should be disqualified from participating in the decision on the case by virtue of that judge's personal or financial interest in any such persons; (B) the case names and docket numbers of all pending appeals to the supreme court or appellate court which arise from substantially the same controversy as the cause on appeal, or involve issues closely related to those presented by the appeal; (C) whether there were exhibits in the trial court; and (D) in criminal cases, whether or not the defendant is incarcerated as a result of the proceedings in which the appeal is being taken. If additional information is or becomes known to, or is reasonably

ascertainable by the appellee, the appellee shall file a docketing statement supplementing the information required to be provided by the appellant.

(4) In all noncriminal matters, except for matters exempt from a preargument conference pursuant to Section 63-10, a preargument conference statement.

(5) In all noncriminal cases, except for: (A) habeas corpus matters based on criminal convictions; (B) pre-and postjudgment orders in matters claiming dissolution of marriage, legal separation or annulment; (C) prejudgment remedies under chapter 903a of the General Statutes; and (D) actions of foreclosure of title to real property, a draft judgment file prepared in the form prescribed by Section 6-2 et seq. If any appellee disagrees in any respect with the draft judgment file, that appellee shall file either a statement specifying the disagreement or a separate draft judgment file within twenty days of the filing of the appellant's draft. The appellate clerk shall transmit the appellant's draft judgment file and any disagreeing statements or other drafts to the trial court clerk. The trial court clerk shall, within twenty days of receipt of such documents and, if necessary, after consultation with the judge who tried the case, file the original judgment file, sending copies to the appellate clerk. The appellate clerk shall send copies to all counsel of record on the appeal. Any objections to the form of the judgment file may thereafter be raised only by a motion for rectification under Section 66-5.

If the trial court clerk fails to file the original judgment file within twenty days as required, the appellant may file with the appellate clerk a notice that the judgment file has not been so filed. The appellate clerk shall notify the trial court clerk and the trial judge of the pending appeal and the fact that the disagreement over the judgment file has not been resolved, after which the trial court clerk shall promptly file the judgment file as prescribed above.

(6) Except for habeas corpus matters based on criminal convictions and all cases in which the attorney general is a party, has appeared on behalf of a party or has filed an amicus brief in proceedings prior to the appeal, in all noncriminal cases where the constitutionality of a state statute has been challenged, a notice identifying the statute, the name and address of the party challenging it, and whether the statute's constitutionality was upheld by the trial court. The appellate clerk shall send a copy of such notice to the Attorney General.

(7) In matters in which documents are under seal, conditionally or otherwise, or limited as to disclosure, a copy of the time, date, scope and duration of sealing order form (JD-CL-76) shall be attached to the appeal form. (See Section 77-2.)

(b) Except as otherwise provided, a party may as of right file amendments to the preliminary statement of issues at any time until that party's brief is filed. Amendments to the docketing statement may be filed at any time. Amendments to the transcript statement may be made only with leave of the court. If leave to file such an amendment is granted, the adverse party shall have the right to move for permission to file a supplemental brief and for an extension of time. Amendments to the preargument conference statement shall not be presented in writing but may be presented orally at the preargument conference, if one is held.

(c)   Failure to comply with this rule shall be deemed as sufficient reason to schedule a case for sanctions under Section 85-3 or for dismissal under Section 85-1.

Historical Note

Derivation:
> 1978 P.B. (1986–97), § 4013
> 1978 P.B., § 3012

Effective July 1, 2013, subsection (a)(2) (concerning designation of pleadings for the printed record) was eliminated and the subsequent subsections renumbered.

Effective January 1, 2012, subsection (a)(5) limited the situations in which a preargument conference statement needs to be filed.

Effective January 1, 2004, subsection (a)(8) was added. Subsections (a)(6) and (a)(7) were added in 1996. Effective October 1, 1992, the first sentences of §§ (a)(2) and (a)(3) were clarified and § (a)(5) and the last sentence of § (b) were added. Effective March 6, 1989, § (a)(3) was amended to refer to the official court reporter rather than to the reporter who actually handled the trial.

Effective May 10, 1988, § 63-4 papers need only be filed in duplicate (formerly triplicate), the designation of contents of record may only include pleadings, the transcript certificate must state in detail what has been ordered and an amended transcript acknowledgment form must be obtained and filed if the transcript is not timely delivered.

Sections (a)(4) and the last paragraph of (a)(1) were added effective October 1, 1986. At the same time, §§ (a)(2) and (a)(3) and the remainder of § (a)(1) were clarified as to when the appellee must file papers.

Effective January 1, 1985, § (a)(1) was amended to expand the right of an appellee to utilize it, in situations when the bill of exceptions previously was used (see, e.g., Farguet v. De Senti, 110 Conn. 367, 372–73, 148 A. 139, 141 (1930)). Section (a)(3) was amended to add the last sentence of the first paragraph and § (b) of the rule was changed to make all amendments to § (a)(3) subject to Supreme Court approval.

Basically this was a new rule effective July 1, 1978, although (a)(1) and (2) resemble old § 612A, (a)(3) bears a vague resemblance to old § 608A, and (b) comes from an old Appellate Session rule § 567B. Effective July 1, 1979, the rule omitted all mention of assignments of errors and findings and expanded the right of the appellee in § (a) to file statements of the issues. Also, in 1979 § (a)(3) required counsel to obtain the reporter's acknowledgment of the transcript order rather than just a certificate by counsel that he has ordered the transcript. In 1979, § (b) was enacted and was similar to repealed § 3035, except that assignments of error could be amended as of right until the case was "ready for assignment for hearing", which was when all briefs were filed. The beginning of the rule was amended effective March 1, 1982 to clarify the appellant's duty.

AUTHORS' COMMENTS

These documents, along with an endorsed copy of the appeal itself, are to be filed with the chief clerk of the Supreme Court in Hartford within ten days of filing the appeal.

(a)(1)

Under the language effective October 1, 1986, failure to raise an issue in the § 63-4 papers will only bar review if the opposition is prejudiced. State v. Marquez, 291 Conn. 122, 126 n.6, 967 A.2d 56, 61 n.6, cert. denied, 558 U.S. 895, 130 S.Ct. 237, 175 L.Ed.2d 163 (2009) (appellant's failure excused); Electrical Contractors, Inc. v. Department of Educ., 303 Conn. 402, 455–56, 35 A.3d 188, 223–24, 192 L.R.R.M. (BNA) 2954, 2012-1 Trade Cas. (CCH) ¶ 77768 (2012) (appellee's failure excused). It is difficult to see how an appellee could ever be prejudiced by an appellant's failure to raise an issue in its preliminary statement of issues because subsection (b) permits amendment of this statement as of right until the brief is filed. The only time prejudice conceivably enters the picture is when the appellee fails to file any § 63-4 papers at all. D'Ulisse-Cupo v. Board of Directors of Notre Dame High School, 202 Conn. 206, 216 n.4, 520 A.2d 217, 222 n.4, 37 Ed. Law Rep. 229, 2 I.E.R. Cas. (BNA) 948, 106 Lab. Cas. (CCH) P 55702 (1987). However, the Supreme Court refused to consider an issue not in the preliminary statement, and no reference was made to prejudice, in Rosenblit v. Danaher, 206 Conn. 125, 136 n.12, 537 A.2d 145, 150 n.12 (1988) (citing pre-1986 law).

The Appellate Court has also mistakenly held that an issue briefed must be raised in the § 63-4 papers. Burns v. Burns, 41 Conn.App. 716, 722, 677 A.2d 971, 975 (1996); but see Chase v. State, Dept. of Motor Vehicles, 45 Conn.App. 499, 501 n.3, 696 A.2d 1299, 1301 n.3 (1997). That is not what § 63-4(a)(1) says. More sensible holdings are Johnson Elec. Co., Inc. v. Salce Contracting Associates, Inc., 72 Conn.App. 342, 356 n.6, 805 A.2d 735, 743 n.6, cert. denied, 262 Conn. 922, 812 A.2d 864 (2002); and Raph v. Vogeler, 45 Conn.App. 56, 58 n.1, 695 A.2d 1066, 1068 n.1, cert. denied, 241 Conn. 920, 696 A.2d 342 (1997) (failure to raise issue in § 63-4 papers immaterial unless appellee prejudiced). See also ATC Partnership v. Town of Windham, 251 Conn. 597, 610 n.11, 741 A.2d 305, 313 n.11 (1999) (issue considered where it was discussed by trial court). The appellate clerk routinely copies the appellant's statement of issues found in the brief for the appellate record as the statement of issues raised on appeal.

The Appellate Court has confused failure to raise an issue in the trial court with failure to raise it in the § 63-4 papers. Woodburn v. Conservation Com'n of Town of Redding, 37 Conn.App. 166, 176 n.8, 655 A.2d 764, 770 n.8, cert. denied, 233 Conn. 905, 657 A.2d 645 (1995). The former implicates the plain error standards of § 60-5; the latter does not.

On the other hand, whether or not an issue is in the preliminary statement, it clearly should be in the statement of issues in the brief. Elm Street Builders, Inc. v. Enterprise Park Condominium Ass'n, Inc., 63 Conn.App. 657, 659 n.2, 778 A.2d 237, 239 n.2 (2001).

The appellee should take advantage of the broad language of subsection (a)(1); State v. Samuels, 273 Conn. 541, 555, 563 n.13, 871 A.2d 1005, 1015–16, 1020 n.13 (2005); and commentary to § 61-8 concerning when to file a cross appeal. Note that, in the absence of a cross appeal, this section is the only authority for the appellee to bring up a separate issue, DiSesa v. Hickey, 160 Conn. 250, 262–63, 278 A.2d 785, 792 (1971); and the failure of the appellee to file a preliminary statement will probably mean that the appellee cannot raise any question of law if the opponent is prejudiced. Windels v. Environmental Protection Com'n of Town of Darien, 284 Conn. 268, 304, 933 A.2d 256, 278 (2007) (appellee was prejudiced by lack of notice and limited opportunity to respond to complex issues in reply brief); Vertex, Inc. v. City of Waterbury, 278 Conn. 557, 563 n.7, 898 A.2d 178, 184 n.7 (2006); State v. Talton, 209 Conn. 133, 142 n.12, 547 A.2d 543, 548 n.12 (1988) (prejudice not mentioned; judgment directed for appellant). A catchall statement in the state's statement of alternate bases to affirm avoided waiver of its res judicata claim in State v. Martin M., 143 Conn.App. 140, 70 A.3d 135, cert. denied, 309 Conn. 919, 70 A.3d 41 (2013). The court rarely finds prejudice, however. See, e.g., Samnard Associates, LLC v. City of New Britain, 140 Conn.App. 290, 294, 58 A.3d 377, 380 (2013). But when the issue is fully briefed and argued, it will no doubt be decided. Connecticut Ins. Guar. Ass'n v. Fontaine, 278 Conn. 779, 784 n.4, 900 A.2d 18, 19 n.4 (2006); Milliun v. New Milford Hosp., 129 Conn.App. 81, 99 n.13, 20 A.3d 36, 47 n.13 (2011) (issue considered where both sides briefed it). The court will not review an alternate basis, however, that is inadequately briefed. Candlewood Hills Tax Dist. v. Medina, 143 Conn.App. 230, 240 n.5, 74 A.3d 421, 427 n.5, cert. denied, 310 Conn. 929, 78 A.3d 856 (2013).

The appellee's right to file a § 63-4(a)(1) statement has not eliminated the duty to have raised the issue in the trial court. City of New Haven v. Bonner, 272 Conn. 489, 497 n.7, 863 A.2d 680, 685 n.7 (2005). Peck v. Jacquemin, 196 Conn. 53, 62 n.13, 491 A.2d 1043, 1048 n.13 (1985).

If the trial court failed to rule on an issue raised by the appellee in the trial court, the appellee's failure to raise it on appeal may mean that the issue has been abandoned. Karls v. Alexandra Realty Corp., 179 Conn. 390, 393 n.1, 426 A.2d 784, 785 n.1 (1980); McHugh v. McHugh, 181 Conn. 482, 488–91 n.4, 436 A.2d 8, 12–14 n.4 (1980); Cf. Beccia v. City of Waterbury, 192 Conn. 127, 132, 470 A.2d 1202, 1206–07 (1984) (appellee excused for not raising issue on first appeal, where first appeal resulted in new trial). But see State v. Martin, 143 Conn.App. 140, 70 A.3d 135, cert. denied, 309 Conn 919, 70 A.3d 41 (2013) (reviewing state's res judicata claim raised for the first time on appeal). Raising of the general verdict rule now appears to be an exception; Pedersen v. Vahidy, 209 Conn. 510, 516–17, 552 A.2d 419, 422–23 (1989); Cuartas v. Town of Greenwich, 14 Conn.App. 370, 373, 540 A.2d 1071, 1073 (1988); but the appellee should file a statement under this rule to be on the safe side since Hall v. Burns, 213 Conn. 446, 484 n.9, 569 A.2d 10, 31 n.9 (1990), leaves the issues in some doubt. See also Logan v. Greenwich Hosp. Ass'n, 191 Conn. 282, 309, 465 A.2d 294, 308 (1983).

What constitutes an alternate basis to affirm has been discussed in State v. Lynch, 21 Conn.App. 386, 393, 574 A.2d 230, 234, cert. denied, 216 Conn. 806, 580 A.2d 63 (1990). If the alternate issue was not ruled on by the trial court, the issue must be one that the trial court would have been forced to rule in favor of the appellee. Any other test would usurp the trial court's discretion. This comment was cited in Zahringer v. Zahringer, 262 Conn. 360, 371, 815 A.2d 75, 81 (2003), and in Metropolitan Dist. Com'n v. American Federation of State, County and Mun. Employees, Council 4, Local 3713, 35 Conn.App. 804, 805 n.1, 647 A.2d 755, 755 n.1 (1994), aff'd, 237 Conn. 114, 676 A.2d 825 (1996).

The Supreme Court may resolve an appeal on an alternate basis even though the trial court did not rule on it and the appellee did not raise it in its preliminary statement of issues if the issue is a question of law and the material facts are not disputed. Grady v. Town of Somers, 294 Conn. 324, 349 n.28, 984 A.2d 684, 701 n.28 (2009). The issue must have been raised in the trial court, however. Perez-Dickson v. City of Bridgeport, 304 Conn. 483, 499–501, 43 A.3d 69, 84–85 279 Ed. Law Rep. 1015, 114 Fair Empl. Prac. Cas. (BNA) 1461 (2012).

Since 1985, the appellee can file a preliminary statement of issues to claim a new trial where the appellant would otherwise be entitled to a directed judgment. Falby v. Zarembski, 221 Conn. 14, 23 n.7, 602 A.2d 1, 5 n.7 (1992). This change overrules Equitable Life Assur. Soc. of U. S. v. Slade, 122 Conn.

451, 465, 190 A. 616, 622 (1937), which would have required the appellee to fie a cross appeal. However, there are still some situations where a cross appeal is required. See comments to § 61-8. This section also can be used to raise adverse rulings in the event there is to be a new trial. Girard v. Weiss, 43 Conn.App. 397, 399, 682 A.2d 1078, 1080 (1996).

If the appellee files a cross appeal when a § 63-4 statement on the appellant's appeal should have been filed, the cross appeal is often considered as an alternate basis to affirm. Pelletier v. Sordoni/Skanska Const. Co., 286 Conn. 563, 589–90 n.36, 945 A.2d 388, 405 n.36 (2008); see also State v. Preston, 286 Conn. 367, 373 n.4, 944 A.2d 276, 282 n.4 (2008) (appeals by both sides); or as an issue to be considered if the appellant is awarded a new trial, Kortner v. Martise, 312 Conn. 1, 59 n.17, 91 A.3d 412, 446 n.17 (2014).

In Cadle Co. v. D'Addario, 268 Conn. 441, 844 A.2d 836 (2004), the Supreme Court dismissed the defendants' appeal because they were not aggrieved but then treated the issues raised in their appeal as an alternate basis to affirm on the plaintiff's appeal.

In Finley v. Inland Wetlands Com'n of Town of Orange, 289 Conn. 12, 18 n.7, 959 A.2d 569, 575 n.7 (2008), the court excused the failure to file a cross appeal and treated the issue as an alternate basis to affirm because the appellant had notice of the claim and was not prejudiced.

The Court may overlook the absence of a cross appeal or § 63-4 statement by the appellee in certain cases, such as where there is no prejudice to the appellant, DiGiovanna v. St. George, 300 Conn. 59, 70, 12 A.3d 900, 907 (2011); Culver v. Culver, 127 Conn.App. 236, 253, 17 A.3d 1048, 1059, cert. denid, 301 Conn. 929, 23 A.3d 724 (2011); Simone v. Miller, 91 Conn.App. 98, 108 n.3, 881 A.2d 397, 404 n.3 (2005); or where the public interest is involved, Peterson v. City of Norwalk, 150 Conn. 366, 382, 190 A.2d 33, 40–41 (1963); or where the issue has been fully briefed and argued; Connecticut Ins. Guar. Ass'n v. Fontaine, 278 Conn. 779, 784 n.4, 900 A.2d 18, 19 n.4 (2006); D'Arcy v. Shugrue, 5 Conn.App. 12, 28, 496 A.2d 967, 975 (1985); Beechwood Gardens Tenants' Ass'n v. Department of Housing, 214 Conn. 505, 509 n.4, 572 A.2d 989, 991 n.4 (1990); or where review of the issue is plenary. Achillion Pharmaceuticals, Inc. v. Law, 291 Conn. 525, 528 n.5, 970 A.2d 57, 59 n.5 (2009). There may also be instances where a judgment will be sustained although entered for the wrong reason, W. J. Megin, Inc. v. State, 181 Conn. 47, 434 A.2d 306 (1980); Kowal v. Hofher, 181 Conn. 355, 359, 436 A.2d 1, 3 (1980). It helps if the alternate ground is related to the trial court's ground, Vasquez v. State, 181 Conn. 130, 434 A.2d 330 (1980). Nevertheless, if the trial court has decided any issue of law adverse to the appellee or has failed to decide an issue of law, a § 63-4(a)(1) statement or a cross appeal under § 61-8 should be filed, for otherwise the Supreme Court may not consider the issue, as in City Council of City of West Haven v. Hall, 180 Conn. 243, 247 n.5, 429 A.2d 481, 483 n.5 (1980); even if the issue would give the reviewing court an alternate basis on which to affirm, State v. Santiago, 8 Conn.App. 290, 306, 513 A.2d 710, 718 (1986). The amendment to § (a)(1) in 1986 has been read by a majority of the Appellate Court to loosen rather than tighten the requirements on the ground that the opponent can always file a reply brief. Cristofaro v. Planning and Zoning Com'n of Town of Burlington, 11 Conn.App. 260, 262 n.4, 527 A.2d 255, 256 n.4, cert. denied, 204 Conn. 810, 528 A.2d 1156 (1987). The authors agree with the dissenting opinion by Judge Bieluch.

If the appellant prevails on the appeal and there are further proceedings, the appellee's failure to raise an issue may not constitute forfeiture in certain circumstances. See Harris v. Bradley Memorial Hosp. and Health Center, Inc., 306 Conn. 304, 316-27. 50 A.3d 841(2012).

Make sure the judgment file refers to all rulings on pleadings which are the subjects of the appeal, for otherwise the Supreme Court will not consider them. Gonirenki v. American Steel & Wire Co., 106 Conn. 1, 3, 137 A. 26, 27 (1927).

If a preliminary issue is not briefed, it is abandoned, State v. Samaha, 180 Conn. 565 n.1, 430 A.2d 1290, 1291 n.1 (1980).

The Appellate Court should not decide a non-jurisdictional issue the parties have not raised, unless the court gives notice to the parties and an opportunity to brief the issue. Sequenzia v. Guerrieri Masonry Inc., 298 Conn. 816, 9 A.3d 322 (2010).

(a)(2) [(a)(3) before July 1, 2013]

For appeals filed after July 1, 2013, the designation of pleadings under old § (a)(2) has been eliminated, and § (a)(3), which was the transcript provision, has now been moved here. A motion to amend the transcript (order form) was granted in Sanborn v. Greenwald, 39 Conn.App. 289, 290 n.1, 664 A.2d 803, 805 n.1 (1995).

The failure to order transcripts can be fatal to a claim that the trial court improperly admitted certain evidence. Wasilewski v. Machuga, 92 Conn.App. 341, 885 A.2d 216 (2005). However, in LeBlanc v. Tri-Town Shelter Services, Inc., 110 Conn.App. 118, 120, 955 A.2d 55 (2008), the appeal was decided without any transcripts because the facts were largely undisputed.

In State v. Adams, 117 Conn.App. 747, 749 n.2, 982 A.2d 187, 188 n.2 (2009), the court granted a pro se defendant's request to take judicial notice of transcripts in his appendix where he failed to designate transcripts pursuant to this subsection. The authors do not recommend trying this tactic.

In Cunniffe v. Cunniffe, 150 Conn.App. 419, 423 n.5, 91 A.3d 497, 503 n.5, cert. denied, 314 Conn. ___, ___ A.3d ___ (2014), the failure to designate transcripts was not fatal where they were made part of the record by the court or as an exhibit.

(a)(3) [(a)(4) before July 1, 2013]

The information provided in the docketing statement assists the appellate clerk in administrating the appeal and also alerts the judges of the Appellate Court and justices of the Supreme Court to conflicts.

The Supreme Court rejected the appellee's argument that the failure to file a docketing statement should preclude review. Monk v. Temple George Associates, LLC, 273 Conn. 108, 122, 869 A.2d 179, 189 (2005).

Listing all parties may save a failure to list a party in the jurisdictional statement on appeal. Brown v. Soh, 280 Conn. 494, 496 n.2, 909 A.2d 43, 45 n.2 (2006).

(a)(4) [(a)(5) before July 1, 2013]

The preargument conference form contains two questions that require careful consideration: whether you want to transfer the case to the Supreme Court and whether you would be willing to waive oral argument. If you want to be in the Supreme Court, check the "yes" box and be prepared to explain to the preargument conference judge why the case warrants the Supreme Court's attention. The conference judge can recommend transfer, which while not binding is helpful.

As for waiving oral argument, the authors advise against it because the reversal rate on cases submitted on briefs is less than half of the rate for those that are argued.

(a)(5) [(a)(6) before July 1, 2013]

See authors' comments to P.B. §§ 6-2 to 6-4 in Horton & Knox, Connecticut Practice Series, Connecticut Superior Court Civil Rules (2009 ed.), for drafting judgment files. The appellate clerk will forward the draft judgment to the trial court clerk, who will review and make changes. Therefore, it is advisable to keep the draft judgment file in your word processing system until the record is filed. If there is some problem in preparing the judgment file, be sure to keep the appellate clerk informed of what is being done to solve it.

While the rule is silent, the authors believe that no draft judgment file is required in workers' compensation cases.

(a)(7) [(a)(8) before July 1, 2013]

The appellate clerk needs to be aware of any sealing orders, including if the file is sealed. Although there should be documentation in the court file, this is not always the case, especially where particular documents are sealed during trial and the only order is oral. In that case, provide a copy of the transcript pronouncing the order or, if this is not available, write a letter to the chief clerk.

(b)

Section (b) is very liberal in allowing amendments as of right until your brief is filed (except for the transcript statement). See (apparently) Skuzinski v. Bouchard Fuels, Inc., 240 Conn. 694, 702 n.6, 694 A.2d 788, 793 n.6 (1997). An untimely amendment can be requested after the brief is filed, but this will annoy the Supreme Court even if the Court grants the motion. Cf. Union Trust Co. v. Stamford Trust Co., 72 Conn. 86, 95, 43 A. 555, 559 (1899) (motion after briefs and record prepared). Be sure to file an original and fifteen copies of any motion under (b). The one document that should not be amended is the draft judgment file. If amendments need to be made, the authors advise sending it directly to the trial clerk.

§ 63-5. Fees

At the time of filing the appeal, the appellant, or one of the appellants, shall, unless the appeal is taken by the state, or the costs have been waived pursuant to Section 63-6 or 63-7, pay to the clerk of the trial court the fees provided by statute. Security for costs is not required to take an appeal, but security may at any time, on motion and notice to the appellant, be ordered by the court. Such security shall be filed with the trial court.

Historical Note

Derivation:
     1978 P.B. (1986–97), § 4015
     1978 P.B., § 3014
     1963 P.B., § 602
     1951 P.B., § 379
     1934 P.B., § 335
     1930 Rule Changes, § 2

This section was amended effective October 1, 1986 to exclude appeals taken by the state, and on May 10, 1988 to reduce the security for costs from $500 to $300. The security was raised to $400 effective October 1, 1992 and eliminated in 1996.

This rule was clarified effective January 1, 1985 to eliminate ambiguities in the form of recognizance.

This rule was rewritten effective July 1, 1978. The security was raised from $150 to $500, the language as to who should be recognized for security was simplified, and the language about the appeal being "void and of no effect" in certain circumstances (which was fatal in The State v. Pallotti, 119 Conn. 70,

74, 174 A. 74, 76 (1934)) has been omitted.

Previously the rule was unchanged since 1963, except that the penultimate sentence was added to be effective October 1, 1976, and there were only minor changes from 1943 to 1963. Prior to 1943, a motion for extension of time to file the appeal, bond or recognizance, and fees could be granted even if the motion was filed after the appeal period had run out. This change is discussed in State ex rel. Baskin v. Bartlett, 132 Conn. 623, 624, 46 A.2d 335, 336 (1946).

Cross References

Form 3001

Maltbie, Conn.App.Proc.2d, § 120

AUTHORS' COMMENTS

1. Fees

When the appeal is filed, the appellant must pay to the trial clerk (fees may change; check with the clerk or on the Judicial Branch website when filing the appeal):

Entry fee of $250.00 in the Appellate Court or the Supreme Court. C.G.S.A. § 52-259.

The Supreme Court record fee (C.G.S.A. § 52-269) was abolished in 1991 by P.A. 91-3, § 167 (June Session); the Appellate Court record fee (C.G.S.A. § 52-259) was abolished in 1994 by P.A. 94-135, § 3.

2. Security

The appellant no longer must automatically post security of $400 in either the Appellate Court or in the Supreme Court. However, security is required in summary process cases under C.G.S.A. § 47a-35a.

If a fee or, if ordered, security is not paid or posted at the proper time, the appeal may be vulnerable to dismissal, Jensen v. Nationwide Mut. Ins. Co., 147 Conn. 722, 723, 161 A.2d 785, 786–87 (1960); Palmer v. Des Reis, 135 Conn. 388, 389, 64 A.2d 537, 538 (1949); although an older case held to the contrary, General Hospital Soc. v. New Haven Rendering Co., 79 Conn. 581, 582, 65 A. 1065, 1066 (1907). However, even in spite of the language of old § 602, the appeal is not "void", but only "voidable," and thus the appellee must file a motion to dismiss within ten days, see the *Palmer* case; Ives v. Finch, 22 Conn. 101, 1852 WL 667 (1852). In light of the rule change in 1978 to eliminate the "void and of no effect" language, the authors' opinion is that *Jensen* and *Palmer* no longer require dismissal if a motion to dismiss is timely filed. Rather the court now has discretion to permit the late filing of security.

If security is ordered to be posted and a recognizance is proper, the authors recommend that the recognizance in unofficial Form 3000.3-A be used. It is simpler than formerly official Forms 3000.3, 3000.4 and 3000.5 and appears to be permitted in Jensen v. Nationwide Mut. Ins. Co., 147 Conn. 722, 726, 161 A.2d 785, 788 (1960), which also holds that a recognizance is defective if it names a specific appellee for protection, but fails to name another one. This problem is avoided by our modified form, which does not mention a specific appellee. See Fogelson v. Fogelson, 39 Conn.Supp. 63, 65, 467 A.2d 1272, 1273 (1983).

If the trial court orders an improper appeal bond the order should be reviewed under § 66-6 rather than on the merits of the appeal. Hartford Federal Sav. & Loan Ass'n v. Tucker, 192 Conn. 1, 8, 469 A.2d 778, 782 (1984).

While there is no case on point the authors are of the opinion, based on the context, that the only security this section refers to is security for costs, not for the underlying judgment. The rule in the older editions of the Practice Book tend to support the authors' opinion, as they go into great detail about security *for costs*. The official commentary to the 1996 amendment abolishing automatic security for costs gives no indication that the definition of "security" is being broadened.

§ 63-6. Waiver of Fees, Costs and Security—Civil Cases

If a party in any case where fees and costs may lawfully be waived is indigent and desires to appeal, that party may, within the time provided by the rules for taking an appeal, make written application, to the court to which the fees required by statute or rule are to be paid, for relief from payment of fees, costs and expenses. The application must be under oath and recite, or it must be accompanied by an affidavit reciting, the grounds upon which the applicant proposes to appeal and the facts concerning the applicant's financial status. Where an application arises out of a habeas corpus proceeding, the application shall be handled pursuant to Section 63-7. Where an application arises out of a child protection matter, the application shall be handled pursuant to Section 79a-4.

The judicial authority shall act promptly on the application for waiver of fees, costs and expenses, if the application is denied in whole or in part, and the applicant wishes to challenge that denial, the applicant shall file a written request for a hearing, pursuant to Section 8-2 within ten days of the issuance of notice of the denial of the application. The court clerk shall assign the application for a hearing within twenty days of the filing of the request and the judicial authority shall act promptly on the application following the hearing.

If the court is satisfied that the applicant is indigent and has a statutory or constitutional right to court appointed counsel or a statutory right to appeal without payment of fees, costs and expenses, the court may (1) waive payment by the applicant of fees specified by statute and of taxable costs, and waive the requirement of Section 63-5 concerning the furnishing of security for costs upon appeal, and (2) order that the necessary expenses of prosecuting the appeal be paid by the state. The court may not consider the relative merits of a proposed appeal in acting upon an application pursuant to this section except that the court may consider the criteria contained in General Statutes § 52-259b.

Before incurring any expense in excess of $100, including the expense of obtaining a transcript of the necessary proceedings or testimony, the applicant shall obtain the permission of the judge who presided at the applicant's trial. The judge shall authorize a transcript at state expense only of the portions of testimony or proceedings which may be pertinent to the issues on appeal.

The sole remedy of any party desiring the court to review an order concerning the waiver of fees, costs and security shall be by motion for review under Section 66-6.

Historical Note

Derivation:
  1978 P.B. (1986–97), § 4017
  1978 P.B., § 3016

Effective September 1, 2014 this section was amended to bring it into compliance with C.G.S. § 52-259b(c).

The third paragraph was revised effective January 1, 2006 to amend the first sentence and to add the last one.

The last paragraph was added effective January 1, 2000.

The second paragraph and the test for entitlement to an appeal in the third paragraph were added effective October 1, 1986. This rule is entirely new effective July 1, 1978. Previously there was no rule permitting waiver of fees in civil cases. In general they were not waivable, Appeal of Dattilo, 135 Conn. 411, 65 A.2d 262 (1949).

Cross References

P.B. § 63-7 and commentary

AUTHORS' COMMENTS

The pre-1978 waiver rule, § 603, referred only to criminal cases, but there was some indication that it applied to certain civil cases. Cooper v. Matzkin, 160 Conn. 334, 340, 278 A.2d 811, 814 (1971), criticized the use of the rule for "unfounded, collateral, civil legal excursions", but left the question open as to non-frivolous appeals. Boddie v. Connecticut, 401 U.S. 371, 91 S. Ct. 780, 28 L. Ed. 2d 113 (1971), held that those desiring divorces need not pay certain trial fees if they are unable to do so, but Robertson v. Apuzzo, 170 Conn. 367, 377-80, 365 A.2d 824, 831-32 (1976), refused to extend *Boddie* to paternity actions. But see Little v. Streater, 452 U.S. 1, 101 S. Ct. 2202, 68 L. Ed. 2d 627 (1981), and Lavertue v. Niman, 196 Conn. 403, 493 A.2d 213 (1985).

The language "is entitled to an appeal" has been construed to mean that the trial court cannot consider the merits of the appeal. In re Jeisean M., 74 Conn.App. 233, 812 A.2d 80 (2002). This rule explicitly so states since 2006. A § 63-6 application was denied based on the applicant's failure to provide an affidavit and other conduct constituting a failure to pursue the appeal in good faith in In the In re Oliver B., 1994 WL 478733 (Conn. Super. Ct. 1994).

One judge has held that the opposing party does not have standing to contest a § 63-6 application; it is a matter solely between the applicant and the court. Ferris v. Clark, 13 Conn. L. Rptr. 134, 1994 WL 702655 (Conn. Super. Ct. 1994).

Small v. State, 101 Conn.App. 213, 218, 920 A.2d 1024, 1026 (2007), has listed various statutes applicable to this situation, such as C.G.S.A. §§ 17a-498, 19a-221, 45a-717(b), 46b-135(b), and 51-296(a).

Note that the sole means to challenge a denial of a motion to provide the transcripts without charge is a motion to review pursuant to P.B. § 66-6. Traylor v. Awwa, 2011 WL 1886490 (Conn. Super. Ct. 2011).

§ 63-7. Waiver of Fees, Costs and Security—Criminal Cases

Any defendant in a criminal case who is indigent and desires to appeal, and has not previously been determined to be indigent, may, within the time provided by the rules for taking an appeal, make written application to the court to which the fees required by statute or rule are to be paid, for relief from payment of fees, costs and expenses. The application must be under oath and recite, or it must be accompanied by an affidavit reciting, the grounds upon which the applicant proposes to appeal and the facts concerning the applicant's financial status.

The application must be sent to the public defender's office for investigation. The judicial authority shall assign the request for waiver of fees, costs and expenses for hearing within twenty days after filing, and the trial counsel, the trial public defender's office to which the application had been sent for investigation and the chief of legal services of the public defender's office shall be notified in writing by the clerk's office of the date of such hearing.

The judicial authority shall act promptly on the application following the hearing. Upon determination by the judicial authority that a defendant in a criminal case is indigent, the court to which the fees required by statute or rule are to be paid may (1) waive payment by the defendant of fees specified by statute and of taxable costs, and waive the requirement of Section 63-5 concerning the furnishing of security for costs upon appeal, (2) order that the necessary expenses of prosecuting the appeal be paid by the state, and (3) appoint appellate counsel and permit the withdrawal of the trial attorney's appearance provided the judicial authority is satisfied that that attorney has cooperated fully with appellate counsel in the preparation of the defendant's appeal as set forth in Section 43-33.

When the judicial authority has appointed an attorney in private practice to represent the defendant upon appeal, the attorney shall obtain the approval of the judicial authority who presided at the trial before incurring any expense in excess of $100, including the expense of obtaining a transcript of the necessary proceedings or testimony. The judicial authority shall authorize a transcript at state expense only of the portions of proceedings or testimony which may be pertinent to the issues on appeal.

The sole remedy of any defendant desiring the court to review an order concerning the waiver of fees, costs and security or the appointment of counsel shall be by motion for review under Section 66-6.

Historical Note

Derivation:
    1978 P.B. (1986–97), § 4018
    1978 P.B., § 3017
    1963 P.B., § 603
    1951 P.B., § 379A

The last paragraph was added effective January 1, 2000.

The reference to P.B. § 43-33 at the end of the third paragraph was added effective September 3, 1996.

The first two paragraphs and the first sentence and item (3) in the third paragraph were added effective October 1, 1986. The rule was rewritten effective July 1, 1978. The only major change is that since 1978 indigency will initially be determined by the public defender's office rather than by the court. Previously, this rule was amended effective September 1, 1970 to change "that the proposed appeal would not be frivolous" to "the applicant is entitled to an appeal", and amended effective October 1, 1972 to add, subject to certain limitations, the following powers to the trial court:

"(2) to appoint counsel to prosecute the appeal without expense to him, and

(3) order that the necessary expenses of presenting the appeal be paid by the State."

This rule was first adopted effective October 15, 1962.

AUTHORS' COMMENTS

Although fees, costs and security may be waived in a criminal case if there is an affidavit as to indigency, the appellant should nevertheless be prepared to present testimony if there is any question about the motion being granted. The reason for this is that in the past the Supreme Court would not review the denial of a motion for waiver in the absence of a finding, State v. Hudson, 154 Conn. 631, 632–633, 228 A.2d 132, 133–134 (1967).

The penultimate paragraph authorizes the indigent to receive the pertinent portions of the transcript. Presumably the court's ruling on what is pertinent can be reviewed under § 66-6. In State v. Clark, 4 Conn. Cir. Ct. 570, 237 A.2d 105 (App. Div. 1967), the Appellate Division of the Circuit Court held that it was illogical to deny waiver of all transcript costs.

The court refused to review a claim on appeal regarding appointment of counsel, following the last sentence of this rule in State v. Jimenez, 127 Conn.App. 706, 14 A.3d 1083 (2011), and State v. Casiano, 122 Conn.App. 61, 998 A.2d 792, cert. denied, 298 Conn. 931, 5 A.3d 491 (2010).

Review of a § 63-7 order is *only* by a § 66-6 motion, not by appeal. State v. Lanasa, 141 Conn.App. 685, 687 n.1,62 A.3d 572, 574 n.1, cert. denied, 308 Conn. 945, 66 A.3d 885 (2013).

This section applies only to the appointment of appellate, not trial, counsel. State v. Francis, 148 Conn.App. 565, 574-75, 86 A.3d 1059, 1064, cert. denied, 314 Conn. ____, ____ A.3d ____ (2014).

§ 63-8. Ordering and Filing of Transcripts

(a) On or before the date of the filing of the Section 63-4 papers, the appellant shall, subject to Section 63-6 or 63-7 if applicable, order, using Form JD-ES-38, from the official reporter a transcript and an electronic version of a transcript of the parts of the proceedings not already on file which the appellant deems necessary for the proper presentation of the appeal. Such order shall specify the case name, docket number, judge's name(s), and hearing date(s), and include a detailed statement describing the parts of the proceedings of which a transcript has been ordered, for example, "the voir dire on Monday, May 25, 1995," or "the entire sentencing proceeding before Smith, J., on June 4, 1995." If any other party deems other parts of the transcript necessary, that party shall, within twenty days from the filing of the appellant's transcript papers, similarly order those parts, and an electronic version of those parts, in writing from the official reporter.

(b) A party must make satisfactory arrangements for payment of the costs of the transcript, pursuant to guidelines established by the chief court administrator. After those arrangements have been made, the official reporter shall send the party who ordered the transcript a written acknowledgment of the order, including an estimate of the date of delivery of, and the number of pages in, the transcript. The ordering party shall file it forthwith with the appellate clerk with certification pursuant to Section 62-7 to all counsel of record. The official reporter shall also immediately send copies of the acknowledgment to the chief court administrator and the appellate clerk. If the final portion of the transcript cannot be delivered on or before the estimated delivery date on the acknowledgment, the official reporter will, not later than the next business day, issue to the ordering party an amended transcript order acknowledgment form (JD-ES-38A) with a revised estimated delivery date and shall also immediately send copies of the amended acknowledgment form to the chief court administrator and the appellate clerk. The ordering party shall file the amended acknowledgment form forthwith with the appellate clerk with certification pursuant to Section 62-7 to all counsel of record.

(c) The official reporter shall cause each court reporter involved in the production of the transcript to prepare a certificate of delivery stating the number of pages in the transcript and the date of its delivery to the party who ordered it, and a certificate stating that an electronic version of the transcript has been produced and delivered in accordance with Section 63-8A. If delivery is by mail, the transcript, including the electronic version of the transcript, shall be mailed first class certified, return receipt requested. The date of mailing is the date of delivery. If delivery is manual, the court reporter shall obtain a receipt acknowledging delivery. The date of the receipt is the date of delivery. Each court reporter shall forward the certificates of delivery to the official reporter with a copy to the chief court administrator. Upon receipt of all the certificates of delivery, the official reporter shall forward to the appellate clerk, with copies to the chief court administrator and the party who ordered the transcript, including an electronic transcript, a certificate of completion stating the total number of pages in the entire transcript and the date of final delivery of the transcript.

(d) Upon receipt of the certificate of completion from the official reporter, counsel who ordered the transcript shall file a certification that a paper copy of the certificate of completion has been sent to all counsel of record in accordance with Section 62-7.

(e) (1) The appellant is required, either before or simultaneously with the filing of the appellant's brief, to file with the appellate clerk one unmarked, nonreturnable copy of the transcript, including a copy of the court reporter's certification page, ordered pursuant to subsection (a).

(2) All other parties are likewise required, either before or simultaneously with the filing of their briefs, to file those additional portions ordered pursuant to subsection (a) but shall not include the portions already filed by the appellant.

(3) The party filing the transcript shall provide the appellate clerk and all opposing counsel with a list of the number, and inclusive dates, of the volumes being filed. Form JD-CL-62, or one similar to it, should be used to satisfy this subsection.

Historical Note

Derivation:
    1978 P.B. (1986–97), § 4019
    1978 P.B., § 3018

The first line of (a) was amended effective January 1, 2013 to make it clear that the transcript order is due the date the § 63-4 papers are filed, not the date the appeal is filed.

Amendments effective January 1, 1996 and November 1, 2002 concern what payment arrangements are "satisfactory" and how to handle the ordering of electronic versions of the transcript.

Effective March 6, 1989, this rule was amended to require that the transcript be ordered from the official court reporter, not from the reporter who actually handled the trial. Now the official court reporter sends out a certificate of completion after receiving all of the transcript completion forms from the individual court reporters.

Effective January 1, 1985, § (b) was clarified to require the reporter to include the dates of the proceedings being transcribed; § (c) was amended to require counsel to send a copy of the certificate of completion of the transcript to all counsel of record.

The beginning of subsection (b) was added effective October 1, 1982. Basically this is a new rule effective July 1, 1978, although it bears a vague resemblance to old § 608A.

AUTHORS' COMMENTS

The timing for filing briefs is governed by § 67-3. The transcript must be filed at the same time. Since the time for filing the appellant's brief does not start to run until the transcript is sent to counsel by the court reporter, it is not necessary to file a motion for extension of time to file the brief or transcript when the appeal is filed. The time for filing the appellant's brief starts to run when the reporter mails the last ordered transcript to counsel, not when counsel receives it. Counsel therefore should arrange for the last transcript to be hand-delivered and for any previously typed transcripts to be delivered as soon as they are finished so that counsel will have as much time as possible to prepare the brief.

Note that the court reporter does not send the transcript to the Supreme Court or Appellate Court; it goes to ordering counsel, whose duty it is when all the transcript are received to send opposing counsel a copy of the 8½" by 11" certificate by the chief court reporter of completion of the transcript, to file a certification with the clerk that the certificate of completion was sent to opposing counsel, and, when filing the brief, to file the transcript. It is not necessary for counsel to file in court or send to other counsel the small (5½" by 8½") transcript delivery certificate received from the individual court reporters who actually prepared the transcript. Note also that counsel does not have to send a copy of the transcript to opposing counsel.

The court reporter will send the electronic version of the transcripts to the court with a copy on disc to the ordering party. Note, however, that the pagination of the electronic version does not always correspond to the printed version. Use the pagination from the printed version for your brief.

Failure to file a transcript where factual or procedural claims are made is likely to be fatal, Creative Masonry & Chimney, LLC v. Johnson, 142 Conn.App. 135, 139–40, 64 A.3d 359, 363, cert. denied, 309 Conn. 903, 68 A.3d 658 (2013); McGaffin v. Roberts, 193 Conn. 393, 399 n.6, 479 A.2d 176, 179 n.6 (1984); see also Buggy v. Buggy, 141 Conn.App. 733, 64 A.3d 778 (2013) (self-represented party failed to file transcripts even after court ordered her to do so). Likewise, a failure to file a transcript of *all* relevant hearings may be fatal, Duart v. Department of Correction, 303 Conn. 479, 495, 34 A.3d 343, 352, 114 Fair Empl. Prac. Cas. (BNA) 363 (2012); Quaranta v. King, 133 Conn.App. 565, 569–71, 36 A.3d 264, 267–69 (2012); Stutz v. Shepard, 279 Conn. 115, 901 A.2d 33 (2006); Calo-Turner v. Turner, 83 Conn.App. 53, 56, 847 A.2d 1085, 1086–87 (2004). Cf. Gilhuly v. Karazulas, 4 Conn.App. 440, 495 A.2d 1077 (1985), where the appellant failed to have the final arguments recorded. It is the appellant's burden to see that there is a proper record for appellate review. And failure to file transcripts with the appellant's brief may lead to their being stricken as untimely filed, which may result in the appeal being lost. Rice v. Housing Authority of City of Meriden, 129 Conn.App. 614, 20 A.3d 1270 (2011); Taylor v. American Thread Co., 200 Conn. 108, 509 A.2d 512 (1986); State v. Mitchell, 8 Conn.App. 598, 605, 513 A.2d 1268, 1272 (1986). The court reviewed the electronic transcript where the pro se litigant failed to file a paper version in Manzi v. Manzi, 134 Conn.App. 333, 38 A.3d 1247 (2012); see also Norton v. Commissioner of Correction, 132 Conn.App. 850, 33 A.3d 819, cert. denied, 303 Conn. 936, 36 A.3d 695 (2012). The authors do not recommend relying on these cases.

Subsection (a) states the detailed information that must be on the order form. In the *Creative Masonry* case, the appellant just requested "trial and short calendar proceedings," resulting in no transcript being prepared. The issue was not reviewed on appeal.

Do not count on the last sentence of § (a) to save an appellant who has failed to order adequate transcripts to provide appellate review. See § 61-10; State v. Spillane, 255 Conn. 746, 760 n.10, 770 A.2d 898, 907 n.10 (2001).

The Supreme Court will not consult an uncertified transcript, Ravitch v. Stollman Poultry Farms, Inc., 165 Conn. 135, 144 n.6, 328 A.2d 711, 716 n.6 (1973), although the Appellate Division of the Circuit Court held that proper certification may be waived, State v. Tode, 1 Conn. Cir. Ct. 308, 312, 23 Conn.Supp. 454, 457–58, 184 A.2d 549, 551 (App. Div. 1962). The failure to file a certified transcript may be fatal, Cocchia v. Paul, 33 Conn.Supp. 730, 732, 369 A.2d 257, 258 (App. Sess. 1976). Note that the trial judge's signature is no longer needed on the transcript, except where such a transcript constitutes the memorandum of decision. See § 64-1. However, if the transcript is inaccurate the trial judge has the right to correct it, Whiteside v. State, 148 Conn. 77, 81–83, 167 A.2d 450, 453–54 (1961). See § 66-5. Certification of the transcript carries with it the certification of the exhibits, Goldblatt v. Ferrigno, 138 Conn. 39, 42, 82 A.2d 152, 154 (1951), although that was decided at a time when the trial judge had to sign the transcript.

If you are reading a transcript but were not at the hearing, it is a good idea to have trial counsel review it for accuracy.

If testimony was not recorded, obviously one cannot obtain a transcript, and this oversight may be fatal. State v. Ridley, 7 Conn.App. 503, 505, 509 A.2d 546, 548 (1986). This may be a problem with sidebar and chambers conferences, final arguments, and voir dire proceedings. Sometimes the testimony can be reconstructed without a transcript; § 66-5 is a possible source of relief.

If the proceedings were recorded but the reporter's notes cannot be transcribed or reconstructed, and if the claim of error cannot be properly reviewed, a new trial may be ordered. C.G.S.A. § 52-268; State v. Aquart, 69 Conn.App. 21, 793 A.2d 1185, cert. denied, 260 Conn. 926, 797 A.2d 521 (2002). However, in State v. Furbush, 131 Conn.App. 733, 27 A.3d 497 (2011), the missing transcript was successfully reconstructed (over the defendant's objection) from various sources, including his own counsel's notes.

Be sure to file the transcripts with your briefs. Make sure any comments you may have written on the margins of the transcripts are removed. See National Pub. Co., Inc. v. Hartford Fire Ins. Co., 94 Conn.App. 234, 237 n.2, 892 A.2d 261, 266 n.2 (2006), judgment rev'd on other grounds, 287 Conn. 664, 949 A.2d 1203 (2008). However, the authors recommend that, whenever a large number of transcripts are filed, especially when there are multiple volumes on the same day, they be numbered chronologically for easy reference in the briefs. The appellate clerk does not object to counsel's typing a volume number on the cover of each transcript.

§ 63-8A. Electronic Copies of Transcripts

(a) Any party ordering a transcript of evidence as part of an appeal, a writ of error, or a motion for review shall, at the same time, order from the court reporter an electronic version of the transcript. If the party already has the transcript to be submitted to the court, the party shall order an electronic version of the transcript within the period specified by these rules for the ordering of a transcript.

(b) Whenever an electronic transcript is ordered in accordance with this section, the court reporter shall produce, on disks provided by the official court reporter, an electronic version of the transcript in Rich Text File (rtf) format.

(c) The court reporter shall file a disk containing the electronic version of the transcript with the appropriate court and with the ordering party, together with a certification that the electronic version of the transcript is accurate and a certificate of delivery.

(d) The electronic version of the transcript shall be filed with the court and delivered to the ordering party at the same time as the paper copy is delivered to the ordering party, provided that if only an electronic version of the transcript is ordered, the electronic version shall be filed and delivered within ten days of its order unless a different time period is specified by the court.

Historical Note

New rule in 2002.

AUTHORS' COMMENTS

Failure to file the electronic version of the transcripts may be fatal. Rice v. Housing Authority of City of Meriden, 129 Conn.App. 614, 20 A.3d 1270 (2011).

The court in Manzi v. Manzi, 134 Conn.App. 333, 38 A.3d 1247 (2012), and Norton v. Commissioner of Correction, 132 Conn.App. 850, 33 A.3d 819, cert. denied, 303 Conn. 936, 36 A.3d 695 (2012), reviewed electronic transcripts where the paper version was not filed. The authors do not recommend reliance on these cases.

§ 63-9. Filing Withdrawals of Appeals or Writs of Error

A withdrawal of an appeal or writ of error shall be filed with the appellate clerk, who shall send a copy to the trial judge and the clerk of the trial court.

Prior to oral argument, an appeal or writ of error may be withdrawn as of right; thereafter it may be withdrawn only on motion to the court in which the appeal is pending.

Unless an appeal or writ of error is withdrawn on the consent of the appellee without costs, costs shall be taxed as if the trial court judgment had been affirmed.

Historical Note

Derivation:
    1978 P.B. (1986–97), § 4038
Derivation (First Paragraph):
    1978 P.B., § 3075
    1963 P.B., § 709
    1951 P.B., § 439
Derivation (Third Paragraph):
    1978 P.B., § 3130
    1963 P.B., § 734
    1951 P.B., § 463
    1934 P.B., §§ 412, 413
    1922 P.B., §§ 61, 62
    1908 P.B., §§ 59, 60
    1899 P.B., §§ 59, 60

The first paragraph is substantially unchanged since it was adopted in 1951.

The second paragraph is new in 1986.

The third paragraph simplifies old § 3130 in 1986. Previously that rule stated:

"If an appeal or writ of error is dismissed, or if an appellant or plaintiff in error withdraws the appeal, the appellee or defendant in error is entitled to a judgment of the supreme court affirming the judgment of the lower court, with costs, to be entered pro forma by the chief clerk of the supreme court upon the filing of a written request therefor."

The prior rule was substantially unchanged since it was adopted in 1899.

AUTHORS' COMMENTS

This rule is subject to the caveat that appellate costs are not taxable if the appeal is dismissed for lack of jurisdiction, Connecticut Light and Power Co. v. Costle, 179 Conn. 415, 424, 426 A.2d 1324, 1329 (1980). If *Costle* does not apply, see the table of appellate costs in § 71-3. Trial court costs should be taxed by the trial court clerk under § 18-5.

In one case the appellee conditionally withdrew his cross appeal if the Supreme Court affirmed on the appeal. Carlino v. City of Meriden, 132 Conn. 394, 396, 44 A.2d 823, 824 (1945). See also Coble v. Maloney, 34 Conn.App. 655, 657 n.4, 643 A.2d 277, 279 n.4 (1994).

With the 1986 change in this rule, the chief clerk no longer has authority to enter a judgment affirming the lower court judgment if the appeal is dismissed or withdrawn. The author's opinion is that the clerk still can prepare a judgment file showing what did happen on the appeal, such as that the appeal was withdrawn or dismissed. Costs should also still be taxable if otherwise permitted. See P.B. § 71-2.

A statute that prohibits the settlement of zoning appeals without court approval only applies to appeals pending in the Superior Court, not in higher courts. Levine v. Town Plan and Zoning Com'n of Fairfield, 25 Conn.App. 199, 203 n.1, 594 A.2d 9, 11 n.1 (1991).

The appellate courts may well grant a motion to withdraw an appeal after oral argument if the opinion has not been sent to the printer. See *Travelers Indemnity Co. v. Tishman Realty & Construction Co. Inc., S.C. 15443* (withdrawal approved almost two months after oral argument).

An alternative to a § 63-9 motion, which is discretionary, is a motion to dismiss for lack of jurisdiction on the ground that the appeal has been settled and is therefore moot. Such a motion was granted in Downes-Patterson Corp. v. First National Supermarkets, 258 Conn. 917, 782 A.2d 1242 (2001).

If litigants settle a case after oral argument and fail to tell the appellate tribunal, the litigants will be estopped to claim the benefit of the subsequent appellate decision. Waterbury Twin, LLC v. Renal Treatment Centers-Northeast, Inc., 49 Conn. L. Rptr. 848, 2010 WL 1999072 (Conn. Super. Ct. 2010).

§ 63-10. Preargument Conferences

The chief justice or the chief judge or a designee may, in cases deemed appropriate, direct that conferences of the parties be scheduled in advance of oral argument. All civil cases are eligible for preargument conferences except habeas corpus appeals; appeals where a party is self-represented; appeals involving juveniles, such as delinquency and termination of parental rights cases; and appeals from the suspension of a motor vehicle license due to operating under the influence of liquor or drugs. A party in an exempt case may request a preargument conference by writing a letter, certified to all parties, to the appellate clerk explaining why the case should not be exempt. The chief justice may designate a judge trial referee or senior judge to preside at a conference. The scheduling of or attendance at a preargument conference shall not affect the duty of the parties to adhere to the times set for the filing of briefs. Failure of counsel to attend a preargument conference may result in the imposition of sanctions under Section 85-2. Unless other arrangements have been approved in advance by the conference judge, parties shall be present at the conference site and available for consultation. When a party against whom a claim is made is insured, an insurance adjuster for such insurance company shall be available by telephone at the time of such preargument conference unless the conference judge, in his or her discretion, requires the attendance of the adjuster at the conference. The conference proceedings shall not be brought to the attention of the court by the presiding officer or any of the parties unless the conference results in a final disposition of the appeal.

The following matters may be considered:

(1)   Possibility of settlement;

(2)   Simplification of issues;

(3)   Amendments to the preliminary statement of issues;

(4)   Transfer to the supreme court;

(5)   Timetable for the filing of briefs;

(6)   En banc review; and

(7)   Such other matters as the conference judge shall consider appropriate.

All matters scheduled for a preargument conference before a judge trial referee are referred to that official by the chief court administrator pursuant to General Statutes § 52-434a, which vests judge trial referees with the same powers and jurisdiction as superior court judges and senior judges, including the power to implement settlements by opening and modifying judgments.

Historical Note

Derivation:
    1978 P.B. (1986–97), § 4013
    1978 P.B., § 3117

The second and third sentences were added effective January 1, 2012.

The last paragraph was added effective January 1, 2000.

What are now the fifth and sixth sentences were added October 1, 1989.

What are now the seventh and eighth sentences were added effective February 4, 1997.

Entirely new rule effective July 1, 1978.

AUTHORS' COMMENTS

Failure to attend a settlement conference is a serious matter. In Esposito v. Presnick, 15 Conn.App. 654, 665–68, 546 A.2d 899, 904–06 (1988), a $500 fine was assessed for failure to attend.

The preargument judge does not have the power to refer a pending appellate motion to substitute a party to the trial court. Systematics, Inc. v. Forge Square Associates Ltd. Partnership, 45 Conn.App. 614, 697 A.2d 701, cert. denied, 243 Conn. 907, 701 A.2d 337 (1997).

Before the settlement conference is even scheduled, the clerk's office often extends the time for filing the appellant's brief until 45 days after the settlement conference. In any event, the settlement judge has the de facto power to extend the time for filing briefs.

CHAPTER 64

PROCEDURE CONCERNING MEMORANDUM OF DECISION

§ 64-1. Statement of Decision by Trial Court; When Required; How
    Stated; Contents
§ 64-2. Exceptions to Section 64-1

§ 64-1. Statement of Decision by Trial Court; When Required; How Stated; Contents

(a) The Court shall state its decision either orally or in writing, in all of the following: (1) in rendering judgments in trials to the court in civil and criminal matters, including rulings regarding motions for stay of execution, (2) in ruling on aggravating and mitigating factors in capital penalty hearings conducted to the court, (3) in ruling on motions to dismiss under Section 41-8, (4) in ruling on motions to suppress under Section 41-12, (5) in granting a motion to set aside a verdict under Section 16-35, and (6) in making any other rulings that constitute a final judgment for purposes of appeal under Section 61-1, including those that do not terminate the proceedings. The court's decision shall encompass its conclusion as to each claim of law raised by the parties and the factual basis therefor. If oral, the decision shall be recorded by a court reporter and, if there is an appeal, the trial court shall create a memorandum of decision for use in the appeal by ordering a transcript of the portion of the proceedings in which it stated its oral decision. The transcript of the decision shall be signed by the trial judge and filed in the trial court clerk's office.

    This section does not apply in small claims actions and to matters listed in Section 64-2.

(b) If the trial judge fails to file a memorandum of decision or sign a transcript of the oral decision in any case covered by subsection (a), the appellant may file with the appellate clerk an original and three copies of a notice that the decision has not been filed in compliance with subsection (a). The notice shall specify the trial judge involved and the date of the ruling for which no memorandum of decision was filed. The appellate clerk shall promptly notify the trial judge of the filing of the appeal and the notice. The trial court shall thereafter comply with subsection (a).

Historical Note

Derivation:

1978 P.B. (1986–97), § 4059

1978 P.B., § 3060B

Effective January 1, 2011, an original and three copies of the notice pursuant to subsection (b) must be filed.

Effective January 1, 1999, numerous changes were made, primarily for clarification.

Effective September 3, 1996, subsection (a)(5) was added and the clause "but do not terminate the proceedings" was added to subsection (a)(6) in order to clarify the breadth of this rule. Previously the rule could have been construed to apply to all judgments in jury trials, a result not intended.

Section (a) was clarified and § (b) was added effective May 31, 1994. The official commentary states: "These amendments [§§ 64-1 and 64-2] clarify under what circumstances a memorandum of decision must be filed by the trial court and provide a mechanism for notifying concerned parties that the decision had not been prepared at the time the appeal was taken."

The reference to criminal cases and the need to file a transcribed decision within ten days of the filing of the appeal were added effective October 1, 1986.

The rule was amended effective October 1, 1980 to clarify that the transcript of the decision (not the evidence) must be transcribed.

Entirely new rule effective July 1, 1979. Prior to 1979, the memorandum of decision was relatively unimportant; rather Supreme Court review was based on the trial court's finding.

The history of this section is discussed in Holmes v. Holmes, 32 Conn.App. 317, 321 n.7, 629 A.2d 1137, 1139 n.7 (1993).

Cross References

P.B. § 6-1

AUTHORS' COMMENTS

This rule mandates that the trial court prepare an oral or written memorandum of decision in virtually every trial to the court. Wells Fargo Bank of Minnesota, N.A. v. Morgan, 105 Conn.App. 856, 860–61, 941 A.2d 943, 945–46 (2008). Because the memorandum of decision usually constitutes the judgment (see § 2 of commentary to § 63-1), it should contain the reasoning of the court in reaching its result. Since the granting of various motions, such as a motion to dismiss or for summary judgment, would result in an appealable judgment, the authors believe this rule requires a memorandum in these cases as well. For an example of an oral decision, see State v. Lo Sacco, 12 Conn.App. 481, 484, 531 A.2d 184, 186 (1987). While P.B. § 16-38 requires a memorandum of decision in jury cases when the verdict is set aside, the authors believe § 64-1(a)(6) also applies when the verdict is sustained. See Boretti v. Panacea Co., 918, 67 Conn.App. 223, 231–32, 786 A.2d 1164, 1170 (2001), cert. denied, 259 Conn. 915, 791 A.2d 565 (2002).

A memorandum should also be written or dictated in rulings on certain other motions that are likely to be reviewable, such as waiver of fees because of indigency, State v. Hudson, 154 Conn. 631, 632–33, 228 A.2d 132,133–34 (1967); setting of bail, State v. Clark, 160 Conn. 555, 556, 274 A.2d 451, 451 (1970); admission of out-of-state attorneys, Silverman v. St. Joseph's Hospital, 168 Conn. 160, 173–79, 363 A.2d 22, 28–31 (1975); and the denial of a motion to open, Gordon v. Gordon, 148 Conn.App. 59, 66-68, 84 A.3d 923, 927–28 (2014).

The obvious purpose of this rule is to abolish the postcard decision in all but small claims and certain other cases referred to in § 64-2. The memorandum aids the appellate court in carrying out its function of judicial review, Rompe v. King, 185 Conn. 426, 441 A.2d 114, 118 (1981). Because the judge will have the option of stating the basis of the decision orally, unnecessary work in routine cases can be avoided. At the same time, all litigants will know the basis of the decision and will be able to make an informed decision as to the prospects of an appeal. In addition, the memorandum of decision can be relied on by the litigants to state the trial judge's views and can no longer be undercut or contradicted by the finding, as often occurred in the past. See, e.g., Devitt v. Manulik, 176 Conn. 657, 658 n.1, 410 A.2d 465, 467 n.1 (1979).

If the trial court fails to prepare a memorandum, the appellant should file a notice with the appellate clerk under subsection (b). Woodbury Knoll, LLC v. Shipman and Goodwin, LLP, 305 Conn. 750, 754, 48 A.3d 16, 20 (2012); Testa v. Geressy, 286 Conn. 291, 303–04, 943 A.2d 1075, 1083 (2008). If nothing happens, the appellant should move under § 60-2(1). Otherwise the issue may not be reviewed. State v. Pressley, 59 Conn.App. 77, 755 A.2d 929, 930 (2000); unless the record is adequate for review; State v. Muhammad, 117 Conn.App. 181, 184 n.1, 979 A.2d 501, 503 n.1 (2009) (unsigned transcript sufficient detailed); Chase Manhattan Mortg. Corp. v. Machado, 83 Conn.App. 183, 187, 850 A.2d 260, 263–64 (2004) (no relevant facts in dispute).

A notice under (b) should be filed *only* when *no* memorandum of decision is filed. If an inadequate one is filed, a motion for articulation is the appropriate remedy. Murphy v. Zoning Bd. of Appeals of City of Stamford, 86 Conn.App. 147, 158–60, 860 A.2d 764, 772–74 (2004), cert. denied, 273 Conn. 910, 870 A.2d 764 (2005); Lucarelli v. Freedom of Information Com'n, 136 Conn.App. 405, 411, 46 A.3d 937, cert. denied, 307 Conn. 907, 53 A.3d 222 (2012) (no decision and no compliance with § 64-1 was fatal); but see Town of Trumbull v. Palmer, 123 Conn.App. 244, 249 n.17, 1 A.3d 1121, 1126 n.7, cert. denied, 299 Conn. 907, 10 A.3d 526 (2010) (treating motion for articulation as a motion to compel compliance with this section).

If there is only an oral decision, make sure the judge signs a transcript of the decision. Filing a transcript not signed by the judge is insufficient. Mikolinski v. Commissioner of Motor Vehicles, 55 Conn.App. 691, 694–96, 740 A.2d 885, 888–90 (1999). The failure of the judge to sign the transcript has been excused in numerous recent cases, such as Manning v. Feldman, 149 Conn.App. 224, 229 n.4, 91 A.3d 466, 470 n.4 (2014); State v. Brown, 133 Conn.App. 140, 145 n.5, 34 A.3d 1007, 1011 n.5, cert. granted, 304 Conn. 901, 37 A.3d 745 (2012), and judgment rev'd on other grounds, 310 Conn. 693, 80 A.3d 878 (2013) (appellant filed a § 64-1 motion to no avail); Kairon v. Burnham, 120 Conn.App. 291, 294 n.6, 991 A.2d 675, 679 n.6,cert. denied, 297 Conn. 906, 995 A.2d 634 (2010); but see In re Diamond J., 121 Conn.App. 392, 996 A.2d 296, cert. denied, 297 Conn. 927, 998 A.2d 1193 (2010) (unsigned transcript did not reveal basis for decision). In State v. Jagat, 111 Conn.App. 173, 176–77, 958 A.2d 206, 208 (2008), the trial court was ordered to sign the transcript when the unsigned transcript varied from the judgment file. The court in In re Paul M., Jr., 148 Conn.App. 654, 659 n.5, 85 A.3d 1263, 1267 n.5, cert. denied, 311 Conn. 938, 88 A.3d 550 (2014), ordered the court to sign the transcript where it was apparent it had not reviewed the unsigned transcript.

If the trial judge, rather than signing a transcript of the oral decision, prepares a written decision, make sure it does not contradict the oral decision. If it does, move for clarification or rectification. State v. Kendrick, 132 Conn.App. 473, 478–79 n.5, 31 A.3d 1189, 1193 n.5 (2011), cert. granted, 303 Conn. 925, 35 A.3d 1076 (2012).

Note that the judge is supposed to sign the transcript *of the decision*, not of the whole day's activities. See official commentary above.

Getting the trial judge to sign the transcript of the court's decision will do no good, however, if the transcript gives no reasons for the decision. Amo v. Pincince, 55 Conn.App. 767, 768, 740 A.2d 895, 895–96 (1999), appeal dismissed, 254 Conn. 861, 760 A.2d 1263 (2000). Articulation is then in order. P.B. § 66-5.

Where the case involves a higher standard of proof than usual, the memorandum should state whether that standard was applied, Lopinto v. Haines, 185 Conn. 527, 441 A.2d 151 (1981). But see Kaczynski v. Kaczynski, 294 Conn. 121, 131, 981 A.2d 1068, 1074–75 (2009) (presuming court applied proper standard in the absence of an articulation).

Superior Court rules §§ 5-1 and 5-2 should be read along with this section. They provide:

Sec. 5-1. Trial Briefs

The parties may, as of right, or shall, if the judicial authority so orders, file, at such time as the court shall determine, written trial briefs discussing the issues in the case and the factual or legal basis upon which they ought to be resolved.

Sec. 5-2. Raising Questions of Law Which May Be the Subject of an Appeal

Any party intending to raise any question of law which may be the subject of an appeal must either state the question distinctly to the judicial authority in a written trial brief under Section 5-1 or state the question distinctly to the judicial authority on the record before such party's closing argument and within sufficient time to give the opposing counsel an opportunity to discuss the question. If the party fails to do this, the judicial authority will be under no obligation to decide the question.

The trial judge may under this rule permit or require the parties to submit briefs. Since the judge does not have to prepare a finding, there will rarely be any need to await the transcript before filing trial briefs. Also, any substantial delay between trial and decision will defeat one purpose of the new appellate rules, which is to permit the judge to render a decision while the case is fresh in his mind. Certainly any claim of law filed after the memorandum of decision is filed is too late, Zeller v. Kugell, 145 Conn. 729, 730, 141 A.2d 240, 241 (1958).

If the trial court improperly refuses to file a memorandum, one should not claim error in that action, but rather make a motion (presumably under § 66-5 or § 60-2) to order the trial court to make a memorandum, Maloney v. Taplin, 154 Conn. 247, 248, 224 A.2d 731, 733 (1966). See Kaplan v. Kaplan, 185 Conn. 42, 46, 440 A.2d 252, 254 (1981). Once the trial judge has resigned, further action by counsel would be futile, so reversal was warranted in Claude v. Claude, 143 Conn.App. 307, 68 A.3d 1204 (2013). In Chapman Lumber, Inc. v. Tager, 288 Conn. 69, 83 n.20, 952 A.2d 1, 13 n.20 (2008), the Supreme Court treated a motion for review from the denial of such a motion for articulation as a motion for compliance with this section. Likewise, if the memorandum is inadequate, a § 66-5 motion is in order, Scherr v. Scherr, 183 Conn. 366, 439 A.2d 375 (1981); Hall v. Hall, 186 Conn. 118, 124, 439 A.2d 447, 450 (1982); Town of Newington v. General Sanitation Service Co., 196 Conn. 81, 83–84, 491 A.2d 363, 365 (1985). Or use subsection (b), which was successfully invoked by the appellate clerk in Federal Home Loan Mortg. Corp. v. Bardinelli, 44 Conn.Supp. 85, 667 A.2d 1315, aff'd, 39 Conn.App. 786, 667 A.2d 806 (1995).

On occasion the trial court will prepare a memorandum accepting as true virtually every fact claimed by the appellee, and rejecting all facts claimed by the appellant. The Appellate Court has repeatedly criticized this practice. Gillon v. Bysiewicz, 105 Conn.App. 654, 657–58, 939 A.2d 605, 607–08 (2008); Grayson v. Grayson, 4 Conn.App. 275, 279-85, 494 A.2d 576, 579–82 (1985), appeal dismissed, 202 Conn. 221, 520 A.2d 225 (1987). It ordered a new articulation when the trial court incorporated one party's memorandum in Doe v. Bridgeport Hosp., 40 Conn.App. 429, 671 A.2d 405 (1996).

The rule requires the trial court to rule on each claim of law raised by the parties in nonjury cases. Cottiero v. Ifkovic, 35 Conn.App. 682, 685–86, 647 A.2d 9, 11, cert. denied, 231 Conn. 938, 651 A.2d 262 (1994). If it does not do so, the Appellate Court may order the court to do so. Busa v. Busa, 24 Conn.App. 426, 589 A.2d 370 (1991). Claims of law should be ruled on in administrative appeals as in other cases, St. John v. Commissioner of Transp., 172 Conn. 234,

235 n.1, 374 A.2d 190, n.1 (1977). Thus the trial court cannot ignore an issue that it thinks is immaterial. The materiality of an issue is initially for counsel and ultimately for the reviewing court to decide. Compare Cappiello v. Haselman, 154 Conn. 490, 491–92, 227 A.2d 79, 80 (1967) (issues), and Watrous v. Sinoway, 135 Conn. 424, 427, 65 A.2d 473, 475 (1949) (facts), both decided under the old rules. If the trial court fails to comply, a motion to the Supreme Court under § 60-2 or to the trial court under § 66-5 would be in order. If the trial court does state its conclusion on each issue but fails to make clear the basis of each conclusion (such as by failing to pass on the credibility of crucial testimony), a motion under the second sentence of § 60-5 and § 66-5 is in order. Pandolphe's Auto Parts, Inc. v. Town of Manchester, 181 Conn. 217, 435 A.2d 24 (1980). However, the rule does not require the trial court to rule on every factual or legal matter raised by the litigants, Gretsch v. Housatonic Cable Vision Co., 8 Conn.L.Trib. No. 14, p. 13 (1981); nor is the court bound to articulate the claims *in haec verba* or in any particular format, Apostles of the Sacred Heart v. Curott, 187 Conn. 591, 600, 448 A.2d 157, 162 (1982).

Certainly a statement such as "the plaintiff proved the essential allegations of his complaint", which was improper under the old rules, see Ford v. Hotel and Restaurant Emp. and Bartenders Intern. Union AFL-CIO Local 159, 152 Conn. 533, 534, 209 A.2d 187, 188 (1965), is even more improper now. On the other hand, a trial judge may not have to rule on improperly prepared claims of law. Claims of law were properly overruled because they were too abstract, Easton v. Easton, 172 Conn. 451, 454–56, 374 A.2d 1090, 1092–94 (1977); others were properly summarized because they were "discursive," Mazzola v. Commissioner of Transp., 175 Conn. 576, 579–80, 402 A.2d 786, 787 (1978).

The 1994 amendment expanding this section to postjudgment modification orders was applied in Gallant v. Esposito, 36 Conn.App. 794, 798 n.3, 654 A.2d 380, 382 n.3 (1995).

§ 64-2. Exceptions to Section 64-1

(a) In any uncontested matter where no aspect of the matter is in dispute, in any pendente lite family relations matter whether contested or uncontested, or in any dismissal under Sec. 14-3, the oral or written decision as provided in Section 64-1 is not required. The trial clerk shall, however, promptly notify the trial judge of the filing of the appeal.

(b) Within twenty days from the filing of an appeal from a contested pendente lite order or from a dismissal under Section 14-3 in which an oral or written decision has not been made pursuant to subsection (a), each party to the appeal shall file a brief with the trial court discussing the legal and factual issues in the matter. Within twenty days after the briefs have been filed by the parties, the court shall file a written memorandum of decision stating the factual basis for its decision on the issues in the matter and its conclusion as to each claim of law raised by the parties.

Historical Note

Derivation:
  1978 P.B. (1989–97), § 4060
  1978 P.B., § 3060C
Entirely new rule effective July 1, 1979.

This rule was amended effective May 31, 1994 to regulate more closely the judicial compliance with this section. See also historical note to § 64-1.

AUTHORS' COMMENTS

This section excepts various routine types of decisions from the requirements of § 64-1, since appeals from such decisions are unusual. If an appeal does occur, subsection (b) essentially requires the parties and the judge to proceed as in § 64-1. Uncontested decisions are not included in subsection (b), since the proper way to challenge a stipulated judgment is by moving to reopen it before appealing. William G. Major Const. Co. v. DeMichely, 166 Conn. 368, 375, 349 A.2d 827, 830–31 (1974). See also Simmons v. Wetherall, 180 Conn. 587, 430 A.2d 1296 (1980).

While the language "uncontested matter where no aspect of the matter is in dispute" is lifted substantially from domestic relations practice, it is not limited to such matters. For example, an uncontested judgment by default or nonsuit would qualify as an exception to § 64-1.

If the court complies with § 64-1 even when it does not have to, then § 64-2(b) is inapplicable. Herrmann v. Summer Plaza Corp., 201 Conn. 263, 513 A.2d 1211 (1986).

CHAPTER 65

TRANSFER OF CASES

§ 65-1. Transfer of Cases by Supreme Court (Applicable to appeals filed before July 1, 2013)

When, pursuant to General Statutes § 51-199(c), the supreme court (1) transfers to itself a cause in the appellate court, or (2) transfers a cause or a class of causes from itself to the appellate court, the appellate clerk shall notify all parties and the clerk of the trial court that the appeal has been transferred. A case so transferred shall be entered upon the docket of the court to which it has been transferred. There shall be no fee on such transfer. The appellate clerk may require the parties to take such steps as may be necessary to make the appeal conform to the rules of the court to which it has been transferred, for example, supply the court with additional copies of the record and the briefs.

§ 65-1. Transfer of Cases by Supreme Court (Applicable to Appeals filed on or after July 1, 2013)

When, pursuant to General Statutes § 51-199(c), the supreme court (1) transfers to itself a cause in the appellate court, or (2) transfers a cause or a class of causes from itself to the appellate court, the appellate clerk shall notify all parties and the clerk of the trial court that the appeal has been transferred. A case so transferred shall be entered upon the docket of the court to which it has been transferred. There shall be no fee on such transfer. The appellate clerk may require the parties to take such steps as may be necessary to make the appeal conform to the rules of the court to which it has been transferred, for example, supply the court with additional copies of the briefs and appendices.

Historical Note

Derivation:
1978 P.B. (1986–97), § 4023
1978 P.B. (1986–97), § 4023

1978 P.B. (1986–97), § 4023
1978 P.B., § 3004A

New rule effective July 1, 1983. Minor changes were made effective September 3, 1996.

Effective May 10, 1988, the substitute recognizance on transfer to the Supreme Court was lowered to $300 from $500; it was eliminated effective October 1, 1992.

AUTHORS' COMMENTS

This section is the workhorse of the Supreme Court's docket. In the twelve months from November 1, 2002 through October 31, 2003, of the cases the Supreme Court disposed of with a reported decision, 70% (111) were decided under this section.

This section was first noted in Fellin v. Administrator, Unemployment Compensation Act, 196 Conn. 440, 441, 493 A.2d 174, 175 (1985). A discussion of the factors that the Supreme Court may consider in deciding whether to transfer a case is found in State v. Ellis, 224 Conn. 711, 722–25, 621 A.2d 250, 255–57 (1993). A lack of clarity in the record convinced a majority of justices to let the Appellate Court sort through the record first.

In Vasquez v. Superior Court, 102 Conn.App. 394, 395 n.1, 925 A.2d 1112, 1116 n.1, cert. denied, 284 Conn. 915, 931 A.2d 935 (2007), the Supreme Court transferred a writ of error to the Appellate Court for decision.

§ 65-2. Motion for Transfer from Appellate Court to Supreme Court

After the filing of an appeal in the appellate court, but in no event after the case has been assigned for hearing, any party may move for transfer to the supreme court. The motion, addressed to the supreme court, shall specify, in accordance with provisions of Section 66-2, the reasons why the party believes that the supreme court should hear the appeal directly. A copy of the memorandum of decision of the trial court, if any, shall be attached to the motion. The filing of a motion for transfer shall not stay proceedings in the appellate court.

If, at any time before the final determination of an appeal, the appellate court is of the opinion that the appeal is appropriate for supreme court review, the appellate court may file a brief statement of the reasons why transfer is appropriate. The supreme court shall treat the statement as a motion to transfer and shall promptly decide whether to transfer the case to itself.

Historical Note

Derivation:
1978 P.B. (1986–97), § 4024, 4135
1978 P.B., § 3004B

Prior to 1996, it was common for a litigant seeking transfer to file a letter rather than a motion.

New rule effective July 1, 1983. Amendments effective October 1, 1996 and October 1, 1997 are noted above. The reference to the memorandum of decision was added effective October 1, 1986. The first sentence was revised effective January 1, 1985 to eliminate the requirement of requesting transfer to the

Supreme Court within 10 days of the filing of the appeal and again effective October 1, 1992 to eliminate the requirement that it be done "as soon as possible."

AUTHORS' COMMENTS

When an appeal is filed, the appellant also must file the Statement for Preargument Conference (JD-AC-6). One of the questions on the Form is whether the case should be transferred to the Supreme Court. This issue is normally considered at the preargument conference. A recommendation by the preargument judge increases the chances of transfer.

If the case is not transferred at this point, it is proper for counsel to file a motion requesting transfer. The best time to do so would be after all the briefs are filed. However, if there is an important motion pending, the motion to transfer should be filed as soon as possible. In *Cashman v. Cashman, S.C. 15629*, a motion to transfer was filed early and granted so that the Supreme Court could rule on a pending motion for review of a stay order. See also State v. McDowell, 241 Conn. 413 n.1, 696 A.2d 977, 978 n.1 (1997). Criminal, juvenile and pro se appeals normally bypass the conference program, so a motion in those cases should be filed early in the appellate process.

The Appellate Court used the second paragraph successfully in Austin-Casares v. Safeco Ins. Co. of America, 310 Conn. 640, 647 n.9, 81 A.3d 200, 206 n.9 (2013); Sharper Image Corp. v. Miller, 42 Conn.App. 310, 678 A.2d 977 (1996), aff'd, 240 Conn. 531, 532 n.1, 692 A.2d 774, 775–76 n.1 (1997), and in State v. Luurtsema, 262 Conn. 179, 182 n.6, 811 A.2d 223, 226 n.6 (2002) (overruled on other grounds by, State v. Salamon, 287 Conn. 509, 949 A.2d 1092 (2008)), and unsuccessfully in State v. Daniels, 42 Conn.App. 445, 681 A.2d 337, cert. denied, 239 Conn. 928, 683 A.2d 397 (1996), and State v. Garrett, 42 Conn.App. 507, 681 A.2d 362 (1996). In J.E. Roberts Co., Inc. v. Signature Properties, LLC, 309 Conn. 307, 71 A.3d 492 (2013), the Supreme Court accepted the case after it had been argued in the Appellate Court.

In Crawford v. Commissioner of Correction, 285 Conn. 585, 940 A.2d 789 (2008), and Johnson v. Commissioner of Correction, 285 Conn. 556, 941 A.2d 248 (2008), the Appellate Court requested the Supreme Court take the cases after the Appellate Court heard argument.

§ 65-3. Transfer of Petitions for Review of Bail Orders from Appellate Court to Supreme Court

Whenever a petition for review of an order of the superior court concerning release is filed in the appellate court pursuant to General Statutes § 54-63g in any case on appeal to the supreme court or where the defendant could appeal to the supreme court if convicted, such petition shall be transferred to the supreme court pursuant to the exercise of the supreme court's transfer jurisdiction under General Statutes § 51-199(c) for review of such order.

Historical Note

Derivation:
    1978 P.B. (1986–97), § 4025
This rule is new effective October 1, 1986.

AUTHORS' COMMENTS

If the underlying charge is not within the Supreme Court's mandatory jurisdiction, it appears that the Supreme Court has no power to transfer review of a bail order to itself. State v. Ayala, 222 Conn. 331, 340, 610 A.2d 1162, 1167–68 (1992). The language of *Ayala* on this point seems to be inconsistent with this section. The language in *Ayala*, however, is dictum, because it concerned a petition after the ruling of the Appellate Court, not a request for transfer before.

In State v. Fernando A., 294 Conn. 1, 5 n.3, 981 A.2d 427, 430 n.3 (2009), the court treated an appeal from a bail hearing as a petition for review of the order and transferred the appeal to itself under this section.

The Supreme Court used this section to transfer a petition for review of an order sealing a grand jury report in In re Investigatory Grand Jury No. 2007-04, 293 Conn. 464, 467 n.2, 977 A.2d 621, 624 n.2 (2009). The authors disagree that this section applies outside bail orders.

§ 65-4. Transfer of Matters Brought to Wrong Court

Any appeal or cause brought to the supreme court or the appellate court which is not properly within the jurisdiction of the court to which it is brought shall not be dismissed for the reason that it was brought to the wrong court but shall be transferred by the appellate clerk to the court with jurisdiction and entered on its docket. Any timely filed appeal or cause transferred shall be considered timely filed in the appropriate court. The appellate clerk shall notify all parties and the clerk of the trial court that the appeal or cause has been transferred. In the event that an appeal or cause is so transferred, no additional fees or security for costs will be due.

Historical Note

Derivation:
    1978 P.B. (1986–97), § 4027
    1978 P.B., § 3076
Entirely new rule effective July 1, 1978. Minor changes were made in 1983 and 1985. Effective October 1, 1992, the need to pay new fees was abolished.

AUTHORS' COMMENTS

In Bortner v. Town of Woodbridge, 250 Conn. 241, 245 n.4, 736 A.2d 104, 107 n.4, 137 Ed. Law Rep. 1019 (1999), the appellants improperly appealed directly to the Supreme Court but no one apparently noticed that fact until the Supreme Court was writing its decision. It treated the appeal as having been filed in the Appellate Court and transferred to the Supreme Court.

In State v. Pink, 274 Conn. 241, 244 n.2, 875 A.2d 447, 450 n.2 (2005), the Supreme Court transferred to itself a case that should have been filed in that court originally but was erroneously filed in the Appellate Court. See also Hong Pham v. Starkowski, 300 Conn. 412, 416 n.3, 16 A.3d 635, 636 n.3 (2011) (appeal from decision holding a statute unconstitutional should have been filed in Supreme Court); A. Gallo and Co. v. Commissioner of Environmental Protection, 309 Conn. 810, 820, 73 A.3d 693, 700 (2013), cert. denied, ___ U.S. ___, 134 S. Ct. 1540, 188 L. Ed. 2d 581 (2014) (same).

CHAPTER 66

MOTIONS AND OTHER PROCEDURES

§ 66-1. Extension of Time

(a) Except as otherwise provided in these rules, the judge who tried the case may, for good cause shown, extend the time limit provided for filing the appeal, except that such extension shall be of no effect if the time within which the appeal must be taken is set by statute and is a time limit that the legislature intended as a limit on the subject matter jurisdiction of the court to which the appeal is taken. In no event shall the trial judge extend the time for filing the appeal to a date which is more than twenty days from the expiration date of the appeal period. Where a motion for extension of the period of time within which to appeal has been filed at least ten days before expiration of the time limit sought to be extended, the party seeking to appeal shall have no less than ten days from issuance of notice of denial of the motion to file the appeal.

For extensions of time to file a cross appeal, see Section 61-8; to file a petition for certification to the supreme court, see Section 84-7; to file a petition for certification to the appellate court, see Section 81-5.

(b) If an appeal has been filed, the time provided for taking any step necessary to prosecute or defend the appeal may be extended by the court in which the appeal is pending.

(c)(1) Extensions shall be granted only upon a written motion filed with the clerk of the trial court, in the case of a preappeal motion, and with the appellate clerk, in the case of a postappeal motion. The motion, only an original of which need be filed, should set forth the reason for the requested extension, and shall be accompanied by a certification that complies with Section 62-7. An attorney filing such a motion on a client's behalf shall also indicate that a copy of the motion has been mailed to each of his or her clients who are parties to the appeal. The moving party shall also include a statement as to whether the other parties consent or object to the motion. A motion for extension of time to file a brief must specify the current status of the brief or preparations therefor, indicate the estimated date of completion, and, in criminal cases, state whether the defendant is incarcerated as a result of the proceeding in which the appeal has been taken.

(2) The appellate clerk is authorized to grant or deny motions for extension of time promptly upon their filing. Motions for extension of time to complete any step necessary to prosecute or defend the appeal, to move for or oppose a motion for reconsideration, or to petition for or to oppose a petition for certification will not be granted except for good cause. Claims of good cause shall be raised promptly after the cause arises.

(3) An opposing party who objects to a motion for extension of time filed pursuant to subsection (b) of this section shall file an objection with reasons in support thereof with the appellate clerk within five days from the filing of the motion.

(4) A motion for extension of time shall be filed at least ten days before the expiration of the time limit sought to be extended or, if the cause for such extension arises during the ten day period, as soon as reasonably possible after such cause has arisen. No motion under this rule shall be granted unless it is filed before the time limit sought to be extended by such motion has expired.

(5) Any action by the trial court judge pursuant to subsection (a) of this section or the appellate clerk pursuant to subsection (c)(2) of this section is reviewable pursuant to Section 66-6.

(6) Postappeal motions for extension of time may be filed, signed or verified by electronic means that comply with procedures and technical standards set forth on the Judicial Branch website. A paper filed by electronic means in compliance with such procedures and standards constitutes a written paper for the purpose of applying these rules. Service and proof of service shall be made pursuant to sections 10-13, 10-14 and 62-7.

Historical Note

Derivation:
  1978 P.B. (1986–97), § 4040
  1978 P.B., § 3097
  1963 P.B., § 665
  1951 P.B., §§ 378, 413, 451
  1934 P.B., §§ 335, 367
Subsection (c) (6) was added in 2009; the provision in (c) (1) that the lawyer

notify the client of the filing of a motion for extension was added in 2006; the exception clause in the first sentence of (a) (2) was added in 1996.

The second paragraph in section (a) was amended effective October 1, 1992.

Section (c)(1) was amended effective May 10, 1988 to change the filing requirement from triplicate to duplicate and effective October 1, 1992 from duplicate to original only.

This rule was substantially rewritten effective October 1, 1986. Old § 3097 stated as follows:

"(a) If an appeal has not yet been filed, the judge who tried the case may, for good cause shown, extend the time provided for filing the appeal, except as may be otherwise provided in these rules. In no event shall the trial judge extend the time for filing the appeal to a date which is more than twenty days from the expiration date of the original appeal period.

"(b) If an appeal has been filed, the time provided for taking any step necessary to perfect the appeal may be extended by the supreme court.

"(c)(1) Extensions shall be granted only upon a written motion filed in triplicate with the clerk of the trial court, in the case of a pre-appeal motion, and with the chief clerk of the supreme court, in the case of a post-appeal motion. A motion should set forth the reason for the requested extension and include certification of service on the other parties as in Sec. 120. No motion for an extension of time shall be granted until the expiration of ten days after it has been filed.

"(2) If during the ten-day period a party who wishes to oppose the motion notifies the clerk of the trial court with respect to a motion filed pursuant to (a) above that he desires to be heard, the motion shall be granted only after a hearing by the trial court upon due notice to all parties, but if all nonmoving parties endorse their consent on the motion, it may be granted immediately.

"(3) A party who objects to a motion filed pursuant to (b) above shall file his reasons for objecting with the chief clerk of the supreme court in accordance with Sec. 3013.

"(4) No motion under this rule shall be granted unless it is filed before the time for filing the appeal or subsequent paper has expired."

The following history refers to old § 3097:

The second sentence of subsection (a) was added effective October 1, 1982 and, unless a § 3007 motion is filed, prevents the granting of any extension of time to take the appeal beyond 40 days of notice of rendition of the judgment. In re Michelle O., 10 Conn.L.Trib. No. 7, p. 13 (1983). The rule effective July 1, 1978 bears very little resemblance to the rule that was in effect and substantially unchanged since 1951. A minor change was made effective October 1, 1980 to clarify that 3 rather than 10 copies of the motion need be filed. Prior to 1978, all such motions were made initially to the trial court. Also prior to 1978, a motion to extend the time to file the appeal or the brief had to be made before the time ran out. An "extraordinary circumstances" exception, added in 1978, was removed effective July 1, 1979. The procedure to be followed in granting extensions was not spelled out in detail prior to 1951, and trial judges often granted extensions before the opposition had a chance to object. MacDonald v. Newman, 112 Conn. 596, 153 A. 296 (1931).

Before 1943, extensions of time for filing any document could be granted by the trial court even if the motion was filed after the time had expired. This was changed in 1943 as to the filing of the appeal and the security for costs, and the payment of fees, and in 1951 as to briefs. The old rule apparently caused a lot of dissatisfaction, since parties never knew when they could close their files, see State ex rel. Baskin v. Bartlett, 132 Conn. 623, 624, 46 A.2d 335, 336 (1946). This commentary was cited in State v. Thomas, 9 Conn.L.Trib. No. 12, pp. 15, 16 (1982).

Prior to 1934, the power to grant extensions was mentioned in passing in various rules.

Cross References

Maltbie, Conn.App.Proc.2d, §§ 287–299

AUTHORS' COMMENTS

Except for the 20-day extension to file the appeal, the motion generally must be filed 10 days before the period expires. The clerk generally rules on the motion immediately if it is consented to, and within a few days if it is not. Note that only the original motion must be filed; copies are not necessary. According to the clerk's office, the statement of the other party's consent or objection should be placed prominently on the front page of the motion, although this requirement is not explicit in the rule.

As of March 1, 2009, it is now proper (but not mandatory) for counsel, if all agree, to file motions for extension and objections solely electronically. Be sure to obtain consent from all recipients to electronic service and to certify that you have received such consent. Also make sure you have the correct email addresses. Failure to do either of these things may lead to rejection of your motion.

The trial court has no power to extend the appeal period for more than an additional twenty days. DeTeves v. DeTeves, 202 Conn. 292, 520 A.2d 608 (1987); Corcoran v. Corcoran, 19 Conn. L. Rptr. 598, 1997 WL 344730 (Conn. Super. Ct. 1997).

The reasons for the extension should be stated in the motion; Chanosky v. City Bldg. Supply Co., 152 Conn. 449, 451, 208 A.2d 337, 338–39 (1965); although a failure to do so at one time was not fatal, see Luth v. Butwill, 119 Conn. 697, 176 A. 552 (1935).

If the motion is late, the motion cannot be granted under this section, although it might be granted by the Appellate Court under § 60-2(6), State v. Stead, 186 Conn. 222, 226–28, 440 A.2d 299, 300–02 (1982); State v. Files, 183 Conn. 586, 588, 441 A.2d 27, 29, 27 A.L.R.4th 208 (1981). See Gordon v. Gordon, 148 Conn.App. 59, 62 n.5, 84 A.3d 923, 925 n.5 (2014).

If an appeal is not timely filed, see §§ 4 and 5 of commentary to § 63-1.

A motion for extension is implicitly granted if a court takes action on the document for which an extension was requested. Cristini v. Griffin Hospital, 134 Conn. 282 n.1, 57 A.2d 262, 263–64 n.1 (1948) (transcript filed late; motion to file it implicitly granted when the trial court certified the transcript); Lesser v. Lesser, 134 Conn. 418, 419 n.1, 58 A.2d 512, 516–17 n.1 (1948).

A motion for extension of time to file the appeal implicitly extends the time to pay the appellate fees. Second Nat. Bank v. Harris, 122 Conn. 180, 181, 187 A. 910, 911 (1936). The *Harris* case is also interesting because of the Supreme Court's lax attitude toward the appellant's counsel who filed the motion with the judge rather than with the clerk and did not give notice to opposing counsel before the first motion was granted.

The authors' opinion is that a motion for extension of time to file a cross appeal is filed with the trial clerk because it is a "preappeal motion" as it pertains to the cross appeal. See § 61-8, second sentence.

§ 66-2. Motions, Petitions and Applications; Supporting Memoranda

(a) Motions, petitions and applications shall be specific. No motion, petition or application will be considered unless it clearly sets forth in separate paragraphs appropriately captioned: (1) a brief history of the case; (2) the specific facts upon which the moving party relies; and (3) the legal grounds upon which the moving party relies. A separate memorandum of law may but need not be filed. If the moving party intends to file a memorandum of law in support of the motion, petition or application, however, such memorandum shall be filed with the motion, petition or application. A party intending to oppose a motion, petition or application shall file a brief statement clearly setting forth in separate paragraphs appropriately captioned the <u>factual</u> and <u>legal grounds</u> for opposition within ten days after the filing of the motion, petition or application. If an opposing party chooses to file a memorandum of law in opposition to a motion, petition or application, that party shall do so within ten days after the filing of the motion, petition or application. Responses to memoranda in opposition are not permitted. Except as provided in subsection (e) below, no proposed order is required.

(b) Except with special permission of the appellate clerk, the motion, petition or application and memorandum of law taken together shall not exceed ten pages, and the memorandum of law in opposition thereto shall not exceed ten pages.

(c) Where counsel for the moving party certifies that all other parties to the appeal have consented to the granting of the motion, petition or application, the motion, petition or application may be submitted to the court immediately upon filing and may be acted upon without awaiting expiration of the time for filing opposition papers. Notice of such consent certification shall be indicated on the first page of the document.

(d) Motions which are not dispositive of the appeal may be ruled upon by one or more members of the court subject to review by a full panel upon a motion for reconsideration pursuant to Section 71-5.

(e) Motions that are directed to the trial court, such as motions to terminate stay pursuant to Section 61-11 or motions for rectification or articulation pursuant to Section 66-5, shall: (1) include both the trial court and the appellate court docket numbers in the caption of the case; (2) state in the first paragraph the name of the trial court judge, or panel of judges, who issued the order or orders to be reviewed; (3) include a proper order for the trial court if required by Section 11-1; and (4) comply with the requirements of Section 66-3. Such motions will be forwarded to the trial court by the appellate clerk.

Cross References

Section 60-4 (definition of motions, petitions and applications)

Historical Note

Derivation:
   1978 P.B. (1986–97), § 4041
   1978 P.B., § 3098
   1963 P.B., § 668
Subsection (e) was added effective January 1, 2011.
Effective January 1, 2013, language in (e) (3) was changed from "pursuant to

§ 11-1" to "if required by § 11-1".

This section now refers to petitions (except for certification, see § 60-4), effective September 3, 1996.

Section (a) was amended effective October 1, 1992 to require that the motion have the three requirements "in separate paragraphs appropriately captioned." The last sentence of (a) was added at the same time.

Section (a) was amended effective October 1, 1986 to eliminate the need to submit a statement separate from the motion. At the same time, the last sentence of section (b) was added, as were present sections (c) and (d). A section about requesting a hearing was added at that time and deleted effective October 1, 1992.

The 14 day period for filing opposing papers was reduced to 10 days effective January 1, 1985.

This rule was new in 1963 (the official 1963 Practice Book erroneously refers to § 438 of the 1951 Practice Book), and extensively revised effective March 1, 1982.

AUTHORS' COMMENTS

Note that motions (including an optional memorandum of law) generally may not exceed 10 pages (§ e). Therefore, it just wastes space to file a separate memorandum.

Note also that motions to dismiss and the like may be denied without a hearing even if one is claimed. Hearings are rarely granted.

Be sure that each motion has separate subheadings labeled "brief history," "specific facts," and "legal grounds". The memorandum in opposition should have separate subheadings labeled "specific facts in opposition" and "legal grounds in opposition."

Papers filed in favor of and in opposition to a motion are usually the only opportunity litigants have to be heard, as hearings by the appellate courts are rarely scheduled (see § 66-4), and evidentiary hearings before the trial court (as on motions for articulation) are not required by due process. State v. Figueroa, 235 Conn. 145, 665 A.2d 63 (1995).

The rule states that a response to the opposition memorandum is not permitted. The Appellate Court dismissed a motion for permission to file a reply memorandum in All Seasons Services, Inc. v. Guildner, 89 Conn.App. 781, 783 n.1, 878 A.2d 370 n.1 (2005). If the opponent files something improper, however, the moving party might try a motion to strike the improper matter under P.B. § 60-2(3).

All motions should comply with § 66-2. It is not proper to tuck a motion to file a late appeal into a statement in opposition to a motion to dismiss the appeal as untimely. Blue Cross/Blue Shield of Connecticut, Inc. v. Gurski, 47 Conn.App. 478, 482-83, 705 A.2d 566, 568, cert. denied, 247 Conn. 920, 722 A.2d 809 (1998).

The court considered a late-filed statement in opposition in Buehler v. Buehler, 117 Conn.App. 304, 310 n.8, 978 A.2d 1141, 1145 n.8 (2009).

The authors believe that the citation format may follow the format in the argument portion of briefs. See P.B. § 67-11(b) and (c).

In Estate of Owens v. CTRE, LLC, 123 Conn.App. 61, 68, 998 A.2d 1285 (2010), the court cited this section for the proposition that the appellant should have filed a motion to reargue (unless the appellant filed a motion for rectification under § 66-5) to fill in a gap in the trial court's decision. The authors disagree with *Owens*. Section 66-5 has nothing to do with a trial court motion to reargue under Practice Book Chapter 11.

§ 66-2a. Supreme Court Briefs on Compact Disc; Hyperlinking

In addition to the filing of the requisite number of printed briefs and the submission of the electronic version of briefs as required by Section 67-2, the supreme court will accept all briefs in an appeal on a single compact disc, read-only memory (CD-ROM). Counsel who wish to file such a CD-ROM should consult with opposing counsel and self-represented litigants who should cooperate in its preparation. If only one party wishes to participate in the preparation of the CD-ROM, that party may prepare the CD-ROM with briefs provided by all parties, as long as (1) those parties consent, (2) all briefs are hyperlinked as described below and (3) all parties who have filed briefs are afforded an opportunity to review the CD-ROM before it is filed.

The CD-ROM briefs shall comply with the current technical specifications available on the Judicial Branch website and shall be identical in content and format to the printed version. The CD-ROM briefs shall be word-searchable and hyperlinked to each other and to the full text of all cases, statutes, rules and treatises cited therein. The disc and its paper sleeve shall be labeled with the title of the case, the docket number and the documents reproduced on the disk.

Twenty copies of the CD-ROM shall be filed in the office of the appellate clerk no later than thirty days after the last paper brief is filed, accompanied by proof of service of at least one disc on each other party.

Historical Note

This is a new rule in 2010. In any event paper briefs still must be filed.

§ 66-3. Motion Procedures and Filing

Except as otherwise provided, the original and fifteen copies of motions, petitions, applications, memoranda of law and stipulations brought to the court shall be filed with the appellate clerk. All papers shall contain a certification that a copy has been served on each other counsel of record in accordance with the provisions of Section 62-7. No motion or other paper mentioned above shall be filed after expiration of the time for its filing, and no amendment to any of these filings shall be filed, except on written motion and by consent of the court. Motions shall be typewritten and fully double spaced, and shall not exceed three lines to the vertical inch or twenty-seven lines to the page. Footnotes and block quotations may be single spaced. Only the following two typefaces, of 12 point or larger size, are approved for use in these motions: arial and univers. Each page of a motion, petition, application, memorandum of law, stipulation and opposition shall have as a minimum the following margins: top, 1 inch; left, 1 and

1/4 inch; right, 1/2 inch; and bottom, 1 inch. A certificate shall be attached to the signed original paper, indicating that it is in compliance with all the provisions of this section.

Historical Note

Derivation:
> 1978 P.B. (1986–97), § 4042
> 1978 P.B., § 3099
> 1963 P.B., §§ 687, 689
> 1951 P.B., § 438
> 1934 P.B., § 397
> 1922 P.B., § 67
> 1908 P.B., § 65
> 1899 P.B., § 65

The last two sentences were added effective January 1, 2004 to make the page formatting of motions and other papers consistent with the format for briefs.

The number of copies of motions was changed from 10 to 15 effective October 1, 1982, back to 10 effective October 1, 1986, and back to 15 effective May 10, 1988. Also, on October 1, 1986 the last sentence was clarified. Several ambiguities in this rule were eliminated effective January 1, 1985, such as the prior reference to one judge of the Supreme Court and to the term of court to which the motion pertained.

The rule effective July 1, 1978 eliminates the reference to various trial clerks but otherwise generally continues old §§ 687 and 689. The reference to § 66-2 was added effective March 1, 1982.

Except for changing the number of copies from eight to ten effective December 12, 1966, this rule is unchanged since 1951, except that the last sentence was added in 1963. Prior to 1951, four copies were to be filed with the Hartford County Supreme Court clerk, except in certain circumstances. Prior to 1932, motions were filed in duplicate.

AUTHORS' COMMENTS

An older case holds that an amendment to a motion relates back to the filing of the motion, State ex rel. Baskin v. Bartlett, 132 Conn. 623, 625, 46 A.2d 335, 336 (1946) (plea in abatement).

Motions for extension of time are filed in the original only (§ 66-1); motions to terminate the stay of execution or for rectification are filed in an original and three copies (§§ 61-11, 66-5), and motions for reargument are filed in an original and fifteen copies (§ 71-5). Note that fully double spaced means just that; do not use one and one-half spacing.

The Appellate Clerk will return papers that do not include a certification that the format of the motion complies. Be sure to cite the proper formatting rule in the certification.

§ 66-4. Hearings on Motions

Hearings on motions will be assigned only upon order of the court and only in exceptional cases. In cases involving parties who are self-represented and incarcerated, hearings on motions may be conducted by videoconference upon direction of the court.

Historical Note

Derivation:

1978 P.B. (1986–87), § 4043
1978 P.B., § 3101
1963 P.B., § 691

The second sentence was added effective January 1, 2012.

The last phrase, "and only in exceptional cases," was added effective September 3, 1996.

A minor deletion was made effective October 1, 1986.

This rule was amended effective October 1, 1992 to delete the provision that counsel could request hearings on various motions.

This rule was new in 1963. (The official 1963 Practice Book erroneously refers to § 438 of the 1951 Practice Book). Changes to conform to the amendment to § 66-2(b) were made effective March 1, 1982.

AUTHORS' COMMENTS

State v. Lopez, 235 Conn. 487, 668 A.2d 360 (1995), holds essentially that this rule is not a violation of due process. Until the late 1970's, it was normal for most motions to be argued orally to the Supreme Court. Since then, that is rare.

In the Appellate Court, motions by counsel are rarely scheduled for a hearing. However, a suo motu motion calendar is held one morning each term. Whether heard orally or on the papers, motions are normally decided by five judges.

Occasionally a cautious lawyer, being uncertain which of two decisions is final, will file a separate appeal from both decisions and move to consolidate them. It makes no sense for the Appellate Court suo motu to put the more vulnerable appeal on its motion calendar and then dismiss it. The cautious lawyer then has to file a petition for certification and, if the Appellate Court chose the wrong appeal to dismiss, the parties may be stuck briefing a redundant jurisdictional issue. The proper result is to allow the consolidation so that the jurisdictional issue can be ignored. That is exactly what the Supreme Court did in State v. Lombardo Bros. Mason Contractors, Inc., 307 Conn. 412, 419–20 n.13, 54 A.3d 1005, 1012 n.13 (2012).

§ 66-5. Motion for Rectification; Motion for Articulation (Applicable to appeals filed before July 1, 2013)

A motion seeking corrections in the transcript or the trial court record or seeking an articulation or further articulation of the decision of the trial court shall be called a motion for rectification or a motion for articulation, whichever is applicable. Any motion filed pursuant to this section shall state with particularity the relief sought.

Except in cases where the trial court was a three judge court, an original and two copies of such motion shall be filed with the appellate clerk. Where the trial court was a three judge court, an original and four copies of such motion shall be filed. Any other party may oppose the motion by filing an original and two or four copies of an opposition with the appellate clerk within ten days of the filing of the motion for rectification or articulation.

The appellate clerk shall forward the motion for rectification or articulation and the opposition, if any, to the trial judge who decided, or presided over, the subject matter of the motion for rectification or articulation for a decision on the motion. If any party requests it and it is deemed necessary by the trial court, the trial court shall hold a hearing at which arguments may be heard, evidence taken or a stipulation of counsel received and approved. The trial court may make such corrections or additions as are necessary for the proper presentation of the issues. The trial judge shall file the decision on the motion with the appellate clerk.

Nothing herein is intended to affect the existing practice with respect to opening and correcting judgments and the records on which they are based. The trial judge shall file any such order changing the judgment or the record with the appellate clerk.

Corrections or articulations made before the appellant's brief and appendix are prepared shall be included in the appellant's appendix. Corrections or articulations made after the appellant's brief and appendix have been filed, but before the appellee's brief and appendix have been filed, shall be included in the appellee's appendix. When corrections or articulations are made after both parties' briefs and appendices have been filed, the appellant shall file the corrections or articulations as an addendum to its appendix. Any addendum shall be filed within ten days after issuance of notice of the trial court's order correcting the record or articulating the decision.

The sole remedy of any party desiring the court having appellate jurisdiction to review the trial court's decision on the motion filed pursuant to this section or any other correction or addition ordered by the trial court during the pendency of the appeal shall be by motion for review under Section 66-7.

Upon the filing of a timely motion pursuant to Section 66-1, the appellate clerk may extend the time for filing briefs until after the trial court has ruled on a motion made pursuant to this section or until a motion for review under Section 66-7 is decided.

Any motion for rectification or articulation shall be filed within thirty-five days after the delivery of the last portion of the transcripts or, if none, after the filing of the appeal, or, if no memorandum of decision was filed before the filing of the appeal, after the filing of the memorandum of decision. If the court, sua sponte, sets a different deadline from that provided in Section 67-3 for filing the appellant's brief, a motion for rectification or articulation shall be filed ten days prior to the deadline for filing the appellant's brief, unless otherwise ordered by the court. The filing deadline may be extended for good cause. No motion for rectification or articulation shall be filed after the filing of the appellant's brief except for good cause shown.

A motion for further articulation may be filed by any party within twenty days after issuance of notice of the filing of an articulation by the trial judge. A motion for extension of time to file a motion for articulation shall be filed in accordance with Section 66-1.

§ 66-5. Motion for Rectification; Motion for Articulation (Applicable to appeals filed on or after July 1, 2013)

A motion seeking corrections in the transcript or the trial court record or seeking an articulation or further articulation of the decision of the trial court shall be called a motion for rectification or a motion for articulation, whichever is applicable. Any motion filed pursuant to this section shall state with particularity the relief sought.

Except in cases where the trial court was a three judge court, an original and two copies of such motion shall be filed with the appellate clerk. Where the trial court was a three judge court an original and four copies of such motion shall be filed. Any other party may oppose the motion by filing an original and two or four copies of an opposition with the appellate clerk within ten days of the filing of the motion for rectification or articulation.

The appellate clerk shall forward the motion for rectification or articulation and the opposition, if any, to the trial judge who decided, or presided over, the subject matter of the motion for rectification or articulation for a decision on the motion. If any party requests it and it is deemed necessary by the trial court, the trial court shall hold a hearing at which arguments may be heard, evidence taken or a stipulation of counsel received and approved. The trial court may make such corrections or additions as are necessary for the proper presentation of the issues. The trial judge shall file the decision on the motion with the appellate clerk.

Nothing herein is intended to affect the existing practice with respect to opening and correcting judgments and the records on which they are based. The trial judge shall file any such order changing the judgment or the record with the appellate clerk.

Corrections or articulations made before the appellant's brief and appendix are prepared shall be included in the appellant's appendix. Corrections or articulations made after the appellant's brief and appendix have been filed, but before the appellee's brief and appendix have been filed, shall be included in the appellee's appendix. When corrections or articulations are made after both parties' briefs and appendices have been filed, the appellant shall file the corrections or articulations as an addendum to its appendix. Any addendum shall be filed within ten days after issuance of notice of the trial court's order correcting the record or articulating the decision.

The sole remedy of any party desiring the court having appellate jurisdiction to review the trial court's decision on the motion filed pursuant to this section or any other correction or addition ordered by the trial court during the pendency of the appeal shall be by motion for review under Section 66-7.

Upon the filing of a timely motion pursuant to Section 66-1, the appellate clerk may extend the time for filing briefs until after the trial court has ruled on a motion made pursuant to this section or until a motion for review under Section 66-7 is decided.

Any motion for rectification or articulation shall be filed within thirty-five days after the delivery of the last portion of the transcripts or, if none, after the filing of the appeal, or, if no memorandum of decision was filed before the filing of the appeal, after the filing of the memorandum of decision. If the court, sua sponte, sets a different deadline from that provided in Section 67-3 for filing the appellant's brief, a motion for rectification or articulation shall be filed ten days prior to the deadline for filing the appellant's brief, unless otherwise ordered by the court. The filing deadline may be extended for good cause. No motion for rectification or articulation shall be filed after the filing of the appellant's brief except for good cause shown.

A motion for further articulation may be filed by any party within twenty days after issuance of notice of the filing of an articulation by the trial judge. A motion for extension of time to file a motion for articulation shall be filed in accordance with Section 66-1.

Historical Note

Derivation:
     1978 P.B. (1986–97), § 4051
     1978 P.B., § 3082
     1963 P.B., § 675
     1951 P.B., § 423
     1934 P.B., § 365
     1930 Rules Change, § 19
     1922 P.B., § 15
     1908 P.B., § 14
     1899 P.B., § 14
     58 Conn. at 585, § 9
     1879 P.B. p. 260, § 5

The fifth paragraph was amended in 2013 to make clear that the appendices should include articulations and corrects made in response to a motion under the rule.

In 2002 the penultimate paragraph extended the deadline if the court sua sponte (but only if sua sponte) extends the time to file the brief. The last two paragraphs were originally added in 1996.

The second paragraph was amended effective January 1, 2000 to refer to a three judge court.

Effective October 1, 1992, motions are to be filed in quadruplicate rather than triplicate.

The first paragraph was added effective October 1, 1986 at which time minor changes were made elsewhere in the rule.

This rule was clarified effective January 1, 1985 to refer explicitly to articulation of the trial court's decision. At the same time, language requiring the trial court to have a hearing before ruling on the motion was removed.

Substantial changes were made in this rule effective July 1, 1978, principally adding the language "the trial court record" in the first line of the second paragraph. The inclusion of this language was one of the very few drafting changes made by the Supreme Court between March 28, 1978, when the tentative draft of the new rules was released, and April 25, 1978, when the final one was released. This addition provided the basis for counsel to ask the trial court to articulate the basis of its decision more fully, until the rule became explicit in 1985.

Previously there was no significant change in this rule since 1934 except that in the 1963 rule, correction of the finding was specifically excluded from this section.

The 1951 rule was entitled "Correction of record".

Prior to 1934, the application for recertification was made directly to the Supreme Court.

Cross References

See § 66-7 for review of decision under this section.

Maltbie, Conn.App.Proc.2d, §§ 281–85.

AUTHORS' COMMENTS

On November 6, 2012, the Supreme Court finally adopted a new subsection (b) in § 61-10 effective January 1, 2013 abolishing the forfeiture practice the appellate courts had followed for many years if a litigant failed to move for articulation of an arguably ambiguous decision. For a discussion how we believe (b) should be applied to the motion for articulation, see Authors' Comments to § 61-10. Because this is such a recent and major change, the following articulation discussion needs to be read with some caution.

a. When to Use this Section

A motion under this section concerns matters that occurred or were raised in the trial court about which the trial judge would be familiar but which the Supreme Court would not be able to resolve without having the trial judge pass on the matter first. In general it is the appellant's duty to invoke this section to make sure that the record is adequate for appellate review of the appellant's case. Stiffler v. Continental Ins. Co., 288 Conn. 38, 52, 950 A.2d 1270, 1280 (2008) (no trial ruling on issue; review denied); Dickinson v. Mullaney, 284 Conn. 673, 680–82, 937 A.2d 667, 672–73 (2007) (no finding on crucial issue; review denied); In re Diamond J., 121 Conn.App. 392, 399–400, 996 A.2d 296, 301, cert. denied, 297 Conn. 927, 998 A.2d 1193 (2010); Miller v. Miller, 124 Conn.App. 36, 40, 3 A.3d 1018 (2010) (matter overlooked by trial judge; review denied); Edmands v. CUNO, Inc., 277 Conn. 425, 436–37, 892 A.2d 938, 947 (2006) (articulation off the record inadequate). But see In re Brian T., 134 Conn.App. 1, 8, 38 A.3d 114, 119 (2012) (suo motu articulation order under §§ 60-2 and 60-5). Articulation is unnecessary if the needed finding is implicit in other findings, Deutsche Bank National Trust Co. v. Perez, 146 Conn.App. 833, 843–44 n.6, 80 A.3d 910. 916 n.6 (2013), cert. granted, 311 Conn. 924, 86 A.3d 1058 (2014); or if a finding is unnecessary because the trial court ruled as a matter of law. MSO, LLC v. DeSimone, 313 Conn. 54, 60-62, 94 A.3d 1189, 1193–94 (2014).

The 2013 amendment to P.B. § 61-10 provides that the failure to seek articulation shall not be the "sole" ground to deny review. While that amendment means the appellate tribunal will probably review more cases on the merits, it does not mean that parties should dispense with motions under this section. For example, the failure to move for rectification may result in a refusal to review if critical documents are missing from the record. State v. Ciullo, 140 Conn.App. 393, 412, 59 A.3d 293, 307 (refusing to review claim that jury instructions varied from written instructions provided to counsel where written version not in record), cert. granted, 308 Conn. 919, 62 A.3d 1133 (2013); State v. Alvarado, 139 Conn.App. 494, 497, 56 A.3d 737, 741 (2012) (record not rectified to include hospital report), cert. denied, 307 Conn. 956, 59 A.3d 1191 (2013).

Further, the reviewing court will normally read an ambiguous record to support rather than undermine the judgment. Synkowicz v. Synkowicz, 140 Conn.App. 525, 532, 59 A.3d 1194, 1199 (2013). Moving for articulation can pin down the trial court's reasoning and avoid this fate. Moreover, if the trial court issues a one-word decision, e.g., "denied," the failure to move for articulation may still result in the court's refusal to review the issue. State v. Henderson, 140 Conn.App. 672, 60 A.3d 294 (2013).

The death of the trial judge who rendered the decision does not excuse the requirement to seek articulation. Lawton v. Weiner, 91 Conn.App. 698, 715–16, 882 A.2d 151, 164 (2005). The authors do not agree with Lawton.

If the issue involves subject matter jurisdiction, the failure to articulate an unclear decision will not prevent review and reversal. LaSalle Bank, Nat. Ass'n v. Bialobrzeski, 123 Conn.App. 781, 788, 3 A.3d 176, 181–82 (2010). The authors do not agree with this exception. After all, jurisdiction in a court of general jurisdiction is supposed to be presumed.

If the issue concerns a cross appeal, the burden is on the cross appellant. Knapp v. Knapp, 270 Conn. 815, 825, 856 A.2d 358, 364 (2004); Yellow Page Consultants, Inc. v. Omni Home Health Services, Inc., 59 Conn.App. 194, 201, 756 A.2d 309, 313 (2000). This burden also applies to an appellee raising an alternate basis to affirm. Aaron Manor, Inc. v. Irving, 307 Conn. 608, 619, 57 A.3d 342, 349 (2013); Olson v. Mohammadu, 310 Conn. 665, 684–85 n.15, 81 A.3d 215, 118 n.15 (2013); Zahringer v. Zahringer, 262 Conn. 360, 370–71, 815 A.2d 75, 81 (2003); Orcutt v. Commissioner of Correction, 284 Conn. 724, 737–39, 937 A.2d 656, 663–64 (2007).

It is also important for appellees to consider using this section if the memorandum of decision is inadequate. The last thing the appellee wants is to have the Supreme Court decide the appeal on a weak supporting record when a stronger record could have been made. Reversals were ordered in Lynn v. Lynn, 130 Conn.App. 319, 23 A.3d 771 (2011) (contempt judgment reversed); Fairfield County Trust Co. v. Thompson, 152 Conn. 718, 719, 210 A.2d 171, 172 (1965); and State v. Ball, 159 Conn. 603, 604, 267 A.2d 441, 442 (1970), because of inadequate factual records. See also Hoyt v. City of Stamford, 116 Conn. 402, 409, 165 A. 357, 360 (1933) (subordinate facts do not support conclusions). On the other hand, the appellee should not rush to rectify the decision, because sometimes the trial court will weaken it factually. See State v. Newman, 127 Conn. 398, 402, 17 A.2d 774, 775 (1940).

b. Excusing Compliance

Even prior to the 2013 amendment to P.B. § 61-10, the failure to seek articulation was sometimes excused, such as when the record is adequate and the facts are not in dispute; Listenes v. Listenes, 102 Conn.App. 642, 646 n.3, 925 A.2d 1249, 1251 n.3 (2007); or if the appellant has filed a motion which is the functional equivalent of a motion for articulation, North Park Mortg. Services, Inc. v. Pinette, 27 Conn.App. 628, 629–30, 608 A.2d 714, 715 (1992) (motion for reargument and for a written decision sufficient), or if review is plenary; Town of Trumbull v. Palmer, 123 Conn.App. 244, 251 n.8, 1 A.3d 1121, 1128 n.8, cert.

denied, 299 Conn. 907, 10 A.3d 526 (2010); although reliance on these cases is risky. In any event, if clarification is needed, do not count on the Supreme or Appellate Court to order a remand for articulation on its own, although it did do so in State v. Kelly, 313 Conn. 1, 12, 95 A.3d 1081, 1089 (2014); Aley v. Aley, 97 Conn.App. 850, 855, 908 A.2d 8, 11–12 (2006), and Urich v. Fish, 261 Conn. 575, 580, 804 A.2d 795, 798 (2002). Suo motu orders for articulation may become more frequent with the 2013 amendment to P.B. § 66-10. Nor is it likely to grant a request in the appellant's brief for such a remand. Phillips v. Phillips, 101 Conn.App. 65, 71 n.1, 922 A.2d 1100, 1104 n.1 (2007). Nor will it treat a motion to set aside order as a motion for articulation. Aquarion Water Co. of Connecticut v. Beck Law Products and Forms, LLC, 98 Conn.App. 234, 241–42 n.6, 907 A.2d 1274, 1279 n.6 (2006).

c. § 64-1 versus § 66-5

If the trial judge fails to issue a statement of decision at all in any circumstance when § 64-1 applies, the proper response is a notice under § 64-1, not § 66-5. Murphy v. Zoning Bd. of Appeals of City of Stamford, 86 Conn.App. 147, 158–60, 860 A.2d 764, 772–74 (2004), cert. denied, 273 Conn. 910, 870 A.2d 1080 (2005). However, in Chapman Lumber, Inc. v. Tager, 288 Conn. 69, 83 n.20, 952 A.2d 1, 13 n.20 (2008), and Town of Trumbull v. Palmer, 123 Conn.App. 244, 249 n.7, 1 A.3d 1121, 1126 n.7 (2010), cert. denied, 299 Conn. 907, 10 A.3d 526 (2010), the courts treated a motion for review of a denial of articulation as a motion for compliance with § 64-1.

d. Various Uses of § 66-5

The following would appropriately be considered under this section:

1. To seek an articulation or a further articulation of the factual basis of the trial court's decision under § 60-5, or to seek a ruling on an issue a party raised but the trial court failed to address. Bauer v. Bauer, 308 Conn. 124, 130–35, 60 A.3d 950, 954–57 (2013) (reconciling discrepancy between findings and orders is permissible use of articulation). The failure to seek articulation has been criticized by the court on numerous occasions. See e.g., Celentano v. Oaks Condominium Ass'n, 265 Conn. 579, 589 n.9, 830 A.2d 164, 172 n.9 (2003); Benedetto v. Wanat, 79 Conn.App. 139, 154 n.13, 829 A.2d 901, 910 n.13 (2003). The appellee should make sure that a correction in the factual basis for the decision does not undermine any of the conclusions, Goodsell v. Brighenti, 128 Conn. 581, 584, 24 A.2d 834, 835 (1942). See Housatonic Valley Pub. Co. v. Citytrust, 4 Conn.App. 12, 15, 492 A.2d 203, 205 (1985). This rule also applies to rulings in criminal cases. State v. Fontanez, 37 Conn.App. 205, 207, 655 A.2d 797, 798 (1995).

However, in order to articulate a decision, it must be unclear; this section cannot be used to change a decision or the reasoning. State v. Wilson, 199 Conn. 417, 434–38, 513 A.2d 620, 630–32 (1986); In re Jason R., 306 Conn. 438, 51 A.3d 334 (2012); Lusa v. Grunberg, 101 Conn.App. 739, 742–43, 923 A.2d 795, 798–99 (2007); Gomes v. Massachusetts Bay Ins. Co., 87 Conn.App. 416, 422 n.7, 866 A.2d 704, 708 n.7 (2005); but see Misthopoulos v. Misthopoulos, 297 Conn. 358, 380, 999 A.2d 721, 735 (2010) (noting that an articulation would allow the trial court "to correct any inconsistencies or miscalculations"); Cappo v. Suda, 126 Conn.App. 1, 13, 10 A.3d 560, 569 (2011) (defendant should have filed motion for rectification to correct factual errors). Nevertheless, it can be used to change a clerical error; Maguire v. Maguire, 222 Conn. 32, 39, 608 A.2d 79, 82–83 (1992); or to clarify why an issue was not properly briefed. Town of Windham v. Freedom of Information Com'n, 48 Conn.App. 522, 524 n.1, 711 A.2d 738, 739 n.1 (1998).

In Wasson v. Wasson, 91 Conn.App. 149, 881 A.2d 356 (2005), the Appellate Court went to great lengths to explain why a trial court's decision providing a third option for dividing a marital estate was a clarification and not a modification. The authors agree with the concurring opinion that the order was a modification but was proper because it was made in response to a § 11-11 motion to reargue. Id. at 167–68, 881 A.2d at 367–68 (Flynn, J., concurring).

If the trial judge uses the articulation process to change a decision, that becomes an appealable order. Miller v. Miller, 16 Conn.App. 412, 547 A.2d 922 (1988). In Sosin v. Sosin, 300 Conn. 205, 242–43, 14 A.3d 307, 329–30 (2011), the Supreme Court made clear that a party may challenge an inconsistent articulation on appeal without first filing a motion for review. Note, however, ordinarily a motion for review, not an appeal, is the proper way to challenge an articulation ruling. Lynn v. Lynn, 145 Conn.App. 33, 37 n.2, 74 A.3d 506, 508 n.2 (2013).

The trial court's failure to provide a detailed analysis does not require articulation if the reviewing court can determine the basis of the trial court's decision. Thus, articulation is not required just because the trial court "did not spell out in detail" its reasoning. Town of Westbrook v. ITT Hartford Group, Inc., 60 Conn.App. 767, 772 n.10, 761 A.2d 242, 245 n.10 (2000). Also, the trial court's precise legal analysis is not essential if review is de novo. Miller's Pond Co., LLC v. City of New London, 273 Conn. 786, 815 n.27, 873 A.2d 965, 984 n.27 (2005); Community Action for Greater Middlesex County, Inc. v. American Alliance Ins. Co., 254 Conn. 387, 392–97, 757 A.2d 1074, 1077–80 (2000); Smith v. Lefebre, 92 Conn.App. 417, 420 n.4, 885 A.2d 1232, 1234 n.4 (2005) (articulation of reason for holding verdict shocked the conscience unnecessary); City of Norwalk v. Farrell, 80 Conn.App. 399, 406 n.10, 835 A.2d 117, 121 n.10 (2003); but see Alter and Associates, LLC v. Lantz, 90 Conn.App. 15, 876 A.2d 1204 (2005) (refusing to review legal question where trial court had not articulated basis and appellant failed to seek review of motion for articulation).

Articulation is also unnecessary if the issue is failure to state a claim; Singhaviroj v. Board of Educ. of Town of Fairfield, 301 Conn. 1, 16–17, 17 A.3d 1013, 1021 (2011); or the duty is on the trial court to do so without any motion, as in explaining any deviation from the child support guidelines. Wallbeoff v. Wallbeoff, 113 Conn.App. 107, 110–13, 965 A.2d 571, 573–74 (2009).

If a decision is clarified after a party has filed a brief, a request for permission to file a supplemental brief would be in order. Purnell v. Purnell, 95 Conn.App. 677, 684 n.3, 897 A.2d 717, 721 n.3 (2006).

A spectacular example of a successful articulation requested by the appellant is Housatonic Valley Pub. Co. v. Citytrust, 4 Conn.App. 12, 15, 492 A.2d 203, 205 (1985), where the trial court clarified its decision by stating the ground on which it made the decision; the Appellate Court has held that that ground was clearly erroneous and directed judgment for the appellant.

If the trial court does articulate its decision, but the moving party is still dissatisfied, that party can seek to have it refined, Grunschlag v. Ethel Walker School, Inc., 190 Conn. 679, 683 n.2, 462 A.2d 1, 3 n.2 (1983).

In light of Kaczynski v. Kaczynski, 294 Conn. 121, 131, 981 A.2d 1068, 1074 (2009), it is now necessary to move for articulation in a civil case if the trial court does not state the standard of proof it applied and the appellant believes the proper standard is higher than preponderance of the evidence. See also Singhaviroj v. Board of Educ. of Town of Fairfield, 301 Conn. 1, 17 n.12, 17 A.3d 1013, 1022 n.12 (2011). Before *Kaczynski*, the presumption without a motion for articulation was that the trial court applied the preponderance standard; now the presumption is that the trial court applied the correct standard. An articulation in In re Jason R., 306 Conn. 438, 51 A.3d 334 (2012), persuaded the majority that the trial court had applied the proper burden of proof to the proper party.

Whether a decision is unclear is itself occasionally unclear. In David Caron Chrysler Motors, LLC v. Goodhall's, Inc., 122 Conn.App. 149, 997 A.2d 647

(2010), the Appellate Court split 2-1 in concluding the decision was unclear and therefore the appellant should have moved for articulation. The Supreme Court disagreed. David Caron Chrysler Motors, LLC v. Goodhall's, Inc., 304 Conn. 738, 743–44, 43 A.3d 164, 168–69 (2012). For appellants there is no safe harbor here, because filing an unnecessary motion for articulation often gives the trial judge a chance to make things worse for the appellant.

2.   To clarify the legal basis for a ruling, Leverty and Hurley Co. v. Commissioner of Transp., 192 Conn. 377, 379, 471 A.2d 958, 959 (1984); Ceslik v. Winer, 62 Conn.App. 650, 652, 772 A.2d 655, 656 (2001).

3.   To show that an oral motion was made in chambers or otherwise is not in the record, State v. McIntyre, 242 Conn. 318, 332–33, 699 A.2d 911, 920 (1997); Fishman v. Scarpa, 149 Conn. 531, 533, 182 A.2d 410, 411 (1962); Leograndis v. Liquor Control Commission, 149 Conn. 507, 511, 182 A.2d 9, 11 (1962); cf. Hasbrouck v. Hasbrouck, 195 Conn. 558, 560, 489 A.2d 1022, 1023 (1985).

4.   To reflect oral argument not on the record, Nair v. Thaw, 156 Conn. 445, 455, 242 A.2d 757, 762 (1968), especially to show that a particular issue was argued to the jury, Syms v. Harmon, 134 Conn. 653, 656, 60 A.2d 166, 167 (1948).

5.   To contradict a finding that the trial court offered to reopen the judgment to correct a mistake but the appellant refused, Levy v. Carter Rice & Co., 136 Conn. 216, 221, 70 A.2d 147, 150 (1949); or to contradict a finding that one of the trial lawyers had certain knowledge relevant to juror disqualification, McCarten v. Connecticut Co., 103 Conn. 537, 539–41, 131 A. 505, 506–07 (1925); or otherwise to contradict the trial court's recollection of something not on the record, Kakalik v. Bernardo, 184 Conn. 386, 390–91, 439 A.2d 1016, 1018 (1981); such as an agreement of counsel as to the scope of the trial, Leventhal v. Town of Stratford, 125 Conn. 215, 217, 4 A.2d 428, 429 (1939); or a stipulation of counsel, Keating v. Glass Container Corp., 197 Conn. 428, 434–435, 497 A.2d 763, 767 (1985).

6.   To show evidence not transcribed, Hirsch v. Vegiard, 137 Conn. 302, 303, 77 A.2d 85, 86 (1950); State v. Benitez, 122 Conn.App. 608, 613–14, 998 A.2d 844, 847–48 (2010) (defendant should have moved to rectify record to show comments made at site visit by jury).

7.   To make corrections in the transcript, Whiteside v. State, 148 Conn. 77, 83, 167 A.2d 450, 453–54 (1961); or to complain if the court makes such corrections, Papallo v. Meriden Sav. Bank, 128 Conn. 289, 22 A.2d 637 (1941).

8.   To correct the printed record or the judgment file, Kakadelis v. DeFabritis, 191 Conn. 276 n.1, 464 A.2d 57 n.1 (1983).

9.   To ask the trial judge to rule on an overlooked matter, such as counsel fees, Wolk v. Wolk, 191 Conn. 328, 335 n.1, 464 A.2d 780, 785 n.1 (1983); or counsel fees and interest, Gennarini Const. Co., Inc. v. Messina Painting & Decorating Co., 5 Conn.App. 61, 66, 496 A.2d 539, 542 (1985); or where the court has failed to rule on a motion, Rahmati v. Mehri, 188 Conn. 583, 588, 452 A.2d 638 (1982), or a claim, McCarthy v. Chromium Process Co., 127 Conn.App. 324, 334, 13 A.3d 715, 723 (2011).

To some extent there is an overlap here with § 60-2. For example, if the trial judge fails to decide a claim of law, a motion to the Appellate Court might well be made under § 60-2. However, § 66-5 is a more tactful way to oversights by the trial judge, who can correct the record before the Appellate Court becomes involved.

10.   To show that a party made a claim of law to the trial judge, Harty v. Cantor Fitzgerald and Co., 275 Conn. 72, 90 n.9, 881 A.2d 139, 151 n.9 (2005); Stabile v. D. & N. Transp. Co., 129 Conn. 11, 13, 26 A.2d 12, 13 (1942).

11.   To show that an overlay was added to an exhibit after the trial, New

York, N.H. & H.R. Co. v. Armstrong, 92 Conn. 349, 355, 102 A. 791, 794 (1918).

12. To show that the trial judge changed a finding of fact from "proven" to "not proven." Morris v. Winchester Repeating Arms Co., 73 Conn. 680, 690, 49 A. 180, 184 (1901).

13. To have an exhibit marked for identification, State v. Irizarry, 95 Conn.App. 224, 239 n.22, 896 A.2d 828, 839 n.22, cert. denied, 279 Conn. 902, 901 A.2d 1224 (2006) (the court had granted a motion to preclude testimony on the report after apparently reviewing it); State v. Calabrese, 279 Conn. 393, 405 n.16, 902 A.2d 1044, 1052 n.16 (2006) (answering machine had been offered but inadvertently not marked for identification).

14. To have a missing document that was before the court made part of the court file; Bauer v. Bauer, 2009 WL 1532343 (Conn. Super. Ct. 2009), aff'd, 308 Conn. 124, 60 A.3d 950 (2013).

15. To correct a transcript cover page to indicate the judge who presided at hearing. State v. Pires, 310 Conn. 222, 226 n.4, 77 A.3d 87, 91 n.4 (2013).

e. Matters off the Record

That this rule can be used for matters not on the record does not mean that it can be used to import into the record matters that were never presented to the trial court, State v. Brunetti, 279 Conn. 39, 55 n.27, 901 A.2d 1, 14 n.27 (2006). Nor can issues be raised for the first time in a motion for articulation. Brandy v. Commissioner of Correction, 89 Conn.App. 387, 394 n.6, 873 A.2d 1061, 1065 n.6 (2005). Also, if the trial court finds that it has no recollection of matters allegedly discussed in chambers, this rule is not much help. Eamiello v. Piscitelli, 133 Conn. 360, 363, 51 A.2d 912, 914 (1947). Appellate courts generally will not consider facts extraneous to the record, McCarthy v. Santangelo, 137 Conn. 410, 412, 78 A.2d 240, 241 (1951), so don't put something in your brief unless the record supports it, State v. McCarthy, 179 Conn. 1, 7, 425 A.2d 924, 929 (1979). However, the Supreme Court has occasionally accepted representations of counsel on marginal or undisputed matters, Connecticut Mobile Home Ass'n, Inc. v. Jensen's, Inc., 178 Conn. 586, 593 n.3, 424 A.2d 285, 289 n.3 (1979); Bates v. Spooner, 75 Conn. 501, 505, 54 A. 305, 307 (1903).

f. Preappeal Matters

Notwithstanding the opening language of § 60-2, the Appellate Court has held that a § 66-5 motion may be filed only after an appeal is filed. Thorsen v. Durkin Development, LLC, 129 Conn.App. 68, 70 n.2, 20 A.3d 707, 710 n.2 (2011); Brycki v. Brycki, 91 Conn.App. 579, 594, 881 A.2d 1056, 1064–65 (2005). Before an appeal, the authors recommend the filing of a motion for clarification (see our commentary to § 11-1), although § 66-6 would not apply to the trial court's ruling on that motion. Thus, once an appeal is filed, a § 66-5 motion would have to be filed anyway.

g. Factual Questions on Motion

If there is a factual question raised by a § 66-5 motion, it is the authors' opinion that the trial judge must resolve it, although the procedure is unclear. See State v. Floyd, 253 Conn. 700, 732, 756 A.2d 799, 818–19 (2000) (trial court order to hold evidentiary hearing on whether there had been a plea agreement when a witness testified). There used to be a specific procedure for depositions to be taken; see Sperandeo v. Aetna Cas. & Sur. Co., 131 Conn. 407, 409, 40 A.2d 280, 281 (1944); cf. Cohn v. Dunn, 111 Conn. 342, 351, 149 A. 851, 854, 70 A.L.R. 740 (1930); Marks v. Dorkin, 104 Conn. 660, 664, 133 A. 915, 917 (1926); but this is no longer so. This section does not afford the parties an automatic evidentiary hearing, and such is not required by due process. State v. Lopez, 235 Conn. 487, 668 A.2d 360 (1995).

h. Review of Articulation Decision

A party who is dissatisfied with the trial court's ruling under § 66-5 may seek review under § 66-7. Where an articulation or rectification is necessary, the party must seek review under § 66-7 or waive the issue, Highgate Condominium Ass'n v. Watertown Fire Dist., 210 Conn. 6, 21, 553 A.2d 1126, 1134 (1989); Ramondetta v. Amenta, 97 Conn.App. 151, 167–68, 903 A.2d 232, 241–42 (2006). Another possible approach, if the articulation itself is unclear, is to move to clarify or to refine it. Eslami v. Eslami, 218 Conn. 801, 817, 591 A.2d 411, 419 (1991); Grunschlag v. Ethel Walker School, Inc., 190 Conn. 679, 683 n.2, 462 A.2d 1, 3 n.2 (1983). The authors do not recommend this approach. Better to move for review and let the Appellate Court sort things out. In any event, simply filing a second, third or fourth motion for articulation with the trial court is improper. Viets v. Viets, 39 Conn.App. 610, 666 A.2d 434 (1995).

i. Workers Compensation Cases

If an appeal bypasses the Superior Court, as in workers' compensation cases, the agency is the "trial court" for the purpose of this rule. Cable v. Bic Corp., 270 Conn. 433, 444–45, 854 A.2d 1057, 1065 (2004); Plati v. United Parcel Service, 33 Conn.App. 490, 636 A.2d 395 (1994). But see Sidella v. Kelly Services, Inc., 41 Conn.App. 116, 675 A.2d 1 (1996) (limiting Plati to compensation cases where the Compensation Review Board is not involved).

j. Time for Filing

The motion generally must be filed at least 10 days before the appellant's brief is due. The existence of a motion for articulation does not automatically entitle a party to an extension of time to file a brief, so be sure to file a timely motion under § 66-1 if needed. Likewise, if a motion for extension of time is requested for the brief, be sure to do so for the articulation motion at the same time, unless you have already filed the motion for articulation. Note that the clerk does not have the authority to grant an extension of time after the deadline has run. Only the judges can do that.

§ 66-6. Motion for Review; In General

The court may, on written motion for review stating the grounds for the relief sought, modify or vacate any order made by the trial court under Section 66-1(a); any action by the appellate clerk under Section 66-1(c)(2); any order made by the trial court, or by the workers' compensation commissioner in cases arising under General Statutes § 31-290a(b), relating to the perfecting of the record for an appeal or the procedure of prosecuting or defending against an appeal or any order made by the trial court concerning a stay of execution in a case on appeal; any order made by the trial court concerning the waiver of fees, costs and security under Sections 63-6 or 63-7; or any order concerning the withdrawal of appointed appellate counsel pursuant to Section 62-9(d). Motions for review shall be filed within ten days from the issuance of notice of the order sought to be reviewed. Motions for review of the clerk's taxation of costs under judgments of the court having appellate jurisdiction shall be governed by Section 71-3.

If a motion for review of a decision depends on a transcript of evidence or proceedings taken by a court reporter, the moving party shall file with the motion either a transcript or a copy of the transcript order form (JD-ES-38). The opposing party may, within one week after the transcript or the copy of the order form is filed by the moving party, file either a transcript of additional evidence or a copy of the order form. Parties filing or ordering a transcript shall order an electronic version of the transcript in accordance with Section 63-8A.

Historical Note

Derivation:
    1978 P.B. (1986–97), § 4053
    1978 P.B., § 3107
    1963 P.B., § 694
    1951 P.B., §§ 411, 435

The addition of §§ 63-6, 63-7 and 62-9(d) to the first sentence were made in 2006. The last sentence was added in 2002. The first sentence was revised in 1997 to clarify that Appellate Court rulings are not reviewable by the Supreme Court under this section. Changes in 1996 clarified that the existence of an appeal is not always a prerequisite to the use of this section.

This section was amended effective October 1, 1986 to include review of orders of the clerk under § 66-2. The first paragraph was redrafted effective January 1, 1985 to clarify bail review and the time period for filing various motions. The second sentence was entirely redrafted effective July 1, 1979 in order to reflect the abolition of the finding system.

The rule effective July 1, 1978 expands the scope of this rule somewhat by explicitly referring to trial court orders concerning extensions of time. Effective June 1, 1971, the second paragraph was added. In 1963 the first sentence of the first paragraph was broadened to include review of trial court action in relation to "the perfecting of the record" and "procedure of * * * defending against the appeal."

Prior to 1951, there was no particular rule concerning reviews of decisions on stays of execution and on bail. However, an application for review of the denial of bail pending appeal had previously been considered, Winnick v. Reilly, 100 Conn. 291, 297, 123 A. 440, 442 (1924).

Cross Reference
    Maltbie, Conn.App.Proc.2d, § 271 (prosecuting appeal)

AUTHORS' COMMENTS

1. Review of Extensions of Time

Even before the 1978 amendment, this section was broad enough to review decisions under old § 665 (now § 66-1(a)), Minnelli v. Poulos, 166 Conn. 666, 316 A.2d 421 (1974). Such review can and should be requested before the appeal is filed. See the first sentence of § 60-2.

If the trial judge denies a motion for extension of time to appeal, the prospective appellant should file both a motion for review under this section and a motion for permission to file a late appeal under § 60-2(6), although granting a § 60-2(6) motion obviously is discretionary in the Appellate Court. The latter motion was granted by the Appellate Court in Kinderman v. Kinderman, 19 Conn.App. 534, 562 A.2d 1151 (1989). The advantage of the § 60-2(6) motion is that it bypasses the abuse of discretion standard that may apply on a § 66-6 motion.

2. Stays of Execution

A motion to review an order concerning a stay of execution must be filed within ten days after the issuance of notice was sent out or announced in open court. Stay rulings are only reviewable pursuant to this section and not by appeal. Clark v. Clark, 150 Conn.App. 551, 575–76, 91 A.3d 944, 957–58 (2014).

A denial of a stay was reversed in Moshier v. Goodnow, 217 Conn. 303, 305 n.4, 586 A.2d 557, 558 n.4 (1991), and in Rosado v. Bridgeport Roman Catholic Diocesan Corp., 60 Conn.App. 134, 758 A.2d 916 (2000). A termination of a stay was reversed in Lopez v. Board of Education, 310 Conn. 576, 686 n.11, 81 A.3d 184, 190 n.11 (2012).

3. Waiver of Fees

This section should be used to review a denial of waiver, rather than raising the issue after the merits of the appeal. State v. Lanasa, 141 Conn.App. 685, 687 n.1, 62 A.3d 572, 574 n.1, cert. denied, 308 Conn. 945, 66 A.3d 885 (2013).

4. Finding

A finding is no longer needed. For prior law, see State v. Clark, 160 Conn. 555, 556, 274 A.2d 451, 451 (1970); Brody v. Dunnigan, 161 Conn. 602, 603, 282 A.2d 913, 913 (1971). See also commentary to § 61-14. Nevertheless, an evidentiary hearing may be necessary and may require a factual determination by the trial court. State v. Floyd, 253 Conn. 700, 732, 756 A.2d 799, 818–19 (2000) (motion for rectification).

5. Review Prior to Appeal

Trial court decisions previously could not be reviewed under this section before the appeal is filed, State v. Audet, 170 Conn. 337, 343, 365 A.2d 1082, 1086 (1976). A change in § 60-2 eliminates this problem.

6. Timeliness

A motion for review must be filed in ten days. A motion filed six days late was dismissed as untimely in Town of Southington v. Pierce, 29 Conn.App. 716, 719 n.3, 617 A.2d 929, 930 n.3 (1992).

7. Withdrawal of Appearance

For review of the trial court's denial of withdrawal of an appellate appearance under § 62-9, see Franko v. Bronson, 19 Conn.App. 686, 563 A.2d 1036 (1989) (abrogated by, Vazquez v. Commissioner of Correction, 88 Conn.App. 226, 869 A.2d 234 (2005)).

8. Bond

An order imposing an appeal bond of $5,000.00 on a contempt appeal should have been reviewed under this section (bail) rather than on the merits of the appeal. Hartford Federal Sav. & Loan Ass'n v. Tucker, 192 Conn. 1, 8, 469 A.2d 778, 782 (1984). See State v. McDowell, 241 Conn. 413, 696 A.2d 977 (1997). This section apparently also applies to review of a summary process bond set under C.G.S.A. § 47a-35a(b). See City of New Haven v. Konstandinidis, 29 Conn.App. 139, 140, 612 A.2d 822, 823 (1992). If this section is applicable, filing an amended appeal under § 61-9 is not a proper alternative. Scagnelli v. Donovan, 88 Conn.App. 840, 871 A.2d 1084 (2005).

9. Review on Merits of Appeal

A litigant who is disappointed with a ruling on a motion for review should consider briefing the matter in the brief on the merits. This almost succeeded in State v. Bergin, 214 Conn. 657, 574 A.2d 164 (1990). See also Barry v. Historic Dist. Com'n of Borough of Litchfield, 108 Conn.App. 682, 687 n.2, 950 A.2d 1, 6 n.2, cert. denied, 289 Conn. 942, 959 A.2d 1008 (2008) (reconsidering a jurisdictional question). While McClintock v. Rivard, 219 Conn. 417, 425, 593 A.2d 1375, 1379 (1991), and State v. Holloway, 22 Conn.App. 265, 272–76, 577

A.2d 1064, 1068–70, cert. denied, 215 Conn. 819, 576 A.2d 547 (1990), discourage such an attempt, they do not completely close the door to such review. However, the Appellate Court did close the door in State v. Casiano, 122 Conn.App. 61, 998 A.2d 792, cert. denied, 298 Conn. 931, 5 A.3d 491 (2010). In those cases the sole remedy was held to be the motion for review. Attempting review on the merits almost certainly will fail in any event if the litigant does not first move for review under this section. State v. Pieger, 42 Conn.App. 460, 467, 680 A.2d 1001, 1005 (1996), aff'd, 240 Conn. 639, 692 A.2d 1273 (1997).

The failure to file a motion for review of a denial of a stay of execution generally does not affect the appealability of the order sought to be stayed. Goodson v. State, 228 Conn. 106, 117–18, 635 A.2d 285, 290 (1993). Where the lack of a stay destroys aggrievement, however, see, e.g., Lichtman v. Beni, 280 Conn. 25, 905 A.2d 647 (2006) (failure to seek stay of discharge of mechanics lien mooted appeal), the party should seek review under this section.

If the appeal is transferred to the Supreme Court after an Appellate Court ruling, a motion for reconsideration might be in order. If untimely, a motion for permission to file would be in order. A timely motion for reconsideration accompanied by a motion for transfer might be the best option. This appears to be essentially what happened (successfully) in Office of Consumer Counsel v. Department of Public Utility Control, 234 Conn. 624, 662 A.2d 1251 (1995).

10. Denial of Request to Appeal

The denial of a request to appeal a habeas corpus decision under C.G.S.A. § 52-470(b) can itself be appealed; prior to the 1996 revisions a motion for review was not the proper remedy. Simms v. Warden, 229 Conn. 178, 186–89, 640 A.2d 601, 606–07 (1994). This aspect of *Simms* apparently is overruled by the revisions. See official commentary. State v. McMillan, 43 Conn.App. 698, 685 A.2d 1138 (1996), which holds that the state must file an appeal rather than a motion to challenge a denial of permission to appeal under C.G.S.A. § 54-96, fails to take account of the 1996 amendments to this section. State v. Avcollie, 174 Conn. 100, 110–11, 384 A.2d 315, 320–21 (1977), relied on by *McMillan*, validates the appeal route but does not consider the motion route.

11. Workers Compensation Appeals

See § i of commentary to § 66-5.

12. Miscellaneous

The Supreme Court cited this rule to transfer a petition for review of the sealing of a grand jury report. In re Investigatory Grand Jury No. 2007-04, 293 Conn. 464, 467 n.2, 977 A.2d 621, 624 n.2 (2009). This seems to be an overly broad reading of this section.

This rule provides the sole means to review an order for use and occupancy payments pending a summary judgment appeal. Brown v. Fenyes, 127 Conn.App. 771, 15 A.3d 1160, cert. denied, 302 Conn. 902, 23 A.3d 1242 (2011).

A motion for review is the sole remedy for review of an order denying appointment of counsel. State v. Jimenez, 127 Conn.App. 706, 14 A.3d 1083 (2011).

§ 66-7. Motion for Review of Motion for Rectification of Appeal or Articulation (Applicable to appeals filed before July 1, 2013)

Any party aggrieved by the action of the trial judge as regards rectification of the appeal or articulation under Section 66-5 may, within ten days of the issuance of notice of the order sought to be reviewed, make a written motion for review to the court, to be filed with the appellate clerk, and the court may, upon such a motion, direct any action it deems proper. If the motion depends upon a transcript of evidence or proceedings taken by a court reporter, the procedure set forth in Section 66-6 shall be followed. Corrections which the court makes or orders made pursuant hereto shall be included in the prepared record in the same way in which, under Section 66-5, corrections made by the trial judge are included.

§ 66-7. Motion for Review of Motion for Rectification of Appeal or Articulation (Applicable to appeals filed on or after July 1, 2013)

Any party aggrieved by the action of the trial judge as regards rectification of the appeal or articulation under Section 66-5 may, within ten days of the issuance of notice of the order sought to be reviewed, make a written motion for review to the court, to be filed with the appellate clerk, and the court may, upon such a motion, direct any action it deems proper. If the motion depends upon a transcript of evidence or proceedings taken by a court reporter, the procedure set forth in Section 66-6 shall be followed. Corrections or articulations which the trial court makes or orders made pursuant to this section shall be included in the appendices as indicated in Section 66-5.

Historical Note

Derivation:
   1978 P.B. (1986–97), § 4054
   1978 P.B., § 3108
   1963 P.B., § 695
   1951 P.B., § 423
   1934 P.B., § 365
   1930 Rules Change, § 19
   1922 P.B., § 15
   1908 P.B., § 14
   1899 P.B., § 14

This rule was amended in 2013 to make clear that articulations or corrections that result from a motion under this rule should be included in the appendix.

Effective October 1, 1992, this rule was revised by requiring the motion to review to be filed within ten days of the issuance of the order to be reviewed.

This rule was clarified effective January 1, 1985 to follow changes made in § 3107 (now § 66-6) at the same time. Prior thereto, factual questions were resolved by reference to a referee under §§ 3103–05. Prior to 1951 rule, factual questions were resolved by affidavits and depositions, rather than by reference to a referee. See Bielan v. Bielan, 135 Conn. 163, 164 n.1, 62 A.2d 664, 665 n.1, 9 A.L.R.2d 1019 (1948). Prior to 1934, a motion for rectification was made directly to the Supreme Court.

Cross References

Maltbie, Conn.App.Proc.2d, §§ 281–85 (in general); § 292 (stays of execution)

AUTHORS' COMMENTS

This is the section to use to order the trial court to articulate its decision.

Wright v. Commissioner of Correction, 106 Conn.App. 342, 344–45, 942 A.2d 438, 439–40, cert. denied, 289 Conn. 901, 957 A.2d 875 (2008).

A party has ten days to file a motion for review under this rule. As to what can be rectified, see commentary to § 66-5. A failure to move for review of an inadequate articulation or a denial of articulation was fatal in Cedar Mountain, LLC v. D & M Screw Machine Products, LLC, 135 Conn.App. 276, 286–87, 41 A.3d 1131, 1138–39 (2012), and numerous other cases. But see Miller v. Town of Westport, 268 Conn. 207, 220 n.21, 842 A.2d 558, 566 n.21 (2004). If, however, the appellant unsuccessfully moves for review, the appellant has complied with § 61-10. Kenny v. Banks, 289 Conn. 529, 532 n.5, 958 A.2d 750, 752 n.5 (2008).

This section is not available for review of a denial of an articulation by the workers' compensation review board as this section limits review to actions by a trial judge. Reising v. General Dynamics Corporation/Electric Boat Div., 38 Conn.App. 637, 661 A.2d 1042 (1995).

This section does not provide a means for reviewing a pre-appeal motion for articulation. Brycki v. Brycki, 91 Conn.App. 579, 593, 881 A.2d 1056, 1064 (2005). The authors disagree with *Brycki*. See Practice Book § 60–2.

For ultimately successful use of this section, see D'Appollonio v. Griffo-Brandao, 138 Conn.App. 304, 311 n.3, 53 A.3d 1013, 1019 n.3 (2012) (articulation ordered by Appellate Court); Town of Southington v. DeMello, 10 Conn.App. 581, 584 n.1, 524 A.2d 1151, 1153 n.1 (1987); State v. Wilson, 199 Conn. 417, 437–38, 513 A.2d 620, 632 (1986) (motion denied without prejudice to renewal; renewed successfully on the merits of the appeal); Biller Associates v. Rte. 156 Realty Co., 52 Conn.App. 18, 725 A.2d 398 (1999), aff'd, 252 Conn. 400, 746 A.2d 785 (2000) (motion denied; decision reversed in opinion on merits); Housing Authority of City of Hartford v. Charter Oak Terrace/Rice Heights Health Center, Inc., 82 Conn.App. 18, 23–25, 842 A.2d 601, 605–06 (2004) (relief denied on motion for review; on merits, remanded for articulation) opinion after remand Housing Authority of City of Hartford v. Charter Oak Terrace/Rice Heights Health Center, Inc., 85 Conn.App. 240, 856 A.2d 529 (2004).

Because this rule provides the sole means to challenge an articulation ruling, a party may not appeal a ruling on an articulation. Burke v. Burke, 94 Conn.App. 416, 892 A.2d 964 (2006). However, a party may claim on appeal that an articulation is inconsistent and should be disregarded. Sosin v. Sosin, 300 Conn. 205, 242–43, 14 A.3d 307, 329–30 (2011).

The trial court's decision regarding whether to hold a hearing pursuant to State v. Floyd, 253 Conn. 700, 756 A.2d 799 (2000) (post trial hearing to determine whether defendant was precluded from perfecting the record because of new information post judgment), is reviewable pursuant to this section. State v. Ouellette, 295 Conn. 173, 182 n.7, 989 A.2d 1048, 1054 n.7 (2010).

§ 66-8. Motion to Dismiss

Any claim that an appeal or writ of error should be dismissed, whether based on lack of jurisdiction, failure to file papers within the time allowed or other defect, shall be made by a motion to dismiss the appeal or writ. Any such motion must be filed in accordance with Sections 66-2 and 66-3 within ten days after the filing of the appeal or the return day of the writ, or if the ground alleged subsequently occurs, within ten days after it has arisen, provided that a motion based on lack of jurisdiction may be filed at any time. The court may on its own motion order that an appeal be dismissed for lack of jurisdiction.

Historical Note

Derivation:
    1978 P.B. (1986–97), § 4056
    1978 P.B., § 3110
    1963 P.B., § 697
    1951 P.B., § 436
    1934 P.B., § 393
    1930 Rules Change, § 38

Prior to September 3, 1996, the title was "Lack of Jurisdiction; Other Defects in Appeal."

Effective January 1, 1985 this rule was revised to distinguish it more clearly from a § 3109 motion. Effective July 1, 1978, the rule was clarified as to where to file the motion based upon the appeal itself if being filed late. Prior to 1951, a plea in abatement or a motion to erase was the proper way to raise a defect in the appeal. Prior to 1934, there was no rule on the time limitation to file such motions, except that the 1930 rule provided that pleas in abatement should be filed by the Friday preceding the first day of the Supreme Court term.

Cross References

Maltbie, Conn.App.Proc.2d, §§ 272–278

AUTHORS' COMMENTS

1. Against Appellant Only

This section provides sanctions only against the appellant. If the appellee fails to file a document on time, a motion for judgment cannot be made under this section, but only under § 85-1.

2. Discretion of Court

If a motion to dismiss is not filed within ten days of the filing of the appeal (not the § 63–4 papers) and the issue does not involve subject matter jurisdiction, the defect claimed will probably have been waived. State v. Lanasa, 141 Conn.App. 685, 687 n.1, 62 A.3d 572, 574 n.1, cert. denied, 308 Conn. 945, 66 A.3d 885 (2013). The court has often said that late or defective appeals are "voidable," State v. Johnson, 301 Conn. 630, 641 n.11, 26 A.3d 59, 66 n.11 (2011); Parlato v. Parlato, 134 Conn.App. 848, 850 n.1, 41 A.3d 327, 328 n.1 (2012); LaReau v. Reincke, 158 Conn. 486, 490–95, 264 A.2d 576, 578–81 (1969) (late appeal); Angier v. Barton, 160 Conn. 204, 207, 276 A.2d 782, 784 (1970) (defective appeal); thus suggesting that a timely motion to dismiss would automatically be granted. However, in every such case, the motion was actually untimely filed, so the lateness was waived.

The dicta in these decisions are almost certainly bad law in light of Kelley v. Bonney, 221 Conn. 549, 559 n.4, 606 A.2d 693, 699 n.4 (1992), expressly holding the timely filing of a motion to dismiss an untimely filed appeal merely invokes the Appellate Court's discretion. However, Nicoll v. State, 38 Conn.App. 333, 661 A.2d 101 (1995) (no further proceedings), makes it clear that timely motions to dismiss untimely appeals are likely to be granted. This strict attitude is enforced in Blue Cross/Blue Shield of Connecticut, Inc. v. Gurski, 47 Conn.App. 478, 481–82, 705 A.2d 566, 567–68, cert. denied, 247 Conn. 920, 722 A.2d 809 (1998) (cross appeal filed eight days late dismissed); Alliance Partners, Inc. v. Voltarc Technologies, Inc., 263 Conn. 204, 820 A.2d 224 (2003) (affirming dismissal of appeal where lawyer misread § 63-2).

It has been the authors' experience that voidable appeals based on defective papers are not dismissed despite timely motions to dismiss if the defect may readily be corrected and there has been no prejudice to the appellee. The appellant should file a motion for permission to amend the appeal to correct any defect prior to the oral argument (if any) on the motion to dismiss. This may put the burden on the appellee to show some prejudice. If a document is late, it should if at all possible be filed before any hearing.

Note that if no appeal is filed on a particular matter, there is nothing to waive and no reason for the appellee to file a motion to dismiss. Sorteberg Controls Corp. v. Field, 2 Conn.App. 413, 415 n.3, 478 A.2d 1051, 1052 n.3, cert. denied, 194 Conn. 806, 482 A.2d 711 (1984).

In general, appellants should not press their luck too hard. Promptness in attending to perfecting the appeal would have avoided the disaster in State v. Ward, 134 Conn. 81, 54 A.2d 507 (1947). If an appellant mistakenly fails to file a document, it should be filed immediately after that fact is brought to the appellant's attention; any further delay may lead to disaster, as in Hession v. Somers, 113 Conn. 780, 158 A. 794 (1931).

An appeal from preliminary orders rather than from final judgment was dismissed in Midland Funding, LLC v. Tripp, 134 Conn.App. 195, 196–97 n.1, 38 A.3d 221, 222 n.1 (2012), but the error was not fatal as the plaintiff had filed an amended appeal from the final judgment, which cured the jurisdictional problem. See P.B. § 61-9. Midland Funding should not be relied on, however, if the appeal is taken from the wrong final judgment (if there was more than one).

3. Time to File

The time requirements are clear when the appeal is not filed on time (wait until the appeal is filed and then move to dismiss within 10 days). Sergeant v. Sergeant, 39 Conn.App. 57, 663 A.2d 445 (1995). After the appeal is filed, if the time for filing a paper (such as a brief) passes, the motion should be filed at that time. If the appellee waits until the paper is later filed by the appellant, the motion to dismiss is untimely, since the ground for the motion would probably be held to have "arisen" when the time passed and not when the paper was filed. Tamarit v. Ottolini, 145 Conn. 586, 589, 145 A.2d 587, 588 (1958); Sager v. GAB Business Services, Inc., 11 Conn.App. 693, 697, 529 A.2d 226, 228–29 (1987).

While a late motion generally waives the defect; see Cowles v. Cowles, 71 Conn.App. 24, 26, 799 A.2d 1119, 1120 (2002); in one case a motion was allowed which was seven days late where the appeal was one year late, First Nat. Bank in Greenwich v. Ferguson, 129 Conn. 374, 377, 28 A.2d 87, 88 (1942). Moreover in Farmers and Mechanics Sav. Bank v. Sullivan, 216 Conn. 341, 356, 579 A.2d 1054, 1061 (1990), where a motion to open judgment was filed after the 20-day appeal period had run, a subsequent appeal from both the judgment and the denial of the motion to correct was held "nonviable" as to the judgment even though there is no mention of a motion to dismiss having been filed. In the authors' opinion this dictum is wrongly decided. In general, however, failure to attack the defect within 10 days waives it. Mailly v. Mailly, 13 Conn.App. 185, 188, 535 A.2d 385, 387 (1988); Bio-Polymers, Inc. v. D'Arrigo, 23 Conn.App. 107, 109 n.2, 579 A.2d 122, 123 n.2, 118 Lab. Cas. (CCH) P 56562 (1990). Of course, if subject matter jurisdiction is involved, the timeliness of the motion is immaterial. In re Elizabeth H., 40 Conn.App. 216, 669 A.2d 1246 (1996) (lack of final judgment).

The common law fugitive felon disentitlement doctrine is not governed by this rule and so the 10-day period does not apply. State v. Brabham, 301 Conn. 376, 21 A.3d 800 (2011).

4. Further Pleadings

The Appellate Division of the Circuit Court has held that no pleading (such as the old demurrer) should be addressed to a motion to dismiss, Procaccino v. Wood & Wood, Inc., 1 Conn. Cir. Ct. 571, 24 Conn.Supp. 288, 289, 190 A.2d 70,

71 (App. Div. 1962). In general, representations of counsel at oral argument on the motion to dismiss are accepted by the court, and pleading to the motion to dismiss can usually be avoided, at least where the sole factual issue is why appellate papers have not been sooner filed.

5. Opinions on Dismissal

Usually the court rules on motions to dismiss without opinion, unless the matter is of considerable importance, as in State v. Avcollie, 174 Conn. 100, 384 A.2d 315 (1977). On several occasions the court denied the motion but then reconsidered the matter after oral argument on the merits of the appeal, Christy Hill Builders, Inc. v. Hall, 184 Conn. 575, 439 A.2d 1065 (1981); Edgewood Village, Inc. v. Housing Authority of City of New Haven, 54 Conn.App. 164, 166 n.3, 734 A.2d 589, 591 n.3 (1999). For that reason, if the question is jurisdictional, the appellant ought at least to mention the issue in the brief on the merits even though the motion was previously denied; cf. State v. Bergin, 214 Conn. 657, 660–63, 574 A.2d 164, 166–68 (1990).

In Burton v. Browd, 258 Conn. 566, 783 A.2d 457 (2001), the Supreme Court reversed an Appellate Court dismissal as an abuse of discretion. In Alliance Partners, Inc. v. Voltarc Technologies, Inc., 263 Conn. 204, 820 A.2d 224 (2003), the Supreme Court affirmed an Appellate Court dismissal of an appeal that was one day late.

6. Contempts

A party who is in contempt pending appeal risks dismissal unless the contempt is purged. Greenwood v. Greenwood, 191 Conn. 309, 464 A.2d 771 (1983) (visitation rights); Nowell v. Nowell, 155 Conn. 713, 229 A.2d 701 (1967) (counsel fees); Bubrosky v. Bubrosky, 129 Conn.App. 338, 20 A.3d 79, cert. denied, 302 Conn. 933, 28 A.3d 344 (2011) (nine contempt findings); Broderick v. Broderick, 20 Conn.App. 145, 146–47, 565 A.2d 3, 4 (1989); Glinski v. Glinski, 26 Conn.App. 617, 618 n.1, 602 A.2d 1070, 1071 n.1 (1992); Mark v. Mark, 40 Conn.App. 171, 669 A.2d 579 (1995) (appeal dismissed for continued pattern of contemptuous conduct.) All six are domestic cases.

7. Lack of Jurisdiction

The rule says that jurisdictional questions may be raised at any time. As to the distinction between a jurisdictional question and "a defect in the process of appeal" (which is waivable), see LaReau v. Reincke, 158 Conn. 486, 492–93, 264 A.2d 576, 579–80 (1969).

Examples of jurisdictional questions, which can be and often are raised by the Supreme Court *suo moto,* are lack of standing to appeal, Kulmacz v. Kulmacz, 177 Conn. 410, 418 A.2d 76 (1979); mootness, Connecticut Foundry Co. v. International Ladies Garment Workers Union, AFL-CIO, 177 Conn. 17, 411 A.2d 1, 104 L.R.R.M. (BNA) 2974 (1979) (disapproved of by, Delevieleuse v. Manson, 184 Conn. 434, 439 A.2d 1055 (1981)); absence of a necessary (indispensable?) party, Jensen v. Nationwide Mut. Ins. Co., 150 Conn. 56, 58–59, 185 A.2d 77, 78 (1962); lack of a final judgment, Prevedini v. Mobil Oil Corp., 164 Conn. 287, 294, 320 A.2d 797, 800–01 (1973); and party not permitted to appeal, such as the state in certain criminal cases, State v. Falzone, 171 Conn. 417, 370 A.2d 988 (1976). For an interesting case concerning mootness in the detention of a person at the Institute for Living, see Hirsch v. Braceland, 144 Conn. 464, 469, 133 A.2d 898, 900 (1957).

The Appellate Court has jurisdiction of an appeal from a final judgment even if the trial court lacked jurisdiction in the first instance. Herasinovich v. Town of Wallingford, 149 Conn.App. 325, 327 n.2, 87 A.3d 1177, 1179 n.2 (2014).

8. Dilatory or Frivolous Appeal

An appeal was dismissed in a mortgage foreclosure appeal where the appeal was purely a dilatory tactic. Connecticut Nat. Bank v. Zuckerman, 31 Conn.App. 440, 624 A.2d 1163 (1993). Likewise in Glenfed Mortg. Corp. v. Crowley, 61 Conn.App. 84, 763 A.2d 19 (2000), the appeal was dismissed as frivolous.

9. Moot Appeal

Ordinarily a moot appeal will be dismissed. There are occasions when the court will vacate the lower court opinion if the appeal is moot. That was done in State v. Singleton, 274 Conn. 426, 439–42, 876 A.2d 1, 8–10 (2005).

CHAPTER 67

BRIEFS

§ 67-1. Brief and Appendix (Applicable to appeals filed before July 1, 2013)

In any brief or appendix, the plaintiff and defendant shall be referred to as such rather than as appellant and appellee, wherever it is possible to do so; on a reservation the plaintiff below shall be regarded as the appellant.

Each brief shall contain a concise statement of the principal issue or issues involved in the appeal. The statement ordinarily should not exceed one page in length and should be on a page by itself. The court may refuse to receive a brief not complying with this requirement.

The evidence referred to in the brief, and in the appendix if one is filed, will be deemed to embrace all testimony produced at the trial material to the issues on the appeal, although the court may, if sufficient cause appears, consult the transcript of evidence on file or the trial court case file to supplement or explain the evidence.

Any party to an appeal from an administrative agency who claims that the record before the agency does not support its decision, shall include in such party's brief or in the appendix thereto such portions of the record or evidence returned by the agency but not included in the record as that party deems material to such claim. If such portions of the record or evidence have already been included in another party's brief or appendix, inclusion in a second brief is not necessary, and reference to such already-filed brief or appendix will be sufficient. Any other party may include or refer to in that party's brief, reply brief or appendix such additional portions of the record or the evidence as such party deems material. The portions of the record returned by the agency contained in the record before the court and in an appendix to a brief, supplemented by such papers returned by the agency as are of such a nature that they cannot be conveniently photocopied, will be deemed to embrace all of the record returned by the agency material to the issues on the appeal. The court may, however, consult any of the papers returned by the agency to supplement or explain the portions contained in the record and briefs.

§ 67-1. Brief and Appendix (Applicable to appeals filed on or after July 1, 2013)

In any brief or appendix, the plaintiff and defendant shall be referred to as such rather than as appellant and appellee, wherever it is possible to do so; on a reservation the plaintiff below shall be regarded as the appellant.

Each brief shall contain a concise statement of the principal issue or issues involved in the appeal. The statement ordinarily should not exceed one page in length and should be on a page by itself. The court may refuse to receive a brief not complying with this requirement.

Historical Note

Derivation:

1978 P.B. (1996–97), § 4064, 4070, 4072, 4074

This rule was amended in 2013 to address redaction of personally identifying information. A third paragraph was transferred to §§ 67-2 and 67-8A in 2014.

For Historical Note and Authors' Comments to the first paragraph, see § 67-2; to the second paragraph, see § 67-4.

Third Paragraph:
　　1978 P.B. (1986–96), § 4074
　　1978 P.B. (1979–86), § 3060R
　　1978 P.B., § 3049
　　1963 P.B. (1975–78), § 628Q
　　1963 P.B., § 721
　　1951 P.B., § 448

This rule was substantially revised as of July 1, 1979 to reflect the new optional appendix rules. The reference to the trial court case file was added effective January 1, 1985.

Prior to October 1, 1974, this rule also applied to jury cases. Otherwise, there has been no change since this rule was adopted in 1951.

Fourth Paragraph:
Derivation:
　　1978 P.B.(1986–96), § 4072
　　1978 P.B. (1979–86), § 3060P
　　1978 P.B. (1978–79), § 3047
　　1963 P.B. (1975–78), § 628N
　　1963 P.B., § 719
　　1951 P.B., § 447A

This rule is substantially revised as of July 1, 1979 to reflect the new optional appendix rules. Also prior to this time, the rule only applied to zoning appeals. Prior to 1979, the rule was substantially unchanged since it was adopted in 1959.

AUTHORS' COMMENTS

Concerning the third paragraph, the appellate courts have in the past been very reluctant to examine the transcript. See, e.g., Baton v. Potvin, 141 Conn. 198, 200–01, 104 A.2d 768, 769–70 (1954); Barnini v. Sun Oil Co., 161 Conn. 59, 283 A.2d 217 (1971); Morningside Ass'n v. Morningside Development, Inc., 172 Conn. 60, 63–64, 372 A.2d 141, 143 (1976). The courts now review the transcripts routinely. See, e.g., State v. Cardwell, 246 Conn. 721, 726 n.6, 718 A.2d 954, 957 n.6, 38 U.C.C. Rep. Serv. 2d 1158 (1998); In re Kaleb H., 131 Conn.App. 829, 838, 29 A.3d 173, 179 (2011), aff'd, 306 Conn. 22, 48 A.3d 631 (2012).

The failure of a brief to contain a statement of issues was criticized in Dauti v. Stop and Shop Supermarket Co., 90 Conn.App. 626, 627 n.1, 879 A.2d 507, 508 n.1 (2005).

§ 67-2. Format; Copies; Electronic Briefing Requirement (Applicable to appeals filed before July 1, 2013)

(a)   Original briefs and appendices shall be typewritten or clearly photocopied from a typewritten original on white 8 1/2 by 11 inch paper. Unless ordered otherwise, the briefs shall be copied on one side of the page only. Appendices may be copied on both sides of the page. The brief shall be fully double spaced and shall not exceed three lines to the vertical inch or twenty-seven lines to the page; footnotes and block quotations may, however, be single spaced. Only the following two typefaces, of 12 point or larger size, are approved for use in briefs: arial and univers.

(b) If constitutional provisions, statutes, ordinances, regulations or portions of the transcript are contained in an appendix, they may be reproduced in their original form so long as the document is not reduced to less than 75 percent of its original form.

(c) Each page of a brief or appendix shall have as a minimum the following margins: top, 1 inch; left, 1 and 1/4 inch; right, 1/2 inch; and bottom, 1 inch.

(d) Pages shall be numbered in the center of the bottom of the page.

(e) Briefs and appendices shall be firmly bound 1/4 inch from the left side, at points approximately 1/4, 1/2 and 3/4 of the length of the page, so as to make an easily opened volume.

(f) Every brief shall designate on the front page the name, address, telephone and facsimile numbers and e-mail address of the individual counsel who is to argue the appeal. The plaintiff and defendant shall be referred to as such rather than as appellant and appellee, wherever it is possible to do so. For the purposes of this rule, on a reservation, the plaintiff below shall be regarded as the appellant.

(g) Briefs and separately bound appendices shall have a suitable front cover of heavy paper in the color indicated: briefs for appellants and plaintiffs in error, light blue; briefs for appellees and defendants in error, pink; reply briefs, white; briefs for amicus curiae, light green. Covers of briefs filed for cross appeals shall be of the same color as indicated for that party on the original appeal briefs. If a supplemental brief is ordered or permitted by the court, the cover shall be the same color as indicated for that party's original brief. A back cover is not necessary; however, if one is used, it must be white.

(h) Briefs and separately bound appendices must bear on the cover, in the following order, from the top of the page: (1) the name of the court; (2) the number of the case; (3) the name of the case as it appears in the judgment file of the trial court; (4) the nature of the brief (e.g., brief of the defendant-appellant; brief of the plaintiff-appellee on the appeal and of the plaintiff-cross appellant on the cross appeal); (5) the name, address and, if they are different from arguing counsel's telephone and facsimile numbers and e-mail address, the telephone and facsimile numbers and e-mail address of the party's counsel of record, and of the arguing counsel, if different. The foregoing shall be displayed in the upper case of an arial or univers typeface of 12 point or larger size.

(i) Sections 67–4, 67–5 and 67–8 should be consulted for guidance as to when an appendix is necessary and for specific requirements regarding appendices.

(j) Every attorney filing a brief shall submit an electronic version of the brief and appendix in accordance with guidelines established by the court and published on the Judicial Branch website. The electronic version shall be submitted prior to the timely filing of the party's paper brief and appendix. A party who is not represented by counsel is not required to submit an electronic version of his or her brief and appendix. Counsel must certify that electronically submitted briefs and appendices: (1) have been delivered electronically to the last known e-mail address of each counsel of record for whom an e-mail address has been provided; and (2) have been redacted or do not contain any names or other personal identifying information that is prohibited from disclosure by rule, statute, court order or case law.

(k) If the appeal is in the supreme court, the original and fifteen legible photocopies of each brief and appendix, if any, shall be filed with the appellate clerk. If the appeal is in the appellate court, the original and ten legible photocopies of each brief and appendix, if any, shall be filed with the appellate clerk.

(l) The original and all copies of the brief filed with the supreme court or the appellate court must be accompanied by: (1) certification that a copy of the brief and appendix has been sent to each counsel of record and to any trial judge who rendered a decision that is the subject matter of the appeal, in compliance with Section 62–7; (2) certification that the brief and appendix being filed with the appellate clerk are true copies of the brief and appendix that were submitted electronically pursuant to subsection (j) of this section; (3) certification that the brief and appendix have been redacted or do not contain any names or other personal identifying information that is prohibited from disclosure by rule, statute, court order or case law; and (4) certification that the brief complies with all provisions of this rule.

(m) A copy of the electronic confirmation receipt indicating that the brief and appendix were submitted electronically in compliance with subsection (j) of this section shall be filed with the original brief.

(n) No argument shall be allowed any party who has not filed a brief or who has not joined in the brief of another party.

(o) Any request for deviation from the above requirements shall be addressed in writing to the appellate clerk.

§ 67-2. Format of Briefs and Appendices; Copies; Electronic Briefing Requirement (Applicable to appeals filed on or after July 1, 2013)

(a) Original briefs and appendices shall be typewritten or clearly photocopied from a typewritten original on white 8 1/2 by 11 inch paper. Unless ordered otherwise, briefs shall be copied on one side of the page only. Appendices may be copied on both sides of the page. The page number for briefs and appendices shall be centered on the bottom of each page. The brief shall be fully double spaced and shall not exceed three lines to the vertical inch or twenty-seven lines to the page; footnotes and block quotations may, however, be single spaced. Only the following two typefaces, of 12 point or larger size, are approved for use in briefs: arial and univers. Each page of a brief or appendix shall have as a minimum the following margins: top, 1 inch; left, 1 and 1/4 inch; right, 1/2 inch; and bottom, 1 inch. Briefs and appendices shall be firmly bound 1/4 inch from the left side, at points approximately 1/4, 1/2 and 3/4 of the length of the page, so as to make an easily opened volume.

(b) When possible, parts one and two of the appendix shall be bound together. In addition, parts one and two of the appendix may be bound together with the brief. When, however, binding the brief and appendix together would affect the integrity of the binding, the appendix shall be bound separately from the brief. When either part of the appendix exceeds one hundred and fifty pages, parts one and two of the appendix shall be separately bound.

(c) An appendix shall be paginated separately from the brief. The appendix shall be numbered consecutively, beginning with the first page of part one and ending with the last page of part two, and preceded by the letter "A" (e.g., A1 . . . A25 . . . A53). An appendix shall have an index of the names of witnesses whose testimony is cited within it. If any part of the testimony of a witness is omitted, this shall be indicated by asterisks. After giving the name of a witness, the party who called that witness shall be designated, and it shall be stated whether the testimony quoted was given on direct, cross or other examination.

(d) If constitutional provisions, statutes, ordinances, regulations or portions of the transcript are contained in an appendix, they may be reproduced in their original form so long as the document is not reduced to less than 75 percent of its original form.

(e) Briefs and separately bound appendices shall have a suitable front cover of heavy paper in the color indicated: briefs for appellants and plaintiffs in error, light blue; briefs for appellees and defendants in error, pink; reply briefs, white; briefs for amicus curiae, light green. Covers of briefs filed for cross appeals shall be of the same color as indicated for that party on the original appeal briefs. If a supplemental brief is ordered or permitted by the court, the cover shall be the same color as indicated for that party's original brief. A back cover is not necessary; however, if one is used, it must be white.

(f) Briefs and separately bound appendices must bear on the cover, in the following order, from the top of the page: (1) the name of the court; (2) the number of the case; (3) the name of the case as it appears in the judgment file of the trial court; (4) the nature of the brief (e.g., brief of the defendant-appellant; brief of the plaintiff-appellee on the appeal and of the plaintiff-cross ap- pellant on the cross appeal); and (5) the name, address, telephone and facsimile numbers and e-mail address of individual counsel who is to argue the appeal and, if different, the name, address, telephone and facsimile numbers and e-mail address of the party's counsel of record. The foregoing shall be displayed in the upper case of an arial or univers typeface of 12 point or larger size.

(g) Every attorney filing a brief shall submit an electronic ver- sion of the brief and appendix in accordance with guidelines established by the court and published on the Judicial Branch website. The electronic version shall be submitted prior to the timely filing of the party's paper brief and appendix pursuant to subsection (h) of this section. A party who is not represented by counsel is not required to submit an electronic version of his or her brief and appendix. Counsel must certify that electronically submitted briefs and appendices: (1) have been delivered electronically to the last known e-mail address of each counsel of record for whom an e-mail address has been provided; and (2) have been redacted or do not contain any names or other personal identifying information that is prohibited from disclosure by rule, statute, court order or case law.

(h) If the appeal is in the supreme court, the original and fifteen legible photocopies of each brief and appendix, if any, shall be filed with the appellate clerk. If the appeal is in the ap- pellate court, the original and ten legible photocopies of each brief and appendix, if any, shall be filed with the appellate clerk.

(i) The original and all copies of the brief filed with the supreme court or the appellate court must be accompanied by: (1) certification that a copy of the brief and appendix has been sent to each counsel of record and to any trial judge who rendered a decision that is the subject matter of the appeal, in compliance with Section 62–7; (2) certification that the brief and appendix being filed with the appellate clerk are true copies of the brief and appendix that were submitted electronically pursuant to subsection (g) of this section; (3) certification that the brief and appendix have been redacted or do not contain any names or other personal identifying information that is prohibited from disclosure by rule, statute, court order or case law; and (4) certifi- cation that the brief complies with all provisions of this rule.

(j) A copy of the electronic confirmation receipt indicating that the brief and appendix were submitted electronically in compli- ance with subsection (g) of this section shall be filed with the original brief.

(k) Any request for deviation from the above requirements shall be addressed in writing to the appellate clerk.

Historical Note

Derivation (as to duplication of briefs):
  1978 P.B. (1996–97), § 4064A
  1978 P.B.(1988–96), § 4070
  1978 P.B. (1986–88), § 4071
  1978 P.B.(1979–86), § 3060M
  1978 P.B., § 3020
  1963 P.B., § 723
  1951 P.B., § 450
  1934 P.B., § 402
  1922 P.B., § 48
  1908 P.B., § 47
  1899 P.B., § 47
  64 Conn. at 583 (1894)
  40 Conn. at 599 (1874)

This rule was amended in 2013 to require parties to file appendices, which will include papers previously contained in the now eliminated printed record. Changes effective September 1, 2014 note that the appendix may be copied on both sides and explain how the brief and appendix must be filed electronically.

Effective January 1, 2011, email addresses must now be on the cover of briefs and appendices, subsection (l) was added, and certain formatting changes were made to (a). In 2009, (j) and (k) were added.

Effective September 1, 2001, only three typefaces are approved. See the new second paragraph and the new last two sentences of the last paragraph of the rule. After June 30, 2002, only Arial and Univers may be used. Numerous formatting changes were made in 1996.

This section was completely revised effective May 10, 1988 to abolish the printing of briefs. From 1874 until 1988 briefs were printed (from 1894 on, the rule mandated 9" ×× 6" size) and copies were sent to all the law libraries in the state and bound in permanent volumes with other records and briefs. Now briefs are to be typewritten on 81/2" ×× 11" paper, double spaced, with certain type, margins and binding requirements. An original and 25 typewritten (previously 70 printed) copies are to be filed. This means that briefs will be available in law libraries in the future only in microfiche.

Entirely new provisions in 1988 include color coded covers (light blue for appellant, pink for appellee and cross appellant, white for reply and cross appellee, light green for amicus curiae) and mandatory information on the cover.

Derivation (as to number of copies):
  1978 P.B. (1996–97), § 4064A
  1978 P.B. (1988–96), § 4070
  1978 P.B. (1986–88), § 4071
  1978 P.B. (1979–86), § 3060N
  1978 P.B., § 3121
  1963 P.B., § 724
  1951 P.B., § 451
  1934 P.B., § 402
  1922 P.B., § 48
  1908 P.B., § 47
  1899 P.B., § 47

Effective October 1, 1992 an original and 20 rather than 25 copies of briefs shall be filed. At the same time, the telephone number requirements concerning arguing counsel were added.

From 1982 to 1988 70 copies of the brief were filed, from 1963 to 1982 55 copies were filed, from 1951 to 1963 40 copies were filed and before 1951 approximately 30 copies were filed. A rule adopted in 1815 required counsel to file three copies of their briefs. 1 Conn. 365.

AUTHORS' COMMENTS

Counsel are advised to pay attention to the technical requirements of this section. The clerk will reject non-complying briefs. Note that only the front cover must be of heavy paper in the correct color. Also, fully double spaced means just that. Do not try to get by with one and one half spacing or you risk having your brief rejected. The words on the cover must have all capital letters.

The Supreme Court has granted, over objection, a motion to file companion CD-ROM briefs and appendices in addition to the typed copies. Buell Industries, Inc. v. Greater New York Mut. Ins. Co., 259 Conn. 527, 791 A.2d 489, 54 Env't. Rep. Cas. (BNA) 1279, 32 Envtl. L. Rep. 20480 (2002) (order entered September 13, 2001).

Make sure the certification of service includes the name and address of the trial judge or judges and a statement that the brief complies with the formatting requirements of this section.

Failure to comply with this rule may cause the court to refuse to consider your brief. Princess H.Q. v. Robert H., 150 Conn.App. 105, 106 n.1, 89 A.3d 896, 897 n.1 (2014). The authors presume the non-compliance in *Princess H.Q.* was egregious.

§ 67-3. Page Limitations; Time for Filing Briefs (Applicable to appeals filed before July 1, 2013)

Except as otherwise ordered, the brief of the appellant shall not exceed thirty-five pages and shall be filed within forty-five days after the delivery date of the transcript ordered by the appellant. In cases where no transcript is required or the transcript has been received by the appellant prior to the filing of the appeal, the appellant's brief shall be filed within forty-five days of the filing of the appeal.

The delivery date of the paper—not electronic—transcript shall be used, where applicable, in determining the filing date of briefs.

Any party whose interest in the judgment will not be affected by the appeal and who intends not to file a brief shall inform the appellate clerk of this intent prior to the deadline for the filing of the appellee's brief. In the case of multiple appellees, an appellee who supports the position of the appellant shall meet the appellant's time schedule for filing a brief.

Except as otherwise ordered, the brief of the appellee shall not exceed thirty-five pages, and shall be filed within thirty days after the filing of the appellant's brief or the delivery date of the portions of the transcript ordered only by that appellee, whichever is later.

The appellant may within twenty days after the filing of the appellee's brief file a reply brief which shall not exceed fifteen pages.

Where there is a cross appeal, the brief of the cross appellant shall be combined with the brief of the appellee, and this brief shall not exceed fifty pages, and shall be filed at the time the appellee's brief is due. The brief of the cross appellee shall be combined with the appellant's reply brief, if any, and this brief shall not exceed forty pages and shall be filed within thirty days after the filing of the original appellee's brief. The cross appellant may within twenty days after the filing of the cross appellee's brief file a cross appellant's reply brief which shall not exceed fifteen pages.

Where cases are consolidated or a joint appeal has been filed, the brief of the appellants and that of the appellees shall not exceed the page limitations specified above.

All page limitations shall be exclusive of appendices, the statement of issues, the table of authorities, the table of contents, if any, and, in the case of an amicus brief, the statement of the interest of the amicus curiae required by Section 67-7. The last page of a brief shall likewise not be counted if it contains only the signature of counsel of record.

Briefs shall not exceed the page limitations set forth herein except by permission of the chief justice or chief judge. Requests for permission to exceed the page limitations shall be made by letter, filed with the appellate clerk, stating both the compelling reason for the request and the number of additional pages sought.

Where a claim relies on the state constitution as an independent ground for relief, the clerk shall, upon request by letter, grant an additional five pages for the appellant and appellee briefs, and an additional two pages for the reply brief, which pages are to be used for the state constitutional argument only.

§ 67-3. Page Limitations; Time for Filing Briefs and Appendices (Applicable to appeals filed on or after July 1, 2013)

Except as otherwise ordered, the brief of the appellant shall not exceed thirty-five pages and shall be filed with the appendix within forty-five days after the delivery date of the transcript ordered by the appellant. In cases where no transcript is required or the transcript has been received by the appellant prior to the filing of the appeal, the appellant's brief and appendix shall be filed within forty-five days of the filing of the appeal.

The delivery date of the paper—not electronic—transcript shall be used, where applicable, in determining the filing date of briefs.

Any party whose interest in the judgment will not be affected by the appeal and who intends not to file a brief shall inform the appellate clerk of this intent prior to the deadline for the filing of the appellee's brief. In the case of multiple appellees, an appellee who supports the position of the appellant shall meet the appellant's time schedule for filing a brief.

Except as otherwise ordered, the brief of the appellee shall not exceed thirty-five pages, and shall be filed with any appendix within thirty days after the filing of the appellant's brief or the delivery date of the portions of the transcript ordered only by that appellee, whichever is later.

The appellant may within twenty days after the filing of the appellee's brief file a reply brief which shall not exceed fifteen pages.

Where there is a cross appeal, the brief and appendix of the cross appellant shall be combined with the brief and appendix of the appellee. The brief shall not exceed fifty pages and shall be filed with any appendix at the time the appellee's brief is due. The brief and appendix of the cross appellee shall be combined with the appellant's reply brief, if any. This brief shall not exceed forty pages and shall be filed within thirty days after the filing of the original appellee's brief. The cross appellant may within twenty days after the filing of the cross appellee's brief file a cross appellant's reply brief which shall not exceed fifteen pages.

Where cases are consolidated or a joint appeal has been filed, the brief of the appellants and that of the appellees shall not exceed the page limitations specified above.

All page limitations shall be exclusive of appendices, the statement of issues, the table of authorities, the table of contents, if any, and, in the case of an amicus brief, the statement of the interest of the amicus curiae required by Section 67-7. The last page of a brief shall likewise not be counted if it contains only the signature of counsel of record.

Briefs shall not exceed the page limitations set forth herein except by permission of the chief justice or chief judge. Requests for permission to exceed the page limitations shall be made by letter, filed with the appellate clerk, stating both the compelling reason for the request and the number of additional pages sought.

Where a claim relies on the state constitution as an independent ground for relief, the clerk shall, upon request by letter, grant an additional five pages for the appellant and appellee briefs, and an additional two pages for the reply brief, which pages are to be used for the state constitutional argument only.

Historical Note

Derivation (as to length of brief):
    1978 P.B. (1996–97), § 4064B
    1978 P.B. (1986–96), § 4071
    1978 P.B. (1979–86), §§ 3060M
    1978 P.B. § 3120
    1963 P.B., § 723

    1951 P.B., § 450
    1934 P.B., § 402

The second paragraph was added effective January 1, 2011. The last paragraph was added in 1996.

Between 1979 and 1986, briefs exclusive of certain pages could not exceed 50 pages except that since 1985 there has been a 15-page limit on reply briefs. From 1978 to 1979 there was no page limit at all. From 1951 to 1978 there was a page limit of 50 pages in non-jury cases and no limit in jury cases. There were no page limits at all before 1951.

Derivation (as to time for filing):
    1978 P.B. (1996–97), § 4064B
    1978 P.B. (1986–96), § 4071
    1978 P.B. (1979–86), § 3060N
    1978 P.B., § 3121
    1963 P.B., § 724
    1951 P.B., § 451
    1934 P.B., § 402
    1922 P.B., § 48
    1908 P.B., § 47
    1899 P.B., § 47
    58 Conn. at 589, § 3 (1890)
    1879 P.B., p. 262, § 3
    43 Conn. at 607 (1876)
    18 Conn. at 564, ch. V (1847)
    2 Conn. at 375 (1817)
    3 Day at 29 (1807)

Effective October 1, 1992, the Appellate Court deadlines were adopted for both courts: 45 days (not 60) for the appellant; 30 days (not 40) for appellees; 20 days for reply. In the case of a cross appeal; 45 days (not 60) for appellant, 30 days (not 40) for appellee-cross appellant; 30 days (not 40) for cross appellee and reply on appeal; 20 days for reply on cross appeal.

This rule was clarified effective January 1, 1985 to indicate exactly when brief filing periods start to run and when briefs are to be filed when there are cross appeals.

The rule was rewritten effective July 1, 1979 in order to standardize the time period for both court and jury cases.

Substantial changes which have expedited the appellate process were made effective July 1, 1978. Previously the appellant's brief was not due until 45 days after the printed record was filed. Effective July 1, 1978, in jury cases, it was 45 days after his transcript was delivered, and in court cases, it was 45 days after the assignment of errors (when no finding) or after the judge's action in correcting the finding. From 1979 until 1986 it was 45 days after the delivery of the transcript in all cases except that it was 45 days after the filing of the appeal where no transcript was ordered. From 1986 to 1992 it was 60 days (except for the Appellate Court, where it remained 45 days).

Prior to September 3, 1968, the appellant had only thirty days, and the appellee twenty days thereafter, to file their briefs. Between 1940 and 1951, the appellant had to file his brief two weeks before the opening of the term of court, and the appellee had to file his brief at least four days before the opening of the term.

Between 1876 and 1940, briefs were simultaneously exchanged by counsel at least three days before oral argument, and counsel had to supply a copy of their briefs to each justice before starting oral arguments. Before 1876, briefs were exchanged and furnished to the justices at the beginning of oral argument. There was no provision for reply briefs before 1951. The 3 Day citation above implies that there were no briefs at all before 1808.

AUTHORS' COMMENTS

For comments on extensions of time, see Commentary to § 66-1. Transcript deliveries should be carefully handled. See Commentary to § 63-8.

Although five-page extensions are routinely granted (but not always; see Franc v. Planning and Zoning Com'n of Town of Bethel, 47 Conn.App. 939, 707 A.2d 1292 (1998)), it is difficult to get more extensive waivers of page limitations. Trying to evade the limitations by putting arguments in lengthy footnotes or in the appendix is risky business. Papic v. Burke, 113 Conn.App. 198, 217 n.11, 965 A.2d 633, 647 n.11, Blue Sky L. Rep. (CCH) P 74760 (2009) (citing this commentary to criticize "roadmap" of arguments in appellate appendices); South Windsor Cemetery Ass'n, Inc. v. Lindquist, 114 Conn.App. 540, 542 n.2, 970 A.2d 760, 762 n.2, cert. denied, 293 Conn. 932, 981 A.2d 1076 (2009) (improperly placing factual statement and procedural history in appendix); State v. Webley, 17 Conn.App. 200, 202 n.2, 551 A.2d 428, 430 n.2 (1988) (footnotes). This also may apply to type-size requirements. See EDC, Inc. v. Navistar Intern. Transp. Corp., 915 F.2d 1082 (7th Cir. 1990).

The court granted extra pages for a reply brief under this section to address an alternate basis to affirm in Housatonic R. Co., Inc. v. Commissioner of Revenue Services, 301 Conn. 268, 275 n.4, 21 A.3d 759, 764 n.4 (2011).

Since the time for filing the appellant's brief does not start to run until the transcript is sent to counsel by the court reporter, it is not necessary to file a motion for extension of time to file the brief when the appeal is filed.

The rule does not state when the appellee's brief is due if there are two appellants' briefs filed on different dates, or when the appellant's reply brief is due if there are two appellees' briefs filed on different days. The authors' opinion is that the later filing controls; a litigant cannot be expected to prepare a brief without knowing all the arguments to the contrary.

The appellant must file the transcript when the brief is filed. P.B. § 63-8.

If there is any problem about who is the appellant, an order may be made to the Supreme Court to determine it, Tough v. Ives, 160 Conn. 577, 271 A.2d 332 (1970). As to the time period for filing amicus curiae briefs, see commentary to § 67-7.

A party who no longer sought relief used this section to give notice of his intent not to file a brief. Private Healthcare Systems, Inc. v. Torres, 278 Conn. 291, 297 n.6, 898 A.2d 768, 773 n.6 (2006).

§ 67-4. The Appellant's Brief; Contents and Organization (Applicable to appeals filed before July 1, 2013)

The appellant's brief shall contain the following:

(a) A concise statement setting forth, in separately numbered paragraphs, without detail or discussion, the principal issue or issues involved in the appeal, with appropriate references to the page or pages of the brief where the issue is discussed, pursuant to subsection (d) hereof. The court may refuse to receive a brief not complying with this requirement. Such statement shall be deemed in replacement of and shall supersede the preliminary statement of issues.

(b) A table of authorities cited in the brief, with references to the page or pages of the brief where the citations to those authorities appear. Citations shall be in the form provided in Section 67-11.

(c) A statement of the nature of the proceedings and of the facts of the case bearing on the issues raised. The statement of facts shall be in narrative form, shall be supported by appropriate references to the page or pages of the transcript or to the document upon which the party relies and shall not be unnecessarily detailed or voluminous.

(d) The argument, divided under appropriate headings into as many parts as there are points to be presented, with appropriate references to the statement of facts or to the page or pages of the transcript or to the relevant document. The argument on each point shall include a separate, brief statement of the standard of review the appellant believes should be applied.

(1) When error is claimed in the trial court's refusal to charge the jury as requested, the party claiming such error shall include in the brief of that party or the appendix thereto a verbatim statement of the relevant portions of the charge as requested and as given by the court and any relevant exceptions to the charge as given and shall recite in narrative form any evidence which it is claimed would entitle that party to the charge as requested, with appropriate references to the page or pages of the transcript.

(2) When error is claimed in the charge to the jury, the brief or appendix shall include a verbatim statement of all relevant portions of the charge and all relevant exceptions to the charge. Unless essential to review of a claimed error, a verbatim statement of the entire charge to the jury should not be included in the brief or appendix. Evidence relevant to the claimed error shall be recited in narrative form with appropriate references to the page or pages of the transcript.

(3) When error is claimed in any evidentiary ruling in a court or jury case, the brief or appendix shall include a verbatim statement of the following: the question or offer of exhibit; the objection and the ground on which it was based; the ground on which the evidence was claimed to be admissible; the answer, if any; and the ruling.

(4) When error is claimed in any other ruling in a court or jury case, the brief or appendix shall include the pertinent motion or pleading as well as any other pertinent documents which are a part of the trial court case file but are not included in the record.

(5) When the basis of an evidentiary or other ruling referred to in subsection (d) (3) or (d) (4) cannot be understood without knowledge of the evidence or proceeding which preceded or followed the ruling, a brief narrative or verbatim statement of the evidence or proceeding should be made. A verbatim excerpt from the transcript should not be used if a narrative statement will suffice. When the same ruling is repeated, the brief should contain only a single ruling unless

the other rulings are further illustrative of the rule which determined the action of the trial court or establish the materiality or harmfulness of the error claimed. The statement of rulings in the brief shall include appropriate references to the page or pages of the transcript.

(e) A short conclusion stating the precise relief sought.

(f) The text of the pertinent portions of any constitutional provision, statute, ordinance or regulation at issue or on which the appellant relies. Such text need not be included in the brief if it is included in the appendix to the appellant's brief.

(g) In appeals filed pursuant to Section 81-4, a statement identifying the version of the land use regulations filed with the appellate clerk.

The brief shall be organized in the following order: table of contents, if any; statement of issues; table of authorities; if the appeal was filed pursuant to Section 81-4, statement identifying version of land use regulations filed with the appellate clerk; if amicus, statement of interest of the amicus curiae; statement of facts; argument; conclusion and statement of relief requested; signature; and certification pursuant to Section 62-7.

§ 67-4. The Appellant's Brief; Contents and Organization (Applicable to appeals filed on or after July 1, 2013)

The appellant's brief shall contain the following:

(a) A concise statement setting forth, in separately numbered paragraphs, without detail or discussion, the principal issue or issues involved in the appeal, with appropriate references to the page or pages of the brief where the issue is discussed, pursuant to subsection (d) hereof. The court may refuse to receive a brief not complying with this requirement. Such statement shall be deemed in replacement of and shall supersede the preliminary statement of issues.

(b) A table of authorities cited in the brief, with references to the page or pages of the brief where the citations to those authorities appear. Citations shall be in the form provided in Section 67-11.

(c) A statement of the nature of the proceedings and of the facts of the case bearing on the issues raised. The statement of facts shall be in narrative form, shall be supported by appropriate references to the page or pages of the transcript or to the document upon which the party relies and shall not be unnecessarily detailed or voluminous.

(d) The argument, divided under appropriate headings into as many parts as there are points to be presented, with appropriate references to the statement of facts or to the page or pages of the transcript or to the relevant document. The argument on each point shall include a separate, brief statement of the standard of review the appellant believes should be applied.

(1) When error is claimed in the trial court's refusal to charge the jury as requested, the party claiming such error shall include in the brief of that party or the appendix thereto a verbatim statement of the relevant portions of the charge as requested and as given by the court and any relevant exceptions to the charge as given and shall recite in narrative form any evidence which it is claimed would entitle that party to the charge as requested, with appropriate references to the page or pages of the transcript.

(2) When error is claimed in the charge to the jury, the brief or appendix shall include a verbatim statement of all relevant portions of the charge and all relevant exceptions to the charge. Unless essential to review of a claimed error, a verbatim statement of the entire charge to the jury should not be included in the brief or appendix. Evidence relevant to the claimed error shall be recited in narrative form with appropriate references to the page or pages of the transcript.

(3) When error is claimed in any evidentiary ruling in a court or jury case, the brief or appendix shall include a verbatim statement of the following: the question or offer of exhibit; the objection and the ground on which it was based; the ground on which the evidence was claimed to be admissible; the answer, if any; and the ruling.

(4) When error is claimed in any other ruling in a court or jury case, the brief or appendix shall include the pertinent motion or pleading as well as any other pertinent documents which are a part of the record of the proceedings below.

(5) When the basis of an evidentiary or other ruling referred to in subsection (d) (3) or (d) (4) cannot be understood without knowledge of the evidence or proceeding which preceded or followed the ruling, a brief narrative or verbatim statement of the evidence or proceeding should be made. A verbatim excerpt from the transcript should not be used if a narrative statement will suffice. When the same ruling is repeated, the brief should contain only a single ruling unless the other rulings are further illustrative of the rule which determined the action of the trial court or establish the materiality or harmfulness of the error claimed. The statement of rulings in the brief shall include appropriate references to the page or pages of the transcript.

(e) A short conclusion stating the precise relief sought.

(f) The text of the pertinent portions of any constitutional provision, statute, ordinance or regulation at issue or on which the appellant relies. Such text need not be included in the brief if it is included in the appendix to the appellant's brief.

(g) In appeals filed pursuant to Section 81-4, a statement identifying the version of the land use regulations filed with the appellate clerk.

(h) The appellant's brief shall be organized in the following order: table of contents, if any; statement of issues; table of authorities; if the appeal was filed pursuant to Section 81-4, statement identifying version of land use regulations filed with the appellate clerk; statement of facts; argument; conclusion and statement of relief requested; signature; and certification pursuant to Section 62-7.

Historical Note

Derivation:
  1978 P.B. (1996–97), § 4064C
  1978 P.B. (1986–96), § 4065
  1978 P.B. (1979–86), § 3060F
  1978 P.B., § 3054
  1965 P.B., § 631A

The last paragraph of the rule added "if any" in 2011 to indicate that a table of contents is optional.

Subsection (e) was added in 2010.

The last sentence of subsection (b) was added effective January 1, 2000.

Subsections (c) and (d) were amended effective October 1, 1992 to change "record" to "relevant document."

Subsection (d)(3) was amended effective May 10, 1988 to require any document referenced to be included in the appendix if it is not already in the appellate record.

The last sentence of § (a) was added effective October 1, 1986, § (d)(1) and (2) added the reference to the appendix § (e) was expanded in scope from just statutes.

Sections (b) and (e) were added effective January 1, 1985, thus relettering original §§ (b) and (c) to (c) and (d). Prior § 631A was enacted effective October 1, 1974 as part of the new appellate rules for jury cases. Minor revisions were made effective July 1, 1979 to make it applicable to both court and jury appeals.

Cross References

P.B. § 67-11 (Table of Authorities; Citation of Cases)

AUTHORS' COMMENTS

A. *Introduction*

The brief is the most important part of the appeal. This rule should therefore be read carefully. Failure to follow this rule makes appellate review extremely difficult, Karanian v. Maulucci, 185 Conn. 320, 440 A.2d 959, 33 U.C.C. Rep. Serv. 677 (1981), and will often, be fatal. State v. Edward B., 72 Conn.App. 282, 298-300, 806 A.2d 64, 75–76 (2002). To see what happens when counsel blatantly disregard the brief rule, see Paoletta v. Anchor Reef Club at Branford, LLC, 123 Conn.App. 402, 1 A.3d 1238, cert. denied, 298 Conn. 931, 5 A.3d 491 (2010).

The failure to brief an issue constitutes an abandonment of that issue, Czarnecki v. Plastics Liquidating Co., Inc., 179 Conn. 261, 262 n.1, 425 A.2d 1289, 1290 n.1 (1979). Also, an inadequately briefed issue will not be considered. Connecticut Coalition Against Millstone v. Connecticut Siting Council, 286 Conn. 57, 87, 942 A.2d 345, 364 (2008) (conclusory assertions, no relevant authority, and minimal record citations were inadequate); State v. Smith, 63 Conn.App. 228, 234 n.12, 775 A.2d 313, 319 n.12 (2001) (mere abstract assertion inadequate); Middletown Commercial Associates Ltd. Partnership v. City of Middletown, 42 Conn.App. 426, 439 n.12, 680 A.2d 1350, 1357 n.12 (1996) (legal citations without analysis inadequate); Fromer v. Freedom of Information Com'n, 36

Conn.App. 155, 156, 649 A.2d 540, 541 (1994) (issue merely mentioned); State v. Holmes, 257 Conn. 248, 252 n.4, 777 A.2d 627, 630 n.4 (2001) (failure to brief state constitutional issue adequately). But see Ward v. Greene, 267 Conn. 539, 546, 839 A.2d 1259, 1259 (2004) (issue considered although not analyzed in depth).

The brief and oral argument was held to be "a mockery of responsible appellate advocacy" in Commissioner of Health Services v. Youth Challenge of Greater Hartford, Inc., 206 Conn. 316, 317, 537 A.2d 480, 480 (1988). For similar criticism and an explanation of the Court's expectations, see Mullen and Mahon, Inc. v. Mobilmed Support Services, LLC, 62 Conn.App. 1, 773 A.2d 952 (2001). But see Potter v. Chicago Pneumatic Tool Co., 241 Conn. 199, 255 n.38, 694 A.2d 1319, 1349 n.38, Prod. Liab. Rep. (CCH) P 14967 (1997) (argument brief but adequate); Cable v. Bic Corp., 79 Conn.App. 178, 179 n.1, 830 A.2d 279, 281 n.1 (2003), aff'd, 270 Conn. 433, 854 A.2d 1057 (2004). See also § B.4.

It is risky, in the authors' opinion, to brief an issue in a footnote, although it was permitted in Glazer v. Dress Barn, Inc., 274 Conn. 33, 86–87 n.37, 873 A.2d 929, 962 n.37 (2005). But see State v. Grant, 221 Conn. 93, 107 n.13, 602 A.2d 581, 588 n.13 (1992); Costello v. Kozlowski, 47 Conn.App. 111, 116 n.5, 702 A.2d 1197, 1199 n.5 (1997).

Be sure to explain why an erroneous ruling is harmful, unless it is self-evident. Saint Bernard School of Montville, Inc. v. Bank of America, 312 Conn. 811, 824-25, 95 A.3d 1063, 1071-72 (2014).

B. *The Brief*

The front page of the brief should contain the information listed in the last paragraph of § 67-4. Section 67-4 also requires that the parties generally be referred to as "plaintiff" or "defendant" rather than "appellant" or "appellee".

After the front page, the brief should have five or six parts.

1. Table of Contents (optional)
2. Statement of Issue(s)
3. Table of Authorities
4. Nature of Proceedings and Facts of Case
5. Argument, which may include the text of Statutes and the like (or put in appendix)
6. Conclusion

Maltbie's Connecticut Appellate Procedure (2d Ed.1957), p. 463, contains an excellent article on brief writing authored by Karl W. Punzak, former professor of legal writing at the University of Connecticut School of Law, entitled "Some Notes on Brief Writing". We highly recommend Professor Punzak's suggestions.

1. Statement of Issues

All issues briefed should be raised in the statement of issues. Raising them in the preliminary statement of issues under § 63-4 is insufficient. Elm Street Builders, Inc. v. Enterprise Park Condominium Ass'n, Inc., 63 Conn.App. 657, 659 n.2, 778 A.2d 237, 239 n.2 (2001). The failure to identify an issue in the statement of issues precluded review in Label Systems Corp. v. Aghamohammadi, 270 Conn. 291, 301 n.9, 852 A.2d 703, 712 n.9, 21 I.E.R. Cas. (BNA) 959, 150 Lab. Cas. (CCH) P 59897 (2004).

Each issue must state the pages in the brief where the issue is discussed. Robert J. Barnabei Contracting, LLC v. Greater Hartford Jewish Community Center, Inc., 127 Conn.App. 507, 517 n.3, 14 A.3d 461, 469 n.3, cert. denied, 301 Conn. 914, 19 A.3d 1260 (2011). The failure to indicate where issues were argued in the brief where the argument sections in the brief did not correlate to the statement of issues precluded review in Carmichael v. Stonkus, 133

Conn.App. 302, 307–08, 34 A.3d 1026, 1029–30, cert. denied, 304 Conn. 911, 39 A.3d 1121 (2012), and Paoletta v. Anchor Reef Club at Branford, LLC, 123 Conn.App. 402, 1 A.3d 1238, cert. denied, 298 Conn. 931, 5 A.3d 491 (2010).

The number of issues raised in the preliminary statement of issues should be reduced to only the most important ones by the time the brief is prepared. A brief with too many issues conceals the most important ones and was criticized in State v. Raguseo, 225 Conn. 114, 117 n.3, 622 A.2d 519, 522 n.3 (1993); and Boccanfuso v. Conner, 89 Conn.App. 260, 263 n.2, 873 A.2d 208, 213 n.2, cert. denied, 275 Conn. 905, 882 A.2d 668 (2005).

There is no prescribed format, except that the statement should be no more than one page long. Some examples of acceptable formats:

    (a) (In a case tried to the jury for personal injuries sustained in an automobile accident from which a verdict for the plaintiff was rendered.)

        1.   Did the trial court err in failing to charge on the seat belt defense?

        2.   Did the trial court err in failing to set aside the verdict as excessive?

    (b) (In a court case involving school finance.)

        1.   Whether the plaintiffs are being deprived of an equal right to a free public education as provided by Article Eighth, Section 1 of the Connecticut Constitution.

        2.   Whether the Court was correct in concluding that the present system of financing public education in Connecticut does not violate the Fourteenth Amendment of the United States Constitution.

        3.   Whether the state system of financing education bears a rational relationship to legitimate state purpose and satisfies Article First, Section 20 of the Connecticut Constitution.

        4.   Whether the doctrine of sovereign immunity is a defense to this action.

    (c) (In a conversion case.)

        1.   The trial court erred in admitting the hearsay testimony of Mr. Hare.

        2.   The trial court erred in sustaining the objection to the testimony of Mr. Hatter on the ground that he was of unsound mind.

A general statement, such as "Did the court err in its findings of fact and conclusions of law?", does not comply with this rule. Verderame v. Trinity Estates Development Corp., 92 Conn.App. 230, 231 n.3, 883 A.2d 1255, 1256 n.3 (2005).

2. Table of Authorities

Subsection (b) requires the printing of a table of authorities with a reference to the page in which they appear in the brief. The authors suggest the alphabetical listing of

    (a) cases and slip opinions with citations
    (b) statutes, regulations and ordinances
    (c) opinions of attorney general
    (d) textbooks, periodicals and articles
    (e) any other authorities.

Some lawyers include a table of contents as well, but this is not required.

See also § 67-11 (Table of Authorities; Citation of Cases).

The table of authorities serves an advocacy purpose. If it rattles on for four or five pages you might consider whether you are citing too many cases. (Obviously this depends on the number and complexity of issues.) Also, the table gives an overview to the court of the age and prestige of the cases cited (e.g., too many old cases, too many trial cases, too many federal citations in an area of state law).

3. **Nature of Proceedings and Facts of Case**

Counsel should set forth the salient facts in the case in narrative form with adequate references to the transcript or exhibits. Failure to do this may be fatal; Carmichael v. Stonkus, 133 Conn.App. 302, 308, 34 A.3d 1026, 1029–30, cert. denied, 304 Conn. 911, 39 A.3d 1121 (2012); Taylor v. American Thread Co., 200 Conn. 108, 112, 509 A.2d 512, 514 (1986); IN Energy Solutions, Inc. v. Realgy, LLC, 114 Conn.App. 262, 278, 969 A.2d 807, 818 (2009) ("The mere recital of claims supposedly supported by the evidence, without directing the court's attention to those specific portions claimed to be relevant and material does not adequately place those claims before the court for its consideration."); Esposito v. Schiff, 38 Conn.App. 726, 728–29, 662 A.2d 1337, 1338–39 (1995) (failure to comply resulted in limited review; at a minimum it makes appellate review very difficult). The Appellate Court used the appellee's record references where the appellant failed to provide them in In re Anthony H., 104 Conn.App. 744, 761 n.8, 936 A.2d 638, 649 n.8 (2007), cert. denied, 285 Conn. 520, 943 A.2d 1100 (2008). See also Dzienkiewicz v. Department of Correction, 291 Conn. 214, 219 n.3, 967 A.2d 1183, 1185 n.3 (2009) (appellee remedied defects by including transcript excerpts in its record). Do not use the appendix to expand the statement of facts, except as explicitly authorized by § 67-8. Facts erroneously included in the appendix may be stricken. State v. Jones, 193 Conn. 70, 74–75 n.2, 475 A.2d 1087, 1091 n.2 (1984).

The statement should never be argumentative in nature; save that for your argument. In fact an argument found only in the statement of facts was disregarded in Grimm v. Grimm, 276 Conn. 377, 391 n.14, 886 A.2d 391, 400 n.14 (2005). The statement should not include the inconsequential. The statement should refer only to evidence on the record. In O'Hara v. State, 218 Conn. 628, 639–40 n.8, 590 A.2d 948, 954 n.8 (1991), the defendant was ordered to refile a brief, deleting all references to a document outside the record. Review the appellate record of a case upon which you rely. The briefs in that case may well help your case.

The statement of facts should be as short as possible, stating only those facts relevant to the issues on appeal.

A good reason not to put unnecessary facts in the appellant's brief is that the court may use any evidence brought before it by the appellant in order to cure any defects in the trial record and thus affirm the judgment, State v. Ferraiuolo, 145 Conn. 458, 463, 144 A.2d 41, 44 (1958); Sosnowski v. Lenox, 133 Conn. 624, 628, 53 A.2d 388, 390 (1947).

Ironically, narrating the evidence in the brief rather than in an appendix returns us to some extent to the procedures in effect prior to 1951. See, e.g., 1934 P.B. § 346. The pre-1951 precedent and briefs may be of some value in preparing briefs today. One sanction for printing evidence verbatim rather than boiling it down into a narrative is that the court may deny costs otherwise permitted, Gaffney v. Pesce, 144 Conn. 17, 19, 126 A.2d 926, 927 (1956).

4. **Argument**

In Kopylec v. Town of North Branford, 130 Conn.App. 146, 148 n.1, 23 A.3d 51, 53 n.1, cert. granted, 302 Conn. 930, 28 A.3d 346 (2011), appeal withdrawn (2012), the court criticized the failure to divide the argument by issues with appropriate headings but afforded review nonetheless.

Each point of law must be specifically and separately briefed by points, starting with a brief statement of the standard of review for each issue. Willow Springs Condominium Ass'n, Inc. v. Seventh BRT Development Corp., 245 Conn. 1, 20–21, 717 A.2d 77, 89 (1998); Cable v. Bic Corp., 79 Conn.App. 178, 179 n.1, 830 A.2d 279, 281 n.1 (2003), aff'd, 270 Conn. 433, 854 A.2d 1057 (2004) (criticizing lack of brief statement of standard of review); Carmichael v.

Stonkus, 133 Conn.App. 302, 308–09, 34 A.3d 1026, 1030, cert. denied, 304 Conn. 911, 39 A.3d 1121 (2012).

a. Standard of Review

There are many possible standards of review. If the issue is a question of law, review is plenary, Rhode v. Milla, 287 Conn. 731, 737, 949 A.2d 1227, 1233 (2008) (whether invocation of Fifth Amendment privilege constitutes admissible evidence is a question of law); Bysiewicz v. Dinardo, 298 Conn. 748, 788 n.38, 6 A.3d 726, 751 n.38 (2010) (plenary review of constitutional claim); In re Emoni W., 305 Conn. 723, 733, 48 A.3d 1 (2012) (plenary review of statutory construction claim); L & R Realty v. Connecticut Nat. Bank, 246 Conn. 1, 8, 715 A.2d 748, 752 (1998), which means that the trial court's ruling has no effect on the appellate review except for its intrinsic persuasiveness. If the issue is one of fact, review is usually limited to clear error. If the issue is one of a discretionary ruling during trial, review is usually limited to abuse of discretion. If the issue is one of mixed law and fact, review is plenary. Friezo v. Friezo, 281 Conn. 166, 180, 914 A.2d 533, 544 (2007) (en banc); Tooley v. Metro-North Commuter R. Co., 58 Conn.App. 485, 492 n.8, 755 A.2d 270, 275 n.8, 168 L.R.R.M. (BNA) 2875 (2000). If the facts are undisputed, review is likely to be plenary. Webster Bank v. Zak, 259 Conn. 766, 773–74, 792 A.2d 66, 70 (2002).

Sometimes it is not clear what is a fact and what is a conclusion, or put another way, what is an issue of fact and what is an issue of law. The Supreme Court is in a bit of a morass. Compare Monti v. Wenkert, 287 Conn. 101, 111 n.2, 947 A.2d 261, 262, 268 n.2 (2008) (abuse of discretion standard applies to mixed questions of fact and law), with Friezo v. Friezo, 281 Conn. 166, 180–81, 914 A.2d 533, 544 (2007) (mixed questions of fact and law subject to plenary review). A useful discussion of this problem is found in State v. Geisler, 222 Conn. 672, 692–94, 610 A.2d 1225, 1235–36 (1992); White Oak Excavators, Inc. v. Burns, 172 Conn. 478, 481, 374 A.2d 1097, 1099–1100 (1977); Davis v. Margolis, 107 Conn. 417, 140 A. 823 (1928); and especially Nolan v. New York, N. H. & H. R. Co., 70 Conn. 159, 39 A. 115 (1898). See Sanchione v. Sanchione, 173 Conn. 397, 402, 378 A.2d 522, 525 (1977) ("a deduction from other facts found . . . is a conclusion"). If there is no question of the credibility of witnesses, such as in the construction of deeds, the clear error test may well not apply. See Marion Road Ass'n v. Harlow, 1 Conn.App. 329, 332, 472 A.2d 785, 787–88 (1984); and Lavigne v. Lavigne, 3 Conn.App. 423, 427, 488 A.2d 1290, 1292 (1985). But see Besade v. Interstate Sec. Services, 212 Conn. 441, 449, 562 A.2d 1086, 1091 (1989) (medical records). A conclusion of fact, that is, one based on subordinate facts, is treated as a conclusion of law. Hadfield v. Tracy, 101 Conn. 118, 125, 125 A. 199, 201, 34 A.L.R. 581 (1924). A "conclusion of fact" appears to mean the same thing as an "ultimate fact." Dziekiewicz v. Caffrey, 101 Conn. 449, 455–56, 126 A. 563, 565 (1924).

What seems to be clear is that, when the trial court determination is based solely on a stipulation of facts and the oral and written arguments of counsel, review is plenary. Hirschfeld v. Hirschfeld, 50 Conn.App. 280, 284, 719 A.2d 41, 43 (1998). Thus if the facts are undisputed on appeal so that the issue is the legal significance of those facts, review is plenary; Webster Bank v. Zak, 259 Conn. 766, 773, 792 A.2d 66, 70 (2002) (facts undisputed); First Federal Sav. and Loan Ass'n of Rochester v. Charter Appraisal Co., Inc., 247 Conn. 597, 724 A.2d 497 (1999); Olson v. Accessory Controls and Equipment Corp., 254 Conn. 145, 156, 757 A.2d 14, 22, 16 I.E.R. Cas. (BNA) 1050, 142 Lab. Cas. (CCH) P 59132 (2000).

b. Suggestions for making your argument

In preparing the appellant's brief, you need to be creative in thinking about ways the trial court may be in error. For example, if a trial court has discretion but fails to exercise it, that is error. Collins v. Anthem Health Plans, Inc., 266 Conn. 12, 47, 836 A.2d 1124, 1146–47 (2003); Higgins v. Karp, 243 Conn. 495, 504, 706 A.2d 1, 6 (1998); Gurliacci v. Mayer, 218 Conn. 531, 557, 590 A.2d 914, 928 (1991); Trumbull v. O'Hara, 68 Conn. 33, 34, 35 A. 764, 765 (1896).

Likewise, if a trial court gives only erroneous reason (a) for a decision, the appellate court will not affirm the decision for reason (b) if that reason is discretionary. Kalams v. Giacchetto, 268 Conn. 244, 263 n.13, 842 A.2d 1100, 1112 n.13 (2004). Sometimes a colloquy with the trial court will show that the court's reasoning was improper. Loughlin v. Loughlin, 280 Conn. 632, 648–50, 910 A.2d 963, 975–76 (2006). An improper reason for exercising discretion is grounds for finding error. State v. Palko, 121 Conn. 669, 678, 186 A. 657, 661 (1936).

Finally, rulings on the merits when the trial court dismisses the case for lack of jurisdiction may be disregarded as "merely advisory." Statewide Grievance Committee v. Rozbicki, 211 Conn. 232, 245–46, 558 A.2d 986, 992 (1989). Ditto for ruling on damages when the defendant wins on liability. Broughel v. Southern New England Tel. Co., 72 Conn. 617, 625, 45 A. 435, 438 (1900).

For review of contract language, see Pesino v. Atlantic Bank of New York, 244 Conn. 85, 709 A.2d 540 (1998), and Tallmadge Bros., Inc. v. Iroquois Gas Transmission System, L.P., 252 Conn. 479, 479–97, 746 A.2d 1277, 1286–88 (2000) (sophisticated commercial parties). For review of the applicability of a statute, see New England Sav. Bank v. Bedford Realty Corp., 246 Conn. 594, 599 n.7, 717 A.2d 713, 717 n.7 (1998). For review of construction of a contested judgement, see Mazziotti v. Allstate Ins. Co., 240 Conn. 799, 806–07, 695 A.2d 1010, 1014 (1997). For a stipulated judgment, see Issler v. Issler, 250 Conn. 226, 234–36, 737 A.2d 383, 389–90 (1999). For review of discretionary rulings, compare Glass v. Peter Mitchell Const. Leasing & Development Corp., 50 Conn.App. 539, 718 A.2d 79, cert. granted, 247 Conn. 938, 723 A.2d 317 (1998) (appeal withdrawn) (abuse of discretion found), with O'Shea v. Mignone, 50 Conn.App. 577, 719 A.2d 1176, cert. denied, 247 Conn. 941, 723 A.3d 319 (1998) (abuse of discretion not found).

The authors suggest that the argument follow the order of the statement of issues. Briefing a point which should have been stated as a separate issue may preclude review. Hirtle v. Hirtle, 217 Conn. 394, 403 n.8, 586 A.2d 578, 582 n.8 (1991); State v. Sweeney, 30 Conn.App. 550, 553 n.5, 621 A.2d 304, 306 n.5 (1993).

An argument addressing issues outside the scope of appeal may be stricken. See Altberg v. Paul Kovacs Tire Shop, Inc., 31 Conn.App. 634, 639, 626 A.2d 804, 807 (1993).

While the rule is unclear, the authors' view is that, unless the specific subsections of § 67-4(d) apply, the argument should generally make factual references to the statement of facts rather than directly to the transcript. Otherwise, the argument and the statement of facts will be duplicative. See Vaiuso v. Vaiuso, 2 Conn.App. 141, 145, 477 A.2d 678, 682, cert. denied, 194 Conn. 807, 482 A.2d 712 (1984). However, if the specific subsections of (d) apply, reference should be made directly to the transcript. Jancura v. Szwed, 176 Conn. 285, 287–288, 407 A.2d 961, 963 (1978). This defect was excused in Jancura.

c. Inadequate Briefing

If an issue is briefed, it should be briefed seriously. Failure to research or brief an issue properly may be deemed an abandonment of an issue. Montagnese v. Spicer, 130 Conn.App. 301, 304 n.2, 22 A.3d 702, 704 n.2 (2011) (lack of analysis); State v. Prioleau, 235 Conn. 274, 294–95, 664 A.2d 743, 755 (1995); State v. Peloso, 109 Conn.App. 477, 503 n.27, 952 A.2d 825, 842 n.27 (2008) (claim made in footnote); Blacker v. Crapo, 112 Conn.App. 795, 802–03 n.6, 964

A.2d 1241, 1245–46 n.6, cert. denied, 291 Conn. 915, 970 A.2d 727 (2009) (failure to provide references to facts and legal analysis); Carmichael v. Stonkus, 133 Conn.App. 302, 309–10, 34 A.3d 1026, 1030, cert. denied, 304 Conn. 911, 39 A.3d 1121 (2012) (lengthy quotations from cases in trial transcripts without analysis improper). Noncompliance was criticized but excused in Labulis v. Kopylec, 128 Conn.App. 571, 583 n.16, 17 A.3d 1157, 1164 n.16 (2011). Merely mentioning an issue is insufficient. Tetreault v. Eslick, 271 Conn. 466, 473 n.7, 857 A.2d 888, 893 n.7 (2004). However, two sentences were apparently sufficient to brief an issue in Bell Atlantic Mobile, Inc. v. Department of Public Utility Control, 253 Conn. 453, 487, 754 A.2d 128, 147 (2000). The Supreme Court considered an issue even though the appellant paid scant attention to it because the issue was important and was a certified issue from the Appellate Court. Sablosky v. Sablosky, 258 Conn. 713, 717 n.3, 784 A.2d 890, 894 n.3 (2001).

A particularly good discussion of what constitutes adequate briefing is found in the 6-1 decision in Electrical Contractors, Inc. v. Department of Educ., 303 Conn. 402, 444 n.40, 35 A.3d 188, 217 n.40, 192 L.R.R.M. (BNA) 2954, 2012-1 Trade Cas. (CCH) ¶ 77768 (2012), and State v. Pearson, 139 Conn.App. 521, 56 A.3d 722 (2012).

In Windels v. Environmental Protection Com'n of Town of Darien, 284 Conn. 268, 304, 933 A.2d 256, 278 (2007), the court declined to find an issue after reversal was already ordered on another issue because the arguments were only a page and half long and were "essentially generic."

Briefing an issue in post-trial proceedings did not authorize the Appellate Court to decide an issue the party did not raise again on appeal. Sequenzia v. Guerrieri Masonry Inc., 298 Conn. 816, 823–24, 9 A.3d 322, 325–26 (2010).

In State v. Ledbetter, 275 Conn. 534, 568, 881 A.2d 290, 312 (2005), the Court approved a survey in the brief of relevant scientific data in the scientific literature.

d. Improper Briefing

An ad hominem attack on the trial judge is likely to get strong criticism from the appellate court. State v. Gemmell, 151 Conn.App. 590, 612 n.9, 94 A.3d 1253, 1266 n.9, cert. denied, 314 Conn. ___, ___ A.3d ___ (2014).

5. Evidentiary Rulings and Charge to Jury

Section (d) causes the principal procedural problems on appeal, for litigants constantly fail to follow the rule.

Evidentiary rulings and the charge must be presented essentially verbatim as discussed in § 67-4(d), unlike federal practice. Thus, the assertion in the brief that evidence was improperly admitted or excluded, coupled with a transcript page reference, is insufficient. Roberto v. Honeywell, Inc., 43 Conn.App. 161, 163, 681 A.2d 1011, 1013 (1996); Mather v. Griffin Hosp., 207 Conn. 125, 148 n.3, 540 A.2d 666, 677 n.3 (1988); State v. Morris, 95 Conn.App. 793, 800 n.7, 898 A.2d 822, 827 n.7, cert. denied, 280 Conn. 939, 912 A.2d 476 (2006). References to the pages of the transcript by themselves are insufficient, State v. Siller, 12 Conn.App. 395, 402, 530 A.2d 1106, 1109 (1987); although necessary, Cable v. Bic Corp., 79 Conn.App. 178, 179 n.1, 830 A.2d 279, 281 n.1 (2003), aff'd, 270 Conn. 433, 854 A.2d 1057 (2004).

Rulings under (d) (3) should be recited in detail along with the questions, objections, offer of proof, claims of admissibility and reference to evidence. Travelers Casualty & Surety Co. of America v. Netherlands Ins. Co., 312 Conn. 714, 762 n.37, 95 A.3d 1031 (2014); Mattie & O'Brien Contracting Co., Inc. v. Rizzo Const. Pool Co., 128 Conn.App. 537, 545, 17 A.3d 1083, 1089, cert. denied, 302 Conn. 906, 23 A.3d 1247 (2011); Wilkes v. Wilkes, 55 Conn.App. 313, 323 n.9, 738 A.2d 758 (1999); Aspiazu v. Orgera, 205 Conn. 623, 636 n.5, 535 A.2d

338, 344 n.5 (1987). General transcript citations will not suffice. Local 84, Theatrical Stage Employees, Moving Picture Technicians, Artists and Relied Crafts of the United States, Its Territories and Canada, AFL-CIO, CLC v. Francis, 138 Conn.App. 77, 91, 51 A.3d 401, 410 (2012). The court excused noncompliance with (d)(3) in *Wilkes*, State v. Gonzalez, 106 Conn.App. 238, 246 n.7, 941 A.2d 989, 995–96 n.7, cert. denied, 287 Conn. 903, 947 A.2d 343 (2008), but it did not in Gorra Realty, Inc. v. Jetmore, 200 Conn. 151, 170–71, 510 A.2d 440, 450 (1986) and Creative Masonry & Chimney, LLC. v. Johnson, 142 Conn.App. 135, 141–42, 64 A.3d 359, 364, cert. denied, 309 Conn. 903, 68 A.3d 658 (2013), and many other cases.

The rule also requires a brief narration or verbatim statement if the ruling cannot be understood without it. The court did the best it could to review a ruling without the narrative in Santangelo v. Middlesex Theatre, 125 Conn. 572, 579–80, 7 A.2d 430, 433 (1939). Sometimes a narrative statement is far better than a verbatim statement. In Soper Lumber Co. v. Halsted & Harmount Co., 73 Conn. 547, 553, 48 A. 425, 428 (1901), the trial court criticized the presentation of some evidentiary rulings as "a wrangle covering nine pages" that could have been presented in one page.

If the answer to the question is not given, the ruling may not be reviewed, Blatt v. Star Paper Co., 160 Conn. 193, 203, 276 A.2d 786, 791 (1970); State v. McLaughlin, 132 Conn. 325, 339, 44 A.2d 116, 123 (1945); if there is no preliminary statement and the ruling could not be understood without it, the ruling may not be reviewed, Morgillo v. Evergreen Cemetery Ass'n, 152 Conn. 169, 175, 205 A.2d 368, 371 (1964); and if each ruling is not put in separate paragraphs, there may be no review, Vachon v. Ives, 150 Conn. 452, 455, 190 A.2d 601, 603 (1963). However, if the issues are sufficiently delineated, the court occasionally overlooks technical defects, Siladi v. McNamara, 164 Conn. 510, 512 n.1, 325 A.2d 277, 279 n.1 (1973).

Citing subsections (c) and (d), the Appellate Court criticized the failure to refer to the return of record in an administrative appeal. Solomon v. Connecticut Medical Examining Bd., 85 Conn.App. 854, 862, 859 A.2d 932, 938 (2004), cert. denied, 273 Conn. 906, 868 A.2d 748 (2005).

In LaBossiere v. Jones, 117 Conn.App. 211, 221, 979 A.2d 522, 529 (2009), the court refused to review a ruling that the plaintiff failed to identify anywhere in the record or transcripts.

6. Pleadings and the Like

For appeals filed prior to July 1, 2013, pleadings, order, and other documents that are in the case file but not in the printed record should be put in the appendix if error is claimed as to a ruling involving the document. § 67-4(d)(4). The printed record, however, is usually not prepared until after the appellant's (and often the appellee's) brief is filed. Thus, any pleading that falls within this subsection and is not listed in the preliminary or revised designation of pleadings should go into the appendix. If you have any doubt as to whether a specific document will go in the printed record, put it in the appendix to be safe or consult the case manager to determine whether it will go in.

7. Statutes and the Like

The text of any relevant statute must now be quoted in the brief unless it is in an appendix. If the text is lengthy it should be put in an appendix.

Although § 67-4(e) does not expressly apply to Practice Book rules or restatement provisions, it is useful to put these in the appendix when they are relevant to the argument.

The court criticized the failure to provide the town charter at issue in Andross v. Town of West Hartford, 285 Conn. 309, 317 n.5, 939 A.2d 1146, 1151 n.5 (2008).

8. Conclusion

The rule now requires a formal conclusion in subsection (e). It should state the precise relief requested. State v. Jimenez-Jaramill, 134 Conn.App. 346, 379, 38 A.3d 239, 260, cert. denied, 305 Conn. 913, 45 A.3d 100 (2012).

9. Length of Brief

Counsel are limited to 35 pages (excluding certain pages) without prior consent of the court. See § 67-3.

There are two schools of thought with reference to a brief. The more effective school is to make the brief short, erring on the side of giving the court the case citations without the attorney's interpretation or interpolations. The other school feels that a full and detailed quotation from the cases relied upon, plus the "ALR" scoreboard, that is, a state by state case citation upholding one's view, is necessary.

If one checks the appellant's brief in McKirdy v. Cascio, 142 Conn. 80, 111 A.2d 555 (1955) (60 pages—no remittitur), with the one in Lengel v. New Haven Gas Light Co., 142 Conn. 70, 111 A.2d 547 (1955) (8 pages—remittitur of $14,000), decided the same day, one can be impressed with the benefits of a shorter brief. The authors obtained a new trial in which their argument covered one and one-half pages in Labatt v. Grunewald, 182 Conn. 236, 438 A.2d 85 (1980).

10. Citation to Record (for appeals filed prior to July 1, 2013)

The record is almost never prepared until after the appellant's brief is filed. The authors suggest citing to the record as follows: "(R. __)" and then sending a letter to the appellate clerk after the record is filed giving the page citations.

11. Test for Harmful Error

See discussion in the authors' comments to § 60-5, subsection C.

C. *The Appendix*

For appeals filed after July 1, 2013, an appendix is mandatory, at least for appellants and cross-appellants, as the printed record no longer exists. Part two of the appendix can be used to comply with § 67-4. Each appendix should begin with an index of the names of the witnesses and any papers placed in the appendix. After giving the name of the witness, and which side called him, one must state whether the evidence was given on direct or cross.

The most effective use of part two of the appendix today is to reproduce exhibits or lengthy portions of statutes that are to be used in oral argument. State v. Shanks, 34 Conn.App. 103, 110–11 n.7, 640 A.2d 155, 159 n.7, cert. denied, 229 Conn. 921, 642 A.2d 1216 (1994).

One thing appendices *cannot* be used for is including transcripts that were not designated under § 63-4(a)(3) or documents that were not marked as exhibits. Doing either of these things makes those portions of the appendix, as well as any references in the brief to them, subject to a motion to strike under § 60-2(3).

D. *Reply Brief*

The appellant may within 20 days after the filing of the appellee's brief file a reply brief. However, a reply brief cannot be used to raise a new issue absent exceptional circumstances, Plante v. Charlotte Hungerford Hosp., 300 Conn. 33, 58–59, 12 A.3d 885, 899–900 (2011); McDonough v. Forrest, 129 Conn.App. 851, 856 n.3, 21 A.3d 546, 549 n.3, cert. denied, 302 Conn. 924, 28 A.3d 340 (2011); or to brief an issue that was inadequately briefed in the main brief, Hurley v. Heart Physicians, P.C., 298 Conn. 371, 378 n.6, 3 A.3d 892, 898 n.6, Prod. Liab. Rep. (CCH) P 18501 (2010). State v. Wilson, 242 Conn. 605, 607–08 n.5, 700

A.2d 633, 635 n.5 (1997). Exceptional circumstances apparently were found in Curry v. Burns, 225 Conn. 782, 789 n.2, 626 A.2d 719, 722 n.2 (1993), because the issue was also raised by the amicus curiae; and in 37 Huntington Street, H, LLC v. City of Hartford, 62 Conn.App. 586, 597 n.17, 772 A.2d 633, 641 n.17, cert. denied, 256 Conn. 914, 772 A.2d 1127 (2001) (same); and in Bennett v. New Milford Hosp., Inc., 300 Conn. 1, 22, 12 A.3d 865, 878 (2011), where the new claim had to be considered to provide a logical construction of the statute at issue on the appeal. See also State v. Jose G., 290 Conn. 331, 341 n.8, 963 A.2d 42, 49 n.8 (2009), where the Appellate Court had given the state permission to file a supplemental brief regarding the issue raised in the reply brief.

Among the issues that cannot be raised for the first time in a reply brief is a claim of plain error. Harty v. Cantor Fitzgerald and Co., 275 Conn. 72, 90–91 n.9, 881 A.2d 139, 151 n.9 (2005). This puts the appellant in the uncomfortable position, if the issue was arguably raised below, of claiming in the opening brief that the issue was raised properly, but, if it was not, the error was plain.

If procedural mistakes are made in the original brief and are raised in the appellee's brief, correcting the errors in the reply brief may succeed. State v. Jones, 8 Conn.App. 177, 183 n.3, 512 A.2d 932, 935 n.3 (1986).

E. *Supplemental Brief*

The appellate courts occasionally ask for supplemental briefs before, at or after oral argument. Recent examples are Flannery v. Singer Asset Finance Co., LLC, 312 Conn. 286, 306 n.22, 94 A.3d 553, 566 n. 22 (2014); In re Joseph W., Jr., 301 Conn. 245, 255, 21 A.3d 723, 729 (2011), and In re Cadle Co., 129 Conn.App. 814, 832–33, 21 A.3d 572, 582–83, cert. denied, 302 Conn. 914, 27 A.3d 323 (2011). In Thompson v. Orcutt, 257 Conn. 301, 306-07, 777 A.2d 670, 674–75 (2001), the Supreme Court allowed the parties an opportunity to file supplemental briefs in response to the trial court's articulation ordered by the court after oral argument. In State v. Klinger, 50 Conn.App. 216, 220, 718 A.2d 446, 448 (1998), the Appellate Court ordered supplemental briefs on mootness before oral argument. In State v. Sanders, 54 Conn.App. 732, 743 n.9, 738 A.2d 674, 681 n.9 (1999), the Appellate Court granted the defendant's request to file a supplemental brief before oral argument. A comprehensive list of cases ordering supplemental briefing is found in Judge Bishop's dissenting opinion in Gosselin v. Gosselin, 110 Conn.App. 142, 159–61 n.4, 955 A.2d 60, 70–71 n.4 (2008).

A motion to file a supplemental brief to comply with § 67-4 was denied in Moulton Brothers, Inc. v. Lemieux, 74 Conn.App. 357, 360 n.5, 812 A.2d 129, 131 n.5 (2002).

F. *Failure to Follow Rule*

As noted throughout this commentary, failure to follow this rule generally results in a refusal of the Court to review the judge's charge or other rulings. However, there are numerous exceptions and it is difficult to predict when the rule will be strictly enforced. Contrast the majority and dissenting opinions in State v. Tryon, 145 Conn. 304, 307, 313, 142 A.2d 54, 56, 59 (1958) ("mere defect in appellate procedure" vs. "If we expect the judges and attorneys to conform to the rules, we should at least set a good example and do so ourselves"). The Appellate Court, with one judge dissenting, opined in refusing to consider an issue: "Either we adhere to the rules or we do not adhere to them." Osborne v. Osborne, 2 Conn.App. 635, 639, 482 A.2d 77, 80 (1984).

§ 67-5. The Appellee's Brief; Contents and Organization (Applicable to appeals filed before July 1, 2013)

The brief of the appellee shall contain, in a form corresponding to that stated in Section 67-4, the following:

(a) A counter statement of any issue involved as to which the appellee disagrees with the statement of the appellant or a statement of any other grounds which were properly raised by an appellee under Section 63-4. Such statement shall be deemed in replacement of and shall supersede the preliminary statement of the issues.

(b) A table of authorities cited in the brief, with references to the page or pages of the brief where the citations to those authorities appear. Citations shall be in the form provided in section 67-11.

(c) A counter statement of any fact as to which the appellee disagrees with the statement of the appellant. The counter statement of facts shall be in narrative form and shall be supported by appropriate references to the page or pages of the transcript or to the relevant document upon which the appellee relies. An appellee may not rely on any fact unless it is set forth in the appellee's counter statement of facts or in the appellant's statement of facts or is incorporated in any brief of the parties in accordance with Section 67-4(d) or with subsection (d) hereof.

(d) The argument of the appellee, divided as provided in Section 67-4(d). The argument on each point shall include a separate, brief statement of the standard of review the appellee believes should be applied. The argument may augment or take exception to the appellant's presentation of rulings or the charge by reference to any relevant part of the court's charge or any other evidence in narrative or verbatim form which is relevant to such question, with appropriate references to the statements of facts or to the page or pages of the transcript or to the relevant document.

(e) Claims, if any, directed to any rulings or decisions of the trial court adverse to the appellee. These shall be made in the manner provided in Section 67-4(d).

(f) A short conclusion stating the precise relief sought.

(g) The text of the pertinent portions of any constitutional provision, statute, ordinance or regulation at issue or upon which the appellee relies. Such text need not be included in the brief if it is included in the appellant's brief or appendix or in the appendix to the appellee's brief.

(h) In appeals filed pursuant to Section 81-4, a statement as to whether the appellee disputes the applicability of the version of the land use regulations filed with the appellate clerk. If the appellee disputes the applicability of such regulations, it shall set forth this basis for maintaining that such regulations do not apply.

The brief shall be organized in the following order: table of contents, if any; statement of issues; table of authorities; if amicus, statement of interest of the amicus curiae; statement of facts; argument; conclusion and statement of relief requested; signature; and certification pursuant to Section 62-7.

(i) When the appellee is also the cross appellant, the issues on the cross appeal shall be briefed in accordance with Section 67-4. In such a case, the briefs shall clearly label which sections of the brief refer to the appeal and which refer to the cross appeal.

§ 67-5. The Appellee's Brief; Contents and Organization (Applicable to appeals filed on or after July 1, 2013)

The brief of the appellee shall contain, in a form corresponding to that stated in Section 67-4, the following:

(a) A counter statement of any issue involved as to which the appellee disagrees with the statement of the appellant or a statement of any other grounds which were properly raised by an appellee under Section 63-4. Such statement shall be deemed in replacement of and shall supersede the preliminary statement of the issues.

(b) A table of authorities cited in the brief, with references to the page or pages of the brief where the citations to those authorities appear. Citations shall be in the form provided in Section 67-11.

(c) A counter statement of any fact as to which the appellee disagrees with the statement of the appellant. The counter statement of facts shall be in narrative form and shall be supported by appropriate references to the page or pages of the transcript or to the relevant document upon which the appellee relies. An appellee may not rely on any fact unless it is set forth in the appellee's counter statement of facts or in the appellant's statement of facts or is incorporated in any brief of the parties in accordance with Section 67-4 (d) or with subsection (d) hereof.

(d) The argument of the appellee, divided as provided in Section 67-4 (d). The argument on each point shall include a separate, brief statement of the standard of review the appellee believes should be applied. The argument may augment or take exception to the appellant's presentation of rulings or the charge by reference to any relevant part of the court's charge or any other evidence in narrative or verbatim form which is relevant to such question, with appropriate references to the statements of facts or to the page or pages of the transcript or to the relevant document.

(e) Claims, if any, directed to any rulings or decisions of the trial court adverse to the appellee. These shall be made in the manner provided in Section 67-4 (d).

(f) A short conclusion stating the precise relief sought.

(g) The text of the pertinent portions of any constitutional provision, statute, ordinance or regulation at issue or on which the appellee relies. Such text need not be included in the brief if it is included in the appellant's brief or appendix or in the appendix to the appellee's brief.

(h) In appeals filed pursuant to Section 81-4, a statement as to whether the appellee disputes the applicability of the version of the land use regulations filed with the appellate clerk. If the appellee disputes the applicability of such regulations, it shall set forth its basis for maintaining that such regulations do not apply.

(i) The appellee's brief shall be organized in the following order: table of contents, if any; statement of issues; table of authorities; statement of facts; argument; conclusion and statement of relief requested; signature; and certification pursuant to Section 62-7.

(j) When the appellee is also the cross appellant, the issues on the cross appeal shall be briefed in accordance with Section 67-4. In such a case, the briefs shall clearly label which sections of the brief refer to the appeal and which refer to the cross appeal.

Historical Note

Derivation:

    1978 P.B. (1996–97), § 4064D
    1978 P.B. (1986–96), § 4066
    1978 P.B. (1979–86), § 3060G
    1978 P.B., § 3055
    1963 P.B., § 632A

The second paragraph of subsection (h) added "if any" in 2011 to indicate that a table of contents is optional.

Subsection (f) was added in 2010. What is now subsection (i) was added in 1996.

"May" was changed to "shall" in (e) effective January 1, 2006.

The last sentence of subsection (b) was added effective January 1, 2000.

Sections (c) and (d) were added effective October 1, 1992 to change "record" to "relevant document."

Section (a) was clarified and § (f) was expanded in scope from just statutes effective October 1, 1986.

Effective January 1, 1985, § (b) and § (f) were added.

Prior § 632A was enacted effective October 1, 1974 as part of the new appellate rules for jury cases. Section (d) was added effective July 1, 1979, at which time the rule became effective for both court and jury appeals.

AUTHORS' COMMENTS

The appellee must state what the standard of review is on each issue, regardless of which side briefs the issue first. If the appellee agrees with the appellant, the appellee may simply so state. An in depth discussion of various standards of review is found in the authors' comments to § 67-4.

The failure of an appellee to respond to an issue raised in the appellants brief is not a concession that the issue is meritorious. Harris v. Commissioner of Correction, 271 Conn. 808, 841 n.24, 860 A.2d 715, 737 n.24 (2004).

In general, the burden is on the appellant to present a proper record on appeal, and the appellee should not correct the appellant's deficiencies, for then they will probably be excused. Gladstone, Schwartz, Baroff and Blum v. Hovhannissian, 53 Conn.App. 122, 123 n.2, 728 A.2d 1140, 1142 n.2 (1999); State v. Thomas, 15 Conn.App. 197, 203 n.2, 543 A.2d 1356, 1359 n.2 (1988). The exceptions to this rule that the burden is on the appellant are discussed below. The appellee *does* need to give transcript or other record references in the statement of facts. State v. Jimenez-Jaramill, 134 Conn.App. 346, 380, 38 A.3d 239, 260, cert. denied, 305 Conn. 913, 45 A.3d 100 (2012).

An appellee who wishes to present an adverse ruling for review must have a counterstatement or statement under § (a). State v. One 1981 BMW Auto., 15 Conn.App. 589, 598, 546 A.2d 879, 884 (1988). The appellee must then comply with the technical requirements of this rule or the issue will not be reviewed. Thompson & Peck, Inc. v. Harbor Marine Contracting Corp., 5 Conn.App. 366, 368 n.1, 497 A.2d 1049, 1050 n.1 (1985), judgment aff'd, 203 Conn. 123, 523 A.2d 1266, 4 U.C.C. Rep. Serv. 2d 152 (1987). Likewise, if the appellee is claiming an alternate basis to affirm; see Jacques v. Carter, 2 Conn.App. 27, 35 n.4, 476 A.2d 621, 625 n.4 (1984); or a subsequent curing of the error; see Hutchinson v. Plante, 175 Conn. 1, 7, 392 A.2d 488, 491 (1978); the burden is on the appellee to present the proper record. At the very least, the appellee cannot expect the Appellate Court to raise an alternate basis to affirm on its own. Mountaindale Condominium Ass'n, Inc. v. Zappone, 59 Conn.App. 311, 319 n.11, 757 A.2d 608, 614 n.11, cert. denied, 254 Conn. 947, 762 A.2d 903 (2000). The appellee must also state the applicable standard of review for each argument. Schwartz v. Milazzo, 84 Conn.App. 175, 178 n.3, 852 A.2d 847, 849 n.3, cert. denied, 271 Conn. 942, 861 A.2d 515 (2004). The appellee must present the alternate basis to affirm as a separate argument. Vertex, Inc. v. City of Waterbury, 278 Conn. 557, 563 n.7, 898 A.2d 178, 184 n.7 (2006).

Under the pre-1978 rules if the appellant claimed there was no evidence to support a factual determination, the appellee's brief or appendix had to refer to such evidence, or the finding could be stricken. Lar-Rob Bus Corp. v. Town of Fairfield, 170 Conn. 397, 399, 365 A.2d 1086, 1088 (1976). The appellee's failure so to do could be fatal, Morningside Ass'n v. Morningside Development, Inc., 172 Conn. 60, 63–64, 372 A.2d 141, 143 (1976).

In general, the appellee's failure to print or refer to evidence to support facts or conclusions attacked in the appellant's brief may in some circumstances be as fatal under the post-1978 rules. Barry v. Posi-Seal Intern., Inc., 40 Conn.App. 577, 581 n.4, 672 A.2d 514, 517 n.4, cert. denied, 237 Conn. 917, 676 A.2d 1373 (1996); Duksa v. City of Middletown, 192 Conn. 191, 196 n.4, 472 A.2d 1, 3, 8 n.4 (1984). At the least, the court is going to rely on the appellant's version of the case, Blakeman v. Tobin, 177 Conn. 597 n.1, 419 A.2d 336 n.1 (1979); Belinsky v. Belinsky, 5 Conn.App. 133, 135, 497 A.2d 84, 85 (1985).

For suggestions on brief writing as it applies to both court and jury cases, see commentary to § 67-4.

§ 67-6. Statutory (§ 53a-46b) Review of Death Sentences

(a)   When a sentence of death has been imposed upon a defendant, following a conviction of a capital felony in violation of General Statutes § 53a-54b and the hearing upon imposition of the death penalty pursuant to General Statutes § 53a-46a, the briefs of the parties shall include a discussion of the issues set forth in General Statutes § 53a-46b(b), to wit, whether (1) the sentence was the product of passion, prejudice or any other arbitrary factor; (2) the evidence fails to support the finding of an aggravating circumstance specified in subsection (h) of § 53a-46a; and (3) the sentence is excessive or disproportionate to the penalty imposed in similar cases, considering both the circumstances of the crime and the character and record of the defendant.

(b) For the purpose of reviewing the issue of disproportionality pursuant to General Statutes § 53a-46b(b), the briefs of the parties shall contain appendices setting forth the circumstances of the crimes that are claimed to be similar to that of which the defendant has been convicted and the characters and records of the defendants involved therein so far as these are ascertainable from the transcripts of those trials and hearings on the imposition of the death penalty or may be judicially noticed. Only those capital felony cases that have been prosecuted in this state after October 1, 1973, and in which hearings on the imposition of the death penalty have taken place, whether or not the death penalty has been imposed, shall be deemed eligible for consideration as "similar cases," unless the court, on application of a party claiming that the resulting pool of eligible cases is inadequate for disproportionality review, shall modify this limitation in a particular case. Any such application shall identify the additional case or cases claimed to be similar and set forth, in addition to the circumstances of the crime and the character and record of the defendant involved, the provisions of the applicable statutes pertaining to the imposition of the death penalty with citations of pertinent decisions interpreting such provisions.

> Any such application shall be filed within thirty days after the delivery date of the transcript ordered by the appellant, or, if no transcript is required or the transcript has been received by the appellant prior to the filing of the appeal, such application shall be filed within thirty days after filing the appeal.

Historical Note

Derivation:
  1978 P.B. (1996–97), § 4064E
  1978 P.B. (1990–96), § 4066A
This rule was new effective July 16, 1990.

AUTHORS' COMMENTS

The first officially reported use of this rule is State v. Ross, 225 Conn. 559, 624 A.2d 886 (1993). Strict—indeed, impossible—compliance with this rule was not required in State v. Cobb, 234 Conn. 735, 742–43, 663 A.2d 948, 952–53 (1995).

While subsection (a)(3) is probably obsolete today because the statute no longer provides for such a review, its language was cited in State v. Rupar, 293 Conn. 489, 514, 978 A.2d 502, 518 (2009).

§ 67-7. The Amicus Curiae Brief

A brief of an amicus curiae in cases before the court on the merits may be filed only with the permission of the court. An application for permission to appear as amicus curiae and to file a brief shall be filed within twenty days after the filing of the brief of the party, if any, whom the applicant intends to support, and if there is no such party then the application shall be filed no later than twenty days after the filing of the appellee's brief.

The application shall state concisely the nature of the applicant's interest and the reasons why a brief of an amicus curiae should be allowed. The length of the brief shall not exceed ten pages unless a specific request is made for a brief of more than that length. The application shall conform to the requirements set forth in Sections 66-2 and 66-3. The amicus application should specifically set forth reasons to justify the filing of a brief in excess of ten pages. A party served with an application may within ten days after the filing of the application file an objection concisely stating the reasons therefor.

All briefs filed under this section shall comply with the applicable provisions of this chapter and shall set forth the interest of the amicus curiae.

An amicus curiae may argue orally only when a specific request for such permission is granted by the court in which the appeal is pending.

With the exception of briefs filed by the attorney general as provided by this rule, all briefs shall indicate whether counsel for a party wrote the brief in whole or in part and whether such counsel or a party contributed to the cost of the preparation or submission of the brief and shall identify those persons, other than the amicus curiae, its members or its counsel, who made such monetary contribution. The disclosure shall be made in the first footnote on the first page of the text.

Except for habeas corpus matters based on criminal convictions, if an appeal in a noncriminal matter involves an attack on the constitutionality of a state statute, the attorney general may appear and file a brief amicus curiae as of right. Notice of the attorney general's intention to appear and file a brief shall be given to the appellate clerk and all parties no later than the date on which the brief of the party the attorney general supports is filed, and the attorney general's brief will be due twenty days after the filing of the brief of the party the attorney general supports.

Historical Note

Derivation:
    1978 P.B. (1996–97), § 4064F
    1978 P.B. (1986–96), § 4067

1978 P.B. (1979–86), § 3060H
1978 P.B., § 3119
1963 P.B., § 714A

The last paragraph was added in 1996 and the next to the last paragraph was added in 2009.

Effective July 27, 1993, the second and third sentences of the second paragraph were added.

The procedures in the second paragraph were greatly simplified effective October 1, 1986. At the same time the last paragraph was added.

The first paragraph was amended effective January 1, 1985 to clarify when an amicus brief shall be filed. Prior to the amendment, amicus briefs generally were expected to be filed simultaneously with the brief of the party the amicus supports. This is apparently what was ordered in Brecciaroli v. Commissioner of Dept of Environmental Protection, 167 Conn. 672, 328 A.2d 427 (1974).

This rule was adopted effective October 1, 1970.

AUTHORS' COMMENTS

Before the mid-1990s, the Supreme Court tended not to be enthusiastic about amicus briefs. Now, however, the attitude has changed. They are now rarely denied if made by an organization with a general interest in the issue. However, the Supreme Court usually denies amicus motions by litigants in other cases. Oral argument is another matter. The authors cannot think of one instance since 1994 (other than perhaps a motion by the attorney general) where an amicus has been granted oral argument.

Amici should not expect the Supreme Court to consider issues not briefed by the parties. In re Bruce R., 234 Conn. 194, 215 n.16, 662 A.2d 107, 118 n.16 (1995); State v. Mercer, 208 Conn. 52, 56 n.4, 544 A.2d 611, 614 n.4 (1988). However, in one case the Supreme Court overruled a case based on the argument of the amicus even though the appellant did not join that argument until she filed her reply brief. Curry v. Burns, 225 Conn. 782, 789 n.2, 626 A.2d 719, 722 n.2 (1993). In another case the Supreme Court expressly referred to the amici's statutory construction argument. West Hartford Interfaith Coalition, Inc. v. Town Council of Town of West Hartford, 228 Conn. 498, 520, 636 A.2d 1342, 1353 (1994). See also Oller v. Oller-Chiang, 230 Conn. 828, 836, 646 A.2d 822, 827–28 (1994).

An amicus brief may properly present scientific studies. State v. Ledbetter, 275 Conn. 534, 569–70, 881 A.2d 290, 313–14 (2005). See also Kerrigan v. Commissioner of Public Health, 279 Conn. 447, 464 n.17, 904 A.2d 137, 149 n.17 (2006).

It is proper to bring the brief along with the application (the clerk will hold it until the application is granted), although that is not required. It is also proper to repeat the interest of the amicus in the brief. This statement is not part of the 10-page limit. See P.B. § 67-3.

In Bender v. Bender, 258 Conn. 733, 741 n.4, 785 A.2d 197, 205 n.4 (2001), the Supreme Court invited amici briefs from two organizations. This is happening more frequently. See also State v. Rigual, 256 Conn. 1, 771 A.2d 939 (2001).

Filing an amicus curiae brief is probably the only way a non-party can participate in an appeal. City of Norwalk v. Farrell, 80 Conn.App. 399, 404-05 n.8, 835 A.2d 117, 120–21 n.8 (2003) (holding that committee in foreclosure case did not have right to participate in appeal as appellee but could have applied to file an amicus brief).

§ 67-8. The Appendix (Applicable to appeals filed before July 1, 2013)

No appendix is required in either a court or a jury case, except where an opinion is cited which is not officially published, in which case the text of the opinion must be included in the appendix. An appendix may be used to excerpt lengthy exhibits or quotations from the transcripts, or to comply with the provisions of Section 67-4 subsections (d) or (e). To reproduce a full transcript or lengthy exhibit when an excerpt would suffice is a misuse of an appendix. If use of any appendix is indicated, all materials must be included in a single appendix.

The appendix shall be prepared in accordance with section 67-2. An appendix shall be paginated separately from the brief, and may be bound with it or separately. Where, however, binding the brief and appendix together would affect the integrity of the binding or where the appendix exceeds one hundred numbered pages, the appendix and brief shall be bound separately. Pages of an appendix shall be numbered consecutively and be preceded by the letter "A" (e.g., A1 . . . A25 . . . A53).

An appendix of any length may be reproduced on both sides of a page; an appendix, however, in excess of fifty numbered pages must be reproduced on both sides of a page. An appendix shall have at its beginning a table of contents of any papers in it and shall also have an index of the names of witnesses whose testimony is cited within it. If any part of the testimony of a witness is omitted, this shall be indicated by asterisks. After giving the name of a witness, the party who called that witness shall be designated and it shall be stated whether the testimony quoted was given on direct, cross or other examination.

§ 67-8. The Appendix, Contents and Organization (Applicable to appeals filed on or after July 1, 2013)

(a) An appendix shall be prepared in accordance with Section 67-2.

(b) The appellant's appendix shall be divided into two parts.

(1) Part one of the appellant's appendix shall contain: a table of contents giving the title or nature of each item included; the docket sheets, a case detail, or court action entries in the proceedings below; in chronological order, all relevant pleadings, motions, requests, findings, and opinions or decisions of the trial court or other decision-making body (see Sections 64-1 and 64-2); the judgment file; the endorsed appeal form, in accordance with Section 63-3; the docketing statement filed pursuant to Section 63-4 (a) (3); any relevant appellate motions or orders that complete or perfect the record on appeal; and, in appeals to the supreme court upon grant of certification for review, the order granting certification and the opinion or order of the appellate court under review. In administrative appeals, part one of the appellant's appendix also shall meet the requirements of Section

67-8A (a). In criminal or habeas appeals filed by incarcerated self-represented parties, part one of the appendix shall be prepared by the appellee. See Section 68-1. In these appeals, the filing of an appendix by incarcerated self-represented parties shall be in accordance with subsection (c) of this rule.

(2) Part two of the appellant's appendix may contain any other portions of the proceedings below that the appellant deems necessary for the proper presentation of the issues on appeal. Part two of the appellant's appendix may be used to excerpt lengthy exhibits or quotations from the transcripts or to comply with other provisions of the Practice Book that require the inclusion of certain materials in the appendix. To reproduce a full transcript or lengthy exhibit when an excerpt would suffice is a misuse of an appendix. Where an opinion is cited that is not officially published, the text of the opinion shall be included in part two of the appendix.

(c) The appellee's appendix should not include the portions of the proceedings below already included in the appellant's appendix. If the appellee determines that part one of the appellant's appendix does not contain portions of the proceedings below, the appellee shall include any such items that are required to be included pursuant to Section 67-8 (b) (1) in part one of its appendix. Where an appellee cites an opinion that is not officially published and is not included in the appellant's appendix, the text of the opinion shall be included in part two of the appellee's appendix. Part two of the appellee's appendix may also contain any other portions of the proceedings below that the appellee deems necessary for the proper presentation of the issues on appeal.

(d) In appeals where personal identifying information is protected by rule, statute, court order or case law, and in appeals that have been ordered sealed in part or in their entirety or are subject to limited disclosure pursuant to Section 77-2, all briefs and appendices shall be prepared in accordance with Section 67-1.

Historical Note

This rule was substantially revised in 2013. It was revised again in 2014 to require electronic filing.

Derivation (first sentence):
    1978 P.B. (1996–97), § 4064G
    1978 P.B. (1986–96), § 4068
    1978 P.B. (1979–86), § 3060J

Entirely new provision effective July 1, 1979. Much of the first paragraph was added in 1996. The reference to § 67-2 was added in 2009.

Derivation (rest of rule):
    1978 P.B. (1996–97), § 4064G
    1978 P.B. (1986–96), § 4069
    1978 P.B. (1979–86), § 3060K

1978 P.B., § 3050
1963 P.B. (1974–78), § 628R
1963 P.B., § 722
1951 P.B., § 449

Prior to July 1, 1979, this was the non-jury rule as to the format of the appendix. Effective July 1, 1979, this rule applies to both court and jury appeals, as it ironically did prior to October 1, 1974 as well.

Cross Reference

See P.B. § 67-2 for formatting of the appendix.

AUTHORS' COMMENTS

This rule was re-written in 2013 in light of the elimination of the printed record, which the appellate clerk previously prepared. Except for criminal and habeas cases filed by incarcerated self-represented parties, part one of the appellant's appendix must include the documents previously included in the printed record. The appellee's appendix should not include documents in the appellant's appendix. The appellee is not required to file a part one appendix unless the appellee believes the appellant's appendix is incomplete or inadequate.

The commentary indicates that the following should not be included in part one of the appendix: papers not necessary for the proper presentation of the appeal; papers not included in the proceedings below; lengthy memoranda in support of motions, objections, and replies; exhibits attached to complaints or motions that are not relevant to the appeal; officer's return or exhibits (unless at issue in the appeal). Affidavits attached to motions for summary judgment and affidavits attached to other motions should be included when relevant to the appeal.

If a party believes that material that should not be included in part one should be included (say, for example, a trial brief to show an issue was raised), such materials can be included in part two of the appendix.

Note that as of September 1, 2014 the appendix may be double sided. Further, while the two parts of the appendix normally should be bound together and may be bound with the brief if doing so will not affect the integrity of the binding, when either part of the appendix exceeds 150 pages, each part of the appendix must be separately bound.

The appendix should be used to highlight certain evidence or statutes and the like. This will improve the effectiveness of oral argument, the entire panel will have access to the evidence as you discuss it. There is another incentive to use it, as the appendix is not counted in the page limitations (§ 67-3). On the other hand, litigants sometimes use the appendix to evade the brief page limitations. Papic v. Burke, 113 Conn.App. 198, 217 n.11, 965 A.2d 633, 647 n.11, Blue Sky L. Rep. (CCH) P 74760 (2009). Such a practice is risky since a statement of facts improperly placed in an appendix may be stricken, leaving the record inadequate for review. State v. Jones, 193 Conn. 70, 74–75 n.2, 475 A.2d 1087, 1091 n.2 (1984).

The court struck portions of an appendix in Janusauskas v. Fichman, 264 Conn. 796, 804 n.6, 826 A.2d 1066, 1072 n.6 (2003), in which the party paraphrased trial transcripts. Appendices should also *not* include transcripts unless they were designated under § 63-4(a)(3), as well as documents unless they were admitted as exhibits.

Counsel were criticized for not complying with the requirement to include unreported cases in State v. Heck, 128 Conn.App. 633, 646 n.6, 18 A.3d 673, 682 n.6, cert. denied, 301 Conn. 935, 23 A.3d 728 (2011); State v. Milotte, 95 Conn.App. 616, 624–25 n.4, 897 A.2d 683, 688 n.4 (2006), appeal dismissed, 281

Conn. 612, 917 A.2d 25 (2007); Murphy v. Commissioner of Motor Vehicles, 60 Conn.App. 526, 532 n.3, 760 A.2d 510, 512 n.3 (2000).

Subsection (c) says that the appellee "shall" include any items in its appendix that the appellant should have but failed to include in the appendix. The authors believe the "shall" is directory, not mandatory. How can the appellees properly be punished for not doing the appellant's job?

§ 67-8a. The Appendix in Administrative Appeals; Exceptions (Applicable to appeals filed on or after July 1, 2013)

(a) Except as provided in subsection (c), in appeals from administrative agencies, part one of the appellant's appendix shall include the materials required by Section 67-8, the part of the return of the administrative agency which identifies the papers returned to the trial court, and also such of the papers returned as consist of: (1) the application or appeal to the agency; (2) the notice of hearing and the affidavit of publication, if they are in issue on the appeal; and (3) any minutes or decision showing the action taken by the agency, the reasons assigned for that action, and any findings and conclusions of fact made by the agency.

(b) The appellee's appendix, if any, shall be prepared in accordance with the provisions of Section 67-8 (c).

(c) Subsection (a) shall not apply to the following administrative appeals:

> (1) Appeals from municipal boards of tax review taken pursuant to General Statutes §§ 12-117a and 12-119.

> (2) Appeals from municipal assessors taken pursuant to General Statutes § 12-103.

> (3) Appeals from the commissioner of revenue services.

> (4) Appeals from the insurance commissioner taken pursuant to General Statutes § 38a-139.

> (5) Any other appeal in which the parties received a trial de novo in the superior court.

The appendices in these matters shall be prepared in accordance with the provisions of Section 67-8.

§ 67-9. Citation of Unreported Decisions (Repealed only as to appeals filed after July 1, 2013)

A decision not officially reported may be cited before the court only if the person making reference to it provides the court and opposing counsel with copies of the decision. If it is cited in a brief, a copy of the text of the decision must be included in the appendix to the brief.

Historical Note

Derivation:

1978 P.B. (1996–97), § 4064H

Cross Reference
P.B. § 5-9

AUTHORS' COMMENTS

The requirement to include unreported decisions in the appendix now appears in § 67-8(b)(2).

§ 67-10. Citation of Supplemental Authorities after Brief is Filed

When pertinent and significant authorities come to the attention of a party after the party's brief has been filed, or after oral argument but before decision, a party may promptly advise the appellate clerk of such supplemental authorities, by letter, with a copy certified to all counsel of record in accordance with Section 62-7. The clerk shall be provided with an original and seven copies of the letter. The letter shall set forth the citations of the authorities. If the authority is an unreported decision, a copy of the text of the decision must accompany the letter. The letter shall concisely and without argument state the relevance of the supplemental citations and shall include, where applicable, reference to the pertinent page(s) of the brief. Any response shall be made promptly and shall be similarly limited.

This section may not be used after oral argument to elaborate on points made or to address points not made.

Historical Note

Derivation:
    1978 P.B. (1996–97), § 4064J
    1978 P.B. (1993–96), § 4071A

This rule was new effective April 10, 1993. The second paragraph was added in 2009, but it does not prevent counsel from correcting errors made in their brief.

AUTHORS' COMMENTS

This rule reverses the apparent criticism of this practice in Tedesco v. City of Stamford, 24 Conn.App. 377, 379 n.5, 588 A.2d 656, 657 n.5 (1991), rev'd on other grounds, 222 Conn. 233, 610 A.2d 574 (1992). Compliance with this rule obviated the need for supplemental briefs in State v. Corrigan, 40 Conn.App. 359, 362 n.2, 680 A.2d 312, 314 n.2 (1996). It is proper to explain the relevance of the case cited. New England Cable Television Ass'n, Inc. v. Department of Public Utility Control, 247 Conn. 95, 119 n.22, 717 A.2d 1276, 1290 n.22, 188 Pub. Util. Rep. 4th (PUR) 555 (1998); Connecticut Ins. Guar. Ass'n v. Drown, 134 Conn.App. 140, 156 n.12, 37 A.3d 820, 830 n.12, cert. granted, 305 Conn. 908, 44 A.3d 183 (2012).

A party was even permitted to raise a new issue in response to a letter from the Supreme Court ordering that a different issue be addressed. Hall v. Gilbert and Bennett Mfg. Co., Inc., 241 Conn. 282, 298, 695 A.2d 1051, 1060 (1997).

In addition to this rule, the courts have occasionally ordered supplemental briefs by the parties after oral argument. See § 67-4, Authors' Comments, § E.

The court ordered supplemental briefs on an issue raised in a § 67-10 letter in Lohnes v. Hospital of St. Raphael, 132 Conn.App. 68, 73, 31 A.3d 810, 813–14 (2011), cert. denied, 303 Conn. 921, 34 A.3d 397 (2012).

This rule was cited in State v. Calabrese, 279 Conn. 393, 413 n.22, 902 A.2d 1044, 1057 n.22 (2006).

The rule does not require that the authority be new, although citing several authorities in existence when your brief was filed should be avoided.

In Red 11, LLC v. Conservation Com'n of Town of Fairfield, 117 Conn.App. 630, 638n.6, 980 A.2d 917, 922 n.6, cert. denied, 294 Conn. 918, 984 A.2d 67 (2009), the court criticized a party for filing a letter with several unbriefed new authorities, noting that the purpose of this section is to identify "genuinely unknown" cases, not file a supplemental brief.

Suggestion of mootness was raised in a § 67-10 letter without criticism by the court. Commissioner of Public Safety v. Freedom of Information Com'n, 301 Conn. 323, 332, 21 A.3d 737, 742 (2011).

The authors' opinion is that anything that would have been properly cited in a brief can be cited in a § 67-10 letter; "authorities" is a broad word.

§ 67-11. Table of Authorities; Citation of Cases

(a) In the table of authorities, citations to state cases shall be to the official reporter first, if available, followed by the regional reporter. Citations to cases from jurisdictions having no official reporter shall identify the court rendering the decision. Citations to opinions of the United States Supreme Court shall be to the United States Reports, if therein; otherwise, such citations shall be to the Supreme Court Reporter, the Lawyer's Edition, or United States Law Week, in that order of preference.

(b) In the argument portion of a brief, citations to Connecticut cases shall be to the official reporter only. Citations to other state cases may be to either the official reporter or the regional reporter. United States Supreme Court cases should be cited as they appear in the table of authorities.

(c) If a case is not available in print and is available on an electronic database, such as LEXIS, Westlaw, CaseBase or LOIS, the case shall be cited to that database. In the table of authorities, citations to such cases shall include the case name; docket number; name of the database and, if applicable, numeric identifiers unique to the database; court name; and full date of the disposition of the case. Screen, page or paragraph numbers shall be preceded by an asterisk. In the argument portion of a brief, such cases shall be cited only by name and database. If such a case is published in a print reporter after the filing of the party's brief, but prior to the case on appeal being orally argued or submitted for decision on the record and briefs, the party who cited the unreported case shall, by letter, inform the chief clerk of the print citation of that case.

Historical Note

This is a new rule effective January 1, 2000.

AUTHORS' COMMENTS

Subsection (c) was noted in State v. Milotte, 95 Conn.App. 616, 624–25 n.4, 897 A.2d 683, 688 n.4 (2006), appeal dismissed, 281 Conn. 612, 917 A.2d 25 (2007).

§ 67-12. Stay of Briefing Obligations Upon Filing of Certain Motions After Appeal Is Taken

As provided in Section 63-1, if, after an appeal has been taken but before the appeal period has expired, a motion is filed that would render the judgment, decision or acceptance of the verdict ineffective, any party may move to stay the briefing obligations of the parties. The chief clerk may grant such motions for up to sixty days. Any further request for stay must be made by motion to the appellate court having jurisdiction prior to the expiration of the stay granted by the chief clerk. Such request must describe the status of the motion in the trial court and must demonstrate that a resolution of the motion is being actively pursued.

After all such motions have been decided by the trial court, the appellant shall, within ten days of notice of the ruling on the last such outstanding motion, file a statement with the appellate clerk that such motions have been decided, together with a copy of the decisions on any such motions. The filing of such statement shall reinstate the appellate obligations of the parties, and the date of notice of the ruling on the last outstanding motion shall be treated as the date of the filing of the appeal for the purpose of briefing pursuant to Section 67-3.

Historical Note

This is a new rule effective January 1, 2000.

§ 67-13. Briefs in Family and Juvenile Matters and Other Matters Involving Minor Children

In family and juvenile matters and other matters involving minor children, counsel for the minor child and/or counsel for the guardian ad litem shall, within ten days of the filing of the appellee's brief, file either: (1) a brief; (2) a statement adopting the brief of either the appellant or an appellee, or (3) a detailed statement that the factual or legal issues on appeal do not implicate the child's interests.

Historical Note

This is a new rule effective January 1, 2005.

AUTHORS' COMMENTS

Where the attorney for the minor child did not agree with either party and had filed a separate appeal, the court considered all the claims together. In re Ryan R., 102 Conn.App. 608, 609 n.2, 926 A.2d 690, 693 n.2, cert. denied, 284 Conn. 923, 924, 933 A.2d 724 (2007).

CHAPTER 68

CASE FILE

AUTHORS' COMMENTS

With the exception of § 68-1, this chapter is obsolete for appeals filed on or after July 1, 2013.

§ 68-1. Responsibilities of Trial Court Clerk Regarding Copying Case File and Additions to Case File Made After Appeal is Taken; Exhibits and Lodged Records (Applicable to appeals filed on or after July 1, 2013)

(a) With the exception of those appeals in which the contents of the case file consist solely of papers filed by electronic means, the clerk of the trial court shall, within ten days of the filing of the appeal, prepare and forward to the appellate clerk one complete copy of the case file, including the case detail page for noncriminal cases and all written requests to charge. No omissions may be made from the case file except upon the authorization of the appellate clerk. The appellate clerk may direct the clerk of the trial court to prepare and to forward a case file in any

249

other instance in which it is needed. The clerk of the trial court shall forward to the appellate clerk one copy of all additions made to the case file after the initial preparation and transmittal of the case file.

(b) (1) In criminal appeals filed by incarcerated self-represented parties, the clerk of the trial court shall forward to the office of the chief state's attorney one complete copy of the case file and all written requests to charge for use in preparing part one of the appendix pursuant to Section 67-8 (b).

(2) In habeas appeals filed by incarcerated self-represented parties, the clerk of the trial court shall forward to either the office of the chief state's attorney or the office of the attorney general one complete copy of the case file, including the case detail page and all written requests to charge for use in preparing part one of the appendix pursuant to Section 67-8 (b).

(3) In criminal and habeas appeals filed by incarcerated self-represented parties, the office of the chief state's attorney or the office of the attorney general and the clerk of the trial court may agree that the copy of the case file be provided by electronic means.

(c) Each document of the case file must be numbered, and the file must include a table of contents listing each item entered in the file according to its number.

(d) In an appeal from an administrative agency, the papers returned by the agency to the trial court, even though annexed to and incorporated by reference in the answer, shall accompany the copies of the file but need not be included in the copies of the file.

(e) All exhibits in the trial court are deemed exhibits on appeal and are deemed in the custody of the appellate clerk while the appeal is pending. The appellate clerk shall notify the clerk of the trial court of the exhibits required by the court in which the appeal is pending. Within ten days of such notice, the clerk of the trial court shall transmit those exhibits to the appellate clerk accompanied by a list of all exhibits in the case. The trial court clerk shall notify all counsel and self-represented litigants of the transmittal and provide them with a copy of the exhibit list. The provisions of this paragraph shall apply to records lodged pursuant to Section 7-4C.

Historical Note

Derivation:
    1978 P.B. (1986–97), § 4084
    1978 P.B., § 3019

Subsection (b) was added in 2013 to make sure that the state's attorney or attorney general receive a copy of the court file for those appeals in which they must prepare part one of the appendix.

The first sentence was added effective March 1, 2013.

The last paragraph was amended in 2002, 2004 and 2010 to emphasize the importance of the exhibits in processing the appeal.

The first sentence was amended effective September 3, 1996 to add reference to written requests to charge. The first paragraph was amended effective January 1, 1985 to require the complete trial court file to be forwarded. This intent was made crystal clear in amended language effective October 1, 1992. The last two paragraphs were transferred at the same time from § 3079 and amended to remove counsel's duty to file a list of exhibits he needs when he files his brief. This is a new rule effective July 1, 1978.

AUTHORS' COMMENTS

The appellant must make sure that exhibits are part of the appellate file by the trial court and that the trial clerk has forwarded them to the higher court. The failure to do this may be fatal, Edward Sutt Associates, Inc. v. D & S Concrete Products, Inc., 3 Conn.App. 179 n.3, 485 A.2d 1358, 1359 n.3 (1985). The inclusion of an exhibit in the record does not necessarily mean that the facts in the exhibit were found to be true by the trial court, Goldblatt v. Ferrigno, 138 Conn. 39, 42, 82 A.2d 152, 154 (1951).

If an exhibit is lost pending appeal, the appellee should make sure other parts of the record explain the nature or contents of the exhibit so that the appellant will not have the basis for a new trial. Neiditz v. Morton S. Fine and Associates, Inc., 2 Conn.App. 322, 325 n.5, 479 A.2d 249, 252 n.5 (1984), judgment set aside on other grounds, 199 Conn. 683, 508 A.2d 438 (1986).

§ 68-2. Record Preparation (Repealed only as to appeals filed on or after July 1, 2013)

As soon as possible after the filing of the appellant's brief, the appellate clerk shall prepare and certify the record for use upon the hearing in the court having appellate jurisdiction of any case the file of which has been delivered to or prepared by such clerk.

Upon certification of the record by the appellate clerk, the appellant shall cause the record to be photocopied in accordance with these rules.

Historical Note

Derivation:
  1978 P.B. (1986–97), § 4085
  1978 P.B., § 3078
  1963 P.B., § 671
  1951 P.B., § 420
  1934 P.B., §§ 373, 377
  1922 P.B., §§ 20, 21
  1908 P.B., §§ 19, 20
  1899 P.B., §§ 19, 20

The first clause in the first sentence was added effective October 1, 1992.

Effective May 10, 1988, the record is now photocopied rather than printed.

The second paragraph was added effective October 1, 1986. Before that time the clerk's office prepared and filed a printed record.

All mention of the trial clerk was eliminated from the rule effective July 1, 1978.

Previously this rule was substantially revised effective September 15, 1975. Before that the New Haven and Bridgeport clerks prepared and printed the record in appeals from their county, but between 1975 and 1978 only the Hartford

County Clerk did it.

Between 1934 and 1975 there appears to have been no substantial change in who was to prepare and print the record (the Hartford County Clerk).

Prior to 1934, the record was prepared and printed by "the clerk of the Supreme Court of Errors for the County in which the case is to be heard * * *." This reflects the fact that prior to 1931, the Supreme Court sat as a matter of course in Hartford, Norwich, New Haven and Bridgeport.

Cross References

Maltbie, Conn.App.Proc.2d, § 284

AUTHORS' COMMENTS

The appellant must file the record according to the appellate clerk's directions. See § 68-7.

The first clause of this section makes it clear that the appellant will not have the appellate record while preparing the brief. The reason appears to be so that the clerk can determine from reading the appellant's brief what the appeal is really about. See § 68-3.

§ 68-3. Record Contents (Repealed only as to appeals filed on or after July 1, 2013)

The appellate clerk, in preparing the record, must study the case with sufficient care, must study the revised designation of specific pleadings, submitted pursuant to Section 63-4(a)(2), and the brief of the appellant, and may confer with counsel, and, if necessary, with the clerk of the trial court, to determine what part of the case file should become the record. The appellate clerk should include nothing in the record which is not necessary for the proper presentation of the statement of issues or for the proper presentation of questions reserved.

No officer's return or exhibit, except as provided herein, shall be photocopied unless it is at issue in the appeal. The record returned to the trial court by an administrative agency shall, even though incorporated by reference in a pleading, not be photocopied except to the extent provided in Section 68-10. In the discretion of the appellate clerk, exhibits annexed to a pleading may be photocopied so far as they are relevant to any issue presented in the appeal and are not excessive in length.

Historical Note

Derivation (1986–97):
 1978 P.B., § 4086
 1978 P.B., § 3080
 1963 P.B., § 673
 1951 P.B., § 421
 1934 P.B., §§ 374, 379, 381
 1922 P.B., §§ 21, 23, 25
 1908 P.B., §§ 20, 22, 24
 1899 P.B., §§ 20, 22, 24

The reference to the Appellate Clerk studying the appellant's brief while preparing the record was added effective October 1, 1992.

The second paragraph was revised effective January 1, 1985 to give the chief clerk more discretion as to what exhibits he prints in the record.

The reference about zoning was added in 1963 and was broadened to include all administrative appeals effective July 1, 1979. The last sentence was revised in 1963, but otherwise there has been no substantial change since 1899, except that as of July 1, 1978, the chief clerk no longer is required to confer with counsel, although the clerk must now consult the § 63-4 designation.

Cross References

Maltbie, Conn.App.Proc.2d, § 284

AUTHORS' COMMENTS

The appellate clerk prepares the record based on the briefs and revised designation of pleadings and sends it to the appellant for copying. The appellant nevertheless bears the responsibility of making sure that the printed record is adequate by including necessary pleadings on the revised designation of pleadings and calling to the clerk's attention any omissions. The appellate clerk will resolve any disputes about what goes into the printed record. See §§ 68-2 and 63-4(a)(2).

§ 68-4. Record Format (Repealed only as to appeals filed on or after July 1, 2013)

Cases brought to the supreme or appellate court otherwise than by writ of error shall be entitled as they were in the judgment of the trial court.

The date when each paper contained in the record was filed must be stated.

The appellant shall prepare a table of contents giving the title or nature of each paper in its order as photocopied.

The record shall be photocopied on white 8½ by 11 inch paper.

The cover of the record shall be yellow.

Historical Note

Derivation:
   1978 P.B. (1986–97), § 4087
   1978 P.B., § 3081
   1963 P.B., § 674
   1951 P.B., § 422
   1934 P.B., §§ 374, 380, 383
   1922 P.B., §§ 21, 24, 27
   1908 P.B., §§ 20, 23, 26
   1899 P.B., §§ 20, 23, 26

This section was amended effective May 10, 1988 to eliminate the technical requirements for printing the record.

There were no substantial changes from 1899 until 1988, except for printing provisions which are now obsolete.

AUTHORS' COMMENTS

Notwithstanding paragraph 3, the clerk in fact prepares the table of contents, which the appellant then is ordered to copy verbatim.

§ 68-5. Record where More than One Appeal (Repealed only as to appeals filed on or after July 1, 2013)

In the discretion of the appellate clerk where more than one appeal is taken in a case, such clerk may prepare only one record.

Historical Note

Derivation:
    1978 P.B. (1986–97), § 4090
    1978 P.B., § 3083
    1963 P.B., § 676
    1951 P.B., § 424
"Prepare" was substituted for "print" effective October 1, 1986.
This rule otherwise is substantially unchanged since 1951.

Cross References
    Maltbie, Conn.App.Proc.2d, § 286
    P.B. § 61-9 and commentary

§ 68-6. Record where Several Cases Present Same Question (Repealed only as to appeals filed on or after July 1, 2013)

In the discretion of the appellate clerk where several cases are pending in which the same question of law is presented, whether between the same or different parties, such clerk may prepare only one record of the pleadings, exhibits, or other papers which are part of the record in more than one of the cases may be included in only one of them, with suitable references to the record in that case made in the records in the other cases.

Historical Note

Derivation:
    1978 P.B. (1986–97), § 4091
    1978 P.B., § 3084
    1963 P.B., § 677
    1951 P.B., § 424
    1934 P.B., § 382
    1922 P.B., § 26
    1908 P.B., § 25
    1899 P.B., § 25
The reference to the clerk printing the record was eliminated effective October 1, 1986.

The rule otherwise is substantially unchanged since 1899, except that the chief clerk was given more discretion effective January 1, 1985. A second paragraph was removed effective January 1, 1985. It gave the parties certain powers not subject to the clerk's control.

Cross References
    Maltbie, Conn.App.Proc.2d, § 286

AUTHORS' COMMENTS

Consolidation was granted under this section in Carroll v. Aetna Cas. and Sur. Co., 189 Conn. 16, 17 n.1, 453 A.2d 1158, 1159 n.1 (1983).

§ 68-7. Record Filing (Repealed only as to appeals filed on or after July 1, 2013)

Within twenty days of the certification of the record by the appellate clerk pursuant to Section 68-2, the appellant shall file the record in accordance with the instructions which accompany it, with a certification attached to the original record only that a copy thereof has been sent to each counsel of record and any trial judge who rendered a decision that is being challenged on appeal.

Historical Note

Derivation:
  1978 P.B. (1986–97), § 4092
  1978 P.B., § 3085
  1963 P.B., § 678
  1951 P.B., § 425
  1934 P.B., § 376
  1930 Rules Change, § 21A

The language about clerk's instructions was added in 1996.

This section was substantively revised effective October 1, 1992, to accord with previous practice. Previously the rule required the appellant to file the record with his brief, but the record was rarely prepared by the appellate clerk by then.

Effective May 10, 1988, the appellant files only the original and 25 photocopies (formerly 70 printed copies) of the record. A second sentence, directing the clerk to send 40 copies to the Supreme Court and 30 copies to the Reporter of Judicial Decisions, was dropped.

This section was completely rewritten effective October 1, 1986. Old § 3085 stated as follows: "Three copies of the printed record in each case shall be sent by the chief clerk of the supreme court to each counsel of record promptly upon the completion of the printing, and thirty copies to the reporter of judicial decisions. The clerk shall retain twenty copies of the printed record for use by the supreme court. The clerk shall mark upon the front page of each copy so sent the date of sending it and shall keep a record thereof."

The following history refers to old § 3085.

This section was revised effective September 15, 1975 to conform to § 671. Previously the clerk responsible for printing the record sent three copies to each counsel (unchanged), ten copies to the Hartford County Supreme Court Clerk, and twenty-five copies to the Reporter of Judicial Decisions.

This section was previously unchanged since 1951. Under the 1930 and 1934 rules, counsel or the court could order argument at a particular term if the printed record was available at the start of the term.

The clerk normally sends the record to the appellant after the appellant's brief is filed. It is appropriate thereafter to send a letter to the clerk giving the page references for the record citations in the brief.

AUTHORS' COMMENTS

The chief clerk prepares and sends to the appellant a certified copy of the record pursuant to § 68-2. The appellant then files the certified record within 20 days. Occasionally, the clerk will impose a shorter deadline, so read the instructions carefully. According to the clerk's office, if problems arise making it unlikely that the record will be filed on time, counsel may call the case manager, rather than filing a motion for extension of time. The clerk's instructions currently require counsel to certify the record to the trial judge as well as to counsel of record. Be sure to list the judge's address as well as counsel's.

§ 68-8. Supplements (Repealed only as to appeals filed on or after July 1, 2013)

After the record has been filed, the appellate clerk shall distribute to each appellate jurist a copy of any supplement to the record.

Historical Note

Derivation:
  1978 P.B. (1986–97), § 4093
  1978 P.B., § 3086
  1963 P.B., § 679
  1951 P.B., § 426
  1934 P.B., §§ 385, 386
  1922 P.B., § 29
  1908 P.B., § 28
  1899 P.B., § 28

Effective May 10, 1988, the reference to printing was eliminated. Otherwise, there has been no significant change in this rule since 1951. Under the 1934 rules, amendments to assignments of error were printed as well; prior to 1934, all pleadings, applications and motions filed in the Supreme Court were printed by the Clerk.

§ 68-9. Evidence Not to Be Included in Record (Repealed only as to appeals filed on or after July 1, 2013)

Evidence of witnesses before a court, including evidence necessary upon an appeal from the denial of a motion to set aside a nonsuit, evidence taken before a committee or state referee and filed in court in connection with exceptions to a report, and, except as hereinafter provided, evidence taken before an administrative officer or board and filed in court in connection with a petition or an appeal, or admitted at a hearing shall not be placed in the record except as it is made a part of a pleading, or of a finding or report in explanation of a ruling made in the course of a hearing, but it may be presented in the brief as provided in Sections 67-1, 67-4 and 67-5. The reproduction of evidence taken before an administrative agency shall be governed by Section 68-10, and the reproduction of evidence contained in exhibits annexed to pleadings shall be governed by Section 68-3.

Historical Note

Derivation:
  1978 P.B. (1986–97), § 4094
  1978 P.B., § 3087
  1963 P.B., § 645
  1951 P.B., § 415

Prior to July 1, 1979, the only administrative proceeding to which this rule was applicable was zoning appeals. Under the 1951 rule, evidence concerning the denial of a motion to set aside a nonsuit was printed in the record. Under the 1963 rule it was not.

Prior to 1951, all material evidence was printed in the court record. See 1934 Practice Book, §§ 346, 369, 370, 370A, 371, 374; 1899 Practice Book, § 20.

Maltbie, Conn.App.Proc.2d, § 317

§ 68-10. Record in Administrative Appeals; Exceptions (Repealed only as to appeals filed on or after July 1, 2013)

(a) Except as provided in subsection (b), in appeals from administrative agencies, the record shall include the part of the return of the administrative agency which identifies the papers returned to the trial court, and also such of the papers returned as consist of (1) the application or appeal to the agency; (2) the notice of hearing and the affidavit of publication, if they are in issue on the appeal; and (3) any minutes or decision showing the action taken by the agency, the reasons assigned for that action, and any findings and conclusions of fact made by the agency. The record shall also contain such other portions of the returned record as the judge who tried the case shall order included or as the appellate clerk finds is needed for the proper presentation of any of the issues on the appeal but in no event, unless the judge who tried the case directs otherwise, the testimony before the agency or the documentary evidence offered at its hearings. Relevant portions of the record before the agency returned by it to the trial court but not included in the record should be reproduced in the brief as provided in Sections 67-1, 67-4 and 67-5.

(b) Subsection (a) shall not apply to the following administrative appeals:

(1) Appeals from municipal boards of tax review taken pursuant to General Statutes §§ 12-117a and 12-119.

(2) Appeals from municipal assessors taken pursuant to General Statutes § 12-103.

(3) Appeals from the commissioner of revenue services.

(4) Appeals from the insurance commissioner taken pursuant to General Statutes § 38a-139.

(5) Any other appeal in which the parties received a trial de novo in the superior court.

The record in these matters shall be prepared pursuant to the rules for the preparation of the record in ordinary civil actions.

Historical Note

Derivation:
   1978 P.B. (1986–87), § 4095
   1978 P.B., § 3088
   1963 P.B., § 647
   1951 P.B., § 415A

Paragraph (b) was added effective October 1, 1979.

Prior to July 1, 1979, this rule applied only to zoning appeals and minor changes were made effective October 1, 1980. Otherwise, this rule is substantially unchanged since it was first adopted in 1959. Prior to 1959, such appeals were governed by the predecessor of § 4094.

AUTHORS' COMMENTS

The implication of this rule is that all § (b) administrative appeals concern trials de novo in the Superior Court. See Kimberly-Clark Corp. v. Dubno, 204 Conn. 137, 145, 527 A.2d 679, 683 (1987).

§ 68-11. Decision to Be Part of Record (Repealed only as to appeals filed on or after July 1, 2013)

The oral or written decision shall become a part of the record on appeal. See Sections 64-1 and 64-2.

Historical Note

Derivation:
    1978 P.B. (1986–97), § 4096
    1978 P.B., § 3089
    1963 P.B., § 650
    1951 P.B., § 407
    1934 P.B., § 361
    1930 Rules Change, § 19B
    1922 P.B., § 24
    1908 P.B., § 23
    1899 P.B., § 23

This rule is substantially changed as of July 1, 1979 to reflect the abolition of the finding system. Between 1969 and 1979, the rule forbade making the memorandum a part of the finding. Between 1930 and 1969, the rule merely discouraged making it a part of the finding, and prior to that the rule said nothing about its function. However, the 1930 rule codified the prior practice giving the memorandum of decision a limited role on appeal, Cummings v. City of Hartford, 70 Conn. 115, 124, 38 A. 916, 919 (1897).

Cross References

Maltbie, Conn.App.Proc.2d, § 152

AUTHORS' COMMENTS

As of July 1, 1979, the written or oral memorandum of decision, not the finding, is the key document on appeal expressing the trial judge's views on the case. Previously the memorandum of decision served a very limited role on appeal, and parties could not rely on it to establish any facts, Pelc v. City of Danbury, 166 Conn. 364, 367, 349 A.2d 825, 826–27 (1974); or conclusions, Fairfield County Trust Co. v. Thompson, 152 Conn. 718, 719, 210 A.2d 171, 172 (1965).

CHAPTER 69

ASSIGNMENT OF CASES FOR ARGUMENT

§ 69-1. Printed Docket

The appellate clerk shall periodically prepare a printed docket of all pending cases which are not on a current assignment list for oral argument and which appear to be ready for assignment under Section 69-2 or have been ordered to be heard by the court and shall send a copy to each appellate jurist, to each counsel appearing in the cases entered on the printed docket, and to the reporter of judicial decisions.

Historical Note

Derivation:
>1978 P.B. (1986–97), § 4100
>1978 P.B., § 3095
>1963 P.B., § 685
>1951 P.B., § 433
>1934 P.B., § 392
>1922 P.B., §§ 36, 37
>1908 P.B., §§ 35, 36
>1899 P.B., §§ 35, 36

This rule was amended effective October 1, 1992 to accord with the practice starting in late 1990 in which the courts did not necessarily start their terms on the first Tuesday of most months. The second paragraph was deleted at the same time. It had stated:

The printed docket should indicate in each case the nature of the proceeding—whether an appeal, writ of error or reservation—and the court from which the proceeding comes, and should show which parties have filed briefs, and the dates upon which the record was mailed to counsel and the briefs were filed.

Prior to September 15, 1975, the printed docket included all pending cases in which the record had been filed.

The rule was amended effective April 12, 1982 to push back the cut-off date for the printed docket from 22 to 36 days before the opening of the term. Effective January 1, 1985, it was moved up to 29 days and changed to include cases ordered to be heard by the Supreme Court.

The portion of the second paragraph beginning with " * * * and should show which parties * * * " was added in 1963.

Prior to October 1931 the Supreme Court sat in various judicial districts, so separate dockets were prepared for each district.

§ 69-2. Cases Ready for Assignment (Applicable to appeals filed before July 1, 2013)

Cases will be considered ready for assignment when the record and all briefs of all parties, including reply briefs, have been filed or, if the record has been filed, the time for filing reply briefs has expired. Any case ready for assignment may be assigned pursuant to Section 69-3. After notice to counsel of a date and time to be heard, the chief justice, the chief judge, or a designee may order the assignment for oral argument of any appeal, notwithstanding the fact that the case on appeal does not appear on the printed docket.

Cases may be assigned for argument on a standby basis in which event counsel will be notified at least forty-eight hours before the time scheduled for oral argument that the standby case is to be heard.

If a case scheduled for oral argument, whether on standby basis or not, is settled or withdrawn for any reason, counsel for the appellant shall notify the appellate clerk of that fact promptly and shall not wait until the time scheduled for oral argument.

§ 69-2. Cases Ready for Assignment (Applicable to appeals filed on or after July 1, 2013)

Cases will be considered ready for assignment when the briefs and appendices of all parties, including reply briefs, have been filed or the time for filing reply briefs has expired. Any case ready for assignment may be assigned pursuant to Section 69-3. After notice to counsel of a date and time to be heard, the chief justice, the chief judge, or a designee may order the assignment for oral argument of any appeal, notwithstanding the fact that the case on appeal does not appear on the printed docket.

Cases may be assigned for argument on a standby basis in which event counsel will be notified at least forty-eight hours before the time scheduled for oral argument that the standby case is to be heard.

If a case scheduled for oral argument, whether on standby basis or not, is settled or withdrawn for any reason, counsel for the appellant shall notify the appellate clerk of that fact promptly and shall not wait until the time scheduled for oral argument.

Historical Note

Derivation:
    1978 P.B. (1986–97), § 4101
    1978 P.B., § 3115
    1963 P.B., § 711
    1951 P.B., § 443
    1934 P.B., § 376
    1930 Rules Change, § 21A

The 2013 amendment provides that appeals are ready for assignment when the briefs are filed.

A 1999 amendment made it clear that a case is ready for assignment when all briefs are filed, even if the record has not yet been prepared.

The second and third paragraphs were added effective October 1, 1986.

The first paragraph was greatly revised effective January 1, 1985 to reflect the backlog of appeals and the court's inability to hear all ready cases. At the same time certain technical language about requesting continuances was eliminated.

The last sentence of the first paragraph was added effective April 12, 1982. Other than that, there has been no substantial change in this rule since 1951. Previously, the case would be assigned to the next term of court starting at least three weeks after the printed record was distributed.

AUTHORS' COMMENTS

In 2008, both the Appellate Court and the Supreme Court stopped assigning cases for argument on a standby basis. Appellate lawyers had been complaining that standby assignments often forced the lawyer to prepare for oral argument twice, thus increasing the costs to the clients. The Appellate Court briefly resumed the practice for in the fall of 2010 and the fall of 2011 then discontinued it again.

§ 69-3. Time for Assignments; Order of Assignment

Assignments of cases for oral argument ordinarily will be made in the order in which the cases become ready for argument pursuant to Section 69-2. Requests for variations from this order, stating the reason therefor, shall be made by letter certified pursuant to Section 62-7, addressed to the appellate clerk and delivered, mailed or sent by facsimile to the clerk's office in time for the appellate clerk to receive it at least two working days on which the clerk's office is required to be open before assignments are made. An attorney making such a request shall also indicate that a copy of the request has been mailed to each of his or her clients who are parties to the appeal.

Assignments for oral argument in the supreme court and appellate court shall take precedence over all other judicial branch assignments.

The appellate clerk will forthwith mail copies of the assignment list to all counsel of record.

Historical Note

Derivation:
    1978 P.B. (1986–97), § 4104
    1978 P.B., § 3118
    1963 P.B., § 712
    1951 P.B., § 444
    1934 P.B., § 400
    1922 P.B., §§ 43, 46, 47
    1908 P.B., §§ 42, 45, 46
    1899 P.B., §§ 42, 45, 46

The last sentence of the first paragraph was added in 2009. The second paragraph was added in 1997.

The first paragraph was deleted effective October 1, 1992. It stated:

Assignment of cases for hearing will be made at the supreme court room in Hartford at 10 a.m., unless notice of a different hour is specially given, on the second Wednesday before the opening of each term of the supreme court. Personal attendance by counsel is not required.

Reference to facsimile was added effective September 3, 1996. The second paragraph was added effective February 4, 1997.

There has been no significant change in this rule from 1932 to 1992 except that in 1952, the date was changed from the first Wednesday to the second Wednesday. Prior to 1932, the docket was called by the Supreme Court at the opening of each term and assignments were made at that time.

AUTHORS' COMMENTS

The deletion of the original first paragraph in 1992 reflects that the practice had been discontinued. Before Ellen A. Peters became chief justice in 1984, it was usual for the chief justice to handle the assignment of cases personally at the appointed hour by conferring at counsel table with any lawyer who showed up.

CHAPTER 70

ARGUMENTS AND MEDIA COVERAGE OF COURT PROCEEDINGS

§ 70-1. Oral Argument; Videoconferencing of Oral Argument in Certain Cases (Applicable to appeals filed before July 1, 2013)

(a) Oral argument will be allowed as of right in all appeals except as provided in subsection (b) of this rule.

(b) In civil cases where: (1) the dispositive issue or set of issues has been recently authoritatively decided; or (2) the facts and legal arguments are adequately presented in the briefs and record and the decisional process would not be significantly aided by oral argument, notice will be sent to counsel of record that the case will be decided on the briefs and record only. This notice will be sent after the record and all briefs have been filed. Any party may request argument by letter addressed to the appellate clerk stating briefly the reasons why oral argument is appropriate and shall do so within seven days of the issuance of the court's notice. After receipt and consideration of such a request, the court will either assign the case for oral argument or assign the case for disposition without oral argument, as it deems appropriate.

(c) In matters involving parties who are self-represented and incarcerated, oral argument may be conducted by videoconference upon direction of the court in its discretion.

§ 70-1. Oral Argument; Videoconferencing of Oral Argument in Certain Cases (Applicable to appeals filed on or after July 1, 2013)

(a)   Oral argument will be allowed as of right in all appeals except as provided in subsection (b) of this rule.

(b)   In civil cases where: (1) the dispositive issue or set of issues has been recently authoritatively decided; or (2) the facts and legal arguments are adequately presented in the briefs and the decisional process would not be significantly aided by oral argument, notice will be sent to counsel of record that the case will be decided on the briefs and record only. This notice will be sent after all briefs and appendices have been filed. Any party may request argument by letter addressed to the appellate clerk stating briefly the reasons why oral argument is appropriate and shall do so within seven days of the issuance of the court's notice. After receipt and consideration of such a request, the court will either assign the case for oral argument or assign the case for disposition without oral argument, as it deems appropriate.

(c)   In matters involving parties who are self-represented and incarcerated, oral argument may be conducted by videoconference upon direction of the court in its discretion.

Historical Note

Derivation:
    1978 P.B. (1986–97), § 4106

This section was revised effective January 1, 2012 to eliminate the absolute right to a hearing before the court denies oral argument on the appeal. In its place a party can send a letter to the clerk explaining why oral argument is appropriate. Also effective January 1, 2012, subsection (c) was added.

This section is new effective October 1, 1986. The first word was changed from "Oral" to "Full" and the phrase "or on an abbreviated time schedule" in (b) was added effective October 1, 1992. "Full" was changed back to "oral" effective September 3, 1996.

AUTHORS' COMMENTS

The Appellate Court aggressively uses this rule to deny oral argument to about 15–20% of its docket. The Supreme Court has never used this rule, as far as the authors can tell.

That the Appellate Court denies oral argument does not mean the appellant will inevitably lose; see, e.g., Passini v. Town of Winchester, 45 Conn.App. 413, 696 A.2d 1021 (1997) (2-1 decision); Sady v. Liberty Mut. Ins. Co., 29 Conn.App. 552, 616 A.2d 819 (1992); Fabiano v. Fabiano, 10 Conn.App. 466, 523 A.2d 937 (1987); although generally that is the case.

Occasionally the Appellate Court considers cases for summary affirmance on the motion calendar if a recent case on point has just been decided. Counsel might consider a motion for summary affirmance or reversal if the court does not *suo motu* do so.

There are nine (ten when one is the chief court administrator) judges who hear Appellate Court appeals on a regular basis. Public Act 97-178, § 3, allows one retired appellate judge to sit, and consent of the parties is no longer required. A dozen or so retired judges sit with some regularity and a majority of the panels include a retired judge. The Appellate Court usually sits in panels of three.

If a lawyer fails to show up for oral argument, the argument will proceed. There is usually no default found. Lauer v. Zoning Com'n of Town of Redding, 246 Conn. 251, 253 n.4, 716 A.2d 840, 841 n.4 (1998); but see In re Shanice P., 64 Conn.App. 78, 779 A.2d 151 (2001) (dismissing appeal where appellant failed to appear at oral argument). However, the failure to appear will be treated as a waiver of the right to oral argument. Statewide Grievance Committee v. Burton, 88 Conn.App. 523, 524 n.2, 871 A.2d 380 n.2 (2005), judgment aff'd, 282 Conn. 1, 917 A.2d 966 (2007).

§ 70-2. Submission Without Oral Argument On Request of Parties

With the permission of the court, counsel of record may, before or after a case has been assigned for a hearing, submit the case for decision on the record and briefs only, without oral argument. No request for submission without oral argument will be granted unless the requesting party certifies that all other parties agree to waive oral argument. This rule applies only to counsel of record who have filed a brief or joined in the brief of another party.

Historical Note

Derivation:
    1978 P.B. (1986–97), § 4102
    1978 P.B., § 3116
The second sentence was added and the first sentence was revised effective January 1, 2012.
Entirely new rule effective July 1, 1978.

§ 70-3. Order of Argument

Counsel for the appellant or plaintiff in error will be entitled to open and close the argument. On a reservation, the plaintiff will open and close, unless the court otherwise directs, except in suits for the construction of wills or of interpleader, when the court will fix the order of argument. If there are cross appeals, the original appellant will open and close unless the court otherwise orders for cause shown. If there are consolidated appeals, the parties in the appeal filed first in the trial court will argue first unless the court otherwise orders.

Historical Note

Derivation:
    1978 P.B. (1986–97), § 4107
    1978 P.B., § 3122
    1963 P.B., § 726
    1951 P.B., § 453
    1934 P.B., § 403
    1922 P.B., § 49
    1908 P.B., § 48
    1899 P.B., § 48
This rule is substantially unchanged since 1899 except that before 1963 the

original plaintiff argued first if there were cross-appeals and except that the last sentence was added in 1996.

AUTHORS' COMMENTS

The Supreme Court ordered the residuary legatee in a will construction case to open and close argument in Appeal of Eliot, 74 Conn. 586, 589, 51 A. 558, 559 (1902). Notwithstanding the second sentence, the defendant was permitted to open and close argument on a reservation in Woodruff v. Baldwin, 72 Conn. 439, 441, 44 A. 748, 749 (1899).

§ 70-4. Time Allowed for Oral Argument; Who May Argue

The time occupied in the argument of any case shall not exceed one-half hour on each side, without special leave of the court, granted before the argument begins. The time thus limited and allowed may be apportioned among counsel on the same side of a case as they may choose. The court may terminate the argument whenever in its judgment further argument is unnecessary.

Except by special permission of the presiding jurist, which permission must be obtained prior to the date assigned for hearing, no more than one counsel shall present oral argument for any one party to the appeal.

No argument shall be allowed any party who has not filed a brief or who has not joined in the brief of another party.

Historical Note

Derivation:
    1978 P.B. (1986–97), § 4108
    1978 P.B., § 3123
    1963 P.B., § 727
    1951 P.B., § 454
    1934 P.B., § 404
    1922 P.B., § 50
    1908 P.B., § 49
    1899 P.B., § 49
    58 Conn. at 589, § 5 (1890)
    1879, P.B., p. 262, § 5
    43 Conn. at 607 (1876)

The requirement that the appellant make "a fair opening of the case" was abolished effective September 3, 1996.

The last paragraph was added effective October 1, 1992. The penultimate paragraph was added effective July 1, 1991.

Effective October 1, 1982, oral argument was lowered from a maximum of one hour to one-half hour. At the same time, the last sentence of the first paragraph was added. Before 1951 each side was allowed two hours. Before 1876, oral argument was apparently unlimited in time.

AUTHORS' COMMENTS

Starting in April 1996, the Appellate Court has interpreted this rule to permit it to allow less than 30 minutes per side. The court has since then been routinely restricting arguments to 20 minutes per side. The authors question whether that is a proper construction of the rule. Except with permission, only one counsel may argue on behalf of a litigant. In Nichols v. Fisk, 93 Conn. 324, 326, 105 A. 624, 624 (1919), the court allowed two but not three counsel to argue for the appellant.

A party who failed to comply with an order to file a brief was not permitted to argue. Cox v. Aiken, 278 Conn. 204, 207 n.3, 897 A.2d 71, 73 n.3.

If there are two different parties on the same side with a common but not identical interest, the court may or may not allow both to be heard. Jones v. Quinnipiack Bank, 29 Conn. 25, 33, 1860 WL 1145 (1860) (no). Even if the answer is yes, the two will almost certainly have to divide up their twenty or thirty minutes.

In the Appellate Court, counsel should arrive at oral argument 30 minutes before the scheduled time to check in with the clerk and to be ready in case a prior appeal folds at the last minute or the argument ends early.

The Supreme Court requires counsel arguing at 10:00 to arrive by 9:30 and counsel arguing after that to arrive one hour prior to argument. Counsel must also provide a cell phone number or other number where they can be reached on the day of argument.

This rule does not apply to an amicus curiae. See § 67-7.

§ 70-5. Points to Be Argued

(a) Oral argument should clarify and focus arguments in the written briefs. The court discourages oral argument read from a prepared text and lengthy quotations from legal precedents, the transcript, or the record.

(b) Counsel should assume that the court has read the briefs in advance of oral argument. No points made in briefs will be considered waived because not argued orally. Rebuttal argument shall be confined to the points presented by the argument of opposing counsel.

Historical Note

Derivation:
    1978 P.B. (1986–97), § 4109
    1978 P.B., § 3124
    1963 P.B., § 728
    1951 P.B., § 455
    1934 P.B., § 405
    1922 P.B., § 51
    1908 P.B., § 50
    1899 P.B., § 50

Effective September 3, 1996, (a) and the first sentence of (b) were added and the requirement for a "fair opening" of the oral argument was abolished. Until 1996, this rule was unchanged since 1934 and substantially unchanged since 1899.

AUTHORS' COMMENTS

Counsel should spend sufficient time preparing oral argument to avoid wasting the court's time. Counsel must be familiar with the yellow-covered record or part of the appellant's appendix. Each justice and judge has read and brings to oral argument the record, the appellant's brief and the appellee's brief. Encourage questions rather than make speeches.

Use the exhibits which accompany the record; make sure the clerk brings the originals to the oral argument if you want them.

Be careful what you say at oral argument, for oral concessions may be used against you if the trial record is silent, Staples v. Palten, 214 Conn. 195, 202 n.1, 571 A.2d 97, 101 n.1 (1990) (citing this commentary). They can also be used in later trial proceedings. Higgins v. Karp, 243 Conn. 495, 501 n.8, 706 A.2d 1, 4 n.8 (1998). On the other hand, counsel will be criticized for making a representation inconsistent with the record. Reid and Riege, P.C. v. Brainerd Cashman Ins. Agency, Inc., 26 Conn.App. 580, 582 n.2, 602 A.2d 1051, 1052 n.2 (1992). Oral arguments are recorded. Harty v. Cantor Fitzgerald and Co., 275 Conn. 72, 84 n.7, 881 A.2d 139, 149 n.7 (2005).

Generally, the court will not consider an issue raised at oral argument that is not in the brief, Jones v. Ippoliti, 52 Conn. App. 199, 201 n.4, 727 A.2d 713, 714 n.4 (1999); Stafford v. Roadway, 312 Conn. 184, 190 n.6, 93 A.3d 1058, 1061 n. 6 (2014) (rebuttal argument).

§ 70-6. Reconsideration when Court Evenly Divided

When the court is evenly divided as to the result, the court shall reconsider the case, with or without oral argument, with an odd number of justices or judges.

Historical Note

Derivation:
    1978 P.B. (1986–97), § 4111
    1978 P.B., § 3073
    1963 P.B., § 705
    1951 P.B., § 442

This provision is substantially unchanged since 1951, when it was adopted, except that before 1996 the rule referred only to 2-2 votes.

The fate of cases where the justices are equally divided has a very interesting history.

Before 1867, the chief justice (before 1808, the governor) had a casting vote if there was a tie. See, for example, Apthorp v. Backus, 1 Kirby 407, 1788 WL 16 (Conn. Super. Ct. 1788) (motion denied on 2-2 vote in Superior Court); Ogden v. Lyman, 1 Day 34, 35, 1802 WL 317 (Conn. 1802) (costs allowed on casting vote of governor); Smith v. Sherwood, 4 Conn. 276, 1822 WL 28 (1822) (2-2 vote on a reservation); Town of Canaan v. Greenwoods Turnpike Co., 1 Conn. 1, 1814 WL 2 (1814) (affirmed on a 4-4 vote); Rotch v. Miles, 2 Conn. 638, 1818 WL 37 (1818) (same); Watson v. Watson, 10 Conn. 75, 1834 WL 71 (1834) (affirmed on a 2-2 vote); Brainard v. Cowdrey, 16 Conn. 498, 1844 WL 513 (1844) (same); Green v. Town of Canaan, 29 Conn. 157, 1860 WL 1164 (1860) (same); Hall v. Hall, 3 Conn. 308, 1820 WL 16 (1820) (reversed on a 2-2 vote); Sage v. Wilcox, 6 Conn. 81, 1826 WL 61 (1826) (same); Goodspeed v. East Haddam Bank, 22 Conn. 530, 1853 WL 786 (1853) (same); Wordin v. Bemis, 33 Conn. 216, 1866 WL 878 (1866) (same); Peters v. Goodrich, 3 Conn. 146, 1819 WL 29 (1819) (overruled in part by, Pond v. Clarke, 14 Conn. 334, 1841 WL 365 (1841)) (partially reversed on a 2-2 vote). In at least one instance, the chief justice did not exercise that right, but put off the case for two years until a full court could rule. Booth v. Booth, 7 Conn. 350, 352, 1829 WL 43 (1829). The chief justice ended up writing the dissenting opinion.

The casting vote arose for two reasons. First, before 1855, the five Supreme Court justices constituted all the judges of the Superior Court. Therefore, there was no one who could fill in to make a full court if one justice was disqualified. This was a particular problem from 1852, when a statute was passed disqualifying the trial judge from sitting on the appeal (see Dodd v. Seymour, 21 Conn. 476, 481, 1852 WL 639 (1852)), until 1855, when for the first time some separate judges were appointed for the Superior Court. Secondly, from 1855 until 1867, Superior Court judges were allowed to substitute for Supreme Court justices only if there were fewer than three qualified Supreme Court justices available to sit. This in fact occurred in Dodd v. City of Hartford, 25 Conn. 232, 233, 1856 WL 974 (1856). Before 1855, two justices constituted a quorum if the other three were disqualified. United Society v. Eagle Bank of New Haven, 7 Conn. 456, 476, 1829 WL 54 (1829).

In 1867 a statute was enacted generally allowing Superior Court judges to sit in place of Supreme Court justices. See C.G.S.A. § 51-207 and its predecessors. This section was first used in 1868, when Superior Court Judge Dwight Loomis sat in place of Justice Butler on two cases. Pease v. Pease, 35 Conn. 131, 1868 WL 955 (1868). Judge Loomis also sat on the reargument in 1874 to break the tie in Bristol Knife Co. v. First Nat. Bank, 41 Conn. 421, 424, 1874 WL 1611 (1874). The Supreme Court raised a slight question about the constitutionality of this statute in State v. Carroll, 38 Conn. 449, 478–79, 1871 WL 1596 (1871). The statute has never subsequently been questioned, and the Supreme Court has often substituted one or more Superior Court judges on Supreme Court cases.

Also in 1867, the predecessor of C.G.S.A. § 51-209 was passed barring the chief justice's casting vote if it resulted in reversal of a judgment. This statute thus preserved his casting vote in Bloodgood v. Beecher, 35 Conn. 469, 1868 WL 1006 (1868), cited in Nolan v. New York, N. H. & H. R. Co., 70 Conn. 159, 175, 39 A. 115, 121 (1898) (reservation to Supreme Court), Hubbard v. Brainard, 35 Conn. 563, 3 A.F.T.R. (P-H) P 3351, 1869 WL 149 (1869), rev'd, 79 U.S. 1, 20 L. Ed. 272, 2 A.F.T.R. (P-H) P 2264, 1870 WL 12779 (1870), (same), Ashburn v. Poulter, 35 Conn. 553, 1869 WL 998 (1869) (affirmance), and Norton v. Phoenix Mut. Life Ins. Co., 36 Conn. 503, 1870 WL 1061 (1870) (same). In *Norton* the senior justice exercised the casting vote since the chief justice had died.

When John Park became chief justice in 1874, he apparently decided not to exercise this power. In *Bristol Knife*, the court ordered reargument even though Park's casting vote on the initial argument would have resulted in affirmance at that time. While only four justices have sat on innumerable appeals since 1874, the authors are not aware of any case since *Norton* in which a casting vote was actually used. Park apparently de facto killed a practice that was sanctioned by C.G.S.A. § 51-209 until 1983. Thus, when § 70-6 was adopted in 1951, the Supreme Court was merely ratifying the position it had taken since 1874. In 1983 the Legislature finally removed the statutory power of the chief justice to use a casting vote to break a tie in favor of an affirmance.

The size of the Supreme Court may explain Park's decision to jettison his casting vote, since it was always possible from his time forward to select a fifth judge to rehear the appeal. This was not always possible before 1870, when for a period of time a full court consisted of only four justices. From 1818 until 1855, five justices sat on the Supreme Court. From 1855 until mid-1858, there were four or five justices, but three constituted a full court. 27 Conn. iii. From mid-1858 until mid-1859, four justices and one superior court judge constituted a full court. 27 Conn. 32 n.; 28 Conn. iii. From mid-1859 until mid-1863, and from the beginning of 1868 until mid-1870, four justices constituted a full court. 28 Conn. 352, n.; 34 Conn. iii. From mid-1870 until 1987, five justices constituted a full court. 31 Conn. iii; 37 Conn. iii. Since 1987, it is five, six or seven; § 51-207.

After the statute was passed curtailing the chief justice's casting power in 1867 and before the size of the full court was returned to five in 1870, one wonders what would have happened if the vote was 2-2 and the chief justice favored reversal. Fortunately, the four times a 2-2 vote occurred between 1868 and 1870, that did not happen.

AUTHORS' COMMENTS

If six Supreme Court Justices sit and are divided 3-3, a lower court judge will be added to the panel *before* decision. The remaining paragraphs of these comments therefore pertain to practice before September 2009. While this rule has theoretical application in the Appellate Court, the authors are unaware of any cases in which that court sat with an even numbered panel.

While this rule was not directly applicable, the Supreme Court denied a nonargued motion on a 3-3 vote in State v. Cobb, 234 Conn. 735, 663 A.2d 948 (1995). Prior to 2009, the authors are aware of only one argued case that was decided by six justices, and that was because the chief justice disqualified himself after oral argument. Pamela B. v. Ment, 244 Conn. 296, n.1, 709 A.2d 1089, n.1 (1998). The vote was 3-1-1-1 as to one of the defendants, but none of the opinions mentioned this rule. Since 2009, numerous cases have been decided by a six-justice panel.

Pesino v. Atlantic Bank of New York, 244 Conn. 85, 709 A.2d 540 (1998), was argued before five justices, one of whom recused himself after oral argument. The remaining four split 2-2, so a new fifth justice was added, without further oral argument, to break the tie. The dissenters protested that further argument should have been allowed on the applicability of C.G.S.A. §§ 51-183e and 51-209, but the majority held that this Practice Book rule applied. 244 Conn. at 85–87, n. 1, 709 A.2d at 542, n. 1, (majority), at 98, n. 1 (dissent), 709 A.2d at 542–43, 548. According to the majority, § 51-183e, requiring reargument, must yield to § 70-6 because it is a procedural matter, and § 51-209 does not apply unless all the justices heard the case. Query: what would happen if the vote was 3-3 because one of the justices disqualified himself after oral argument (see Pamela B.). The authors' opinion is that § 51-209 would then apply (in Pamela B. the tie breaker would be the senior justice, see Norton in the Historical Note).

§ 70-7. Appellate Court Consideration En Banc and Reargument En Banc

(a) Before a case is assigned for oral argument, the chief judge may order, on the motion of a party or sua sponte, that a case be heard en banc.

(b) After argument but before decision, the entire court may order that the case be considered en banc with or without further oral argument or with or without supplemental briefs. The judges who did not hear oral argument shall have available to them the electronic recording or a transcript of the oral argument before participating in the decision.

(c) After decision, the entire court may order, on the motion of a party pursuant to Section 71-5 or sua sponte, that reargument be heard en banc.

Historical Note

Derivation:
    1978 P.B. (1991–97), § 4112
As of January 1, 2011, this rule no longer applies to the Supreme Court, which since September 2009 has been sitting en banc in all cases.

This section was amended effective January 1, 2000 to clarify the procedure after argument but before decision. After decision, however, the Supreme Court cannot reconsider the case en banc without argument. Paige v. Saint Andrew's Roman Catholic Church Corp., 250 Conn. 14, 734 A.2d 85 (1999) (order entered October 27, 1998). If the purpose of the amendment was to overrule the Paige order in the authors' opinion the amendment failed to do so. However, the Supreme Court apparently does not agree. See Town of Groton v. United

Steelworkers of America, 254 Conn. 35, 36 n.1, 757 A.2d 501 n.1 (2000).

New rule effective July 1, 1991. Until 1996, the entire rule read as follows:

With or without oral reargument, as the court may direct, the court may reconsider a submitted case en banc.

AUTHORS' COMMENTS

Before mid-2009, the Supreme Court usually sat in panels of five, with the chief justice ordering an en banc hearing only a few times a year, and the court as a whole ordering after oral argument that the case be decided en banc a few more times a year. All that changed in mid-2009. As of September 1, 2009, this rule became obsolete as to the Supreme Court because that Court adopted a policy effective then of hearing all cases en banc. The rule is still effective as to the Appellate Court, but that court rarely sits en banc, once or twice a year at most.

If in the Supreme Court less than five justices are qualified or available to sit, the Supreme Court will call up Appellate Court judges on a rotation based on seniority. Once all have been called up, the rotation starts over again.

The Appellate Court has a policy of not overruling its own decisions except en banc. Consiglio v. Transamerica Insurance Group, 55 Conn.App. 134, 138 n.2, 737 A.2d 969, 971 n.2 (1999). Parties seeking to override a decision of the Appellate Court should request an en banc hearing. See Fernandez v. Commissioner of Correction, 139 Conn.App. 173, 175 n.1, 55 A.3d 588, 590 n.1 (2012), cert. granted, 307 Conn. 947, 60 A.3d 960 (2013); State v. DiFano, 109 Conn.App. 679, 687, 952 A.2d 848, 852, cert. denied, 298 Conn. 937, 958 A.2d 1246 (2008).

In Neuhaus v. Decholnoky, 83 Conn.App. 576, 850 A.2d 1106 (2004), aff'd in part, rev'd in part, 280 Conn. 190, 905 A.2d 1135 (2006), the court sat en banc but decided not to overrule a prior decision.

§ 70-8. Special Sessions

The Supreme Court will be deemed in special session whenever the justices meet for consultation; but the presence of the clerk or judicial marshal will not be required, unless specially directed.

Historical Note

Derivation:
    1978 P.B. (1986–97), § 4115
    1978 P.B., § 3127
    1963 P.B., § 731
    1951 P.B., § 460
    1934 P.B., § 411
    1922 P.B., § 60
    1908 P.B., § 58
    1899 P.B., § 58

There has been no substantial change in this rule since 1899, except that in 2002 "judicial marshal" replaced "sheriff".

§ 70-9. Coverage of Court Proceedings by Cameras and Electronic Media

(a) Except for those matters enumerated in subsection (c) of this rule, all judicial courtroom proceedings in the supreme and appellate courts are presumed to be subject to coverage by cameras and electronic media.

(b) (1) All such proceedings may be broadcast, televised, videotaped, audio recorded or photographed unless: (A) the panel of jurists grants a motion by a party or a victim in a case requesting the limitation or preclusion of such coverage, or (B) the panel of jurists, on its own motion, limits or precludes such coverage. The right to permit or exclude coverage, whether partially or totally, at any time in the interests of the administration of justice shall remain with the panel of jurists.

(2) Any party or victim who desires to file a motion to limit or preclude coverage shall do so not later than one week before the start of the term for which the case is subject to being assigned, as indicated on a printed docket pursuant to Section 69-1. The party or victim shall mail a copy of such motion to each counsel or self-represented party and to any other victim in the case. The party or victim shall give notice to any such victim by notifying the state's attorney in a criminal case, the attorney or guardian ad litem for a minor child in cases involving a minor victim or child represented by an attorney or guardian ad litem, and to any other victim or child by notifying the Connecticut Victim Advocate. Endorsed on the motion shall be certification of such mailing. The appellate clerk shall refer any such notion to the panel of jurists for review as soon as the panel is determined. The panel of jurists may consider a late motion to limit or preclude coverage. Prior to acting on such motion, the panel of jurists shall provide any media outlet expected to cover the proceeding an opportunity to respond in writing to the motion.

(3) In acting on such motion or on its own motion, the panel of jurists will apply the presumption that all judicial courtroom proceedings in the supreme and appellate courts are subject to coverage by cameras and electronic media. In addition, it will be guided by the principles that such coverage should be limited only if there is good cause to do so, there are no reasonable alternatives to such limitations, and the limitation is no broader than necessary to protect the competing interests at issue.

(4) In acting on such motion or its own motion, the panel of jurists will conclude that the presumption in favor of coverage by cameras and electronic media has been overcome only if it is satisfied that good cause exists for a limitation or preclusion on coverage. If the panel of jurists orders a limitation or preclusion on coverage, it will provide a statement of its reasons. A statement may be written or stated on the record in open court.

(c) (1) The presumption in favor of coverage shall not apply to cases involving: (A) sexual assault; (B) risk of injury to, or impairing the morals of, a child; (C) abuse or neglect of a child; (D) termination of parental rights; and (E) contested questions of child custody or visitation.

(2) In cases to which the presumption in favor of coverage does not apply, any person may request such coverage by filing a motion not later than one week before the start of the term for which the case is subject to be assigned, as indicated on a printed docket pursuant to Section 69-1. The applicant shall mail a copy of such written request to each counsel or self-represented party and to any victim or child in the case. The application shall give notice to any such victim by notifying the state's attorney in a criminal case, the attorney or guardian ad litem for a minor child in cases involving a minor victim or child represented by an attorney or guardian ad litem, and to any other victim or child by notifying the Connecticut Victim Advocate. Endorsed on the motion shall be a certification of such mailing. The appellate clerk shall refer any such motion to the panel of jurists for review as soon as the panel is determined. The panel of jurists may consider a late motion requesting coverage. Prior to acting on such motion, the panel of jurists shall provide the parties, any such minor children and any victims of the offense an opportunity to respond in writing to the motion. The panel of jurists shall grant the motion only if it is satisfied that the need for such coverage outweighs the privacy interests involved in the case.

(d) The supreme and appellate courts shall establish appropriate protocols governing the number, location and use of all forms of coverage consistent with these rules.

(e) As used in this rule, "panel of jurists" means the justices or judges assigned to hear a particular case.

Historical Note

Derivation:
    1978 P.B. (1992–97), § 4116A
Completely rewritten effective June 1, 2007 to incease the ability of the public to view appellate court proceedings.

Effective January 1, 2004, the laundry list of factors to be taken into account was repealed. In 1982 this section and § 70-10 were added to the Code of Judicial Conduct on a temporary basis. Similar provisions were approved by the Appellate Court in 1983. Several technical changes were made and the provisions were made permanent for both courts effective October 1, 1984. These provisions were transferred here effective October 1, 1992.

Canon 3.A.(7C) applied to the Supreme Court. Canon 3.A.(7D) applied to the Appellate Court.

AUTHORS' COMMENTS

Full oral arguments have been televised in a number of cases such as Sullivan v. McDonald, 281 Conn. 122, 913 A.2d 403 (2007) (legislative subpoena to Justice Sullivan); Sheff v. O'Neill, 238 Conn. 1, 678 A.2d 1267, 111 Ed. Law Rep. 360 (1996) (de facto segregation in public schools); and Benjamin v. Bailey, 234 Conn. 455, 662 A.2d 1226 (1995) (legislative assault on so-called assault weapons). The first live broadcast of oral argument took place in 2004 in Office of Governor v. Select Committee of Inquiry, 269 Conn. 850, 850 A.2d 181 (2004), opinion issued, 271 Conn. 540, 858 A.2d 709 (2004), concerning the possible impeachment of Governor Rowland. The first live broadcast with more than one camera (there were three) took place on May 14, 2007 in Kerrigan v. Commissioner of Public Health, 289 Conn. 135, 957 A.2d 407 (2008) (en banc), a case challenging the exclusion of same sex couples from marriage.

§ 70-10. Cameras and Electronic Media; Coverage of Supreme and Appellate Court Proceedings by News Media [Repealed effective June 1, 2007]

CHAPTER 71

APPELLATE JUDGMENTS AND OPINIONS

§ 71-1. Appellate Judgment Files

Judgments of the court may be embodied in judgment files, to be drawn upon request and signed by the appellate clerk. Unless the court otherwise directs, a judgment shall be deemed to have been rendered on the date an opinion or memorandum decision appears in the Connecticut Law Journal; except that if an opinion or decision is issued by slip opinion or by oral announcement from the bench, the judgment shall be deemed to have been rendered on the date that appears as the officially released date in the slip opinion or the date that the oral announcement is made. In the case of an order on, for example, a motion or petition, the order shall be deemed to have been made on the date that the appellate clerk issues notice of the order to the clerk of the trial court and to all counsel of record. Judgments or orders shall be entered as of the appropriate date.

Historical Note

Derivation:
  1978 P.B. (1986–97), § 4117
  1978 P.B., § 3128
  1963 P.B., § 732
  1951 P.B., § 461
  1934 P.B., §§ 411, 419
  1922 P.B., §§ 60, 68
  1908 P.B., §§ 58, 66
  1899 P.B., §§ 58, 66

This rule was clarified effective January 1, 2011 as to the effective date of appellate decisions. Prior clarifications on the subject were made in 2009. Prior to 1951, this first sentence did not specify the clerk to draw the judgment file. Also prior to 1951, judgments ordinarily were entered as of the date of their rendition by the Supreme Court in special session (see § 70-8).

AUTHORS' COMMENTS

Previously, this rule was somewhat misleading in that the only orders that normally appear in the Law Journal are Supreme Court orders on petitions for certification. Some unfortunate language in State v. Moore, 98 Conn.App. 85, 89–90, 908 A.2d 568, 570–71 (2006), suggested (wrongly, in the authors' view) that the order on a petition for certification did not go into effect until it was published in the Law Journal. The 2009 amendment clarified that this is not the case.

The reference to slip opinions being mailed or orally announced implies that the release of a slip opinion on the Judicial Branch Website is not the official release date, unless so-designated in the decision.

If the Superior Court judgment is affirmed, the judgment is effective retroactive to the date of its entry; if a Superior Court judgment is reversed and a different judgment is directed by the Supreme Court, it is effective as of the date of the appellate judgment. Varley v. Varley, 181 Conn. 58, 61 n.4, 434 A.2d 312, 313 n.4 (1980); Preisner v. Aetna Cas. and Sur. Co., 203 Conn. 407, 415, 525 A.2d 83, 88 (1987); Protect Hamden/North Haven from Excessive Traffic and Pollution, Inc. v. Planning and Zoning Com'n of Town of Hamden, 220 Conn. 527, 541–542, 600 A.2d 757, 765–66 (1991); Connecticut Bank and Trust Co., Inc. v. Winters, 225 Conn. 146, 156–61, 622 A.2d 536, 541–43 (1993). Query whether the latter date is the date that the Supreme Court opinion is issued, or the date the Superior Court enters the new judgment in accordance with the Supreme Court opinion. Query also what is the rule if the Superior Court judgment is modified only in part. See Bower v. D'Onfro, 45 Conn.App. 543, 696 A.2d 1285 (1997), which authorized an award of post-judgment interest from the date judgment was originally entered after trial even though that judgment was somewhat modified upon appeal. *Varley* concerned when a judgment was entered for the purpose of determining when a petition for a new trial could be brought.

§ 71-2. Costs Included in Judgments

Except as otherwise provided herein, in all appeals or writs of error which go to judgment in the supreme or appellate court including an order for a new trial, costs shall be taxed to the prevailing party by the appellate clerk, in the absence of special order to the contrary by the court. On all reservations the mandate which follows the opinion of the court will specify what costs shall be taxed. A bill of costs shall be filed with the appellate clerk no more than thirty days after the notice of the appellate decision, or, of the denial of a motion for reconsideration, or, of the denial of a petition for certification by the supreme court of this state, whichever is latest.

Historical Note

Derivation:
　　1978 P.B. (1986–97), § 4118
　　1978 P.B., § 3129
　　1963 P.B., § 733
　　1951 P.B., § 462
　　1934 P.B., § 415
　　1922 P.B., § 64
　　1908 P.B., § 62
　　1899 P.B., § 62

The deadline for filing a bill of costs was added in 1996.

Effective May 10, 1988, this section was amended to remove references to taxing printing expenses.

This section was clarified effective October 1, 1986 so that the record fee is taxed to the appellant when a new trial is ordered as well as when judgment is directed.

Prior to 1934 costs on appeal were provided by rule only when "error" was found.

Cross References

P.B. § 63-9 (costs on withdrawal of appeal)

AUTHORS' COMMENTS

If the Supreme Court directs judgment on an appeal from the Appellate Court, the winner is entitled to costs in both courts. Petrowski v. Norwich Free Academy, 199 Conn. 231, 506 A.2d 139, 31 Ed. Law Rep. 485 (1986) (order on bill of costs). *A fortiori,* the winner of a directed judgment would also be entitled to costs in the Superior Court.

No costs are allowed if the appeal is dismissed for lack of jurisdiction; Connecticut Light and Power Co. v. Costle, 179 Conn. 415, 424, 426 A.2d 1324, 1329 (1980); but this exception does not apply if the Supreme Court dismisses a certified appeal as improvidently granted, Grayson v. Grayson, 202 Conn. 221, 520 A.2d 225 (1987) (unreported order after appeal decided), or if there are factual issues on the jurisdictional claim, Sisk v. Meagher, 82 Conn. 483, 74 A. 880 (1909), or if the case is decided on the basis of res judicata, Rosenfeld v. McCann, 33 Conn.App. 760, 638 A.2d 631 (1994). Costs are discretionary on reservations and when a new trial is granted. C.G.S.A. § 52-257. However, if *Beit* is still good law, the failure of the Supreme Court to mention costs in its opinion requires the clerk to tax costs, even discretionary ones, to the prevailing party.

An appellant who is successful in any of claims of error, is entitled to a bill of costs. McQueeney v. Norcross Bros., 75 Conn. 381, 382 n.*, 54 A. 301 n.* (1903) (per curiam); Walzer v. Walzer, 173 Conn. 62, 376 A.2d 414 (1977) (decision by Bills, Asst. Clerk), citing *McQueeney*. *Walzer* taxed costs on both the appeal and the cross appeal. See also State ex rel. Bonoff v. Evarts, 115 Conn. 98, 99, 160 A. 294, 294 (1932) (error only on trial costs makes appellant the prevailing party).

If several appeals are consolidated and only one record and set of briefs are filed, the authors' opinion is that only one $100 fee can be taxed as "all proceedings." See Avery v. Studley, 74 Conn. 272, 274, 50 A. 752, 752 (1901). The petition for certification fee is taxable when the Supreme Court simultaneously grants the petition and remands the case to the Appellate Court for further consideration, even when the appellant ultimately loses. Blancato v. Randino, S.C. 14781 (clerk's order entered January 24, 1994).

Transcripts are not taxable. To this extent the authors agree with Aparo v. United Technologies Corp., 1 CSCR 920 (1986). Since the passage of Public Act 95-176, § 3 (now C.G.S.A. § 52-257(d)(2)), the costs of photoduplicating briefs is now taxable up to $200.00. The authors believe that this would include the expense of copying the appendix. Costs are not taxable against the state unless a statute specifically so states. The State v. Anderson, 82 Conn. 392, 73 A. 751 (1909); State v. Chapman, 176 Conn. 362, 407 A.2d 987 (1978).

Table of Normal Appellate Costs

Entry Fee (if paid)   250.00

Brief Photoduplicating Expenses	up to 200.00
All Proceedings	100.00
Motion for Reargument Fee (if paid)	125.00
Petition for Certification Fee (if paid)	75.00

§ 71-3. Motion to Reconsider Costs

Any party may within ten days after the issuance of the decision on the taxation of costs file a written motion, in accordance with the provisions of Sections 66-2 and 66-3, that the court review the clerk's taxation of costs under its judgment. Any such motion must be submitted without oral argument.

Historical Note

Derivation:
   1978 P.B. (1986–97), § 4119
   1978 P.B., § 3113
   1963 P.B., § 706
   1951 P.B., § 457
   1934 P.B., § 407
   1922 P.B., § 53
   1908 P.B., § 51A
   4 Day 119, 120 (1809)

A last sentence referring to briefs was removed effective January 1, 1985.

Except to change "after the decision is announced" in 1963 to "after the taxation of costs is announced", and then later in 1972 to "after the issuance of the decision on the taxation of costs", there has been no significant change in this rule since 1951. Prior to 1951, there was no specific time period for filing such a motion.

Cross References

C.G.S.A. §§ 52-257, 52-259, 52-259c
P.B. §§ 84-4, 81-1; see also § 85-2 (Sanctions)

AUTHORS' COMMENTS

Trial costs should be taxed by the clerk of the trial court under § 18-5, with review by the trial court, and appellate costs should be taxed by the clerk of the Supreme Court, with review under this section. Rossignol v. Danbury School of Aeronautics Inc, 156 Conn. 646, 237 A.2d 697 (1968).

This section has been narrowly construed to permit motions only when the clerk has misapplied the rule. Where counsel wish the court to exercise discretion in awarding or denying costs, mention of costs should be made in the brief on the merits; Beit v. Beit, 135 Conn. 413, 65 A.2d 171 (1949); Cassidy v. City of Waterbury, 130 Conn. 237, 246–47, 33 A.2d 142, 146, 147 (1943); although this may not be the attitude today of the Supreme Court, which rarely mentions costs in its opinions on the merits (except for reservations).

§ 71-4. Opinions; Rescripts; Notice; Official Release Date

(a) After the court hands down an opinion in any case other than a case involving a question certified from a federal court, the reporter of judicial decisions shall send a copy of the opinion and the original rescript to the clerk of the trial court and shall send a copy of the rescript to the appellate clerk. Notice of the decision of the court shall be deemed to have been given, for all purposes, on the official release date that appears in the court's opinion.

(b) Notices of decisions upon motions and of orders of the court shall be given by the appellate clerk to the clerk of the trial court and to all counsel of record.

(c) The official release date of an opinion or memorandum decision appears in the court's opinion or memorandum decision. In the case of an order on, for example, a motion or petition, the official release date is the date that the appellate clerk issues notice of an order to the clerk of the trial court and to all counsel of record.

(d) The opinions of the court in the bound volumes of the Connecticut Reports and the Connecticut Appellate Reports are the official opinions. The appellate clerk is authorized to furnish official copies of those opinions and, until the bound volumes are published, of the opinions as they appear in the Connecticut Law Journal.

Historical Note

Derivation:
    1978 P.B. (1986–97), § 4120
    1978 P.B., § 3131
    1963 P.B., §§ 735, 736
    1951 P.B., §§ 464, 465
    1934 P.B., § 414
    1922 P.B., § 63
    1908 P.B., § 61
    1899 P.B., § 61

The last sentence of (a) was completely rewritten effective September 3, 1996 because of the advent of the electronic bulletin board in early 1996 to notify counsel of decisions before publication in the Law Journal. This section was amended effective October 1, 1986 to exclude questions certified by a federal court.

Effective July 1, 1978, § (a) was clarified to adopt the prior practice that official notification of a decision is generally made by publication in the Connecticut Law Journal. Otherwise, the rule is substantially unchanged since 1951. In the 1934 rules, the Hartford County Clerk notified counsel except for New Haven and Fairfield County cases. Prior to 1934, there was no special rule as to notice.

Section (b) was revised effective July 1, 1983 to eliminate the role of the reporter of judicial decisions.

Section (b) was first adopted in 1949.

AUTHORS' COMMENTS

Supreme and Appellate Court opinions are published in the Connecticut Law Journal each Tuesday. The opinions are usually available as slip opinions prior to publication in the Connecticut Law Journal at the Judicial Branch website (h ttp://www.jud.ct.gov./) under advanced release opinions in the pertinent court. At oral argument, counsel must provide an email address to receive notice that the decision will be available on the website. The Reporter of Judicial Decisions will send an email a day or two ahead of the appearance of the decision. The Reporter no longer sends paper notices. The decision usually appears on the website several days before the case is published in the weekly Law Journal. Prior to 166 Conn., the opinion gave the date it was decided, which means when the judges voted on the opinion, usually in conference; since then it generally gives the date it is published in the Law Journal, which is a few weeks later. However, since 1996 the opinion occasionally gives the date it was released electronically. The deadline for taking further action depends on whether the Connecticut Law Journal or electronic publication date is given in the opinion.

Beginning in June 2008, the notice no longer includes the rescript. Unlike trial court practice, the appellate clerk is not required to and in fact usually does not send a copy of the opinion to counsel. Oakland Heights Mobile Park, Inc. v. Simon, 40 Conn.App. 30, 668 A.2d 737 (1995). But see 2012 commentary to P.B. § 79a-11 (noting that decisions in child protection matters are generally emailed to counsel).

The Supreme Court usually issues full written opinions, even when they are per curiams. However, a thus far unique one-liner is State v. Alexander, 241 Conn. 691, 696 A.2d 982 (1997). The Appellate Court frequently issues very short per curiams, which are found in the back of the volumes. Often these are one-liners ("The judgment is affirmed.")

Written opinions have been regularly issued by the Supreme Court since 1810. 4 Day 129, 130 n. Before then, the Supreme Court generally issued opinions only when it reversed the Superior Court. However, the Superior Court regularly issued written opinions starting in 1785. Kirby iii–iv.

Before mid-1990, instead of "affirmed", the rescript usually said "no error"; instead of "reversed" or "vacated", the rescript usually said "error, further proceedings", "error, new trial" or "error, judgment directed". Where a judgment is reversed, no new trial is to be held unless the rescript explicitly so states. Lamenza v. Shelton, 96 Conn. 403, 411–14, 114 A. 96, 99–100 (1921). See also Coughlin v. McElroy, 72 Conn. 444, 44 A. 743 (1899). If the rescript says "further proceedings" it may mean as much as a whole trial, as little as making mathematical calculations, or something in between. The rescript, or mandate, directed to the lower court, defines the scope of the lower court's authority, if any, to proceed with the case. Hurley v. Heart Physicians, P.C., 298 Conn. 371, 381 n.9, 383, 3 A.3d 892, 900 n.9, 901, Prod. Liab. Rep. (CCH) P 18501 (2010).

Where there is error on only one aspect of a case, such as damages but not liability, the court may order a new trial on that one issue only, Harewood v. Carter, 63 Conn.App. 199, 204–07, 772 A.2d 764, 767–68 (2001); Herrera v. Madrak, 58 Conn.App. 320, 327, 752 A.2d 1161, 1166 (2000). However, the court has cautioned that it hesitates before ordering only a restricted new trial; George v. Ericson, 250 Conn. 312, 332–33, 736 A.2d 889, 900 n.9, 901 (1999); Fazio v. Brown, 209 Conn. 450, 551 A.2d 1227, 5 A.L.R.5th 1176 (1988); Sunbury v. Sunbury, 210 Conn. 170, 553 A.2d 612 (1989). This hesitancy was not evident in Zarrelli v. Barnum Festival Soc., Inc., 6 Conn.App. 322, 505 A.2d 25 (1986).

Where the defendant wins a reversal on part of the case, sometimes the interests of justice for the plaintiff requires reversal of another part of the case favorable to the defendant on the ground of inconsistency even if the plaintiff did not appeal. Magnan v. Anaconda Industries, Inc., 193 Conn. 558, 577–78, 479 A.2d 781, 791, 117 L.R.R.M. (BNA) 2163, 101 Lab. Cas. (CCH) P 55485 (1984). The court also noted and ordered correction of an illegal sentence even though not raised in State v. Tabone, 279 Conn. 527, 545, 902 A.2d 1058, 1068 (2006).

If a judgment is set aside on appeal, the judgment no longer exists and it is as if there were never a judgment. Hurley v. Heart Physicians, P.C., 298 Conn. 371, 383, 3 A.3d 892, 901, Prod. Liab. Rep. (CCH) P 18501 (2010). Where error is found and the trial court's factual statement would support a directed judgment to the contrary, sometimes the Supreme Court will order a new trial instead on the ground that the trial court's attention may not have been sufficiently directed to the fact in question. Guillara v. Liquor Control Com'n, 121 Conn. 441, 446–47, 185 A. 398, 400, 105 A.L.R. 563 (1936). Likewise, if a judgment for the defendant on liability is reversed, the judge's hypothetical opinion on damages may also be reversed. Broughel v. Southern New England Tel. Co., 72 Conn. 617, 625, 45 A. 435, 438 (1900). Cf. Statewide Grievance Committee v. Rozbicki, 211 Conn. 232, 246, 558 A.2d 986, 992 (1989).

On certified appeals where the Appellate Court does not decide all issues but the issue it does decide is reversed by the Supreme Court, the case is normally remanded to the Appellate Court to decide the other issues. State v. Wohler, 231 Conn. 411, 416, 650 A.2d 168, 171 (1994), on remand, 38 Conn.App. 277, 661 A.2d 103 (1995).

Where there is an unrestricted new trial, any rulings made at the first trial, whether or not reviewed on appeal, are subject to reconsideration. Purdy v. Watts, 91 Conn. 214, 217–18, 99 A. 496, 498 (1916); State v. Darwin, 161 Conn. 413, 419, 288 A.2d 422, 425 (1971). But see id., 161 Conn. at 422–23, 288 A.2d at 427, concerning a jurisdictional ruling before the first trial. In addition, failure to raise an issue on appeal from the first trial will not bar review later. Beccia v. City of Waterbury, 192 Conn. 127, 132, 470 A.2d 1202, 1206–07 (1984). An admission of fact at the first trial is admissible, but not necessarily conclusive, at the second trial. Perry v. Simpson Waterproof Mfg. Co., 40 Conn. 313, 317, 1873 WL 1426 (1873). A reversed judgment has no collateral estoppel effect. Daly v. County Obstetrics and Gynecology Group, 40 Conn. L. Rptr. 158, 2005 WL 2857623 (Conn. Super. Ct. 2005).

When a case is remanded for a new trial, it goes back to the same docket (jury or non-jury) as before. Hartford Nat. Bank and Trust Co. v. DiFazio, 6 Conn.App. 576, 578, 506 A.2d 1069, 1075 (1986).

Occasionally the Supreme Court has released opinions it has prepared even though the case was settled in the meantime. McManus v. Jarvis, 128 Conn. 707, 22 A.2d 857 (1939). Dissenting opinions are not so frequent as in U.S. Supreme Court cases.

In a mortgage foreclosure case, if the law day has passed pending the appeal, the fact that the Supreme Court finds no error does not bar the Superior Court from thereafter extending the law day. Brooks v. Benham, 70 Conn. 92, 99, 38 A. 908, 911 (1897).

The trial court must not deviate from an appellate court reversal order even if a new statute intervenes. Flanagan v. Blumenthal, 40 Conn. L. Rptr. 805, 2006 WL 574261 (Conn. Super. Ct. 2006), aff'd, 100 Conn.App. 255, 917 A.2d 1047 (2007).

Where a judgment is reversed, C.G.S.A. § 51-183c prohibits the same judge from retrying the case. Judge Flynn has held that this statute only applies if there is an actual retrial. L & G Associates, Inc. v. City of Danbury Zoning Bd. of Appeals, 12 Conn. L. Rptr. 276, 1994 WL 421454 (Conn. Super. Ct. 1994). This narrow definition of "trial" is clearly wrong in light of Higgins v. Karp, 243 Conn. 495, 500 n.7, 706 A.2d 1, 4 n.7 (1998). But see State v. Miranda, 260 Conn. 93, 131–32, 794 A.2d 506, 529 (2002) (trial judge who was reversed may decide resentencing issue).

Where an appeal is dismissed as moot, the appellant may be able to get the lower court judgment vacated. In re Jessica M., 250 Conn. 747, 738 A.2d 1087 (1999). But see In re Alex M., 59 Conn.App. 389, 757 A.2d 66 (2000).

The Supreme Court and the Appellate Court often issue replacement pages for their decisions a few weeks after the decision is announced. Usually these pages correct minor mistakes, but sometimes they make major changes. One such change led to a blast from the dissent and persuaded one member of the majority to change sides. State v. Porter, 241 Conn. 57, 90, 164, 165, 698 A.2d 739, 757, 793–95 (1997). In another case, the replacement page changed the rescript, which led to dismissal of a subsequent appeal. State v. James, 63 Conn.App. 697, 778 A.2d 987 (2001).

Generally, three judges decide Appellate Court cases and, since September 2009, seven decide Supreme Court cases. If a judge is disqualified or dies after oral argument, consent is required for two or four judges to decide the appeal. Otherwise the case is reargued before a full panel, as in State v. Casanova, 54 Conn.App. 714, 715 n.1, 738 A.2d 668, n.1 (1999), rev'd on other grounds, 255 Conn. 581, 767 A.2d 1189 (2001). But see cases such as Burritt Mut. Sav. Bank of New Britain v. City of New Britain, 146 Conn. 669, 154 A.2d 608 (1959), decided shortly after Chief Justice Daly died.

C.G.S.A. § 51-198(c) allows a justice who sat on a case before age 70 to decide it thereafter. See State v. Cole, 254 Conn. 88, 755 A.2d 202 (2000) (statute applies to Chief Justice Callahan, who retired June 2000). The Supreme Court upheld the constitutionality of § 51-198(c) in Honulik v. Town of Greenwich, 293 Conn. 641, 980 A.2d 845 (2009).

§ 71-5. Motions for Reconsideration; Motions for Reconsideration En Banc

A motion for reconsideration will not be entertained unless filed with the appellate clerk, accompanied by a receipt showing that the fee was paid or waived, within ten days from the date when the decision or any order being challenged is officially released. The fee may be paid to the clerk of any trial court in the state.

The motion for reconsideration shall state briefly the grounds for requesting a reconsideration.

A party may also request reconsideration en banc by placing "en banc" in the caption of the motion and requesting such relief as an alternative to reconsideration by the panel.

Whenever reconsideration en banc is sought, the motion shall state briefly why reconsideration is necessary (for example, to secure or maintain uniformity of decision or because of the importance of the decision) and shall also state the names of the decisions, if any, with which the decision conflicts. A motion for reconsideration shall be treated as a motion for reconsideration en banc when any member of the court which decided the matter will not be available, within a reasonable time, to act on the motion for reconsideration.

Historical Note

Derivation: (first and second paragraphs)
 1978 P.B. (1986–97), § 4121
 1978 P.B., § 3111A
 1963 P.B., § 703

1951 P.B., § 441
1934 P.B., § 399
1930 Rules Change, § 42
1922 P.B., § 42
1908 P.B., § 41
1899 P.B., § 41

The third paragraph was added in 1996.

The references to "reargument" in the caption and the text were deleted effective January 1, 2000.

This section was renumbered from § 4122 and amended effective October 1, 1992 to refer to dispositive orders as well as decisions.

This section was amended in 1986 to add motions for reconsideration (such as when there was no argument) and to change the number of copies from 9 to 10 to conform with § 4014.

Except for referring explicitly to the justices who heard the case rather than to all justices effective January 1, 1985, except for filing the motion with the chief clerk of the Supreme Court effective July 1, 1978, and except for abolishing summer rules in 1969 and 1973, and changing the period for filing from two weeks to ten days in 1943, there has been no significant change in this rule since 1934. Prior to 1934, there was no provision similar to the second sentence, and prior to 1930, the motion had to be filed before the opening of the next term of the Supreme Court.

Derivation (third paragraph):
1978 P.B. (1996–97), § 4121
1978 P.B. (1983–96), § 4122

The reference to the importance of the decision and the last sentence were added effective October 1, 1986.

Entirely new rule effective August 23, 1983.

Derivation (fourth paragraph)
1978 P.B. (1996–97), § 4121
1978 P.B. (1978–96), § 4123 (second paragraph)

Cross References

Maltbie, Conn.App.Proc.2d, § 320.

C.G.S.A. § 52-259c(b) ($125.00 civil case filing fee effective July 1, 2009). (The appellate clerk is applying this statute to reconsideration as well as reargument motions.)

AUTHORS' COMMENTS

The motion to reargue is rarely granted by the Supreme Court and, when it is, the decision may be the same. Lexington Ins. Co. v. Lexington Healthcare Group, Inc., 311 Conn. 29, 84 A.3d 1167 (2014) (same result on an en banc review of 5-justice decision); Travelers Ins. Co. v. Namerow, 261 Conn. 784, 807 A.2d 467 (2002) (same result, but decided on merits). See also State v. Ray, 290 Conn. 602, 966 A.2d 148 (2009) (same result); Kiniry v. Kiniry, 79 Conn.App. 378, 830 A.2d 364 (2003) (same result); State v. Perez, 82 Conn.App. 100, 842 A.2d 1187, cert. denied, 269 Conn. 904, 852 A.2d 734 (2004) (same result).

In fact, since 1978 only four motions under this section have succeeded in the Supreme Court where the same panel that heard the appeal heard the motion to reconsider. In Pelletier v. Sordoni/Skanska Const. Co., 264 Conn. 509, 825 A.2d 72 (2003), the same panel reconsidered its earlier decision and reached the opposite result, and in Williams v. Best Cleaners, Inc., 237 Conn. 490, 677 A.2d 1356 (1996), reargument by the same panel also yielded an entirely different result. In Cheshire Mortg. Service, Inc. v. Montes, 223 Conn. 80, 612 A.2d 1130 (1992), although the Court denied the motion to reargue, it withdrew its original opinion and issued a different opinion ordering a reversal rather than an affirmance of a foreclosure judgment and in Jaconski v. AMF, Inc., 208 Conn. 230, 235 n.4, 543 A.2d 728, 730 n.4 (1988), the winning party successfully moved for reargument to modify the language of a footnote favoring the losing party.

The rarity of success contrasts sharply with the Maltbie era (1930's and 40's), when reconsideration was granted a few times every year.

Between the fall of 1987 and the fall of 2009, the seven justices normally sat in panels of five. A number of 3-2 decisions in that era were reconsidered en banc. In addition during that time, the Supreme Court on several occasions ordered reargument en banc before decision. State v. Wilson, 242 Conn. 605, 606 n.1, 700 A.2d 633, 635 n.1 (1997); Haynes v. Yale-New Haven Hosp., 243 Conn. 17, 19 n.1, 699 A.2d 964, 965 n.1 (1997) (supplemental briefing and reargument en banc); State v. Sawyer, 279 Conn. 331, 334 n.1, 904 A.2d 101, 104 n.1 (2006) (overruled on other grounds by, State v. DeJesus, 288 Conn. 418, 953 A.2d 45 (2008)) (same); Gore v. People's Sav. Bank, 235 Conn. 360, 370 n.12, 665 A.2d 1341, 1346 n.12 (1995); Barrett Builders v. Miller, 215 Conn. 316, 576 A.2d 455 (1990); State v. Belle, 215 Conn. 257, 576 A.2d 139 (1990).

The Appellate Court has occasionally granted such motions, State v. Elson, 125 Conn. App. 328, 9 A.3d 731 (2010) (same result rev'd), 311 Conn. 726, 91 A.3d 862 (2014), State v. Flanagan, 102 Conn. App. 105, 925 A.2d 385 (2007) (same result enbanc), rev'd, 293 Conn. 406, 978 A.2d 64 (2009); State v. Lawrence, 91 Conn.App. 765, 882 A.2d 689 (2005) (reargument en banc; reversal becomes affirmance), aff'd, 281 Conn. 147, 913 A.2d 428 (2007); State v. Martin, 2 Conn.App. 605, 482 A.2d 70 (1984) (same result); Davis v. Yudkin, 3 Conn.App. 576, 495 A.2d 714 (1985) (more favorable result for nonmoving party—he wins on the merits rather than on jurisdiction); Fishman v. Middlesex Mut. Assur. Co., 4 Conn.App. 339, 494 A.2d 606 (1985) (same result); Hayward v. Hayward, 53 Conn.App. 1, 752 A.2d 1087 (1999) (summary affirmance reversed); Farley v. T.R.W., Inc., 4 Conn.App. 191, 493 A.2d 268, Prod. Liab. Rep. (CCH) P 10689 (1985) (moving party wins reversal of original decision).

Reargument before decision was ordered in State v. Barber, 64 Conn.App. 659, 781 A.2d 464, cert. denied, 258 Conn. 925, 783 A.2d 1030 (2001); and City of Bridgeport v. Barbour-Daniel Electronics, Inc., 16 Conn.App. 574, 548 A.2d 744, cert. denied, 209 Conn. 826, 552 A.2d 432 (1988). The court also sat en banc in the initial hearing in In the Matter of Presnick, 19 Conn.App. 340, 563 A.2d 299 (1989); in State v. Geisler, 22 Conn.App. 142, 576 A.2d 1283 (1990), cert. granted, judgment vacated, 498 U.S. 1019, 111 S. Ct. 663, 112 L. Ed. 2d 657 (1991).

If the time for reargument has passed, possibly try a writ of error coram nobis, State v. Wojculewicz, 143 Conn. 118, 119 A.2d 913 (1956) (criminal case); Greenberg v. Harrison, 143 Conn. 731, 127 A.2d 827 (1956) (civil case). The writ of error coram nobis is also discussed in State v. Grisgraber, 183 Conn. 383, 439 A.2d 377 (1981). See also State v. Medina, 227 Conn. 456 (1993), on reconsideration, 228 Conn. 281, 636 A.2d 351 (1994), involving the disqualification of Justice Norcott. The motion for reargument was granted although it was filed very late. However, a tardy motion for reconsideration was barred in Richards v. Stewart, 2 Day 328, 338, 1806 WL 197 (Conn. 1806). The 10-day rule is not jurisdictional. Novak v. Levin, 287 Conn. 71, 951 A.2d 514 (2008).

If a case is reconsidered and a new opinion is issued, the previous practice was that the first opinion was withdrawn from permanent publication. The new practice is that both opinions are published. Town of Groton v. United Steelworkers of America, 254 Conn. 35, 36 n.1, 757 A.2d 501, 504 n.1 (2000). Sanstrom v. Strickland, 11 Conn.App. 211, 525 A.2d 989 (1987). The authors applaud this change.

A motion to reconsider the denial of a petition for certification was granted on a petition filed six months late, shortly after Supreme Court opinion was issued arguably conflicting with the Appellate Court decision. Barry v. Posi-Seal Intern., Inc., 235 Conn. 901, 664 A.2d 1124 (1995). A petition for certification was also granted on reconsideration in State v. Burke, 254 Conn. 202, 203–04, 757 A.2d 524, 524–25 (2000), and in Spears v. Garcia, 263 Conn. 22, 818 A.2d 37 (2003). See also Caruso v. City of Milford, 75 Conn.App. 95, 100, 815 A.2d 167, cert. denied, 263 Conn. 907, 819 A.2d 838 (2003). In Usowski v. Jacobson, 261 Conn. 902, 802 A.2d 856 (2002), the Supreme Court granted a petition on sua sponte reconsideration.

A reconsideration of a sanctions order prohibiting the filing of any papers must be made in seven rather than the usual ten days. P.B. § 85-2.

§ 71-6. Stay of Proceedings

Unless the chief justice or chief judge shall otherwise direct, any stay of proceedings which was in effect during the pendency of the appeal shall continue until the time for filing a motion for reconsideration has expired, and, if a motion is filed, until twenty days after its disposition, and, if it is granted, until the appeal is finally determined. If no stay of proceedings was in effect during the pendency of the appeal and the decision of the court having appellate jurisdiction would change the position of any party from its position during the pendency of the appeal, all proceedings to enforce or carry out the decision of the court having appellate jurisdiction shall be stayed until the time for filing a motion for reconsideration has expired, and, if a motion is filed, until twenty days after its disposition, and, if it is granted, until the appeal is finally determined. (See also Section 61-11.)

Historical Note

Derivation:
    1978 P.B. (1986–97), § 4123
    1978 P.B., § 3112
    1963 P.B., § 704
    1951 P.B., § 441
    1934 P.B., § 399
    1922 P.B., § 42
    1908 P.B., § 41
    1899 P.B., § 41

The automatic stay was extended from ten days to twenty days effective January 1, 2000.

There has been no substantial change in this rule since 1899. In addition to the changes effective September 3, 1996, the phrase "ten days after" was added effective October 7, 1996.

AUTHORS' COMMENTS

Since 1986, § 61-12 must be used for administrative appeals, contempts, injunctions and the like. If the Appellate Court denies a stay or denies relief on a § 66-7 motion for review query whether the Supreme Court can enter the stay while the appeal is pending in the Appellate Court. The authors believe that the first sentence of § 60-2 permits it. The U.S. Supreme Court often exercises such power. Stern & Gressman, Supreme Court Practice, 5th Ed. § 17.19.

An appeal bond expires when the appeal is finally disposed of. State v. Walzer,

208 Conn. 420, 425, 545 A.2d 559, 562 (1988) (petition for certification denied by Supreme Court and no further action taken by counsel under this rule).

The automatic stay provision was cited in RAL Management, Inc. v. Valley View Associates, 278 Conn. 672, 899 A.2d 586 (2006).

In the authors' opinion, this section trumps § 61-11(d).

§ 71-7. Stays of Execution Pending Decision by United States Supreme Court

When a case has gone to judgment in the state supreme court and a party to the action wishes to obtain a stay of execution pending a decision in the case by the United States supreme court, that party shall, within twenty days of the judgment, file a motion for stay with the state supreme court. The filing of the motion shall operate as a stay pending the state supreme court's decision thereon.

When the state supreme court has denied a petition for certification from the appellate court, any stay in existence at the time of such denial shall remain in effect for twenty days. Any party to the action wishing to extend such stay of execution or to otherwise obtain a stay of execution pending a decision in the case by the United States supreme court shall file a motion for stay with the appellate court. The filing of the motion shall operate as a stay pending the appellate court's decision thereon.

Historical Note

Derivation:
  1978 P.B. (1986–97), § 4050
  1978 P.B., § 3068

The automatic stay was extended from ten days to twenty days effective January 1, 2000.

The three-day stay in the second paragraph was changed to a ten-day stay effective October 1, 1992. At the same time, the ten-day deadline in the first paragraph was added.

In 1986, the original first paragraph was eliminated. It stated:

When an order of a court or administrative agency is not stayed by an appeal in accordance with Secs. 3065 and 3066, or by operation of statute, or when relief has been denied below, any party may file a motion with the supreme court for a stay of execution pending decision in the supreme court or the court below.

The original paragraph was an entirely new rule effective July 1, 1978 and was applied in Garrison v. Garrison, 190 Conn. 173, 183 n.7, 460 A.2d 945, 950 n.7 (1983), and Laurel Park, Inc. v. Pac, 194 Conn. 677, 684 n.11, 485 A.2d 1272, 1276 n.11 (1984). The paragraph was amended effective January 1, 1985 to clarify when it may be used. While there had previously been no similar rule, the Supreme Court did on one occasion grant a motion for a stay, Beit Havurah v. Zoning Board of Appeals of Town of Norfolk, 174 Conn. 809, 386 A.2d 1135 (1978).

What are now the first and second paragraphs were added effective October 1, 1980 to clarify how stays of execution are requested pending decision by the United States Supreme Court.

AUTHORS' COMMENTS

If a stay is not requested within twenty days, the previous stay, if any, automatically expires. F.D.I.C. v. Caldrello, 79 Conn.App. 384, 388 n.5, 830 A.2d 767, 771 n.5 (2003).

CHAPTER 72

WRITS OF ERROR

§ 72-1. Writs of Error; In General

(a) Writs of error for errors in matters of law only may be brought from a final judgment of the superior court to the supreme court in the following cases: (1) a decision binding on an aggrieved nonparty; (2) a summary decision of criminal contempt; (3) a denial of transfer of a small claims action to the regular docket; and (4) as otherwise necessary or appropriate in aid of its jurisdiction and agreeable to the usages and principles of law.

(b) No writ of error may be brought in any civil or criminal proceeding for the correction of any error where (1) the error might have been reviewed by process of appeal, or by way of certification, or (2) the parties, by failure timely to seek a transfer or otherwise, have consented to have the case determined by a court or tribunal from whose judgment there is no right of appeal or opportunity for certification.

Historical Note

Derivation:
  1978 P.B. (1986–97), § 4143
  1978 P.B., § 4143
  1978 P.B., § 3090

This rule was modernized in 2004 to make clear when it applies and how it should be processed.

This rule was amended effective May 31, 1994 to bring it into compliance with *State v. Sims* (discussed in Authors' Comments). Effective February 1, 1988, the state can no longer file a writ of error where it has been denied permission to appeal under C.G.S.A. § 54-96. This section was completely rewritten effective October 1, 1986. Old § 3090 stated as follows: "An aggrieved party may file a writ of error in the supreme court only to review the final judgment of a judge or court in a case where no unqualified statutory right of appeal has been provided. A writ of error may be used only to review errors apparent on the face of the record."

The following history refers to old § 3090.

Entirely new rule effective July 1, 1978. This new rule follows various prior decisions of the Supreme Court, State v. Audet, 170 Conn. 337, 365 A.2d 1082 (1976); State v. Falzone, 171 Conn. 417, 370 A.2d 988 (1976); State v. Assuntino, 173 Conn. 104, 376 A.2d 1091 (1977).

Cross References
C.G.S.A. §§ 52-272 to 52-278 (repealed in 2003)
Form 3000.24-A

AUTHORS' COMMENTS

The writ of error is the traditional common law method of review by the Supreme Court. There also was a statutory writ until 2003. Now everything about the writ of error is found in this chapter. The history of the writ is discussed in some detail in State v. Caplan, 85 Conn. 618, 622–24, 84 A. 280, 282 (1912). Prior to the advent of the statutory right of appeal in 1882, a statutory motion in error, a short substitute for a writ of error, normally served the purpose of the writ of error. 1870 Rules, 37 Conn. 619, § IV.

The writ is not a mere relic; it is the only means of review of summary criminal contempt judgments, Vasquez v. Superior Court, 102 Conn.App. 394, 404–05, 925 A.2d 1112, 1120–21, cert. denied, 284 Conn. 915, 931 A.2d 935 (2007); Martin v. Flanagan, 259 Conn. 487, 494, 789 A.2d 979, 983–84 (2002). See § 1(iv) of commentary to § 61-1. It is also viable in a case where the legislature does not provide for an appeal. State v. Falzone, 171 Conn. 417, 370 A.2d 988 (1976); State v. Audet, 170 Conn. 337, 341 n.1, 365 A.2d 1082, 1085 n.1 (1976); (certain criminal appeals by the state); Cannavo Enterprises, Inc. v. Burns, 194 Conn. 43, 48, 478 A.2d 601, 604 (1984) (small claims) (but see comments below); State v. Rupar, 293 Conn. 489, 978 A.2d 502 (2009) (sentence review division).

Until Hardy v. Superior Court, Judicial Dist. of Fairfield, 305 Conn. 824, 48 A.3d 50 (2012), was decided, several decisions had said that Supreme Court review of summary criminal contempt judgments was restricted to jurisdictional or face-of-the-record issues. *Hardy* eliminated that restriction.

Note, however, a writ of error is not a vehicle to review the merits of a decision by the sentencing review decision, but can be used to review the procedure by which the division decided the matter. State v. Rupar, 293 Conn. 489, 502, 978 A.2d 502, 511–12 (2009).

De facto reprimand of a non-party lawyer in the Appellate Court can be reviewed on a writ of error (and only on a writ of error, in the authors' opinion). State v. Perez, 276 Conn. 285, 288 n.2, 885 A.2d 178, 181 n.2 (2005).

Today, the most important use of the writ is to review a trial court ruling as to a nonparty. Examples are Perry v. Perry, 312 Conn. 600, 618-621, 95 A.3d 500 (2014); Seymour v. Seymour, 262 Conn. 107, 809 A.2d 1114 (2002) (subpoena for discovery); Thalheim v. Town of Greenwich, 256 Conn. 628, 636, 775 A.2d 947, 954–55 (2001) (lawyer who files an amicus brief without permission sanctioned); B & B Bail Bonds Agency of Connecticut, Inc. v. Bailey, 256 Conn. 209, 770 A.2d 960 (2001) (bail bond issue); State v. Sheriff, 301 Conn. 617, 21 A.3d 808 (2011) (same); Nanni v. Dino Corp., 117 Conn.App. 61, 978 A.2d 531 (2009) (administratrix challenged order binding her in her individual capacity when she did not appear individually in action); Conte v. Conte, 45 Conn.App. 235, 236, 695 A.2d 32, 33 (1997) (fine levied against plaintiff's attorney); Yamin v. Savarese and Schefiliti, P.C., 58 Conn.App. 171, 753 A.2d 388 (2000) (same); Bergeron v. Mackler, 225 Conn. 391, 623 A.2d 489 (1993) (disqualification of a lawyer for a witness); Kennedy v. QVC Network, Inc., 43 Conn.App. 851, 686 A.2d 997 (1996) (order against non-party); State v. Salmon, 250 Conn. 147, 735 A.2d 333 (1999) (disapproved of by, Board of Educ. of City of New Haven v. Tavares Pediatric Center, 276 Conn. 544, 888 A.2d 65, 205 Ed. Law Rep. 752 (2006)) (same).

The writ should not be used if the issues can be raised by appeal; State v.

Dellacamera, 110 Conn.App. 653, 955 A.2d 613 (2008); State v. One or More Persons Over Whom Courts Jurisdiction Has Not Yet Been Invoked, 107 Conn.App. 760, 946 A.2d 896, cert. denied, 289 Conn. 912, 957 A.2d 880 (2008) (denial of motions for return of seized property should have been appealed); State v. Marro, 68 Conn.App. 849, 854, 795 A.2d 555, 558–59 (2002) (appeal by state—a party—concerning bail bond); Cary v. Phoenix Ins. Co., 83 Conn. 690, 696–97, 78 A. 426, 429 (1910); nor can it be used to raise issues previously disposed of by an appeal; Leopold v. State, 114 Conn. 729, 159 A. 660 (1932). The writ cannot, in the authors' opinion, be used to avoid finality issues.

The writ will also not avoid a jurisdictional problem on an appeal. Crone v. Gill, 250 Conn. 476, 736 A.2d 131 (1999) (disqualified attorney lacks standing to file writ of error); Green Rock Ridge, Inc. v. Kobernat, 250 Conn. 488, 736 A.2d 851 (1999) (deponent can't file writ of error from discovery order unless first held in contempt); State v. Ross, 272 Conn. 577, 596–98, 863 A.2d 654, 665–66 (2005) (lack of aggrievement).

Interesting questions about possible conflicts between this section and C.G.S.A. § 52-273 were raised but not resolved in Walker v. Commissioner of Correction, 223 Conn. 411, 413 n.3, 611 A.2d 413, 414 n.3 (1992).

The addition of § 72-1(b)(1) in 1986 made clear that the State as well as the prisoner must obtain the trial court's permission to file an appeal under § 61-1. Laws v. Warden, State Prison, 218 Conn. 479, 590 A.2d 436 (1991), overruled by Simms v. Warden, 229 Conn. 178, 640 A.2d 601 (1994). However, until revised effective May 31, 1994, this subsection was inconsistent with the governing statute, C.G.S.A. § 52-470(b), and therefore could not be used if the statutory certification to appeal was denied. Simms v. Warden, 229 Conn. 178, 640 A.2d 601 (1994). According to *Simms*, the remedy for a denial of certification to appeal would be an appeal from the denial, with the threshold issue being whether the court abused its discretion in denying certification.

Previous dicta to the contrary notwithstanding, a defendant can file a writ of error from a default judgment if the other conditions for filing a writ are met. Cannavo Enterprises, Inc. v. Burns, 194 Conn. 43, 48, 478 A.2d 601, 603–04 (1984).

The addition of (b)(2) in 1986 greatly reduces the use of the writ of error in small claims cases, but the Appellate Court has been very creative in getting around it by relying on § 60-1. In Veterans Memorial Medical Center v. Townsend, 49 Conn.App. 198, 712 A.2d 993 (1998), no small claims hearing was held at all, and this was held a proper basis for a writ. In Safe Home Sec., Inc. v. Lewis, 52 Conn.App. 780, 727 A.2d 1289 (1999), no notice of the pendency of a counterclaim was sent to the plaintiff, so this was also held a proper basis for a writ. See also Newtown Pool Service, LLC v. Pond, 140 Conn.App. 514, 59 A.3d 378 (2013) (writ allowed when the defendant presses counterclaim over jurisdictional limit at trial). However, in Nielson v. Docker, Supreme Court No. 13486, the trial judge dismissed a small claims case and the plaintiff filed a writ of error on the theory that (b)(2) only applies when the case is determined on the merits. The Supreme Court dismissed the writ in May 1989. See also Esposito v. Tony's Long Wharf Services, LLC, 96 Conn.App. 571, 901 A.2d 82 (2006). There is no question that a writ of error can raise a *Cannavo*-type issue, in which the trial court denied a timely motion by the defendant to transfer the case out of small claims. Such a case is Burns v. Bennett, 220 Conn. 162, 595 A.2d 877 (1991).

A writ of error, like an appeal, requires a final judgment, State v. Ross, 189 Conn. 42, 51, 454 A.2d 266, 270 (1983); Finch v. Ives, 24 Conn. 387, 1856 WL 937 (1856).

The writ of error generally cannot be used to review a judgment entered after the Supreme Court gave advice to the Superior Court on a reservation. Smith v. Lewis, 26 Conn. 110, 117, 1857 WL 932 (1857).

An early case holds that harmless error will not save a judgment attacked by a writ of error. Stalker v. State, 9 Conn. 341, 344, 1832 WL 95 (1832).

§ 72-2. Form

The writ shall contain in numbered paragraphs the facts upon which the petitioner relies and a statement of the relief claimed.

Historical Note

Derivation:
    1978 P.B. (1996–97), § 4143A
This is a new rule effective September 3, 1996. The reference to security for costs was deleted effective January 1, 2011.

AUTHORS' COMMENTS

The Supreme Court held in Morrison v. Parker, 261 Conn. 545, 552–53, 804 A.2d 777, 780–81 (2002), that the trial court has discretion to reject a writ that does not comply with this section.

§ 72-3. Applicable Procedure (Applicable to appeals filed before July 1, 2013)

(a) Upon payment in the trial court of the filing fee, the writ, if in proper form, shall be allowed and signed by a judge or clerk of the court in which the judgment or decree was rendered. The writ shall be presented for signature within twenty days of the date notice of the judgment or decision complained of is given but shall be signed by the judge or clerk even if not presented in a timely manner. Failure without cause to present the writ in a timely manner may be ground for dismissal of the writ by the supreme court.

(b) The writ shall be served and returned as other civil process, except that (1) the writ shall be served at least ten days, before the return day, and (2) shall be returned to the appellate clerk at least one day before the return day. The return days of the supreme court are any Tuesday not less than twelve nor more than thirty days after the writ is signed.

(c) If the writ is brought against a judge of the superior court to contest a summary decision of criminal contempt by that judge, the defendant in error shall be the superior court. In all other writs of error, the writ shall bear the caption of the underlying action in which the judgment or decision was rendered. All parties to the underlying action shall be served in accordance with chapter 8 of these rules.

(d) The writ shall be deemed filed the day it is returned. The appellate clerk shall forthwith give notice to all parties of the filing of the writ.

(e) Within twenty days after filing the writ, the plaintiff in error shall file with the appellate clerk two copies of such documents as are necessary to present the claims of error made in the writ, including pertinent pleadings, memoranda of decision and judgment file, accompanied by a certification that a copy thereof has been served on each counsel of record in accordance with Section 62-7.

(f) In the event a transcript is necessary, the plaintiff in error shall follow the procedure set forth in Sections 63-8 and 63-8A.

(g) Within ten days of the filing by the plaintiff in error of the documents referred to in subsections (e) and (f) of this rule, the defendant in error may file two copies of such additional documents as are necessary to defend the action, accompanied by a certification that a copy thereof has been served on each counsel of record in accordance with Section 62-7.

(h) Answers or other plea shall not be filed in response to any writ of error.

§ 72-3. Applicable Procedure (Applicable to appeals filed on or after July 1, 2013)

(a) Upon payment in the trial court of the filing fee, the writ, if in proper form, shall be allowed and signed by a judge or clerk of the court in which the judgment or decree was rendered. The writ shall be presented for signature within twenty days of the date notice of the judgment or decision complained of is given but shall be signed by the judge or clerk even if not presented in a timely manner. Failure without cause to present the writ in a timely manner may be ground for dismissal of the writ by the supreme court.

(b) The writ shall be served and returned as other civil process, except that (1) the writ shall be served at least ten days before the return day, and (2) shall be returned to the appellate clerk at least one day before the return day. The return days of the supreme court are any Tuesday not less than twelve nor more than thirty days after the writ is signed.

(c) If the writ is brought against a judge of the superior court to contest a summary decision of criminal contempt by that judge, the defendant in error shall be the superior court. In all other writs of error, the writ shall bear the caption of the underlying action in which the judgment or decision was rendered. All parties to the underlying action shall be served in accordance with chapter 8 of these rules.

(d) The writ shall be deemed filed the day it is returned. The appellate clerk shall forthwith give notice to all parties of the filing of the writ.

(e) Within twenty days after filing the writ, the plaintiff in error shall file with the appellate clerk one copy of such documents as are necessary to present the claims of error made in the writ, including pertinent pleadings, memoranda of decision and judgment file, accompanied by a certification that a copy thereof has been served on each counsel of record in accordance with Section 62-7.

(f) In the event a transcript is necessary, the plaintiff in error shall follow the procedure set forth in Sections 63-8 and 63-8A.

(g) Within ten days of the filing by the plaintiff in error of the documents referred to in subsections (e) and (f) of this rule, the defendant in error may file one copy of such additional documents as are necessary to defend the action, accompanied by a certification that a copy thereof has been served on each counsel of record in accordance with Section 62-7.

(h) Answers or other pleas shall not be filed in response to any writ of error.

Historical Note

Derivation:
> 1978 P.B. (1986–97), § 4144
> 1978 P.B., § 3091
> 1963 P.B., § 681
> 1951 P.B., § 429
> 1934 P.B., § 389
> 1922 P.B., § 33
> 1908 P.B., § 32
> 1899 P.B., § 32

This rule was substantially revised in 1996 and 2004 to eliminate much of the archaic language pertaining to the writ of error. The last clause of (g) was added effective January 1, 2011.

This section was completely rewritten effective October 1, 1986. Old § 3091 stated as follows: "The procedure for filing, prosecuting and defending a writ of error shall be in accordance with the rules for appeals except that:

"(a) The writ must be allowed and signed by a judge of the superior court, or by a judge or clerk of the court in which the judgment or decree was rendered, within two weeks after the rendition of the judgment or degree; and

"(b) The writ shall be made returnable to the next return day or next but one to which it can be made returnable."

The following history refers to old § 3091:

The new rule effective July 1, 1978 bears virtually no resemblance to the prior procedure. Writ of error provisions can be found in the 1847 rules, 18 Conn. 562, 571–72, and even in an 1804 rule, 1 Day 330.

AUTHORS' COMMENTS

The 2-week (now 20-day) filing period is not jurisdictional, even though it used to be set by statute, under C.G.S.A. § 52-273. Banks v. Thomas, 241 Conn. 569, 698 A.2d 268 (1997); B & B Bail Bonds Agency of Connecticut, Inc. v. Bailey, 256 Conn. 209, 211-12 n.5, 770 A.2d 960, 962 n.5 (2001) (untimely writ reviewed in view of no prejudice to or objection by the state).

The signing of a writ of error is a purely ministerial act. Morrison v. Parker, 261 Conn. 545, 804 A.2d 777 (2002). One should carefully note that the writ must be signed by a judge or clerk within 20 days of notification of the decision. The writ must be made returnable to the Supreme Court in the time period mentioned in (b).

Do not be misled by this rule; the writ of error is not procedurally similar to an appeal. The writ is an independent action, with its own return date. It is served by marshal and returned to the Supreme Court. Failure to follow the mandates for service and return of process may be fatal. Wakefield v. Chevalier, 85 Conn. 374, 82 A. 973 (1912).

For a suggested form for the writ, use the separate writ of error form (unofficial form 3000.24-A) rather than the appeal form. The history of "allowing" a writ of error is thoroughly discussed in Haylett v. Commission on Human Rights and Opportunities, 207 Conn. 547, 541 A.2d 494, 46 Fair Empl. Prac. Cas. (BNA) 1876, 47 Empl. Prac. Dec. (CCH) P 38164 (1988).

The writ of error requires a $250.00 filing fee. C.G.S.A. § 52-259.

§ 72-4. Applicability of Rules

Except as otherwise provided by statute or rule, the prosecution and defense of a writ of error shall be in accordance with the rules for appeals.

Historical Note

Derivation:
1978 P.B. (1996–97), § 4145
1978 P.B. (1986–97), § 4144
1978 P.B., § 3092
1963 P.B., § 682
1951 P.B., § 430
1934 P.B., § 390
1922 P.B., § 34
1908 P.B., § 33
1899 P.B., § 33

Effective January 1, 2004, the words "once filed" after writ of error were deleted.

"Need" was replaced by "shall" effective October 1, 1986. Prior to 1979, responsive pleadings were permitted.

Cross References

Maltbie, Conn.App.Proc.2d, §§ 237–40

AUTHORS' COMMENTS

This rule was followed in CB Commercial/Hampshire, LLC v. Security Mut. Life Ins. Co., 61 Conn.App. 144, 146, 763 A.2d 32, 34 (2000).

CHAPTER 73

RESERVATIONS

§ 73-1. Procedure; Form (Applicable to appeals filed before July 1, 2013)

(a) Any reservation shall be taken to the supreme court or to the appellate court from those cases in which an appeal could have been taken directly to the supreme court, or to the appellate court, respectively, had judgment been rendered. Reservations in cases where the proper court for the appeal cannot be determined prior to judgment shall be taken directly to the supreme court.

(b) All questions presented for advice shall be specific and shall be phrased so as to require a Yes or No answer.

(c) Before any question shall be reserved by any court, counsel shall file in that court a stipulation which shall clearly and fully state the question or questions upon which advice is desired; that their present determination by the appellate court having jurisdiction would be in the interest of simplicity, directness and economy in judicial action, the grounds for such allegation being particularly stated; that the answers to the questions will determine, or are reasonably certain to enter into the final determination of the case; and that the parties request that the questions be reserved for the advice of the appellate court having jurisdiction. The stipulation shall also designate the specific pleadings in the trial court case file which are necessary for the presentation of the question or questions sought to be reserved and shall state the undisputed facts which are essential for determination of the question or questions sought to be reserved. With the stipulation the parties shall file a joint docketing statement in the format specified in Section 63-4(a)(4) for regular appeals.

(d) Upon the ordering of a reservation by the superior court, the clerk of the trial court shall send notice of the reservation to the appellate clerk and to all parties of record. The date of issuance of this notice shall be deemed the filing date of the appeal for purposes of the brief filing deadlines of Section 67-3. No entry fee shall be paid to the superior court and no costs shall be taxed in favor of any party. With the notice of reservation, the clerk of the trial court shall send to the appellate clerk two copies each of the stipulation, its accompanying joint docketing statement, the superior court's order of reservation, and the docket sheet (DS1) listing the counsel for all parties.

(e) The court will not entertain a reservation for its advice upon questions of law arising in any action unless the question or questions presented are such as are, in the opinion of the court, reasonably certain to enter into the decision of the case, and it appears that their present determination would be in the interest of simplicity, directness and economy of judicial action.

(f) The advice of the appellate court on a reservation may be reviewed by the supreme court only upon the granting of certification as provided in chapter 84.

§ 73-1. Procedure; Form (Applicable to appeals filed on or after July 1, 2013)

(a) Any reservation shall be taken to the supreme court or to the appellate court from those cases in which an appeal could have been taken directly to the supreme court, or to the appellate court, respectively, had judgment been rendered. Reservations in cases where the proper court for the appeal cannot be determined prior to judgment shall be taken directly to the supreme court.

(b) All questions presented for advice shall be specific and shall be phrased so as to require a Yes or No answer.

(c) Before any question shall be reserved by any court, counsel shall file in that court a stipulation which shall clearly and fully state the question or questions upon which advice is desired; that their present determination by the appellate court having jurisdiction would be in the interest of simplicity, directness and economy in judicial action, the grounds for such allegation being particularly stated; that the answers to the questions will determine, or are reasonably certain to enter into the final determination of the case; and that the parties request that the questions be reserved for the advice of the appellate court having jurisdiction. The stipulation shall state the undisputed facts which are essential for determination of the question or questions sought to be reserved. With the stipulation, the parties shall file a joint docketing statement in the format specified in Section 63-4 (a) (3) for regular appeals.

(d) Upon the ordering of a reservation by the superior court, the clerk of the trial court shall send notice of the reservation to the appellate clerk and to all parties of record. The date of issuance of this notice shall be deemed the filing date of the appeal for purposes of the brief and appendix filing deadlines of Section 67-3. The plaintiff in the court that ordered the reservation shall be deemed the appellant, and the defendant in such court shall be deemed the appellee for purposes of these rules, unless otherwise ordered by the court.

(e) No entry fee shall be paid to the superior court and no costs shall be taxed in favor of any party. With the notice of reservation, except in appeals in which the contents of the case file consists solely of papers filed by electronic means, the clerk of the trial court shall send to the appellate clerk one copy each of the stipulation, its accompanying joint docketing statement, the superior court's order of reservation, and the case detail page listing the counsel for all parties.

(f) The court will not entertain a reservation for its advice upon questions of law arising in any action unless the question or questions presented are such as are, in the opinion of the court, reasonably certain to enter into the decision of the case, and it appears that their present determination would be in the interest of simplicity, directness and economy of judicial action.

(g) The advice of the appellate court on a reservation may be reviewed by the supreme court only upon the granting of certification as provided in chapter 84.

Historical Note

Derivation:
>   1978 P.B. (1986–97), §§ 4146, 4147
>   1978 P.B., §§ 3133, 3134
>   1963 P.B., §§ 738, 739
>   1951 P.B., §§ 469, 470
>   1934 P.B., §§ 421, 422
>   1922 P.B., §§ 71, 72
>   1908 P.B., §§ 70, 71

This rule was rewritten to make it more user-friendly in 1996.

Reservations have been permitted by rule apparently since the early 1800's and have been permitted by statute since 1855. Sargent & Co. v. New Haven Steamboat Co., 65 Conn. 116, 128, 31 A. 543, 547 (1894).

This section was reorganized with little change in substance effective October 1, 1986.

Cross References
>   C.G.S.A. § 52-235

AUTHORS' COMMENTS

Unless C.G.S.A. § 51-199 is applicable, all reservations should be taken to the Appellate Court. The Supreme Court may then transfer the case to itself if it wishes. See Izzo v. Colonial Penn Ins. Co., 203 Conn. 305, 306 n.1, 524 A.2d 641, 642 n.1 (1987).

The reservation rules were used to determine which party got the top line on the ballot, Republican Party of Connecticut v. Merrill, 307 Conn. 470, 55 A.3d 251 (2012); to test the legality of the replacement of the locally elected board of education with a state-appointed board in Pereira v. State Bd. of Educ., 304 Conn. 1, 37 A.3d 625, 278 Ed. Law Rep. 347 (2012); constitutionality of Good Friday laws; Griswold Inn, Inc. v. State, 183 Conn. 552, 441 A.2d 16 (1981); the automobile blue law; Fair Cadillac-Oldsmobile Isuzu Partnership v. Bailey, 229 Conn. 312, 640 A.2d 101 (1994); the legality of certain ATM charges, Burke v. Fleet National Bank, 252 Conn. 1, 742 A.2d 293 (1999); an offset to UM/UIM coverage, Hartford Cas. Ins. Co. v. Farrish-LeDuc, 275 Conn. 748, 882 A.2d 44

(2005); and whether a statute replaced certain fees, Small v. Going Forward, Inc., 281 Conn. 417, 915 A.2d 298 (2007) (en banc); whether a narrower construction of a criminal statute applies retroactively, Luurtsema v. Commissioner of Correction, 299 Conn. 740, 12 A.3d 817 (2011), and whether an indigent criminal defendant who represents himself has a right to publicly funded experts and investigators. State v. Wang, 312 Conn. 222, 92 A.3d 220 (2014).

The most important point about a reservation is that it does not require a final judgment, although the Supreme Court may in its discretion decline to consider it without one. Texaco Refining and Marketing Co., Inc. v. Commissioner of Revenue Services, 202 Conn. 583, 587, 522 A.2d 771, 774 (1987). The Supreme Court often declines reservations before a final judgment. State v. Ross, 237 Conn. 332, 677 A.2d 433 (1996). A reservation has been held premature when there are other unresolved issues which may dispose of the case, Rothkopf v. City of Danbury, 156 Conn. 347, 350, 242 A.2d 771, 773 (1968) (defense of res judicata pending); Barr v. First Taxing Dist. of City of Norwalk, 147 Conn. 221, 158 A.2d 740 (1960) (trial inevitable regardless of how questions answered); and improper when the same issue is before the federal courts, Hoblitzelle v. Frechette, 156 Conn. 253, 268, 240 A.2d 864, 870–71 (1968); or has already been decided in another proceeding, ASL Associates v. Zoning Com'n of Town of Marlborough, 18 Conn.App. 542, 547–48, 559 A.2d 236, 239 (1989). However, it can be used for an ancillary proceeding that would qualify as appealable under § 61-1, Potter v. Appleby, 136 Conn. 641, 643, 73 A.2d 819, 820 (1950) (validity of attachment).

If the factual stipulation is inadequate to render final judgment, the Supreme Court may refuse to answer the questions reserved. Lehrer v. Davis, 214 Conn. 232, 571 A.2d 691 (1990); Capel v. Plymouth Rock Assur. Corp., 141 Conn.App. 699, 62 A.3d 582 (2013); Duggins v. H.N.S. Management Co., Inc., 34 Conn.App. 863, 644 A.2d 376 (1994). In addition, if the record is defective, the Supreme Court can and often does refuse to answer the questions. State v. Zach, 198 Conn. 168, 179, 502 A.2d 896, 902 (1985).

The questions must be framed so that each one raises "a definite point of law to which the court can give a categorical * * * answer". Rothkopf v. City of Danbury, 156 Conn. 347, 351, 242 A.2d 771, 773 (1968). "Whether or not" is not a proper format. Herzig v. Board of Ed. of Town of West Hartford, 152 Conn. 144, 152, 204 A.2d 827, 830 (1964).

The court has criticized the use of the "will construction" format in reservations concerning declaratory judgments and has noted that form 3000.20 should be used. Hardware Mut. Cas. Co. v. Premo, 153 Conn. 465, 472–73, 217 A.2d 698, 702–03 (1966); Kellems v. Brown, 163 Conn. 478, 480–82, 313 A.2d 53, 54–57 (1972), appeal dismissed 409 U.S. 1099, 93 S. Ct. 911, 34 L.E.2d 678 (1973).

If the rights of nonparties will be affected, the questions will not be answered. Congress & Daggett, Inc. v. Seamless Rubber Co., 145 Conn. 318, 322, 142 A.2d 137, 140 (1958). The Court has also refused a reservation where the parties were not adverse at the time of hearing. Greenwich Trust Co. v. Brixey, 117 Conn. 663, 166 A. 918 (1933).

Questions of fact cannot be resolved by a reservation, as this is the function of the trial court. Wiegert v. Pequabuck Golf Club, Inc., 150 Conn. 387, 190 A.2d 43 (1963); Fox v. First Bank, 8 Conn.L.Trib. No. 19, pp. 19, 20 (1982). For this reason State v. Zach, 198 Conn. 168, 502 A.2d 896 (1985), was remanded for trial, although the merits of the dispute were discussed in detail. Likewise, a reservation is improper if there is no question of law in the case, but merely an issue as to the proper judgment to be entered on the facts agreed to. Harrison v. Harrison, 96 Conn. 568, 114 A. 681 (1921). *Harrison* also stands for the proposition that a reservation should not be used if the case is not ready for a final judgment upon issuance of the Supreme Court decision. However, for an example of a successful reservation when the case was not ready for final judgment, see Carroll v. Socony-Vacuum Oil Co., 136 Conn. 49, 52, 68 A.2d 299, 301–02 (1949).

A reservation concerning the sufficiency of service of process was refused in Ingle v. Case, 46 Conn. 240, 1878 WL 1575 (1878), on the ground that it did not relate to the merits of the case, subject matter jurisdiction, or the sufficiency of pleadings.

Advice given by the appellate court on the reservation is binding. Thus, after the trial court enters judgment in accordance with the advice, the loser cannot file an appeal raising the issue on which the advice was given. Nichols v. City of Bridgeport, 27 Conn. 459 (1858).

The reservation (and presumably the stipulation) need only be agreed to by the appearing parties. State Bank v. Bliss, 67 Conn. 317, 320, 35 A. 255, 256 (1896).

Note that once the trial court approves the reservation, it can be filed like any other appeal without any approval by the Supreme Court.

In Clini v. New Haven Brewing Co., 119 Conn. 556, 177 A. 745 (1935), the trial judge reserved the case to the Supreme Court and then sat in the Supreme Court on the case.

CHAPTER 74

APPEALS FROM JUDICIAL REVIEW COUNCIL

§ 74-1. Time to Take; Form; Filing; Costs

Appeals from decisions of the judicial review council shall be taken within twenty days from the date the decision appealed from is received by the respondent judge.

The appeal shall be directed to and filed with the supreme court and shall be accompanied by a certification that a copy thereof has been served on the chair or executive director of the judicial review council in accordance with the provisions of Section 62-7. No fee shall be required to be paid. The appellate clerk shall docket the appeal, note thereon the date and time of the filing, affix the docket number assigned to the appeal and send a copy to the judicial review council and to each appearing party.

Historical Note

Derivation:
    1978 P.B. (1986–97), § 4150
    1978 P.B. § 3168
New rule effective October 1, 1979.

§ 74-2. Papers to Be Filed

The respondent judge shall submit, as set forth in Section 61-5, to the appellate clerk at the time the appeal is filed:

(a)   a copy of the decision of the judicial review council appealed from, and

(b)   the submissions required by Section 63-4.

Historical Note

Derivation:
    1978 P.B. (1986–97), § 4151
    1978 P.B., § 3169
New rule effective October 1, 1979.

§ 74-3. Costs and Security Not Required

Statutory fees, taxable costs and the requirement for furnishing security for costs are waived.

Historical Note

Derivation:
    1978 P.B. (1986–87), § 4152
    1978 P.B., § 3170
New rule effective October 1, 1979.

§ 74-4. Decision of Council; Remand by Supreme Court

The judicial review council shall state its decision in writing on the issues of the case and, if there are factual issues, the factual basis for its decision. The judicial review council shall state in its decision its conclusion as to each claim of law raised by the parties. If the supreme court deems it necessary to the proper disposition of the cause, it may remand the case to the judicial review council for clarification of the basis for its decision.

Historical Note

Derivation:
    1978 P.B. (1986–97), § 4153
    1978 P.B., § 3171
New rule effective October 1, 1979.

§ 74-5. Parties

The parties shall be referred to as the judicial review council and the respondent.

Historical Note

Derivation:
    1978 P.B. (1986–97), § 4154
    1978 P.B., § 3172
New rule effective October 1, 1979.

§ 74-6. Applicability of Rules

All proceedings subsequent to the filing of the appeal shall be governed by the rules applicable to appeals and appeals from administrative agencies.

Historical Note

Derivation:
    1978 P.B. (1986–97), § 4155
    1978 P.B., § 3173
New rule effective October 1, 1979.
The reference to the finding system was omitted effective October 1, 1980.

§ 74-7. Action on Recommendation when No Appeal

In the event that the respondent judge does not appeal a decision by the judicial review council to recommend to the supreme court such judge's suspension or removal, the council shall, at the expiration of the time to appeal, forward to the appellate clerk a certified copy of its decision together with those parts of the record and transcript as it deems necessary for a proper consideration of its recommendation.

The appellate clerk shall note the date of filing on the documents, notify the chief justice that they have been filed, and prepare sufficient copies for the members of the supreme court. That court shall, as soon as practicable, review the filed documents and render a decision on the recommendation of the council.

Historical Note

Derivation:
    1978 P.B. (1986–97), § 4156
    1978 P.B., § 3174
New rule effective October 1, 1979.

§ 74-8. Initiation of Action by Supreme Court

In the event that the supreme court, on its own motion, wishes to initiate proceedings against a judge, it shall refer the matter to the judicial review council or, if the judge to be investigated is a member of that council, to a committee of three state referees for investigation and hearing.

The council or the committee shall render a decision pursuant to Section 74-4 and forward a copy of its decision to the respondent judge and to the appellate clerk.

The decision may be appealed by the respondent judge pursuant to the provisions of this chapter. If the respondent judge fails to appeal within the time provided, the decision shall be final, unless it was rendered by a committee or contains a recommendation for suspension or removal of the judge, in which case, at the expiration of the time to appeal, the council or committee shall file pertinent parts of the record and transcript with the appellate clerk pursuant to Section 74-7 and the supreme court shall render a decision thereon.

Historical Note

Derivation:
    1978 P.B. (1986–97), § 4157
    1978 P.B., § 3175
New rule effective October 1, 1979.

CHAPTER 75

APPEALS FROM COUNCIL ON PROBATE JUDICIAL CONDUCT

§ 75-1. Time to Take; Form; Filing; Costs

Appeals from decisions of the council on probate judicial conduct to reprimand or censure shall be taken within twenty days from the date that notice of the reprimand or censure is received by the respondent judge.

The appeal shall be directed to and filed with the supreme court, and shall be accompanied by a certification that a copy thereof has been served on the chair or secretary of the council on probate judicial conduct in accordance with the provisions of Section 62-7. No fee shall be required to be paid. The appellate clerk shall docket the appeal, note on the form the date and time of the filing, affix the docket number assigned to the appeal and send a copy to the council on probate judicial conduct and to each appearing party.

Historical Note

Derivation:
  1978 P.B. (1986–97), § 4159
  1978 P.B., § 3177
New rule effective June 7, 1983.
The first appeal under this chapter is Council on Probate Judicial Conduct re Council on Probate Judicial Conduct re Kinsella, 193 Conn. 180, 476 A.2d 1041 (1984).

§ 75-2. Papers to Be Filed

The appellant shall submit, as set forth in Section 62-7, to the appellate clerk at the time the appeal is filed:

(a) a copy of the decision of the council on probate judicial conduct appealed from, and

(b) the submissions required by Section 63-4.

Historical Note

Derivation:

1978 P.B. (1986–97), § 4160
1978 P.B., § 3178
New rule effective June 7, 1983.

§ 75-3. Costs and Security Not Required

Statutory fees, taxable costs and the requirement for furnishing security for costs are waived.

Historical Note

Derivation:
    1978 P.B. (1986–97), § 4161
    1978 P.B., § 3179
New rule effective June 7, 1983.

§ 75-4. Decision of Council; Remand by Supreme Court

The council on probate judicial conduct shall state its decision in writing on the issues of the case. Within two weeks of receipt of notice of an appeal, the council shall file a finding of fact and conclusions therefrom. If the supreme court deems it necessary to the proper disposition of the cause, it may remand the case to the council on probate judicial conduct for clarification of the basis of its decision.

Historical Note

Derivation:
    1978 P.B., § 4162
    1978 P.B., § 3180
New rule effective June 7, 1983.

§ 75-5. Parties

The parties shall be referred to as the council on probate judicial conduct and the respondent.

Historical Note

Derivation:
    1978 P.B. (1986–97), § 4163
    1978 P.B., § 3181
New rule effective June 7, 1983.

§ 75-6. Applicability of Rules

All proceedings subsequent to the filing of the appeal shall be governed by the rules applicable to appeals and appeals from administrative agencies.

Historical Note

Derivation:
    1978 P.B. (1986–97), § 4164
    1978 P.B., § 3183
New rule effective June 7, 1983.

CHAPTER 76

APPEALS IN WORKERS' COMPENSATION CASES

§ 76-1. Applicability of Rules

Except as otherwise noted in Sections 76-2 through 76-6, the practice and procedure for appeals to the appellate court (1) from a decision of the compensation review board (board), or (2) from a decision of a workers' compensation commissioner acting pursuant to General Statutes § 31-290a(b) (§ 31-290a commissioner), shall conform to the rules of practice governing other appeals.

Historical Note

Derivation:
    1978 P.B. (1992–97), § 4165
    1978 P.B. (1983–97), § 2015
The reference to the two types of appeal was added in 1996.

Effective October 1, 1980, appeals were taken from the compensation review division of the agency to the Appellate Session of the Superior Court pursuant to §§ 1080–87. Appellate Court §§ 2015–22 displaced these rules effective August 23, 1983.

This section was adopted effective August 23, 1983 and is substantially the same as predecessor § 1081, adopted effective October 1, 1980.

Cross References
C.G.S.A. § 31-301b

AUTHORS' COMMENTS

Since appellate rules are entirely different from trial court rules, and since these appeals are no longer heard by the trial court, pre-1980 decisions on trial court procedure in this area are probably obsolete.

In Cleveland v. U.S. Printing Ink, Inc., 218 Conn. 181, 184–85, 588 A.2d 194, 196–97 (1991), the Supreme Court held in dictum that only final judgments can be appealed under C.G.S.A. § 31-301b even though the statute states no such limitation. The Supreme Court relied on this section for its holding. But how can a court rule impose a finality requirement not found in the statute?

The failure of the commissioner to address issues directed in a remand from the Supreme Court meant there was no final judgment in Matey v. Estate of Dember, 85 Conn.App. 198, 856 A.2d 511 (2004). Concerning when the decisions of the Board are appealable, see Byars v. Whyco Chromium Co., 33 Conn.App.

667, 637 A.2d 805 (1994); Ericson v. Perreault Spring and Equipment Co., 38 Conn.App. 71, 658 A.2d 982 (1995), and Mulligan v. F.S. Elec., 231 Conn. 529, 534 n.4, 651 A.2d 254, 257 n.4 (1994). Fantasia v. Tony Pantano Mason Contractors, Inc., 54 Conn.App. 194, 732 A.2d 822, cert. denied, 250 Conn. 927, 738 A.2d 655 (1999), concerns an unsuccessful attempt to bypass the Board.

A late appeal was allowed in Dowling v. Slotnik, 244 Conn. 781, 712 A.2d 396 (1998). Note, however, that the twenty-day period set forth in C.G.S.A. § 31-301(a) to appeal to the compensation review board is jurisdictional. Stec v. Raymark Industries, Inc., 299 Conn. 346, 10 A.3d 1 (2010).

§ 76-2. Filing Appeal

The appeal shall be filed with the appellate clerk accompanied by a certification that a copy thereof has been served on each party of record and on the board or the § 31-290a commissioner, as appropriate, in accordance with the provisions of Section 62-7.

The appellate clerk shall stamp or note on the appeal the date and time of filing, shall docket the appeal, shall affix to the appeal the docket number assigned to it, and shall send one copy to the board or the § 31-290a commissioner, as appropriate, and one copy to each appearing party.

Historical Note

Derivation:
    1978 P.B. (1992–97), § 4165.1
    1978 P.B. (1983–92), § 2016
Adopted effective August 23, 1983 and substantially the same as predecessor § 1082, adopted effective October 1, 1980.

§ 76-3. Record; Preparation of Case File; Exhibits

Within ten days of the issuance of notice of the filing of an appeal, the board or the § 31-290a commissioner, as appropriate, shall cause to be filed with the appellate clerk two complete copies of the case file. No omissions may be made from the case file except upon the authorization of the appellate clerk. Each document of the case file must be numbered and the file must include a table of contents listing each item entered in the file according to its number.

All exhibits before the board or the § 31-290a commissioner are deemed exhibits on appeal. The appellate clerk shall notify the board or the § 31-290a commissioner of the exhibits required by the court. It shall be the responsibility of the board or the § 31-290a commissioner to transmit those exhibits promptly to the appellate clerk.

§ 76-3. Preparation of Case File; Exhibits

Within ten days of the issuance of notice of the filing of an appeal, the board or the § 31-290a commissioner, as appropriate, shall cause to be filed with the appellate clerk one complete copy of the case file. No omissions may be made from the case file except upon the authorization of the appellate clerk. Each document of the case file must be numbered, and the file must include a table of contents listing each item entered in the file according to its number.

All exhibits before the board or the § 31-290a commissioner are deemed exhibits on appeal. The appellate clerk shall notify the board or the § 31-290a commissioner of the exhibits required by the court. It shall be the responsibility of the board or the § 31-290a commissioner to transmit those exhibits promptly to the appellate clerk.

Historical Note

Derivation:
   1978 P.B. (1992–97), § 4165.2
   1978 P.B. (1983–92), § 2017
Adopted effective August 23, 1983 and substantially the same as predecessor § 1083, adopted effective October 1, 1980.

§ 76-4. Fees and Costs

On appeals from the board or the § 31-290a commissioner, or upon the reservation of a workers' compensation case by the compensation review board, no entry fee shall be paid, and no costs shall be taxed in favor of either party provided that if an appeal is found by the court either to be frivolous or to be taken for the purpose of vexation or delay, the court may tax costs in its discretion against the person so taking the appeal.

Historical Note

Derivation:
   1978 P.B. (1992–97), § 4165.4
   1978 P.B. (1983–92), § 2019
Adopted effective August 23, 1983 and substantially the same as predecessor § 1085, adopted effective October 1, 1980.

§ 76-5. Reservation of Case

When, in any case arising under the provisions of this chapter, the Compensation Review Board is of the opinion that the decision involves principles of law which are not free from reasonable doubt and which public interest requires shall be determined by the Appellate Court, in order that a definite rule be established applicable to future cases, the Compensation Review Board may, on its own motion and without any agreement or act of the parties or their counsel, reserve such case for the opinion of the Appellate Court. Upon a reservation so made, no costs or fees shall be taxed in favor of either party. Upon the filing of such a reservation, the question shall come before the Appellate Court as though an appeal had been taken, and that court shall thereupon reserve the case for the opinion of the Supreme Court in the manner herein indicated; but if, in the opinion of the Appellate Court, the principles of law involved in the decision are in fact free from reasonable doubt and the public interest does not in fact require that they be determined by the Supreme Court, the Appellate Court may, in its discretion, hear and determine the controversy as in other cases. Any reservation under this rule may be transferred to the Supreme Court on its own motion pursuant to General Statutes § 51-199 (c) or on the motion of any party pursuant to Section 65-2.

Historical Note

Derivation:
    1978 P.B. (1992–97), § 4165.5
    1978 P.B. (1983–92), § 2020
This section was entirely rewritten, presumably for clarity, effective January 1, 2000.

Adopted effective August 23, 1983 and substantially the same as predecessor § 1086, adopted effective October 1, 1980.

AUTHORS' COMMENTS

C.G.S.A. § 31-324 generally requires the Appellate Court to reserve these cases for Supreme Court review. Dixon v. United Illuminating Co., 36 Conn.App. 150, 649 A.2d 538 (1994). The merits of the controversy were resolved in Id., 232 Conn. 758, 657 A.2d 601 (1995). See also Barton v. Ducci Elec. Contractors, Inc., 248 Conn. 793, 730 A.2d 1149 (1999).

§ 76-6. Definitions

With regard to appeals from the board or the § 31-290a commissioner, references in the rules of appellate procedure to trial court or trial judge shall, where applicable, be deemed to mean the individuals who comprised the board which rendered the decision from which the appeal was taken, or the § 31-290a commissioner, as appropriate.

Historical Note

Derivation:
    1978 P.B. (1992–97), § 4165.6
    1978 P.B. (1983–92), § 2021
Adopted effective August 23, 1983 and substantially the same as predecessor § 1087, adopted effective October 1, 1980.

CHAPTER 77

REVIEW OF COURT CLOSURE ORDER

§ 77-1. Expedited Review of an Order Concerning Court Closure, or an Order That Seals or Limits the Disclosure of Files, Affidavits, Documents or Other Material

(a) Except as provided in subsection (b), any person affected by a court order which prohibits the public or any person from attending any session of court or any order that seals or limits the disclosure of files, affidavits, documents or other material on file with the court or filed in connection with a court proceeding, may seek review of such order by filing an original and fifteen copies of a petition for review with the appellate court within seventy-two hours after the issuance of the order. The petition shall fully comply with Sections 66-2 and 66-3. The petition shall not exceed ten pages in length, exclusive of the appendix, except with special permission of the appellate court. An appendix containing the information or complaint, the answer, all motions pertaining to the matter, the opinion or orders of the trial court sought to be reviewed, a list of all parties with the names, addresses, telephone and facsimile numbers and, if applicable, the juris number of their counsel, the names of all judges who participated in the case, and a transcript order acknowledgment form (JD-ES-38), shall be attached to each copy of the petition.

Any person filing a petition for review pursuant to this rule shall serve a copy of the petition and appendix upon (1) all parties to the case and (2) any nonparty who sought the closure order or order sealing or limiting disclosure by facsimile or hand delivery on the same day as the petition is filed. Any party or nonparty who sought such order may file a written response within ninety-six hours after the filing of the petition for review. Failure to file a written response shall not preclude that party or nonparty who sought the order under review from participating in the hearing on the petition.

The filing of any petition for review of a court order which prohibits the public or any person from attending any session of court shall stay the order until the final determination of the review. The filing of any petition for review of an order that seals

313

or limits the disclosure of files, affidavits, documents or other material on file with the court shall not stay the order during the review.

The appellate court shall hold an expedited hearing on any petition for review on the fifth business day next following the day upon which the certificate of completion provided for by Section 63-8(c) has been filed with the appellate clerk. After such hearing the appellate court may affirm, modify or vacate the order reviewed.

(b) This section shall not apply to court orders concerning any session of court conducted pursuant to General Statutes §§ 46b-11, 46b-49, 46b-122, 54-76h, and any order issued pursuant to a rule that seals or limits the disclosure of any affidavit in support of an arrest warrant or any other provision of the General Statutes under which the court is authorized to close proceedings.

Historical Note

Derivation:
 1978 P.B. (1992–97), § 4166
 1978 P.B. (1983–92), § 2022

The reference to sealing and disclosure limitation orders in the caption and the text were added effective January 1, 2000. The second paragraph of (a) was added in 1996.

Section (a) was completely revised effective October 1, 1992 to provide for review by motion rather than appeal.

Adopted effective August 23, 1983 and substantially the same as predecessor old § 1088. Subsection (a) was adopted effective October 1, 1981 and subsection (b) was added effective 1, 1982.

AUTHORS' COMMENTS

For decisions under this rule, see State v. Manfredi, 4 Conn.App. 247, 493 A.2d 242 (1985), in which the court sat en banc; and State v. Kelly, 45 Conn.App. 142, 695 A.2d 1 (1997), and Bank of New York v. Bell, 120 Conn.App. 837, 993 A.2d 1022, cert. dismissed, 298 Conn. 917, 4 A.3d 1225 (2010).

This section does not apply when the trial judge denies a motion for closure, State v. Gates, 38 Conn.Supp. 546, 453 A.2d 781 (App. Sess. 1982).

This rule includes orders that parties may appear anonymously. Vargas v. Doe, 96 Conn.App. 399, 900 A.2d 525, cert. denied, 280 Conn. 923, 908 A.2d 546 (2006).

If a closing order is not covered by this section (such as in family and juvenile cases, see subsection (b)), there apparently is no general right to appeal under § 61-1. Wendt v. Wendt, A.C. 16592 (appeal of closing in family case dismissed January 15, 1997).

Doe v. Hartford Roman Catholic Diocesan Corp., 51 Conn.App. 287, 721 A.2d 154 (1998), discusses P.B. §§ 11-20 and 13-5 (sealing files and protective orders) and expedites appellate review from the former but not the latter.

Query whether 72 hours is the same thing as three days. To be safe, an appeal on the third day should be taken before the time of the ruling.

§ 77-2. Sealing Orders; Treatment of Lodged Records

(a) When, by order of the trial court or by operation of a statute, a trial court file is sealed or is subject to limited disclosure, all filings with the appellate clerk in that matter shall be treated similarly unless otherwise ordered by the court having appellate jurisdiction. Any sealing or limitation on disclosure ordered by the trial court or required by operation of statute as to any affidavit, document or other material filed in the trial court shall continue throughout the appellate process.

(b) If a claim is raised on appeal challenging the denial of a motion to seal or limit disclosure pursuant to section 7-4B(d), a lodged record shall remain conditionally under seal in the court having appellate jurisdiction and shall be treated as an exhibit pursuant to the provisions of Section 68-1.

Historical Note

This rule is new effective January 1, 2004.

CHAPTER 78

REVIEW OF GRAND JURY RECORD OR FINDING ORDER

§ 78-1. Review of an Order concerning Disclosure of Grand Jury
   Record or Finding

§ 78-1. Review of an Order concerning Disclosure of Grand Jury Record or Finding

Any person aggrieved by an order of a panel or an investigatory grand jury pursuant to General Statutes § 54-47g may seek review of such order by filing a petition for review with the appellate court within seventy-two hours after the issuance of the order. The filing of any such petition for review shall stay the order until the final determination of the petition. The appellate court shall hold an expedited hearing on such petition. After such hearing, the appellate court may affirm, modify or vacate the order reviewed.

Historical Note

Derivation:
   1978 P.B. (1992–97), § 4166A
   1978 P.B. (1989–92), § 2037
This section was amended effective October 1, 1992 to provide for review by motion rather than by petition.
The section was new effective August 1, 1989.

AUTHORS' COMMENTS

The Appellate Court has jurisdiction to review the denial of disclosure of the investigatory report and the suspect is an aggrieved party even though the state made the request. In re Judicial Inquiry No. 2005-02, 104 Conn.App. 398, 934 A.2d 248 (2007), judgment rev'd on other grounds, 293 Conn. 247, 977 A.2d 166 (2009).

CHAPTER 78A

REVIEW OF ORDERS CONCERNING RELEASE ON BAIL

§ 78a-1. Petition for Review of Order Concerning Release on Bail

§ 78a-1. Petition for Review of Order Concerning Release on Bail

Any accused person or the state, aggrieved by an order of the superior court concerning release, may petition the appellate court for review of such order. Any such petition shall have precedence over any other matter before the appellate court and any hearing ordered by the court shall be held expeditiously with reasonable notice.

Petitions for review of bail must conform to the requirements for motions for review set forth in Section 66-6 and are subject to transfer to the supreme court pursuant to Section 65-3.

Historical Note

Entirely new Chapter effective January 1, 2006.

Cross Reference

Conn. Gen. Stat. Anno. § 54-63g. See State v. Crosby, 125 Conn.App. 775, 781–82, 9 A.3d 794, 798 (2011).

CHAPTER 79

APPEALS IN JUVENILE MATTERS [REPEALED]*

§ 79-1. Time to Take; Form; Filing; Costs [Repealed]

[Repealed effective February 1, 2012; see new Chapter 79a]

§ 79-2. Clerk's Duties [Repealed]

[Repealed effective February 1, 2012; see new Chapter 79a]

§ 79-3. Inspection of Records [Repealed]

[Repealed effective February 1, 2012; see new Chapter 79a]

§ 79-4. Hearings; Confidentiality [Repealed]

[Repealed effective February 1, 2012; see new Chapter 79a]

§ 79-5. Briefs [Repealed]

[Repealed effective February 1, 2012; see new Chapter 79a]

---

*Repealed effective February 1, 2012; see new Chapter 79a.

CHAPTER 79A

APPEALS IN CHILD PROTECTION MATTERS

§ 79a-1. Child Protection Appeals Defined

Child protection appeals in juvenile matters include all appeals from judgments in all proceedings concerning uncared for, neglected or abused children and youth within this state, termination of parental rights of children committed to a state agency, petitions for transfers, removal or reinstatement of guardianship and contested matters involving termination of parental rights or removal of guardian transferred or appealed from the probate court.

Historical Note

New Chapter replacing Chapter 79 effective February 1, 2012.

AUTHORS' COMMENTS

The 2012 Commentary to this rule notes that this section includes appeals from orders of temporary custody, citing In re Shamika F., 256 Conn. 383, 773 A.2d 347 (2001).

This chapter was enacted in 2012 to streamline child-protection appeals so that the subject children could secure a permanent placement without delay.

§ 79a-2. Time to Appeal

(a) General Provisions

Unless a different period is provided by statute, appeals from judgments of the superior court in child protection matters shall be taken within twenty days from the issuance of notice of the rendition of the decision or judgment from which the appeal is taken. The judge who tried the case may, for good cause shown, extend the time limit provided for filing the appeal. In no event shall the trial judge extend the time for filing the appeal to a date which is more than twenty days from the expiration date of the initial appeal period. Where a motion for extension of the period of time within which to appeal has been filed at least ten days before expiration of the time limit sought to be extended, and such motion is denied, the party seeking to appeal shall have no less than ten days from issuance of notice of the denial of the motion for extension in which to file the appeal.

(b) When appeal period begins

If notice of the judgment or decision is given in open court, the appeal period shall begin on that day. If notice of the judgment or decision is given only by mail, the appeal period shall begin on the day that notice of the judgment or decision is mailed to counsel by the clerk for juvenile matters. The failure to give notice of judgment to a nonappearing party shall not affect the running of the appeal period.

(c) How a new appeal period is created

If a motion is filed within the appeal period that, if granted, would render the judgment or decision ineffective, then a new twenty day appeal period for filing the appeal shall begin on the day that notice of the ruling is given on the last such outstanding motion. Such motions include, but are not limited to, motions that seek: the opening or setting aside of the judgment; a new trial; reargument of the judgment or decision; or any alteration of the terms of the judgment. Motions that do not give rise to a new appeal period include those that seek: clarification or articulation, as opposed to alteration, of the terms of the judgment or decision; a written or transcribed statement of the trial court's decision; or reargument or reconsideration of a motion listed in this paragraph.

If, within the appeal period, any application is filed, pursuant to Section 79a-4, seeking waiver of fees, costs and security or appointment of counsel, a new twenty day appeal period or statutory period for filing the appeal is not created. If a party files, pursuant to Section 66-6, a motion for review of the denial of any such application, a new appeal period shall begin on the day that notice of the ruling is given on the motion for review.

(d) What may be appealed during new appeal period

If a new appeal period is created under Section 79a-2 (c), the new appeal period may be used for appealing the original judgment or decision and/or for appealing any order that gave rise to the new appeal period. Such period may also be used for amending an existing appeal pursuant to Section 61-9 to challenge the ruling that gave rise to the new appeal period. Rulings on applications for waiver of fees, costs and security or motions for appointment of counsel may not be appealed during the new appeal period but may be challenged by motion for review in accordance with Section 66-6.

(e) Limitation of time to appeal

Unless a new appeal period is created pursuant to Section 79a-2 (c), the time to take a child protection appeal shall not be extended past forty days (the original twenty days plus one twenty day extension for appellate review) from the date of issuance of notice of the rendition of the judgment or decision.

Historical Note

The second, third and fourth sentences of (a) were added effective August 1, 2014.

AUTHORS' COMMENTS

Subsection (e), which limits the appeal period to 40 days, is consistent with P.B. § 35a-21(c).

§ 79a-3. Filing of the Appeal

(a) General Provisions

If counsel of record files an appeal with the clerk for juvenile matters, counsel of record shall then file with the appellate clerk two copies of the endorsed appeal form, accompanied by those papers required by Section 63-4, within ten days of the filing of the original appeal form. All filings shall contain a certification in accordance with Section 62-7 that a copy has been served on all counsel or self-represented parties of record.

(b) Appeal by indigent party

If a trial attorney who has provided representation to an indigent party through the Division of Public Defender Services declines to pursue an appeal and the indigent party expressly wishes to appeal, the trial attorney shall within twenty days of the decision or judgment simultaneously file with the court before which the matter was heard a motion for an additional twenty day extension of time to appeal, a sworn application signed by the indigent party for appointment of an appellate review attorney and a waiver of fees, costs and expenses, including the cost of an expedited transcript, and shall immediately request an expedited transcript from the court reporter in accordance with Section 79a-5, the cost of which shall be paid for by the Division of Public Defender Services.

Any party who is indigent who wishes to appeal and was not provided with representation by the Division of Public Defender Services during the proceeding which resulted in the decision or judgment from which an appeal is being sought shall, within twenty days of the decision or judgment, simultaneously file with the court before which the matter was heard a motion for an additional twenty day extension of time to appeal, a sworn application signed by the indigent party for appointment of an appellate review attorney and a waiver of fees, costs, and expenses, including the cost of an expedited transcript. The indigent party shall immediately request an expedited transcript from the court reporter in accordance with Section 79a-5, the cost of which shall be paid for by the Division of Public Defender Services.

(c) **Review by the Division of Public Defender Services**

(1) If the appellate review attorney determines that there is merit to an appeal, that attorney shall file the appeal in accordance with Section 79a-3 (a).

(2) If the reviewing attorney determines that there is no merit to an appeal, that attorney shall make this decision known to the judicial authority, to the party and to the Division of Public Defender Services at the earliest possible moment. The reviewing attorney shall inform the party, by letter, of the balance of the time remaining to appeal as a self-represented party or to secure counsel who may file an appearance to represent the party on appeal at the party's own expense. A copy of the letter shall be sent to the clerk for juvenile matters forthwith.

(d) **Duties of clerk for juvenile matters for cases on appeal**

At the time of the filing of the appeal, the clerk for juvenile matters shall endorse the appeal form and return a copy of the endorsed appeal form to the filing party, send a copy of the endorsed appeal form and the case information form to the commissioner of children and families, to the petitioner upon whose application the proceedings in the superior court were instituted, unless such party is the appellant, to any person or agency having custody of any child who is a subject of the proceeding, the Division of Public Defender Services, the appellate clerk and to all other interested persons; and if the addresses of any such persons do not appear of record, such juvenile clerk shall call the matter to the attention of a judge of the superior court who shall make such an order of notice as such judge deems advisable.

AUTHORS' COMMENTS

Subsection (d) is derived from P.B. § 79-2. The balance of this section was new in 2012.

An *Anders* brief is not required to support a determination pursuant to subsection (c)(2) that there is not merit to an appeal. In re Isaiah J., 140 Conn.App. 626, 59 A.3d 842, cert. denied, 308 Conn. 926, 64 A.3d 333 (2013).

§ 79a-4. Waiver of Fees, Costs and Security

(a) Any written application to the court for appointment of an appellate review attorney or the waiver of fees, costs and expenses must be personally signed by the indigent party under oath and include a financial affidavit reciting facts concerning the applicant's financial status. The judicial authority shall act without a hearing on the application. If the court is satisfied that the applicant is indigent and has a statutory right to the appointment of an appellate review attorney or a statutory right to appeal without payment of fees, costs and expenses, the court may without a hearing: (1) waive payment by the applicant of fees specified by statute and of taxable costs, and (2) order that the necessary expenses of reviewing or prosecuting the appeal be paid by the Division of Public Defender Services in accordance with Section 79a-3 (c). If the court is not satisfied that the applicant is indigent and has a statutory right to the appointment of an appellate review attorney or a statutory right to appeal without payment of fees, costs and expenses, then an immediate hearing shall be scheduled for the application. If an application is untimely filed, the court may deny the application without hearing. The court may not consider the relative merits of a proposed appeal in acting upon an application pursuant to this section.

(b) The filing of the application for the appointment of an appellate review attorney or waiver of fees, costs and expenses will not extend the appeal period. A denial of the application may be addressed solely by motion for review under Section 66-6. See Section 79a-2 (c).

§ 79a-5. Ordering Transcripts

Transcripts in child protection appeals and in cases reviewed by the Division of Public Defender Services shall be ordered expedited and delivered to the ordering party no later than the close of the fifth business day following the date the order is placed.

§ 79a-6. Format and Time for Filing Briefs (Applicable to appeals filed before July 1, 2013)

Briefs shall be prepared and submitted in accordance with

Chapter 67 of these rules except that the time for filing briefs shall be strictly observed and abbreviated as set forth below.

(a) Except as otherwise ordered, the appellant's brief shall be filed within forty days after the delivery of the transcript ordered by the appellant. In cases where no transcript is required or the transcript has been received by the appellant prior to the filing of the appeal, the appellant's brief shall be filed within forty days of the filing of the appeal.

(b) Except as otherwise ordered, the brief of the appellee shall be filed within thirty days after the filing of the appellant's brief or the delivery date of the portions of the transcript ordered only by that appellee, whichever is later.

(c) Counsel for the minor child and/or counsel for the guardian ad litem shall, within ten days of the filing of the appellee's brief, file either: (1) a brief, (2) a statement adopting the brief of either the appellant or an appellee, or (3) a detailed statement that the factual or legal issues on appeal do not implicate the child's interests.

(d) The appellant may file a reply brief within ten days of the filing of the appellee's brief.

(e) Except as otherwise ordered, the case shall be deemed ready for assignment by the court after the filing of the appellee's brief.

(f) The unexcused failure to file briefs in accordance with this schedule may result in a dismissal of the appeal pursuant to Section 85-1, a refusal of the court to accept the late brief and/or an assignment of the case without the delinquent brief.

§ 79a-6. Format and Time for Filing Briefs and Appendices (Applicable to appeals filed on or after July 1, 2013)

Briefs and appendices shall be prepared and submitted in accordance with Chapter 67 of these rules except that the time for filing briefs and appendices shall be strictly observed and abbreviated as set forth below.

(a) Except as otherwise ordered, the appellant's brief and appendix shall be filed within forty days after the delivery of the transcript ordered by the appellant. In cases where no transcript is required or the transcript has been received by the appellant prior to the filing of the appeal, the appellant's brief and appendix shall be filed within forty days of the filing of the appeal.

(b) Except as otherwise ordered, the brief and appendix of the appellee shall be filed within thirty days after the filing of the appellant's brief or the delivery date of the portions of the transcript ordered only by that appellee, whichever is later.

(c) Counsel for the minor child and/or counsel for the guardian ad litem shall, within ten days of the filing of the appellee's brief, file either: (1) a brief, (2) a statement adopting the brief of either the appellant or an appellee, or (3) a detailed statement that the factual or legal issues on appeal do not implicate the child's interests.

(d)   The appellant may file a reply brief within ten days of the filing of the appellee's brief.

(e)   Except as otherwise ordered, the case shall be deemed ready for assignment by the court after the filing of the appellee's brief and appendix.

(f)   The unexcused failure to file briefs and appendices in accordance with this schedule may result in a dismissal of the appeal pursuant to Section 85-1, a refusal of the court to accept the late brief and/or an assignment of the case without the delinquent brief.

§ 79a-7. Motions for Extension of Time

Motions for extension of time filed in the appellate court shall be filed in accordance with Section 66-1 and, if filed, shall be presented to a judge of the appellate court for determination. Such motions may be granted only for good cause shown.

AUTHORS' COMMENTS

The 2012 commentary provides that this section applies only to motions for extension filed in the Appellate Court. It does not apply to such motions in the Supreme Court. Note that what constitutes good cause for extensions in other appeals probably will not suffice in child protection appeals. Be prepared to adhere to the deadlines set out in the Rules.

§ 79a-8. Docketing Child Protection Appeals for Assignment

The supreme court and appellate court may assign child protection matters without the case appearing on the printed docket. See Sections 69-1 and 69-2.

Notwithstanding the provisions of Section 69-3, child protection appeals shall ordinarily take precedence for assignment for oral argument.

§ 79a-9. Oral Argument (Applicable to appeals filed before July 1, 2013)

(a)   Oral argument will be allowed as of right except as provided in subsection (b) of this rule.

(b)   In child protection appeals as defined by Section 79a-1 where: (1) the dispositive issue or set of issues has been recently authoritatively decided; or (2) the facts and legal arguments are adequately presented in the briefs and record and the decisional process would not be significantly aided by oral argument, notice will be sent to counsel of record that the case will be decided on the briefs and record only. This notice will be sent after all briefs and appendices have been filed. Any party may request argument by letter addressed to the appellate clerk stating briefly the reasons why oral argument is appropriate and shall do so within seven days of the issuance of the court's notice. After receipt and consideration of such a request, the court will either assign the case for oral argument or assign the case for disposition without oral argument, as it deems appropriate.

(c)　In matters involving parties who are incarcerated and self-represented, oral argument may be conducted by videoconference upon direction of the court in its discretion.

§ 79a-9. Oral Argument (Applicable to appeals filed on or after July 1, 2013)

(a)　Oral argument will be allowed as of right except as provided in subsection (b) of this rule.

(b)　In child protection appeals as defined by Section 79a-1 where: (1) the dispositive issue or set of issues has been recently authoritatively decided; or (2) the facts and legal arguments are adequately presented in the briefs and the decisional process would not be significantly aided by oral argument, notice will be sent to counsel of record that the case will be decided on the briefs and record only. This notice will be sent after all briefs and appendices have been filed. Any party may request argument by letter addressed to the appellate clerk stating briefly the reasons why oral argument is appropriate and shall do so within seven days of the issuance of the court's notice. After receipt and consideration of such a request, the court will either assign the case for oral argument or assign the case for disposition without oral argument, as it deems appropriate.

(c)　In matters involving parties who are incarcerated and self-represented, oral argument may be conducted by videoconference upon direction of the court in its discretion.

AUTHORS' COMMENTS

The 2012 commentary indicates that video conferencing will not automatically occur where a pro se party is incarcerated.

§ 79a-10. Submission without Oral Argument on Request of Parties

With the permission of the court, counsel of record may, before or after a case has been assigned for a hearing, submit the case for decision on the record and briefs only, without oral argument. No request for submission without oral argument will be granted unless the requesting party certifies that all other parties agree to waive oral argument. This rule applies only to counsel of record who have filed a brief or joined in the brief of another party.

§ 79a-11. Official Release Date

A judgment in child protection appeals shall be deemed to have been rendered on the date an opinion or memorandum decision appears in the Connecticut Law Journal; except that if an opinion or memorandum decision is issued by slip opinion, the official release date is the date indicated in the slip opinion, and the parties shall be notified and sent the opinion or memorandum decision by the reporter of judicial decisions via electronic mail. If any of the parties who participated in the appeal has not provided the reporter of judicial decisions with an electronic mail address, then the slip opinion or memorandum decision shall be mailed to the parties by the appellate clerk on the date indicated in the slip opinion.

If a judgment in a child protection appeal is given by oral announcement from the bench, then the judgment shall be deemed to have been rendered on the date the oral announcement is made.

The official release date of decisions upon motions, petitions and of orders of the court shall be the date the appellate clerk issues notice to the parties.

See Sections 71-1 and 71-4 and General Statutes §§ 51-213 and 51-215a.

AUTHORS' COMMENTS

The 2012 commentary notes that slip opinions generally will be sent by email to the parties.

§ 79a-12. Inspection of Records

The records and papers of any juvenile matter shall be open for inspection only to counsel of record and to others having a proper interest therein only upon order of the court. The name of the child or youth involved in any appeal from a juvenile matter shall not appear on the record of the appeal.

AUTHORS' COMMENTS

This rule was formerly P.B. § 79-3.

§ 79a-13. Hearings; Confidentiality

(a) For the purpose of maintaining confidentiality, upon the hearing of an appeal from a juvenile matter, the court may exclude any person from the court whose presence is unnecessary.

(b) All proceedings shall be conducted in a manner that will preserve the anonymity of the child or youth.

AUTHORS' COMMENTS

This rule was formerly P.B. § 79-4.

§ 79a-14. Motions Filed with the Appellate Clerk

All motions filed with the appellate clerk in child protection matters shall include a statement on the first page by the moving party as to whether the other parties consent or object to the motion.

§ 79a-15. Applicability of Rules

The rules governing other appeals shall, so far as applicable, and to the extent they have not been modified by this chapter, be the rules for all proceedings in child protection appeals.

CHAPTER 80

APPEALS IN HABEAS CORPUS PROCEEDINGS FOLLOWING CONVICTION

§ 80-1. Certification to Appeal; Procedure on Appeal

§ 80-1. Certification to Appeal; Procedure on Appeal

In any habeas corpus proceeding where the party desiring to appeal is required by statute to petition the trial court for certification that a question is involved in the decision which ought to be reviewed by the appellate court, the petition for such certification shall be made to the judge who tried the case or, if such judge is unavailable, a judge of the superior court designated by the chief court administrator, within ten days after the case is decided. The appeal shall be filed within twenty days from the issuance of the notice of decision on the petition for certification, unless an application for waiver of fees, costs and security is filed pursuant to Section 63-6, in which event the appeal shall be filed within twenty days from the decision on the application.

Historical Note

Derivation:
  1978 P.B. (1992–97), § 4166C
  1978 P.B. (1983–92), § 2028
Adopted effective August 23, 1983.

AUTHORS' COMMENTS

The Supreme Court excused an inordinate delay in appealing in Ramos v. Commissioner of Correction, 248 Conn. 52, 727 A.2d 213 (1999); and in Parker v. Commissioner of Correction, 117 Conn.App. 727, 980 A.2d 930, cert. denied, 294 Conn. 917, 983 A.2d 851 (2009).

CHAPTER 81

APPEALS TO APPELLATE COURT BY CERTIFICATION FOR REVIEW IN ACCORDANCE WITH GENERAL STATUTES CHAPTERS 124 AND 440

§ 81-1. Petition; Where to File; Time to File; Service; Fee

(a) A petition for certification in accordance with chapters 124 and 440 of the General Statutes shall be filed by the party aggrieved by the decision of the trial court in the trial court within twenty days from the issuance of notice of the decision of the trial court. If within this period a timely motion is filed which, if granted, would render the trial court judgment ineffective, as, for example, a motion for a new trial, then the twenty days shall run from the issuance of notice of the decision thereon.

> The petitioner shall file the original and one copy of the petition with, and pay a filing fee to, the clerk of the trial court. The clerk shall endorse on the original petition the date and time of filing and the receipt, or waiver, of fees. The clerk shall return the original endorsed petition to the petitioner, who shall promptly file it, together with fifteen additional copies, with the appellate clerk. The petitioner shall serve a copy upon every other party in the manner set forth in Section 62-7.

(b) Any other party aggrieved by the decision of the trial court may file a cross petition within ten days of the filing of the original petition. The filing of cross petitions, including the payment of the fee, service pursuant to Section 62-7, the form of the cross petition and all subsequent proceedings shall be the same as though the cross petition were an original petition.

(c) The filing of a petition or cross petition by one party shall be deemed to be a filing on behalf of that party only.

Historical Note

Derivation:
1978 P.B. (1992–97), § 4142
1978 P.B. (1986–92), § 2030

This rule was adopted effective October 1, 1986 and was amended effective October 1, 1992 in the same way as § 4129. Subsection (b) was added in 2005.

Sections 4142 through 4142.4 apply to zoning, and since October 1, 1995, inland wetlands appeals. C.G.S.A. §§ 8-8(o), 8-9, 8-30a, 22a-43.

The fee for filing a petition is $75.00. C.G.S. § 52-259.

AUTHORS' COMMENTS

On petitions filed in the 2013-2014 fiscal year the Appellate Court granted 11 out of 32, about one-third; a few years ago the grant rate was around 50%. Unlike the Supreme Court, the Appellate Court does not limit certified appeals to issues stated in the order granting certification.

Two of the nine judges must vote in favor for a petition to be granted. C.G.S.A. § 8-8o. Failure to file a petition where required will result in dismissal of a appeal. Christensen v. Zoning Bd. of Appeals of Town of Avon, 78 Conn.App. 378, 827 A.2d 716 (2003).

This Chapter applies to affordable housing appeals (§ 8-30g). Ensign-Bickford Realty Corp. v. Zoning Com'n Town of Simsbury, 245 Conn. 257, 715 A.2d 701 (1998).

One complication, unresolved in Murphy v. Zoning Bd. of Appeals of City of Stamford, 86 Conn.App. 147, 860 A.2d 764 (2004), is what a petitioner should do if the trial court's decision needs to be articulated. The authors recommend pointing out the problem in the petition and assuring the Appellate Court that a motion for articulation will be filed if the petition is granted.

§ 81-2. Form of Petition

(a) A petition for certification shall contain the following sections in the order indicated here:

(1) A statement of the questions presented for review, expressed in the terms and circumstances of the case but without unnecessary detail.

(2) A statement of the basis for certification identifying the specific reasons why the appellate court should allow the extraordinary relief of certification. These reasons may include but are not limited to the following:

(A) The court below has decided a question of substance not theretofore determined by the supreme court or the appellate court or has decided it in a way probably not in accord with applicable decisions of the supreme court or the appellate court.

(B) The decision under review is in conflict with other decisions of the court below.

(C) The court below has so far departed from the accepted and usual course of judicial proceedings, or has so far sanctioned such a departure by any other court, as to call for an exercise of the appellate court's supervision.

(D) A question of great public importance is involved.

(3) A summary of the case containing the facts material to the consideration of the questions presented, reciting the disposition of the matter in the trial court, and describing specifically how the trial court decided the questions presented for review in the petition.

(4) A concise argument amplifying the reasons relied upon to support the petition. No separate memorandum of law in support of the petition will be accepted by the appellate clerk.

(5) An appendix containing the operative complaint, all briefs filed by all parties, the opinion or order of the trial court sought to be reviewed, a copy of the order on any motion which would stay or extend the time period for filing the petition, and a list of all parties to the appeal in the trial court with the names, addresses, telephone and facsimile numbers, and if applicable, the juris numbers of their counsel.

(b) The petition shall not exceed ten pages in length, exclusive of the appendix, except with special permission of the appellate clerk. The petition shall be typewritten and fully double spaced and shall not exceed three lines to the vertical inch or twenty-seven lines to the page. Footnotes and block quotations may be single spaced. Only the following two typefaces, of 12 point or larger size, are approved for use in petitions: arial and univers. Each page of a petition shall have as a minimum the following margins: top, 1 inch; left, 1 and 1/4 inch; right, 1/2 inch; and bottom, 1 inch. A certificate shall be attached to the signed, original petition, indicating that it is in compliance with all the provisions of this rule.

Cross References
Authors' suggested Form 3000.23-A

Historical Note

Derivation:
    Effective January 1, 2013, subsection (a)(5) was amended to add the operative complaint and all trial briefs.
    Effective January 1, 2004, the second to the last sentence was added to subsection (b).
    1978 P.B. (1992–97), § 4142.1
    1978 P.B. (1986–92), § 2031
Effective April 15, 2002, the last four sentences of (b) were added to make the petition conform more closely with briefs. The clerk's authority in the first sentence of (b) was added in 1999.
Effective September 3, 1996, the last two sentences of (b) were revised to stop evasion of the page limitations. This rule is new effective October 1, 1986.

AUTHORS' COMMENTS

Be sure to include a certification stating that the format of the petition complies with this section, P.B. § 62-7.

§ 81-3. Statement in Opposition to Petition

(a) Within ten days of the filing of the petition in the trial court, any party may file a statement in opposition to the petition. The original statement in opposition, together with fifteen additional copies, shall be filed with the appellate clerk. The statement shall disclose any reasons why certification should not be granted by the appellate court and shall be presented in a manner which is responsive, in form and content, to the petition it opposes. The statement in opposition shall not exceed ten pages in length, except with special permission of the appellate clerk. The statement in opposition shall be typewritten and fully double spaced and shall not exceed three lines to the vertical inch or twenty-seven lines to the page. Footnotes and block quotations may be single spaced. Only the following two typefaces, of 12 point or larger size, are approved for use in the statement in opposition: arial and univers. Each page of a statement in opposition to a petition shall have as a minimum the following margins: top, 1 inch; left, 1 and 1/4 inch; right, 1/2 inch; and bottom, 1 inch. A certificate shall be attached to the signed, original statement in opposition, indicating that it is in compliance with all the provisions of this rule.

No separate memorandum of law in support of the statement in opposition will be accepted by the appellate clerk.

(b) The statement in opposition shall be served in the manner set forth in Section 62-7.

(c) No motion to dismiss a petition for certification will be accepted by the appellate clerk. Any objection to the jurisdiction of the court to entertain the petition shall be included in the statement in opposition.

Historical Note

Derivation:
    Effective January 1, 2004, the second to the last sentence of paragraph (a) was added.
    1978 P.B. (1992–97), § 4142.2
    1978 P.B. (1986–92), § 2031A

Effective April 15, 2002, the last two sentences of the first paragraph of (a) were added to make the opposition statement conform more closely with briefs. Effective October 1, 1992, this rule was amended to require the filing of the statement in opposition with the appellate clerk and service in accordance with § 4014. This rule is new effective October 1, 1986.

AUTHORS' COMMENTS

Be sure to include a certification stating that the format of the statement in opposition conforms to this rule. See P.B. § 62-7.

§ 81-4. Proceedings after Certification by Appellate Court

Within twenty days from the issuance of notice of certification, the petitioner, who shall be considered the appellant, shall file the appeal in the manner provided by Section 63-3, take all other steps as may be required by Section 63-4, and in accordance with Section 63-5 shall pay the appropriate fees and give security. The clerk of the trial court must forward the case file to the appellate clerk in accordance with Section 68-1. Except as otherwise noted in Section 81-6, all proceedings subsequent to the filing of the appeal shall be governed by the rules applicable to appeals and appeals from administrative agencies.

Historical Note

Derivation:
    1978 P.B. (1992–97), § 4142.3
    1978 P.B. (1986–92), § 2033
This rule is new effective October 1, 1986.

§ 81-5. Extensions of Time

Motions for extensions of time for purposes of filing a petition for certification or a statement in opposition thereto shall be filed with the appellate clerk and shall be governed by Section 66-1.

Historical Note

Derivation:
    1978 P.B. (1992–97), § 4142.4
    1978 P.B. (1986–92), § 2034
This rule is new effective October 1, 1986.

§ 81-6. Filing of Regulations

The appellant's brief shall be filed simultaneously with one complete copy of the local land use regulations that were in effect at the time of the hearing that gave rise to the agency action or ruling in dispute. The regulations shall be certified by the local zoning or equivalent official as having been in effect at the time of the hearing. The appellant need not serve a copy of such regulations on other counsel of record.

Historical Note

New rule in 2002

CHAPTER 82

CERTIFIED QUESTIONS FROM COURTS OF OTHER JURISDICTIONS

Historical Note

This Chapter is new in 1986 and implements C.G.S.A. § 51-199a. Public Act 99-107 repealed § 51-199a and replaced it with a much broader law permitting the Supreme Court to accept questions not only from the federal courts but also from the highest courts of tribes and other states. In addition, the law for the first time allowed the Supreme Court itself to certify questions to the highest court of a tribe or another state. The implementing rules in this chapter refer only to § 51-199a.

§ 82-1. Certification of Questions from Other Courts

The supreme court may answer questions of law certified to it by a court of the United States or by the highest court of another state, as defined in General Statutes § 51-199b, or by the highest court of a tribe of Native Americans recognized by federal law when requested by the certifying court if the answer may be determinative of an issue in pending litigation in the certifying court and if there is no controlling appellate decision, constitutional provision or statute of this state.

Historical Note

Derivation:
    1978 P.B. (1986–97), § 4168
"Native Americans" was added in 2005 to conform with a statutory change.

AUTHORS' COMMENTS

Issues certified should generally be close calls and of general importance. L. Cohen & Co., Inc. v. Dun & Bradstreet, Inc., 629 F. Supp. 1419 (D. Conn. 1986). From 2001 to 2011, federal courts certified 25 cases to the Connecticut Supreme Court. Three were withdrawn and the other 22 were accepted by the Supreme Court. Certification is discussed in detail in Erik Sandler and John Cerreta, *"Certifying State Law Questions to the Connecticut Supreme Court,"* Connecticut Lawyer (October 2013) pp. 20-25.

§ 82-2. Method of Initiating [Repealed effective January 1, 2005]

§ 82-3. Contents of Certification Request

A certification request shall set forth: (1) The questions of law to be answered; (2) a finding or stipulation approved by the court setting forth all facts relevant to answering the questions certified and showing fully the nature of the controversy in which the questions arose; (3) that the receiving court may reformulate the questions; and (4) the names and addresses of counsel of record and self-represented parties.

The questions presented should be such as will be determinative of the case, and it must appear that their present determination would be in the interest of simplicity, directness and economy of judicial action.

All questions presented shall be specific and shall be phrased so as to require a Yes or No answer, wherever possible.

Historical Note

Derivation:
    1978 P.B. (1986–97), § 4170
This was a new rule effective October 1, 1986 and was amended in 2005 to conform to changes in C.G.S.A. § 51-199b.

§ 82-4. Preparation of Certification Request

The certification request shall be prepared by the certifying court, signed by the judge presiding at the hearing, and forwarded to the supreme court by the clerk of the certifying court under its official seal. The certification request shall be submitted together with eight copies thereof and also eight copies of any briefs or other documents relating to the questions certified. Upon receipt of the certification request, the appellate clerk shall notify the parties who shall be allowed a period of ten days from the date of mailing such notice to file objections to the acceptance of the certification request. The Supreme Court shall either preliminarily accept or decline the certification request. An order of preliminary acceptance shall not prevent the Supreme Court from rejecting the certification if it should later appear to have been improvidently ordered.

The Supreme Court may decline to answer the questions certified whenever it appears that the questions have been improperly framed, the necessary facts have not been fully set forth, or, for any other reason, certification has been improvidently ordered. The Supreme Court may also request the certifying court to provide additional facts required for a decision upon the questions certified, and also to clarify such questions when necessary. The Supreme Court may require the original or copies of all or of any portion of the record before the certifying court to be filed with the certification order, if, in the opinion of the Supreme Court, the record or portion thereof may be necessary in answering the questions.

Historical Note

Derivation:
    1978 P.B. (1986–97), § 4171
New rule effective October 1, 1986. Effective October 1, 1992, eight rather than six copies of the certification request must be submitted.

AUTHORS' COMMENTS

The certification request must include a stipulation or finding of facts. But see Capstone Building Corp. v. American Motorists Ins. Co., 308 Conn. 760, 765 n.4, 67 A.3d 961, 969 n.4 (2013) (summary judgment facts may suffice).

Even if the request is in proper form, the Supreme Court may reject it, as it did in Connecticut Performing Arts Foundation, Inc. v. Brown, 801 F.2d 566 (2d Cir. 1986). Or it may accept one question and decline another as it did in Avis Rent A Car System, Inc. v. Liberty Mut. Ins. Co., 203 Conn. 667, 526 A.2d 522 (1987).

§ 82-5. Receipt; Costs of Certification

Upon issuance of an order of preliminary acceptance, the appellate clerk shall docket the order, affix to the order the docket number assigned, and shall send notice of issuance of such order, with the docket number assigned, to the certifying court and to all parties. Within twenty days of receipt of such notice, the fees and costs shall be paid equally by the parties, unless otherwise ordered by the certifying court in its order of certification. In addition, within twenty days of preliminary acceptance, the parties shall file a docketing statement in the format specified in Section 63-4(a)(4). No security or recognizance shall be required, and no costs shall be taxed in favor of either party.

Historical Note

Derivation:
    1978 P.B. (1986–97), § 4172
New rule effective October 1, 1986. The third sentence was added effective September 3, 1996.

§ 82-6. Briefs and Argument

The plaintiff in the court that requested certification shall be deemed the appellant, and the defendant in such court shall be deemed the appellee for purposes of these rules, unless otherwise ordered by the court.

Briefs filed by the parties shall conform to the rules here. The time for filing briefs shall commence from the mailing of notice of preliminary acceptance of the certification order.

Oral argument shall be as provided for by the rules here, unless otherwise ordered by the court.

§ 82-6. Briefs, Appendices and Argument

The plaintiff in the court that requested certification shall be deemed the appellant, and the defendant in such court shall be deemed the appellee for purposes of these rules, unless otherwise ordered by the court.

Briefs and appendices filed by the parties shall conform to the rules here. The time for filing briefs and appendices shall commence from the mailing of notice of preliminary acceptance of the certification order.

Oral argument shall be as provided for by the rules here, unless otherwise ordered by the court.

Historical Note

Derivation:
    1978 P.B. (1986–97), § 4173
This was a new rule effective October 1, 1986 and was amended in 2005 to conform to changes in C.G.S.A. § 51-199b.

§ 82-7. Opinion

Upon publication thereof, the written opinion of the supreme court in response to the question or questions certified shall be sent by the appellate clerk to the certifying court. Unless otherwise ordered by the supreme court, official notification to counsel of record shall be the publication of the opinion in the Connecticut Law Journal.

Historical Note

Derivation:
    1978 P.B. (1986–97), § 4174
New rule effective October 1, 1986.

§ 82-8. Certification of Questions to Other Courts

The supreme court, on its own motion or motion of a party, may certify a question of law to the highest court of another state, as defined in General Statutes § 51-199b, or to the highest court of a tribe of Native Americans recognized by federal law if the pending case involves a question to be decided under the law of the other jurisdiction; the answer to the question may be determinative of an issue in the pending cause; and the question is one for which no answer is provided by a controlling appellate decision, constitutional provision, or statute of the other jurisdiction. The procedures for certification from the supreme court to the receiving court shall be those provided in the statutes or rules of the receiving court.

Historical Note

New rule effective January 1, 2006.

CHAPTER 83

CERTIFICATION PURSUANT TO GENERAL STATUTES § 52-265a IN CASES OF SUBSTANTIAL PUBLIC INTEREST

§ 83-1. Application; In General

Prior to filing an appeal pursuant to General Statutes § 52-265a, the party seeking to appeal shall, within two weeks of the issuance of the order or decision of the superior court, submit an original plus three copies of an application for certification by the chief justice. The application shall contain: (1) the question of law on which the appeal is to be based; (2) a description of the substantial public interest that is alleged to be involved; (3) an explanation as to why delay may work a substantial injustice and; (4) an appendix with: (A) the decision or order of the superior court sought to be appealed and (B) a list of all parties to the case in the superior court with the names, addresses, telephone and facsimile numbers, e-mail addresses and, if applicable, the juris numbers of their counsel.

Using an expeditious delivery method such as overnight mail or facsimile or other electronic medium, the party submitting the application shall provide the trial judge, the trial court clerk, and all counsel of record with a copy of the application. This requirement is in addition to the customary certification requirements of Section 62-7.

Historical Note

Derivation:
   1978 P.B. (1986–97), § 4177
The first paragraph was revised for clarity and (4) was added effective March 1, 2013.
New section effective October 1, 1986. In 2001, expeditious notice to the opposition was added.

AUTHORS' COMMENTS

C.G.S.A. § 52-265a first was litigated in State ex rel. Kelman v. Schaffer, 161 Conn. 522, 290 A.2d 327 (1971) (overruled on other grounds by, Serrani v. Board of Ethics of City of Stamford, 225 Conn. 305, 622 A.2d 1009 (1993)), concerning whether a citizen between the age of 18 and 21 can hold public office. While the case was dismissed on another ground, the Court took the opportunity to make it clear that any attempts to expedite an appeal should be brought under § 762 (now § 60-3) of the Practice Book, and not under C.G.S.A. § 52-265a.

> "Following the enactment by the legislature of § 52-265a the Supreme Court amended § 762. * * * Implicit in the adoption of this amendment to the appellate rules of procedure is a recognition of the possible constitutional infirmity of the statute * * *." 161 Conn. at 530, 290 A.2d at 331.

While most lawyers appear to have read *Kelman* to mean that C.G.S.A. § 52-265a is probably unconstitutional under the separation-of-powers doctrine, which was later elaborated upon in State v. Clemente, 166 Conn. 501, 353 A.2d 723 (1974), the judgment of the trial court was a final judgment under anyone's definition of the term, so § 52-265a did not have to be employed to give the Supreme Court jurisdiction. Rather the second half of the statute, which mandated certain procedures after the appeal was filed (such as in effect ordering the Supreme Court to drop everything else to attend to this appeal), was apparently what concerned the Court. 161 Conn. at 529, 290 A.2d at 331. But see Wrinn v. Dunleavy, 186 Conn. 125, 132–35, 440 A.2d 261, 265–66 (1982), where somewhat similar statutory commands were followed without comment. See also Town of Westport v. State, 204 Conn. 212, 527 A.2d 1177 (1987).

The Supreme Court has used the statute a couple times a year since *Kelman*. Examples are Kinsella v. Jaekle, 192 Conn. 704, 709 n.6, 475 A.2d 243, 247 n.6 (1984) (possible probate judge impeachment); Fernandez v. Fernandez, 208 Conn. 329, 545 A.2d 1036 (1988) (diplomatic immunity in divorce case); Moshier v. Goodnow, 217 Conn. 303, 305 n.3, 586 A.2d 557, 558 n.3 (1991) (authority of selectman over budget); State v. Ayala, 222 Conn. 331, 341–42, 610 A.2d 1162, 1168 (1992) (revocation of bail); Moore v. Ganim, 233 Conn. 557, 560 n.3, 660 A.2d 742, 744 n.3 (1995) (right to minimal level of subsistence under Connecticut Constitution); Metropolitan Life Ins. Co. v. Aetna Cas. and Sur. Co., 249 Conn. 36, 730 A.2d 51 (1999) (discovery order); State v. Ross, 251 Conn. 579, 742 A.2d 312 (1999) (capital case); Honulik v. Town of Greenwich, 290 Conn. 421, 963 A.2d 979, 185 L.R.R.M. (BNA) 3063 (2009), superseded on reconsideration en banc, 293 Conn. 698, 980 A.2d 880, 187 L.R.R.M. (BNA) 2408, 158 Lab. Cas. (CCH) P 60879 (2009) and on reconsideration, 293 Conn. 641, 980 A.2d 845 (2009) (collective bargaining dispute).

Certification to appeal has been denied in numerous unreported orders. Such an order, entered by the senior associate justice, was mentioned in Serrani v. Board of Ethics of City of Stamford, 225 Conn. 305, 307 n.3, 622 A.2d 1009, 1011 n.3 (1993) (holding modified by, Batte-Holmgren v. Commissioner of Public Health, 281 Conn. 277, 914 A.2d 996 (2007)).

The chief justice in effect waived the statutory two-week filing deadline by treating an appeal as a request for certification under C.G.S.A. § 52-265a in Hall v. Gilbert and Bennett Mfg. Co., Inc., 241 Conn. 282, 300–01, 695 A.2d 1051, 1062 (1997). He also did so for a cross appeal in Pamela B. v. Ment, 244 Conn. 296, 306 n.10, 709 A.2d 1089, 1096 n.10 (1998). *Hall* is also interesting because the underlying ruling was by the Compensation Review Board, not the Superior Court. *Hall*, 241 Conn. at 298-301, 695 A.2d at 1060-62.

The court treated a petition for certification from the Appellate Court's denial of relief on a motion for release as a § 52-265a petition from the trial court order at issue in State v. Heredia, 310 Conn. 742, 745 n.2, 81 A.3d 1163, 1165 n.2 (2013).

State v. Komisarjevsky, 302 Conn. 162, 25 A.3d 613 (2011), treated an appeal from order to disclose a witness list as a late application under C.G.S.A. § 52-265a.

This section was referred to in Moore v. Ganim, 233 Conn. 557, 560 n.3, 660 A.2d 742, 744 n.3 (1995).

There is no fee for filing an application. The appeal fee of $250.00 is paid if the application is granted.

§ 83-2. Application Granted

If any application is certified pursuant to General Statutes § 52-265a by the chief justice, the usual rules of procedure shall apply except as modified by the supreme court pursuant to Sections 60-2 or 60-3. The party certified to appeal shall have such additional time as the order of certification allows to file the appeal.

Historical Note

Derivation:
   1978 P.B. (1986–97), § 4178
New section effective October 1, 1986.

§ 83-3. Application Denied

If an application pursuant to General Statutes § 52-265a is denied by the chief justice, the denial shall be deemed to terminate all proceedings relating to the appeal.

Historical Note

Derivation:
   1978 P.B. (1986–97), § 4179
New section effective October 1, 1986.

§ 83-4. Unavailability of Chief Justice

If the chief justice is unavailable or disqualified, the most senior associate justice who is available and is not disqualified shall rule on the application for certification.

Historical Note

Derivation:
   1978 P.B. (1986–97), § 4180
New section effective October 1, 1986.

AUTHORS' COMMENTS

This section was applied in State v. Fernando A., 294 Conn. 1, 981 A.2d 427 (2009); State v. Marsh and McLennan Companies, Inc., 286 Conn. 454, 457 n.2, 944 A.2d 315, 318 n.2, 2008-1 Trade Cas. (CCH) ¶ 76173 (2008); State v. Solek, 242 Conn. 409, 413, 699 A.2d 931, 934 (1997); and Packer v. Board of Educ. of Town of Thomaston, 246 Conn. 89, 96–97, 717 A.2d 117, 123–24, 129 Ed. Law Rep. 400 (1998).

CHAPTER 84

APPEALS TO SUPREME COURT BY CERTIFICATION FOR REVIEW

Historical Note

As of July 1, 1983, certification by the Supreme Court applies only to decisions of the Appellate Court, C.G.S.A. § 51-197f; certification by the Appellate Court applies only to decisions of the Superior Court in zoning cases under C.G.S.A. §§ 8-8, 8-9, 8-28 and 8-30; C.G.S.A. § 51-197b.

This chapter has a tortuous history as to administrative appeals. Since July 1, 1983, administrative appeals, except for zoning appeals under §§ 8-8, 8-9, 8-28 and 8-30, are appealable as of right to the Appellate Court, C.G.S.A. § 51-197b. From July 1, 1981, to June 30, 1983 all administrative appeals were appealable as of right to the Appellate Session, P.A. 81-416. Between July 1, 1978 and June 30, 1981, all administrative appeals were appealable only to the Supreme Court and only on certification. Prior to that time, administrative appeals other than zoning appeals were appealable like other civil actions. However, from 1971 to 1978, zoning appeals were appealable to the Supreme Court and only on certification. Prior to 1971, zoning appeals were appealable like other civil actions, as the flood of zoning appeals during the 1960s attests.

This chapter is a consolidation of former chapters 38 and 38A as of July 1, 1978. From January 1, 1975 to July 1, 1978, Chapter 38 applied to appeals from the Appellate Session; Chapter 38A applied to zoning appeals from the Superior Court to the Supreme Court.

Between October 1, 1972 and December 31, 1974, old Chapter 38 was entitled "Appeals from Appellate Division of Court of Common Pleas". Prior to October 1, 1972, it was entitled "Appeals from Appellate Division of Circuit Court".

Old Chapter 38 was originally adopted effective January 1, 1961 as sections 470A.1 to 470A.19 of the 1951 Practice Book. It was on that date that the Circuit Court went into operation. Old Chapter 38A was originally adopted effective September 4, 1973 and repealed old § 738A, entitled "Application of

Rules to Petitions for Certification in Zoning Cases", which had been in effect since September 1, 1971.

Because of changes in the names of the trial and appellate courts, slight changes have been made in most of the rules simply to refer to the proper name of the court. These changes are not noted after each rule.

AUTHORS' COMMENTS

For certification rules in zoning and similar cases to the Appellate Court, see §§ 81-1 to 81-6.

This chapter is not authority for filing a petition to the Supreme Court from the denial of certification by the Appellate Court in a zoning case. Ingersoll v. Planning and Zoning Com'n of Town of Salisbury, 194 Conn. 277, 479 A.2d 1207 (1984); Grieco v. Zoning Com'n of Town of Redding, 226 Conn. 230, 627 A.2d 432 (1993). It is also not authority for filing a petition from an interlocutory ruling. State v. Ayala, 222 Conn. 331, 338–40, 610 A.2d 1162, 1166–68 (1992) (revocation of bail).

§ 84-1. Certification by Supreme Court

An appeal may be taken to the supreme court upon the final determination of an appeal in the appellate court where the supreme court, upon petition of an aggrieved party, certifies the case for review.

Historical Note

Derivation:
  1978 P.B. (1986–97), § 4126
  1978 P.B., § 3135
  1963 P.B., § 740
  1951 P.B., § 470A.1

This section was adopted in 1961 and was greatly revised effective July 1, 1983 in light of P.A. 83-29, § 7, June Session. No longer can the Appellate panel force the Supreme Court to take a case. As of 1997 there is no longer any provision for the Appellate Court even to request the Supreme Court to take the case.

AUTHORS' COMMENTS

Any appeal that is finally disposed of by the Appellate Court is subject to a petition for certification even if the Appellate Court decision will require further proceedings in the Superior Court. Gold v. Town of East Haddam, 290 Conn. 668, 675–77, 966 A.2d 684, 688–89 (2009). Thus finality in the Appellate Court is not the same as finality in the Superior Court for the purpose of an immediate appeal.

§ 84-2. Basis for Certification

Certification by the supreme court on petition by a party is not a matter of right but of sound judicial discretion and will be allowed only where there are special and important reasons therefor. The following, while neither controlling nor fully measuring the court's discretion, indicate the character of the reasons which will be considered:

(1) Where the appellate court has decided a question of substance not theretofore determined by the supreme court or

has decided it in a way probably not in accord with applicable decisions of the supreme court.

(2)   Where the decision under review is in conflict with other decisions of the appellate court.

(3)   Where the appellate court has so far departed from the accepted and usual course of judicial proceedings, or so far sanctioned such a departure by any other court, as to call for an exercise of the supreme court's supervision.

(4)   Where a question of great public importance is involved.

(5)   Where the judges of the appellate panel are divided in their decision or, though concurring in the result, are unable to agree upon a common ground of decision.

Historical Note

Derivation:
   1978 P.B. (1986–97), § 4127
   1978 P.B., § 3137
   1963 P.B., § 742. Compare § 761C
   1951 P.B., § 470A.2

This rule is substantially unchanged since it was adopted in 1961.

The background and purpose of this rule is discussed in State v. Cullum, 149 Conn. 728, 176 A.2d 587 (1961).

AUTHORS' COMMENTS

For the calendar year 2013, the authors for the first time did an extensive analysis of the certification grant rate broken down by types of cases and whether they were filed pro se or by a lawyer. Their findings were published in W. Horton & K. Bartschi, "2013 Connecticut Appellate Review," 87 Connecticut Bar Journal 275, 275–77 (2014). The principal findings were that, if criminal and habeas petitions and all petitions filed by pro se parties are eliminated, the certification grant rate is over 35%.

Three votes are needed to grant a petition. C.G.S.A. § 51-197f. Before 1996, only two were needed. The grant rate was over 30% in the early 1990s.

Justice Berdon was the first justice to have written an opinion dissenting from a denial of certification. State v. Weber, 221 Conn. 84, 87, 602 A.2d 963, 964 (1992) (Berdon, J. dissenting). He did so frequently in his eight years on the Supreme Court bench, but the other justices rarely dissent at all. But see Brown v. Commissioner of Correction, 277 Conn. 908, 894 A.2d 989 (2006) (two justices dissenting from denial). In *Brown*, the court subsequently changed its mind and granted certification. Brown v. Commissioner of Correction, 277 Conn. 922, 895 A.2d 795 (2006).

When the Appellate Court decides an appeal on the merits summarily, the Supreme Court rarely grants certification. But it does happen. See State v. Sullivan, 44 Conn.App. 902, 688 A.2d 368 (1997), aff'd, 244 Conn. 640, 712 A.2d 919 (1998) (3-2 decision); Eldridge v. Eldridge, 45 Conn.App. 904, 692 A.2d 1320 (1997), aff'd in part, rev'd in part, 244 Conn. 523, 710 A.2d 757 (1998) (en banc) (5-2 decision).

Normally, no dissents are noted if a petition is granted. But in State v. Komisarjevsky, 301 Conn. 920, 21 A.3d 465 (2011), opinion after grant of certification, 302 Conn. 162, 25 A.3d 613 (2011), the order granting certification in a capital case noted that three justices dissented.

§ 84-3. Stay of Execution

In any action in which a stay of proceedings was in effect during the pendency of the appeal, or, if no stay of proceedings was in effect, in which the decision of the appellate court would change the position of any party from its position during the pendency of the appeal, proceedings to enforce or carry out the judgment shall be stayed until the time to file the petition has expired. If a petition by a party is filed, the proceedings shall be stayed until the supreme court acts on the petition and, if the petition is granted, until the final determination of the cause; but if the presiding judge of an appellate panel which heard the case is of the opinion that the certification proceedings have been taken only for delay or that the due administration of justice so requires, such presiding judge may, up to the time the supreme court acts upon the petition, upon motion order that the stay be terminated. If such presiding judge is unavailable, the most senior judge on such panel who is available may act upon such a motion for termination of the stay.

Historical Note

Derivation:
  1978 P.B. (1986–97), § 4128
  1978 P.B., § 3138
  1963 P.B., § 744. Compare § 761D
  1951 P.B., § 470A.4

This section was amended in 1996 to make this stay rule similar to that for a motion for reconsideration.

The sentence referring to the presiding judge's unavailability was added effective October 1, 1986. At the same time a reference to the trial judge was deleted.

This rule is otherwise substantially unchanged since it was adopted in 1961 except that prior to 1973 the stay lasted only five days. Certain redundant language was removed effective January 1, 1985.

AUTHORS' COMMENTS

In the authors' opinion, this section, because it specifically covers certified appeals, trumps § 61-11(d).

In State v. Oral H., 125 Conn.App. 276, 7 A.3d 444 (2010), cert. denied, 300 Conn. 902, 12 A.3d 573, cert. denied, ___ U.S. ___, 131 S. Ct. 3003, 180 L. Ed. 2d 831 (2011), the court held that the automatic stay requirement pursuant to this section applied to an Appellate Court decision declaring a criminal statute to be unconstitutional where the Supreme Court ultimately upheld the statute.

In State v. Jordan, 151 Conn.App. 1, 16 n.9, 92 A.3d 1032, 1050 n.9, cert. denied, 314 Conn. ___, ___ A.3d ___ (2014), the court held that an appellate court decision has little precedential value when the Supreme Court grants certification in light of this rule. The authors do not agree with *Jordan*.

§ 84-4. Petition; Time to File; Where to File; Service; Fee

(a) A petition for certification shall be filed by the petitioner within twenty days of (1) the date the opinion is officially released as set forth in Section 71-4 or (2) the issuance of notice of any order or judgment finally determining a cause in the appellate court, whichever is earlier. If within this period a timely motion is filed which, if granted, would render the appellate court order or judgment ineffective, as, for example, a motion for reconsideration, or if within this period an application for waiver of fees is filed, then the twenty days shall run from the issuance of notice of the decision thereon.

The petitioner shall file the original and one copy of the petition with, and pay a filing fee to, the clerk of the trial court. No fee shall be required in cases where a waiver of fees, costs and expenses under Section 63-6 or 63-7 was previously granted. The fee, if not waived or exempted by statute, may be paid to the clerk of any trial court in the state. The clerk shall endorse on the original petition the date and time of filing and the receipt, or waiver, of fees. The clerk shall return the original endorsed petition to the petitioner, who shall promptly send it, with fifteen additional copies of the petition, to the appellate clerk. The petitioner shall serve a copy upon every other party in the manner set forth in Section 62-7. If the fee was paid at a location other than the original trial court, then the petitioner shall also attach a separate certification indicating that a copy has been served upon the clerk of the original trial court.

In cases where a waiver of fees, costs and expenses under Section 63-6 or 63-7 was granted or a statutory provision exempts the petitioner from paying the required fee, the petitioner may file the original petition and fifteen additional copies of the petition directly with the appellate clerk. Any petition for certification filed directly with the appellate clerk shall include a certification indicating the name of the judge granting the waiver of fees, costs and expenses and the date such waiver was granted, or the specific statutory section exempting the petitioner from paying the required fee. The petitioner shall serve a copy of the petition for certification upon every other party in the manner set forth in Section 62-7 and shall also attach a certification indicating that a copy has been served upon the clerk of the original trial court.

In workers' compensation cases, the petitioner shall file the original petition and fifteen additional copies of the petition directly with the appellate clerk. The petitioner shall serve a copy upon every other party in the manner set forth in Section 62-7, and upon the trial commissioner in a General Statutes § 31-290a appeal and upon the compensation review board in an appeal from that board. No fee is required in workers' compensation cases.

(b) Any other party aggrieved by the judgment of the appellate court may file a cross petition within ten days of the filing of the original petition. The filing of cross petitions, including the payment of the fee, service pursuant to Section 62-7, the form of the cross petition, and all subsequent proceedings shall be the same as though the cross petition were an original petition.

(c) The filing of a petition or cross petition by one party shall not be deemed to be a filing on behalf of any other party.

Historical Note

Derivation:
  1978 P.B. (1986–97), § 4129
  1978 P.B., § 3139
  1963 P.B., § 745. Compare § 761E
  1951 P.B., § 470A.5

The third paragraph of subsection (a) was added effective October 1, 2013.

The last sentence of the second paragraph of subsection (a) was rewritten to add the "separate certification" language effective January 1, 2013.

Subsection (b) was added in 1996. In 1999 (a) was clarified concerning workers' compensation cases, and in 2002 (a) was clarified to indicate that the petition is "filed" with a trial court but "sent" to the appellate clerk. This rule was completely revised effective October 1, 1992 to raise the filing fee from $10.00 to $75.00, to abolish cross petitions and to require the original petition to be filed with and endorsed by the trial court before it is filed with the appellate clerk.

The second paragraph of (a) and section (b) were added effective October 1, 1986. As for section (a), the first paragraph was completely rewritten effective January 1, 1985 to clarify the time period for filing.

Between 1961, when the rule was adopted, and 1973 a notice of petition had to be filed within five days of the judgment under § 743, and then within another ten days the petition itself had to be filed under § 745.

Prior to 1973, only eight copies of the petition had to be filed and, prior to 1966, only six copies had to be filed.

AUTHORS' COMMENTS

The fee is $75.00. C.G.S. § 52-259.

Prior to 1992 this rule was a trap. You had to remember to file a copy of the petition, with the filing fee, in the trial court clerk's office within the petition time period. Cf. Van Mecklenburg v. Pan American World Airways, Inc., 196 Conn. 517, 519, 494 A.2d 549, 550 (1985). Now, one may go to a trial clerk anywhere in the state first and that clerk can endorse on the original petition that the fee was paid. A copy of the petition, however, must still be sent to the original trial clerk's office.

The authors' opinion is that the 20-day deadline for filing is met if the petition is filed in the trial court on the twentieth day, even if the endorsed original is not filed with the appellate clerk until the next day or so. This is the (to be sure, risky) implication of "promptly" in the second paragraph.

A conditional cross petition (to be considered only if the opposition petition is granted) is permissible. Barry v. Posi-Seal Intern., Inc., 237 Conn. 918, 676 A.2d 1373 (1996). A conditional cross petition should have been filed in Jones v. Crystal, 242 Conn. 599, 603–04, 699 A.2d 961, 963 (1997).

§ 84-5. Form of Petition

(a) A petition for certification shall contain the following sections in the order indicated here:

(1) A statement of the questions presented for review, expressed in the terms and circumstances of the case but without unnecessary detail. The supreme court will ordinarily consider only those questions squarely raised, subject to any limitation in the order granting certification.

(2)   A statement of the basis for certification identifying the specific reasons, including but not limited to those enumerated in Section 84-2, why the supreme court should allow the extraordinary relief of certification.

(3)   A summary of the case containing the facts material to the consideration of the questions presented, reciting the disposition of the matter in the appellate court, and describing specifically how the appellate court decided the questions presented for review in the petition.

(4)   A concise argument amplifying the reasons relied upon to support the petition. No separate memorandum of law in support of the petition will be accepted by the appellate clerk.

(5)   An appendix containing:

(A)   the opinion or order of the appellate court sought to be reviewed,

(B)   if the opinion or order of the appellate court was a summary affirmance or dismissal, a copy of the trial court's memorandum of decision that was entered in connection with the claim raised by the petitioner before the appellate court, or, if no memorandum was filed, a copy of the trial court's ruling on the matter,

(C)   a copy of the order on any motion which would stay or extend the time period for filing the petition,

(D)   a list of all parties to the appeal in the appellate court with the names, addresses, telephone and facsimile numbers, and if applicable, the juris numbers of their trial and appellate counsel.

The appendix may be reproduced on both sides of a page.

(b)   The petition shall not exceed ten pages in length, exclusive of the appendix, except with special permission of the appellate clerk. The petition shall be typewritten and fully double spaced, and shall not exceed three lines to the vertical inch or twenty-seven lines to the page. Footnotes and block quotations may be single spaced. Only the following two typefaces, of 12 point or larger size, are approved for the use in petitions: arial, and univers. Each page of a petition shall have as a minimum the following margins: top, 1 inch; left, 1 and 1/4 inch; right, 1/2 inch; and bottom, 1 inch. A certificate shall be attached to the signed, original petition, indicating that it is in compliance with all the provisions of this rule.

Historical Note

Derivation:
 1978 P.B. (1986–87), § 4130
 1978 P.B., § 3140
 1963 P.B., § 746. Compare § 761F
 1951 P.B., § 470A.6
Effective January 1, 2004, the second to the last sentence of subsection (b)

was added. In 1999, subsection (a)(5)(B) was added.

Effective April 15, 2002, the sentence just before (b) and the last four sentences of (b) were added to make the petition conform more closely with briefs.

Effective September 3, 1996, the last two sentences of (b) were revised to stop evasion of the page limitations.

Effective October 1, 1992, (a)(5) was amended to order an extension of time and the last sentence of (b) was added.

This section was completely rewritten effective October 1, 1986. Old § 3140 stated as follows: "A petition for certification shall be in the form of a brief and shall contain a summary and short statement of the matter involved, questions presented, and the reasons and basis upon which it is contended that the supreme court should allow the extraordinary relief of certification. Only the questions specifically brought forward by the petition will be considered. Individual counsel for the petitioner shall sign the petition, stating counsel's address, and shall certify that the petition presents a substantial question meriting certification and that it is filed in good faith and not for purposes of delay."

The following history refers to old § 3140:

This rule is substantially unchanged since it was adopted in 1961 except that prior to 1973 the last sentence read in part: "Counsel for the petitioner shall sign the petition and shall certify that it presents * * * ".

Cross References

Authors' suggested Form 3000.23-B

AUTHORS' COMMENTS

Be sure to include a certification stating that the format of the petition conforms to this rule. See P.B. § 62-7.

§ 84-6. Statement in Opposition to Petition

(a) Within ten days of the filing of the petition in the trial court, any party may file a statement in opposition to the petition. The original statement in opposition, together with fifteen additional copies, shall be filed with the appellate clerk. The statement in opposition shall disclose any reasons why certification should not be granted by the supreme court and shall be presented in a manner which is responsive, in form and content, to the petition it opposes. The statement in opposition shall not exceed ten pages in length except with special permission of the appellate clerk.

The statement in opposition shall be typewritten and fully double spaced and shall not exceed three lines to the vertical inch or twenty-seven lines to the page. Footnotes and block quotations may be single spaced. Only the following two typefaces, of 12 point or larger size, are approved for the use in the statement in opposition: arial and univers. Each page of a statement in opposition to a petition shall have as a minimum the following margins: top, 1 inch; left, 1 and 1/4 inch; right, 1/2 inch; and bottom, 1 inch.

A certificate shall be attached to the signed, original statement in opposition, indicating that it is in compliance with all the provisions of this rule.

No separate memorandum of law in support of the statement in opposition will be accepted by the appellate clerk.

(b) The statement in opposition shall be served in the manner set forth in Section 62-7.

(c) No motion to dismiss a petition for certification will be accepted by the appellate clerk. Any objection to the jurisdiction of the court to entertain the petition shall be included in the statement in opposition.

Historical Note

Derivation:
    1978 P.B. (1986–97), § 4131
    1978 P.B., § 3141
    1963 P.B., § 747; compare § 761G
    1951 P.B., § 470A.7

Effective January 1, 2004, the second to the last sentence in paragraph 2 of section (a) was added.

Effective April 15, 2002, the second paragraph of (a) was added to make the opposition statement conform more closely with briefs.

Effective October 1, 1991, (b) was amended to require the filing of the statement in opposition with the appellate clerk and service in accordance with § 4014.

This section was completely rewritten effective October 1, 1986. Old § 3141 stated as follows: "Within ten days of the service of the petition upon him, the respondent shall serve and file his brief in the manner specified in Sec. 3139. The brief shall be filed in the same manner as a petition and shall be considered an opposition to a petition for purposes of Sec. 3098."

"Any respondent aggrieved by the decision of the appellate court may file a cross petition for certification within ten days of the filing of the petition. The filing and form of cross petitions, including the payment of the record fee, and all subsequent proceedings shall be the same as though the cross petition were an original petition."

The following history refers to old § 3141:

This rule was adopted in 1961. The second sentence in the first paragraph and the second paragraph were added effective January 1, 1985.

AUTHORS' COMMENTS

Be sure to include a certification stating that the format of the statement in opposition conforms to this rule. See P.B. § 62-7.

Failure to file a cross petition can get an appellee into trouble if the Supreme Court grants certification on the petition. D'Ulisse-Cupo v. Board of Directors of Notre Dame High School, 202 Conn. 206, 216 n.4, 520 A.2d 217, 222 n.4, 37 Ed. Law Rep. 229, 2 I.E.R. Cas. (BNA) 948, 106 Lab. Cas. (CCH) P 55702 (1987); Jones v. Crystal, 242 Conn. 599, 603–04, 699 A.2d 961, 963 (1997).

§ 84-7. Extensions of Time

Motions for extensions of time for purposes of filing a petition for certification or a statement in opposition thereto shall be filed with the appellate clerk and shall be governed by Section 66-1.

Historical Note

Derivation:

1978 P.B. (1986–97), § 4132
1978 P.B., § 3142
1963 P.B., § 747A. Compare § 761H

This section was greatly simplified effective October 1, 1986 by referring to the procedure in § 4040.

This rule was adopted effective September 4, 1973 and was slightly revised effective January 1, 1985.

AUTHORS' COMMENTS

If the time has already expired, move for permission to file a late petition under § 60-2 and § 60-3. These are liberally granted, at least in habeas cases. Janulawicz v. Commissioner of Correction, 310 Conn. 265, 273-74, 77 A.3d 113, 119 (2013).

§ 84-8. Grant or Denial of Certification

A petition by a party shall be granted on the affirmative vote of three or more justices of the supreme court. Upon the determination of any petition, the appellate clerk shall enter an order granting or denying the certification in accordance with the determination of the court and shall send notice of the court's order to the clerk of the trial court and to counsel.

Historical Note

Derivation:
1978 P.B. (1986–97), § 4136
1978 P.B., § 3152A
1978 P.B., § 3146
1963 P.B., § 750. Compare § 761M
1951 P.B., § 470A.10

Minor revisions were made effective October 1, 1986. The change from two to three votes was made effective October 29, 1996 to accord with the statutory change in P.A. 96-179, § 8.

Reference to a request from the appellate panel and certain other minor changes were added effective January 1, 1985.

Prior to 1966, a petition could be granted only if three of the justices voted in favor of it. The rule was adopted in 1961.

AUTHORS' COMMENTS

The denial of certification does not mean that the Supreme Court approves of either the opinion or the result of the lower court opinion. State v. Chisholm, 155 Conn. 706, 707, 236 A.2d 465, 466 (1967); State v. Doscher, 172 Conn. 592, 376 A.2d 359 (1977); Mandanici v. Zoning Bd. of Appeals of City of Shelton, 50 Conn.App. 308, 311, 717 A.2d 287, 288, cert. denied, 247 Conn. 935, 719 A.2d 1174 (1998); Pagano v. Board of Educ. of City of Torrington, 4 Conn.App. 1, 5–6, 492 A.2d 197, 200, cert. denied, 197 Conn. 809, 499 A.2d 60 (1985).

Until 1987, the court's practice was generally either to grant or deny certification without qualification. Now it uniformly grants certification limited to certain issues.

It is possible to move for reconsideration on a denial of a petition. State v. Burke, 254 Conn. 202, 203–04, 757 A.2d 524, 524–25 (2000) (petition granted on reconsideration). See also Caruso v. City of Milford, 75 Conn.App. 95, 100, 815 A.2d 167, cert. denied, 263 Conn. 907, 819 A.2d 838 (2003).

§ 84-9. Proceedings after Certification; Appeals Deemed Pending

Whenever certification is granted by the supreme court, the cause shall be deemed pending on appeal in the supreme court and the appellate clerk shall enter the case upon the docket. Where a petition has been granted, the petitioner shall be considered the appellant. The appellant shall pay the filing fee to the clerk of any trial court within twenty days from the issuance of notice of certification. No fee shall be required, however, in workers' compensation cases or in cases where a waiver of fees, costs and expenses under Section 63-6 or 63-7 was previously granted. The appellant shall certify to all other counsel and to the clerk of the trial court from which the cause arose that the fees have been paid or that no fees were required. Security for costs is not required to take an appeal pursuant to a grant of certification, but security may at any time, on motion and notice to the appellant, be ordered by the supreme court. Such security, if ordered, shall be filed with the trial court. The appellant shall also file with the appellate clerk the docketing statement required by Section 63-4(a)(4). The appellant's brief shall be filed within forty-five days from the issuance of notice of certification, and thereafter the time limits for filing the appellee's brief and the reply brief, if any, shall be in accordance with Section 67-3.

The issues which the appellant may present are limited to those raised in the petition for certification, except where the issues are further limited by the order granting certification.

Historical Note

Derivation:
> 1978 P.B. (1986–87), § 4138
> 1978 P.B., § 3154
> 1963 P.B., §§ 758, 759
> 1951 P.B., §§ 470A.16, .17

Various changes were made in 1997 and 2002 concerning the payment and waiver of fees. Effective October 1, 1992, the 60-day period for the appellant to file his brief was reduced to 45 days.

Effective May 10, 1988, the provision regarding security for costs was changed so that the cross appellant waits until after the appellant files the security.

Effective October 1, 1986 the fees and security are due 20 rather than 14 days from notice of certification, and the last sentence of the first paragraph was added.

Language clarifying who is the appellant was added effective January 1, 1985. The last paragraph was added at the same time.

This rule was adopted in 1961.

AUTHORS' COMMENTS

The authors recommend filing a new appeal form with the filing fees, although it is not required. This gives the trial court clerk a form to endorse, indicating payment has been made. The jurisdictional statement should identify the action which constitutes the final judgment as the judgment of the Appellate Court upon the granting of certification. The appellant must also file a new docketing statement under this section, and the clerk normally orders the filing of a new designation of pleadings as well.

If issues other than those certified by the Supreme Court occur to the appellant, they may possibly be considered under §§ 60-3 or 60-5. State v. Torrence, 196 Conn. 430, 433–34 n.5, 493 A.2d 865, 867 n.5 (1985); Merlo v. Planning and Zoning Com'n of Town of Wethersfield, 196 Conn. 676, 680 n.3, 495 A.2d 268, 270 n.3 (1985). The court will consider questions of subject matter jurisdiction even if they are not certified. Citibank, N.A. v. Lindland, 310 Conn. 147, 159, 75 A.3d 651, 659 (2013). Sometimes a non-certified issue will be considered in the interest of judicial economy. Carpenter v. Commissioner of Correction, 274 Conn. 834, 842 n.6, 878 A.2d 1088, 1092 n.6 (2005). In general, however, the Supreme Court will only consider those issues squarely raised in the petition; Queach Corp. v. Inland Wetlands Com'n of Town of Branford, 258 Conn. 178, 189 n.19, 779 A.2d 134, 142 n.19 (2001); Fernandes v. Rodriguez, 255 Conn. 47, 53 n.4, 761 A.2d 1283, 1286 n.4 (2000) (but trial court invited to re-examine issue on remand). But see Levey Miller Maretz v. 595 Corporate Circle, 258 Conn. 121, 127, 780 A.2d 43, 47 (2001); State v. Hodge, 201 Conn. 379, 517 A.2d 621 (1986); Rametta v. Stella, 214 Conn. 484, 491 n.6, 572 A.2d 978, 982 n.6 (1990); Nardini v. Manson, 207 Conn. 118, 119 n.1, 540 A.2d 69, 70 n.1 (1988), where issues not certified were considered, in *Hodge* and *Rametta* to affirm on an alternate basis, in *Levey* and *Nardini* to reverse. In *Levey* the majority in a 3-2 decision considered an uncertified issue because it undermined the factual predicate of the certified issue. See also Center Shops of East Granby, Inc. v. Planning and Zoning Com'n of Town of East Granby, 253 Conn. 183, 195 n.10, 757 A.2d 1052, 1059 n.10 (2000). The certified issue should not be read narrowly if the Supreme Court's purpose in combining the issues was to avoid redundancy. Total Recycling Services of Connecticut, Inc. v. Connecticut Oil Recycling Services, LLC, 308 Conn. 312, 335, 63 A.3d 896, 909 (2013).

If the petition is denied, it is possible to move for reconsideration. It succeeded in Barry v. Posi-Seal Intern., Inc., 235 Conn. 901, 664 A.2d 1124 (1995); State v. Burke, 254 Conn. 202, 203–04, 757 A.2d 524, 524–25 (2000).

In Olson v. Accessory Controls and Equipment Corp., 254 Conn. 145, 169 n.10, 757 A.2d 14, 28 n.10, 16 I.E.R. Cas. (BNA) 1050, 142 Lab. Cas. (CCH) P 59132 (2000), the Court decided to address a crime-fraud exception as sufficiently related to the certified issue, but declined to review a work product issue as neither the trial court nor the appellate court had considered it.

In Bernstein v. Commissioner of Correction, 272 Conn. 904, 863 A.2d 698 (2004), the court granted the petition for certification and remanded for reconsideration in light of another recent decision. The court waived the provisions of this rule due to the lack of further proceedings in that court.

§ 84-10. Record (Applicable to appeals filed before July 1, 2013)

Those portions of the record on appeal to the appellate court relevant to the issue certified by the supreme court shall constitute the record on appeal to the supreme court and shall be prepared and distributed in the same manner as in other appeals to the supreme court. In addition, the record shall include the appellate court order or decision on the order granting certification and, to the extent the appellate clerk deems appropriate, any papers subsequently filed pursuant to Section 84-11.

The argument, if any, before the appellate court shall not be considered part of the record on appeal to the supreme court, except upon motion by a party showing special and important reasons therefor.

§ 84-10. Record (Repealed only as to appeals filed on or after July 1, 2013)

Historical Note

Derivation:
    1978 P.B. (1986–97), § 4139
    1978 P.B., § 3156
    1963 P.B., § 760
    1951 P.B., § 470A.18

In 1996 this rule was clarified concerning what goes into the record. Effective October 1, 1992, this section was changed to make the record in both courts the same.

The reference to the clerk printing the record was changed to "prepared" effective October 1, 1986.

This rule was adopted in 1961. Minor changes were made effective January 1, 1985.

§ 84-11. Papers to Be Filed by Appellant and Appellee

(a) Upon the granting of certification, the appellee may present for review alternative grounds upon which the judgment may be affirmed provided those grounds were raised and briefed in the appellate court. Any party to the appeal may also present for review adverse rulings or decisions which should be considered on the appeal in the event of a new trial, provided that such party has raised such claims in the appellate court. If such alternative grounds for affirmation or adverse rulings or decisions to be considered in the event of a new trial were not raised in the appellate court, the party seeking to raise them in the supreme court must move for special permission to do so prior to the filing of that party's brief. Such permission will be granted only in exceptional cases where the interests of justice so require.

(b) Any party may also present for review any claim that the relief afforded by the appellate court in its judgment should be modified, provided such claim was raised in the appellate court either in such party's brief or upon a motion for reconsideration.

(c) Any party desiring to present alternative grounds for affirmance, adverse rulings or decisions in the event of a new trial or a claim concerning the relief ordered by the appellate court shall file a statement thereof within fourteen days from the issuance of notice of certification. Parties shall not file other Section 63-4 papers on a certified appeal without permission of the supreme court.

Historical Note

Derivation:
    1978 P.B. (1986–97), § 4140

This section is new effective October 1, 1986.

AUTHORS' COMMENTS

On rare occasions, the Supreme Court grants certification and immediately remands the case for reconsideration in light of a recent Supreme Court decision. See, e.g., Bernstein v. Commissioner of Correction, 272 Conn. 904, 863 A.2d 698 (2004); Forsberg v. New Hampshire Ins. Co., 220 Conn. 922, 598 A.2d 364 (1991).

On several occasions, the court, after full briefing and oral argument, summarily affirmed or dismissed the appeal, Brennan v. Burger King Corp., 244 Conn. 204, 707 A.2d 30 (1998) (affirmed on the opinion of Appellate Court); Metro Mobile CTS of Fairfield County, Inc. v. Department of Public Utility Control, 243 Conn. 235, 702 A.2d 1179 (1997) (dismissed for lack of jurisdiction because of mootness); Lawler v. Lawler, 212 Conn. 117, 561 A.2d 128 (1989) (dismissed because record unclear; complication due to another recent decision). Often the Supreme Court dismisses the appeal as "improvidently granted." Weeks v. Kramer, 244 Conn. 203, 707 A.2d 30 (1998); Sheehan v. Balasic, 245 Conn. 148, 710 A.2d 770 (1998). This may mean that the factual predicate for an important legal issue is found to be inadequate. F.D.I.C. v. Bombero, 236 Conn. 744, 674 A.2d 1324 (1996). Therefore, the appellee can move to dismiss a certified appeal if the proper occasion arises.

Occasionally, the Supreme Court reformulates the certified question in its decision. State v. Brown, 242 Conn. 389, 401, 699 A.2d 943, 949 (1997).

An adverse ruling raised by an appellee as of right in a certified appeal succeeded in Tremaine v. Tremaine, 235 Conn. 45, 48 n.2, 663 A.2d 387, 389 n.2 (1995); and in Commissioner of Labor v. C.J.M. Services, Inc., 268 Conn. 283, 292–94, 842 A.2d 1124, 1130–31 (2004). See also Gibson v. Capano, 241 Conn. 725, 729–30, 699 A.2d 68, 70 (1997).

In State v. Winot, 294 Conn. 753, 988 A.2d 188 (2010), the court reviewed the defendant-appellee's claim for a modification of the Appellate Court judgment under this section even though the court had denied his petition for certification, where it had granted the state's petition.

In Dickinson v. Mullaney, 284 Conn. 673, 682 n.4, 937 A.2d 667, 673 n.4 (2007), and Anatra v. Zoning Board of Appeals, 307 Conn. 728, 756, 59 A.3d 772, 787 (2013), the court reviewed alternate bases to affirm that were not raised under this section but were raised in the Appellate Court and fully briefed in the Supreme Court.

Alternate bases to affirm must be raised in a statement filed with the Supreme Court (not just in the brief). Olson v. Mohammadu, 310 Conn. 665, 684-85 n.15, 81 A.3d 215, 228 n.15 (2014). They were raised in Grimm v. Grimm, 276 Conn. 377, 382 n.5, 886 A.2d 391, 394 n.5 (2005); State v. Samuels, 273 Conn. 541, 562 n.12, 871 A.2d 1005, 1019 n.12 (2005). An alternate basis to affirm succeeded in Caminis v. Troy, 300 Conn. 297, 12 A.3d 984 (2011). The Supreme Court granted the appellee's right to review certain issues in Santorso v. Bristol Hospital, 308 Conn. 338, 344-45, 354, 63 A.3d 940, 945, 950 (2013) and State v. Lee, 229 Conn. 60, 63, 640 A.2d 553, 555 (1994). The authors do not understand why the appellee had to request permission to do so since in *Lee* the issues apparently were raised in the Appellate Court. Section 63-4(a)(1) is used by analogy here. Russell v. Mystic Seaport Museum, Inc., 252 Conn. 596, 600 n.3, 748 A.2d 278, 281 n.3 (2000). In Dougan v. Dougan, 301 Conn. 361, 21 A.3d 791 (2011), the court permitted the defendant to raise an alternate basis she had not raised in the Appellate Court. The issue, concerning judicial estoppel, succeeded.

If alternate bases to affirm are poorly briefed, the Supreme Court may leave those issues to the Appellate Court to decide if a remand is ordered. Gajewski v.

Pavelo, 229 Conn. 829, 838, 643 A.2d 1276, 1280 (1994), on remand, 36
Conn.App. 601, 652 A.2d 509 (1994), aff'd, 236 Conn. 27, 670 A.2d 318 (1996).
An appellee's related claims were addressed by the Supreme Court in State v.
Brown, 242 Conn. 445, 447, 700 A.2d 1089, 1090 (1997), and Murphy v. Commis-
sioner of Motor Vehicles, 254 Conn. 333, 335 n.2, 757 A.2d 561, 566 n.2 (2000).
But in Wright Bros. Builders, Inc. v. Dowling, 247 Conn. 218, 221 n.3, 720 A.2d
235, 236 n.3 (1998), where the appellee's claim was not raised under this sec-
tion even though it was briefed, the claim was neither considered by the
Supreme Court nor explicitly referred to the Appellate Court to consider.

An alternate basis to affirm will not preserve an issue that the appellee
should have raised in the Appellate Court on a cross appeal. Gagne v. Vaccaro,
311 Conn. 649, 661-62, 90 A.3d 196 (2014).

In Carrano v. Yale-New Haven Hosp., 279 Conn. 622, 655, 904 A.2d 149, 172
(2006), the court reviewed, in unusual circumstances, a questionable alternate
basis to affirm even though it denied certification on a proper cross petition. Another unusual review is found in Vine v. Zoning Bd. of Appeals of Town of
North Branford, 281 Conn. 553, 568–69 n.11, 916 A.2d 5, 15 n.11 (2007).

An alternate basis to affirm failed in State v. Silas S., 301 Conn. 684, 691 n.8,
22 A.3d 622, 627 n.8 (2011), where the defendant conceded the issue in his main
brief in the Appellate Court and only briefly raised it in his Appellate Court
reply brief.

§ 84-12. Applicability of Rules

The rules governing other appeals shall, so far as applicable,
and to the extent they have not been modified by this chapter, be
the rules for all proceedings subsequent to the granting of
certification.

Historical Note

Derivation:
   1978 P.B. (1986–97), § 4141
   1978 P.B., § 3158
   1963 P.B., §§ 761, 761Q
   1951 P.B., § 470A.19

The proviso "to the extent they have not been modified by this chapter" was
added effective October 1, 1986.

Otherwise, this rule is substantially unchanged since it was adopted in 1961
as to appeals from appellate panels and in 1973 as to zoning appeals, except
that effective January 1, 1985, the first sentence refers to the granting of certification rather than to printing the record.

If the appeal is withdrawn after certification, notice is given in the Connecticut Law Journal. This procedure was instituted in the Law Journal dated February 1, 1994, page 55.

CHAPTER 84A

MATTERS WITHIN SUPREME COURT'S ORIGINAL JURISDICTION IN WHICH FACTS MAY BE FOUND

Historical Note

Entirely new Chapter effective January 1, 2006.

§ 84a-1. Application of Rules

These rules apply only to an action within the original jurisdiction of the supreme court in which facts may be found.

These rules do not apply to (1) a motion to invoke the court's supervisory powers under Section 60-2 of the rules of practice, or (2) certified questions of law from court of other jurisdictions under chapter 82 of the rules of practice.

Historical Note

New rule effective January 1, 2006.

AUTHORS' COMMENTS

This Chapter appears to apply only to certain types of reapportionment cases. See Constitutional Amendments, Art. 16, § 2.

§ 84a-2. Pleadings and Motions

Unless otherwise ordered in a particular case, the form of pleadings and motion prescribed in the rules of practice should be followed in an original action in the supreme court. In other respects, those rules, when their application is appropriate, may be taken as a guide to procedure in an original action in this court.

Historical Note

New rule effective January 1, 2006.

§ 84a-3. Discovery

The rules of practice pertaining to discovery shall not apply in original actions in the supreme court except to the extent expressly authorized by the court in a particular case.

Historical Note

New rule effective January 1, 2006.

§ 84a-4. Reference of Issues of Fact

(a) Reference

Issues of fact closed on pleadings in an original action in the supreme court may be referred, by order of the chief justice or his or her designee, to a senior judge, justice or judge trial referee or, should the parties agree, to any other person or persons, which referral may contain such provisions as the court deems available.

(b) Procedure

Unless otherwise ordered by the court, if any reference is made pursuant to subsection (a), the rules of practice pertaining to references in chapter 19 of the rules of practice shall apply.

(c) Costs of References

The court may allocate the costs of the reference in its discretion.

Historical Note

New rule effective January 1, 2006.

§ 84a-5. Evidence

The Connecticut Code of Evidence may be taken as a guide to the admission of evidence in an original action in the supreme court.

Historical Note

New rule effective January 1, 2006.

§ 84a-6. Other Officers

The court may appoint such other officers as the court deems advisable in carrying out its original jurisdiction. The costs of such officers shall be taxed in accordance with 84a-4(c) above.

Historical Note

New rule effective January 1, 2006.

CHAPTER 85

SANCTIONS

§ 85-1. Lack of Diligence in Prosecuting or Defending Appeal

If a party shall fail to prosecute an appeal with proper diligence, the court may dismiss the appeal with costs. If a party shall fail to defend against an appeal with proper diligence, the court may set aside in whole or in part the judgment under attack, with costs, and direct the entry of an appropriate final judgment by the trial court against the party guilty of the failure. If that party is a defendant in the action, the directed judgment may be in the nature of a judgment by default for such amount as may, upon a hearing in damages, be found to be due. If that party is a plaintiff in the action, the directed judgment may be one dismissing the action as to that plaintiff, and the judgment shall operate as an adjudication upon the merits. The statutory provisions regarding the opening of judgments of nonsuit and by default shall not apply to a judgment directed under the provisions of this rule.

Historical Note

Derivation:
    1978 P.B. (1996–97), § 4184A
    1978 P.B. (1986–96), § 4055
    1978 P.B., § 3109
    1963 P.B., § 696
    1951 P.B., § 436A

This rule was new in 1958 and was amended effective September 4, 1973 to eliminate any reference to writs of error.

Cross References

Maltbie, Conn.App.Proc.2d, § 276
P.B. § 66-8

AUTHORS' COMMENTS

Since 1985, it has been clear that any motion under this section, whether for dismissal or judgment, may be filed at any time. However, if the appellee is delinquent, the Supreme Court does not reverse the judgment as a penalty. Rather, if for example, the appellee does not file a brief, the Supreme Court decides the case on the appellant's brief only. Pac v. Altham, 49 Conn.App. 503, 506–07, 714 A.2d 716, 717 (1998) (appellee denied right to oral argument); East Hartford Housing Authority v. Morales, 67 Conn.App. 139 n.1, 786 A.2d 1134,

1135 n.1 (2001) (case considered on appellant's brief and record); Fromm v. Fromm, 108 Conn.App. 376, 383 n.3, 948 A.2d 328, 332 n.3 (2008) (same, but appellee simply did not show up); Rhode v. Milla, 287 Conn. 731, 733 n.3, 949 A.2d 1227, 1231 n.3 (2008) (same, but appellee did not even file a brief although ordered to do so) (judgment affirmed). However, in Papagorgiou v. Anastopoulous, 29 Conn.App. 142, 613 A.2d 853, cert. denied, 224 Conn. 919, 618 A.2d 527 (1992), the Appellate Court dismissed the defendants' appeal as rendered moot by the defendants' failure to file a cross-appellees' brief despite a representation that one would be filed, which resulted in a judgment for the plaintiff on her cross appeal. The Appellate Court did not reach the merits on either the appeal or the cross appeal.

Parties are not safe from this section because motions for extension have been granted under § 66-1; actually, the more such motions for extension are filed and granted, the more likely is action under this section, Chanosky v. City Bldg. Supply Co., 152 Conn. 449, 451–52, 208 A.2d 337, 338–39 (1965), although that case concerned extensions granted by the trial court rather than by the Supreme Court. See also Tamarit v. Ottolini, 145 Conn. 586, 145 A.2d 587 (1958). In State v. Files, 183 Conn. 586, 441 A.2d 27, 27 A.L.R.4th 208 (1981), a new trial was ordered because of the state's thirteen month delay in preparing its brief after three extensions had been granted by the Supreme Court, and in Bronson v. President, etc., of Mechanics' Bank of New Haven, 83 Conn. 128, 75 A. 709 (1910), the appeal was dismissed after the appellant delayed having the record printed promptly.

Note that the ultimate sentence of this section is the only area of the Supreme Court rules where the constitutional supremacy of the judiciary in rule making is explicitly stated. Compare State v. Clemente, 166 Conn. 501, 353 A.2d 723 (1974).

One problem that frustrates appellees is the appellant who simply will not give up and keeps filing motions and delaying resolution of the case. In Mortgage Electronic Registration Systems, Inc. v. Book, 110 Conn.App. 833, 956 A.2d 609 (2008), cert. denied, 290 Conn. 909, 964 A.2d 546 (2009), the Appellate Court entered an elaborate set of orders directing the appellate clerk not to accept certain papers or further appeals filed by the defendant before first getting permission from the Appellate Court. Without such permission, the clerk was directed to return the papers to the defendant.

§ 85-2. Other Actions Subject to Sanctions

Actions which may result in the imposition of sanctions include, but are not limited to, the following:

(1)   Failure to comply with rules and orders of the court.

(2)   Filing of any papers which unduly delay the progress of an appeal.

(3)   Presentation of unnecessary or unwarranted motions or opposition to motions.

(4)   Presentation of unnecessary or unwarranted issues on appeal.

(5)   Presentation of a frivolous appeal or frivolous issues on appeal.

(6)   Presentation of a frivolous defense or defenses on appeal.

(7)   Failure to attend preargument settlement conferences.

(8)   Disregard of rules governing withdrawal of appeals.

(9)   Repeated failures to meet deadlines.

Offenders will be subject, at the discretion of the court, to appropriate discipline, including the prohibition against appearing in the court or filing any papers in the court for a reasonable and definite period of time, the imposition of a fine pursuant to General Statutes § 51-84, and costs and payment of expenses, together with attorney's fees to the opposing party.

The sanction of prohibition against filing any papers in the court shall not prevent an offender from filing a motion for reconsideration of that sanction within seven days.

Offenders subject to such discipline include both counsel and self-represented parties and, if appropriate, parties represented by counsel.

Historical Note

Derivation:
   1978 P.B. (1996–97), § 4184B
   1978 P.B.(1986–96), § 4184
   1978 P.B. (1979–86), § 3114A

This rule was completely revised effective July 16, 1990 to incorporate much of the language of the now repealed Appellate Court § 2036. The prior rule stated as follows:

The presentation to the court of unnecessary motions and the unwarranted opposition to motions, or the presentation to the court of a frivolous appeal or frivolous issues and defenses on appeal or the failure to comply with rules and orders of the court or the filing of any papers which unduly delay the progress of an appeal, will subject an offender, at the discretion of the court, to appropriate discipline, including the imposition of a fine pursuant to Gen.Stat. Sec. 51-84, and costs and payment of expenses including attorney's fees to the opposing party. Offenders subject to such discipline include both counsel and self-represented parties.

Actions which may result in the imposition of sanctions include, but are not limited to, failure to attend preargument conferences, disregard of rules governing withdrawal of appeals and repeated failure to meet deadlines.

This section was strengthened effective October 1, 1986. The old § 3114A stated as follows: "The presentation to the court of unnecessary motions and the unwarranted opposition to motions, or the presentation to the court of frivolous issues and defenses on appeal, which in either case unduly delay the progress of an appeal, will subject an offender, at the discretion of the court, to appropriate discipline, including the imposition of costs and payment of expenses including attorney's fees to the opposing counsel or party. Failure of counsel to comply with the rules and orders of the court may subject counsel to discipline."

The following history refers to old § 3114A:

Entirely new rule effective July 1, 1979. The rule was greatly strengthened effective January 1, 1985 to refer to frivolous issues and defenses and to add the last sentence.

AUTHORS' COMMENTS

Note that reconsideration of a sanctions order prohibiting the filing of any paper must be made in seven days rather than the usual ten.

The test whether an appeal is frivolous under this rule is the same as that under Rule 3.1 of the Rules of Professional Conduct. Texaco, Inc. v. Golart, 206

Conn. 454, 463–464, 538 A.2d 1017, 1021–1022 (1988). A motion to dismiss an appeal as frivolous, although not listed as a possible remedy in the rule, was granted in Connecticut Nat. Bank v. Zuckerman, 31 Conn.App. 440, 624 A.2d 1163 (1993); and in Glenfed Mortg. Corp. v. Crowley, 61 Conn.App. 84, 763 A.2d 19 (2000). It was denied in Knutson Mortg. Corp. v. Salata, 55 Conn.App. 784, 785 n.2, 740 A.2d 918 n.2 (1999).

The respondent father's appeal was dismissed because he failed to appear for oral argument in In re Shanice P., 64 Conn.App. 78, 779 A.2d 151 (2001).

Sanctions of $500 were imposed for failure to attend a settlement conference in Esposito v. Presnick, 15 Conn.App. 654, 665–68, 546 A.2d 899, 904–06 (1988). A $750 sanction for that offense was imposed in Feuerman v. Feuerman, 39 Conn.App. 775, 667 A.2d 802 (1995). In Srager v. Koenig, 42 Conn.App. 617, 681 A.2d 323 (1996), the Appellate Court ordered the plaintiff's attorney to pay the defendant's attorney over $1,300 in attorneys' fees and costs for abuse of the judicial process.

The Appellate Court has held that sanctions must be claimed by motion, and not raised for the first time in the brief on the merits. Hernandez v. Dawson, 109 Conn.App. 639, 643, 953 A.2d 664, 667 (2008); Main v. Main, 17 Conn.App. 670, 677, 555 A.2d 997, 1001, cert. denied, 211 Conn. 809, 559 A.2d 1142 (1989). The authors disagree with this decision. If the appeal or parts of it are truly frivolous, why put extra roadblocks in the way of imposing sanctions? If the issue is raised in the appellee's brief, the appellant has an opportunity to respond in the reply brief. See Adamsons v. Wharton, 771 F.2d 41, 43 n.4, 27 Ed. Law Rep. 73 (2d Cir. 1985). On the other hand, Bove v. Bove, 128 Conn.App. 811, 818 n.7, 20 A.3d 31, 35 n.7, cert. denied, 302 Conn. 904, 23 A.3d 1244 (2011), surprisingly suggests, contrary to *Hernandez* and *Main*, that the appellee should have raised the issue on a cross appeal. The authors do not understand the reference to a cross appeal, as the challenged action is the party's frivolous appeal, not a decision of the trial court. Why is the court even thinking of these roadblocks when it can act on its own under § 85-3?

If sanctions must be claimed by motion, the authors suggest that a motion to dismiss would be appropriate. If the appeal is truly frivolous, why put the appellee to the time and expense of going through the entire appellate process?

The reference to "frivolous issues on appeal" was originally added to the old Appellate Court rule in 1988 following the decisions in Falls Mills Associates, Ltd. v. Maruzo, 13 Conn.App. 119 n.1, 534 A.2d 912 n.1 (1987). It was added to this section in 1992. However, *Bove* denied a motion for sanctions when it found that one of the issues was not frivolous.

The Appellate court has occasionally dismissed an appeal and barred the appellant from filing any further appeals or motions concerning a particular case. See, e.g., Lee v. Palumbo, A.C. 23073 (Order entered June 19, 2002).

§ 85-3. Procedure on Sanctions

Sanctions may be imposed by the court, on its own motion, or on motion by any party to the appeal. A motion for sanctions may be filed at any time. Before the court imposes any sanction on its own motion, it shall provide notice to the parties and an opportunity to respond.

Historical Note

Derivation:
    1978 P.B. (1996–97), § 4184C
The last sentence was revised to eliminate the need for a hearing effective

March 1, 2013.

This rule was new effective September 3, 1996.

CHAPTER 86

RULE CHANGES; EFFECTIVE DATE; APPLICABILITY

§ 86-1. Publication of Rules; Effective Date
§ 86-2. Rule Changes; Applicability to Pending Appeals

§ 86-1. Publication of Rules; Effective Date

Each rule hereafter adopted by the justices of the supreme court and the judges of the appellate court shall be promulgated by being published once in the Connecticut Law Journal. The rule shall become effective at such date as the justices and judges shall prescribe, but not less than sixty days after its promulgation. The justices and judges may waive the sixty day provision if they deem that circumstances require that a rule or a change in an existing rule be adopted expeditiously.

Historical Note

Derivation:
  1978 P.B. (1986–97), § 4188
  1978 P.B., § 3165
  1963 P.B., § 763

This rule was new in 1963, and substantially unchanged since then, except that the last sentence was added in 2005.

Cross Reference

P.B. § 1-9(a)

AUTHORS' COMMENTS

The final published rule does not have to track in haec verba the language of the proposed rule, nor do the subscribers to the Journal actually have to receive it within 60 days. Sweet v. Sweet, 190 Conn. 657, 666–67, 462 A.2d 1031, 1037 (1983). The Supreme Court and the Appellate Court have not complied with this section on a number of occasions. See 49 Conn.L.J. No. 45, p. 3B (no advance notice at all given); 44 Conn.L.J. No. 49, p. 1C; 44 Conn.L.J. No. 52, p. 1C; 45 Conn.L.J. No. 8, p. 1C. In some cases § 60-3 was referred to. The Supreme Court apparently considers C.G.S.A. § 51-14, which requires public hearings before the adoption of rules, to be unconstitutional.

§ 86-2. Rule Changes; Applicability to Pending Appeals

Whenever a new rule is adopted or a change is made to an existing rule, the new rule or rule change shall apply to all appeals pending on the effective date of the new rule or rule change and to all appeals filed thereafter. Appellate papers filed prior to the effective date of any new rule or rule change need not be refiled.

Any difficulty occasioned by the application of a new rule or rule change to appeals taken prior to the effective date thereof shall be resolved in the spirit of Section 60-1.

Historical Note

Derivation:
  1978 P.B. (1986–97), § 4189
  1978 P.B., § 3166

This section was updated for the rules effective October 1, 1986 and then again for the rules effective October 1, 1992 and effective September 3, 1996.

Similar language was enacted effective July 1, 1978 and January 1, 1985 to accommodate the numerous technical changes taking effect then.

A different transitional provision was enacted when the finding system was abolished effective July 1, 1979.

AUTHORS' COMMENTS

This provision saved the day in McKeon v. Lennon, 131 Conn.App. 585, 611, 27 A.3d 436, 452, cert. denied, 303 Conn. 901, 31 A.3d 1178 (2011), by applying the amendment to P.B. § 61-9 (amended appeal from final judgment provides appellate jurisdiction even if original appeal dismissed for lack of final judgment).

This rule does not apply to the July 1, 2013, revisions pertaining to the elimination of the printed record.

FORMS*

If a form is inconsistent with a rule of law, the form, even though it is officially approved by the judges, must yield to the rule, Altman v. Hill, 144 Conn. 233, 238–39, 129 A.2d 358, 361–62 (1957). Cf. State v. Grant, 176 Conn. 17, 404 A.2d 873 (1978). "Furthermore, the forms for appeal and amended appeals do not in any way implicate subject matter jurisdiction." Pritchard v. Pritchard, 281 Conn. 262, 275, 914 A.2d 1025, 1033 (2007).

---

*Used with permission of the Connecticut Judicial Branch, Copyright © 2011, Secretary of State, State of Connecticut.

Form JD-SC-28. Non-Criminal Appeal Form (Annotated)

APPEAL - CIVIL
JD-SC-28   Rev. 12-09
P.B. §§ 3-8, 62-8, 63-3, 63-4, 63-10
C.G.S. §§ 31-301b, 51-197f, 52-470

(Page 1 of 2)

See Instructions on Back/page 2

☐ **To Supreme Court**   ☐ **To Appellate Court**

Name of case *(State full name of case as it appears in the judgment file)*

Classification							Other *(Specify)*
☐ Appeal	☐ Cross appeal	☐ Joint appeal	☐ Amended appeal	☐ Stipulation for reservation	☐ Corrected/amended appeal form	☐	

Trial Court History

Tried to   Trial court location
☐ Court   ☐ Jury

Trial court judges being appealed   List all trial court docket numbers, including all location prefixes

All other trial court judge(s) who were involved with the case

Judgment for *(Where there are multiple parties, specify any individual party or parties for whom judgment may have been entered.)*
☐ Plaintiff   ☐ Defendant   ☐ Other: _____

Judgment date of decision being appealed	Date of issuance of notice on any order on any motion which would render judgment ineffective	Date for filing appeal extended to

Case type
☐ Juvenile — Termination of Parental Rights   ☐ Juvenile — Order of Temporary Custody   ☐ Juvenile — Other _____
☐ Civil/Family: Major/Minor code _____   ☐ Habeas Corpus   ☐ Workers compensation   ☐ Other _____

For habeas corpus or zoning appeals indicate the date certification was granted: _____

Appeal

Appeal filed by *(Where there are multiple parties, specify the name of the individual party or parties filing this appeal.)*
☐ Plaintiff(s) _____   ☐ Defendant(s) _____   ☐ Other _____

From *(the action which constitutes the appealable judgment or decision):* _____

If to the Supreme Court, the statutory basis for the appeal *(Connecticut General Statutes section 51-199)*

By *(Signature of attorney or self-represented party)* ▶	Telephone number	Fax number	Juris number *(If applicable)*

Type name and address of person signing above *(This is your appearance; see Practice Book section 62-8)*   E-mail address

Appearance

"X" one if applicable
☐ Counsel or self-represented party who files this appeal will be deemed to have appeared **in addition to** counsel of record who appeared in the trial court under Practice Book section 62-8.
☐ Under Practice Book section 3-8, counsel or self-represented party who files this appeal is appearing **in place of:**   Name of counsel or self-represented party   Juris number *(If applicable)*

Certification (Practice Book section 63-3)

I certify that a copy of this appeal was mailed or delivered to all counsel and self-represented parties of record as required by Practice Book section 62-7 on:*   Signed *(Individual counsel/self-represented party)* ▶

* Attach a list with the name, telephone number and fax number of each counsel and self-represented party and the address where the copy was mailed or delivered.

To Be Completed By Trial Court Clerk   Fees, Costs, and Security waived by Judge   Court Use Only
☐ Entry Fee Paid   ☐ No Fees Required   ☐ *(enter judge's name below)*   Date and time filed

Judge   Date waived

Signed *(Clerk of trial court)*   Date

The clerk of the original trial court, if different from this court, was notified on _____ that this appeal was filed.
In habeas matters, a copy of this endorsed appeal was provided to the Office of the Chief State's Attorney, Appellate Bureau, on _____

Documents to be given to the Appellate Clerk with the endorsed Appeal form

The following documents must be filed with the Appellate Clerk when filing the endorsed appeal form; Practice Book sections 63-3 and 63-4.
1. Preliminary Statement of the Issues
2. Preliminary Designation of Pleadings
3. Court Reporter's Acknowledgment/Certification re transcript
4. Docketing Statement
5. Statement for Preargument Conference (form JD-SC-28A)
6. Draft Judgment File
7. Constitutionality Notice (if applicable)
8. Sealing Order form, if any
9. List of counsel of record in trial court (DS1 received from clerk)
10. Proof of receipt of the copy of the endorsed appeal form by the original trial court clerk or the clerk of the court or courts where the case was transferred, if the case was in more than one trial court

Certification

I certify that a copy of the endorsed appeal and all documents to be given to the Appellate Clerk with the endorsed Appeal form were mailed or delivered to all counsel and self-represented parties of record* as required by Practice Book section 63-3 on: Signed *(Individual counsel or self-represented party)* ▶

* Attach a list with the name, telephone number and fax number of each counsel and self-represented party and the address at which the copy was mailed or delivered.

[PRINT]   [RESET]

AUTHORS' COMMENTS

Note: This form is only for non-criminal cases. Attached to it is JD-SC-28A (Statement for Preargument Conference).

1. See § 61-8 and comments.

2. See § 61-7 and comments.

3. See § 61-9 and comments.

4. See § 73-1 and comments.

5. This should not be used when filing an amended appeal under § 61-9. It is used when corrections to the original appeal form are made.

6. This whole form is inappropriate for the writ of error (see § 72-3). The authors recommend using our unofficial form.

7. If the notice of judgment is sent out after judgment is entered, the appeal period runs from the notice date. See § 63-1 and comments. Why the form refers to the date of judgment is difficult to see.

8. See § 63-1 and comments.

9. See § 66-1 and comments.

10. See Form 103.1.

11. Do not say "et al." Name all appellants.

12. This could be an intervening party, a third party plaintiff or defendant, or a petitioner, respondent, guardian ad litem, or minor child. For a nonparty, use a writ of error.

13. Unless some specialized statute is involved, language from P.B. § 61-1 should be used. When in doubt, always include the word "judgment". If there is more than one judgment in the file, the judgment being appealed should be specified. Any judgment other than the one specified will not be considered unless the appeal is amended. Rocque v. DeMilo and Co., Inc., 85 Conn.App. 512, 527, 857 A.2d 976, 986 (2004).

14. Make reference to the appropriate subsection of C.G.S.A. § 51-199(b).

15. Ask the trial court clerk to fill out these boxes in your presence when you file the appeal.

16. Give the trial court clerk an extra copy of the appeal form so he can stamp it for your records.

Form JD-SC-28A. Statement for Preargument Conference (Annotated)

STATEMENT FOR PREARGUMENT CONFERENCE
JD-SC-28A New 12-09

Settlement Material - Confidential

CONNECTICUT JUDICIAL BRANCH
APPELLATE CLERK
231 CAPITOL AVENUE
HARTFORD CT 06106

Instructions

1. Fill out this form by using a typewriter or computer and mail or deliver a copy to all other parties or their attorneys if they are represented by an attorney. (See Practice Book Section 62-7 for more information).
2. List on the back of this form the names and addresses and, if known, e-mail address of all parties and attorneys that a copy of this form has been mailed or delivered to as required in instruction number 1 above.
3. If you are the party who is appealing (appellant), you must attach to this form a copy of the trial court's written decision or a transcript of the trial court's decision if that decision was not in writing. (See Practice Book Section 64-1 for more information).
4. Give the original and one copy of this form to the Appellate Clerk at 231 Capitol Avenue, Hartford, CT 06106.
5. Keep a copy of this form and bring it to the preargument conference.

Name of case(s)	For Court use only (Docket Numbers)
Case type 1	
Briefly describe the final judgment/ruling appealed	
Party or parties appealing	

Attorney or self-represented party filing statement for preargument conference/juris number	Telephone number

Address *(Number, street, town, state and zip)*

Filing status *(Check all that apply)*
☐ Attorney   ☐ Self-represented party   ☐ Appellant   ☐ Cross appellant

1. State the issues you intend to present on the appeal or cross-appeal or, alternatively, attach a copy of your Preliminary Statement of the Issues to this form (Practice Book Sections 61-8, 63-4). Continue on separate page if necessary.

2. If this appeal was filed in the Appellate Court, should it be transferred to the Supreme Court?   ☐ Yes *(Explain below)*   ☐ No 2

3. Would you be willing to waive oral argument in this case?   ☐ Yes   ☐ No 3

4. Have you attached a copy of the memorandum of decision or a transcript of oral decision?   ☐ Yes   ☐ No 4

Notice To Counsel And Self-represented Parties

If you do not file this form, or do not come to a preargument conference, sanctions may be imposed (Practice Book Sections 85-2, 85-3). It is the duty of counsel and self-represented parties to communicate with each other to assure attendance at the conference.

I certify that a copy of the above was mailed to all counsel and self-represented parties of record, Practice Book Section 62-7. 5

Signature of individual counsel/self-represented party	Date signed

AUTHORS' COMMENTS

Note: This form must be filed in all non-criminal cases along with other § 63-4 papers.

1. See Superior Court Form 103.1.

2. See §§ 65-1 and 65-2. This is an important tactical decision. This box should be filled in only after considerable thought is given to which court is likely to give your case the more favorable reception. The judge assigned to handle the settlement conference recommends cases for transfer. The recommendation then goes to retired Justice David Borden, who is authorized to make the final decision on transfer.

3. See § 70-1. Checking "yes" may signal that the appeal is weak.

4. The appellant must attach the memorandum or transcript. See instruction three at the top of the form. If there is neither, see P.B. §§ 64-1 and 64-2.

5. This certification does not comply with § 62-7. See instruction number 2. Also include telephone and fax numbers.

Form JD-SC-29. Criminal Appeal Form (Annotated)

APPEAL - CRIMINAL
JD-SC-29   Rev. 12-09
P.B. §§ 3-8, 62-7, 62-8, 63-3, 63-4
C.G.S. §§ 51-197f, 52-470

(Page 1 of 2)

See Instructions on Back/page 2

☐ To Supreme Court   ☐ To Appellate Court

Name of case

Classification						
☐ Appeal	☐ Cross 1 appeal	☐ Joint 2 appeal	☐ Amended 3 appeal	☐ Stipulation for reservation	☐ Corrected/amended 4 appeal form ☐	Other *(Specify)* 5

Trial Court History

Tried to   ☐ Court   ☐ Jury   ☐ Magistrate   Trial court location

Trial court judges being appealed   List all trial court docket numbers, including all location prefixes

All other trial court judge(s) who were involved with the case

Judgment for   ☐ State of Connecticut   ☐ Defendant

Judgment date of decision being appealed 6	Date of issuance of notice on any order on any motion which would render judgment ineffective 7	Date for filing appeal extended to 8

Case type   ☐ Infraction   ☐ Juvenile   ☐ Felony/Misdemeanor
☐ Other *(Specify)*

Appeal

Appeal filed by   ☐ State of Connecticut   ☐ Defendant 9 _____   ☐ Other 10 _____

From *(the action which constitutes the final judgment)*: 11

If this appeal is taken by the State of Connecticut, give name of Judge granting permission to appeal and date of order

If to the Supreme Court, the statutory basis for the appeal *(Connecticut General Statutes section 51-199)* 12

By *(Signature of attorney or self-represented party)* ▶	Telephone number	Fax number	Juris number *(If applicable)*

Type name and address of person signing above *(This is your appearance; see Practice Book section 62-8)*   E-mail address

Appearance

"X" one if applicable
☐ Counsel or self-represented party who files this appeal will be deemed to have appeared **in addition** to counsel of record who appeared in the trial court under Practice Book section 62-8.
☐ Under Practice Book section § 3-8, counsel or self-represented party who files this appeal is appearing **in place of**:   Name of counsel or self-represented party   Juris number *(If applicable)*

Certification (Practice Book section 63-3)

I certify that a copy of this appeal was mailed or delivered to all counsel and self-represented parties of record as required by Practice Book section 62-7 on:*   Signed *(Individual counsel/self-represented party)* ▶

* Attach a list with the name, telephone number and fax number of each counsel and self-represented party and the address where the copy was mailed or delivered.

To Be Completed By Trial Court Clerk

☐ Entry Fee Paid   ☐ No Fees Required   ☐   Fees, Costs, and Security waived by Judge 13, 14 *(enter judge's name below)*

For Appellate Clerk's Office Use Only

Judge   Date waived

Signed *(Clerk of trial court)*   Date

The clerk of the original trial court, if different from this court, was notified on _____ that this appeal was filed.

A copy of this endorsed appeal was provided to the Office of the Chief State's Attorney, Appellate Bureau, on _____ .

Documents to be given to the Appellate Clerk with the endorsed Appeal form

The following documents must be filed with the Appellate Clerk when filing the endorsed appeal form; Practice Book section 63-4.
1. Preliminary Statement of the Issues
2. Preliminary Designation of Pleadings
3. Court Reporter's Acknowledgment/Certification re transcript
4. Docketing Statement
5. Constitutionality Notice (if applicable)
6. Sealing Order form, if any

Certification

I certify that a copy of the endorsed appeal and all documents to be given to the Appellate Clerk with the endorsed Appeal form were mailed or delivered to all counsel and self-represented parties of record* as required by Practice Book section 63-3 on: Signed *(Individual counsel or self-represented party)* ▶

* Attach a list with the name, telephone number and fax number of each counsel and self-represented party and the address at which the copy was mailed or delivered.

AUTHORS' COMMENTS

1. See § 61-8 and comments.

2. See § 61-7 and comments.

3. See § 61-9 and comments.

4. This should not be used when filing an amended appeal under § 61-9. It is used when corrections to the original appeal form are made.

5. This whole form is inappropriate for the writ of error (see § 72-3). The authors recommend using unofficial form 3000.24-A.

6. If the notice of judgment is sent out after judgment is entered, the appeal period runs from the notice date. See § 63-1 and comments.

7. See § 66-1 and comments.

8. See § 63-1 and comments.

9. Do not say "et al." Name all appellants.

10. Who this might be is unclear, perhaps the victim.

11. Unless some specialized statute is involved, language from P.B. § 61-1 should be used. When in doubt, always include the word "judgment". In most cases it is sufficient to simply say "from the final judgment". If there is more than one judgment in the file, the judgment being appealed should be specified.

12. Make reference to the appropriate subsection of C.G.S.A. § 51-199(b).

13. Ask the trial court clerk to fill out these boxes in your presence when you file the appeal.

14. Give the trial court clerk an extra copy of the appeal form so it can be stamped for your records.

Form 3000.1-A. Model Appeal by Plaintiff and Cross Appeal by Defendant in Court or Jury Case*

Plaintiff's Appeal

Prepare Form JD-SC-28 or JD-SC-29.

Preliminary Statement of Issues

[to be filed within 10 days of appeal, §§ 63-3, 63-4(a)(1)]

Pursuant to P.B. § 63-4(a)(1), the plaintiff intends to present the following issues on this appeal:

1. Did the court err in overruling the plaintiff's motion to strike the second special defense?

2. Did the court err in concluding that the defendant's negligence was not a substantial factor in causing the plaintiff's injuries?

3. Did the court err in concluding that the plaintiff was negligent in failing to wear his seat belt at the time of the collision?

[Section 3000.1-A]

*Supplemental Form supplied—not P.B. Form.

4.   Did the court err in concluding that the plaintiff's negligence, if any, in failing to wear a seat belt was a substantial factor in causing his injuries?

5.   Did the court err in admitting the testimony of the defendant's expert concerning the effect of the plaintiff's failure to wear a seat belt on his injuries?

Plaintiff

by
his attorney.
Filed July 13, 2015.

Designation of Pleadings
[to be filed within 10 days of appeal, §§ 63-3, 63-4(a)(2)]

Pursuant to P.B. § 63-4(a)(2), the he plaintiff designates the following pleadings which he deems necessary to include in the appellate record:

1.   The complaint;

2.   The answer filed [date]; (DS-#) [get docket entries from trial court computer]

3.   Motion to strike the second special defense filed [date]; (DS-#)

4.   Ruling denying motion to strike the second special defense filed [date]; (DS-#)

5.   Memorandum of decision filed [date]; (DS-#)

6.   Judgment file;

7.   Appeal.

Plaintiff

by
his attorney.
Filed July 13, 2015.

Transcript Order Form
[to be filed within 10 days of appeal, §§ 63-3, 63-4(a)(3); see also § 63-8]

[File Form JD-ES-38]

Filed July 13, 2015.

Docketing Statement
[to be filed with appeal, § 63-4(a)(4)]

[give required information]

Plaintiff

by
his attorney.
Filed July 13, 2015.

Preargument Conference Statement
[to be filed within 10 days of appeal, § 63-4(a)(5)]

[fill out form attached to appeal form]
Filed July 13, 2015.

Draft Judgment File
[to be filed with in 10 days of appeal, §§ 63-3, 63-4(a)(6)]

[Prepare in accordance with P.B. §§ 6-2, 6-3]
Filed July 13, 2015.

Notice Re Constitutionality of State Statute
[If applicable, to be filed within10 days of appeal, §§ 63-3, 63-4(a)(7)]

[Prepare proper notice]
Filed July 13, 2015.

Defendant's Cross Appeal
[to be filed within ten days of appeal, § 61-8]
Prepare Form JD-SC-28.

Filed July 13, 2015.

Preliminary Statement of Issues on Cross Appeal
[to be filed with cross appeal, §§ 61-8, 63-4(a)(1)]
Pursuant to P.B. § 63-4(a)(1), the defendant intends to present the following issue on this cross appeal:

1. Did the court err in failing to assess attorney's fees against the plaintiff for bringing a frivolous action?
Defendant

by
his attorney.
Filed July 23, 2015.

Designation of Pleadings on Cross Appeal
[to be filed within 10 days of cross appeal, §§ 61-8, 63-4(a)(2)]

Pursuant to P.B. § 63-4(a)(2), the defendant designates the following pleadings which he deems necessary to include in the printed appeal record:

1. The defendant's motion for attorney's fees filed [date]; (DS-#)

2. The ruling denying the motion for attorney's fees filed [date]. (DS-#)
Defendant

by
his attorney.
Filed July 23, 2015.

Transcript Order Form
[to be filed within 10 days of cross appeal, §§ 61-8, 63-3, 63-4(a)(4)]

[File Form JD-ES-38]
Filed July 23, 2015.

Docketing Statement on Cross Appeal
[to be filed within 10 days of cross appeal, §§ 61-8, 63-3, 63-4(a)(4)]

[give required information]
Defendant

by
his attorney.
Filed July 23, 2015.

Documents to be filed by Appellee

Preliminary Statement of Issues by Appellee

[optional]

[to be filed within 20 days of filing of appellant's preliminary statement, § 63-4(a)(1)]

The defendant wishes to present for review the following alternate ground upon which the judgment may be affirmed:

1. Did the court err in concluding that the defendant was negligent in operating his vehicle at the time of the collision?

The defendant further wishes to present for review the following adverse ruling of the court which should be considered on appeal in the event the plaintiff-appellant is awarded a new trial:

1. Did the court err in granting the plaintiff's motion to strike the first special defense alleging an unavoidable accident?

Defendant

by

his attorney.

Filed August 3, 2015.

Designation of Pleadings by Appellee
[optional]

[to be filed within 20 days of filing of appellant's designation, § 63-4(a)(2)]

The defendant designates the following pleadings which are necessary to include in the appellate record:

1. The plaintiff's motion to strike the first special defense filed [date]; (DS-)

2. The ruling on the motion to strike the first special defense filed [date]. (DS-)

The defendant further objects to item 1 in the plaintiff's designation on the grounds that it is immaterial to the issues raised on appeal.

Defendant

by

his attorney.

Filed August 3, 2015.

Transcript Order Form by Appellee
[optional]

[to be filed within 20 days of filing of appellant's designation,
§ 63-4(a)(3)]

[File Form JD-ES-38]

Filed August 3, 2015.

Docketing Statement
[if necessary]

[to be filed within 20 days of filing of appellant's designation,
§ 63-4(a)(4)]

[give required information]

Defendant

by
his attorney.
Filed August 3, 2015.

[The parties now await the transcript. After it is sent to him, the appellant has 45 days (§ 67-3) to file his brief and the record.]

Documents to be filed with appellant's brief

Certification Re Brief

[to be filed with appellant's brief]

I hereby certify that the foregoing brief complies with the formatting requirements set forth in P.B. § 67-2 and that the font is [Arial/Univers] 12.

I further certify that a copy of the plaintiff's brief was mailed on November 5, 2015 to the [list trial judge or judges, P.B. § 67-2] [list names, addresses, and telephone and facsimile numbers of all counsel of record].

Plaintiff

by
his attorney.
Filed November 5, 2015.

Notice of Filing Transcript
[to be filed with appellant's brief]

[File Form JD-CL-62]

Documents to be filed with appellee's brief

Revised Designation of Pleadings

[to be filed with appellant's brief]

[File revisions to original based on what issues are actually
briefed]

Certification Re Brief
[to be filed with appellee's brief]

I hereby certify that a copy of the defendant's brief was mailed
on October December 5, 2015 to [list the trial judge or judges,
P.B. § 67-2] [list names, addresses, and telephone and facsimile
numbers of all counsel of record].

I further certify that the foregoing brief complies with the
formatting requirements set forth in P.B. § 67-2 and that the font
is [Arial/Univers] 12.
Defendant

by
his attorney.
Filed December 7, 2015.

[Thereafter, cases will generally be scheduled for oral argument in the order in which the last brief was filed.]

Form 3000.1-B. Caption of Documents Filed before Appellate Docket Number Assigned*

(Superior Court No. 157898)
Barnaby Rudge   Appellate Court [or Supreme
                          Court]

[Section 3000.1-B]

*Supplemental Form supplied—not P.B. Form.

vs.
Uriah Heep   July 13, 2015

Designation of Pleadings

Form 3000.1-C. Caption of Motion Addressed to Appellate or Supreme Court*

A.C. 10986
Barnaby Rudge   Appellate Court [or Supreme
                                 Court]
vs.__   August 3, 2015
Uriah Heep

Motion to Dismiss
    The plaintiff-appellee moves that the Appellate Court dismiss the appeal on the ground that * * *.

Form 3000.1-D. Caption of Document or Motion Addressed to Trial Court Under Appellate Rules*

[such as motion to terminate stay of execution, motion for rectification of appeal]

No. A.C. 10986 (CV 92-
0045678)
Barnaby Rudge   Appellate Court [or Supreme
                                 Court]
vs.   Fairfield Judicial District
Uriah Heep   August 3, 2015

Motion to Terminate Stay of Execution
    The plaintiff-appellee moves, pursuant to § 61-11, that the trial judge (Smith, J.) terminate * * *.

Form 3000.1-E. Certification to Counsel and Pro Se Parties Pursuant to P.B. § 62-7

[Section 3000.1-C]
    *Supplemental Form supplied—not P.B. Form.
[Section 3000.1-D]
    *Supplemental Form supplied—not P.B. Form.

CERTIFICATION

I hereby certify that the foregoing complies with the form and font requirements of P.B. § 66-3 and that the font used is Arial 12. I further certify that a copy of the foregoing was mailed on August 3, 2015 to the following counsel of record [list names, addresses, and telephone and facsimile numbers] by first class mail, postage prepaid [or by hand, or by express U.S. Mail]:

Kenneth J. Bartschi
HORTON, SHIELDS & KNOX, P.C.
90 Gillett Street
Hartford, CT 06105
(860) 522-8338
Fax (860) 728-0401

Form 3000.3-A. Security for Costs*

(Caption)

Recognizance

You, (name and residence—a non-party), deemed by me to be of sufficient responsibility, acknowledge yourself to be bound in this action in a recognizance in the sum of $_____ that (name of the appellant), the appellant, will prosecute the foregoing appeal to full effect and pay any costs for which judgment may be rendered against him.

Dated at (place and date).

_____

Commissioner of the Superior
Court

AUTHORS' COMMENT

This is the security form the authors use, in lieu of prior official forms 3000.3, 3000.4, or 3000.5 (all of which are unnecessarily complicated), when a recognizance is necessary. See commentary to § 63-5. On the filing of an appeal or cross appeal, a recognizance is no longer necessary.

Note that the bottom of the form must be signed by the lawyer and certified to all counsel of record. See § 63-8.

Form JD-CL-62. Notice of Filing Transcript

_____

[Section 3000.3-A]

*Supplemental Form supplied—not P.B. Form.

**NOTICE OF FILING OF
TRANSCRIPT OR LAND
USE REGULATIONS**
JD-CL-62 Rev. 9-02
Pr. Bk. §§ 63-8, 81-6

**STATE OF CONNECTICUT
APPELLATE CLERK'S OFFICE**

INSTRUCTIONS

NOTE: *Transcripts and land use regulations are non-returnable and will be destroyed after completion of appeal process.*

1. Type or print legibly.
2. Submit completed form along with the transcript(s) or land use regulations filed.
3. This document need not be certified under Practice Book Section 62-7. The accuracy of the information will be verified when the transcript or land use regulation is filed in the appellate clerk's office and notice to all concerned will be sent at that time.

☐ AC #
☐ SC # _____   _____

V.

_____

The ☐ appellant
    ☐ appellee   *(Name:)*   _____

☐ is filing: _____ non-returnable volume(s) of **transcript** in the above-captioned appeal on *(date)*: _____

☐ is filing: _____ non-returnable volume(s) of **land use regulations** in the above-captioned appeal on *(date)*: _____

NAME AND MAILING ADDRESS OF COUNSEL OR PRO SE PARTY FILING TRANSCRIPT OR LAND USE REGULATIONS

FOR COURT USE ONLY
NOTICE OF FILING SENT

Form JD-AC-8. Withdrawal

WITHDRAWAL
JD-AC-8 Rev. 9-03
Pr. Bk. §§ 63-9, 63-10

STATE OF CONNECTICUT
SUPREME COURT
APPELLATE COURT
www.jud.ct.gov

COURT ☐ SUPREME ☐ APPELLATE	DOCKET NO.	DATE
NAME OF CASE *(First Named Plaintiff and Defendant)*		

vs.

This appeal/cross-appeal is withdrawn as to:

☐ all parties without costs.

☐ the below-named plaintiff(s) only, without costs

☐ the below-named defendant(s) only, without costs.

By: _____   ☐ Appellant   ☐ Cross-appellant

Type or print name of person signing above   *Law firm affiliation*

This appeal/cross-appeal is withdrawn as a result of:

☐ the settlement conference program *(Pr. Bk. § 63-10)*

☐ some activity BEFORE the case was assigned to the settlement program.

☐ some activity AFTER the settlement program, not related to the settlement program.

For Office Use Only

PRINT   RESET

Illustrations of the Presentation of Rulings on Evidence in a
Brief

A

Jane Stiles, a witness called by the plaintiff, testified that for a
number of months prior to June 27, 1962, she had occupied the
apartment upon the second floor of said tenement house (*transcript* 247) and upon cross-examination by the defendant's counsel
the following occurred (*transcript* 248):

Q. Did the light in the hallway upon the third floor shine down
the stairs?

Mr. Fenn: I object. The time when the witness was upon the
premises was three months prior to the accident.

Mr. Smith: We shall prove that the same conditions continued
up to the time of the accident.

The Court: Upon that assurance I will allow the testimony.

A. It shone almost to the bottom and the stairway was well
lighted by it.

Thereafter the defendant offered no testimony that the conditions testified to by the witness continued unchanged to the time
of the accident, but the plaintiff did not thereafter move to have
the testimony stricken from the record, or request the court to
charge the jury to disregard it, and the court did neither.

B

One of the issues in the trial of this case was whether or not
the defendant was the owner of the car involved in the collision,
and as evidence that he was the plaintiff testified to a conversation she claimed to have had with him in which she testified that,
in answer to a question she put to him as to whether he owned
the car, he answered: "Well, I did." (*transcript* 18) In cross-
examination of the plaintiff she testified (*transcript* 19) that a
third person whose name was unknown to her was present and
took part in this conversation and that he appeared to be a friend
or employee of the defendant. The defendant, as a witness in his
own behalf, testified on direct examination (*transcript* 25) that he
did have a conversation with the plaintiff but denied that
anything was said about the accident or his ownership of the car.
He further testified that the third person present at the conversation was John Smith, who was then employed by him but who
had left his employment six months before the trial.

The following then occurred (*transcript* 26):

Q. Do you know where Smith is now?

A. No.

Q. Have you made efforts to find him?

Mr. Jones: I object. That is entirely irrelevant to any issue in the case.

Mr. Fenn: I claim it. My brother will argue that my failure to produce Smith indicates that if here, his testimony would be hostile to the interests of my client. I want to beat him to it by showing we tried our best to find this man, that he has left Hartford for parts unknown and we just can't locate him.

The Court: Admitted.

A. Yes.

Q. What have you done?

Mr. Jones: Same objection.

Mr. Fenn: Claimed for the purpose I have just stated.

The Court: I think you have gone far enough. Excluded.

Mr. Fenn: Exception. [obsolete]

Later in the trial, John Ray, a police officer of the city of Hartford, called by the defendant, testified on direct examination (*transcript* 32), that he had had a warrant for the arrest of John Smith in his possession for three months and had repeatedly searched for him in Hartford, but had been unable to find him.

Historical Note

Derivation:

1963 P.B., Form 604

1951 P.B., Form 560

1934 P.B., Form 646

Cross References

See §§ 67-4, 67-5.

Form 3000.15. Motion for Review of Decision Concerning Rectification of Appeal

1. On the trial of this case to the jury, the defendant offered evidence that a storm, which occurred on a day shortly before the plaintiff's fall, caused a deposit of ice and snow throughout the city, which would have cost the city many thousands of dollars to remove from the roadways and sidewalks, had the city undertaken to remove it from the sidewalks within a day or two.

2. In his argument counsel for the defendant pointed out, as relevant to the issue of the requirements of reasonable care in making its sidewalks reasonably safe, the great burden this storm placed upon it.

3. In the closing argument the counsel for the plaintiff said in

substance: "The city of New Haven is telling you that they employ 1000 men and 400 trucks, and if they had to clean all the sidewalks in the city they would have to employ 10,000 men, all the king's horses and all the king's men; they are asking you for sympathy. The city can well take care of itself. If there is any sympathy, gentlemen of the jury, it should be for this poor unfortunate woman. Do you want to see her become a public charge? Do you want to see her pass her remaining days on charity, a cripple, just because the officers of the city were not willing to exert themselves a little to protect poor people who, like her, were compelled to walk to their work?"

4.   Counsel for the defendant objected and requested the court to instruct the jury to disregard the portion of the argument above stated; but the court did not in any way instruct the jury in reference to the matter.

5.   The argument of counsel was not taken by the stenographer.

[or]

There is appended hereto, a transcript of said argument as taken by the stenographer.

6.   The trial court was requested to rectify the appeal by including the above facts in the record, but it refused to do so.

The defendant respectfully moves that the supreme court correct the record, so that the above stated facts will appear therein.

Defendant,

by
his attorney.

(P.B.1963, Form 609; see Rules, Sec. 66-7.)

Historical Note

Derivation:

1963 P.B., Form 609

1951 P.B., Form 565

1934 P.B., Form 653

Cross References

See § 66-7. See also format requirements of § 66-2.

Notice of Appeal and Reservation of Right to Appeal From Judgment Disposing of Part of Issues

(Caption)

The plaintiff (*or* defendant) in the above entitled action respectfully represents

1. A judgment was entered in this action on *(date)* which disposed of certain issues between the parties *(or a part or all of the issues between some of the parties)* in such a manner as to be final, but not terminating the litigation.

2. He therefore exercises his option to reserve his appeal from such judgment until final judgment is rendered which disposes of the cause for all purposes and as respects all parties.

Wherefore, within twenty days after the issuance of notice of rendition thereof, notice of appeal from this judgment disposing of part of the issues is hereby given.

(P.B.1963, Form 612; see Rules, Sec. 61-5.)

Reservation

STIPULATION

The parties herein unite in requesting the court to reserve the above entitled action for the advice of the supreme court upon the questions arising therein, and stipulate and agree as follows:

1. The facts upon which the questions arise are as follows: *(insert agreed statement of facts or finding of the court).*

2. The questions upon which advice is desired are as follows: *(state clearly and fully the questions upon which advice is desired).*

3. The answers to the questions will determine, or are reasonably certain to enter into the determination of, the case.

4. The present determination of the questions will be in the interest of simplicity, directness and economy in judicial action because *(state reasons).*

Plaintiff,

by
his attorney.

Defendant,

by
his attorney.

RESERVATION

At the request and with the consent of all the parties to the above entitled cause, the court reserves the questions stated in the foregoing stipulation for the consideration and advice of the supreme court.

By the Court (_____, J.)

(P.B.1963, Form 614; see Rules, § 73-1.)

Historical Note

Derivation:

1963 P.B., Form 614

1951 P.B., Form 570

1934 P.B., Forms 658, 659

Reservation in Workers' Compensation Case on Motion of Compensation Review Division*

The Workers' Compensation Division is of the opinion that the decision of this matter involves principles of law which are not free from reasonable doubt and which public interest requires shall be determined by the Appellate Court in order that a definite rule be established applicable to further cases.

The Workers' Compensation Division, therefore, upon its own motion reserves the case for the opinion of the Appellate Court.

By the Compensation Review
Division

AUTHORS' COMMENTS

This form is in accord with C.G.S.A. § 31-324 in effect since July 1, 1983.

Petition to Appellate Court for Certification for Review*

(Caption)

PETITION FOR CERTIFICATION

The Plaintiff petitions the Appellate Court for certification to appeal from the judgment of the Superior Court in this case.

1. The questions presented for review are as follows:

a.

[Section 3000.15]

*Supplemental Form supplied—not P.B. Form.

*Supplemental Form supplied—not P.B. Form.

b.

c.

2. The basis for certification is as follows:

   [make brief statement of grounds under § 81-2(a)(2)]

3. Summary of Case

   [state facts, disposition of trial courts, and how trial court decided the questions presented above]

4. Argument

   [amplify reasons justifying certification]

5. Appendix

   [include trial court decision, list all parties with names and addresses of counsel]

   [Petition exclusive of appendix must not exceed 10 pages]

                                        Plaintiff

                                        by
                                        his attorney.

[order and certification to counsel]

AUTHORS' COMMENTS

This unofficial form tracks the language of § 81-2.

Petition to Supreme Court for Certification for Review From the Appellate Court*

(Caption)

PETITION FOR CERTIFICATION

The Plaintiff petitions the Supreme Court for certification to appeal from the judgment of the Appellate Court in this case.

1. The questions presented for review are as follows:

   a.

   b.

   c.

2. The basis for certification is as follows:

   [make brief statement of grounds under § 84-2, if possible]

---

*Supplemental Form supplied—not P.B. Form.

3. Summary of Case

[state facts, disposition by Appellate Court, and how Appellate Court decided the questions presented above]

4. Argument

[amplify reasons justifying certification—do not submit separate memorandum of law]

5. Appendix

[include Appellate Court decision, list all parties to the appeal in Appellate Court with names and addresses of counsel]

[Petition exclusive of appendix must not exceed 10 pages]

Plaintiff

by
his attorney.

AUTHORS' COMMENTS

This unofficial form tracks the language of § 84-5.

Writ of Error*

WRIT OF ERROR TO SUPREME COURT

To the marshal, his deputy or any constable of the town of Hartford, within said county, Greeting:

By authority of the State of Connecticut you are hereby commanded to summon John Rudd, of the town and county of Hartford, State of Connecticut, to appear before the supreme court of the State of Connecticut, to be held in the town and county of Hartford, in said state, on the first Tuesday of October, 2005, then and there to answer unto the State of Connecticut, in this writ of error, wherein the State of Connecticut complains and says:

1. On May 1, 2005, the State, acting through Richard Fenn, an assistant state's attorney of the Superior Court, G.A. # 14 in said county, brought an information against the defendant in error, a copy of which is hereto annexed as part of the record hereinafter mentioned.

2. On May 10, 2005, upon being arraigned on said warrant and information, said accused filed a motion to strike said information.

---

*Supplemental Form supplied—not P.B. Form.

3. On August 1, 2005, said court by one of its judges, namely Honorable Robert Paine, granted said motion upon the ground that the provision of the General Statutes with the violation of which the accused was charged was unconstitutional and void and found the accused not guilty, all of which proceedings more fully appear in a copy of so much of the record thereof as is pertinent hereto and annexed and made a part hereof as Exhibits A, B, C, and D.

4. The State applied to the said court for permission to appeal, but such permission was denied. The State has moved for review of this denial, but the motion has not yet been acted upon by the Appellate Court.

5. The provisions of the General Statutes giving the right of appeal to the state in criminal cases does not include cases in which permission to appeal has been denied, and this writ of error is brought to present a matter of law, viz., the constitutionality of the provision of the statute with the violation of which the accused was charged, to the supreme court which matter of law cannot be raised by an appeal by the State unless the appellate court vacates the trial court's order denying the motion to appeal.

6. Said court in rendering said judgment erred in the following aspects, namely, in declaring said provision of said statute unconstitutional and void.

The plaintiff in error claims:

That said erroneous judgment be reversed and set aside.

Hereof fail not but due service and return make.

Allowed and signed at Hartford, this fifteenth day of August, A.D.2015.

[s/s Judge or Clerk of the trial court]

Cross References

See §§ 72-1 to 72-4 and § 1 of commentary to § 61-1.

C.G.S.A. §§ 52-572 to 578.

AUTHORS' COMMENTS

This is a revised version of Form 573 of the 1951 Practice Book. The writ must be signed by a judge or clerk. See § 72-3. Note that writs of error should be filed in the Supreme Court (not in the Appellate Court) in all cases.

Table of Laws and Rules

UNITED STATES CODE ANNOTATED

28 U.S.C.A.	Sec.
1292(a)(1)	61-1

FEDERAL RULES OF APPELLATE PROCEDURE

Rule	Sec.
2	60-3

FEDERAL RULES OF CIVIL PROCEDURE

Rule	Sec.	Rule	Sec.
51	60-5	52	60-5

CONNECTICUT CONSTITUTION

	Sec.
Art. 16, § 2	61-1

CONNECTICUT GENERAL STATUTES

Sec.	Sec.	Sec.	Sec.
2-16	61-1	17a-696	61-1
4-183(j)	61-1	19a-221	63-6
8-8	61-1, 83-4	22a-43(d)	61-1
8-8(o)	81-1	31-118	61-1, 63-1
8-9	61-1, 83-4	31-290a	61-1
8-28	83-4	31-290a(b)	66-6, 76-1
8-30	83-4	31-301(a)	63-1, 76-1
8-30a	61-1	31-301b	61-1, 76-1
9-323	61-1	31-324	76-5, Form 3000.15
9-325	61-1	37-3a	61-1
12-103	67-8A, 68-10	38a-139	67-8A, 68-10
12-117a	67-8A, 68-10	42-110h	61-1
12-119	67-8A, 68-10	45a-65	61-1
14-321	61-1	45a-186	61-1
17a-498	63-6	45a-186(f)	61-11
17a-695	61-1	45a-717(b)	63-6

CONNECTICUT GENERAL STATUTES—Continued

CONNECTICUT GENERAL STATUTES—Continued

CONNECTICUT PUBLIC ACTS

CONNECTICUT PRACTICE BOOK

CONNECTICUT PRACTICE BOOK—Continued

CONNECTICUT PRACTICE BOOK—Continued

CONNECTICUT PRACTICE BOOK—Continued

CONNECTICUT PRACTICE BOOK—Continued

CONNECTICUT PRACTICE BOOK—Continued

CONNECTICUT PRACTICE BOOK—Continued

CONNECTICUT RULES OF APPELLATE PROCEDURE

CONNECTICUT RULES OF APPELLATE PROCEDURE—Continued

CONNECTICUT FORMS OF APPELLATE PROCEDURE

CONNECTICUT RULES OF PROFESSIONAL CONDUCT

Table of Cases

A

C

Connecticut Bank and Trust Co., Inc. v. Winters, 225 Conn. 146 (1993)—60-5, 71-1

Connecticut Bank and Trust Co., N.A. v. Reckert, 33 Conn.App. 702 (1994)—61-2

Connecticut Business and Industries Ass'n, Inc. v. Commission on Hospitals and Health Care, 214 Conn. 726, 573 A.2d 736 (1990)—61-1

Connecticut Coalition Against Millstone v. Connecticut Siting Council, 286 Conn. 57 (2008)—67-4

Connecticut Emp. Union Independent, Inc. v. Connecticut State Emp. Ass'n, Inc., 183 Conn. 235, 439 A.2d 321 (1981)—60-5

Connecticut Foundry Co. v. International Ladies Garment Workers Union, AFL-CIO, 177 Conn. 17, 411 A.2d 1, 104 L.R.R.M. (BNA) 2974 (1979)—66-8

Connecticut Ins. Guar. Ass'n v. Drown, 134 Conn.App. 140, 37 A.3d 820 (2012)—61-1, 67-10

Connecticut Ins. Guar. Ass'n v. Fontaine, 278 Conn. 779 (2006)—63-4

Connecticut Light and Power Co. v. Costle, 179 Conn. 415, 426 A.2d 1324 (1980)—61-1, 63-9, 71-2

Connecticut Light and Power Co. v. Lighthouse Landings, Inc., 279 Conn. 90, 900 A.2d 1242 (2006)—60-1, 60-2, 63-1

Connecticut Mobile Home Ass'n, Inc. v. Jensen's, Inc., 178 Conn. 586 (1979)—66-5

Connecticut Mortgage & Title Guaranty Co. v. Di Francesco, 112 Conn. 673, 151 A. 491 (1930)—63-1

Connecticut Nat. Bank v. Giacomi, 242 Conn. 17 (1997)—60-5

Connecticut Nat. Bank v. L & R Realty, 40 Conn.App. 492, 671 A.2d 1315 (1996)—61-1

Connecticut Nat. Bank v. Rytman, 241 Conn. 24 (1997)—61-2

Connecticut Nat. Bank v. Zuckerman, 31 Conn.App. 440, 624 A.2d 1163 (1993)—66-8, 85-2

Connecticut Performing Arts Foundation, Inc. v. Brown, 801 F.2d 566 (2d Cir. 1986)—82-4

Connecticut Pharmaceutical Ass'n, Inc. v. Milano, 191 Conn. 555 (1983)—61-1

Connecticut Post Ltd. Partnership v. South Cent. Connecticut Regional Council of Governments, 60 Conn.App. 21, 758 A.2d 408 (2000)—61-1

Connecticut Resources Recovery Authority v. Planning and Zoning Com'n of Town of Torrington, 46 Conn.App. 563, 699 A.2d 314—61-1

Connecticut Sav. Bank v. Howes, 9 Conn.App. 446, 519 A.2d 1216 (1987)—61-11

Connecticut State Medical Society v. Connecticare, Inc., 272 Conn. 482 (2005)—61-8

Connelly v. Doe, 213 Conn. 66 (1989)—63-1

Connole v. Babij, 140 Conn.App. 494 (2013)—61-8

Conrad v. Erickson, 12 Conn. L. Rptr. 543, 1994 WL 590579 (Conn. Super. Ct. 1994)—61-11

Consiglio v. Transamerica Insurance Group, 55 Conn.App. 134 (1999)—70-7

Consumer Counsel, Office of v. Department of Public Utility Control, 234 Conn. 624, 662 A.2d 1251 (1995)—66-6

Conte v. Conte, 45 Conn.App. 235 (1997)—61-1, 72-1

Continental Nat. Am. Group v. Majeske, 30 Conn.Supp. 567, 305 A.2d 291 (C.P. App. Div. 1973)—63-1

Conway v. City of Hartford, 60 Conn.App. 630 (2000)—61-1

D

E

F

G

H

Harris v. Commissioner of Correction, 271 Conn. 808 (2004)—67-5

Harris v. First Nat. Bank & Trust Co. of New Haven, 139 Conn. 749 (1953)—61-1

Harrison v. Harrison, 94 Conn. 280, 108 A. 800 (1920)—61-1

Harrison v. Harrison, 96 Conn. 568, 114 A. 681 (1921)—73-1

Hartford Acc. and Indem. Co. v. Ace American Reinsurance Co., 279 Conn. 220, 901 A.2d 1164 (2006)—61-1

Hartford Acc. and Indem. Co. v. Ace American Reinsurance Co., 284 Conn. 744 (2007)—61-3

Hartford Cas. Ins. Co. v. Farrish-LeDuc, 275 Conn. 748, 882 A.2d 44 (2005)—73-1

Hartford, City of v. Hartford Elec. Light Co., 172 Conn. 13 (1976)—61-11

Hartford, City of v. Hartford Elec. Light Co., 172 Conn. 71, 372 A.2d 131 (1976)— 60-1, 60-2

Hartford Federal Sav. and Loan Ass'n v. Bowen, 3 Conn. Cir. Ct. 86 (App. Div. 1964)—61-1

Hartford Federal Sav. & Loan Ass'n v. Tucker, 192 Conn. 1 (1984)—61-11, 63-5, 66-6

Hartford Kosher Caterers, Inc. v. Gazda, 165 Conn. 478 (1973)—61-1

Hartford Nat. Bank and Trust Co. v. DiFazio, 6 Conn.App. 576 (1986)—71-4

Hartford Nat. Bank and Trust Co. v. Tucker, 181 Conn. 296, 435 A.2d 350 (1980)— 61-11

Hartford Nat. Bank and Trust Co. v. Tucker, 195 Conn. 218 (1985)—61-1

Hartford Steam Boiler Inspection and Ins. Co. v. Underwriters at Lloyd's and Companies Collective, 121 Conn.App. 31, 994 A.2d 262—60-5

Hartford Steam Boiler Inspection and Ins. Co. v. Underwriters at Lloyd's and Companies Collective, 271 Conn. 474 (2004)—61-1

Harty v. Cantor Fitzgerald and Co., 275 Conn. 72 (2005)—66-5, 67-4, 70-5

Hasbrouck v. Hasbrouck, 195 Conn. 558 (1985)—66-5

Hayes Family Ltd. Partnership v. Planning and Zoning Com'n of Town of Manchester, 98 Conn.App. 213 (2006)—62-5

Haylett v. Commission on Human Rights and Opportunities, 207 Conn. 547, 541 A.2d 494, 46 Fair Empl. Prac. Cas. (BNA) 1876, 47 Empl. Prac. Dec. (CCH) ¶ 38164 (1988)—72-3

Haynes v. Power Facility Evaluation Council, 177 Conn. 623 (1979)—61-1

Haynes v. Yale-New Haven Hosp., 243 Conn. 17 (1997)—71-5

Hayward v. Hayward, 53 Conn.App. 1, 752 A.2d 1087 (1999)—71-5

Health Services, Commissioner of v. Youth Challenge of Greater Hartford, Inc., 206 Conn. 316 (1988)—67-4

Heard v. Heard, 116 Conn. 632 (1933)—60-2

Hendel's Investors Co. v. Zoning Bd. of Appeals of the Town of Montville, 62 Conn.App. 263 (2001)—61-1

Henderson v. U.S., __ U.S. __, 133 S. Ct. 1121, 185 L. Ed. 2d 85 (2013)—60-5

Herasinovich v. Town of Wallingford, 149 Conn.App. 325 (2014)—66-8

Heritage Village Master Ass'n, Inc. v. Heritage Village Water Co., 30 Conn.App. 693 (1993)—61-1

Hernandez v. Dawson, 109 Conn.App. 639 (2008)—85-2

Herrera v. Madrak, 58 Conn.App. 320, 752 A.2d 1161 (2000)—60-5, 71-4

Herrmann v. Summer Plaza Corp., 201 Conn. 263, 513 A.2d 1211 (1986)—64-2

I

J

K

L

M

N

Princess H.Q. v. Robert H., 150 Conn.App. 105 (2014)—67-2

Prishwalko v. Bob Thomas Ford, Inc., 33 Conn.App. 575, 636 A.2d 1383 (1994)—60-5

Pritchard v. Pritchard, 281 Conn. 262, 914 A.2d 1025 (2007)—61-1, 86-2

Private Healthcare Systems, Inc. v. Torres, 278 Conn. 291 (2006)—67-3

Probate Judicial Conduct re Council on Probate Judicial Conduct re Kinsella, Council on, 193 Conn. 180, 476 A.2d 1041 (1984)—75-1

Procaccino v. Wood & Wood, Inc., 1 Conn. Cir. Ct. 571, 24 Conn.Supp. 288 (App. Div. 1962)—66-8

Prokolkin v. General Motors Corp., 170 Conn. 289 (1976)—61-8

Protect Hamden/North Haven from Excessive Traffic and Pollution, Inc. v. Planning and Zoning Com'n of Town of Hamden, 220 Conn. 527 (1991)—71-1

Pryor v. Tavana, 49 Conn. L. Rptr. 657, 2010 WL 2106225 (Conn. Super. Ct. 2010)—61-11

Psaki v. Karlton, 97 Conn.App. 64 (2006)—61-4

Public Safety, Commissioner of v. Freedom of Information Com'n, 301 Conn. 323 (2011)—67-10

Purdy v. Watts, 91 Conn. 214 (1916)—71-4

Purnell v. Purnell, 95 Conn.App. 677 (2006)—66-5

Putman v. Kennedy, 279 Conn. 162 (2006)—61-1

Putnam, Coffin & Burr, Inc. v. Halpern, 154 Conn. 507 (1967)—61-1

Q

Quaranta v. King, 133 Conn.App. 565 (2012)—61-10, 63-8

Queach Corp. v. Inland Wetlands Com'n of Town of Branford, 258 Conn. 178 (2001)—84-9

Quinlan v. City Nat. Bank of South Norwalk, 105 Conn. 424 (1926)—61-11

R

Racial Disparity, In re Claims of, 135 Conn.App. 756, 42 A.3d 401 (2012)—61-1

Rahmati v. Mehri, 188 Conn. 583, 452 A.2d 638 (1982)—66-5

RAL Management, Inc. v. Valley View Associates, 278 Conn. 672, 899 A.2d 586 (2006)—61-1, 61-9, 61-11, 61-14, 63-1, 71-6

Ralto Developers, Inc. v. Environmental Impact Com'n of City of Danbury, 220 Conn. 54 (1991)—60-5

Rametta v. Stella, 214 Conn. 484 (1990)—84-9

Ramondetta v. Amenta, 97 Conn.App. 151 (2006)—66-5

Ramos v. Commissioner of Correction, 248 Conn. 52, 727 A.2d 213 (1999)—60-5, 80-1

Ramsdell v. Union Trust Co., 202 Conn. 57 (1987)—61-1

Raph v. Vogeler, 45 Conn.App. 56, 695 A.2d 1066—63-4

Raudat v. Leary, 88 Conn.App. 44 (2005)—61-1

Ravitch v. Stollman Poultry Farms, Inc., 165 Conn. 135 (1973)—60-2, 63-8

Reappointment Commission, In re Petition of, 303 Conn. 798, 36 A.3d 661 (2012)—61-1

Reapportionment Commission, In re Petition of, S.C. 16642—61-1

S

State v. Kelley, 206 Conn. 323 (1988)—61-6
State v. Kelly, 45 Conn.App. 142, 695 A.2d 1 (1997)—77-1
State v. Kelly, 208 Conn. 365 (1988)—61-1
State v. Kelly, 313 Conn. 1, 95 A.3d 108 (2014)—66-5
State v. Kemp, 124 Conn. 639, 1 A.2d 761 (1938)—61-1
State v. Kendrick, 132 Conn.App. 473 (2011)—60-5, 64-1
State v. King, 187 Conn. 292 (1982)—60-5
State v. Kitchens, 299 Conn. 447, 10 A.3d 942 (2011)—60-5
State v. Klinger, 50 Conn.App. 216 (1998)—67-4
State v. Knight, 29 Conn.App. 675 (1992)—60-5
State v. Komisarjevsky, 301 Conn. 920, 21 A.3d 465 (2011)—84-2
State v. Komisarjevsky, 302 Conn. 162, 25 A.3d 613 (2011)—61-1, 83-1
State v. Kreske, 130 Conn. 558 (1944)—60-3
State v. Lafferty, 191 Conn. 73, 463 A.2d 238 (1983)—60-5
State v. Lanasa, 141 Conn.App. 685, 62 A.3d 572 (2013)—61-1, 63-7, 66-6, 66-8
State v. Lawler, 30 Conn.App. 827 (1993)—60-2
State v. Lawrence, 91 Conn.App. 765, 882 A.2d 689 (2005)—71-5
State v. Ledbetter, 275 Conn. 534 (2005)—67-4, 67-7
State v. Lee, 229 Conn. 60 (1994)—84-11
State v. Legnani, 109 Conn.App. 399, 951 A.2d 674—61-9
State v. Leslie, 166 Conn. 393, 349 A.2d 843 (1974)—61-1
State v. Linarte, 107 Conn.App. 93, 944 A.2d 369 (2008)—61-10
State v. Lloyd, 185 Conn. 199 (1981)—61-1
State v. Lombardo Bros. Mason Contractors, Inc., 307 Conn. 412 (2012)—61-7, 66-4
State v. Lonergan, 16 Conn.App. 358 (1988)—60-5
State v. Longo, 192 Conn. 85, 469 A.2d 1220 (1984)—61-1
State v. Lopez, 235 Conn. 487, 668 A.2d 360 (1995)—66-4, 66-5
State v. Lo Sacco, 12 Conn.App. 481 (1987)—64-1
State v. Lugo, 266 Conn. 674 (2003)—61-10
State v. Luurtsema, 262 Conn. 179 (2002)—65-2
State v. Lynch, 21 Conn.App. 386, 574 A.2d 230—63-4
State v. Madigosky, 291 Conn. 28 (2009)—60-5
State v. Malave, 47 Conn.App. 597 (1998)—60-5
State v. Malcolm, 257 Conn. 653 (2001)—61-1
State v. Malm, 143 Conn. 462, 123 A.2d 276 (1956)—61-1
State v. Manfredi, 4 Conn.App. 247, 493 A.2d 242 (1985)—77-1
State v. Marquez, 291 Conn. 122, 967 A.2d 56 (2009)—63-4
State v. Marro, 68 Conn.App. 849 (2002)—72-1
State v. Marsh and McLennan Companies, Inc., 286 Conn. 454, 2008-1 Trade Cas. (CCH) ¶ 76173 (2008)—83-4
State v. Martin, 2 Conn.App. 605, 482 A.2d 70 (1984)—71-5
State v. Martin, 189 Conn. 1 (1983)—60-5
State v. Martinez, 295 Conn. 758, 991 A.2d 1086 (2010)—60-2
State v. Martin M., 143 Conn.App. 140, 70 A.3d 135 (2013)—63-4
State v. Marzbanian, 2 Conn. Cir. Ct. 312, 198 A.2d 721—61-1

T

U

V

W

Waterbury Teachers Ass'n v. Freedom of Information Com'n, 230 Conn. 441, 645 A.2d 978 (1994)—61-1

Waterbury Trust Co. v. Porter, 130 Conn. 494 (1944)—61-1

Waterbury Twin, LLC v. Renal Treatment Centers-Northeast, Inc., 49 Conn. L. Rptr. 848, 2010 WL 1999072 (Conn. Super. Ct. 2010)—63-9

Waterford, Town of v. Connecticut State Bd. of Ed., 148 Conn. 238 (1961)—60-5

Waterworks v. Audet, 29 Conn.App. 722, 617 A.2d 932 (1992)—61-1

Watrous v. Sinoway, 135 Conn. 424 (1949)—64-1

Watson v. Howard, 138 Conn. 464 (1952)—61-1

Watson v. Watson, 10 Conn. 75, 1834 WL 71 (1834)—70-6

Web Press Services Corp. v. New London Motors, Inc., 203 Conn. 342 (1987)—63-1

Webster Bank v. Zak, 259 Conn. 766 (2002)—67-4

Webster Trust v. Mardie Lane Homes, LLC, 93 Conn.App. 401 (2006)—61-11

Weeks v. Kramer, 244 Conn. 203, 707 A.2d 30 (1998)—84-11

Weigel v. Planning and Zoning Commission of Town of Westport, 160 Conn. 239, 278 A.2d 766 (1971)—61-1

Weiner v. E. M. Loew's Enterprises, 120 Conn. 581 (1935)—60-5

Weinstein v. Weinstein, 275 Conn. 671 (2005)—63-1

Weisman v. Kaspar, 233 Conn. 531 (1995)—60-5

Welles v. Schroeder, 67 Conn. 257, 34 A. 1051 (1896)—61-1

Wells Fargo Bank of Minnesota, N.A. v. Jones, 85 Conn.App. 120, 856 A.2d 505 (2004)—61-1, 63-1

Wells Fargo Bank of Minnesota, N.A. v. Morgan, 98 Conn.App. 72, 909 A.2d 526 (2006)—63-1

Wells Fargo Bank of Minnesota, N.A. v. Morgan, 105 Conn.App. 856 (2008)—61-10, 64-1

Wells Laundry & Linen Supply Co. v. ACME Fast Freight, 138 Conn. 458 (1952)—61-1, 61-2

Wesley v. Schaller Subaru, Inc., 277 Conn. 526, 893 A.2d 389 (2006)—60-4, 60-5, 61-8

Westbrook, Town of v. ITT Hartford Group, Inc., 60 Conn.App. 767 (2000)—61-1, 66-5

West Hartford Interfaith Coalition, Inc. v. Town Council of Town of West Hartford, 228 Conn. 498 (1994)—60-2, 60-5, 67-7

West Hartford, Town of v. Willetts, 125 Conn. 266 (1939)—61-1

West Haven, City Council of City of v. Hall, 180 Conn. 243 (1980)—63-4

West Haven Housing Authority v. Simmons, 5 Conn. Cir. Ct. 282 (App. Div. 1968)—61-11

West Haven Sound Development Corp. v. City of West Haven, 207 Conn. 308 (1988)—60-5

Westover Park, Inc. v. Zoning Bd. of City of Stamford, 91 Conn.App. 125, 881 A.2d 412 (2005)—61-1

Westport, Town of v. State, 204 Conn. 212, 527 A.2d 1177 (1987)—83-1

Whitaker v. Howard, AC 21046 (2000)—61-11

White v. Edmonds, 38 Conn.App. 175 (1995)—61-1

White v. Howd, 66 Conn. 264 (1895)—61-1

Index